The Case
That Never Dies

The Case That Never Dies

THE LINDBERGH KIDNAPPING

LLOYD C. GARDNER

RUTGERS UNIVERSITY PRESS
NEW BRUNSWICK, NEW JERSEY, AND LONDON

Library of Congress Cataloging-in-Publication Data

Gardner, Lloyd C., 1934–
    The case that never dies : the Lindbergh kidnapping / Lloyd C. Gardner.
        p. cm.
Includes bibliographical references and index.
    ISBN 0-8135-3385-6 (hardcover : alk. paper)
    1. Lindbergh, Charles Augustus, 1930–1932—Kidnapping, 1932.
2. Kidnapping—New Jersey—Hopewell. 3. Lindbergh, Charles A.
(Charles Augustus), 1902–1974. 4. Hauptmann, Bruno Richard, 1899–1936.
I. Title.
    HV6603 .L5G37 2004
    364.15'4'0974965—dc22
                                                              2003018870

British Cataloging-in-Publication information for this book is available from
the British Library.

The publication of this book has been made possible, in part, by a gift from
Anne Moreau Thomas.

Manufactured in the United States of America

For
Richard P. McCormick
Friend and Colleague
For All These Years . . .

Contents

Acknowledgments

From the beginning, this book was a team effort. It originated in a series of conversations with a dear friend, Bill Mooney, whose own take on the Lindbergh case has now been presented to audiences on land and sea in his role as actor-folklorist extraordinaire. Bill and his wife, Val, sustained me with their friendship through this journey, which began with the new millennium.

Working on the project has brought many rewards, and several new friends, especially Mark Falzini, Siglinde Rach, and Dolores Raisch. I value their contributions to the book, but above all their friendship. Mark Falzini is the archivist at the New Jersey State Police Museum in West Trenton. His dedication has made the museum a perfect place to do research. But beyond that, he has produced a number of invaluable compendia on a variety of subjects so that researchers can grasp the complexities involved in understanding the challenges presented by conflicting statements and testimony. He seems to know what document you need before you know you need it. He was also the one who discovered how the holes in the ransom notes perfectly fit over a table found in 1948. And he plays a mean bagpipe.

Siglinde Rach has no peer when it comes to knowledge of the geography of the case, from New Jersey to New York to Germany. She also applies her keen intelligence to the problem of understanding the relationships of all the major and minor players in this drama played out on an international stage. I log on each morning, hoping there will be another E-mail from Sigi—because I know it will pose a new question to be answered.

Dolores Raisch has been at this longer than any of us. Her knowledge of the collections housed in the museum is unsurpassed. Dolores found documents tucked away in places one might overlook, and she loaned me her own personal files on the case. She rightly insists, however, that one must not forget the original investigations still raise the key questions. Dolores is also the translator of the steno shorthand notebooks of the investigations, an important new source for researchers.

Kurt Tolksdorf allowed me to use his voluminous files on the case, while Steve Lehman provided me with copies of his well-researched and ably argued essays on the ladder evidence and eyewitness testimony.

All of the above form the "State Street Irregulars," who meet when they can or via E-mail to discuss the case.

Several people gave needed assistance in understanding the era and the locations, especially Flemington, New Jersey, in the mid-1930s. They include Richard P. McCormick, to whom the book is dedicated with great thanks for our long friendship and his knowledge of New Jersey life and politics; Thomas Hartmann, whose friendship and knowledge of Princeton (especially the "Balt") are invaluable; Anne Thomas, whose family owns the *Hunterdon County Democrat,* and whose memories of the trial helped to make vivid its impact on the town and environs; Jean Parker and Vern Williamson, for the same reason. Ryman Herr, Jr., the son of Lloyd Fisher's law partner, shared his memories of the way Fisher operated in the courtroom to defend his clients' interests.

Freeholder George Muller arranged a special tour of the Old Flemington Cemetery and Courthouse, and the jail. Judge Sam Chiarvalli recalled for me his experiences as a young law clerk at the lawyers' table in the Union Hotel across the street from the courthouse, and his memories of Hauptmann and Lindbergh at the trial. Hope Nelson, Governor Harold Hoffman's daughter, took time to talk with me about her father's efforts. So many people have told me in casual conversations about how the case affected their families. Thanks to all of them.

Two stalwart and patient researchers, Katherine Elias and Joseph Groshong, worked their way through the FBI files. State Troopers Walter Babecki and Anthony Ceravolo gave me some real "clues" to work on about evidence and how it is (or should be) handled by professional investigators. Michael Melsky shared his ideas with me unselfishly while he worked on is own Lindbergh study.

My agent and friend Gerry MacCauley believed in this project, and so did Marlie Wasserman, director of the Rutgers University Press. My editor, Victoria Haire, is simply tops, one of the best I have ever worked with during my career. My wife, Nancy, a close reader of every page (through all the revisions), has practically lived with it as I did from conception to realization. Even the title was her idea. It is a much better book because of her insight and sympathy for all the victims of this crime.

Finally, to the Swan Bar, in Lambertville, thanks for letting the "Irregulars" occupy that corner table under the framed newspaper Front Page Story of the Lindbergh flight while the "seminar" worked out all the "details."

Lloyd C. Gardner
Newtown, Pennsylvania
September 2003

The Case
That Never Dies

INTRODUCTION

It couldn't be true, could it? Edmund DeLong, a reporter for the *New York Sun,* living in Princeton, New Jersey, put down the phone, and asked his wife, Bea, where the Lindbergh house was. He had to get over there and see what had happened, see if it was true. The man on the phone said the Lindbergh baby had been kidnapped! Bea could drive him. She had been there recently to tea, and knew the way along those country roads to the house where the colonel and Anne lived. DeLong was the first reporter there. Soon after he arrived, the place was covered with reporters like a watermelon rind with ants after a summer picnic. Years later, the *Sun* reporter told his grandchildren that he thought his fingerprints were probably all over that ladder found about seventy-five-feet from the house—everyone was picking it up, curious to see just how it might have figured in the crime.[1]

How the ladder was used has never been satisfactorily explained, but that was only the beginning. Journalists and forensic experts, Freudian psychiatrists and novelists, have all written about the Lindbergh kidnapping. There are enough theories about how the crime was carried out to fill a set of volumes only a few short of the most recent edition of the *Encyclopaedia Britannica.* Until now, however, no historian has ventured into the overgrown maze of evidence and speculation.

I was fortunate to secure some directions through the maze from newly available FBI records, as well as from many previously neglected files at the New Jersey State Police Museum. The only way to understand the enduring significance of the case, moreover, is to put it into the context of a United States entering its third year of the Great Depression. It was a time when the nation seemed to have lost its grip on the future—something unheard of in past days when the West was being "won." The Depression saw a steady increase of state power at all levels, while Americans watched with shocked fascination as the underworld rose to the surface to challenge civic authority in cities and countryside.

From the outset investigators and the public believed the crime must have been the work of "foreigners," uninvited aliens plotting their evil in the nation's midst. Suspicion fell first on the Lindbergh servants. Most of them were from other countries but were not the sort of immigrants Americans feared as threats to society. Indeed, when the English maid Violet Sharp committed suicide, the press singled out police bullying as the proximate cause of her desperate act. Perhaps this complex attitude was best captured in Agatha Christie's *Murder on the Orient Express,* a novel obviously about the Lindbergh case without using the name.

Arguably the greatest of all mystery writers, Christie is certainly the most widely read around the world. *Murder on the Orient Express* was published in 1933, a year before the arrest of Bruno Richard Hauptmann. The plot concerns the murder of a man traveling on the Orient Express under an assumed name. Belgian detective Hercule Poirot discovers that the victim was actually Casetti, head of the gang that kidnapped Colonel Armstrong's daughter. Suspicion had originally fallen on one of the servants, however, who then committed suicide. Casetti's murder was thus an act of revenge by her friends. In an unusual ending, Poirot excuses the killing and forgives the perpetrators. Christie's novel, and her choice of an Italianate villain, mirrored common prejudices and nativist feelings of the day. These would emerge starkly at Hauptmann's trial in 1935.

The Lindbergh case began when little Charlie—Charles Augustus Lindbergh, Jr.—was taken from his crib on March 1, 1932. Lindbergh was adamant that there be no police "interference" beyond a rather perfunctory questioning of the servants. The New Jersey State Police, led by Colonel H. Norman Schwarzkopf (the father of the commander of U.S. forces in the first Gulf War), followed Colonel Lindbergh's wishes and did not pursue the kidnapper until the body was found on May 12, 1932. To many, Lindbergh's behavior was understandable but regrettable.

The first negotiations were carried out by a shady figure who traveled back and forth between two worlds, boasting that the Lindberghs had authorized him to deal with Al Capone's New York counterpart, Owney Madden, owner of the already famous Cotton Club, and a crime kingpin. It seemed for a moment that the power of the underworld to negotiate terms had reached new heights, threatening to usher in an era of lawless anarchy.

Lindbergh also adamantly opposed the efforts of J. Edgar Hoover's Bureau of Investigation (later renamed the Federal Bureau of Investigation) to follow an independent line of inquiry. Actually, since kidnapping was not yet a federal crime—the Lindbergh case led to legislation making it a federal offense—there was little Hoover could do about the situation anyway.

Over the next two years, however, Hoover and Schwarzkopf became dedicated and determined rivals in the struggle to bring the perpetrator or perpetrators to justice. At times they even kept evidence from each other. This aspect of the story has not been told until now, but it is of great significance, for the Lindbergh case became inextricably linked with the FBI's rapid growth and its quest for public recognition under Hoover's very focused leadership.

The emotional strain on the Lindberghs, of course, was intense, both at the time of the kidnapping and in its aftermath, when they had to deal not only with their grief but with the press's continuing obsession with the case. As the first anniversary of the kidnapping approached at the end of February 1933, Anne wrote in her diary: "I am sick of clothes and gewgaws and bags and advertisements and newspaper clippings and society pages and the new *Vogue* and fittings and the main floors of department stores and the radio—jazz and magazines and hairdressers. I am sick sick to death of them. But I clutch at them madly, like smoking or drinking—anything to keep from thinking."[2]

Although the present book does not deal at length with this emotional strain, as do the Lindberghs' biographies, it will no doubt be apparent to the reader as the story develops day to day, week to week, year to year. In order to tell the story as it happened, I constructed each chapter around the one person most responsible for, or closest to, the immediate events of the crime and what followed, so the book is organized both topically and chronologically.

The argument over Hauptmann's guilt or innocence is crucial to understanding the way the trial developed, but it is only part of the Lindbergh case. It continues to intrigue us because so many people were involved—far beyond the principals in the case. Since I began this book, many people who were children at the time have told me of their parents' fears that they would be stolen away, too. The kidnapping shocked Americans because it could happen to a national hero, whose fate foretold their own worst fears, and because it suggested something had gone very wrong with American society. It suggested, in fact, that the Great Depression was much more threatening than an economic crisis. When Lindbergh left the country in December 1935, seeking to restart an interrupted life, Bruno Richard Hauptmann was still awaiting execution in his death-house cell in Trenton, New Jersey. It seemed there was no end to the case, even when the sentence was finally carried out.

1 SUDDEN FAME

Yes, aviation has great power, but how fragile are its wings!
When all goes well in flying, one can soar through the sky
like a god, letting the planet turn below—remaining aloof or
partaking of its life as one desires. But how slight an error
can bring one tumbling down; how minute are the pitfalls of
the air—a microscopic flaw in a fitting, a few crystals of ice
in a venturi tube, the lack of an hour's sleep.

—CHARLES LINDBERGH, *The Spirit of St. Louis*

In May 1927 Charles Augustus Lindbergh astonished the world by
being the first man to fly solo across the Atlantic from New York to
Paris. When he finally landed at Le Bourget airport thirty-three hours
after takeoff, crowds engulfed his plane, *The Spirit of St. Louis,* and
"parts of the ship began to crack from the pressure of the multitude."
Lindbergh started to climb out of the cockpit. "But as soon as one foot
appeared through the door I was dragged the rest of the way without
assistance on my part . . . For nearly half an hour I was unable to touch
the ground, during which time I was ardently carried around in what
seemed to be a very small area, and in every position it is possible to
be in. Every one had the best of intentions but no one seemed to know
just what they were."[1]

Lindbergh's flight provided a world hungry for heroes after the
Great War with someone to worship. His story sold newspapers like
nothing ever had before. It required an estimated twenty-five thousand
extra tons of newsprint to satisfy readers' appetites for everything
about "Lucky Lindy's" flight. After the president of the French Republic
pinned the Legion of Honor on the lapel of Lindbergh's borrowed suit,

and kissed him on both cheeks, Ambassador Myron Herrick declared to the world, "This young man from out of the west brings you better than anything else the spirit of America."[2]

"There's nothing I can't do with *The Spirit of St. Louis,*" Lindbergh exulted. "It's truly a magic carpet, as though it came directly out of the tale of the Arabian Nights to take me anywhere at all. When I'm ready to leave Europe, I can step into its cockpit again and fly on around the world, through Egypt, and India, and China, until I reach the West by flying east. There's no place on earth I can't go."[3]

Instead, President Calvin Coolidge sent a cruiser, the *Memphis,* to bring him home. A squadron of fifty pursuit airplanes maneuvered overhead in tribute as his ship neared the American coast. Waiting to greet him, the president and Mrs. Coolidge stood on a high stand in front of the Washington Monument. "Our messenger of peace and good-will," Coolidge addressed him. "In less than a day and a half he had crossed the ocean over which Columbus had traveled for sixty-nine days and the Pilgrim Fathers for sixty-six days on their way to the New World. It is our great privilege to welcome back to his native land, on behalf of his own people, who have a deep affection for him and have been thrilled by his splendid achievement, a Colonel of the United States Officers' Reserve Corps, an illustrious citizen of our Republic, a conqueror of the air and strength for the ties which bind us to our sister nations across the sea." As men in shirtsleeves turned the handles of newsreel cameras, Coolidge pinned the Distinguished Flying Cross on Lindbergh's lapel.[4]

It was only the beginning. Adoring crowds everywhere cheered the "Lone Eagle" as a hero, a pioneer of the wonders of the air age and American technology, and a gift to promoters of the aviation industry. Propelled from obscurity to head the pantheon of modern world heroes, the twenty-five-year-old barnstormer from the Midwest had landed *The Spirit of St. Louis* smack-dab in the highest circles of American society. Ambivalent about the emotional displays, as befitted his Swedish heritage, he liked the role of ambassador for aeronautics.

In the first month after the flight, Lindbergh received offers totaling more than $5 million. The most extravagant came from William Randolph Hearst, baronial ruler of a vast media empire that stretched from coast to coast, and which included Cosmopolitan Pictures. He offered Lindbergh $500,000 to star in a picture about aviation opposite Hearst's mistress, Marion Davies—and 10 percent of the gross. Hearst pleaded with him to accept the offer not merely for selfish reasons but to serve "as an inspiration to others."[5]

Doubtful about the idea of going into the movies, and even more so about Hearst's style, Lindbergh discussed the plan with friends Henry Guggenheim and Colonel Henry Breckinridge, a lawyer who would become his closest confidant. The discussion went on until three in the morning, with both Henrys warning him Hearst wanted to use Lindy's fame to promote Davies—just as he used everyone else. The episode introduced Lindbergh to a side of American society that he would come to hate and fear. Hearst accepted his refusal with good grace, but it was the only time they would meet on friendly terms.[6]

Assured by his new friends that many paths were open to him to achieve great things, Lindbergh was soon launched on a writing career in addition to aviation. He received nearly $200,000 for *"WE,"* an autobiographical account of events culminating in the flight itself.

That October Lindbergh received an invitation to the New York apartment of Dwight B. Morrow, a former J. P. Morgan partner, recently appointed ambassador to Mexico. President Plutarco Calles's determination to carry out the Constitution of 1917 and exercise complete sovereignty over natural resources, especially oil, had produced new tensions with Mexico's neighbor to the north. Calles had closed churches, canceled American oil leases, and was threatening to repudiate foreign debts. Undaunted by the challenge, Morrow thought he could calm things down by a display of goodwill, and he wanted Lindbergh to help him out.[7]

Accordingly, on December 13, 1927, *The Spirit of St. Louis* lifted off from Washington's Bolling Field on a nonstop flight to Mexico City. As Morrow had hoped, the Mexicans hailed Colonel Lindbergh, just as the French had greeted his arrival in Paris. At the embassy he met Anne Morrow, the ambassador's daughter, a bookish young college student. A romance flourished, somewhat to the dismay of the Morrow family, as Anne was eager to shed her protective chrysalis and join Charles in his daring pursuits. She found him just the opposite of the callow young men in her social circle and fell completely in love with the aviator from another world. "There are some things she is going to lose," her worried mother wrote, "but he is a romantic figure & a fine virile man who has conquered her imagination. I can't imagine it—but I must."[8]

They married in May 1929. Pregnancy and childbirth did not diminish Anne's determination to become her husband's full partner in pioneering air exploits. She even flew a long cross-country route at high altitudes when seven months pregnant. Charles Augustus Lindbergh, Jr., was born on June 22, 1930, and immediately dubbed "the Little Eaglet." In a short time Anne was back in the cockpit, playing an increasingly important role in her husband's ambitions. High on their priority list was an air tour of the Orient. The ostensible goal was to find the shortest air route between New York and Tokyo, but Anne later admitted it was to experience the "glamour and magic" of the Orient, the thrill and expectations of seeing new and previously inaccessible territory.[9]

There was "glamour and magic" on the trip but also great danger. Placing Charlie in the care of a nursemaid from Scotland, Betty Gow, they began the journey in the summer of 1931. On the first leg of the trip, Charles had difficulty landing because of fog over Kamchatka and was forced down on a small island. After two weeks in Japan they flew on to flood-stricken China, where Lindbergh landed in a submerged rice paddy hoping to distribute medical supplies, only to be driven off by hungry and desperate peasants demanding food and money. Charles chased the Chinese away by waving a pistol in the air. No previous peril in the air had been so frightening, and it underscored that certain challenges were beyond the reach of technology and planning.[10]

The death of Anne's father cut short the Lindberghs' adventures in the Orient. Dwight Morrow's death at fifty-eight came as a shock to the family, and to Republican leaders who saw the recently elected senator as future presidential material. Relations between Charles and his father-in-law had been generally harmonious, but there was a somewhat unpleasant situation involving the will. Three and a half months after the wedding, Dwight had attempted to have Anne agree to a stipulation that in the event of her premature death, her inheritance would be divided between Charles, the widower, and her three siblings. If there were children, her money would go into a professionally administered trust. In that case, the Morrows would effectively control the children's education and upbringing. Charles objected strongly and said he would rather Anne forsake her inheritance altogether. To keep the peace, that is exactly what she did. A new trust was set up in her name anyway, encompassing the provisions the senator had desired. This situation rankled the young, headstrong flier, who valued independence, and hesitated to take advice about his private life and household from anyone.[11]

Charles and Anne now divided their time between an apartment in Manhattan and the Morrow home in Englewood, New Jersey—Next Day Hill—while they scouted an area near Princeton known as the Sourlands Mountains to find an agreeable place to build their own home. His major prerequisite was that there be room for an airstrip. "Land in the Sourlands was cheap because it was rocky, unfertile, and wooded," Lindbergh wrote of the place years later. "Even where fields had been cleared on the property we bought, the soil was so poor that cropping had been discontinued years before. But those fields were long enough to make an airplane landing strip, with only a little labor spent in clearing, I would be able to taxi right into a small hangar that I planned to have constructed next to our garage. There were wonderful views across the valley, and endless trails for walking through the woods."[12]

It was the ideal place. As the house outside Hopewell neared completion, the Lindberghs spent weekends there, arriving on Friday or Saturday, and departing on Sunday or Monday. Charles worked in New York City, often with Dr. Alexis Carrel, a brilliant and controversial scientist, whose ideas were either far ahead of his time or amazingly reactionary—depending on the subject. "I learned," Lindbergh wrote about Carrel, "about the problems of infection, the sensitivity of blood, the complicated character of living tissue, the hereditary qualities in every cell." Carrel was powerfully influenced, in turn, by eugenics. He wanted to set up a foundation, he wrote Lindbergh, to study the use of voluntary eugenics to build up a stronger human race and establish conditions "indispensable to the life of an elite."[13]

Anne relished weekends in the new house and looked forward to spending more time there and getting reacquainted with her son, a process she could accomplish best without the nursemaid's presence. "I take care of him more and do not take Betty [Gow, the nurse] down to Princeton so that he'll know me better," she wrote her mother-in-law. "It is such a joy to hear him calling for 'Mummy' instead of 'Betty'! And she understands just how I feel about it and helps me."[14]

The home had already become a refuge for the Lindberghs, far from the madding crowd. Across the nation, however, the Great Depression had settled over the land like a toxic fog. The Roaring Twenties—filled with flappers and fun, speakeasies and soaring stock market—had become the Dismal Thirties—burdened with apathy, dead ends, and a dust bowl. A stricken people looked around and saw the American dream shriveled into the mocking smirk of gangsterland.

Whatever it was called, gangsterland, the underworld, the mob, American society seemed poised on the edge of a terrible precipice. Even before the Crash, Prohibition had spawned a new style of criminal who catered to the needs of the rich, fought territorial wars with machine guns, and whose exploits made antiheroic legends in Hollywood films. At the highest levels, the "firms" caricatured modern principles of business efficiency, complete with cost-accounting bookkeepers wearing eyeshades. Kidnapping had become a major source of revenue in the Depression, with hundreds of snatches carried out each year.

"So long as the organized crime underworld characters were just kidnapping and killing one another, and the small-time underdog gangsters were winging an occasional banker or shooting up the place in the course of a robbery, it was looked upon as a sort of interesting sidelight during otherwise drab times. Such events actually provided a vicarious thrill of sorts for much of the public."[15]

At first, gangs kidnapped members of rival gangs, but soon the idea spread outside the dark alleys to respectable neighborhoods. Now the crime of kidnapping took on a new urgency. The question on everyone's lips was, Could the nation protect its citizens? The *New York Times* ran a series of front-page articles—"Progress of Kidnap War," "The Drive on Crime," and "The Kidnapping Situation"—complete with running summaries like baseball boxscores. Lloyd's of London introduced ransom insurance for wealthy American customers. Bing Crosby and Marlene Dietrich were among the first in Hollywood to sign on. Applicants had to have sterling reputations and not be known to consort with shady characters. The identities of policyholders were kept confidential in order not to provide an incentive to kidnappers.[16]

Attorney General Homer S. Cummings warned the nation that it faced a "war with the organized forces of crime." It was a dark moment in the nation's history. "It is conservative to say that there are more people in the underworld carrying deadly weapons than there are in the Army and Navy of the United States."[17]

On Saturday afternoon, February 27, 1932, a Morrow chauffeur drove Anne and Charlie from Englewood to Hopewell, where caretakers Olly Whateley and his wife, Elsie, greeted them and took their things inside. Later that evening the baby seemed to be coming down with a cold. . . .

2 BETTY GOW'S JOURNEY

I was born in Glasgow, Scotland, February 12, 1904. I resided
with my parents at 30 Nithsdele Street, Glasgow. I attended
school until I was about fourteen and started to work as a
salesgirl in various stores in Glasgow. My last position was
with A. L. Scott & Son, Glasgow, shoe dealers. I worked for
them for four years up until I left Scotland, April 28, 1929, to
come to America.

—BETTY GOW, March 10, 1932

The telephone call late that Tuesday morning did not come as a
complete surprise. Betty Gow knew the baby had taken ill with
a cold over the weekend. The Lindberghs always returned to
the Morrow estate on Sunday night or Monday morning. But this time
Charles and Anne had decided to stay over at their new home near
Princeton to see if their son's cold would improve. It did—some—but
now Anne had a cold, too. Between caring for the twenty-month-old and
her own condition—she had just completed the first trimester of her
second pregnancy—she felt exhausted. So around 10:30 she asked the
butler, Olly Whateley, to call Betty and instruct her to come down from
the Morrow home to help out.[1]

The weather had turned rainy and windy. Anne's mother, Elizabeth
Morrow, decided that instead of having Betty take a train, a chauffeur,
Henry Ellerson, should drive Charlie's nursemaid down to Hopewell.

Ever since the colonel and Mrs. Lindbergh had been spending time
at the new house, Betty had her weekends free. Even on weeknights she
was often able to leave between 7 and 10 P.M. The colonel had issued
strict rules about the upbringing of his son. No one was allowed to
enter the nursery during those hours. For Betty, that meant she could

go out with her boyfriend, Henrik Finn Johnson, nicknamed "Red," almost any night so long as she was back by 10 P.M. to take the baby for his last trip to the bathroom. She had planned a special date for this Tuesday night, the last date for a while, because Red was going to see his brother in Hartford, Connecticut, the next morning.

But now Betty had to cancel her plans. She hurriedly packed a case and left a message with her boyfriend's landlady that Red should call her at the Morrow house. She asked another servant, Marguerite Junge, to take the call when it came and explain matters to Johnson. Then she dashed out through the rain to the Chevrolet roadster, where Henry Ellerson sat waiting. On the way out of town they made one brief stop at a drugstore so that Betty could pick up some candy or cold medication for Charlie.

Ordinarily, the trip from north Jersey down to the Lindbergh house took no more than ninety minutes. But the rain was coming down harder now, blowing in gusts as they reached the main highway, Route 1, and turned south toward New Brunswick and Princeton. As she watched the windshield wipers sweep back and forth, Betty felt depressed—not only because of the weather and the canceled date with Red, but by the prospect of an extended stay at the Lindberghs' new home. The place gave her "the blues," she told Ellerson; she felt "confined" there. This time it might only be for a day or two. But what of the future—when the family moved there permanently? Devoted to Charlie, she had to think about what was ahead for her. At twenty-eight, she was three years older than Mrs. Lindbergh and on the verge of spinsterhood. What kind of life would she have, as a single woman, when the colonel and his family settled permanently into their home in the woods? Who would even know she was there?[2]

Betty Gow had come to the United States hoping to find a different future from what awaited a shopgirl in Scotland. A pretty, petite, dark-haired woman, Betty possessed a ready wit and cool demeanor. She worked for about a year as a nursemaid for a family in Teaneck, New Jersey, near where her brother, William, and his family lived. Then she moved to Detroit to find out what she really thought about an old boyfriend from Scotland who was working in the Ford plant. "I was feeling restless and wanted a change and I thought I would . . . see if I really liked this boy well enough to marry him."[3]

But he didn't seem to have much ambition. He was quite content just to go out now and then, putting Betty no higher than his other girlfriends. Well, she was not going to stand for that. And, besides, he had no mind to save money. "I don't want to work after I am married," she told him, and made up her mind to go back to New Jersey. She got ready by reading books on child care. "Her sole ambition," said her Detroit landlord, "was to fit herself for a position as a nurse maid in a wealthy family."[4]

Back in New Jersey a friend who worked in the Morrow household told her about a position opening up with the Lindberghs. After a brief interview with Colonel Lindbergh, she was hired. Lindbergh retained two caretakers for the new house, Olly and Elsie Whateley, in equally casual fashion. Olly had no previous experience as a caretaker; he had owned a jewelry shop in his home town of Birmingham, England. "We only have three servants," Lindbergh said, "and I have complete faith in them."[5]

More than twenty servants worked with Betty Gow at Next Day Hill in Englewood, however. An estate of more than fifty-six acres, it included the Morrow home, lovely gardens, a swimming pool, and a tennis court. Even when the Morrows were away at their summer home on North Haven Island, Maine, the house was often filled with guests. For when Dwight Morrow had become a senator, he had taken on a whole new set of social ambitions and burdens.

Many of the employees had come to the United States from other places, just as Betty had, in search of a better life. Unlike his son-in-law, the senator had a strong paternal instinct about the servants. Mrs. Rhoderick Cecil Henry Grimes-Graeme, as Mrs. Morrow's social secretary, enjoyed special privileges that others, such as Betty's friend Marguerite Junge, did not. Marguerite's designation was seamstress, but she claimed much higher origins on the social scale in Germany before her family lost its fortune as the world depression swept away the Weimar Republic. Septimus Banks, the butler, had a notorious reputation for drunkenness but through the intercession of Mrs. Morrow kept his position. When the senator died, Banks was not included in the will, but it was understood he would be taken care of through an allowance.

Betty entered the household in February of 1931, when little Charlie was less than a year old. Whatever she had heard about the famous Colonel Lindbergh and Anne could hardly have prepared her to be left virtually alone with the baby for an extended period—as she was when the couple flew off that summer on a pioneering voyage north across the Bering Sea to Asia.

Left to care for the baby at the North Haven summer home, she felt abandoned. Then she met a young Norwegian sailor, Red Johnson, who worked as a deckhand on a neighbor's yacht belonging to Thomas Lamont, another Morgan partner. Red's future was even more uncertain than Betty's. He was an illegal immigrant who had jumped ship in 1927.

But for now, at least, he was fun. They went to dances and beach parties—and talked a lot about the Lindberghs and Charlie.

"[Betty] would tell me of different little things the baby would do," Johnson later remembered, "and words the baby would say at different times." On one occasion, he also recalled, she was "quite upset because the newspaper reporters took a picture of the baby. I would say that Betty Gow was very much devoted to the Lindbergh baby."[6]

Red's interest in Betty blossomed quickly into a serious romance, at least on his side.[7] Betty's growing interest in Red is a little more difficult to understand. Loneliness? They had dated for only a few weeks when Red Johnson and the neighbor's yacht left North Haven for winter harborage near New York. They wrote to each other, and after a single visit to Betty in Englewood, Red decided to move to a rooming house near the Morrow estate. He held no steady job and was apparently content to wait for the new yachting season to begin simply to be near Betty.

She liked him quite a lot. But his prospects were hardly encouraging for a long-term commitment. His shaky status as an illegal immigrant, and his footloose existence as a seasonal deckhand, hardly made him a better bet than the discarded Detroit beau. Betty probably didn't know that he had fathered an illegitimate child before he came to the United States. Red was also younger, by a year, and had other problems—perhaps unknown to Betty. Theirs was a sexually intimate relationship, but Johnson had been diagnosed with a venereal disease and had been advised not to marry until it had been treated successfully. Red and Betty were seeing one another three times a week. How much longer could that have continued without Betty learning about his condition?[8]

She was very much alone in the United States. Her brother in New Jersey had been electrocuted the previous fall working on high power lines, and his family had returned home to Scotland. Betty had written to her mother that she would return home in the summer for her vacation. She had a "premonition" that "something was going to happen" in the Lindbergh family, her mother told a British newspaper; but she was sure her daughter "never dreamed of the baby being kidnapped."[9]

Senator Morrow's death had, according to Marguerite Junge, increased tensions among the servants. Maybe that was the reason Betty wanted to get away for a time and take stock. But she faced nothing better for the long term than the life of an anonymous nursemaid locked away in a country home.[10]

That rainy afternoon, the car exited the highway and wound its way along small county roads, finally reaching the gravel lane Lindbergh had pushed through the woods for more than half a mile until it opened into a clearing. Even in bright sunshine, the house—later called High-fields—was more than a little forbidding.

"The house stands in a secluded spot," read an FBI description, "on the summit of Sorrel Hill, in the Sourland Mountains, in a region sparsely inhabited, difficult of access, thickly wooded and clogged with underbrush." Another report added, "There are numerous unimproved country roads going in every direction and it is a very easy matter for a stranger to become lost." Lindbergh had selected the four-hundred-acre site from the air precisely because it offered such privacy, more than enough land for a rambling two-story French provincial–style farmhouse and a private airstrip. Here, he and his family could be absolutely alone.[11]

Many of the locals had not welcomed the arrival of the Lindberghs. "It is known that the territory purchased by Colonel Lindbergh had been a favorite hunting ground for many of the natives. After this purchase . . . Colonel Lindbergh barred everyone, which further added to the feeling against him. The Sourland Mountains are inhabited largely by uneducated people who keep much to themselves, many of them earn their livelihood by making applejack."[12]

Lindbergh had not put a manned gatehouse at the entrance, however. Senator Morrow, according to Marguerite Junge, had not approved of his son-in-law's decision in this regard. He did not think the family was safe. She recalled him saying, "Sometime the baby would be kidnapped if they didn't have better protection." His warning took on added significance because of a kidnap-blackmail threat a few years earlier against his youngest daughter, Constance.

During the week, the house stood empty except for the two care-takers. Like Betty, the Whateleys' often felt confined and isolated living at Highfields.

The very isolation of Highfields seemed to attract celebrity hunters, who relished the challenge of finding the place. Olly Whateley had recently chased off a couple in a green car, but not before the woman had taken several photographs of the house, focusing especially on the nursery windows. Olly did not always chase off strangers, however, especially when the Lindberghs were not around. Sometimes he gave strangers house tours.

(According to Ambrose Titus, the local man who sat in for the Whateleys when they played hooky, they went away "several times." The last time was only a few days earlier, on February 26. That day, a man and woman suddenly appeared asking if Mrs. Lindbergh was there. No, she was not, Titus answered. Well, the man persisted, they were friends of the family and would like to know when the Lindberghs were expected. They were probably up in Englewood, Titus said. And where was Englewood? asked this supposed friend. That raised Titus's eyebrows.)[13]

Betty and Red had enjoyed a Whateley tour as well. Indeed, the couple was there alone with the caretakers on three occasions. Olly walked them through the house and then took Red outside for a trek around the grounds. Betty never said much about these visits, but her boyfriend was far from reticent. Each time they came in Red's car and stayed for several hours. On the most recent visit, just two weeks earlier, Johnson parked his car in the garage. Sometime after that, he later recalled, he left the others in the living room and went alone to the garage to pour an extra can of oil into the engine. It took him twenty minutes because the weather was cold. Before returning to the living room, he went to the second-floor toilet in the servants' quarters to wash his hands. Of the outsiders, then, Red Johnson probably knew the house better than anyone else.[14]

This detail isn't as significant as it might seem at first. There were the unauthorized Whateley tours, for one thing; and it was quite possible that when they were away somebody could slip by Ambrose Titus to take a very private, unaccompanied, look-see. Moreover, one did not have to go inside the house, to become familiar with the comings and goings of those who moved about from room to room, turning lights on and off. "The house is a big house," Jersey City police inspector Harry Walsh said, "and it is an easy matter for anyone standing just a short distance from the house to conceal himself and become acquainted with the movements of the family by reason of the fact that no window in the house has shades or curtains." At night Highfields was a huge glowing lantern shining through the woods.[15]

This end-of-February weekend, however, the movements of the lady of the house were anything but routine. Because of Charlie's cold, Anne broke her husband's rules. She made "frequent visits" to the nursery Saturday night to see if he was still covered. She also left the lights on in the bathroom next to the nursery. Sunday night was not so unusual in terms of visits. The colonel did not return to Highfields from New York on Monday night but stayed near the city at Next Day Hill. Concerned for Charlie, Anne left all the doors open between the nursery and her bedroom. The nursery was in the southeast corner of the second floor. Next to it was a bathroom and beyond that the Lindberghs' bedroom, all connected by interior doors. One did not have to go in the hall. "During the night," Anne later recalled, "I went in several times to see if the baby was all right." In other words, someone standing outside the house in the dark would have noticed more lights on than usual. But despite Harry Walsh's statement, there were shutters on all the windows, and those on the nursery windows were closed each night. It would have been impossible to tell, therefore, how many visits Anne made to the nursery or how long she stayed.

This point became significant because a watcher simply observing the routine, as argued at Hauptmann's trial, could not have known of a "safe" time to put a ladder up against the house and climb into the nursery—unless he had specific knowledge no one would be entering the child's room. Two alternatives appear: the kidnapper succeeded by pure chance—or there was inside help.

Ellerson and Betty arrived that Tuesday between 1:30 and 2 P.M. After a late lunch, the nursemaid went upstairs to tend to Charlie, just now waking from his afternoon nap. Off the hall opposite the nursery was Betty's room and another bathroom. The Whateleys slept in a rear bedroom also on the second floor. A second set of stairs led up from the kitchen to near their quarters.

Ellerson left the house around 3 P.M. At the end of the drive he encountered a green Ford coupe partially blocking his way. He blew his horn, but the driver did not budge. "I had to drive my car around his to get by." Such intrusions by celebrity hunters were so frequent, however, that they hardly caused a comment.

When Charlie awoke, Betty spent time playing with him in the nursery. Anne, meanwhile, had taken advantage of a temporary break in the weather to "walk down the road." When she returned, she stood outside the house under the nursery window, throwing pebbles up to attract Betty's attention until she brought the child to the window to wave to his mother. Anne had tried to stay on the narrow catwalk still in place around that side of the yet unfinished house, which also lacked landscaping. Nevertheless, at times she stepped in places "where it was quite muddy." She was sure she left footprints underneath the window. Given the placement of the catwalk, it would have been awkward for her to throw pebbles at the window otherwise.[16]

Later in the afternoon, Betty brought Charlie downstairs, where he ran about the kitchen in search of his dog, "Wahgoosh." Variously described as high-strung and apt to bark at any strange occurrence, the dog could be totally indifferent to his surroundings at other times. There was another dog, Charlie's little black Scotty called "Scium." Usually, he went down to the new house with the family. But this time he remained at Next Day Hill. He had gone for a stroll in the park, according to Marguerite Junge, and the colonel could not wait for him. "This is another fact that so many people do not know and ask puzzled, why just that night was the watchdog not sleeping under Charlie's bed?"[17]

Soon enough, Betty scooped Charlie up from his gamboling expedition round and round the kitchen table and escorted him upstairs to the nursery, where he had his dinner at a small table in the center of the room. Anne entered the nursery just as he was finishing, and the two began to prepare him for bed. "This was shortly after six o'clock," Betty said.[18]

It was now near dusk on a moonless cloudy night with the wind rising. Out on the main road seventeen-year-old Sebastian "Ben" Lupica was driving home from prep school in Princeton and had reached his family's mailbox directly across from the entrance to Highfields. Lupica retrieved a letter and got back into his car. He continued on his way northwards, trying to read the letter and drive at the same time. Coming around a bend toward him appeared a dark sedan. Seeing Lupica, the driver veered off diagonally to the left side of the road and stopped. He appeared to be waiting for Ben to pass him on his right side, thereby placing himself somewhat out of Lupica's direct line of vision. The sedan was a dark blue or black Dodge. Lupica later said he felt sure, also, that it had a New Jersey license plate on the front. The plate began with the letter *L,* designating Mercer County, and indicating a local owner. Lupica noticed two stacked ladders, stretching diagonally from the rear window across the front seat to the windshield. The ladders partially blocked his view of the driver. He looked to be about thirty-five to forty years old, Ben estimated, wearing a dark fedora and overcoat. "He had a thin face and long features." And he was dressed "after the manner of a resident in a city." It struck Lupica he might be a window washer. But that was odd. Why would a window washer be dressed that way, and why would he be out here this time of year, driving around the hills near Hopewell—where hardly anyone lived? Maybe he was nervous about being seen, and that's why he wanted Ben to pass him on the far side. And yet he made no attempt to cover his face. As Ben watched in his rearview mirror, the Dodge started up again and slowly moved on. He could see there was a spare wheel on the trunk.[19]

In the nursery, Betty and Anne continued preparing Charlie for bed, going around the room closing the three windows and shutters. The shutter on the east wall to the rear was warped, however, and could not be locked with the heavy sliding bolt, even though they both tried. Extra measures for the baby's comfort prolonged the bedtime ritual. Betty rubbed his chest with Vicks, a popular decongestant salve. Then, to cover his chest, she fashioned an extra little flannel shirt out of an old petticoat, sewing a decoration around the edge with blue thread.

Snug in one of his Dr. Denton sleeping suits, Charlie was placed in his crib around 7:30.[20]

Anne and Betty briefly discussed which window should be reopened for ventilation. "I went out of the room before Betty," Anne later recalled, "so that I did not see which window she was opening." Usually, Anne opened the French window on the south wall, but it depended on which way the wind was blowing. In any event, a portable screen shielded the bed against drafts—and would have partially blocked an intruder's view. [21]

Anne had already left the nursery when Betty secured Charlie's thumb guards—complicated wire affairs with shoestring-like ties to wrap around the outside of the sleeping suit. Used to prevent a child from sucking its thumb during the night, these would certainly not come off easily. One was later discovered far away from the house toward the main highway—in the opposite direction from where the kidnap ladder was found. The other was never found. Shown the thumb guard at the trial, Anne remembered, "That night I did not put it on." She did not see Betty put it on, either. Could they have been left off intentionally? All we have is Anne's somewhat cryptic testimony. "I don't remember seeing it on."[22]

Having left Betty to finish tucking Charlie in for the night, Anne went downstairs to work at her desk in the living room. Her husband phoned to say he would be late arriving from New York. He was supposed to be much later that night but had forgotten about a speaking engagement, something very unusual for a man who prided himself on details. Anne did not leave her desk, did not go into the corner library directly below the nursery; nor did she open the door between the living room and the library. No light shone through to the outside from the library until Colonel Lindbergh entered that room later in the evening. Such little things, meaningless on any other night.

Betty remained upstairs for a while after Anne left. She would explain to police that she opened the French window halfway, with the shutter locked behind it. Then she worked for a time in the bathroom between the nursery and her own bedroom, washing out some of the baby's garments before making a final check to see if Charlie was asleep yet. She saw that he was resting easily and pinned the blankets down to the mattress with two large safety pins near his head.[23]

About eight o'clock she appeared at the door of the living room to report that the baby had "gone to sleep unusually quickly" and was breathing easily. Then she went to the kitchen to eat dinner with the Whateleys. "The wind was howling around the house," Anne noticed. "Once I thought I heard the sound of car wheels on gravel but thought

I was mistaken because it was at least fifteen minutes later when I heard Colonel Lindbergh's car and his horn. He put the car into the garage and came into the house through the garage, back hall and kitchen. It was about 8:25."[24]

Ten minutes later they sat down to dinner. While they were eating, the phone rang. Olly Whateley answered. Someone wanted to speak to Betty. He did not know who was calling, or at least did not tell her who it was. Betty told Elsie after she hung up that it was Red Johnson telling her he was sorry they had not been able to keep their date. Red told friends that Betty chided him for calling her while she was at Highfields, fearing the Lindberghs would not like it. Yet the conversation went on for some time. Johnson asked if the baby was better and when Betty might return. He also asked if he should delay his visit to his brother in Connecticut in order to see her. Betty said she thought she would be back the next day, but he should not disappoint his brother. They would write while he was gone, and she would see him when he got back. She even took time to ask after their friends Marguerite and Johannes Junge. Then she wished Johnson a good trip, told him to drive carefully and be a good boy.[25]

Johnson's phone call that night triggered suspicions that it was in reality a coded message between kidnap conspirators. When Johnson's movements that day were investigated, however, it was clear that he had been working on a friend's car until late in the afternoon and could not have received Betty's message to call until 4 P.M. That fact, in itself, does not rule out other possibilities of a connection. Between 6 and 6:30, Johnson was seen in Englewood by a young friend, William Boland; then he drove around, parked awhile, and went to the Junges' apartment about 8 P.M. to find out more about Betty's trip to Hopewell. He decided to call her, turning down Marguerite Junge's offer to use their phone, and walked to a nearby drugstore. Returning to the apartment, Johnson suggested they all go for coffee, and then he would take Marguerite back to the Morrow house, where she slept most nights. The evening ended with a pleasure drive along the Hudson River, after which Johnson dropped off Marguerite at the Morrow household around 11:30.

Still, it was curious that Red did not give his name to Whateley when he called—"I asked him if I could speak to Betty Gow but did not tell my name"—and that Whateley apparently did not recognize the Norwegian accent of the man who had visited the house on at least three occasions for several hours at a time. Could someone else have placed that call from the telephone?[26]

Red's various explanations for why he was planning a visit to his brother also raised questions. He was broke, or nearly so, with only seven dollars to last until he could go back to work on the Lamont yacht, he said, and he could live for free at his brother's apartment for a couple of weeks. He told the young man who saw him around 6 P.M., however, that it was getting "monotonous" hanging around doing nothing, so he might as well leave until work started. That was not very flattering to Betty, to be sure. This young man, William Boland, moreover, was the only person to see Red between 6 and 10 P.M., aside from the Junges, until the three entered an Englewood coffee shop.[27]

When the Lindberghs finished eating about 9 P.M. they went into the living room. A few minutes later Charles heard a noise. "What is that?" he asked Anne. It sounded like an orange crate or wooden box falling off a chair in the kitchen. But Anne had not heard anything. What no one knew except a few intimate friends and the servants was that Anne had a hearing problem.[28]

Two men living on a farm nearby also noticed something unusual around that time. A few minutes after the hour, John Kristofeck's dog started barking. From the sound of it, Kristofeck figured the dog was heading toward the Lindbergh estate. His brother-in-law heard the same thing: "I followed the sound of his bark and he seemed to be running toward the Lindbergh estate near the chicken coops. He barked for about four or five minutes and there were sharp yelps as though he was chasing somebody."[29]

Wahgoosh stayed in his bed in the kitchen, however, seemingly unperturbed by anything he heard inside the house or the neighbor dog raising a ruckus about something going on outside.

Red's phone call established an alibi for him at almost precisely that time. It could not have happened earlier, he told the police, "because I spoke to the nurse around 9:00 P.M." and she "did not tell me anything of the kind." Johnson was straining here, because Betty had left the nursery shortly after 8 P.M. and did not return until 10. The points that fix the crime at 9 P.M., then, were not completely convincing to investigators.[30]

After dinner, Anne and Charles went upstairs to draw baths, while Elsie Whateley and Betty Gow chatted about Elsie's new dress in the Whateleys' bedroom at the rear on the second floor, and Olly sat alone reading in the servants' sitting room on the first floor. About 9:30 Charles came back downstairs to work in the library. "No ladder could have been put up *then*," Anne would insist. And yet a ladder could have been there for some time, as the placement of the ladder to the right of the library and nursery windows was the only spot where someone sitting at his desk could not have seen it.[31]

At 9:57, Betty suddenly looked at her watch. "It is nearly ten o'clock," she announced to Elsie. "I have got to go to the baby." Leaving the Whateleys' bedroom, Betty headed toward the nursery down the hall—but not into the baby's room right away. Instead, she entered the bathroom between her room and the nursery and turned on the electric heater. Exiting this bathroom a few minutes later, she encountered Elsie Whateley in the corridor outside the Lindbergh bedroom. Elsie explained that Mrs. Lindbergh had asked for hot lemonade before she went to bed. She was going downstairs to put a kettle on to heat the water. The timing of their meeting in the hall suggests that Betty had taken quite a while simply to turn on the heater in her bathroom. "Where is Mrs. Lindbergh?" Betty asked Elsie. "I wonder if she wants to see the baby." Anne usually accompanied her when she checked on the baby at ten o'clock.[32]

"She is taking a bath," Elsie replied.

"All right, I won't disturb her," Betty said. "If she wants to see the baby, she can go through the connecting door."

Satisfied that Anne would meet her there if she wished, Betty turned around and finally entered the nursery leaving the door open a crack, so that light spilling from the passageway would illuminate the room just enough to see what she was doing. She crossed first to the French window and closed it, turned on the electric heater, waited a moment for the room to lose its chill, and moved close to the bed. Standing still, she listened for Charlie's breathing but began to sense something was wrong. She heard nothing. Reaching over the side rails into the crib, she felt all around. The baby was gone![33]

Without pausing to turn on the light in the nursery, she rushed into the corridor and ran to the Lindberghs' bedroom. "Do you have the baby, Mrs. Lindbergh?"

"No," Anne replied, not sure what Betty meant.

"Perhaps Colonel Lindbergh has him then," Betty said. ("She thought C. had taken him for a joke," Anne later wrote in a letter.) Betty found Lindbergh in the library. "Colonel Lindbergh," she implored him, "have you got the baby[?]—please don't fool me."

"The baby?" said Lindbergh. "Isn't he in his crib?" From the expression on her face, he knew the answer. Taking the steps two at a time, he sprinted upstairs. After a quick look at the bedclothes, he went into the bedroom he shared with Anne, who stood there bewildered, and took a rifle out of his closet. "Anne," he told her, "they have stolen our baby." How could Lindbergh instantly be so sure of what had happened? Had the toddler never "escaped" from his crib? Surely a rambunctious child of that age would have made his way out of bed before.

Major Thomas Lanphier, one of Lindbergh's closest friends and business associates, gave FBI director J. Edgar Hoover a significantly different version of these events. According to Lanphier, Betty Gow came into the Lindberghs' bedroom and said that she believed Colonel Lindbergh had taken the child and hidden him. "Major Lanphier stated that Colonel Lindbergh is noted for his playing of jokes and at many times his jokes are rather extreme, but it is almost an obsession with him." Irritated at her husband for doing this while the child was sick, Anne went to the top of the stairs and called down to ask him why he had taken the child when he knew it had a cold. Lindbergh's penchant for "rather extreme" jokes like hiding Charlie is not discussed in any recorded statement made to New Jersey police, but Betty Gow also confirmed a previous incident, something that had happened when her predecessor, Marie Cummings, was the baby's nursemaid. Lindbergh had hidden Charlie in a clothes closet for forty minutes before he was found.[34]

But this was no joke. Lindbergh ordered Betty to go downstairs and send Whateley to him. Betty came running down to the kitchen—her face white as a sheet—saying over and over again, "The baby is gone." Elsie Whateley feared "the baby had died." No, no, said Betty. "They have taken him away—he has been kidnapped."

Elsie's initial reaction suggests that Charlie's health was of more concern to the household than a simple cold.[35]

Lindbergh and Whateley searched the house from cellar to attic to confirm what had been feared: Charlie had been stolen away.

Back in the nursery, Lindbergh spotted a white envelope on the southeast windowsill, the window with the supposedly faulty shutter. Displaying remarkable restraint, he left it unopened and told Whateley to call the Hopewell police and the New Jersey State Police. Then he called Colonel Henry Breckinridge, his lawyer and close confidant. Breckinridge rushed down from New York to be with him and became, in effect, Lindbergh's emissary to the outside world. Everyone who came to Highfields, however, from local Hopewell police to the commander of the New Jersey State Police, Colonel Norman Schwarzkopf, obeyed Lindbergh's orders. Recovering his child was all that mattered. Once he had his son back, but not until then, the authorities could go after the kidnappers.

Lindbergh told everyone he wanted to handle the situation in the safest way possible. And yet before the envelope was opened, he had already informed the police. Once Whateley placed that telephone call, the Lindbergh kidnapping was no longer a private matter.

The condition of the nursery posed a series of puzzles. Betty said she had not paused to turn on the light when she rushed into the Lindberghs' bedroom. She supposed, she said, that Colonel Lindbergh turned it on when he first came into the room. But Anne saw the light on when she entered the nursery—before Charles and Betty returned from the library. Anne later remembered that "the French window at the rear of the house was closed, that the electric heater was on and that the light was on."[36]

Standing there, Betty now also saw something she had missed before in the semidarkness: dirt markings on the baby's sheets. She had felt all around the crib but had not turned on the light. That would explain why she had not seen the smudges earlier. Only Betty seemed to notice the marks, however. When State Trooper Frank A. Kelly arrived, he observed the covers "were disarranged in the crib." But "there was no indication of any prints."[37]

Other questions were more troubling to investigators. Which nursery window—if any— had been left open? "Colonel Lindbergh surveyed the nursery," writes Jim Fisher, "and saw that the right-hand shutter on the southeast window was standing open—and the window was up. He could feel the night air seeping into the room." But was that really so? When the state police arrived, Trooper Lewis Bornmann asked Colonel Lindbergh about the windows. "He said he wasn't quite sure how the windows had been, but he would call Betty Gow." Betty pointed to the same window and declared "she discovered" it had been opened and later closed. How could she know that?[38]

Of course, if the kidnapper closed the window behind him, that would explain why the ransom note left on the sill had not blown away. But why would a kidnapper, trying to get out of the window with the child in one arm and fishing around with his feet to find the ladder, attempt to close the window?

Perhaps Betty closed the window herself, realizing she would be blamed for leaving open the only entryway into the nursery from outside the house. Or did Lindbergh close the window? He gave orders that no one was "to enter the nursery or to walk around the house until the police arrived." But had he ignored his own orders and so jeopardized evidence?

No marks were found on the outside of the window, which meant that the kidnapper had not used a jimmy to pry it open. When a government agent asked Anne if the window had been locked, she replied no. "Come up to the nursery," she told him. "I will show you exactly how the window was." What else Anne told the agent we do not know—but the question was never resolved.[39]

No doubt Lindbergh was confused about what to do. He started searching the area but realized he had no flashlights and sent Olly Whateley off to find some. On his way out to the main road, Olly encountered Hopewell police chief Harry Wolfe and deputy Charles Williamson, and escorted them the rest of the way up to the house.

Lindbergh greeted the two with a warning not to touch anything in the nursery, especially not the envelope on the windowsill. (Like others that night, Wolfe and Williamson marveled at Lindbergh's restraint. And like others ever since, they wondered if he had done the right thing.) Williamson remarked on several blurred smudges on the floor leading from the window to the crib. Wolfe, however, was surprised at what he did not see. He never forgot the feeling he had that night, his sense there should be more to be seen—more of everything. There were no muddy footprints on the floor of the nursery leading back to the window, nor any handprints or blood anywhere and the screen around the crib was undisturbed. Other than the few smudges, there was no sign of a forced entry—nothing at all.

Wolfe looked hard at the windowsill. There was a chest pushed up against it, so an intruder would have had to launch himself about three feet to get into the room—an awkward feat. And do so without moving the chest. Yet there was no sign it had been budged even an inch. On top of the chest was a suitcase and a Tinkertoy rabbit—also undisturbed. Getting back out with the baby would have been even harder. "The culprit would have pushed it around in order to gain a secure foothold," said Wolfe, and "he certainly would not have taken time to push the chest back into place, especially if he had a baby in his arms and was in the act of a desperate crime. But bear in mind—the chest had not been moved."[40]

When they went outside with Lindbergh, the two policemen could see plainly where a ladder had been placed against the wall somewhat to the right of the windows of the library and nursery. Could a kidnapper have learned, simply by lurking about outside, that this was the only place where a ladder could not be observed by a person working at the desk in the library below the nursery? Williamson also saw three or four footprints in the soft mud "leading toward the ladder." As the policemen swung their flashlights around, the beams of light fell on three sections of a ladder some 75 feet away, apparently abandoned in the getaway.[41]

State troopers began to arrive about forty-five minutes later, between 11:15 and 11:30 P.M. Wolfe and Williamson were soon sent off to do "guard duty" out near the entrance to the estate. The Hopewell officers had limited police experience, mostly directing traffic through the village, but they were the first observers on the scene, and resented being treated as little better than junior G-men. Well, now the case was Colonel Schwarzkopf's headache—not theirs.

Troopers Nuncio DeGaetano and Lewis Bornmann reached the estate first. They concentrated on the scene outside, where the ladder had been placed against the wall. DeGaetano immediately noticed three kinds of footprints. The first was a single print definitely made by a man's shoe "pointing towards the house near the temporary board-walk." Approximately eighteen inches to the right of that print "was an impression presumed to have been made by a heavy woolen stocking as the impression of the ridges were distinctly shown." Also nearby was a woman's footprint, which Chief Wolfe told the troopers had been made by Anne Lindbergh the previous afternoon.[42]

Lindbergh rejoined the search with DeGaetano and Bornmann near where the ladder had been left behind. Together, they traced prints "made by rubber boots or overshoes on an abandoned road which lead[s] to the chicken coop and an old abandoned house at the entrance to the Lindbergh estate. In certain sections there were also a dog's prints near those of the boots or overshoes." From there the footprints "went across the road and appeared to stop alongside some impressions that appeared to be from an automobile and then further trace ceased." A search of the abandoned house yielded nothing.[43]

A third trooper, Corporal J. A. Wolf, went over much of the same muddy area where landscapers had leveled the ground to a distance of about ninety feet to the east and the south of the house. He saw "two sets of fresh foot prints leading off in a southeast direction." From these signs, he concluded: "The Kidnappers consisted apparently of a party of at least two or more persons. They are believed to have driven to the vicinity of the Lindbergh home in a car and parked the car as close as possible without being detected. Apparently two members of the party proceeded on foot to the east side of the Lindbergh residence and assembled a three piece home made extension ladder which they had brought along."[44]

The ground, in places, was little better than slick mire. How someone carrying the twenty-month-old made it across the distance from the ladder to the car without a flashlight and without falling was yet another mystery.[45]

It was after midnight now; at least three hours had elapsed since the kidnapping. While several troopers continued to ponder the footprints, back inside the nursery Trooper Frank Kelly carefully scooped up the plain envelope that bore no name and slit it open with a borrowed nail file. A preliminary test for fingerprints revealed only smudges.

"Dear Sir!" the note began in a bold flourish. But all at once his nerve seemed to falter, and the rest of the message continued in shaky pen strokes:

> Have 50.000 $ redy 25 000 $ in
> 20$ bills 1.5000 $ in 10$ bills and[?]
>   10 000 $ in 5 $ bills. After 2–4 days
> we will inform you were to deliver
> the Mony [or money?].
>   We warn you for making
> anyding public or for notify the Pol[remainder blurred]
>   the child is in gut [gute?] care.
> Indication for all letters are
> singnature.
>
>   (Symbol)
>   and 3 hohls. [or holds]⁴⁶

The identifying symbol consisted of two interlocking hollow circles with a smaller red solid center, wavy vertical lines, and three perforated holes. The purpose of such a complicated "singnature" on all the notes might seem clear enough. Once the news was out, there would be scores (if not hundreds) of opportunists eager to cash in on the deal.

Despite all the care taken with the note, it is not easy to say who actually read the kidnapper's first message. Trooper Kelly reported that besides Lindbergh and himself, several New Jersey State Police officers saw it, as had Hopewell officer Charles Williamson. One report claimed Olly Whateley looked over Lindbergh's shoulder and read it. Any of them could have told someone else, who then told a reporter, who then told his editor. At Lindbergh's request, police denied knowledge of its existence, but within the next two days rumors of a ransom note demanding $50,000 or $500,000 appeared everywhere.⁴⁷

"The amount demanded was a matter of speculation," reported the *Hunterdon County Democrat,* published in nearby Flemington, "$50,000 being given the greatest credence." The Lindberghs, it added, were ready to meet the kidnapper's demand, as set forth in a note left in the crib. The *New York Times* reported that Lindbergh was "ready and anxious to pay the $50,000 ransom demanded" in a note left pinned to the windowsill. And the *Trenton Times* added that Lindbergh had already conveyed to the kidnapper through an intermediary that he would pay the ransom, speculated to be in the range of $50,000 upward.⁴⁸

Highfields was soon under siege. After the state troopers police from all over New Jersey arrived. Legions of reporters came by car from the "big city," and from small-town papers located on Main Street, USA. Gawking onlookers, seeking a walk-on role in the "crime of the century," tramped across the estate, turning it into a fairgrounds midway complete with sideshows. All that was missing was a barker: "Over here, ladies and gentlemen, the original ladder—take a good look now!" Clues were trampled into the mud.

At 10:46 P.M., the New Jersey State Police issued their first bulletin about the kidnapping: "Colonel Lindbergh's baby was kidnapped from Lindbergh home in hopewell nj sometime between 7-30 pm and 10-00 pm this date. baby is 19 months old and a boy. is dressed in a sleeping suit. request that all cars be investigated by police patrols. authority state police trenton NJ."

By eleven o'clock, checkpoints had been set up at the new Holland Tunnel, the George Washington Bridge, and all ferry terminals along the Hudson River. Every vehicle coming into New York was stopped, the license number of each car and truck recorded.[49]

The dragnet had some gaping holes, however. Lloyd Fisher, an attorney from Flemington, New Jersey, left Madison Square Garden (where he had been watching a six-day bicycle race) between one and two in the morning, got in his car, and drove through the Holland Tunnel to reach the "super-highway" toward his home. "I was stopped by about fifty policemen, armed with revolvers, rifles and machine guns," he later reported. "Motorcycles clogged and effectually barred the highway, their motors running and their headlights glaring." The fact that he was headed into the state and not the other way did not seem to make any difference. Nearer to Hopewell, however, the roads were clear: "I never saw another State policeman!"[50]

All through that first night, Lindbergh roamed the area, sometimes searching with police, sometimes mingling with the crowd. "Dressed in a leather jacket, an old cap and a worn pair of trousers, his shoes caked with the sour mud which gives name to the region," reported the *New Brunswick Daily News,* "he tramped most of the night, seeking some clue to his lost namesake." It seemed odd behavior, even contradictory. On the one hand, Lindbergh wanted to give the kidnappers every opportunity to make a safe contact, yet at the same time he joined the search—and made himself appear in national news reports to be the leader in the hunt.[51]

Lindbergh's search party, which included several troopers, began waking neighbors to ask them about anything suspicious they might have seen the previous day. They visited several homes—speaking to the Lupica family, Nelson Wyckoff, Millard Whited, and others—all with negative results. Whited reacted strongly to the visit. "I know what you are after," he said, "you're after those tires that were stolen." He was questioned briefly but said he had seen no one that day or night.[52]

Come daylight, all the roads leading to Highfields, reported the *New York Times,* "were black with cars filled with sight-seers. Above the house large passenger air-liners circled and banked so that the occupants could gaze from above at the house on a hilltop, its lawns dotted with hurrying blue-coated figures of the police and the less colorfully dressed newspaper men and photographers who swarmed to the scene."[53]

By now, the ladder had been taken inside the house. But it had been hours since it was discovered. During all that time police had made no effort to keep reporters, Edmund DeLong and numerous others, from handling the most important clue police had found. It was an amazingly crude instrument if designed specifically for the kidnapping. The rungs were much farther apart than those on a normal ladder, making it difficult to ascend, and even harder to climb down. In one respect, however, it was a clever contraption. Dowels running through the side rails allowed the sections to be unfolded quickly against the wall. But—and here was another curious thing—it had been built in three sections, yet only two were used. Someone who had been scouting the estate, and locating the nursery through field glasses (if not getting closer), presumably would have known how tall a ladder he needed.

The side rails on the second section—the top one used in the entry—had split near the dowel attachment—perhaps causing the noise Lindbergh had heard, and which had provoked the neighbor dog to start barking and running across the grass toward the house. But there was no sign on the muddy ground near the nursery that it had tipped someone over.[54]

Besides the discovery that the third section had not been used, there was the question of why the kidnapper bothered to remove the ladder from the wall and carry it away—burdened as he supposedly was with a twenty-pound child under the other arm—for even seventy-five feet? Perhaps it was a manageable task until the dog came on the scene. Perhaps. Yet there was something curious about the third, unused section. It contained a rail unlike the other wood in the rails or rungs.

There was also a three-quarter-inch wood chisel discovered at a distance from where the ladder had been. Exactly when it was discovered is not clear, but it was outside on the wet ground until morning. Police first assumed it had been brought to jimmy open the shutters and/or lever up the window. The shutters on the window used for entry were warped, however, and could not be locked. So there were no marks on the window. In fact, a chisel that size would do no good against a locked or closed window of that type, or to open the shutters if the sliding bolt had been in place. At the trial, the prosecution advanced a new use for the chisel: a murder weapon to bludgeon Charlie to death. Since it was not found under the window, as was later claimed, nor near the ladder, such theories remain highly speculative, and it is entirely possible the chisel may not have even belonged to the kidnapper.[55]

Fingerprint evidence was completely missing. Trooper Kelly, the fingerprint expert, had arrived at Highfields around 11:15 and spent the entire night carrying out tests for latent fingerprints. He found none on the ladder. By dawn, he had discovered only one smudge on the envelope, nothing on the crib, the windowsill, the window itself inside and out, the sunlamp near the head of the baby's bed, the screen around the crib, or the French window. The powder technique he used was probably not sophisticated enough, but the absence of *any* detectable fingerprints of members of the family was remarkable nonetheless.[56]

By far the most interesting search carried out that first night and the next morning involved a local woodsman, Oscar Bush. Part Indian, Bush spent a great deal of his time trapping small game in the Sourlands Mountains. Tall, with a ruddy complexion, Bush was well known to county officials. He lived with a New York woman (who "kept house" for him) in a rickety hotel in an area bordering on the Delaware and Raritan Canal known as the Princeton Basin.

Among all those milling about the estate was a special police officer whose full-time job was in a local eatery. A reporter for the *Philadelphia Bulletin* overheard him talking about Ol' Oscar Bush, the best tracker around, and promptly set out to find Ol' Oscar.[57] The reporter and a Bush relative, James Wyckoff, caught up with the trapper in the wee hours—he was staying with a friend for a night up in the mountains—and rushed him off to Highfields.

Bush met Lindbergh about 4 A.M. and was immediately dispatched to follow the trail of the odd footprints the colonel and state troopers had discovered earlier. Bush made several additional discoveries. He started under the nursery and followed the muffled prints to where the ladder had been found. From that point he pursued what appeared to be two sets of tracks through a field to Featherbed Lane, where they ended—as others had also observed. "The person that made them never crossed the road, neither did he walk in it," said Bush, "for if he had the road itself was muddy and the prints of his feet would still have been there."

From marks in the bushes and grass he concluded that a car made its way there. "Half way up the Featherbed Lane I finds a place where the bushes has been barked by a car backing in. The bark is off them just on one side, so that looking at them you can see how far the car got." Bush's findings tallied with other reports of a car being seen in and near the old abandoned road posted with signs, "Road Impassable—Drive at your own risk."[58]

Featherbed Lane ran roughly parallel to the gravel road down to the house. More important, the field behind the Lindbergh house had been cleared of heavy growth in preparation for the planned airstrip. Someone not well acquainted with the vicinity would hardly have known about Featherbed Lane. But the woodsman believed that the footprints and tire marks definitely indicated two cars had been on the old road that night, and that, therefore, at least two individuals had been present at the scene of the crime.[59]

As for the tracks, Bush said that one set was made by a "smallish man with a crooked small toe on [his] right foot, one that rested on top of another." It was known to a few people close to Lindbergh that Charlie also had a toe that overlapped another. Having made his report, Bush was dismissed. He had never been a welcome addition so far as the New Jersey State Police were concerned, even though most of his findings tallied with the initial investigations their troopers carried out earlier. Bush weakened his credibility with the police by suggesting the baby would be found up in the hills somewhere because of the difficulty of a clean escape by car without detection.[60]

Oscar Bush was no stranger to Lindbergh. The two had had a run-in over some land Bush owned and the colonel desired to purchase to add to his estate. Perhaps that accounted for Oscar's desire to suggest that locals had been involved, as a rebuke of sorts to the aviator's "invasion" of "their" land.

The next day, as police tried to reconstruct the crime, there was a new arrival at Highfields—someone from the opposite end of the social spectrum. New Jersey governor A. Harry Moore arrived to offer moral support—and to announce that the state had posted a $25,000 reward for the apprehension of the criminals.

Lindbergh was horrified! You are risking my son's life, he declared, and demanded the governor rescind the notice. Moore readily agreed to do so.

Coming out of the house to meet reporters, the governor answered their questions.

Did the Lindberghs think the baby would be returned soon, even today?

No one could say, Moore answered, but Colonel Lindbergh expected something to happen "any minute."

How come?

"Oh, I guess it's just psychic," Moore replied. He may have meant the remark as a joke, but inevitably a parade of psychics would appear to claim to have learned the whereabouts of the kidnapped child from the spirit world.

Moore went on to tell reporters the police's theory of how the crime had been committed. "The nursery window is pretty narrow, and police have decided that it would have been pretty difficult for anyone to climb through it while holding a baby. They think one of the kidnap[p]ers entered the nursery and the other waited at the top of the ladder. Then the baby was handed through the window to the man outside."[61]

The theory apparently originated with Lindbergh himself. It would have been extremely difficult to get in without disturbing the chest or the suitcase with the Tinkertoy rabbit on top of it, Lindbergh related to Major Lanphier. Getting back out with a child would have been impossible—unassisted. There must have been at least two people involved in the crime. One climbed up into the nursery, picked up the child, and handed him out to a second party standing on a ladder. The first person then closed the window, left the note, and walked out of the house. To accomplish this undetected would have been hard. He would have had to pass by several doors where there were people in the rooms. Therefore, Lindbergh believed, the crime had to have taken place earlier, in the short interval between the time the child was put to bed and his arrival at about 8:25 P.M., because later on there was too much activity and movement from room to room.[62]

When Lanphier disclosed Lindbergh's theory to J. Edgar Hoover, the FBI director rejected it—in part. Hoover did not doubt that more than one person had participated in the crime, but "it was rather ridiculous to believe that a stranger would have taken a chance by having to leave by a downstairs exit when he could have left the note in the crib and have left by the window through which he is believed to have entered." Lanphier agreed with Hoover that there must have been "some assistance from inside." "The suspicion attaches first to Betty Gow and, of course, the other servants should be considered."[63]

Hoover's pursuit of his theory eventually brought him into conflict with Lindbergh. The two men never completely trusted each other after Lindbergh interrupted one of Hoover's special agents as he attempted to question Betty. Just before he entered the room, the FBI man had accused her of lying about what she knew.

"I was promised I wouldn't be touched," she shouted at him.

"Who promised you?"

"Col. Lindbergh."

There was to be no more questioning of the servants, Lindbergh then insisted, unless one of Colonel Schwarzkopf's men was present. Hoover thought Lindbergh carried this concern for his employees to "an extreme eccentricity," but nothing would shake him.[64]

Hoover created a "Lindbergh Squad" to work with the New Jersey State Police and the New York City Police; but he and the national hero never got along. Hoover's relations with the other police agencies involved were scarcely better. In fact, they all distrusted one another, and even kept back evidence at various times. One of Hoover's men, Leon Turrou, would write that his boss thought states' rights were unimportant in the face of a threat to the prestige and honor of the whole nation. "Not since Paris abducted Helen and precipitated the Trojan War has a kidnapping had so many repercussions. This was the crowning touch to an unprecedented era of American lawlessness. It was more than a kidnapping; it was a catastrophe."[65]

For Betty Gow, however, the kidnapping was a lifelong catastrophe. Her journey from Glasgow shopgirl with aspirations for a new life in the United States had, by the time of the kidnapping, already looked more like a dreary, repetitive existence confined to Highfields or North Haven Island. But on the morning of March 2, 1932, she now faced a never-ending ordeal of questions and suspicions about herself and Red Johnson.

Three days after the kidnapping, Johnson was arrested in Hartford, Connecticut, where he had gone to visit his brother. Police questioned him for hours, using third-degree methods, but his alibi for the night of March 1, 1932, held up—even after he was penned up in a small cell and physically abused. He was detained anyway as an illegal alien while deportation proceedings began.[66]

Betty and Red never met again. The case followed him back to Norway, and Betty back to Scotland. Would she have listened to Red Johnson describe what might be with only a little risk—and no harm to the baby? Who left the window open?—for it must have been. Who made the phone call? Who turned on the light in the nursery? Who wiped the room clean of fingerprints?—for none were found. Betty's prospects, meanwhile, had shrunk to the size of a police stenographer's notebook.

MICKEY ROSNER'S GAME

I was promised fame and fortune if I succeeded. I said that if the underworld had this baby it would be back in its crib in 48 hours, but there was no baby to get back. They said they did not have it, and they said not to give the money up.

—MORRIS ROSNER, testimony, 1932

The morning after the kidnapping, Morris "Mickey" Rosner was testifying in a civil suit when he noticed Robert Thayer, a young attorney from Colonel William Donovan's law firm, giving him a high sign. When Rosner finished, the lawyer was waiting outside in the corridor. He had already guessed what Thayer would say. Could he help the Lindberghs? "I told him that I could."[1]

Rosner resembled movie star George Raft, and, like Raft's movie characters, he lived a glamorous but precarious life, somewhere between society and the underworld. He often boasted about his connections. And Donovan, the future head of the World War II supersecret spy agency, the Office of Strategic Services (OSS), occasionally needed help from someone with Rosner's special talents. Mickey had often taken Donovan's protégé, Thayer, a bit of a playboy, on special tours of his favorite underworld hangouts. On one memorable occasion, Thayer got to meet the fabulous Jack "Legs" Diamond, whose exploits were the stuff of fiction—only better. A sometime partner of Al Capone in the rum-running business, Diamond survived a gangland war with "Dutch" Schultz and four assassination attempts before someone sneaked into his rooming house in Albany, New York, late one night and put him out of business permanently. Some said Legs was the model for F. Scott Fitzgerald's *Great Gatsby,* the classic novel of the rise and fall of a gangster with real style. But Legs always protested this reputation; "I'm just a young fellow trying to get ahead."[2]

Remember what you told me once, Thayer said to Rosner that day, "if any friends of mine were ever involved in a kidnapping case," you "would be able to help them out considerably." Sure, sure, Rosner replied, he knew the ropes. He already had the Lindbergh kidnapping all doped out. Somebody knew where that baby was, and Mickey Rosner was the man to get Charlie back and reap the glory.[3]

Let's not raise any false hopes, "Wild Bill" Donovan cautioned. But Rosner was calling his office every hour. Hey, he said, he already had a hot lead on a "certain underworld character" who had mysteriously disappeared. All he needed was $2,500 for "expenses" and an absolute guarantee of no interference from the police or secret service, and he would produce results.[4]

Donovan felt he had to pass on the offer to his close friend, Henry Breckinridge. He couldn't vouch for Rosner's honesty, but he laid out the terms, and Breckinridge could decide for himself what to do. The Lindberghs were "absolutely in the dark," Breckinridge replied, and "they would go to any lengths to get the proper information." Well, just don't make a final decision, Donovan cautioned again, until you talk to Rosner face-to-face.

Accompanied by one of his private eyes, Captain William Galvin, and the required $2,500 "expense" money, Breckinridge arrived in New York at 3 A.M. on March 3. With Thayer at his side, Rosner took the money, peeled off $500, and stuffed half into each of his trouser pockets. There were two men waiting in a back room for this, he said, and then, in a stage whisper, confided that one of them was "Scarface" Al's lieutenant. Yep, he had one of Al Capone's men standing by for instructions. The notorious Capone currently occupied a cell in Chicago's Cook County Jail while awaiting transfer to a federal penitentiary to serve an eleven-year term for income tax evasion.[5]

These guys would be on their way to Chicago that night, Rosner promised. Now, he said, could he and Thayer go back with Breckinridge and Galvin to Hopewell to question the Whateleys and Betty Gow? An excellent idea, agreed Breckinridge.

Later that morning at Highfields, Rosner and Thayer interrogated the servants together and discovered there were many things the servants had not told the police. Thayer sensed they, too, suspected the kidnapping had been an inside job and must, therefore, have involved "some of their friends." All was not sweetness and light, for example, between Olly and Betty.[6]

When they went to the nursery, Betty pointed out to Rosner and Thayer that Charlie must have been pulled out from the top of the crib because the sheets were torn whereas the safety pins remained fastened. The child, she told them, was "not friendly by nature and would cry out if any unfamiliar person approached it or attempted to touch it." She was the only person he would not cry out at—"he would even cry when Mrs. Lindbergh came near him at first." Why did she feel able to confide in Rosner and Thayer this way?

At least three people took part, Betty continued. But how could that be if the baby was so easily alarmed? She did not say. "It would not have been possible for anyone to have taken the child in their arms" and "stepped through the window and descend without outside aid."

What about Red Johnson's telephone call? "She was sure that he could not have had anything to do with the kidnapping since he had called her up from Englewood at nine o'clock in the evening, which would have made it impossible to be at the house at the time the kidnapping had occurred."[7]

Rosner agreed, at least, that the kidnapping had required two men and, quite probably, a woman as well to carry the baby to the car. But it could not have been pulled off without one of the trio having an intimate knowledge of the inside of the house. Betty's statement about Charlie's fears pointed in this direction. And she also told them there was no smell of ether or chloroform in the room, another fact seemingly left out of all the statements, including those of the Lindberghs, to police.

Lindbergh bristled at any suggestion of inside help. Not the slightest suspicion could attach to any of the servants, he insisted. Well, replied Rosner, who was not convinced, there wasn't much more he could do in Hopewell. He noticed the police weren't doing much either: "Some were looking up trees, and some spent most of the time looking at each other." Clues left behind must have been obliterated by this time because of terrible police confusion and blundering. "I thought that it would be best to go back to New York where I could digest the unusual investigation that I had made, and determine for myself the definite procedure for action."[8]

Before going back to New York, however, he wanted to look at the ransom note. When he met Breckinridge, Rosner had asked if there were any particular marks "such as skull and bones, the black hand or similar emblems." Nothing like that, only "some very funny scriptic symbols." Well, he ought to have a copy of the note, then, to take with him. With no apparent regard for the possible consequences, Breckinridge ordered Thayer to make Rosner a copy. "I went up to Colonel

Lindbergh's room," the lawyer later told New Jersey State Police officials, "and made with pencil on a long yellow sheet of paper as exact a copy as I could of the note, attempting wherever possible to make the letters in my copy look like the letters in the original, and in copying the signature I indicated with an arrow the portion that was in colors and where the holes were." He put the signature in a different place, however, so that it would not really be an "exact" copy.[9]

When Rosner's activities became known—and ever since—speculations about exact copies of the note have fueled all sorts of theories about two separate crimes: the kidnapping and the extortion. Copies were said to be available all over New York. But the kidnappers had planned well with the signature-sign. They had created something almost impossible to copy, even if one had the original in hand.

Taking Thayer's drawing with him, Rosner left at once for the city. "I immediately set out to find a man by the name of Owney Madden," Rosner would write in his unpublished memoirs, "a man I have had occasion to know for a great many years, and I consider him very trustworthy, and the proper man to advise me in such a matter." And so Rosner commenced his search, Thayer in tow, for the answer to the crime of the century.[10]

The trustworthy Mr. Madden, sometimes known as "Owney the Killer," was Al Capone's New York counterpart, if not quite so famous as the Chicago crime baron. Madden had come to the United States from England at any early age and lost little time getting acquainted with the justice system of his new country. Thus far he had been arrested forty-four times—an unchallenged record. A rare survivor of the 1930s gangland wars, Madden eventually retired in Hot Springs, Arkansas, where he died a natural death in 1965.

But he was having a little trouble at the moment fending off efforts to send him back to prison for parole violations. In 1932 he owned the city's most celebrated jazz nightspot, the Cotton Club in Harlem. After some difficulty making contact, Rosner was told Madden would be at a fight promoter's office at Fourth and Broadway around midnight. Madden would see him there.

Wait outside in the car, Rosner told Thayer. If I don't come out in an hour and a half, you come up and demand to see me. With that, Rosner disappeared up the darkened stairs. Waiting at a table under a strong light sat Owney Madden. Hollywood could hardly have set the scene any better.[11]

Producing his copy of the ransom note, Mickey anxiously awaited the reaction. Madden studied the yellow sheet for a time. Finally, he looked up. So this is about the Lindbergh case? Rosner nodded. Did

Owney want to help? "Mickey, if that is the situation, you can have my body and soul, and have every aid that I have at my command, and make use of me in any way that you think could help in this picture."[12]

Owney studied the note once more but couldn't come up with a quick answer about who snatched the kid. No mobs he knew used that signature. "He could not tell whether they were Wops or Jews or Irish as he had never seen anything like it before." But he would get working on it. Meanwhile, here were three telephone numbers where he could be reached day and night.[13]

What a coup he had pulled off! He could hardly wait to tell the Lindberghs. Owney knew "all about the kidnapping," Rosner assured Thayer as they sped off back to Hopewell. But certain conditions had to be met before Madden could begin negotiations for the child's return. Waiting to hear what these were, Colonel Breckinridge met them in the Baltimore Lunch in Princeton.[14]

Even at 4 A.M. the "Balt" was filled. Located at the center of town on Nassau Street, the only spot for fifty miles around open twenty-four hours a day, it was a magnet for college students, as well as locals and taxicab drivers—all addicted to the Balt's old-fashioned mugs of coffee. Now there were reporters jammed in as well, scraping chairs, pouring a little something extra out of flasks.

When Thayer and Rosner arrived, they found Colonel Breckinridge waiting in a back booth, unnoticed by the noisy crowd behaving almost like revelers at an all-night party. Sliding into the booth, Rosner gave his report on the meeting with Owney Madden. He was eager to help. But there were conditions. First, no police involvement of any kind; second, Rosner was to have a secure telephone line inside the house (where, it seemed, he would now take up residence until the case was over); and, third, the Lindberghs were to give out a public statement that if Charlie was returned there would be absolutely no attempt to pursue or punish the kidnappers. And there was a fourth condition: Rosner had promised help for Madden with the parole board.[15]

The reporters milling around had finally begun to take notice. Hearst reporter Laura Vitray figured there must be a story brewing there with the coffee. That "good-looking, dark-haired young man" sitting next to you, she told Breckinridge, was obviously not a tennis partner. He's my shadow, Breckinridge joked. How's Mrs. Lindbergh's health? she asked. She ought to know better than to ask. He couldn't say anything about that, Breckinridge tut-tutted. "But why don't you ask my friend here? He is responsible for the information that comes out of the Lindbergh home now."

"Is that so?" Vitray asked. "What is your name?"

Rosner and Breckinridge both laughed. By this time others had gathered around the booth to hear the answer, and someone popped off a flash picture. But all they learned was that the "young gentleman was a new Power who had arisen in the Great Lindbergh Kidnapping Mystery."[16]

Breckinridge's teasing manner aside, Rosner's role was a troubling sign of the times. FBI director Hoover found it incredible that Lindbergh would even contemplate entrusting an underworld figure with a copy of the original ransom note. That he would engage such a man to negotiate with the child's abductors demonstrated what Hoover and many others feared was a national crisis brought even closer to anarchy by the Lindbergh kidnapping. Ransom kidnapping had reached near epidemic proportions in the United States—and was a hotly debated topic in Congress at the very moment the "Little Eaglet" was stolen away. On February 26, 1932, the House Committee on the Judiciary had heard testimony on a bill to make kidnapping a federal crime. "We get reports of conferences that have been held among these criminals," said the witness, former House member Cleveland A. Newton, "where the leaders will say to the younger fellows, 'Do not fool with "whiskers."' That is the way they put it—'Do not fool with "whiskers."' 'Whiskers' means Uncle Sam."[17]

Police officials seldom opened up in public about the link between Prohibition and the rise of gangsterism, and the evolution of kidnapping from criminals preying upon criminals to bolder and bolder assaults on wealthy and prominent citizens. But others were not so inhibited. "We find ourselves revolving in a circle of impotence," Walter Lippmann wrote, "in which we outlaw intolerantly the satisfaction of certain persistent human desires and then tolerate what we have prohibited. Thus we find ourselves accepting in their lawless forms the very things, which in lawful form we repudiate, having in the end to deal not only with all the vices we intended to abolish but with the additional dangers which arise from having turned their exploitation to the underworld."[18]

The opinions of Lippmann, already the most famous public intellectual of his time, carried much weight. Prohibition, he said, fostered an oddly symbiotic relationship with the underworld. Society decried the power criminals wielded over local governments, but tolerated those who supplied the prohibited goods. This desensitized the public, wealthy and poor alike, to the "grosser crimes of the underworld . . . remote from our lives." And the result was to blur "the sharp distinction between civilized society and the underworld."

Popular culture, particularly Hollywood gangster movies, accurately reflected the public's ambivalence. Depression-era Hollywood films such

as *Little Caesar, Scarface,* and *Public Enemy* portrayed low-life characters achieving, at least for a time, the life of penthouses and swimming
pools. And even a measure of respectability. True, the antiheroes all
came to a bad end, but often the retribution was too late. Police cor-
ruption and bungling were epidemic as well in Dashiell Hammett's
cynical best-sellers, *Red Harvest,* featuring the Continental Op, and *The
Maltese Falcon,* with protagonist Sam Spade. There was more than a hint
in all this that gangsters were now the real go-getters in a society bogged
down in Depression. "The *New York Post,*" observes one historian, "recognized the bent success ethic of the gangster, dubbing *Little Caesar* 'an
Horatio Alger tale transferred to the underworld.'"[19]

Film images of modern-day gangsters crossing the boundary into
high society, decked out in tuxedos and furs, and propelled on their
way by huge profits from bootlegging, were one thing. But the mundane
reality of criminal organizations mirroring the activities and managerial
skills of legitimate enterprise was a truer picture of the era. Al Capone
was never convicted for any of the murders his organization carried out
in plain sight on Chicago's streets, but for income tax evasion—like any
other misbehaving businessman. That was a remarkable commentary
on local law enforcement, and what Lippmann had rightly feared had
been wrought by Prohibition's double standard. At Al Capone's trial,
Edward G. Robinson, who portrayed a Capone-like mobster in *Little
Caesar,* showed up as a spectator. He was there, he quipped, "to give
Snorky a few pointers on how a real gangster should act."[20]

There were some generally held ideas about how the snatch racket
had evolved into a "business" specialty of the underworld. Considered
an Italian specialty, ransom notes had taken on many aspects of normal
business letters. The first Lindbergh note, for example, began "Dear
Sir," a typical business salutation. It specified the price and said instructions would be forthcoming about where "to deliver the money." Notes
back to the kidnapper from a Lindbergh negotiator, moreover, would talk
about the "goods" and the "package," along with other commonly used
business expressions. Dealing with the underworld now often seemed
the best and, perhaps, the only way of getting a loved one back. Thus
the Mickey Rosner types were thought to be indispensable.

Lindbergh had already experienced a previous extortion demand. In
April 1929, Constance Morrow, Anne's younger sister, a student at the
Milton Academy in Dedham, Massachusetts, had received a letter demanding $50,000. Her father had plenty of money it said; but if he tried
to set a trap, the same thing would happen to her as had happened to
other girls recently. (Two girls had disappeared, and one of their bodies

had been found in the Connecticut River.) The letter was regarded as a crank threat until precise instructions for delivering the money arrived in a second note. No one doubted its seriousness then. Constance was spirited away to North Haven Island by Lindbergh, and police watched as her stand-in dropped a package containing no money behind a wall— and hurried away, half running, never looking back.[21]

But no one approached the wall. Police continued to watch the next day. Two cars passed the site slowly but neither stopped. The stand-in had acted her part extremely well, but it was impossible to tell if the extortionist recognized she was not Constance Morrow, and that a clever trap had been set.

While it was highly unlikely that the threat to his sister-in-law and the kidnapping of his son were at all related, Lindbergh could not eliminate the possibility. Charlie's abductors might well have known something about the earlier incident—and how the Morrow family had reacted. Was it just a coincidence that the would-be extortionist and the kidnappers had both asked for $50,000? If some person or persons had it in mind that the Morrow wealth could be "tapped," they might also have decided that just making threats was not enough—something much more risky had to be undertaken. And did they determine that was the only way to persuade the family, this time, not to bring in the police?

Thus, Rosner's promise to enlist Owney Madden, even if gangland had nothing directly to do with the kidnapping, would seem to offer a way to reassure the "real" kidnappers, whoever they were, that the Lindberghs were ready to deal on those terms.

After a long conference, which included a very unhappy Colonel Norman Schwarzkopf, Lindbergh made the decision to comply with Owney Madden's conditions. Breckinridge gave the required statement to startled reporters the afternoon of March 4, 1932.[22]

> Mrs. Lindbergh and I desire to make a personal contact with the kidnap[p]ers of our child.
>
> Our only interest is in his immediate and safe return and we feel certain that the kidnap[p]ers will realize that this interest is strong enough to justify them in having complete confidence and trust in any promises that we may make in connection with his return.
>
> We urge those who have the child to select any representatives of ours who will be suitable to them at any time and at any place they may designate.
>
> If this is accepted, we promise that we will keep whatever arrangements that may be made by the representative

and ours strictly confidential and we further pledge ourselves
that we will not try to injure in any way those connected with
the return of the child.[23]

Breckinridge—the very model of an American aristocrat—presented the
statement as nothing less than a proposed contract between gentlemen
of roughly equal stature. "We are counting upon the personal statement
to create a feeling of confidence in the minds of the persons who now
have the baby," he said, "so they will feel free to establish a contact with
us. Colonel Lindbergh is not afraid. Certainly the kidnap[p]ers cannot
believe he would trifle with them in a matter of such extreme importance to him. *He will meet them anywhere, under any conditions they may
wish to lay down, even going into the underworld itself, to meet the men
who have his baby and arrange for his return.*"[24]

New Jersey governor A. Harry Moore didn't like what he was hearing. And he was not alone. "No one can give a pass to break the law," he
thundered. "A law is a law." But in his very next words, he backed down
at least partway. "Only a grand jury by refusing to indict, can grant
immunity." A reporter asked about rumors the Lindberghs were making
arrangements with underworld go-betweens? Moore did not know anything about that, he claimed. All he could say was that crime experts he
had consulted had provided some "very good suggestions" for solving
the case.[25]

One of them was a famous local detective, Ellis Parker, known as
the Sherlock Holmes of Burlington County. He had even offered to take
charge of the investigation. Hopped-up drug fiends, he told reporters,
were the most likely suspects. "Once those dope fiends get loaded up,
they'll do anything—they'll try to lift a locomotive off a track." And they
were probably still in the area somewhere. "People carrying a baby
around can't stay free too long. After they've been arrested, I think
shooting's too good for them."[26]

State police officials actually did send for Parker the first night of
the kidnapping but dismissed him after a few words. His reputation for
dealing with suspects and getting confessions *his* way might recom-
mend him to certain people—but not to the Lindberghs, nor even to
Colonel Schwarzkopf, at least while there was a chance the child might
still be alive. Angry at being toyed with, Parker would go ahead with his
private investigation, and, as we shall see, kept Moore and his successor,
Harold G. Hoffman, interested in his progress. In Hoffman's case, Parker
made too much of an impression. But that was all in the future. Parker's
ambition to solve the case, and burning hatred for Schwarzkopf, knew
no limits—and resulted in a terrible fall from grace.[27]

Police officials from all over feared the Lindbergh case might tip the balance in favor of legitimizing private dealings with the under-world—and usher in a fateful twilight era in the nation's history. Prohibition and the Great Depression had all but undermined confidence in fundamental institutions; and now even in Lindbergh, as the last hero of sturdy pioneer values and self-confidence from a bygone time. "The Old World is used to shocks," editorialized the London tabloid *Daily Mirror,* "but it will sit up and gasp at this. The crime illustrates that gangdom in the United States is now virtually in control."[28]

In a category by himself, German filmmaker Fritz Lang's 1931 *M* had the look of a surreal documentary—made before the fact—about the Lindbergh kidnapping. It almost predicted Lindbergh's decision to summon Mickey Rosner, to send him as an emissary to Owney Madden, to take counsel with the underworld when police authority failed to protect the citizenry. Lang set the film in a nervous Berlin during the last years before Hitler came to power; in Lang's Germany, as in the United States, many believed a fundamental shift in the balance of forces had given unprecedented power to ruthless men and organized crime. *M* suggested as well as that when the police failed, the rulers of organized crime would seek to ferret out vicious criminals—such as those who would steal a child—simply to protect their "business" interests. Here again, the movie imitated life.

In *M* the Berlin police are stymied by a child abductor and killer who leaves no fingerprints, witnesses, or any other clues. The film opens with the beleaguered police chief trying to justify himself to the public but he succeeds only in showing how powerless he and his men are to find the murderer: "The police have followed up . . . more than fifteen hundred clues in this case. . . . We have put all our men onto it to systematically comb all the areas around the town. . . . Every thicket, every piece of undergrowth, every clearing is carefully examined. . . . The best trackers have been put onto the weak scents we have found . . . without any result."[29]

Finally, the underground, with its network of thieves, safebreakers, con men, phony beggars and blind men, meet in appropriately half-lit cellars to take up the challenge—out of the instinct for survival. Their leader arrives in a chalk-stripe suit, dark tie, and black leather gloves. He raps the meeting to order: "We all know why we are here. Someone who is not a member of the Union is messing up our affairs. The new measures taken by the police, the daily raids in our areas to find this child murderer, interfere with our business activities in a quite unbearable way. . . . This state of affairs must not be allowed to continue. We'll have to put things right again or we'll be destroyed."[30]

When M is apprehended, the underground leader acts as prosecutor at his "trial." "We must put him down like a mad dog!" screams a prostitute, but the leader halts the outcry: "Everything will be done according to the rule of law." Nevertheless, M's "defense attorney" cannot prevent the assembled group from surging toward the murderer to take the "law" into their own hands—interrupted at the very last minute by the appearance of the police.

M was predictive not simply of the Lindbergh crime's aftermath but of countries balanced on the knife-edge.

While police stood around waiting for Lindbergh's permission to question the servants, and were shut out of the "inner circle," Mickey Rosner enjoyed privileged access to a special phone line inside the house. As Breckinridge had said in a joking manner, Rosner had become the link to the outside world. Using this privilege, Rosner established contact with yet another New York operator, the bootlegger Salvatore "Salvy" Spitale. "If I was as successful with Spitale as I was with Madden," Mickey told himself, "I would pretty well cover any Italian mobs if they had anything to do with the kidnapping."[31]

Even as he thought about how well things were lining up, Lindbergh brought him a new ransom note he himself had plucked out of the mound of mail that had arrived that morning. Postmarked "Brooklyn, N.Y. 2, Mar 4, 9PM," it was addressed to "Mr. Col. Lindbergh Hopewell N.J." The form of address, using both titles—that is, "Mr. Col."—was typically German, and it didn't read much like a mob message:

> Dear Sir. We have warned you not[e?] to make
> anyding Public also notify the Police
> now you have to take the consequence. ths
> means we will hold the baby until everything
> is quiet. We can note make any appointment
> just now. We know very well what it
> means to us. It is rely necessary to
> make a world affair out off this, or to
> get your baby back as soon as possible
> to settle those affair in a quick way
> will better for both seit [side?]. Don't be
> afraid about the baby two ladys
> keeping care of it day and night.
> She also will feed him
> according to the diet. (Symbol)
> Singtuere on
> all letters.

We are interested to send him back in
gut health. ouer ransom was made aus
for 50000 $ but now we have to take
another person to it and probable have
to keep the baby for a longer time as we
expected. So the amount will be 70,000 $
20.000 in 50 $ bills 25.000 $ in 20 $ bills
15000 $ in 10 $ bills and 10.000 in 5 $ bills.
dont mark any bills. or tacke them
from one serial nonmer. We will
inform you latter were to deliver hte
mony. but we willn note do so
untilk the Police is out of ths case
and the Pappers are quiet.
    The Kidnaping was preparet
    for years. so we are preparet
for everyding.[32]

When Lindbergh passed the note around to various people, Rosner "turned very white and started trembling all over." One can imagine several reasons why—but the most reasonable answer is that he suddenly saw glory slipping away. He pleaded with Lindbergh not to give the note to the state police. Instead, he said, he should take it at once to Colonel Breckinridge, who had gone back to New York. Lindbergh agreed, and Rosner left—escorted by a phalanx of state troopers "riding shotgun."

Meanwhile, Breckinridge was closeted with Owney Madden in the Park Avenue office of a famous New York defense attorney, Dudley Field Malone. Rosner now had an additional reason to be concerned, as Malone also claimed to have good contacts. Rosner liked it even less when Madden took charge. After reading the note, Madden folded it up and returned it to Breckinridge, "Please in the name of God, if ever another note comes in, don't show it to me, don't show it to Malone, don't show it to Mickey, don't show it to anybody in the world; try to follow the advice that is given you in this letter because these ruthless bastards are about to take you on a series of increases in ransom and get to a point where nobody would be able to live up to them."[33]

What was next? Were Madden and Malone planning a squeeze play to eliminate Rosner from the game? Obviously, he would have to keep a close eye on their doings, Rosner thought to himself as he left Malone's office for a date with Spitale. If Madden caught Rosner two-timing him, on the other hand, well, that might not be so good either. Better go carefully here. But Mickey Rosner was never one to underplay his hand, nor doubt his abilities as an escape artist.

He met Spitale and his confederate, Irving Bitz, at the Cadillac restaurant, on Broadway, between Forty-third and Forty-fourth Streets. "I ha[ve] to be very careful with my next move," he warned himself, as he told them about Madden's involvement. But Spitale and Bitz were all smiles. Don't worry, said Spitale, "on their words of honor," they were very friendly with Madden.

Relieved, Rosner produced his copy of the first ransom note and then the original of the second note, which he had apparently gotten back from Breckinridge for the purpose of this rendezvous. What did they make of them? Like Madden, Spitale had no idea, but if they could find out, the Lindberghs would never know the ransom was paid because *they* would pay it out of their own pockets.

> Mickey, this search for the Lindbergh baby is costing the "mobs" throughout the country hundreds of thousands of dollars. Police are stopping every vehicle on every road in the country, and searching them very thoroughly, and by doing so they are intercepting truckloads of booze which are being transported from state to state, and to be very truthful, the joke is on us. Only last night we lost two truckloads of liquor on the highways which resulted in a net cost to us of $30,000.00, so you readily see that it would be better for us to pay the ransom and to continue doing our business as in the past.[34]

Could Rosner believe his ears? Were Salvy Spitale and Irving Bitz really about to put up the mob's money (or theirs) to retrieve little Charlie? The flip side of the offer was that Rosner realized "that no Regular Organized Mob had anything to do with the kidnapping," because anyone could have predicted just how much it was costing in lost business and would have returned the child by now. But maybe they could help in the search anyway. Rosner certainly hoped so. He phoned Breckinridge for instructions. The colonel welcomed their aid. He would send his chauffeur to the restaurant, he said, to bring the three of them to F. D. Bartow's home on the Upper East Side at 57 East Sixty-sixth Street. Breckinridge would meet them there.[35]

F. D. Bartow was a J. P. Morgan partner, just like Dwight Morrow. Working fast, Bartow had already assembled the $70,000 the kidnapper demanded, and had it ready to send down to Hopewell, in exactly the denominations the kidnapper specified, and not marked or from a single serial series. Now he greeted Spitale and Bitz like long-lost friends. "Mr. Bartow rose from his chair, shook Spitale and Bitz by the hand and stated that it was more than a pleasure to meet them, in fact he considered it a privilege to shake the hand of two men whom the world held out in a different light than he, and promised that these men if they carried out their end of the job as they promised they would, that he hoped some day that he would be able to personally show his appreciation." Breckinridge was equally effusive, and they all sat down as good friends would. "I don't know how tired you fellows are," Bartow enthused, "but I do know that it has been days and nights since my friend Colonel Breckinridge and Rosner have had any sleep at all, or even food, so I insist that all of you join me in some sandwiches and drinks."[36]

After food and drink, Bartow suggested they all go down to Hopewell together, so that Colonel Lindbergh could also express his appreciation. That was too much for Rosner. He could see bad things ahead for his scheme. He was supposed to be the contact man, and what would Owney Madden think of this? Not a good idea. But there was no stopping the impetuous banker, nothing he could say to dampen Bartow's enthusiasm for a ride with the "boys" to deliver the money to Highfields. Escorted by New Jersey state troopers, a three-car caravan set off for the Lindbergh estate. Bartow even insisted Spitale and Bitz ride with him. He would not miss their company, he told Rosner, "for anything in the world."

Along the way, the banker kept asking his companions to explain almost every other word they uttered in gangland-ese. At one point Bitz expressed concern that he was riding in a car with all that money and no gun for protection. Why don't you carry one? Bartow asked. "I am not allowed to carry a gun, because I have a 'record.'" Please explain what a "record" is, Bartow then asked. Someone who has been in jail has a record, Bitz replied. Unfazed by this revelation, Bartow continued to delight in his companions until the car turned into the Lindberghs' lane.[37]

Once they arrived at Highfields, Bartow introduced his new friends to Lindbergh, who joined in yet another round of high praise for their unselfish offer to do all that was possible to bring the baby home. Brimming with pride, Spitale declared that "as far as he and Bitz were concerned, they did not care what sacrifices they had to make, in order to make it known to these abductors that they were in the case, and were willing to act as intermediaries." Then he suggested that Lindbergh make their offer known to the newspapers.[38]

This feigned altruism infuriated Rosner. He knew they were after immunity from prosecutions—just as Madden had wanted help with the parole board. He also knew Madden would be irate when he heard about their pilgrimage. But the idea of a new press release, to be signed by both the colonel and Anne, had taken hold, and nothing could be done except go along. Besides, reasoned Rosner, maybe the abductors would accept them as official go-betweens, "especially if they should happen to be Italians." He could still claim a good share of the glory if they did.[39]

The notice designating Spitale and Bitz as official intermediaries appeared in newspapers on Sunday, March 6. The *New York Times* headline declared: "LINDBERGHS IN MESSAGE TO ABDUCTORS NAME TWO MEN TO REPRESENT THEM IN NEGOTIATIONS FOR RETURN OF BABY." The notice itself read: "If the kidnappers of our child are unwilling to deal directly, we fully authorize "Salvy" Spitale and Irving Bitz to act as our go-betweens. We will also follow any other method suggested by the kidnappers that we can be sure will bring the return of the child."

Reactions to this latest Lindbergh "shock" brought the first criticism of the family's response to the crisis, although much of it was muted and indirect. Someone suggested that the warden of the famous Sing Sing Prison in New York, Lewis E. Lawes, would be better suited to the job. After all, he probably knew many—if not more—of the same underworld figures and could offer the same promise of immunity. Asked if he would serve, he said, "Certainly, I would. Anybody would." Lawes pointed out, however, that he and his inmates, who were following the case with great interest, doubted if there were any "professionals" involved. Professionals would have asked for a lot more money, and, besides, "from their viewpoint, it hurts everybody and everything."[40]

Princeton president John Grier Hibben and his wife announced, nevertheless, that they would be willing to entertain the two "underworld characters" in their home. "I'll be delighted if they would come," said Mrs. Hibben. "Who wouldn't do anything in his power to help the Lindberghs?" Would she be afraid? "I should say not," she snapped. "I'm sure I wouldn't be."[41]

Anne recorded her quite remarkable reactions to the entrance of the "underworld characters" onto the scene. "Charles is buoyant and had good rest last night. I met the two underworld kings last night. Charles, Col. Henry, and I feel convinced they are sincere and will help us. Isn't it strange, they showed more sincerity in their sympathy than a lot of politicians who've been here." Charles was indeed buoyant about the chances of getting his son back unharmed, and, recorded Robert Thayer, commenced doing "practical jokes all evening."[42]

Knights-errant Spitale and Bitz returned to New York and did—nothing. Scarcely twenty-four hours after they received the Lindbergh "commission," Spitale was spotted at Madison Square Garden taking in a hockey game. A reporter asked him what he was doing in regard to the Lindbergh case. "Well," he mused, "it's this way. . . . If professionals have got a hold of him they know where to get in touch with me in five minutes, day or night, rain or shine. But I'm no cop, see? Now get me straight; I'm no cop; I don't look in cellars."

He thought some more and then went on. "I'm kinda sorry I got mixed up in this thing. The papers are printing pictures of my kids and my family, and my policy of keeping out of the papers has been knocked for a row of milk bottles. *Why listen, fella, I'm up in the news bigger'n the Shanghai War, or wherever it's goin' on.*"[43]

Asked later what help he had rendered, besides making himself visible at the fights, Spitale replied indignantly, "They knew where my address was; they could come in contact with me. I couldn't go and approach five thousand people." A few days after that, however, Spitale's and Bitz's connection with the Lindbergh case played the major role in having a bootlegging charge dismissed in court.[44]

Rosner's game was about to take several unexpected twists. He had set up "headquarters" at Highfields, making hourly phone calls to Madden and others, announcing that he was "X," and asking if there were any messages for him. He was also screening calls, telling anyone who asked for Colonel Lindbergh that he was Lindbergh's secretary, or that he was Colonel Breckinridge, or even that he was Mrs. Morrow's secretary. His presence in the inner circle of advisers, second only to Breckinridge, infuriated state police officials. Rosner would have to trip himself up before things changed in the Lindbergh house.

On March 6 he selected a telegram from the stack of messages:

> MRS. ANNE LINDBERGH
> HOPEWELL, NEW JERSEY
> COMMUNICATE WITH ME AT ONCE REGARDING YOUR BOY'S WHERE-
> ABOUTS.
> FOR FULL PARTICULARS TELEPHONE HARLEM ———
> REVEREND [PETER BIRRITELLA]

Rosner gave the telegram to Breckinridge, saying it looked as if there might be something to it. There had been a nationwide appeal to ministers the night before; perhaps someone had responded. But why this particular telegram? Rosner took note that the reverend was an Italian. (Italians were always favorite suspects in a kidnapping.) Could that fact have prompted Rosner to urge responding to the message?

For days the house had been inundated with calls from spiritualists and messengers from God. (Someone identified only as 89.118 told

Lindbergh to take a rooster up in an airplane and watch carefully which direction he crowed. After that the colonel should land, take the rooster in a truck, and drive in that direction. When the rooster crowed again, that would be the spot where Charlie could be found.)[45] Clairvoyants from all corners of the United States had rushed to the scene; a few had even gained entrance to Highfields, complete with paraphernalia. Communications from the spirit world about the case were in great supply—Schwarzkopf, for example, kept a whole file of séance revelations in his desk—for there was always the chance such "messengers" had real connections with the crime.

After a phone call to the Harlem number by Rosner, the reverend agreed to come out on the first train.

When Breckinridge and Rosner met Birritella at the Princeton Junction train station, the reverend had in tow his medium, Mary Cerrita, "a plumply pretty" young woman with "small feet and hands, and smiling eyes that glow[ed] darkly." Cerrita announced that she wished to be taken to the Lindbergh house and be seated in the nursery. Breckinridge nixed that idea and took them to a room at the Princeton Inn.[46]

Reverend Birritella began the proceedings by reading a chapter from the Bible, recited the Lord's Prayer, and finally undertook to put Cerrita into a trance. As he did this, with much moaning and groaning, Breckinridge lay on the bed, his face buried in a pillow to keep from laughing out loud. The spirits told Cerrita that the baby was in a house only a few miles from Highfields, watched over by an old woman. Then she spoke of a tree on the estate. There really was such a tree, but this might have been a good guess on her part. Still, it got Breckinridge to pay more attention. She also said that there were too many police around, too many reporters, for the abductors to make contact. Breckinridge listened carefully because this comment sounded like the complaints in the second ransom note.[47]

Breckinridge began questioning Cerrita about details. Rattled a bit, she asked in reply if "the light had broken through;" had he received any message? Breckinridge decided to conceal knowledge of the second note. When might they receive some word about the baby? he asked.

Within two weeks, intoned Cerrita.

"Two weeks will be too late," Breckinridge exploded. "There are two things that will be of no use. One is to send a live baby to a dead mother, the second is to send a dead baby to a live mother."

"Jesus Christ," wailed a suddenly awakened Cerrita, "we are innocent people, know nothing of the baby, and can only tell you what the spirits tell us."

"Well," said Breckinridge, "you better tell the spirits to hurry up."

"We can't give orders to the spirits. We can only tell what the spirits tell us. But we might pray and when we pray hard enough the light may break through." Cerrita was searching for something to calm Breckinridge. "Perhaps by next Saturday."[48]

"That is too late, the mother may be dead."

Rosner meanwhile was talking with Peter Birritella, who tried to take over for Cerrita, suggesting that he *also* had psychic powers. After a few moments of "silent communication" with another spirit guide, Birritella promised they would receive word without question "by the very next morning." With this, the séance was over.

Rosner and Breckinridge offered to buy the couple dinner, but they wanted to get back. "I then took them to the Princeton railroad station," Breckinridge later wrote. "Birritella asked if his tickets were good from that station. I said, 'No, but they are good from Princeton Junction.' He said, '*They bought us* round trip tickets to Princeton Junction.'" Breckinridge didn't think too much about that at first and offered to give them the small additional fare. Birritella responded that he was not interested in material things, but repeated, "*they bought us* round trip tickets to Princeton Junction."[49]

However, Breckinridge thought a great deal about what they had said when at 1 P.M. the next day a letter arrived addressed to "Mr. Co. Henry L. Breckenridge, 25 Broadway, N.Y." The message was in two parts. It began: "Please handel inclosed letter to Col. Lindbergh. It is in Mr. Lindberg interest not to notify the Police." The letter for Lindbergh asked if he had received the mail sent from Brooklyn on March 4—thus identifying the second ransom note. "We know Police interfere with your privatemail, how can we come to any arrangements this way. In the future we will send ouer letters to Mr. Breckenbridge at 25 Broadway. We belive Polise captured our letter and did not forwardit to you."[50]

Here were three points that echoed the Birritella-Cerrita performance in Princeton. First, the letter writer had sent his message the next day, as Birritella had said would happen; second, it came to 25 Broadway, where Cerrita had said Breckinridge should be; and third, Breckinridge is referred to as Breckenbridge in the letter to Lindbergh, as Cerrita had called him during the séance. The letter also tried to reassure the Lindbergh family, moreover, about the health of the baby, perhaps a response to Breckinridge's dire warnings about Anne's perilous health. "There is no worry about the Boy. He is very well and will be feed according to the diet. Best dank for Information about it. We are interested to send your Boy back in gud Health." The kidnappers even said that they had delayed carrying out the kidnapping for a year, because "we was afraid the boy would not be strong enough." This double emphasis on the baby's health to assuage fears of the family made an even stronger case that Birritella and Cerrita were involved, at least to the extent of acting as messengers.

To make sure that the light had finally come through, the author of the letter asked that Lindbergh put a short notice in the *New York American* indicating it had been received. But it cautioned that there would be no further communications until the police were out of the case and the newspapers quiet.

The remainder of note number three reiterated the demand made in the previous communication, raising the sum to $70,000, and specifying the same denominations.

Rosner placed the required notice in the *New York American*. It ran on March 8 and 9, and read: "Letter received at new address. Will follow your instructions. I also received your letter mailed to me March 4, and was ready since then. Please hurry on account of mother. Address me to the address you mention in your letter. Father."

A Treasury agent named Frank Wilson later discovered that Peter Birritella had opened a savings account on March 7, the day after his trip to Princeton, with a $35 deposit. Later on, small deposits were added to this account, which, however, never went above a total of $250. Another coincidence? Wilson did not think so and urged Schwarzkopf to conduct a full investigation of Birritella and Cerrita—and Peter's brother, John. The two made their living running a neat con game with spiritualism and faith healing. Sometimes Mary, soon to be Peter's wife, would send a "client" to Peter for further "counseling," which, with her approval, also included sexual therapy. The usual take per day was hardly more than $5 or $10, so a $35 fee (plus tickets) would constitute an average week's work.[51]

Rosner also investigated the couple. He used Owney Madden, and Spitale and Bitz, as his investigators. "One day," Mary would tell a reporter, "Mickey and Mr. Madden called for Peter and me in a big car, and took us out to Hopewell to see if we could find the little house. . . . We drove and drove and drove, but of course it didn't do any good."[52]

Rosner was about to be edged out of all the negotiations, however.

Unknown to Rosner, yet another underworld figure, Al Capone himself, had been in touch with Lindbergh to volunteer his services—if he could be sprung from Cook County jail. "It's the most outrageous thing I have ever heard of," Capone declared from his cell, offering $10,000 for information. He even sent his bodyguard, Frankie Rio, to Hopewell with a message for the Lindberghs. "I know a lot of people who might be valuable in finding the child," the message read. "There's nothing I can do here behind the bars, but I'm pretty sure there would be if I could get out for a while."[53]

Trying to get publicity for his offer, Capone then got word to Arthur Brisbane, a famous Hearst columnist, who was allowed to interview him in the jail. Brisbane's interview made headlines across the nation: Capone thought he knew who did it! A former member of his own gang, Bob Conroy. He would send his brother Mitzi as a hostage for his return to jail. "There isn't a mob that wouldn't trust me to pay that money, if the relations of the kidnapped child wanted me to pay it, and there isn't anybody would think I would tell where I got the child or who had it."[54]

At first blush, Capone's offer seemed to fit all the requirements set out in the ransom notes. Lindbergh decided to call "his friend" Ogden Mills, secretary of the treasury, for advice. That brought treasury agents, who had spent so much of their time over the past years trying to nail Capone, rushing to Hopewell to put an end to all such talk of letting their man loose, even for a day, even for an hour. "Capone doesn't know who has the child, Colonel Lindbergh," Agent Elmer Irey urged. "He is simply trying to get out of jail."[55]

Whether he also thought the Capone offer was bogus, or out of civic duty, Lindbergh responded bravely, "Mr. Irey, I wouldn't ask for Capone's release if—even if it would save a life." If Capone had not actually been convicted and in jail at the time, there is no reason to think that Lindbergh would not have dealt with him as he was already doing with Madden and company. In fact, Lindbergh had previously spent three hours with Spitale and Bitz discussing Capone's price for helping to recover Charlie. They did not tell Lindbergh that Capone had the child or even that he knew of the Little Eaglet's whereabouts. But his power was so great, they said, that "he would find [Charlie] if he once started to put his forces into action." He would even pay the ransom himself—but all this was contingent upon a full pardon and no time in jail.[56]

Frank Wilson in particular feared that Lindbergh would deal with Capone, because even he suspected that Capone might have engineered the kidnapping to bring pressure on the government. "Knowing that the Cook County jail was then a kind of underworld Chess & Rummy Club, I arranged for one of my gangster informers in Chicago to worm his way in and talk to Al. Within twenty-four hours he had seen Capone and was on the wire, saying 'No dice. The big fellow knows nothing about it.' I knew that information was good as gold."[57]

J. Edgar Hoover then received a message from a local attorney, William Leahy, requesting a meeting. Leahy denied he represented Al

Capone, but said he had agreed to forward a message. If Capone were released to work on the Lindbergh kidnapping, and recovered the child, he would be willing to drop his appeal in the tax evasion case, provided the feds would grant him parole after serving one-third of his sentence.[58]

Hoover took the proposal to the attorney general, after giving Leahy notice that he did not see any way the Capone offer could be taken up. And when he saw the attorney general, Hoover was told that "publicly the Department could not announce that it would not listen to any of the Capone suggestions or propositions because of the hysteria that existed at the present time for the recovery of the child, but that no one could give serious consideration to the proposition of releasing Capone, that he would have to go to jail and be treated as anyone else would be treated."

Nervousness about the impact of the Lindbergh case on respect for law and order is more than subliminal in this exchange—it's right in the open. Ever since publication of Brisbane's interview with Al Capone, the nation revealed itself as deeply divided on the issue. Connecticut senator Hiram Bingham minced no words. The kidnapping of the nation's most celebrated baby, he said, was a "colossal plot to get the country's most celebrated criminal, Alphonse Capone, out of jail in Chicago."[59]

Elements of the Capone offer, garbled in some respects, made it to the tabloid newspapers. The *Daily Mirror* in New York published a headline story on March 9 to the effect that Capone agents had kidnapped the child in a desperate bid to free their chief, and, more ominous, that Spitale and Bitz had not been selected by Rosner but were also Capone front men: "The appointment by Col. Lindbergh of 'Salvy' Spitale and Irving Bitz, New York racketeers, to act as go-betweens in eventual negotiations for recovery of the child was seen as the first of a long series of slowly developing negotiations to lead up to the final statement of terms proposed by the 'invisible government' of the country to the visible one: *'Give us Capone and take the child.'*"[60]

Colonel Schwarzkopf, despite his intense admiration for Charles Lindbergh, deeply resented his exclusion from the inner circle negotiating with the underworld for the baby's return. Finally, on March 22 he went to New Jersey's attorney general to discuss the situation. What action should he take, he asked, "with regard to Colonel Breckinridge, Mrs. Breckinridge, Morris Rosner, Robert Thayer, Mr. Fogarty [one of Breckinridge's private eyes], and anyone else who had been in conference with the members of the household?" Specifically, Schwarzkopf wanted advice "as to who should be held on charges of conspiracy, compounding a felony or anything else of this kind in case the payment of the ransom was negotiated and the child returned." Hardly wishing to challenge Lindbergh, the attorney general only promised to "look this matter up."[61]

Soon enough, however, Mickey Rosner's game would be played out. First, on March 8, Owney Madden paid a visit to Hopewell, and there was a conference to which Rosner was not invited. The next day, Rosner returned from New York and talked briefly about developments in the case before going off to bed. At about 10 A.M., Colonel Breckinridge rushed into his room. He wanted, he said, to introduce Rosner "to a gentleman who is a professor in a university in New York City." Breckinridge and Lindbergh had been in conference with the professor "almost all night, which was both interesting and profitable." It appeared that this professor had asked his pupils to write essays on the Lindbergh case, and, as a result, a reporter for the *Bronx Home News* had asked to interview him. In the course of the interview, the professor had offered $1,000 of his own money, in addition to the ransom demanded, if the kidnappers would return the baby through him. He had put that in a letter to the paper and had "obtained some very important information which he [Breckinridge] and Col. Lindbergh hoped would help to solve the case."[62]

Breckinridge introduced the professor to Rosner as "Dr. Stice." "I was more than certain," wrote Rosner later, "that the name of Dr. Stice was only a pseudo nym [*sic*]. I thought that I had made him understand it when I looked him square in the face and held onto his hand, when he in turn looked quickly away and I will never forget that he never looked at me again, nor I at him. I cannot explain the feeling that came over me as I saw this professor face to face."

Well, it was really not that difficult to explain. Rosner's game was all but over. In a futile attempt to regain his position in the Lindbergh hierarchy, he had done some very foolish things. He had rallied Spitale and Bitz to return to Hopewell to present Lindbergh with a proposal to contact Capone directly—which set off the furor reported in the *Daily Mirror*. Rosner explained to Robert Thayer that he had "[gotten] them to do this as an ace in the hole if the kidnappers refused to continue negotiations as a result of the mistake caused by Colonel Breckinridge's refusal to take Rosner into his confidence about Dr. Stice."[63]

Rosner had figured out what cheered Breckinridge and Lindbergh— a fourth note from the kidnappers that this Dr. Stice knew about somehow. Evidently, Rosner was to be kept in the dark about details. Breckinridge's seeming elation at having heard Dr. Stice's presentation sent

Rosner into a tailspin. Desperate at being left out at the payoff, Rosner told reporters on March 12 that he had "definite knowledge that the baby was safe and well and would be returned to his parents in a few days."[64]

Lindbergh was furious. Rosner tried to explain that he had been misquoted, when all he said was that they all *hoped* the baby was safe. But Robert Thayer saw exactly what had happened: "I told [Rosner] frankly that his remarks and actions throughout the case and especially lately had convinced me that he was trying to negotiate things in such a way that he would get personal credit for the return of the child." It is surprising that Thayer had not seen that from the beginning—at least from the time that the two of them had interrogated the servants at Highfields.

There was an ironic coda to Mickey Rosner's game. Months later a newspaper, the *Jersey Journal,* printed a series of articles on the case written by Jersey City police inspector Harry Walsh. According to the story, Colonel Breckinridge had phoned Hoover and asked him to send the "best informer at his command" to the Lindberghs. "The following morning one Morris Rosner, a known character in police circles . . . arrived." Hoover issued a public statement calling the story bogus, and declaring that his contacts with the case had been exclusively through Colonel Schwarzkopf. Walsh responded by saying that he had written only what he knew about from his official contacts. "Reading Mr. Hoover's statement does not change my recollection of the facts." Hoover was truly incensed by Walsh's know-it-all sneer. "There is no doubt in my mind now," he scrawled across his agent's report on the story, "that Walsh *deliberately* lied in the first instance."[65]

These exchanges were an omen of antagonisms during the ensuing investigation. From the near euphoric atmosphere in the Lindbergh house, on the other hand, Mickey Rosner knew that they all thought the professor would succeed where he had failed.

4 MAN OF MYSTERY

So casually that none of us realized then its terrific portent, did Doctor John F. Condon, educator, retire from the Lindbergh case to be replaced by the "Man of Mystery"—Jafsie.

—JOHN F. CONDON

At the time of the kidnapping, Dr. John Francis Condon was a seventy-one-year-old semiretired educator who had lived all his life in the Bronx, the "most beautiful borough in the world." A familiar figure striding down the streets of his neighborhood in a three-piece black suit and derby, Condon would stop passersby to ask them if they knew the answer to his latest puzzle. He loved mathematical mysteries. An elementary school principal at P.S. #12, for nearly three decades, Condon organized a school fife-and-drum corps and marched at their head whenever there was a parade in the Bronx.

Leading parades was something of a sacrament for Condon. Outraged by the decision of Bronx authorities to cancel a children's parade in 1914 because of the outbreak of World War I, he organized his own parade to Pelham Bay Park. He even had a part in designing the banner that would be carried aloft and fly over the borough offices as the Bronx flag—the first in any of the New York boroughs.[1]

After retiring from P.S. #12, he did not slow down. He lectured at Fordham University and the College of New Rochelle and published a steady stream of patriotic poems and essays under various pseudonyms in a local newspaper, the *Bronx Home News*. His alter egos included L. O. Nestar, P. A. Triot, and J. U. Stice, Parson Weems–style writers who celebrated the heroic deeds of Washington and Lincoln, and who remembered "The Martyrs Who Died on the *Maine*." Condon chronicled

American heroism in voluminous scrapbooks he was happy to show visitors—along with clippings of his own educational achievements and athletic prowess, and those describing medals awarded him for life saving.

He was a large man, over six feet tall and weighing well over two hundred pounds. One local sportswriter had once hailed him as the "Tremont Peach," the best ballplayer since Ty Cobb. Condon continued to take the field until he turned sixty. But in recent years he stood behind the plate, an umpire whose fairness and accuracy earned him the title "Old American Eagle Eye." In short, he was the very antithesis of Mickey Rosner and Owney Madden.[2]

Condon always put in a long day—finished off practically every night after eleven with a trip to a favorite spot, Bickford's Restaurant in Fordham Square, for coffee and companionship. Condon was well known to the waitresses, both for his brief lectures on timely topics and for never leaving a tip. On the night of March 1, 1932, he held forth as usual—the Bronx Socrates—to a table of young male admirers.

The subject for the evening was crime, and the relative merits of the world's most famous police organizations in fighting the forces of evil. Votes were cast for the French Sureté and Scotland Yard, while Condon and "Red" Brown, a New York police officer, stoutly defended "[their] own Department of Justice." All of a sudden there was a commotion outside. "Wextra! Wextra! Lindbergh . . ." Condon bought a newspaper and gripped it in a state of shock. How could it be? And to think that they had been talking all evening about crime and criminals!

At another table sat four men, "swarthy of face." "Their words were heavy with accent," Condon later remembered. One of the four, louder than the rest, began to revile the United States. "Your Department of Justice," he sneered. "Your Secret Service. What can they do? In my country, such a crime could never happen."[3]

"If you feel that way," retorted the patriotic educator, "then you should take that thick-soup accent of yours back to its own country. You should be ashamed to talk, as you're talking, of the country that feeds and clothes you." Both men got to their feet. "If he wanted to talk with his fists, that was all right with me." But the blasphemer's companions held him back, recorded Condon, and saved him from the beating he so richly deserved.[4]

The incident set a pattern. From the outset John Condon perceived the Lindbergh kidnapping as directed against the whole nation. Behind the deed he saw shadowy alien forces, especially Italians, dedicated to destroying the Lone Eagle's happiness, yes, but also harboring an evil desire to tear down American honor. Condon brooded over this terrible injustice all the way home that night, and for the next several days. When he learned the Lindberghs had named Salvatore Spitale and Irving Bitz as their trusted go-betweens, he was sick at heart. Why must this second calamity befall the nation? "By golly," he spluttered at the dinner table. "By golly, Uncle Sam *will* solve it, and I'll help him."

Condon's family had doubts about his latest crusade, especially his wife and two sons, John and Lawrence. Only his daughter, Myra, supported him and later became something of a protector when he was under pressure from reporters' and police questions.

Resolved to save Lindbergh from two such scoundrels, he rose from the table and marched off to his study to find the proper voice for this crisis. He did not emerge until three in the morning, clutching a letter he had written to the editor of the *Bronx Home News,* his usual outlet. "In addition to the $50,000 offered by the Colonel, I offer $1000, which I have saved from my salary if the one who handed the Colonel's son out of the window to the man on the ladder, (~~surmise~~) will go to a 'Catholic Priest' and confess his or her transgressions giving the child unharmed to any priest whom the kidnap[p]er will name." But there was a more important offer than money. "I stand ready in person at my own expense to go anywhere, alone on land or water to give the kidnap[p]er the extra money, and promise never to utter his or her name to anyone."[5]

Never to utter his or her name? To anyone? He might be the antithesis of Rosner and Owney Madden, but his terms were practically the same. He probably realized, one could argue, that a letter in the *Home News,* with a circulation of only 150,000 in a city of several million, would never reach the kidnapper or kidnappers but would provide a new clipping for the scrapbooks. Unless, of course, he had some good reason to think otherwise. And he did, as he explained later to the Lindberghs.

The letter, with its appeal to "the greatest criminal in the world" to show that even he "ha[d] a bright spot in his heart," appeared in the *Home News* on March 8, 1932. When he returned home the next evening, there were some twenty letters waiting for him in the dining room beneath the bronze Tiffany clock. He shuffled through them in routine fashion until he came to one in a long white envelope addressed to "Mr. Dr. John Condon."

"I could feel the rush of blood from my face," he recalled the moment, "an emptiness in the pit of my stomach and a heavier hammering of the heart than is good for a man in his seventies."[6]

Somehow he got the letter open and read, "Dear Sir: If you are will-ing to act as go-between in the Lindbergh cace pleace follow stricly instruction." After another pause to steady a shaking hand, he read on.

Handel inclosed letter *personaly* to Mr. Lindbergh. It will ex-plain everything. Don't tell anyone about it. As soon we find out the Press or Police is notified everything are cansell and it will be a further delay.

Affter you gett the mony from Mr. Lindbergh put these 3 words in the *New-York American.*
Mony is redy
Affter not [that or notice] we will give you further instruction. Don't be affrait we are not out for your 1000$ keep it. Only act strickly. Be at home every night between 6–12 by this time you will hear from us.[7]

Inside was a smaller envelope, wrote Condon in *Jafsie Tells All,* on which was printed: "Dear Sir: Please handel inclosed letter to Col. Lindbergh. It is in Mr. Lindberg interest not to notify the Police." Actually, this brief message, on a separate piece of paper, was never sent to Condon. It had been mailed to Colonel Breckinridge accompanying the message the kidnapper sent him. Why Condon or his ghostwriter wished to claim the message may not be terribly important in itself, but it certainly goes to the heart of the issue of Condon's reliability. It is curious, also, that *please* is spelled incorrectly in Condon's letter, and correctly in the brief note, as if there were two writers trying to imitate each other, and not doing a completely successful job of it.

How did the kidnapper expect Condon to establish his credentials as the chosen go-between? There was no coded signature on his letter. Did he just assume that Condon would open the letter to Lindbergh and reveal its contents over the telephone, including the signature? The kid-napper had already established a solid contact through Breckinridge, so the decision to respond to Condon's public letter seems a risky propo-sition—narrowing, as one must imagine, the area for police surveillance. Evidently, he or they took Lindbergh at his word that the family would not involve the police.

In some accounts Condon would claim he immediately called High-fields to advise Colonel Lindbergh. In others, however, he reported that he took it for a "crank" letter and decided to go off for coffee to see what some of his friends thought, especially Al Reich, a former prizefighter and frequent companion. He did not find Al at their usual meeting place,

Rosenhain's restaurant, but he told the owner, Max Rosenhain, and Milton Gaglio about the strange message he had received. They both encouraged him to call Lindbergh. An FBI report states that Condon had both letters "open" before he made the call—and that Gaglio saw the symbol at that time. It was never clear whether that was so. It turned out to be an issue of great significance, for why else should Condon believe that this one letter out of all those he received—or would receive—should be important enough to trouble the Lindberghs about? And why, even if he saw the strange symbol, would Condon have any reason to know what it was?[8]

When Condon gave a statement to Bronx assistant district attorney Edward F. Breslin about the inside letter, he added something else of crucial significance: "It was addressed to Colonel Lindbergh. It was inside, and in order to insure that genuineness, they said I was to see the symbol that they left on the window sill, or in the crib, the night of the kidnapping." Who is "they" here? Condon had few equals for bent syntax, but it certainly sounds as if he had been informed by someone what was inside the supposedly unopened letter to Lindbergh.[9]

According to Robert Thayer, who answered the phone near midnight, Condon first read the letter addressed to him. And when Thayer asked how it was signed, "he stated that it was signed with the sign of the Mafia." There was no special signature on the letter addressed to him, so where did Condon come up with that notion? Open the enclosed letter to "Mr. Colonel Lindbergh, Hopewell," Thayer instructed him, and read it as well. (Condon always thought he had talked to Lindbergh personally.)[10]

"Dear Sir," it began,

> Mr. Condon may act as go-between. You may give him the 70,000$. make one packet the size will be about [and here was a drawing of the proposed packet].
>
> We have notified you already in what kind of bills. We warn you not to set any trapp in any way. If you or someone els will notify the Police ther will be a further delay. Affter we have the mony in hand we will tell you where to find your boy. You may have a airplane redy it is about 150 mil. awy. But before telling you the adr. A delay of 8 houers will be between.[11]

When Condon described the coded signature, his listener urged him "to get into a car as quickly as he could and come down to Hopewell bringing the letter with him." It was after two in the morning when Condon, accompanied by Gaglio and Rosenhain, arrived in Princeton at the Baltimore Lunch to ask directions to Highfields.[12]

Condon handed over the note, but it was the "chain of reasoning" that convinced Henry Breckinridge they must deal with this eccentric old man if there was to be a chance of getting the child back safely. The daily newspapers, Breckinridge explained later, had indicated that a seaman had something to do with the kidnapping, a man called Red Johnson, a friend of Betty Gow's, who was then under arrest. Johnson had worked on a yacht, and many sailors spent a great deal of time on City Island—where Condon had a real estate office. Condon pointed out that the hinterland of City Island was not Manhattan but the Bronx. Sailors going to the movies in the Bronx, for example, would have several chances to see him, and know who he was. Over 40,000 schoolchildren had come through his school, moreover, and would also know he could be trusted. "That was the basis of his chain of reasoning that made him offer himself as an intermediary and that offer was accepted by the kidnappers."[13]

Condon reiterated this story about sailors and Red Johnson many times, embellishing it a bit each time to emphasize how perspicacious he had been from the beginning. He got his clue from a newspaper report that Red Johnson had been seen taking a baby into New York, he said, when it came to him all in a flash—someone, not Red Johnson, must have followed that route from Highfields and was still close by.

"A man supposed to be Red Johnson had taken a baby in an automobile through the Hudson Tunnel to City Island," he recalled for the Bronx district attorney's office. "Naturally, I said, 'that's my bailiwick.' That strengthened my idea that I could be of service in the case." Therefore his letter to the *Home News* prompted a response because, while the accusation against Red Johnson was baseless, the Bronx was the most logical place to begin the search.[14]

After they talked for many hours on the night of March 9, Lindbergh arranged a bed for Condon in the nursery, the only vacant spot in the house. Kneeling by the crib, the old man invoked the deity's aid in his sacred quest to restore the baby to its mother's arms. Awaking after a few hours' sleep, he studied the room and believed he saw vital clues others had missed: footprints leading away from the crib and a partial handprint near the window where the kidnapper had braced himself before exiting down the ladder. "I thought I saw where a man's hand had been on the window framing," he told Lindbergh, "and where he had climbed out the window."[15]

When Lindbergh entered the nursery that morning, he discovered Condon on the floor in front of the child's toy box, examining small wooden animals. Could he take these? he asked. They would provide positive identification of any child presented to him—if he could pronounce their names the way Charlie did. It was a somewhat convoluted explanation, but Lindbergh thought it a fine idea. Condon also took from the crib the safety pins that had held the baby's blanket to the mattress. He had taken these, he added, to help identify any contact as the real kidnapper. "I know how bazaar [*sic*] it is. I don't mind it. I had an object in view," he later contended to a grand jury, searching for one of the pins in his pocket. "I was in such earnest *that I determined to have at least something.*"[16]

Even after this strange behavior, Lindbergh gave him a signed note authorizing Condon to conduct the negotiations. But that was not enough. They must devise a code name he could use. As Condon later recalled, "Suddenly one occurred to me that I had never before employed. 'By putting my initials together,' I exclaimed, 'I get one: J.F.C.—Jafsie.'"[17]

Lindbergh sent Breckinridge back to New York with Condon to monitor developments and watch over the old man. There was another almost live-in guest, *Home News* editor Gregory Coleman. Condon gave the favored reporter a full briefing on Saturday morning, March 12, and Coleman promised to keep Jafsie's identity secret. Henceforth, Coleman enjoyed special access to everybody in the house. The old man had found his Boswell along with everything else.[18]

As the kidnapper had instructed, Jafsie put the notice, "Money is Ready," in the *New York American*. Fifty thousand dollars was also placed at Condon's disposal, although it is not clear if this was the same money originally transported down to Highfields. This money traveled first to a Bronx bank, then to Condon's home, and eventually to the Fordham Branch of the Corn Exchange Bank. It had been decided, for the time being at least, to ignore the demand for an additional $20,000.[19]

The notice appeared on March 11, 1932. Almost at once the phone started ringing, beginning at 9 A.M. Mrs. Condon informed the caller, a man with a Scandinavian or German accent, that her husband would be at home after 7 P.M. Condon himself took the third call. The man spoke in low guttural tones. Cordon's original impression, and that of his wife, was that the man could have been Scandinavian or German; in later accounts it was beyond doubt "a German voice." In at least one version of the phone-call story, the caller "announced himself as John." Later, however, in face-to-face meetings, Jafsie supposedly will have to ask his name, and will, still later, say that *he* named his interlocutor John when the man refused to give his name.[20]

Where was he calling from? demanded Condon.

From "Westchester."

Then, according to Condon, the following exchange took place.

"Doktor Condon, do you write sometimes pieces for the papers?"

Puzzled at this strangely irrelevant question, Condon nevertheless answered promptly. "Yes, I sometimes write articles for the papers."

The voice became muffled, as the speaker apparently turned to his companions. *"He say sometimes he writes pieces for the papers."* Finally, the voice turned back to order him to stay at home nights between six and twelve to receive the next message. "You will receive a note with instructions. Ect *(act)* accordingly or all will be off." Then Condon heard yet another voice call out, "Statti citto!" which he took to be the Italian equivalent of shut up.[21]

The next night, Saturday, March 12, 1932, Joseph Perrone, a taxicab driver, had been driving east down Gunhill Road to Knox Place when a man ran out from the sidewalk and stood in front of his cab with a hand up signaling him to stop. Perrone rolled down a window. Did he know where 2974 Decatur Avenue was? Yes, Perrone knew. "How much would it be over there—it only cost about 50¢ wouldn't it?" That would be about what the clock would say, confirmed Perrone. The man reached into his overcoat pocket and pulled out a letter. "How would you like to deliver a letter for me for a dollar?" Perrone agreed. The man handed over the letter and a one-dollar bill and moved quickly to the rear of the cab, where he appeared to be marking down the license number. Then he backed up the street and was gone.[22]

At first the man spoke with a German or Scandinavian accent, Perrone later remembered, but when he mentioned a particular street— 201st Street—he seemed not to have an accent. He was about thirty-five years old and five-foot-nine, wearing a brown overcoat and hat. He made no attempt to cover his face. His hair was dark blond. The only other special thing Perrone noticed was the man seemed to be looking at a car on the other side of the street as they talked.[23]

When he arrived at Condon's house, shortly after 8 P.M., and handed over the letter, Perrone was put through his paces. Where did he get the letter? Condon asked in a whisper. Could he describe the man? Condon was especially curious about whether he wore gloves and if he were German. Finished with his questions, Condon called Milton Gaglio to come into the room and take down all this information, along with Perrone's name and address and badge number.[24]

The letter read:

Mr Condon

We trust you, but we will note come in your Haus it is too
danger. even you can note know if Police or secret servise is
watching you

   follow this instruction. Take a car and drive to the last
supway station from Jerome Ave line [or here?] 100 feet from
the last station on the left seide is a empty frank-further
stand with a big open Porch around. you will find a notise in
senter of the proch underneath a stone. this notise will tell
you where to find us [or uss].

   act accordingly.

   after ¾ of a houer be on the place. bring mony [or money]
with you.[25]

According to Jafsie, Breckinridge burst out in despair, "'Bring the
Money!' But we haven't the money." "No matter," Condon replied. "The
important thing will be to get in touch with the kidnapper, to follow
his instructions, show him we are anxious to work with him. There isn't
much time. I'll have to hurry."[26]

Where *was* the money? Supposedly, it had been put at Condon's
ready disposal, whether actually in his house that night or in a bank.
Gregory Coleman's narrative of the negotiations, "Vigil," asserted that
Lindbergh had given Condon a letter authorizing him to deliver $50,000
to the kidnapper "if he sees [his] child."[27]

Condon and Al Reich then sped off to the rendezvous. The note
was precisely where the telephone caller had said it would be. It read:
"cross the street and follow the fence from the cemetery. direction to
233rd Street. I will meet you."

There was no symbol on this note, and all the words were spelled
correctly, but Condon said he recognized the handwriting as the same.
(Condon's handwriting expertise, of course, like all of his other qualifications, was highly suspect. The seeming ability of the kidnapper to
spell correctly when he chose to has always been a challenge to the
lone-wolf theory of the crime.) Arriving at Woodlawn Cemetery, Condon
walked around in a lighted plaza, trying to make himself conspicuous
by reading the note. No one came. He walked back to the car. "There's
no one there," he told his friend. "Are you sure we were on time?" Reich
assured him they were.

Walking toward Reich's car, "a Calabrese Italian" suddenly appeared.
"[He was] short and swarthy, wearing a cap," and holding a handkerchief over his face. Who was this? Maybe a lookout, they told each other,
trying to see if Condon had come alone.[28]

Going back to the plaza a second time, Condon now saw a man waving a white handkerchief between the bars of entrance gate. "I see you," Condon announced and walked over to the gate. The man asked immediately if Jafsie had the money.

From here on, we are in uncertain territory. The only other witness that night was a guard, Robert Riehl, who remembered seeing a man sitting on top of the gate, and speaking with a man outside. But the man he saw standing outside did not fit descriptions of Condon. Was someone else, a third person, there that night?[29]

Jafsie remembered Riehl, however, because the man on the gate took fright at the guard's approach, clambered up and over the gate, and ran off across 233rd Street to Van Cordlandt Park. What's wrong with him? the guard asked. Condon answered in general terms that he was "ok" and was with him—and gave chase. Finally, he "caught up" with him, grasping his arm. "You are my guest," Jafsie admonished, "nobody will interfere with you." Condon then looked around for a safe place to continue their conversation. "I escorted him back to . . . a little shack that is up there in the park used for—well, I saw a man sleeping in it, and saw some boys dressing in it for the athletic sports up there—only one room."[30]

He checked out the shack, saw no one was there, and invited his "guest" to join him on a bench, where they resumed their conversation, interrupted just after the man had asked if he had brought the money. No, Condon replied, but he could get it in ten minutes or so, once he had "evidence in regards to the baby." He couldn't take Condon to the baby, said the man, because the "gang" wouldn't stand for it; "they will scratch me out." The pair sat there, sparring over the conditions for the baby's return for nearly an hour—or perhaps even longer. Condon asked what name he should call him. "Call me John," the man said, and he was hereafter known as "Cemetery John."[31]

In one record of this conversation, however, Condon states that the man refused to give his name. "I will call you John," Condon tells him. "His coat collar was turned up and his cap was pulled down over his eyes. I said to him, 'Come, now don't hide your face. You have nothing to fear from me. I am not disguising myself.' He complied and I saw his face clearly. I would know him again. He was obviously a Scandinavian."[32]

Several times during the conversation the man asked if he would "burn" if the baby were dead, protested that he had only gotten involved because the gang had something on him, and cowered—with a tear in his eye—before Condon's grade-school principal's dressing-down. How would his mother feel about what he had done? She would not like it, Condon's new "pupil" confessed. "She would cry."

That a kidnapper facing a possible death sentence would risk spending an hour in Condon's confessional staggers belief. We have only Condon's word, of course, that the conversation did last that long, and that Cemetery John dutifully answered question after question about his role in the crime. Determined to know if he was dealing with a genuine representative of the gang, Jafsie withdrew from his pocket a small leather pouch, in which he had placed the safety pins taken from the baby's crib. "Yes I know," John said. "A blanket was pinned to the baby's sleeping suit and we had to take two pins off to get the baby out of the crib."[33]

Showing the pins assured the kidnapper, asserted Condon, that he was the designated negotiator. But that is hardly all there is to the story of the safety pins. In *Jafsie Tells All,* Condon related that they were the "clue" that, had he grasped its significance the night he spent in the nursery, would have "effected the capture of the man responsible for the grisly crime" when he came to Woodlawn Cemetery. The blankets at the foot of the crib had been disturbed, Condon wrote, and there was the clue. The pins had not been removed; instead the baby had been strangled and then pulled out feet first. Ergo, John's statement that the pins had been taken out was a lie.[34]

Betty Gow, it will be remembered, had asserted exactly the opposite when Rosner questioned her, that the evidence demonstrated the child had been taken out at the top of the crib. Condon did not always insist, moreover, that he had even shown the pins to the kidnapper.

A second crucial point in the conversation was John's promise to send the child's sleeping suit as proof that he was the real kidnapper. Condon argued with him that the money could not be paid over until he saw the "package." Cemetery John countered it was too risky to move the baby or to allow Condon to see it before the money changed hands. After much back-and-forth, Cemetery John said they would send Condon the sleeping suit the baby wore that night to prove they had the child.

There was also much discussion about Red Johnson and Betty Gow. In some versions, Condon asks Cemetery John to clear their names; in others, it is John who seeks Condon's aid to convey a message that the two are "innozent." "Red Johnson is innozent. He must be freed. The girl, too." Condon professed to being surprised at first about Cemetery John's fervent defense of the wronged couple. Then he realized that if Johnson and Gow continued to be suspects, it would delay payment of the ransom, and certainly cut him out as the chosen instrument for the child's return to its mother.

At this time, Red was still incarcerated for further questioning, pending deportation proceedings. Betty, however, was with the Lindberghs.

John complained to Condon, nevertheless, that they had both received "mean" treatment from the authorities. It is hard to accept this at face value, or at all. From the start it was Condon who claimed that concern about Red and Betty pushed him into the case—in addition, of course, to his worries about Lindbergh's reliance on men like Spitale and Bitz. Condon was adept at rationalization whenever questions arose about his veracity or memory.[35]

Condon also claimed to have noticed several things about Cemetery John that are absent in later accounts, for example, the "hacking cough" that is a telltale sign of pulmonary disease. In all of his 1932 statements, Condon observes Cemetery John coughing continually and displaying signs of an unnamed disease, which might, one supposes, have been the ravages of tuberculosis. How all this was so evident to Jafsie in the dark on the bench, when Cemetery John held his *black* coat up around his face for all but a minute is never explained. Perrone, of course, had observed that the man who gave him the note for Condon wore a *brown* coat only hours before Cemetery John turned up in a *black* coat, coughing and hacking away.[36]

Condon would tell police that the man he negotiated with had a lump at the base of his thumb on his left hand—the sign of a carpenter or mechanic. In *Jafsie Tells All,* the print he supposedly saw on the wall of the nursery—which everyone else missed—was recognizable to Condon as being made by the man with "the thenar eminence or ball of the thumb."[37]

John also said that he was a sailor from north of Boston, that four men and two women were involved, and that the baby was on a boat several hours away—but that he, John, could signal quickly from a shore point nearby. And he promised that when the money was paid, there would be no double cross. *"Nobody else shall ever get the baby but you, and you can put that baby's arms around Mrs. Lindbergh's neck."* John's language perfectly replicated Condon's repeated vows. In his original letter to the *Home News,* Condon pledged "to bring back to her bosom the tender offspring, with his tiny arms around her neck." In the introduction to *Jafsie Tells All,* he wrote, "My one desire, my only thought from the first has been to place that baby's arms again around its mother's neck." One wonders if John had somehow been eavesdropping all the while before their first encounter.

Sometimes Condon recalled shaking hands with the man as a parting gesture; sometimes he did not. The first meeting concluded with Cemetery John's promise to send the sleeping suit. For his part, Condon promised to confirm for the rest of the gang that he had met their representative and had agreed to the deal by placing a new notice in the newspapers: "Baby Alive and Well—Money is Ready." Cemetery John said he needed this because Condon had failed to get the money. The notice was put in the *Home News* on Sunday—apparently Condon's choice—though the *New York American* had been the previous vehicle for the "Money is Ready" message. A second ad promising there would be no police or secret service appeared a day later.

What happened next, like so many other sequences in the case, remains controversial. Condon said he received a phone message on Monday morning, March 14, telling him there had been a delay in sending the sleeping suit. Then on either Tuesday or Wednesday—Condon was never clear which, and there was no date stamp to help—a brown oblong package with a ten-cent stamp on it arrived in the 10:30 mail— although Condon shifted ground on this point, as well as who was present when it was found—either in the mailbox or on top of the box. There were two addresses on the package: one printed, and one written in hand, not on opposite sides, but very close together. Colonel Breckinridge would say later that he was there when it arrived; but Condon claimed he called him on the phone to tell him. In some accounts, Condon said he opened it right away; in others that he waited for Breckinridge. Certainly, others saw the package and saw it open that day, including Gregory Coleman of the *Bronx Home News*.[38]

Inside was the sleeping suit, wrapped in a lighter-colored paper, with either one or two notes from the kidnapper, again something that was never clarified. One note, two-sided, was certainly there and may have confused the issue. It declared that there would be no more negotiations, and even complained about incurring an additional expense of three dollars to purchase the child another sleeping suit to replace that one! A trifling remark to put in an ultimatum, apparently intended to show frustration, along with a complaint that the Lindberghs did not seem to credit him with being the man who held the child captive. "You have ouer singnature," it read. "It is always the same as the first one specialy them 3 hohls."[39]

In a statement to New York police on May 14, 1932, Condon said there was a letter addressed to him inside that read, "This is Colonel Lindbergh's baby's sleeping suit I talked to you about; I don't think there will be any trouble about that. Send it to Colonel Lindbergh and tell him the longer he delays the amount will be bigger." Since this was an oral statement, it is perfectly possible that Condon simply collapsed various messages into a brief explanation—but it is so different from what was written in the actual note with the sleeping suit that it raises questions about whether there was, indeed, not a second note in the sleeping suit, or at least more to the phone message that Condon had received on Monday, March 14. Condon also said to the police that day, May 14, that the "package was covered with two-cent stamps." That was what one might expect, because the kidnapper was more likely to have that denomination on hand, as he had used two-cent stamps before. But it was not so. The presence of a ten-cent stamp suggests that he had had the package weighed at the post office, in order to ensure the precise postage, a risky enterprise—or that the outside wrapper was mailed by someone other than the kidnapper, an accomplice.

While they waited for Colonel Lindbergh to arrive—a long wait as he could not manage to elude would-be tails until late in the evening— Condon went upstairs to write a poem for St. Patrick's Day, "Emmet's Epitaph," to ease the tension.

> By the souls of your martyrs and patriot dead
> Make your vows for neglect to atone
> With deeds that are worthy of your honored sires
> Carve the epitaph on that cold stone.

He immediately mailed the poem to the *Home News,* instructing that it be published on the Irish holiday. Could it have been a coded message?

(At the trial, Condon would become even more confused—or accurate?—about certain parts of the sleeping-suit episode, telling the court that he thought there definitely were two messages in the package, and that the handwritten address looked like his handwriting. But he now said that he did not remember who was present when it arrived, and that Colonel Lindbergh was there when it was first opened. These answers, of course, allowed him to avoid a discussion of the day's events.)

Lindbergh finally arrived after midnight, wearing amber-colored glasses, and bundled in a long coat and cap to complete the disguise. "You are quite sure, Colonel," the solicitous Condon asked, "that you wish—that you can bear—to inspect the child's garment." Lindbergh nodded yes and followed Condon to the living room, where the package—closed again—rested on a paisley shawl on the piano. It took Lindbergh some moments to reopen it. He inspected it front and back, Condon later wrote in a magazine article, "with the quiet precision of a scientist. Aware of the exquisite torture of this moment in his life, I marveled at this seeming control—absolute control over his emotions."[40]

"This is my son's sleeping suit," Lindbergh announced. "It is the one he wore the night he was taken." Was there no room for doubt? Several of these Dr. Denton sleeping suits were in Englewood, and more than one was available at Highfields. What had been the reason for the delay after Cemetery John promised delivery Monday morning? Even

Lindbergh wondered why "they went to the trouble of having it cleaned." Why, indeed, in a related way, did the kidnappers say they had to purchase another garment to replace this one? Why clutter up the note that way, unless there was a special point to be made about the suit they sent as *the* one? There would always remain questions about the sleeping suit, whether it was Charlie's, and if so, when it had been removed?[41]

Colonel Norman Schwarzkopf told a strategy session of the New Jersey State Police on May 18, 1932, "This suit had one button off and it had apparently been washed and was not accepted as conclusive; it was accepted as being the same kind of a suit but as for being *the* suit, there was nothing to positively identify it."[42]

According to one authority, Jim Fisher, Lindbergh's experience with the sleeping suit crystallized his determination to pay the ransom. "We must pay the ransom as soon as possible," Fisher has Lindbergh declare. "There should be no delays." Fisher cites *Jafsie Tells All* as a source for this statement. What Lindbergh actually said, however, in reply to Condon's urging caution and further negotiations to see the baby, was: "Yes, of course, if it can possibly be arranged that way. But we must not let negotiations go on too long."[43]

According to Schwarzkopf, moreover, Lindbergh told him that the decision to pay the ransom was *not* due to the appearance of the sleeping suit, but rather the urging of his financial advisers, who warned him that he could not gain control of the situation, because the kidnappers had the baby, and "[he would] have to meet [their terms] somewhere along the line." In particular there was a letter from the kidnappers threatening to raise the ransom to $100,000 if the transaction had not been completed by April 8.

At Condon's house the night the sleeping suit was received, he entertained his guests at a late-night supper with a "magic box." There was no opening to be seen on any side. Turning it over and over, Condon said the case was not unlike this magic box. One had to find the key first and then the keyhole. The trick was to move sliding panels until the key fell out, and then move more panels until the concealed keyhole appeared. It took Breckinridge seven minutes, Al Reich six, and Lindbergh only two.

Condon took the box back and, looking around the table, solemnly explained the meaning of his little experiment. The key to the kidnapping case, he announced, was the return of the sleeping suit and the letters. Lindbergh got the point—it had been returned to Condon, the man the kidnappers trusted—and repeated, yet again, that he was satisfied that Condon would restore his child to him. It was an eerie moment. As the author of "Vigil" makes plain, Condon wanted to discourage Lindbergh from dealing with anyone else. Morris Rosner had recently made his blundering comment that he was sure the baby was about to be returned, and Condon was aware—vaguely at least—that others had approached Lindbergh. They must not be allowed to interfere. "They haven't got a thing," he declared to Coleman in private. "There's a lot of gangs who might make it appear that they have the child for the purpose of hi-jacking the ransom money. It's easier than holding up a bank."[44]

How could Condon be so sure of that? What if Cemetery John had rivals? Maybe he hadn't been able to hold his "gang" together. No, Condon insisted, Lindbergh must not be misled. In a vehement letter to the *Home News,* P. A. Triot, one of Condon's alter egos, denounced any further dealings with underworld figures. Why should he take time to write such a letter in the midst of the negotiations, except to keep himself at the center?

At Condon's urging, a new notice was placed, essentially restating old terms: "I accept. Money is Ready. You know they won't let me deliver without getting the package. Let's make it some sort of C.O.D. transaction. Come. You know you can trust me."

It is as if he must constantly reassure both sides in the negotiation that he is the honest broker—the only one they can both trust. And it is quite possible that Condon believed Cemetery John himself might have chosen to widen his options by bringing in other people. His notice calling for a "C.O.D. transaction" is almost a plea for attention.

Other notices were placed in both the *Home News* and the *New York American*: "I accept. Money is Ready. John, your package is delivered and is O.K. Direct Me. Jafsie." These ran for two days but drew no response. Jafsie drafted a third to run in the newspapers on March 20: "Inform me how I can get important letter to you. Urgent. Jafsie."

If Cemetery John had his doubts about Condon at this point, so did Lindbergh. The day after the sleeping suit arrived, he asked his friend Major Thomas Lanphier to do some checking. Lanphier went to the FBI, which carried out a cursory check, an interview with an official at Fordham. This man knew about Condon's interest in civic movements and his fondness for organizing baseball teams, and had heard something strange. "You will be interested in knowing, perhaps, that I have taken a personal interest in this Lindbergh case," Condon had told him, "and that I am personally offering a reward of $1,000 for the return of the baby." He doubted anything would come of the offer, as who could imagine John Condon seriously involved in such an important case?[45]

Who indeed. Cemetery John's silence might mean he was fed up with the delays working through Jafsie and would seek another way. Condon obviously feared that was the case. Maybe the kidnappers were having a difficult time figuring out how to return the baby. If so, he needed to devise a plan whereby they could do so safely. But he still expected to be the one man to return little Charlie to his mother. Introducing Coleman to the bank manager where the money was being kept, he declared the reporter would accompany him when he came to pick up the ransom. You will be the one, he said, turning to Coleman, to drive us down to Hopewell with the baby![46]

That was a strange vow. Where was Lindbergh supposed to be all this time?

By now, Condon's flirtations with surreal happenings, mystical appearances, and strange voyages had already become a common phenomenon. On Saturday, March 19, he attended the opening of a charity bazaar in a store at 194 East 200th Street. He had brought with him several violins to sell. Sometime in the middle of the afternoon a "short middle-aged woman with the oval face and olive skin of an Italian, came into the bazaar." She seemed nervous and kept looking around in a furtive manner. Finally, she asked to see one of the violins, an excuse to get close enough to whisper a message. "Nothing can be done," she supposedly said, "until the excitement is over. There is too much publicity. Meet me at the depot at Tuckahoe Wednesday at five in the afternoon." Then she vanished.[47]

Condon always believed the mystery woman was a messenger from the kidnappers. Keep the appointment, Breckinridge advised. And so he did—but no one showed up.

She was certainly an enigma. In another Condon description, the lady is younger, gypsy-like, more smartly attired, and wearing a heavy veil. And in a third description given to the FBI, she is even younger— no more than twenty-five years old—and taller, "of medium height, dark complexion, black hair, bobbed and worn in somewhat of a 'Gypsy' fashion . . . coming well down on the forehead and down on the ears and possibly with spit-curls."[48]

In some versions she changes her mind and does show up at Tuckahoe; in others she does not. And in one account—Condon's testimony to the grand jury in the Bronx on May 20, 1932—Condon does not show up himself. At the time of this testimony, Condon had begun to come under suspicion as part of the "gang," a possible reason for his denial that he ever made the trip. The last word goes to Gregory Coleman: "The woman was there all right," he would write, "but she merely announced, 'you will get a message later—keep advertising in the *Home News* until you hear' and she hastened away."[49]

"What is the true explanation of her?" Condon asks readers of his memoirs. "To this day I do not know. Of the many mysterious fantastic incidents that occurred in the famous Lindbergh case, this one ranks high among those that have baffled students of the case."[50] If Condon wished to keep attention focused on his essential role, introducing "Our Lady of Tuckahoe," as investigators knew her, was certainly one good way of going about it. Perhaps she was a product of his inventiveness, a hologram to astound and distract those seated in the darkness.

She may have been, he suggests, simply a partly deranged woman who wandered into the bazaar, played a game on a gullible-looking old man, and wandered out again. There is yet another intriguing possibility. All of Condon's descriptions, albeit with some stretching to suit his ego, would fit Mary Cerrita, Peter Birritella's companion, the medium who accompanied him to Princeton and delivered the spirit messages to Colonel Breckinridge. She was perfectly capable of playing such a role to the hilt. If there was some delay or division and it became necessary to offer reassurance to Condon that things were still on track, someone watching his movements could not have picked a better time.

The evening the woman appeared at the bazaar, a letter was mailed from Station N in New York; it arrived at Condon's home on Monday, March 21. This would be the last communication, the author warned, until the notice accepting his terms had appeared in the paper. "You have to come to us anyway." Why should Mrs. and Mr. Lindbergh suffer any longer? Had Condon failed to send on the sleeping suit? The police wouldn't have any luck searching for them, or the child. "Mr. Linbergh [is] only wasting time with his search."[51]

Breckinridge and Condon did not like the new tone in this letter. After some discussion, Jafsie had the last word on what response to make. The notice they placed was not the one the letter writer expected. "Thanks," it read. "That little package you sent me was immediately delivered and accepted as real article. See my position. Over 50 years in business and can I pay without seeing goods? Common sense makes me trust you. Please understand my position. Jafsie."

Both the kidnappers and Jafsie had something new to worry about, however. Newspapers carried the story on March 24, 1932, that Lindbergh was negotiating with three noted citizens from Norfolk, Virginia, for the return of his son—John Hughes Curtis, Rear Admiral Guy H. Burrage, and the Reverend H. Dobson-Peacock. The "Curtis" angle of the Lindbergh case, a major distraction to students of the crime of the century, was at the time a powerful stimulus to a final settlement. The longer the negotiations went on, the more messages, the greater the risk of being captured, or from the Lindbergh side, the greater the supposed risk that the child would be killed.

In any event, the COD notice was now replaced with a new version: "Money is ready. Furnish simple code for us to use in paper. Jafsie." The kidnapper's response arrived on March 30. It was not necessary to furnish any code. "You and Mr. Lindbergh know ouer Program very well." They would keep the child in a safe place until the money was paid. But if the money was not paid by April 8, they would demand $30,000 more, making a total of $100,000. "How can Mr. Lindbergh follow so many false clues?" they asked when he knew they had to be the right people. "But if Mr. Lindbergh likes to fool around for another month—we can help it." Yet "if he keep's on waiting we will double ouer amount."[52]

Experts in the psychology of kidnapping observed at the time and later that the notes carried no threats to harm the child, only threats to keep on raising the ransom unless it was paid soon. The absence of threats to the child could not be taken as "good news," alas, but as an indication Charlie had already been killed. The kidnapper's direct address to "Mr. Lindbergh," phrased in American-style jargon ("if Mr. Lindbergh likes to fool around for another month—we can['t] help it"), almost seemed to come from someone listening outside the door where the negotiations with John Hughes Curtis were being discussed.

The reference to Lindbergh's fooling around for a month indicated willingness, on the other hand, to play the game out—however long it took. Condon had held out for continuing negotiations. But Lindbergh had delayed approximately a month, hoping, like Condon, to get his son back at the time of the ransom payment. "After consulting with his friends and associates he finally decided it would be advisable on account of the safety of the child and on account of the physical condition of the mother, to comply with the terms of the kidnappers."[53]

The latest communication from the kidnappers brought Lindbergh hastening back to New York for a final late-night conference. This time Condon's efforts to string out the negotiations were overruled, and the next day a new notice in the *Home News* stated, "I accept. Money is ready. Jafsie." The notice appeared on March 31.

Colonel Breckinridge had advised Condon, meanwhile, to have a box made according to the specified dimensions given in one of the ransom notes. Condon's almost loving description of what he had in mind for the box suggests his idea was to copy a box he owned that had long ago belonged to the lieutenant-governor of the State of New York. "When I order this box made tomorrow," he said to Breckrinridge, "I'll specify that it is to be of five-ply veneer. We'll use different types of wood in its construction. Maple, pine, tulip-wood will be good—spruce might warp—and a couple of other varieties of wood. Five different kinds in all." Breckinridge was all for it. "I'll have that box made so that it could be identified in one hundred years from now by anyone acquainted with its construction."[54]

No question was more vexed than the making of the box to contain the ransom money. Condon would contend at various times that his son-in-law, Ralph Hacker, had drawn up plans for its construction and a friend named Frank Peremi had made it. When FBI agents investigated, however, they found that Peremi had died in October of 1931—leaving a mystery about who really had made the box, and why Condon's memory on such a key point was faulty, and even if he were deliberately withholding the truth.[55]

The kidnappers had not asked for the money to be placed in a box, only that a "packet" of a certain size be fashioned to hold the money. It was made to hold $50,000, even though the kidnappers had specified the size of a packet to hold $70,000. It supposedly had a lock placed on it, with a key to be kept in Condon's possession. Condon even told the FBI, on November 21, 1933, that the box was a "family heirloom," without making any effort to reconcile his previous statement about its having been made by a friend. Later, a man named Frank Samuelsohn immediately recognized Condon, when FBI agents took him to Samuelsohn's shop, and said he had charged three dollars for the box. As for Condon's memory and assertion that it was made of several kinds of wood for identification purposes, Samuelsohn stated simply that it was made of five-ply maple veneer. Despite all the tales he had told about the box, perhaps Condon had never wanted it to be identified.

On April 1, 1932, the kidnapper's latest response arrived.

> Dear Sir: have the money ready by Saturday evening. we will inform you where and how to deliver it. have the money in one bundle we want you to put it in on a sertain place. Ther is no fear that somebody else will tacke it, we watch everything closely. Please lett us know if you are agree and redy for action by Saturday evening—if yes—put it in the paer
>
> Yes everything O.K.
>
> It is a very simble delivery but we find out very sun if there is any trapp. after 8 houers you gett the adr. from the boy, on the place you finde two ladies. the are innocence.

If it is to late to put it in the *New York American* for Saturday evening put it in *New York Journal.*[56]

As if on cue, to seal the question of whether to pay the ransom, on April 1, Betty Gow and Elsie Whateley found one of Charlie's metal thumb guards. They were taking their usual walk down to the main entrance along the gravel road, and had just turned back to the house, when Betty noticed something in the center of the drive. "I recognized it immediately," she would testify, and took the object to Colonel Lindbergh. It was the thumb guard later produced at the trial, still tied with the bowknot, just as it had been put on the baby that night. How had it been missed for a month with state troopers scouring the grounds for any clue? And with Betty and Elsie walking there day in and out?[57]

The discovery could not have been timed better to add emotional urgency to a decision to pay the ransom, and topped the list of suspicious coincidences. The original bills that had made up the first $50,000, meanwhile, were now replaced with bills whose serial numbers had been recorded, Lindbergh's only concession to police entreaties. The new package also contained a large proportion of gold certificates, easier to recognize because of the seal they bore to the left of the portrait of Alexander Hamilton. Treasury Department official Elmer Irey believed the United States would sooner or later, perhaps sooner, go off the gold standard. When that happened, the kidnapper would be stuck with a bundle of money he would have to exchange for greenbacks or try to spend in inconspicuous places. Either way, he would face a big risk.[58]

Then the wait began. Al Reich picked up the $50,000 at F. D. Bartow's and delivered it to Condon's home Saturday afternoon, April 2, 1932. Breckinridge brought a separate package of $20,000 in fifty-dollar gold certificates. These would be the easiest to spot. When Lindbergh tried to squeeze the money into the box, it split and had to be tied together with a string. The $50,000, wrapped in individual packages with a brown paper band around the center, was placed on edge in the bottom of the box. The additional $20,000 was placed flat on top of the other bills.

About 7:45 or 8 P.M., someone appeared at the door with a note for Condon. The person was never identified, nor was it ever clear how he had arrived on Condon's doorstep. Unknown to anyone at the time, Lanphier had asked that FBI agents be placed near Condon's home. One was in a room directly across the street, and two more were nearby down the block. They saw no car. New York police were also covering the house that day, and tapping Condon's phone—and they did not observe any car or other vehicle arrive that night.

All day long reporters kept calling. One, Arthur O'Sullivan of the *Daily News,* offered Condon $1,000 for the first "break" in the story. Condon refused. Gregory Coleman called, and Condon promised him the first break. Around 2 P.M., reporters from the United Press called; Al Reich told them that nothing had happened yet. A little later, Condon called the United Press and asked for one of the reporters, a man named Bender, and promised him the first break.[59]

In Jafsie/Condon's soul the desperate struggle between altruistic patriotism and boastful self-promotion never ceased. Only he could have let the press in on the preparations for the ransom payment; and, as the phone taps revealed, only he courted their attention with flirtatious promises of the big story. What actually happened has never been resolved—not even partially. To begin with, no information was taken from this messenger, unlike the careful debriefing of Joseph Perrone. Condon explained the lapse by saying he was too excited to bother asking the messenger's name. With nothing to go on, police never discovered his identity.[60]

During one interrogation Condon admitted he had briefly engaged the man in conversation. The messenger said he had received the note at the corner of 188th Street and Marion Avenue from someone not richly dressed, wearing a brown fedora. This is quite remarkable, given that in other accounts, Condon arrived at the door only to glimpse a figure over his daughter Myra's shoulder disappearing down the porch steps. Yet he was able to notice that the man, who appeared to be about five-foot-six and wore long "sideboards" in a Jewish style, had on a taxi hat and returned to a "cab."[61]

And there was more. He said later that he quite deliberately did not allow the man to enter the house. "I opened the door and *kept him out.* I didn't call the taxi man in."[62]

Condon's extraordinary behavior was temporarily forgotten when the note was opened. It read: "Dear Sir: take a care and follow tremont Ave to the east until you reach the number 3225 east tremont Ave. It is a nursery. Bergen Greenhauses florist there is a table standing outside right on the door, you find a letter undernead the table covert with a stone, read and follow instruction." On the other side of the piece of paper, there were further instructions: "don't speak to anyone on the way. If there is a ratio alarm for policecar, we warn you, we have the same equipment. have the money in one bundle. We give you ¾ of a houer to reach the place."

After a hurried conversation, in which Condon expressed some doubt about the wisdom of Lindbergh's accompanying him, the two left in Reich's car for the appointed rendezvous at the Bergen Greenhouse.

Condon got out of the car, went to the table, and found the note exactly where it was supposed to be under a rock. He returned to the car, and, as he later recounted to police, they read the contents of the note with a flashlight.

Lindbergh described what happened next.

> [Condon] said that he was taking an unnecessary long time and standing outside the car for a purpose. He indicated that his reason was to give the kidnappers an opportunity to identify him. Several people had passed by on the sidewalk when a man appeared walking along the sidewalk opposite to the direction in which the car was stationed. He walked with an unusual gait rather awkwardly and with a pronounced stoop. His hat was pulled down over his eyes. As he passed the car he covered his mouth and the lower part of his face with a handkerchief, and looked at Doctor Condon and at me. He continued along Tremont and passed out of sight.[63]

But that was not to be the last of this man with the awkward gait, a man who resembled the supposed lookout at the first meeting between Jafsie and Cemetery John. The note under the rock instructed Condon to "cross the street and walk to the next corner and follow *Whittemore* Ave to the soud take the money with you. come alone and walk I will meet you."

Like the note delivered to Condon's home that evening, it contained the symbol-signature by which the kidnaper had always identified himself. The "directional" notes, however, all shared two characteristics that set them apart from the "demand" notes. They contained fewer spelling errors, and the writing was smoother, almost as if the author had felt more at ease and less concerned with disguise.

Condon took the note and headed for the corner of Tremont and Whittemore, near the entrance to St. Raymond's Cemetery. There he encountered a man and a little girl. They exchanged a few words about directions, and Condon continued on toward St. Raymond's. As had been the case at Woodlawn, at first there appeared to be no one there, and he turned back toward the car. At that moment, Lindbergh heard a voice calling from the cemetery, "Ay Doctor." "I could hear the call distinctly and the Doctor was pronounced with a definite accent."[64]

Condon walked to the cemetery wall and peered over in among the monuments. It was too dark to see anything. "Where are you?" he called. The voice had seemed to come from behind a tomb, but Condon continued walking along until the voice came again. "Here I am."

From this point on, we are once again faced with Jafsie's varying accounts. The dialogue that follows is taken from one account for the Bronx grand jury in May 1932.

When Condon went over to where the wall met a low hedge, he heard the voice again. "Here, have you got the money?"

"No, I didn't know where [whether?] you were going to be here or not, I have no evidence, I could not give it to you."

"Where is it?"

"Up in the automobile." (In some versions the man asks who is in the automobile, and Condon explains that it is Colonel Lindbergh, and that he is alone.)

"Get it."

"I can't get it without a receipt." (He wanted to "see the handwriting," Condon explained to the grand jury.)

The man said he could get the receipt in two minutes. But during the police interrogation Condon added that the man complained he had already sent the sleeping suit. He would send the directions for finding the child after six hours, "in order that [the kidnappers] might have a getaway."

They debated the issue for a few minutes before it was agreed the money would be exchanged for the directions. But Condon then added a new condition. Times were hard, he said. Lindbergh had only been able to scrape together $50,000, not $70,000. By now in a highly agitated state, according to Condon, the man practically jumped at the offer. "I suppose we will have to let it go for fifty."[65]

"Naturally," Condon congratulated himself, "I felt happy over that, then I went back to the Colonel and he handed [me] the $70,000." Condon then gave him the good news that it would only take $50,000. Taking out the package of fifty-dollar bills, Lindbergh handed him the box. "Thanks, Doctor Condon," Lindbergh supposedly said. "Saving that amount helps a lot. Sure you'll be all right going back there alone?"

"Quite sure," he answered. "The kidnapper's alone. I could handle two like him."

Whether this radio serial dialogue Condon recorded in *Jafsie Tells All* ever happened is doubtful. Only one thing is certain: Lindbergh and Condon went to St. Raymond's with a box, tied about with string, which originally contained $70,000, and Condon gave the man in the cemetery $50,000. Surely a man of Lindbergh's acumen would have realized that the "large bills," the fifty-dollar bills that made up the second package, were ones that could be the most easily traced. How much more time would it have taken to remove stacks of smaller denominations, even $10,000, and keep half of the package of fifty-dollar bills in the box?

From the very first, the way the money was handled, and *mis*handled, seemed incomprehensible to investigators.

"I am glad I can serve you," Condon said modestly. Taking the box, he returned to the cemetery, passing out of Lindbergh's sight for a significant time, and later giving at least three different explanations for why that had occurred.

Then Jafsie confronted the man with an odd statement: "I never saw you before did I, where did I ever see you before?"

"I am the one who spoke to you at the other cemetery."

"Well, I can't see you." Stand up, ordered the schoolmaster.

The man did as he was told, then asked, "Got the money?"

"Yes, where is the receipt?"

"His voice seemed to change and his English changed," noted Condon, but also interesting here is the term *receipt*. He stated that the man had gone away to write it while he got the money. But where could he have written it? Perhaps he anticipated that he would have to provide instructions to find the child in order to get the money. The handwriting in this note is the smoothest of all and does suggest that it had been prepared earlier, not scrawled on top of a tombstone. Both Perrone and Condon noticed that the man who spoke to them changed his accent at times. But Condon does not concern himself very much with the appearance of the receipt.[66]

When the exchange took place, note for money, the man heaped praise on Jafsie, telling him twice how "perfet" his work had been and how much the whole gang thought of him. But that was hardly the end of it. "Vait a minute," Condon related the man said, dropping down to open the box. "I want to see if it is all right."

"John!" Condon exclaimed. "If these bills are marked or serial, I know nothing about it, John. I had nothing to do with it and I didn't see them."

But John reassured him again he had done well. "Oh. The crowd thinks you're fine."

Condon's account abruptly changes direction at this point, as he perhaps realized how chummy it sounded. "I don't know what he meant."[67]

Even so, Condon continued to take credit for carrying out the mission in his statements to authorities and his memoirs. "Well, I kept my word," he said he told the man, since the "truth should be carried out if it is stated to anybody."

The man stood up and pulled his coat around him, Condon continues his account, but this time "he didn't have the great black coat with him." What great black coat? At Woodlawn, Condon had said, Cemetery

John wore only a thin coat. The hacking cough that indicated the onset of a pulmonary disease had also disappeared as well.

Everyone trusts you, rambled on the man who seemed in no great hurry to get away. Well, replied clever Jafsie, "bring them out."

Oh, no, that was much too dangerous; "it is 30 years, John he would be in an awful position." (Who, in heaven's name, was Condon talking to—if not John?) "Would you not like to meet John?" the man teased. "You know they all like you."

At the Woodlawn meeting Jafsie had asked John twice, once in German and once in English, if he were German. The response had been no, he was a Scandinavian. Now he listened carefully for a German accent. And asked yet again if he were German. The man replied no—as before. Condon seemed to agree.

"No, you can't speak German. Scandinavian, [it] was the same man." And from that, he concluded, "it seemed to me positively that it was the same man that had given me the signatures on the letters that I met up at Woodlawn cemetery."[68]

In this mixed-up account of Condon's, what stands out is that Jafsie comes away from two meetings with the man called Cemetery John convinced that he is not German but Scandinavian. Yet there are so many blind alleys in his accounts that one seems to emerge from them as if from a maze—where one has not found the center.

Before Condon returned to the car with the "receipt," Lindbergh had another long look at the man with the handkerchief. It was about fifteen minutes after Condon passed out of sight on his return trip to the cemetery with the money, said Lindbergh, that he saw him. This time he was running down Tremont Avenue toward Whittemore. When he came to that street, he hesitated, looked all around, and then doubled back. "As he passed the car he covered his face with a handkerchief and blew his nose so loudly that it could be distinctly heard across the street where I was parked and undoubtedly a considerably greater distance." Then he dropped the handkerchief.[69]

Police recovered the handkerchief, but it yielded no clues.[70]

Condon's circuitous routes to and from the cemetery were likewise never explained to the satisfaction of federal investigators. As Lindbergh noted:

> It is not known to Colonel Lindbergh or Colonel Breckinridge nor has Condon explained it satisfactorily just why he went one block further down the cemetery before he returned and entered it, to contact "John" the second time on the night of April 2nd. This particular angle has been discussed with Dr.

Condon by Agent J. J. Manning of the New York Office during the course of which Condon has given at least three explanations of the above. Condon states that on his second trip back to the cemetery on the night of April 2nd in passing the entrance he thought he saw some shadows behind the tombstones and thinking possibly that someone had concealed himself there, he would "stick him up" and take the ransom money from him, he walked down another block to give this matter serious thought before he turned around and entered the cemetery. Condon's second explanation for his walking the extra block is that he did so to give him sufficient time in which to say a prayer. His third explanation is in substance that he was confused, and did not know exactly where he was going, since he may have been a little excited at the time.[71]

All three explanations, however, do have a common thread: delay. *Serious thought, prayer, confused*—these are the key words in Jafsie's explanations. They describe a man deeply troubled over what he is about to do.

The man warned Jafsie not to open the note for several hours, but Condon claims he convinced a reluctant Lindbergh there was no injunction against someone else opening it as soon as possible. A mile from the cemetery they stopped the car near a house Condon said he owned, and opened the note:

> the boy is on Boad Nelly
> it is a small Boad 28 feet
> long, two person are on the
> Boad, the are innosent.
> you will find the Boad between
> Horseneck Beach and gay Head
> near Elizabeth Island.[72]

They then returned to Condon's home for a brief conference with Breckinridge. One FBI agent, Leon Turrou, who was on the scene, later recalled that "only Dr. Condon was smiling."

"There's nothing to worry about now," Condon said. "Everything will be fine."

"You should not have argued with him," Lindbergh commented.

"Who argued? I outsmarted him, that's all."

Turning to Turrou, Jafsie described his triumph. "I said to our friend in there, 'Now look here, John, the colonel's not a plutocrat. Seventy thousand is a God-awful lot of money. He just doesn't have it. Some people in this rich and wonderful country have it, and they're lucky, but the colonel—well the answer's no. Fifty thousand is all he could get together. We don't begrudge it. Take it and be satisfied.'"

Turrou looked at Lindbergh for his reaction. "That's what happened," Lindbergh said noncommittally.

"Saved Lindy twenty thousand." Condon said, beaming. "Good day's work, I call it."

"But really, Doctor— "

"Oh, no need to thank me, Colonel. That's what I'm here for."[73]

In a few minutes they left for the Morrow apartment in Manhattan. The Treasury agents were appalled at Condon's stupidity. When they entered the apartment, Jafsie was talking to someone. "Jafsie was always speaking," wrote Agent Elmer Irey, "so I must admit we weren't paying too much attention to him."

"Well, I talked him out of $20,000."

"What?"

"Yes, sir. I saved $20,000. Look."

Before their horrified eyes, Condon produced four hundred fifty-dollar gold certificates. "We could have shot the well-meaning meddler," grumbled Irey. These certificates would have caused any teller or merchant to take notice. Still beaming with pride, Condon presented the money—Lindbergh's money—to one of the agents. That was a lot of cash, said the surprised agent, and he was unarmed. "I'll fix that," said Jafsie. He went to his overcoat and returned with two antique horse pistols, from "Jafsie's long-gone youth."[74]

Lindbergh chartered a seaplane and insisted that Condon accompany him on the flight over the waters around the Elizabeth Islands between Martha's Vineyard and Cape Cod, where Cemetery John had said in the receipt the boat *Nelly* with Charlie on board would be found. They searched for two days (while Condon spouted quotations from the Bible and Shakespeare)—and found nothing. "Now I'll tell you," Condon told Turrou and other agents, "I'm really surprised, and that's the truth. I thought he was playing fair and square. Why shouldn't he? He's got the money, and we didn't touch him. Now that I call being dishonest."[75]

A new series of Jafsie notices appeared in the newspapers: "What is wrong? Have you crossed me? Please, better directions." Within a few days all the newspapers that did not already know the identity of the mysterious Jafsie now knew who had paid over the money to an unknown man in St. Raymond's Cemetery. Gregory Coleman broke the "story" in the *Bronx Home News,* giving details of the notes and conversations. Smelling more hot stories in Condon's kitchen, newspaper reporters by the dozens came trooping to the house on Decatur Avenue. Given that the search for Charlie was still under way, Coleman's story was more than inappropriate—it bordered on the criminal.

The mob around his house apparently upset even Condon. "Get off my property," he shouted from his front porch, a hand in his pocket as if holding a weapon. "I don't know you. You might be the kidnappers."[76] One time he came out of the house and began waving an American flag, as if to ward off evildoers. If he told what he knew, he admonished the crowd, the baby would be dead in twenty-four hours. Or he would be. "I had contacts with the kidnappers and have direct contacts with them still. I have never identified them nor said a word against them. I value my life as they value theirs, and I know that my life would not be worth anything if I said anything against them."[77]

Condon kept to his academic schedule, nevertheless, teaching classes at the College of New Rochelle. He told students in one class that he had recognized the penmanship in all the notes "as the handwriting of a former pupil." He recognized it, he said, because of a peculiarity: the letter *t* was never crossed.

Reporters caught up with Condon in Pelham Park, as he was about to umpire a charity baseball game. Between innings he was "prevailed upon" to speak a few words for the newsreel cameras. "We are in contact with the kidnappers and the baby will be returned soon, I hope." But then he spoke as if he knew Charlie was dead. He would not give up the search, he said, until "the most dastardly crime of modern times," carried out by "an extremely shrewd gang," had been solved.[78]

On April 19, 1932, Condon attempted to demonstrate to the world how the extortionist made good his escape from St. Raymond's with the money. From a dock on City Island bordering on Pelham Bay, Condon and another man dragged a small skiff fifty feet to the water and began rowing across the waters of lower Long Island Sound, stopping at Throggs Neck, then continuing until his boat tipped in the oily waters near a factory wharf close to Ferry Point. Condon nearly drowned. But he achieved his purpose—keeping the press focused on his new mission to hunt down the kidnapper.[79]

Declaring he was in mortal danger, Condon carried an automatic pistol under his coat at all times. In addition to his dip in the bay, Condon had had another adventure—or so he told the reporter Arthur O'Sullivan, perhaps to make up for denying him the big story on the day the ransom was paid. Condon asserted he had been rowed out to a vessel off Throggs Neck, blindfolded, about a week after the meeting at Woodlawn cemetery. When he was taken on board, he found himself confronted by five armed men. He knew two of the men as "John" and "Doc." "John" was a German and was the same man who later received the ransom payment. He was about thirty-five, five-foot-eight, blond, with an athletic build. The second man, "Doc," was Italian, the third, Spanish, and the two others were shadowy figures in the background. Put down your guns, fearless Jafsie ordered, and they all obeyed but one, "Doc," who kept his weapon pointed at him. The baby had been moved ashore, said the leader, for safety reasons. They would now send the sleeping suit. The day after O'Sullivan's articles on Condon's adventure appeared in the *New York Daily News* and the *Newark Evening News,* Condon denied the whole thing. Condon's denial rings hollow. The incident never happened, but he was given to such flights of fancy at the tip of a reporter's hat.[80]

With the exception of his daughter, Condon's family had been opposed to his getting involved in what was now becoming a lifestyle for Jafsie. His wife told FBI agents that her sons, John and Lawrence, were very much upset by his activities. And she was never able to understand why he had offered a $1,000 reward for the safe return of the Lindbergh child. Her only explanation was that he was a "generous philanthropist."[81]

Jafsie's pursuit of the man who had betrayed him took a new turn after the discovery of Charlie's body ten weeks after the kidnapping. On May 12, 1932, a drizzly afternoon, a truck driver stepped into the woods to answer a call of nature. He looked down in the underbrush and saw a half buried, badly decomposed corpse. Amazingly, the site was less than two miles from Hopewell. State troopers and volunteers had scoured the area more than once. Equally amazing, the body was found less than one hundred yards off the road between Hopewell and Princeton. Colonel Norman Schwarzkopf had kept a running log of all the searches. On April 7, 1932, for example, he had written, "a re-check of all the surrounding area was made by experienced detectives in a minute search of the territory for a radius of at least five miles."[82]

Police removed a piece of cloth from the body and took it to the Lindbergh house, and Betty Gow identified it as the little nightshirt she had sewn with blue thread. Unlike the sleeping suit, this was powerful evidence the body was Charlie's. Colonel Lindbergh was away searching at sea off Cape May, New Jersey, so Betty accompanied the men back to the local morgue to spare Anne the pain of seeing the decomposed remains of her firstborn. She emerged from the autopsy room after only a few seconds. "There has not been any mistake. Those are the remains of Charles A. Lindbergh, Jr.!"[83]

"We were now entitled to know the whole story of the kidnapping," wrote J. Edgar Hoover to an aide, not just tidbits picked up from Major Lanphier or Colonel Breckinridge. He wanted to question the servants and Mickey Rosner. "We will certainly want to question Condon." But while New Jersey and New York authorities questioned Condon over and over again, the FBI never got its chance to compare Jafsie's 1,001 stories.[84]

At the heart of the Jafsie mystery, two things stand out above the rest: first, the messenger who slipped away unquestioned—almost unseen—from the house on Decatur Street on the night of the ransom payment, even though police, FBI, and, finally, nearly a dozen reporters stood watch at points along that narrow street day and night.[85] Did a New York taxi arrive at the door, or was the note conveyed by someone else, a person Jafsie did not want admitted to the house? And second, there were the lengthy negotiations at St. Raymond's that night, during which Jafsie seemed to "warn" Cemetery John that the money might be marked. All the most easily traceable bills were removed, moreover, as a result of Condon's bargaining. No one has ever discovered the answer to these mysteries.

5 INTERROGATIONS

This is a brilliant opportunity for every policeman. The cop who arrests the murderer of the Lindbergh baby is made for life. Why, he could get fifty-two weeks' booking at $10,000 a week.

—GOVERNOR A. HARRY MOORE of New Jersey, May 14, 1932

It was a dreary, dismal day—Friday, May 13. A crowd had gathered in front of the Trenton mortuary. Soon a familiar car appeared. A tall, hatless young man got out and pushed his way through the crowd to enter the mortuary. Although he had been assured that the largely decomposed body on the examining table was that of his son, Colonel Lindbergh demanded the sheet be removed so that he could see for himself. After a brief examination of the teeth and toes, he left the room in silence. "I am perfectly satisfied that is my child," he told the county prosecutor.[1]

Dr. John F. Condon stood in the rain under a tree watching the scene from across the street. "I had no desire," Condon would write, "to see the pathetic spectacle inside." Yet he somehow obtained and kept a picture of the corpse, displaying it to an FBI agent in 1934. The trip to the mortuary may have been some sort of "courtesy" arranged for the loyal Jafsie, or it may have been to test his reactions, as he was also taken to see where the body had been discovered, half buried in the undergrowth. In any event, Condon's presence there that day was not entirely voluntary. He and Morris Rosner had been summoned to High-fields, along with John Hughes Curtis, a prominent businessman from Norfolk, Virginia, who claimed to be in contact with the true gang.

After Lindbergh viewed the body, it was placed in a small oak coffin and driven to Rosehill Cemetery and Crematorium in Linden, New Jersey. There the ashes would remain until Lindbergh could take them aloft and scatter them from his plane. He resolved never to be so naive again. "Everything is chance," he said. "You can guard against the high percentage of chance but not against chance itself." Anne felt Charlie's death, nevertheless, had made something "tremendous" out of their marriage that could never be changed. "And for the world, too, perhaps, the sacrifice will bring something."[2]

Lindbergh felt not only deceived but also degraded, and, according to biographer Scott Berg, was beginning to feel that the United States had become so barbaric that he and his family could no longer live there. The cruelest hoaxer had been John Hughes Curtis, who kept Lindbergh occupied for three weeks with a charade about kidnappers on board a ship off Cape May, a tale which suggested as well that the family had been betrayed by the servants. The kidnapping plot originated, said Curtis, "in the household." The kidnappers had been shown the plans of the Hopewell house and had been there three times. They gained entrance, if this were so, through Olly Whateley. And Lindbergh wrote down, "Family job—indicate Whateley." They made their escape, then, by taking the child down the steps to the front door, one of them securing the getaway by locking the pantry door so they could pass out of the house unseen. This "information" intrigued Lindbergh, who wondered how the key got there. Ultimately, under heavy questioning in the basement at Highfields, Curtis was forced to admit that his "Gang of Five" was a hoax.[3]

Rosner, Curtis, and Condon were kept in separate rooms at Highfields, while questioners moved back and forth, comparing notes. Soon the trio started pointing fingers at one another. As usual, the most vocal was Jafsie. He accused Curtis of spoiling his negotiations with Cemetery John. "I knew all along that this Curtis was a faker," Condon complained to reporters after his Highfields interrogation; yet he was the one who suffered ridicule for his efforts. Pulling a newspaper clipping from his coat pocket, Condon showed them a story that claimed Lindbergh had given Curtis the authority to pay over $100,000 for the return of the baby. That did it, he said. "They believed that I, too, had received $100,000 and that I had held out $50,000 on them."[4]

Did Condon believe, then, that Cemetery John's gang, learning of the Lindbergh "offer" to Curtis, had refused the "better instructions" he kept pleading for in newspaper notices? And then killed the child? It is hard to fathom his meaning, since by the time he made this statement he knew the baby had been dead for a long time—and had suspected it even as he paid over the money. Indeed, that was one reason he tried to "save" Colonel Lindbergh $20,000. How could he now argue, "[Curtis's interference] severed my connections with the real kidnappers, coming as it did a short time after I had paid over $50,000 ransom money to them"? Something is seriously wrong here.

Why in the world would Condon still think, finally, after the body was found in the condition it was, that any sort of useful contacts had been severed? The old man's rambling discourses had begun to suggest he was losing control—or that he knew more than he was telling.

Rosner, of course, had been suspicious of Condon since their first meeting at Highfields; even more so after learning that the elderly teacher had been waving around copies of the ransom notes—and perhaps originals as well—in public places such as restaurants. Indeed, a woman had seen Jafsie talking with two men on a subway platform, while displaying a newspaper and a picture of the Lindbergh child, the very night he returned from his first visit to Hopewell.[5]

Even as he engaged in the negotiations—promising fealty to the Lindberghs—Jafsie had told a class of high school girls at the College of New Rochelle exactly what he was doing—and why. He could hardly wait to do so. It was March 14, the Monday after his first meeting with Cemetery John. "He had sworn that he would return the baby to his mother's arms," one of those present reported. "How often he repeated that phrase!" He went on to explain the derivation of his secret persona, Jafsie, and why he had offered himself as go-between. "He said participation in this affair was the greatest thing that had ever happened to him—the motivation of his whole existence—and that he would not fail."

He began class with an "object lesson," as he put it, putting several words on the blackboard "in different handwritings" and asking how they might be identified as from the same person. No one volunteered an answer. He did not expect anyone would. Condon took up his own challenge and pointed out that the *t*s were uncrossed and the *i*s undotted. So these habits, and the way certain letters were formed, proved they were all "written by the same hand." Apparently, some of the students were skeptical about what they were hearing. After all, from the first class meeting Condon had seemed to them "egotistical and conceited." To substantiate his claim, "he called upon a girl in the front row and gave her three letters to read. Two of them were ransom notes and the third a letter from Lindbergh authorizing him, Dr. Condon, to act as intermediary." Once this performance was over, "he asked us with childlike simplicity to promise solemnly that whatever he said that afternoon would be held by us in absolute secrecy."[6]

Mercer County prosecutor Erwin Marshall reported what the interrogators at Highfields had learned from Jafsie so far. "Condon did not tell me his name, only his surname [Cemetery John]. He described the man he saw as very active and of the Scandinavian type." He was about thirty-five years old "and had tight lips, sharp chin, and bulging forehead."

New Jersey governor Harry Moore, meanwhile, tried to shield Colonel Schwarzkopf from charges by Ellis Parker that the whole investigation by the state police had been bungled. "Failure to make a thorough search of the entire community within a wide radius of the Lindbergh home immediately after the kidnapping," said the Burlington County detective, "is inexcusable and shameful." Nonsense, said Moore, he had been informed Condon had even seen the baby. Condon had said no such thing, however, and the autopsy report indicated the child had been dead for at least ten weeks. "Well," huffed Moore, "you know what these examinations are [like;] you can't be sure, especially considering weather conditions, whether the child was dead three or ten weeks."[7]

However self-serving, the governor's statement did touch on an issue not so easily resolved—not how long ago death occurred but how long the body had been there. "Two weeks after the crime had been committed," a farmer who lived near the spot told reporters, "the troopers were all over the place. I believe they were right around the little grave. Of course, they may not have seen it. The underbrush is thick there, and now that the trees are in leaf, it is hard to see more than ten yards ahead."

"I believe the body was placed there lately," said the farmer, Robert Buffet. "I haven't seen any buzzards flying around." A grim statement, lacking empathy, but it called attention to a problem with the accidental discovery of Charlie's corpse by the truck driver. Had the body been there since March 1, or was it moved there from some other location? And if so, why?[8]

The autopsy report, made after a hasty examination the day Charlie's body was discovered, noted first the "marked decomposition" and the missing limbs, the left leg, left hand, and right forearm. "Body shows evidence of prolonged exposure and usual decomposition that would occur in the course of approximately two or three months time, depending on climatic and other conditions that might produce such a result."

The cause of death was identified as "a fractured skull due to external violence." The fracture began at the fontanel and ran down the left side of the skull to a point behind the left ear, where it bifurcated into two distinct fractures. But there was no real clue as to how that had happened, no finding of the classic sort favored in fact and fiction, "Death caused by a blow from a blunt instrument." And there were other things in the report that were apparently not immediately connected with Charlie's death: "Unusually high and prominent forehead and cranium, apparently greater in circumference than would be found in a child of this age. First toe of the right foot completely overlaps the large toe and the second toe of the right foot partially overlaps the large toe." In addition: "The fontanel was not closed, the opening in the skull at this point being about one inch in diameter." Such a large opening was not usual in a two-year-old, as the fontanel should be closed by that age.[9]

Emerging from a three-hour session looking at "rogue's gallery" pictures in New York, the next day, Condon predicted the kidnapper would soon be apprehended. He knew his name, he told a crowd of reporters outside his house, and what he looked like. As he spoke, he fingered a sheaf of papers, inviting more questions. Were those the ransom notes? the reporters asked. He would not say. But he assured them he could "pick him out of a thousand." Little wonder crowds swarmed around his house, waiting to hear the Bronx oracle's latest words. Police stood guard as he emerged from time to time to greet his "admirers."[10]

Small boys seeking an autograph came up to him with a piece of paper as he sat on his front porch. He signed it "Dr. Condon" and, underneath, "Jafsie." FBI agents asked mail carriers what they observed about Condon's behavior. They all agreed he was "a fiend for notoriety," who, when he did not receive any mail, would hail them from half a block away to ask if they were sure there were no letters for him. Prior to the case, he received little mail. "Since the advent of this case he has received a tremendous amount of mail and he makes himself seen more and more and tries to appear much more important."[11]

But it was said he was suffering from fatigue. After testifying before the grand jury on May 20, 1932, Condon sped off in a car driven by a neighbor, Walter Goodwin. Two New York detectives followed, and behind them trailed a caravan of reporters. No one had any idea where Condon and his friend were going, but they wanted to be there to hear Jafsie's latest pronouncements.[12]

Outside Danbury, Connecticut, Condon and his friend stopped at a roadhouse for lunch. Everyone followed them inside. Smiling in mock exasperation, Condon shrugged and said, "I just can't seem to get away for a quiet little jaunt by myself." Then he launched into yet another prophecy so as not to disappoint his fellow travelers. "I have received a communication," the weary titan announced, "and expect to receive other communications along the way." With a piercing look at his audience, he once more vowed, "I want to bring those scoundrels to justice."[13]

Goodwin thought he had lost the reporters. But when they arrived at his camp on a lake near Becket, Massachusetts, the journalists were waiting at the entrance. No sooner was he unpacked than Condon began a new round of revelations, claiming to have received the promised further communications. He had a "message" for "John," he said, and proceeded to read it out loud: "John: Money I gave you is useless. You can't get rid of it. Return to Colonel Lindbergh in time. Get your $25,000 reward." He had signed the note "Jafsie."[14]

Goodwin was alarmed at Condon's behavior. His friend was not willing to admit it, he explained, but he was nearly exhausted. The message to John, however, was only the first of many bizarre utterances from "Center Pond," the Goodwin hideaway. According to Condon's latest story the gang that had kidnapped Charlie consisted of three men and two women. "Their leader is very smart and a high public official. I do not know what his position is. I saw no native Americans."

The money had been "parked," he now said some fishermen had told him, near New Bedford. That's where he would look if he were a policeman. He was expecting a "mystery message," he said. And a little later: "I received the message and it was very important." Could it be, asked reporters, that this message referred to Jack "Bugs" Marston, a member of the infamous Detroit Purple Gang, known to visit nearby Pittsfield on business—stealing automobiles? Pittsfield police officers came to Condon one morning with a picture of Marston Yes, said Condon, that's the man; that's the one he had paid the money to. Go find him. Marston, it turned out, was catching lobsters in the waters off Long Island. By evening, Condon had cooled on Marston—but still thought he should be apprehended.[15]

After an interview or two, Pittsfield police chief John L. Sullivan had cooled on Jafsie as well—warning reporters that he was indeed near a breakdown, and writing Colonel Schwarzkopf that he might do injury to the case if some of his statements were taken at face value. "His sentences and his talk sometimes didn't coordinate."[16]

Yet there were some nuggets of real information buried in Condon's rambling discussions with the importuning reporters. He gave them a plausible reason for Cemetery John's willingness to accept $50,000 instead of the $70,000 he had demanded. "They finally agreed to deliver the baby for $50,000 and the promise of immunity." There was more. John had told Jafsie that the actual kidnapper on the ladder that night was a man from Boston. "Whether the same man was the fiend who so needlessly snuffed out the innocent little life has not been disclosed, for Dr. Condon has not heard from 'John' since the discovery of the child's body."[17]

Condon's efforts to separate John from the rest of the gang, to imply, as he did here, that he had separate contacts with him—perhaps besides the two cemetery meetings—could suggest many things. It could suggest, for example, that Condon was truly on the verge of a complete breakdown, not surprising for a man of his age who had been through what he had in the past few weeks. It could also suggest, however, an unwillingness to accept what had happened as final. And, together with the mention of a supposed discussion of immunity, a relationship that went beyond the immediate events of the kidnapping. "I saw his face clearly," Condon told the reporters. "I would know him again. He was obviously a Scandinavian, and I asked his name. He would not tell me, and I said: 'I will call you John.' He assented."[18]

Inspector Harry Walsh of the Jersey City Police, for one, yearned to know which of Condon's stories approximated what really happened. For the time being, Walsh had become Schwarzkopf's interrogator-in-chief. On June 2, using a pretense that Condon was to look at some more pictures, Walsh had him brought to state police headquarters at Alpine, New Jersey. According to Cordon, the inspector entered the room at Alpine, walked over to him, arms folded, and stood toe-to-toe. "All, right Condon," he snapped, "it's about time that you started to confess."[19]

Police minutes have a somewhat different take on the opening salvo. What did he mean, Walsh said, by promising to keep the confidence of the kidnappers? Throughout the exchanges that followed, Walsh kept coming back to this issue of Condon's assurances that he would not betray the kidnappers—and did he feel the same way now that the baby had been found dead? This, he thought, was the most vulnerable place to begin a serious examination of this sly old codger who had pulled the wool over everyone's eyes.[20]

It took several questions to elicit a simple acknowledgment from Condon that he did not have—or ever had, presumably—any obligations of that sort to the kidnappers. Well, if that were so, what was the meaning of the statement in the second ransom note that their demand had been raised to $70,000, because they had to take in another party? "The person whom they took in and who made it necessary to elevate the ransom money twenty thousand evidently became aware of the fact that the baby was dead and couldn't be produced and said that he didn't want any of this money," Walsh asserted. "That person couldn't have been anybody but you."[21]

"That is a mistake. It is not true," Condon protested. Switching to "good" cop, Walsh tried to ease the old man into a confession of sorts. "I don't believe you had anything to do with it. I believe that you entered into this thing, that you wanted to be a good Samaritan to two people, the kidnap[p]ers and the Lindberghs."[22]

Walsh had threatened him, Condon would claim, both physically and mentally during the four-hour interrogation. "Get your hat," the inspector ordered. "Do you know how to play croquet?" He was an expert, Condon replied, but preferred boxing. Ignoring the sarcasm, Walsh took him for a walk. "Our path led us along New Jersey's glorious Palisades, with their sheer, occasional drops of 700 feet." Maybe it was a psychological trick, Condon wrote, because Walsh put him nearest the edge. If so, it would fail, as did all other attempts to intimidate courageous Jafsie, beginning with the swarthy man in the restaurant the night of the kidnapping, then with Cemetery John, and now with Inspector Walsh.

It was Walsh, Condon reported, who feared heights and drew back from the edge of the abyss. "Come back here," Walsh supposedly said in frustration at his botched ploy, and his "voice held genuine worry." Then Condon turned and smiled at him. "I have nothing to confess, Inspector," he assured him. "And I do not plan to commit suicide."[23]

Walsh could not bring the wily schoolmaster to confess any part in the kidnapping, even when he threatened Condon with exposure of accusations of sexual impropriety with a young female pupil. He admitted the accusation but said, "I was exonerated," and that was the end of it.[24]

Retreating from earlier ambivalence about the nationality of Cemetery John, Condon now insisted the man he had confronted was Scandinavian, *not* German. What made you think that? Walsh pressed. "He told me, and his accent." Why did you believe him, persisted Walsh, when you have been deceived about the baby from beginning to end? "That might be," conceded Condon. Could you really say he was Scandinavian, persisted Walsh, from your own knowledge? "I figure he was not a German and I figure he was what he said he was from the way I've heard them speak and from the way that he spoke to me."[25]

Condon also added another snippet of hitherto unknown conversation from the encounter at St. Raymond's. When the money changed hands, Cemetery John said, "Let me see this, let me count this, let me investigate to see if it is all right. They would smack me out if they think I had gypped some of the money." Since this session at the Alpine headquarters took place only a week after he returned from Massachusetts, the revelation that John feared the gang's retribution fits nicely with his recent statements to reporters. It does not fit comfortably, however, with Condon's later recollections in *Jafsie Tells All* that Cemetery John's instant willingness to accept $50,000 instead of the demanded $70,000 proved to him that the kidnapper was a lone wolf.[26]

Near the end of the session, Condon gave Walsh the fullest description yet of Cemetery John.

> About 5'8", about 158 or 160 lbs. I think a little thick through the shoulders. Then he had when I saw him a black coat of thin material and one button at the top and he held that up over his chin. When I asked him to take it down he did for a moment and when he did I saw that he had a very narrow chin. The eyes were on the axis straight, his nose pretty well formed and well formed mouth. The skin was smooth and it gave me the impression that disease had started its inroads into his body. He had a hacking cough. . . . His eyes were almond shaped and quite distant from the nose, but the eyes he never opened wide. They seemed to be rather semi-closed. Not big eyes. The cheek was smooth, from the high cheekbone right down to the chin. Where disease sets in it would affect the cheeks and it would affect the face opposite the mouth . . . very agile and active. His hair was sort of dirty blond.[27]

The taxicab driver, Josph Perrone, had given police a similar description of the man who appeared out of nowhere with a letter for Condon. During a sesson of the grand jury, however, Perrone described him as having "kind of light brown eyes," a very significant difference from Condon's description of Cemetery John's eyes, and from his own later descriptions of the man's eyes as blue. He talked with a German or Scandinavian accent, said Perrone, probably more like the former. He particularly noticed the man said "Vare" instead of "Where." But when he mentioned 201st Street, Perrone recalled, he did not seem to have an accent at all. A member of the grand jury pressed the cabbie on that point. Did he indicate that he was someone of foreign extraction?

"Well, it looked like he was putting on [an accent]."

"In other words you believe him to be native born and had feigned this accent in the speech to mislead you?"

"Yes."

Here was an important point, as Condon had noticed the same thing at St. Raymond's: the man who took the ransom payment seemed able to slip in and out of his accent when he chose to do so.

Perrone was quite sure about the way the man was dressed. He had on a heavy, double-breasted brown overcoat and brown fedora hat. Condon, of course, remembered very well that the man he met that night at Woodlawn Cemetery wore a lightweight, black coat, with one button fastened at the top.

The place where the man stopped Perrone was not far at all from the cemetery. Indeed, it was quite close. A car parked facing toward the Moshulu Parkway could turn either right or left on that road, and then double back north to Woodlawn. Was there someone waiting in the car? Or did the man who gave the driver the letter change coats at some point, before making his way to the entrance gate of the cemetery?

When Perrone reached Condon's home, and handed over the letter, there was something else that might have caught one's attention. Condon called his young protégé, Milton Gaglio, to come downstairs and take "good care of this young man and give him something." It had already been ascertained that Perrone received the message at Gun Hill and Knox Place, but Gaglio immediately asked, "Where did you get this note, Bainbridge and Gunhill Road?"

"No," responded Perrone, "I got it at Knox Place and Gunhill Road."

Gaglio wanted to know everything about the man who gave him the letter and so Perrone repeated the description. But Gaglio's question about Bainbridge Avenue and Gunhill—a location much closer to the cemetery than Knox Place—had struck Perrone as funny. In a case filled with so many coincidences, Gaglio had hit upon a transfer spot nearer to where Cemetery John would be found scarcely over an hour later. Knox Place was a short street, not a place where cabs cruised for fares. Bainbridge was a much more likely place, coming off a main thoroughfare, Jerome Avenue, south from the cemetery—especially if one expected a meeting there later.

Without prompting, Perrone told FBI agents that he wondered if Gaglio did have prior knowledge of where the contact would be made. When Gaglio was questioned, however, he claimed not to remember if he had made such a statement to the cabbie. The only way to get to the bottom of this, said the agent in his report, was to bring all three of the participants together: Condon, Perrone, and Gaglio. But that was never done. Indeed Condon seemed uninterested in talking with Perrone about his contact, or with the second unknown "taxi man" who brought him the note giving directions for the ransom payment.[28]

Still more curious, in mid-April Gaglio sought out Perrone in a restaurant in the middle of the night near his hack stand on Moshulu Parkway. Gaglio seemed not to recognize him, however, and had to ask if he were the one who had brought the letter to Condon's house. "Yes, I am the fellow." Gaglio produced some cards and said, "Now listen, Inspector [Henry] Bruckman will try to get in touch with you and we don't want them to bother with you yet, is there any possible way that you could leave the house for three days?" Perrone just stared at him and refused. "If the police want me, they know where I am."

The very next day Gaglio showed up at his home, this time with some photographs, to ask if he recognized any of the subjects as the man who had given him the letter for Condon. He took Perrone to his car, where a woman waited, and they drove around for some time. Eventually, Gaglio took the cabbie to a drugstore, where he showed him these pictures in a phone booth. None of them resembled the man. Later, outside the grand jury room, Gaglio behaved again as if he scarcely knew Perrone.[29]

Gaglio denied much of Perrone's story, especially that he had ever tried to persuade him to get out of town and lay low for a while. His explanation for his attempt to find Perrone was that news reporters wanted him to show the cabbie some rogue's gallery pictures to see if Perrone could identify any of them, and Condon asked him to carry out the mission. An FBI agent pressed him on both these points: Had he said anything like what Perrone had reported? Well, said Gaglio, he might have misunderstood him about the pictures. "I might have said to him that I didn't want him to say anything about it to anybody especially to his cab-driver friends because the thing might get out in the papers, and they would indicate who the contact man was." Pressed to elaborate, Gaglio added, "I figured that if it came out in the papers that they might locate the contact man . . . the contact would cease."[30]

Gaglio and Perrone told two very different stories. It would be hard, indeed, to reconcile their accounts. What is also interesting, and perhaps more important, is Condon's reluctance to have Perrone found too soon, and, for all of his protestations about an undying search for the kidnapper, that he never insisted they sit down together and compare notes.

Although Perrone did not recognize any of the photos Gaglio showed him in the drugstore phone booth, over the next two years he would pick out photos of several men he thought closely resembled the mysterious figure in the brown, double-breasted coat. He spotted men on the street from his cab, and at social gatherings. On another occasion, Special Agent John Seykora even asked him how Colonel Schwarzkopf compared to the man; on yet another, Special Agent Thomas Sisk told Perrone that Condon had said the man to whom he had paid the ransom money looked like a Chinaman.[31]

Joe Perrone must have had a real time of it keeping track of what this man looked like. His "suspects" ranged in height from five-foot-six on up to near six feet and in age from early thirties to late forties. He chased several of them in his cab, alighting on occasion to summon police to aid him. One of them rode in his taxi and impressed him with his "conversational likeness" to the man who gave him the note. Shortly after the grand jury proceedings of May 1932, Perrone took a fare out to City Island and there observed Condon talking to a man whom "he thought was the man who gave him the note."[32]

Of all the men Perrone thus identified, however, one stood out. His name was Rhinehold Giirndt, but he used the alias Otto Steiner or Steinert. Steiner had been arrested in the Bronx for stealing stable equipment, and because of the vicinity, police showed Steiner's picture to Perrone. It was, he said, the nearest likeness. The picture reminded him, he said, of one he had picked out at Hopewell when he had been taken there. Steiner was thirty-two, five-foot-nine, and weighed 185 pounds, with blue eyes, medium light complexion, and dark blond hair. He had been born in Germany. Police photographs of Steiner show a man with a full face, wearing a hat in the same style as the man who gave Perrone the note. There were two things about the man Perrone always emphasized through many interrogations: a brown double-breasted coat and a full face. (Condon's Cemetery John wore a black coat and had a narrow face.) The Steiner identification never panned out, but Perrone's insistence on these details throughout the investigation is remarkable.

Over the next two years, Perrone would make himself familiar to New Jersey State Police officers, discovering men who looked like the man coming out of hotels and even in groups walking around the city. He was on a first-name basis with at least one trooper, Sergeant Zapolsky. "Dear Zappy," he wrote on December 21, 1932. "If you should happen to be in the neighborhood stop in to see me, as I have something to tell you." He enclosed license plate numbers of suspicious automobiles. "Zappy I saw these three cars parked at Knox Pl & Gunhill Rd at 11:30 P.M. Dec 23rd." He was the most eager of all the eyewitnesses to help out the police—and collect the reward.[33]

FBI agents wondered if Condon had ever searched for the second taxi driver. A strong case can be made that it was John Birritella, brother of Peter, the spiritualist minister who had brought Mary Cerrita to Princeton for the séance with Henry Breckinridge. John Birritella was a licensed taxicab driver but not a regular driver for any company. Most recently, he had been employed by the American Railway Express Company.

Police discovered he had worked on March 1, 1932, but not the next day, and had been discharged for petty thievery. "The subject," read Sergeant E. A. Hausling's report, "was a good dresser, apparently always having ready cash, [and] a convincing talker."[34]

State police investigators took pictures of John Birritella to Condon for identification purposes. Condon stated that the picture "did not in any way resemble the man with whom he had contact during the Lindbergh Case." When one remembers the various accounts Jafsie gave of meeting the second cabbie, this later comment is another deflection, by a grand master of the art. The picture, he said, did not resemble "the man with whom he had contact," in other words, "Cemetery John." And so it was left at that—the person who brought the second note whether by car or on foot was never to be identified.[35]

The FBI eventually learned of an earlier contact that also possibly related to the Birritellas. A taxi driver had brought a woman to Condon's home on March 7, 1932. When asked about this mysterious visit, Condon replied that the woman was going down to Atlantic Highlands in New Jersey to open a boardinghouse for children, "and wanted Dr. Condon to help her get children for her boarding house for the summer months." The interviewing agent noted only, "An effort will be made to locate this woman."[36]

It can be argued that this woman had a different message. She might have brought an example of the "singnature," so that Condon would recognize which of the letters he received was genuine. Such speculations are not as wild as they might seem at first glance.

Two days after the discovery of the body, on May 12, 1932, Jafsie met with Arthur O'Sullivan of the *New York Daily News* and gave him the first of several confidential interviews. On one occasion when they were sitting together in the living room of his house, Condon spun out a new version of how he first became involved in the case. "Supposing," Condon began, "there were a family in which most of the members were bad but one of them was very good and, suppose that the good one came to you and went down on her knees, asking your protection. Wouldn't you do everything to shield her name?" O'Sullivan tried to find out more, asking for the name of the woman. Condon drew back: "No, I'll carry her name a secret to the day I die."[37]

Any connection with O'Sullivan was always denied by Condon, but an FBI agent later conducted an interview with Jafsie and was surprised when he pulled a morgue picture of Charlie from a large envelope on which was written "H. C. Sullivan, New York, *Daily News*." Condon explained that a newspaperman must have stolen it from the morgue. But he did not say how he got it if he had no close dealings with O'Sullivan.[38]

Was there a trade involved? The picture for a scoop? However that may be, O'Sullivan's recounting of what took place in Jafsie's living room one afternoon in May 1932 is no more unbelievable than Condon's other accounts of how he first became involved. If the woman came to him before he wrote the letter to the *Bronx Home News,* as he told O'Sullivan, that would mean she came to him close on the heels of the visit of Peter Birritella and Mary Cerrita to Princeton and the séance that Sunday afternoon.

Frank Wilson, a Treasury agent, had long wondered about the couple's role, and he also wondered about Condon's. The part Jafsie played in this case was a most exacting one, he wrote his superiors, and perhaps exceedingly dangerous. "I believe that the strain has affected him and that it would not be advisable to depend too strongly on further assistance from him. . . . The fact that the kidnappers acted to select him within twenty-four hours after he offered through the *Bronx Home News* to act as intermediary indicates to me that one of them at some time knew him personally or by reputation. His circle of acquaintances is very large and in passing upon all suspects, an effort should be made to ascertain whether they knew him. . . . Dr. Condon shows a natural desire to solve this case but as his efforts appear to be misdirected, I did not consider it advisable to encourage them."[39]

Condon managed to keep himself center stage, nevertheless. Police showed him hundreds of pictures. As he went through one batch, he picked out a man named Vaclav Simek. "Boys," he declared. "You are hot. I want to see that man." Simek had been convicted a decade earlier for kidnapping threats against Edsel Ford's baby and deported to Czechoslovakia. Told about Simek's record, Condon's excitement grew: "Of all the photos examined by him this was the only one he had found that so closely resembled John."[40]

Alas, Simek—a much-traveled international criminal—was in the Dominican Republic at the time of the kidnapping. But the police had more books of photos to show Condon. It was a dreary business for all concerned, as the investigation seemed to be descending to farce. On one occasion, the pictures were shuffled like a deck of cards, and, in the second round, Condon said a man he had previously identified as a look-alike bore no resemblance to Cemetery John at all.[41]

Even Lindbergh grew weary of Condon's erratic behavior and refused to intervene when New York authorities denied his request to visit state penal institutions to interview inmates.

In New Jersey, meanwhile, police officials believed they had better leads, especially if they concentrated on Morrow maid Violet Sharp.

She had received the phone call from Highfields that rainy morning and passed the information to Betty Gow. Inspector Walsh came to believe she was the key to the whole case. He was determined to break her story down. "I am convinced that Violet Sharp deceived us," he said, "and that she did so deliberately. I am convinced that she was the informant—the agent—of the kidnappers."[42]

Like Betty Gow, Violet Sharp had emigrated from Great Britain. Leaving their home in the English countryside, she and her younger sister, Emily (or Edna as she was also called), came first to Canada. Violet then left for New York and eventually applied for employment in the Morrow household. She was interviewed by the butler, Septimus Banks, and hired at a salary of $100 a month, plus room and board.

She also found work for her sister, Edna, with Constance Chilton, a friend and business partner of Elisabeth Morrow, Anne's sister, in the running of a private school for young children.

A not unattractive, dark-haired woman, Violet had something of a flirtatious manner about her—outside the Morrow household. She also had an independent spirit and was willing to run small (and not so small) risks to break out of the humdrum of daily routine. She also had secrets.

Violet expressed her fears and romantic ambitions through poetry, which she kept hidden away in a diary.

> I'm only a scullery maid, I'm wat they call low bred
> But [lord?] if you could see, I got big things in my head.
> I don't mean waht you mean I mean, I got imaginations
> Romantic; I can kid meself I'm *leaps* above me station.[43]

According to one report, she had married a George Payne in the winter of 1929–30 a few months before coming to North America in April of 1930. Her sister confirmed that she had married this man. When questioned by a Scotland Yard detective, Payne admitted that he had known Violet for nearly six years, had taken her out to movies occasionally, and corresponded with her after she went to the United States. But they had never married. He had been married to another woman for thirty-six years. In the United States, moreover, she always went by her maiden name.[44]

Soon it was being rumored that Banks and Violet Sharp were romantically involved—and marriage was in the future. There were other rumors, however, that Violet would not have Banks unless he stopped drinking and stayed sober for a given period of time. He had come close to being fired on several occasions. And police found a note in her room recording that Banks had promised her to be straight for twelve months, meaning he would not get drunk.

Like Betty Gow, she had come to an age, nearly twenty-eight, when women of this era and with limited prospects needed to take account of where they stood. Returning to rural England and the crowded family home she had left was a grim option, but what awaited her here? Was that future any better?

When the questioning began after the kidnapping, her immediate responses to the police were snappish and less than fully cooperative. Walsh concluded her reluctance had less to do with fears about the disclosure of sexual affairs than with something connected with the Lindberghs' privacy after Charlie's birth, such as selling photos of the child.

Violet singled herself out by her behavior during questioning. In seeking to protect her secrets, she only encouraged police suspicions. Violet's first interrogation took place at the Morrow home on March 10, 1932, and was conducted by two Newark detectives. Asked about her movements on the evening of the kidnapping, she explained only that she had met a man while out walking on February 28, 1932, and he had requested her address and telephone number. This man, whose name she could not remember, asked if she would like to go to the movies one night. Violet indicated that she might. When he telephoned at 8 P.M., on March 1, 1932, she told him she would meet him after work, around 8:30—at the place where they had met.

Instead, he showed up at the pantry door in a car with another couple—people she had never met before. They went to a movie in Englewood, she said, and came straight back. He parked the car and walked her back to the house. He made a date for March 6 but never called back. And that was it. She offered no names, and nothing else about the evening. Violet's vagueness was disturbing, obviously, and there were scraps that suggested there might be more to the story—for example, how was it that the mysterious date arrived at the pantry door, instead of meeting her at the appointed place?[45]

The second interrogation, which occurred a month later at Englewood, was quite a different story. Harry Walsh conducted this one—and subsequent interrogations. According to Walsh's later account, Violet could not remember the name of the theater in Englewood or even the name of the movie. Moreover, she did not remember the names of any of the others, except her escort, "Ernie." She thought he was a bus driver. Walsh found Violet a "cold, abrupt, defiant and surly individual, who frequently grinned at a question regardless of its importance."[46]

Violet finally admitted that the foursome went to a speakeasy, the Peanut Grill, located in one of the Oranges, near Newark. She described her three companions in detail, right down to the "little black tam hat" the other woman wore—but still could remember no names. And Ernie's name, she insisted, she only knew because when he called for a second date he jogged her memory. Walsh found that hard to swallow. She did not keep that date, she now said, because it was raining too hard that day.[47]

Walsh began scouring New York and New Jersey records for either a bus driver or a taxi driver named Ernie. He reported to Colonel Lindbergh that Violet's story just didn't hold up. He wanted another go at questioning her. He wanted to know, for example, how a housemaid earning $100 a month had accumulated over $1,600 in a savings account in the relatively short time of her employment.

The interrogations were taking their toll on Violet. She lost weight and by the end of April had developed infected tonsils. When she saw a physician, he recommended they be removed. But the weight loss worried the doctor. It caused him to order a chest X-ray to determine if there was a more serious underlying condition. None showed up on the X-ray, and the tonsils were removed on May 10, 1932. She did not recover right away, yet she seemed anxious to get out of the hospital and discharged herself, against her physician's advice, on May 14, two days after Charlie's body was discovered.[48]

A week later, on May 21, 1932, Walsh interviewed Violet again—this time at Highfields. "It is impossible for me or anyone else to mimic her condition." he would write. "Her entire body shook and she could not talk coherently." Two police physicians were called in and found that she had a slight fever and a high pulse rate of 120. They called a halt to the interview. No more questioning, the doctors told Walsh, for at least twenty-four hours.[49]

The next interview was held on May 23 shortly after 7 P.M. Present when she entered the room were Colonel Schwarzkopf and one of his aides—as well as Colonel Lindbergh. Apparently surrounded by "accusers," Violet came up with a variety of responses: half-apologies for her previous stories, weak denials, plaintive appeals, and silences. At the outset Violet admitted that "Ernie" had called her, not at 7:45 P.M. on the night of March 1, but at 1 P.M., only a couple of hours after Anne had called from Highfields to instruct Betty Gow to come down to take charge of the baby's care.[50]

Alarm bells went off. If Violet had had a conversation with this Ernie at 1 P.M., there would have been plenty of time for someone to set up the kidnapping. Why hadn't she told the police this the first time? And why hadn't she tried to find out more about this man when she knew that police would be looking for anyone connected with the Lindberghs or Morrows on that fateful night? Hard questions, and she had no answer.

"You told me that you went to a moving picture show when I first questioned you?" Walsh asked.

"Yes," Violet replied.

"You also told the Newark Police that?"

"Yes."

"Will you explain why you told a lie about that?"

"I could not explain why, I don't know."

All right, Walsh moved on, now what about that large sum of money in her bank account, $1,600?

From time to time, she said, she sent money home to her parents, but she could not say how often or how much.

What about the man she had gone out with, the newspaper photographer for the *Daily News*?

Yes, she had gone out with him—several times. And, yes, she admitted, he had offered her a large sum of money, maybe as large as $10,000, for a picture of the Lindbergh baby. But she wouldn't have done that, she said.

If she had not accepted any money for a picture, Walsh persisted, why did her bank records show a $500 deposit the previous October?

She had saved up for a couple of months, and that was why it was so much.

Was it in cash or checks?

"I really could not tell you, I don't know."

Then it was back to Ernie. She did not know where he lived, how to get in touch with him, or what he did—although she thought, as she had said before, that he might be a bus driver.

Well, then, Walsh went on, "how did this man happen to be in Englewood the first time he picked you up?"

"I don't know," she replied.

There was more to that than Walsh could have known at the time, information Violet's sister, Emily, would supply to Scotland Yard's investigator, information that could tie in Violet—not as a participant in the crime but as an unwitting accomplice. When Violet saw the man passing in the car as the two were out walking, she waved, according to Emily. He stopped immediately. "I am sorry," Violet said. "I thought you were one of the workmen at Morrow's." "Well," came the reply, "that's where you come from." "Yes," answered Violet, and they fell into conversation. He called her Violet. Emily wondered about that. "He must have heard me call my sister by her Christian name," but the way she put that point made it seem she was not sure. They talked for a quarter of an hour, Emily remembered, then the women got in the car and rode with him to downtown Englewood. It was a strange meeting, to say the least.[51]

Asked to describe this Ernie, Violet said he was a tall man, who wore a blue suit, a gray overcoat, and a soft felt hat. His complexion was more dark than fair. "Was his hands rough or smooth?" Walsh asked. "Dirty looking," she replied. Violet's statements left few doubts that she had not been entranced with her date—who, it also came out, foisted her off on another man. She may have accepted the date only to irritate Septimus Banks, who went out that afternoon and returned, "sick," to his room.

However that may be, Walsh was highly dissatisfied with Violet's renditions of her evening out with Ernie and his friends. During the questioning, he had ordered a thorough search of Violet's room. Police found among her things a business card for the Post Road Taxicab Company of White Plains. The former owner of this two-cab outfit, it emerged, was a shady character named Ernest Brinkert. Here was a real clue at last—and a chance to see if she was telling the truth. Walsh obtained a photograph of Brinkert and set the stage for the confrontation he truly hoped would break the case wide open.

Producing the photograph from his pocket, the inspector asked if that was the man.

"Yes, it is."

Why didn't she tell police, then, that that was the man?

"I didn't know."

"Yes you did, you knew how to locate him and you was in possession of his business card."

"I did not!" she shot back. "My sister . . ."

"All I want to know," the inspector roared, "is, is it or is it not the man you were with that night?"

"Yes, I guess it is. It looks like him."

"All right," ended Walsh, "we will pick him up and let you see him in the flesh."

Violet spun away from her accuser and headed out of the room. "As she was going through the door," recalled Laura Hughes, a Morrow secretary, "she looked at me, sitting at my desk, smiled and winked." Another Morrow secretary, Arthur Springer, also took note of this wink and told the FBI later that it was because she believed she had fooled Walsh, that she had only pretended to recognize the picture.[52]

Thinking he had a positive identification, Walsh went immediately to the state police headquarters at Alpine, New Jersey. There he met with Schwarzkopf, Lindbergh, and Frank Wilson of the Treasury Department. According to Walsh, it was Colonel Lindbergh himself who suggested Violet be brought to Alpine "in the hope of obtaining information that would lead to the apprehension of the perpetrators."[53]

Walsh arranged for a physician to be present during the questioning; then he sent Lieutenant Arthur Keaten and two other officers to the Morrow home to pick up Violet on the morning of June 10. He had phoned ahead to Arthur Springer, to ask that she be ready to make the trip. When the officers arrived, Springer advised Mrs. Morrow they were waiting in his office for Violet to come down. After half an hour, Lieutenant Keaten finally pressed the issue. Springer left, only to return immediately with the news that Violet "had apparently fainted in the Butler's Pantry and that he had sent for a doctor." Keaten phoned Walsh, who arrived shortly thereafter, bringing with him the physician he had planned to have present at the questioning. Only then did the officers proceed to the study, where Colonel Lindbergh and a Dr. Phillips met them and told them Violet was dead.[54]

Colonel Lindbergh had found a "partially filled can of Cyanide of Potassium Crystals on the shelf in Miss Sharp's room," along with a glass containing the remaining undissolved crystals and a discolored spoon. Walsh proceeded to the room and saw the glass for himself. Violet had apparently committed suicide.

Schwarzkopf rushed to claim he was close to a solution to the kidnapping and death of Charles Augustus Lindbergh, Jr. It was a tragically foolish statement, given without a thought to Violet Sharp's reputation or memory—and it brought down a hailstorm of criticism on the state police. "The suicide of Violet Sharp," it read, "strongly tends to confirm the suspicions of the investigating authorities concerning her guilty knowledge of the crime against Charles A. Lindbergh, Jr." But he did not end the statement there. Violet had identified Ernest Brinkert, it went on, as "her associate on the night of the kidnapping." He all but accused Violet and Brinkert of the crime and promised that vigorous efforts were being made to find this man.[55]

News reports of Violet's suicide portrayed a young woman absolutely terrified of getting the third degree from police, and who had vowed that she would never be taken from the Morrow house to be questioned. "They'll never take me from this house again. They'll never question me again," she supposedly told the other servants the previous night. The next morning, when Arthur Springer delivered Keaten's summons, Violet ran pleading to Septimus Banks: "Walsh wants to question me, but I won't go." She seized a glass and ran upstairs to pour out the poison and drink the deadly potion.[56]

Violet's death stunned the nation and brought a counterstatement from Mrs. Morrow, full of implied criticism of Harry Walsh and the ham-fisted police treatment the young woman had suffered. "Violet was always a good girl. She was timid, diffident, with an unknown but persistent fear of the police. She reacted differently from the other servants, and the fact that she was of this nervous temperament, and constantly laboring under the strain of suspicion directed toward her, caused her to kill herself."

In England, Emily told reporters that police had questioned her sister for hours and hours on end. Her brother, Charles, produced a letter from Violet: "I don't know whether I'll be able to come home. They're still looking for the guys that killed that poor little baby. Mrs. Lindbergh's expecting another in August, so I hope they'll look after it better."[57] "Does that look like she had a crime on her mind?" her brother demanded.

New Jersey police made excuses, without retreating from their assumption that Violet was somehow in on the crime. The autopsy report showed no traces of any serious diseases "or impending motherhood." Harry Walsh was certainly unrepentant: "Someone had to serve as tip-off on the Lindbergh home to the kidnappers and we shall continue to assume that that someone was Violet Sharp." She stuck to that story of hers about going out with men whose names she never knew, he went on, stuck to it until the baby was found. "Then she went all to pieces—a bundle of jumpy nerves." Referring to the business card of the Post Road Taxi Company, which had been found in her room, he speculated, "Maybe that small piece of cardboard will yet prove to be the solution of the Lindbergh case."[58]

Tips from the FBI enabled police to locate Ernest Brinkert in New Rochelle, New York. They subjected him to the sharpest questioning of any of the suspects thus far—and got nowhere. Brinkert had not known Violet, had no idea why the Post Road Taxi Company's card had turned up in her room, and had a strong alibi. He was with his "wife" that day and evening, and all the next day. Brinkert had an unsavory reputation, to be sure; he was a suspect police would have loved to nail, having done prison time for robbery, cracked a rival's head with a wrench, and lied about being divorced so he could "marry" his current companion. When Condon was shown his picture, he said there was some resemblance to Cemetery John. When he saw Brinkert in person, however, he shook his head and remarked, "This man is too short."[59]

There might have been some holes in Brinkert's story about where he was the day of the kidnapping, but they seemingly became irrelevant when an Ernest Miller came forward, along with his friends Katherine Minners and Elmer Johnson, to say that he was the Ernie who had met Violet and her sister as they were walking along the street on February 28, 1932; that he was the man who had asked Violet for a date; and, most important, that he was the one who had called that afternoon of March

1 to make arrangements. "I did not know where she lived." His basic story, confirmed by the other two, tallied with Violet's statement that they had gone to a place called the Peanut Grill in Orangeburg, New York, for a few drinks and to dance, then returned to the Morrow estate near 11 P.M.[60]

There were minor discrepancies in their statements, but nothing the police could find, certainly, that would have tied Violet to the actual kidnapping. It was true Emily Sharp had said that "Ernie" announced that he knew the women worked at Next Day Hill, hardly more than a "pick-up line," one could say, but still intriguing. Why, then, did she take her life? Was it embarrassment, and fear of losing her job with no place to go? Elizabeth Morrow had stood by Septimus Banks when her husband wanted to fire him for drunkenness; would she not stand by Violet? Newspaper reports of police methods made it appear that her innocent dalliances had been blown up to such an extent that she felt friendless and abandoned. In an oft-quoted letter to an English friend on June 7, 1932, Violet had written, "Gee, life is getting so sad I really dont think there is much to live for any more."[61]

The same letter included a reference to the impending return to North Haven Island, Maine, after Anne Lindbergh had her second child. It is certainly possible that the strain of contemplating life close to Anne, after all that had happened, and the suspicion cast on her role, was a lot to bear. The police had recovered from her room not only the business card that seemed to implicate Ernest Brinkert, but also several ribald poems, either written by Violet or copied from racy magazines. Her personal life had become the stuff of vulgar gossip, not just in the servants' hall but in daily headlines as well.[62]

But was she really in danger of losing either her job or Septimus Banks? And why, since so many elements of her story could be confirmed as an innocent date, no matter her small deceptions, did fear of such exposure cause her to commit suicide? Betty Gow had been subjected to much the same treatment. Perhaps she was made of sterner stuff.

Ernest Miller told police that he had called Violet "that afternoon," a call she had not disclosed in the early questioning—and which seemed to be the most sensitive issue of all. Walsh had presented her with a picture of Ernest Brinkert, which she had pretended to identify. The inspector then threatened to bring him to her "in the flesh." The prospect of that confrontation loomed. She would be forced to admit another lie, and there would be more questioning about phone calls on March 1, 1932. If she really could not identify Ernie Miller, who looked nothing like Brinkert, that would have been one thing—but Violet had admitted there had been other calls after the kidnapping, and a date arranged, if not kept. She knew the police would want to know about "Ernie," Walsh insisted, so why didn't she try to find out more? Violet had no answer.

In the end, Violet Sharp's suicide remains a mystery. The only mistake Walsh would admit to was not taking her into custody. Despite the Brinkert contretemps, he continued to believe she knew something— and would rather die than reveal what that was. If Violet believed that she had supplied someone with information, the question of the phone calls goes beyond what was said to Ernie Miller about where to meet her that evening. It may be that she would *rather* have confronted Brinkert than Miller for fear of what police would find out about Miller that she did not know, but quickly realized that avenue offered no way out either.[63]

Much later, information surfaced that Violet had spent the night of June 9, 1932, crying, trying to write a letter she never finished even though she stayed up all night. The letter was never found. When she complained to him of a headache, Septimus Banks, according to this source, sent Marguerite Junge to Violet with an aspirin. Did Banks want to get her out of the way? That hardly seems likely, but the question whether she took the poison or it was administered to her under some pretense is not entirely resolved by the fact that the can of poison was found in her room afterward. Remember that Lieutenant Keaten and the other policemen were kept waiting for half an hour in Arthur Springer's office before they protested the time it was taking to bring Violet down for the trip to Alpine. Only then did Springer report that Violet was in the butler's pantry ill or fainted, and that a doctor had been summoned.[64]

An avalanche of criticism followed Violet's suicide. Questions were raised in the House of Commons, and Governor Moore was hard-pressed this time to defend Schwarzkopf and Walsh. The Republican leader of the state senate, Emerson L. Richardson, demanded a legislative probe into the conduct of the investigation. Walsh was a political hack, a Democratic favorite in Jersey City, he declared, and as for the state police, they were never competent enough "to handle any case bigger than that of a speeding motorist." As soon as he got Walsh on the job, scoffed Richardson, Schwarzkopf took to his bed in Princeton. And see what had happened as a result! "The thing to reckon with now is the looming possibility that, in their disgrace, the police blunderers will attempt something desperate to salvage what remains of their pomposity."[65]

The investigation had bogged down in New Jersey. J. Edgar Hoover derided Schwarzkopf's stubbornness and his inability to mount an effective investigation. "He will do just as he pleases," he scrawled on a letter from the commander of the New Jersey State Police, "which usually is wrong."[66]

"The relation of this Bureau to the investigation," he wrote to handwriting expert Albert D. Osborn, "has been of an extremely minor and subordinate character. . . . We offered our services originally, but have been doing nothing except working on specific minor details."[67] Rivalry and ambition provided enough fuel for Hoover to stoke his anger for the duration of the investigation. "More energy was expended in Trenton," he groused as early as March 17, 1932, "in getting the proper pose for the movies than in solving the crime. I still bear the bruises incurred from the Jersey City Mayor's party in the rush for the cameras."[68]

Violet's suicide left police without a lead to investigate. The case passed to the hands of experts—whose opinions fashioned a picture of the culprit out of handwriting and wood slivers.

EXPERT OPINIONS: MONEY, HANDWRITING, AND A LADDER

On that March morning after the Lindbergh baby had been kidnapped, I looked across the breakfast table at my smallest child, a baby son, and I suppose I shuddered. Then I read further in the newspaper about that homemade ladder left behind by the fellow who had done the crime and I grew excited. You see, that ladder, because it was made of wood, seemed just like a daring challenge.

—ARTHUR KOEHLER, April 1935

The credo of any police investigation is that the criminal or criminals always leave something at the scene and always take something away. In the Lindbergh case, the abductor had left a ladder and perhaps a chisel—though that was far from clear—as well as the first ransom note and some muddy smudges on the floor of the nursery. There were difficult questions about footprints outside. What had not been left, apparently, were usable fingerprints. And there was very little evidence of either entry or exit except the smudges and of course the empty crib. The child had been taken and then left half buried in some undergrowth in a nearby woods. And there had been the $50,000 ransom delivered to an anonymous man crouching behind a hedge in St. Raymond's Cemetery on the night of April 2, 1932.

The first thing to do was to see if the ladder found outside the house really had been the means of entry to the nursery. Columnist Walter Winchell, fast becoming the tabloid insider of the era, wrote that New York police officials had the best theory of the crime, "that it was an inside job—and that the ladder was put there as a 'prop' to serve as a subterfuge. . . . How in the world did the guilty one get into the room (where no clues or footmarks were found) and with one wing free—get down that unusually wide-runged ladder without breaking his neck?"[1]

State troopers quickly found Sebastian "Ben" Lupica, the student who claimed to have seen a man, near the entrance to the Lindbergh estate around six o'clock the night of the kidnapping, driving a car with a ladder laid diagonally from rear to front. The troopers brought Lupica into the house to identify the ladder discovered on the grounds. He was helpful but not positive. "My best recollection and judgment is that the ladders I saw in the Dodge car could have been the same ladders found at the Lindbergh home, but I could not say positively that they were actually the same ladders."[2]

Lupica did not much impress higher-ups in the state police. In a conversation with FBI liaison Thomas Sisk, Schwarzkopf and Lieutenant Arthur Keaten both complained, "He changed his story so many times and built it up so much that they placed no confidence in him."[3]

As for the ladder itself, the state police believed that it most resembled the type a window cleaner would use. "They stated that the ladder would hold a weight of 150 pounds." An earlier FBI report, however, by E. J. Connelley, had estimated that it would hold only 125 pounds. A very simple way of estimating the weight of the abductor by measuring the depth of the holes had been ignored when "test" ladders were placed down in the very same holes as those discovered on the ground.

Various tests were carried out in the first few days after the kidnapping, when the police tried to see if similar ladders they built would work, and what weight they would sustain. Marks had been found some thirty inches below the nursery window, and to the right. These identified where the original had supposedly rested against the wall, making the top rung of the middle section the "jumping off" point and the "returning point"—an acknowledged difficult feat. Several state troopers clambered up and down these ladders for a look-see, including Schwarzkopf himself.

The first reenacter was tracker Oscar Bush, who had pointed out the trail of footprints leading off to Featherbed Lane. Bush also thought the original ladder was probably too weak to hold anyone weighing over 125 pounds and had been used as a ruse to distract attention from the real methods of the abductors. To investigate the possibilities for gaining entrance to the nursery, he climbed up another ladder. He noticed immediately how thick the wall and windowsill were, and the presence of the toddler's toy wooden rabbit on top of the leather suitcase. He marveled at the dexterity of a man who could get across that width without leaving a footprint, and slipping to the nursery floor without even grazing the toy bunny.

"Coming back, like going in, the kidnapper must have left that cedar chest and suitcase and tinker toy, with the child weighing forty or fifty pounds in his arms. And he did it without leaving the smallest smudge from his foot or hands on the window frame." Charlie weighed much less than that, but the difference did not weaken Bush's point. Even more remarkable, the kidnapper perched himself on the ladder with the boy slung over his shoulder, took out the note, placed it on the sill, and then closed the window to descend the rest of the way. "Most of us mountaineers is pretty lightfooted—but the guy who accomplished that trick could get a job as a circus acrobat any time."[4]

The "kidnap" ladder had split along both rails where it was joined to the lower section, causing the whole apparatus to jam against the side of the outer wall. The third section of the kidnap ladder had been found somewhat apart from where the lower two had been left. This top section had not been used during the crime—or probably ever, since the whole thing was never meant for any purpose than the crime. It was too flimsy, to start with, but in no way did it resemble a working ladder. The rungs were too far apart, eighteen inches, as compared to standard twelve-inch spacing. Constructed from odd pieces of board, several of the rails had nail holes. In the bottom section, the rungs had been nailed across the rails, while in the upper two they had been mortised.

Each section was somewhat over six feet in length, designed to fit together for easy transport inside an automobile. If the ladder was merely planned as a false clue, then, its builder had gone to considerable trouble to ensure authenticity—at least on that score. On the other hand, would a person who knew anything about carpentry build a ladder so close to the margins? A person planning to steal the most famous child in the United States, and who had devised a foolproof signature, had neglected to ensure his most important accessory for the crime—how likely was that? Little wonder that both police and reporters expressed skepticism about what the ladder was doing out there on the muddy ground a good distance from the house.

The reenactors could not use the original kidnap ladder, of course. All the experiments over the next several days were carried out either on ladders found on the property or built specially to resemble the original. A ladder found in the Lindbergh garage, for example, did not have any of the same characteristics as the original, yet it was used in some experiments.

All the tests, as well, were conducted under conditions quite different from those confronting the kidnapper on that windy, rainy night. To start with the obvious, they were conducted in daylight. We do not know how many police officers, or other officials, or even household members tried out the ladders, or how many ladders broke. According to Jim Fisher's book on the case, Lindbergh looked on as Colonel Schwarzkopf made one of the tests, carrying out of the nursery a sandbag that weighed the same as the child. This ladder split in exactly the same place as the original ladder. Assistant Attorney General Robert Peacock described another experiment with a duplicate ladder. Police lieutenant John J. Sweeney, a former fireman, entered the nursery, Peacock wrote, emerged with a package weighing the same as the victim, "and at the same rung the ladder broke; hurling Sweeney and the package to the ground."[5]

Except that it never happened that way. Sweeney was only able to show that it was possible to enter the nursery by a man approximately his height, standing on a ladder roughly in the same position, and to exit again. During his testimony and cross-examination, there was considerable confusion over the ladders, since both prosecution and defense proved somewhat careless in talking about the original ladder and the garage ladder as they stood close together in the courtroom. It was clear that Sweeney used the sturdier garage ladder and not one of the duplicates, as these had not been constructed at the time he climbed into the window.[6]

Sweeney also admitted that when he climbed the garage ladder it was broad daylight and the window was open. Yet to make his entrance, he had had to put his hand at least partly inside the window to gain purchase. From Sweeney's account, the way the intruder must have exited was feet first, stepping up to the windowsill and then, after getting his legs out, sitting there for a moment before pivoting to the ladder. Then this:

"And what would you do with your right arm?"

"Hold on to the window case."

"What did you do with your left arm?"

"Hold on to the window sill."

"Both arms were busy."

"Yes sir."

What happened, then, to the baby while Sweeney was fishing around with his legs trying to find the top rung of the ladder?

Moreover, he was probing around for the much more solid garage ladder. "You never went up this ladder," he was then asked, as another questioner pointed to the original ladder, "and went into the window, did you?

"No sir."

"You never went out the window with a bundle in your arm and swung on to this ladder."

"No."[7]

So Oscar Bush's estimate of how difficult it would have been to enter and exit the nursery was never put to the test.

The proliferation of ladders did not, on the other hand, appear to cloud the identification of the kidnap ladder itself. After it was finally brought inside and dusted for fingerprints, first by New Jersey State Police officers—who found none—and then by a volunteer, Dr. Erastus M. Hudson, who brought out hundreds of impressions by newer methods already being used in Europe, the ladder underwent a series of "deconstructions," in an analytic sense as well as actual deconstructions.

Squire Johnson, New Jersey's assistant director of construction and architecture, carried out the first examination of the kidnap ladder. Johnson believed two people had made the ladder, one of them left-handed. The saw cuts and splintering on the rungs of the upper two sections convinced him that was the case. These marks did not appear in the same way on the bottom section. A different saw, moreover, was used on that section. (The placement of the ladder on the right side of the nursery window further indicated a left-handed abductor.) Given the ladder was designed so its sections nested together, Johnson noted also that the largest (bottom) section was the only one likely to have come in contact with anything on its journey, and it showed signs of having made contact with a surface "bearing oil or grease during said transit." The chisel found at the scene, he said, was the same size as one probably used in its construction, and might, in fact, have been the tool itself.[8]

"This would be an extremely difficult and if not impossible ladder for a short person or a tall person unversed in climbing to have negotiated," Johnson believed. "It is considerably more difficult to descend a ladder of this description than to ascend; particularly if both hands are not free."[9]

Johnson attempted to find wood like that in the ladder at the nearby Skillman Institute—a state hospital for epileptics—and then zeroed in on a shack close to the Lindbergh home occupied by a man named Charles Schippell. He found wood there that looked like what had been used in the ladder, along with Buck Brothers chisels, the same make as the one found at Highfields. Missing from the set was the three-quarter-inch size, the same size as the one left at the crime scene. Covered up in a lean-to built against the shack he discovered a dark green Paige sedan that resembled a car seen near the Lindbergh house that night. Inside the car were burlap bags similar to ones found near the body.[10]

"[Schippell] is a powerful man," Johnson reported, "probably of German extraction and is psychopathic. He has unusual and weird obsessions and hallucinations and is possessed of a wild and violent temper." If anyone could have scampered up and down this ladder, he added, it was an ambidextrous man such as Schippell who used a saw with his left hand and "boast[ed] of his ability to climb anything 'like a monkey.'"[11]

Police investigated Schippell, but nothing came of it, except that he was indeed a very strange man with shady characters for friends. Johnson never gave up on the idea that he was involved at least as an accessory before the fact. Johnson's report on the ladder, moreover, contained a series of findings not addressed in later investigations, such as the contention that at least part of the ladder had been made by a man wielding a saw in the left hand, or indications that the bottom section had rubbed up against a greasy or oily surface during transportation.

The ladder yielded few other direct clues after it was examined in Washington. An expert in the Department of Agriculture concluded, "There is nothing either in the construction or the material used that would identify it either by locality or profession of the maker." But there was something suggestive about the differences in the way the three sections had been made. The bottom section had the rungs nailed over the rails, not mortised like the other two. That could have meant the third section was made at a different time, "and perhaps as an afterthought, but since the material appears to be the same it suggests it was made rather hurriedly by the same person."[12]

Hoover saw the report from the specialists at the Department of Agriculture and lamented, "It is a crime how the State Police handled this piece of evidence. It was originally the most valuable clue & by bungling was made almost valueless." His experts were especially interested in the soils embedded in the side rails. As for the chisel found near the ladder, however, there was no way to tell if it had been used in the construction. "In fact, no significance as to the finding of the chisel could be attached." The nails in the rungs had been taken out and replaced by state troopers so many times that marks on the nails and, presumably, the rails had been altered. As for fingerprints, the first method the police used, powders, had turned up nothing. When the silver nitrate process was employed later, three or four potentially useful prints had been found, but this was only after any number of people had handled the ladder. (Hoover noted at this point, "Terrible mishandling.") The footprints outside had been staked out, and photographs had been taken. "No one was permitted to touch them." But since the kidnapping there had been snows and rain, "so that earth from another place adhering to the shoes of the person making these prints would be so mingled at the present time that nothing could be done."[13]

In another place in the federal government, however, work on the ladder was only beginning. A few days after the kidnapping, Arthur Koehler, of the Forest Products Laboratory in Madison, Wisconsin, wrote to Lindbergh offering his services as a wood expert who could help in identifying the ladder's sources. "For me the world perhaps has too limited boundaries," he explained his eagerness to become involved, "fixed by its kinds of trees and the wood they produce." Lindbergh did not answer his letter, but Koehler could well understand why. Thousands were writing him; how could anyone expect Lindbergh to sift through all the chaff to find the few valuable grains? But eventually someone thought of the balding bureaucrat out in Madison, where Lindbergh had attended the university for one year, and asked him to identify "some slivers" from the ladder left behind in Colonel Lindbergh's yard. It would prove to be the biggest job Koehler ever undertook.[14]

Ransom bills, meanwhile, had started to show up in increasing numbers. The first twenty-dollar bill was identified by a teller in the East River Savings Bank at 96th Street and Amsterdam Avenue, on April 4—only two days after the Saturday-night meeting at St. Raymond's. At this time, only banks had lists of serial numbers. But that soon came to an end when a New Jersey newspaper announced it had obtained the information. Not only did that warn off the kidnapper; it might have hindered the search by scaring innocent holders of the bills. In a Greenwich, Connecticut, pastry shop, for example, a well-dressed, attractive woman tried to pay for an order with a twenty-dollar bill the proprietor thought was on a list of the ransom bills. "Why, that's one of the Lindbergh bills," she exclaimed. But before she could be sure, the woman snatched back the money and darted out of the shop to a chauffeur-driven green sedan and sped off in the direction of New Haven.[15]

In only a few instances did anyone get a satisfactory description of the individual who tendered a note. Despite Lindbergh's offer of a two-dollar reward for anyone who spotted a bill, bank tellers proved particularly disappointing as lookouts. They couldn't afford to spend the time it took to check a bill against the ransom list, printed in tiny letters and numbers. An easier-to-read chart replaced the first unwieldy list of serial numbers, but with more than four thousand numbers to check, and impatient customers, the tellers simply failed to check every bill.

Lieutenant James J. Finn of the New York City Police Department, who had served as Lindbergh's bodyguard on his return from the "Lone Eagle" flight, devoted himself to mapping out the locations where bills were passed. As soon as one turned up and could be traced back, Finn rushed to the location to interview the person receiving the bill. He estimated later that he had interviewed over six hundred persons in this quest. On May 19, 1932, a five-dollar bill was tendered to Bickford's Restaurant at 225 West Forty-second Street. The cashier told Finn the man might "possibly" have been Italian, Irish, or American; was about thirty, around five-foot-eight, and approximately 150 pounds, with dark brown hair and eyes, a flabby face, and dark complexion; and looked as if he might be a chauffeur. He failed to recognize anybody from police photographs. A few days later, a cashier at the Brilliant Cafeteria at the corner of Canal Street and the Bowery received another five-dollar bill. This time police described Cemetery John according to Condon's description to the restaurant employee. Yes, she said, there was a man answering that description who came to the cafeteria every other day! The next time William Heilewertz showed up for his usual coffee and cake, policed nabbed him. But despite his physical similarities to Condon's interlocutor, it quickly became apparent he was not their man.[16]

One man almost demanded to be noticed. On Sunday night, November 26, 1933, just in time for the last showing, a man in a dark hat "with the front brim pulled down," wearing a dark suit, walked up to the cashier at the Sheridan Square movie theater in Greenwich Village and tossed down a five-dollar bill. The man's attitude, and the way the bill was folded, drew the cashier's attention. He was about five-foot-eight or five-foot-nine tall, she thought, thirty to thirty-five years old, with a slender build, light brown hair, "high cheek bones; broad shoulders; apparently American." The cashier, Cecile Barr, thought she would recognize him if she ever saw him again.[17]

Finn kept adding pins to a map he had started to show where bills showed up. What began with a few scattered pins here and there around the city, by late 1933 began to resemble a miniature forest. There were thickets of black indicating the fives, along with clusters of red representing ten-dollar notes, and a single green pin for the only twenty that had shown up. "The pins were thickest along the subway and streetcar routes running north and south in the northeast sector of the city: along . . . Lexington and Third [A]venues in upper Manhattan and the German-speaking district of Yorkville; across the Harlem River and the great bosom of the Bronx."[18]

By drawing fine lines between each and every pin, Finn believed he had a large noose encircling the area where the man lived. Such a map did not rule out the possibility that there was more than one person distributing bills. And not all the money turned up neatly inside the target area. Treasury officials had anticipated President Franklin D. Roosevelt's decision to call in all gold and gold certificates, and had made sure the ransom packet contained $35,000 in such notes. FDR's order required holders of gold certificates to exchange them for greenbacks by May 1, 1933. Between April 27, 1933, and May 1, 1933, an aggregate sum of $3,980 of ransom money in gold certificates was exchanged for "greenbacks" at three New York banks within a few blocks of one another.

Anticipating an effort to exchange gold notes, New Jersey authorities had asked the New York City Police Department to station officers in major banks on that last day. And, indeed, a customer walked up to teller James P. Estey at the Federal Reserve Bank, bold as you please, on May 1, 1933, and shoved across a stack of bills and a deposit slip in the amount of $2,980, signed "J. J. Faulkner, 537 West 149th Street." A very busy man, Estey failed to notice what "Faulkner" looked like or what he wore. This was not one of the largest deposits that day, but it included nearly three hundred bills—and Estey did not notice what he looked like! There were extenuating reasons for this failure. Not only was this the last day that exchanges could be made; it was also the day when government employees cashed their checks. The Federal Reserve was the busiest bank in the city, and Estey was the busiest teller, because he was also responsible for tallying deposits from armored cars.

When questioned, Estey raised the possibility that the depositor might have been a woman. Cemetery John had once told Condon a high government official and two women were involved. Who would know better the opportune time to change money than a government official, and who better to send it with than a woman? In addition to their frustration with Estey, New Jersey police were upset that the New York City Police Department had failed to station men in the banks to be on the watch this special day for persons who looked like Cemetery John.[19]

Faulkner's $2,980 fell outside the geographic parameters of Finn's design. If the money had been divided, there was more than a possibility that the "gang" had split up as well, with some more frightened than others of spending Lindbergh ransom money. But at least there was now an address to run down.

Searching for the mysterious J. J. Faulkner turned up some odd coincidences. No one by that name lived at the address on the deposit slip, but, years before, a Jane Faulkner had lived there. She had married a man, Carl Giessler, whose handwriting was tentatively identified as being the same as that on the deposit slip. Further examination eliminated Giessler as a suspect, but Treasury agent Frank Wilson noted something of possible significance about the episode. "We were of the opinion that some one knowing him or Mrs. Giessler when she was single and residing at 537 West 149th Street, had used the name J. J. Faulkner on the ticket and that it might have been an enemy of the family, a friend or some slight acquaintance of the family."[20]

Once again, as so often happened, Condon's name popped up. Giessler's son had lived on Decatur Avenue, one block from Jafsie's residence. Giessler's daughter had married a man named Henry C. Liepold, whose close associates were also supposedly linked with Condon's son-in-law, Ralph Hacker. It turned out that the man in question was instead Rudolph Hacker, with no connection to Condon. Joe Perrone told police, however, that Liepold resembled a man who had given him a fifteen-cent fare to take him to the place near where he had received the note for Condon. Sitting in an unmarked police car outside Giessler's floral shop on Madison Avenue, Perrone even claimed he saw the ransom note man himself emerge from the shop—then disappear into the heavy pedestrian traffic.

Police grilled Liepold, supposedly the weakest of the Giessler family, and believed they were onto something that would solve the case sooner or later. Lieutenant James Finn now asserted, "Some persons who may have known Dr. Condon very well, may have double-crossed him and actually received the $50,000." FBI agents also believed the break would come when Condon made "certain remarks, possibly carelessly, which [would] supply the link."

Liepold did crack under the pressure; he committed suicide by shooting himself with a rifle on August 20, 1933. (The parallel with Violet Sharp's end was an uncomfortable reminder that the Lindbergh case produced extreme behavior.) Liepold's father-in-law told police that he had been afraid, not of the inquiries about the kidnapping, but of the possible disclosure of his affair with another man's wife years earlier. The Giessler-Faulkner connection would continue to be investigated, nevertheless, right up to the arrest of another suspect—and then it was dropped cold.[21]

There was another Condon angle to the J. J. Faulkner investigation. New Jersey State Police officers found a John J. Faulkner had been living with his mother at 1336 Balcom Avenue, the Bronx, less than a block away from St. Raymond's cemetery. This J. J. Faulkner had been a pupil of Condon's at P.S. #12. His mother had had her son committed to something called the Catholic Protectory in 1914, after lodging a complaint that he had burglarized her home. In recent years, Mrs. Faulkner's daughter, a Mrs. Otis, lived at this address with her children, but the postal carrier remembered delivering mail to a man named Faulkner. As the house stood on a hill overlooking the cemetery, and the mailbox at the foot, the carrier did not often observe goings-on there and could not say anything more about the man. It does not appear that police asked Condon about his former pupil, but a psychiatrist worth his salt probing Condon's quotidian inconsistencies and gnarled logic might well have wondered about the schoolmaster's memory of an errant pupil. In *Jafsie Tells All*, finally, Condon remarks that he believed that Cemetery John went to a house nearby to obtain the "receipt" he had demanded, and that he had even told reporters that he recognized the handwriting as that of one of his pupils.[22]

The handwriting in the ransom notes intrigued everyone. The doyen of American handwriting experts, Albert S. Osborn, was very anxious to become involved in the Lindbergh case. His son and associate, Albert D. Osborn, wrote J. Edgar Hoover, "We are naturally interested in the case, and I am sure I can say frankly that, from the reports at least, the so-called experts and graphologists who have been looking at the letters not only do not know anything about this subject but are unreliable." Hoover sympathized. He wrote back that if his bureau had been handling the matter, "they would certainly have been referred to you long ere this."[23]

After a discussion with FBI agent E. J. Connelley, Schwarzkopf agreed to submit the notes to the Osborns. Accordingly, Connelley and Trooper Russell Snook delivered the kidnapper's messages to the Osborns on May 20, 1932. As they did so, Connelley stressed the first question to answer was whether they had all been written by the same person. Three days later, Albert S. Osborn said he could say, informally, that, yes, the notes all did emanate from the same person. The individual was possibly someone born and educated in Germany. He was particularly struck with the "double hyphen," a German characteristic. "Informally, he believed that the notes were the result of an experienced person in this operation."[24]

Two things pop out here. First, the FBI agent's original question was whether one person had written all the notes, and second, Osborn's assumption from a brief examination of the notes that they were dealing with "an experienced person in this operation."

More than twenty pages long, Osborn's formal report on May 27, 1932, reiterated his conviction that all the notes had been written by the same person, from the nursery note to the final directional note. There were several ways to tell that this was so, he went on, beginning with his conclusion that the first and second notes were originally part of the same sheet of paper, as indicated by carefully placing the sheets together and observing the pattern created along the edges. Beyond that, however, it would be "practically impossible that three days after the kidnapping some other party in Brooklyn would be able to write letter No. 2 containing this device on the same kind of paper and in the same kind of envelope as contained the original ransom note."[25]

Thus far in his report, Osborn had not demonstrated that one person had written all the notes, only that they came from the same source—which could have been one person or several.

The signature, he said, was "ingenious," and "this careful preparation, anticipating a future use, points to a careful design and probably experience in similar undertakings." This statement was more of a graphologist's conclusion, of course, an estimate of what was in the writer's mind, and how the ransom notes supposedly revealed "experience in similar undertakings."

Jumping around from one note to another, Osborn asserted that while they were all disguised to a certain extent, only in the first was there a truly serious effort to conceal natural handwriting. The appearance of German words or phrases might have been part of the disguise, but Osborn was inclined to think not. "The writer . . . did not feel that it was necessary in these letters to disguise his handwriting, or his language." That was certainly a bit confusing: on the one hand, the signature design conveyed to Osborn careful planning and experience, but at the same time the writing suggested that he did not feel it necessary to disguise his language. Later on in his report, he changed his mind: "I am inclined to think that there are certain errors which are perhaps a part of a disguise where words are spelled phonetically but the word 'Signature' is consistently misspelled throughout."

Osborn noted, however, that the writing instrument used in the first note was different from the pen used in all the others. "When it is carefully examined it will be seen that it contains the most distinctive identifying characteristics. It is possible it may have been written in an automobile or under circumstances where it was difficult to write as perfectly as on an ordinary desk." That conclusion, of course, raises again the matter of the final directional note. Where in St. Raymond's Cemetery would the kidnapper have found a place to write such a smooth note?

Moreover, how was it logical to say in the same report—if not quite in the same breath—that the first note, the nursery note, showed signs of being written under duress yet was the most successfully disguised? In the final paragraph of his report, the graphologist emerged again, asserting that one person must have written all the notes, not because the handwriting told him so, but because it would have been too dangerous to involve the "two ladies" mentioned in one of them. Besides, he said, this person had probably planned the murder ahead of time, so there would be no need of accomplices to help with care for the child. All of that, even the degree of planning, he could supposedly tell from the handwriting.

He was quite an expert, no doubt. But his assumptions about the kidnapper's state of mind were just that, assumptions, which inevitably raises the issue whether the rest of his analysis was shaped by those beliefs. Although the report did contain many illustrations of how the writing matched up from note to note, it was marked, throughout, by Osborn's indecision about the disguise, what forms it took, and did not take. And in a "Supplemental Suggestion" attached to his report, Osborn added, "It is not probable that successful identification will be made of this writer from only the last communication and a portion of the next to last one that have been published in the newspapers."[26]

Unknown to Osborn or J. Edgar Hoover, Schwarzkopf had sent Lieutenant Snook on another mission earlier. On May 7, 1932, Snook had taken the ransom notes to Washington, D.C., to Dr. Wilmer Souder in the Bureau of Standards in the Commerce Department. Souder assured Snook at their first meeting that everything would be kept secret, and assigned the case a number, T-67194, known only, even to members of the bureau, as the "Adamson case" about a fictitious bank failure. Snook was then introduced to other members of the bureau as "Mr. Martin from New York."[27]

Souder concluded from the writing that the man was a German familiar with the Bronx and might have lived at one time near the Lindbergh home, that he was perhaps a workman skilled in the use of ladders, and that he probably had a criminal record. The cramped writing suggested a former prison inmate used to not having much paper available. "It was thought that the holes in the paper were made by some blunt instrument punched through the paper using something under the paper as a gauge, such as a hole in a belt a shoe or some other ordinary article which would least attract attention."

Souder speculated that the man had a personal liking for Jafsie. "It is possible that he either knows Jafsie personally or knows him by reputation for honesty and integrity."

Souder's conclusions, like those of Osborn, went far beyond handwriting analysis, except for his statements about how the signature was made, by placing something under the paper. Neither expert had said anything, finally, that would rule out the notes being dictated to the writer by someone else. As Osborn said of the eighth note, "although containing numerous errors in spelling, [it] is in composition an excellent piece of work and indicates, I think, that the writer in some of these letters has purposely used clumsy language."

And Treasury agent Frank Wilson wrote in his November 1933 report: "The notes also indicate that the person who composed them had an excellent command of the English language and probably had at

least a high school education. It was their [the handwriting experts']
opinion that the person who wrote the notes did not compose them as
the penmanship appeared to be that of a poorly educated person."[28]

To someone besides a handwriting expert, finally, it would certainly seem odd that if the man were a German, he would purposely use
"clumsy language" to indicate his nationality and help the police to
track him down.

In October FBI agents traced a five-dollar ransom bill to a David Bari,
who turned out to be a carpenter born in Austria. Twenty-eight years
old, he was a short man, a little over five-foot-two, and weighed around
135 pounds. He lived with an older brother who was near forty, about
five-foot-seven, and 160 pounds. These men interested the FBI, as
combining between them various characteristics noticed by Condon
and Perrone. Two agents visited David Bari early in the morning of
October 11, 1932, roused him from bed, and searched him. And then
he "voluntarily" agreed to accompany them to the New York office for
questioning.[29]

He was questioned for two days and asked to write some of the
ransom notes from dictation. These copies were sent to the Osborns
for comparison. They bore the closest resemblance of any previous
submissions to date, came the reply. The dictation went on until four
copies of each note were obtained, with breaks between each writing
session—to divert his mind. The Osborns reported still more enthusi-
astically that, "in addition to the pronounced racial characteristics, etc.,
[the writing] bore many points of resemblance to the writing appearing in the original Lindbergh notes." Still, a comparison was difficult,
they admitted, because "it was impossible to determine just how much
disguise was being used in each of the writings." But there were, indeed,
very significant resemblances. For the record, however, the Osborns
wanted to note that one of the features in the original notes, the *2* with
a curlicue bottom, did not occur in Bari's writing—except for one instance where he did write it that way. He should be kept for a considerable time, they said, and made to write all the notes.

After all this, when the agents asked Albert S. Osborn outright if
Bari should be charged with the crime, the expert waffled. No, he said,
but he should be kept under surveillance. In a lengthy discussion of his
art, Osborn gave the agents a remarkable statement about the problems an expert faced: "considering the similarities in the two writings,
it would not be impossible for a person of some intelligence to so disguise his handwriting during the six months which have elapsed since
the last Lindbergh note, so as to eradicate certain of the characteristics

found in the Lindbergh ransom notes and not found in the handwriting specimens of David Bari."[30]

Osborn hated to let go of the Bari investigation. Sometimes, he said, given the similarities they had found, it would turn out to be the handwriting of another member of the family. In one instance, he related to FBI agents, anonymous notes to New York judges turned out to have been written by a brother of the principal suspect in the case. He did not doubt "for a minute," Osborn told Agent E. A. Tamm, that "any prosecuting attorney in the State of New Jersey, with the possible exception of Newark, and any group of police officers would immediately" proceed to prosecute Bari upon the evidence supplied by his handwriting specimens, and the possession of the five-dollar bill.[31]

The agents called Lieutenant Finn down to have a talk about Bari. Finn said he attributed no particular significance to the Bari bill other than the appearance of several bills in the locality where this one was found.

While investigating the Lindbergh case, Finn had been working closely at times with the psychiatrist Dudley Shoenfeld, a highly regarded physician at Mount Sinai Hospital. Leigh Matteson, science editor of the International News Service, served as go-between for Shoenfeld and Finn. The psychiatrist and the police officer had first met in April of 1932 and shared a belief that the police were on the wrong track. Matteson thought Shoenfeld could convince them that the kidnapping was the work of no "gang," but rather the fiendish scheme of a "lone wolf."[32]

A confirmed Freudian, Shoenfeld gleaned from newspaper reproductions of the ransom notes yet another portrait of their author. The signature contained a definite psychological clue about the kidnapper's motivation. "The symbol used as the identifying mark," Shoenfeld wrote to Lieutenant Finn, "must be classified as an indication of homosexuality in the life of the writer of the letters."[33]

(Condon, however, interpreted the signature as an Italian sign, the Trigamba, which carried a deadly warning to whoever received a note signed that way. He had not studied symbolism, Jafsie told an FBI agent, but had researched "some books in his own library" and talked with Italians. He did not remember any names, however, "just some he met here and there." They all recognized the signature as the Trigamba—a danger signal. "Anyone who received a Trigamba was in danger of death or some great punishment if he did not carry out instructions to the letter. Condon interpreted this as a warning to him to carry out instructions in the ransom notes to the letter.")[34]

Finn told Shoenfeld that many of the recovered bills appeared to have been folded just like the one tossed at the movie cashier Cecile Barr. What did Shoenfeld make of that? He folded the bill that way, said the psychiatrist, for both reassurance and as a sign of power. He would always have only one ransom bill on his person, and it would always be creased in that fashion. FBI agents were skeptical. In the first place, many of the bills in the original packet had been in circulation prior to being used as ransom money. Such "floaters," as they were called, often showed the same creases. Second, by no means all of the bills showed special wear in that way. As the FBI laboratory in New York reported on August 7, 1934, "It is believed that the creases indicating the three-way fold of *some* of the bills, are without any particular significance because they have been noted on bills in general circulation, however this is only an opinion."

Lieutenant Finn continued to insist, despite this report, that *all* of the bills showed this characteristic. "It appears," read an FBI rebuttal, "that most of the individual bills discovered were 'floaters' and also that nearly every old bill has the same creases. The theory of Lieutenant Finn that the guilty person or persons are making the creases therefore appears to be largely speculation."[35]

According to Shoenfeld's theory, Charles Lindbergh represented the despised younger brother who had achieved everything his elder sibling had always wished to do, but had been denied. "The proved laws of physics, as applied to magnetism, show that opposites attract and likes repel."

> Thus, a working basis of possible antagonism to Lindbergh could be sought in this premise. Lindbergh was, in the world of reality, all-powerful, omnipotent. Another person, inferior in the world of reality, but with an unconscious drive and phantasies of being powerful and omnipotent, would see in him an enemy. A successful attack on this "enemy" would, in the reasoning of the inferior individual, immediately evoke a feeling of adequacy in that the great one had been attacked and made humble.[36]

If he could view the actual ransom notes, he could establish the theory beyond all reasonable doubt. Even what had been published in the press revealed—to the psychiatrist's eye—that these were not run-of-the-mill ransom notes. They were too long, too verbose, and, most important, contained no dire threats to mutilate or kill the child if the demands were not met. Instead, the writer offered constant reassurances that the child was well and was being treated even better than it had been by the family—at least in terms of diet. To Matteson and Shoenfeld, the hidden message was that the baby was already dead and had been from the moment of the kidnapping or very soon thereafter.

A circular put out by the New Jersey State Police on May 26, 1932, included the text of the last ransom note, the so-called receipt Condon had demanded from Cemetery John. In this final message the kidnapper had said the baby would be found near Gay Head on board the "Boad Nelly." But was that really what he was telling us? By using a magnifying glass, Shoenfeld and Matteson thought they saw something else: the kidnapper had originally written *Road,* not *Boad,* and then painstakingly corrected his "slip." One can almost hear Shoenfeld exclaim to Matteson with Holmesian pride, "My dear fellow, there was no boat 'Nelly' to find. That was only a secret code word for 'Nearly,' telling us where we would discover the child's body. The baby had been left 'nearly' on the 'road.'"

Driven by his unconscious, the note writer had even tried to tell the world where he lived. Look here, Shoenfeld said, the words *Gay Head* had originally been *Gun Hill,* the very neighborhood where Condon had first met Cemetery John. What sort of person would produce these enciphered messages? Obviously, they were dealing with someone who suffered from a serious mental illness—a delusional form of insanity that evokes in its victim both feelings of inadequacy and omnipotence. And remember Condon's evidence: at first Cemetery John ran away, but then he allowed himself to be caught in order to spend an hour exulting in his exploit, and himself, as the center of the world's attention. Then there was an apparently incorrect statement in another ransom note: "Is it really necessary to make a *word* affair out of this?" What he actually meant, deep in his unconscious, was "It is really necessary to make a *world* affair out of this."[37]

In early November 1932, Shoenfeld finally met Colonel Lindbergh and brought along enlargements of the reproductions. The only other witnesses to this "showing" were New Jersey State Police representatives and Treasury agent Frank Wilson. Shoenfeld spread out his exhibit on the library floor of the Morrow home and began his explanation of the kidnapper's code. At first Lindbergh resisted the "lone wolf" theory and thought the idea the "singnature" revealed homosexual tendencies fanciful. Once again, however, Shoenfeld went over the supposed changes in the final note. Three times, the psychiatrist argued, the man had written *Road,* when he tried to write *Boat,* and he had transformed *Gun Hill* into *Gay Head.* It was enough, anyway, for Lindbergh to ask that copies of the other ransom notes be given Shoenfeld so that he might make a line-by-line examination.[38]

Four days later, on November 10, 1932, the psychiatrist delivered his full report to Finn. He was not a handwriting expert or criminologist, he admitted, but could offer expertise "in the functioning of the unconscious." The report combined conclusions from his own examinations of the ransom notes with Condon's recollections of his conversations with Cemetery John. It was commonly accepted, he wrote, that all the notes exhibited heavy Germanic influence, not just occasional German words but the pervasive "Germanic phraseology." To an untrained observer, it might appear to be poor English grammar. If one "translated" the English back into German, however, the notes revealed an author who "had the ability to think correctly along German lines and thus we are forced to the conclusion that he is a German."[39]

One letter in the ransom notes leaped out more than any of the others. The writer's *x* looked like two *ees*. Knowing the author was German should make it easy to find a driver's license application on which someone of that nationality had used the word *Bronx,* the most likely place for the "Wolf's Lair," as Matteson put it. While it was quite natural for a kidnapper, sane or an insane, to use some symbol or code to ensure payment to himself and no one else, this writer's signature had to be understood in the "light of the new psychology": For the present he was fully functional in society, probably even the sort of individual who was careful to obey traffic laws, pay taxes, abide by rules and regulations. But sometime in the past he must have spent time, even if briefly, in an institution for the insane. What was Shoenfeld's diagnosis, then? Dementia praecox, he said, an already somewhat old-fashioned term for schizophrenia.[40]

Matteson was ready to go. "To hell with the police until we need them," he argued. "Let's take a few hundred dollars and see if we can get access to the duplicate driver's license applications."

"There is a man living in the Bronx who has a license to drive an automobile," he said, "the automobile in which he carried that kidnap ladder to Hopewell, the automobile which he used to carry that child's body to that point along the Hopewell-Princeton Road, where he buried it. This man is a crazy German workman. . . . The man's handwriting has well-defined characteristics that should be easily recognizable on automobile drivers' license applications. . . . Above all, he makes an 'X' as nobody ever saw an 'X' before. This 'X' can be made to mark the spot where the fellow tripped up and literally fell into the arms of the police."[41]

Finn listened to this recitation and assured Matteson that someone must have been checking out the drivers' applications, and if not, he would see that it was done. But apparently it was not. Later, Finn admitted they had not checked: "We slipped up on that angle."

"But, for Christ's sake, how and why?"

"Well," Finn admitted, "the boss thought no man would be so dumb as to use his car on a job like that. He wouldn't believe it was possible."

Shoenfeld believed that once police had their man, they should allow Condon "to 'work' on the prisoner in his own broadly eccentric, pedagogically earnest, passionately naive fashion." As Matteson later recalled, "The psychiatrist was of the opinion that the aged Bronx educator-go-between had a natural flair for breaking down the reserve of a defectively emotional type. . . . He had given evidence of this power in evoking several amazing emotional responses from 'John' during their first conversation, at Woodlawn cemetery."[42]

Although Shoenfeld and Finn "expressed complete confidence in [Condon's] honesty and integrity," they knew that putting him on the stand posed a risk. "We felt . . . that his personality would not be understood and that when the guilty one or ones eventually were apprehended, it would be subject to attack. As a psychiatrist, I predicted that if Dr. Condon were alive when the perpetrator of the crime came to trial, his age, coupled with a past history of eccentricities, would make his testimony extremely vulnerable to attack by the defense on the basis of mental competency."[43]

Despite these worries, Shoenfeld relied to a remarkable degree on Condon's veracity in reporting both sides of the conversations with the presumed abductor. Still, as Shoenfeld said of his conversations with Frank Wilson, "Both of us expressed the opinion that a suspect should be arrested only on evidence so strong and of such a nature that he could be tried without the supporting testimony of Condon."[44]

As time went on, Condon's efforts to keep himself in the case became more and more bizarre. In early 1934, for example, he wrote letters to absolute strangers, calling upon them to supply him with information about the case. In one instance a woman had written to ask if he were interested in purchasing an antique violin. Condon replied: "What about the *violin*? I received only one letter with inclosures [*sic*], and I am attending to it carefully. If you know anything about the baby, box, boodle or bana. let me know. Respt. in haste."[45]

Condon initiated a series of letters to Hoover that raised all sorts of questions about his potential as a witness on any issue. On January 12, 1933, he wrote to say that he had completed most of the "work assigned to [him]" in the "dastardly Lindbergh horror," and had finished his lectureships at Fordham and the College of New Rochelle. "It occurred to me that I would like to work under your supervision and instruction. In all my life, I have never disobeyed a superior's order." In

May he wrote again to ask about a position, not only for himself but for Al Reich as well. In October he wrote to the attorney general, Homer S. Cummings, to explain that he had not tossed the $50,000 over any wall but had handed it directly to the kidnapper, in exchange for a "(sealed) note" which he turned over to Colonel Lindbergh.

"My home was invaded by scribblers and unauthorized, irresponsible reporters," he noted on another occasion. Most of them, as we know, were invited to Condon's house. In January 1934, Condon wrote that he had always done his best to solve the "most dastardly crime of all time." "Does our great 'United States' ever recognize effort such as I have made?" He was not interested in a monetary reward, but perhaps there was something for someone who had suffered such abuse for the honor of opposing the "niggardly gangsters, who would cast a stain upon the Flag of [his] country. Do the authorities ever pin a button upon a fellow, who fought his battle without a uniform? Should you sanction such an honor for my humble work? E.G: a ribbon, a medal, certificate? *No money!*" Condon enclosed a method he had discovered for using glass disks to fashion the signature on the ransom notes. "I have done all that I can possibly accomplish to bring these scoundrels to Justice. I must now try to obtain a position."[46]

Condon even wrote President Franklin D. Roosevelt to secure a picture. A White House secretary asked Hoover for his opinion. "I am of the opinion," the director wrote back, "that he is possibly reaching a somewhat senile state, although in full possession of all his faculties." If the president did send him a photograph, there should be nothing attached but his signature. "Doctor Condon does seem to have a faculty of being in the headlines, and . . . anything sent to him by the President would soon reach the front pages of the press."[47]

Hoover, meanwhile, had Condon placed under surveillance. It was not expected much would turn up. Whatever connections he had had with the kidnappers—if any—were in the area of guilty knowledge, not as an ongoing accomplice. When Agent Sisk talked with Schwarzkopf and Keaten, he found they did not agree on Condon's involvement. Schwarzkopf thought he might have a slight acquaintance with John or had seen him around the Bronx prior to the crime and intended to work it out for himself. Condon had confidence, said the colonel, that one day he would find the man and then "grab" him and become a hero. Keaten wasn't buying that theory. Condon was "wacky" and—if he wasn't involved—mentally deranged. He and Harry Walsh had taken down Condon's statements and noticed how he contradicted himself at times. "He picked out any number of pictures, some of which do not look like each other at all." On one occasion he had been so positive that the police carried out a full investigation and discovered the person had been nowhere near New Jersey that night. So they put the photo in a stack of other pictures to test Condon's memory. This time he said none of the men looked anything like John. "They therefore place no reliance at all in Dr. Condon."[48]

Keaten confirmed one Jafsie statement, however. When Harry Walsh had him at Alpine in June 1932, he had indeed taken him out to the Palisades and made him stand on a high cliff, "and then asked him if he did not feel like jumping into the river." On the other hand, the New Jersey State Police had discovered Condon had kept one of the ransom notes for eight months. Asked why he had retained the note, "he stated he did not know he had it; that he had discovered it out in the bushes in front of the house." Keaten said the truth of the matter probably was that Condon, a great souvenir hunter, had wanted to keep it as a memento. He already had the crib safety pins, Charlie's toys, and a picture from the morgue.[49]

There is more to the story—as there always was whenever Condon was confronted with one of the "gaps" in his various narratives. He now told police investigators that there was a second note enclosed with the sleeping suit—the one recently supposedly found in the bushes—which asked, "Did you Got the note which was thrown in your garden?" Condon looked all over his garden he said, but turned up no other note. But about five weeks earlier, sometime in September 1932, he had received yet another note with the symbol signature—which was the missing one from the garden. It had been thrown on the front lawn, and that was why he missed it. "The above story," wrote the investigators, "is not quite clear to the undersigned, due to the fact that we do not understand how Dr. Condon knows that the note he received about five weeks ago, is the same one that was supposed to have been thrown in his garden, and which he now claims was thrown on his front lawn."[50]

Condon's reports of receiving additional notes from the kidnappers bearing the secret signature are intriguing, if for no other reason than there appears to be no record of whether the handwriting was ever examined.

Meanwhile, out in Madison, Wisconsin, Arthur Koehler was on the trail of the ladder maker. By now all the rungs and rails had been assigned numbers for easy reference. Koehler had been sent three rungs and three side rails, along with one of the dowels. The dowel seemed to have been cut from a much longer piece somewhat smaller in diameter than the ordinary broom handle. It had a relatively smooth surface and was covered with a thin film of some fatty or oily substance. Koehler thought the dowels were originally part of a "wand," commonly used by gym instructors—which would explain the thin oily surface as resulting human contact on a regular basis.

The rails were made from two different woods, Douglas fir and southern yellow pine, woods not grown in New Jersey but readily available across the area. Rail 16, the top left side rail, was entirely different from all the other pieces in the ladder. It appeared to have come from an older building, as evidenced by the moisture content and four nail holes probably made by old-fashioned cut rectangular nails.[51]

The conglomeration of wood types, evidence that certain pieces had been in soil other than that around Highfields, and the presence of black mineral matter like cinders embedded here and there in the wood, had led H. S. Betts, a specialist at the Department of Agriculture, to conclude: "The indications are that the lumber for making the ladder was not obtained from a lumber yard because of the mixture of species and non-standard thickness. It might have been taken from a miscellaneous accumulation of pieces. The moisture content of the one piece that was tested indicated that it had been under cover for some time."[52]

There matters stood. As Koehler put it, "Troopers of the New Jersey State Police had carried the tongue-tied ladder to many places always hoping it could be made to speak."[53]

Koehler was armed to the teeth, as he tells us, with microscopes, calipers, scales, and even X-ray machines for his mission to extract the truth. For days he gazed down the barrel of his microscope so that nothing would escape attention. The first thing that jumped out at Koehler were the plane marks on the rungs (or cleats) on the bottom section of the ladder, and on both edges of the aforementioned rail 16. These marks had been made by a dull wood plane, nicked in such a way that it left behind a "signature" in the ridge pattern on the wood. "Magnified, those ridges stood up from the smoothness of a board almost as prominently as do the steel rails that form a railroad track." Koehler's posttrial musings on the ridges became almost theological: "Strangely, too, he had planed some faces quite needlessly, as if he planed in reverie, or if—as I would like to think—some Force outside himself tricked him into leaving tell-tale marks." In his original report, dated March 1933 however, the plane marks are simply said to be readily identifiable, and "might possibly assist" in detecting where the work was done and by whom.[54]

As for the chisel marks left behind by the builder where the recesses were made in the rails for the rungs, he wrote: "The chisel used in making the mortises for the cleats evidently was a sharp chisel, since it cut the wood smoothly along the grain and left no scratches. It is not even possible to determine the width of the chisel used." Later he would claim that he could identify at least one mark of a three-quarter-inch wood chisel on the ladder, and how it was wielded, in ways "a good carpenter would not do."[55]

In his 1933 report, Koehler also wrote, "The spacing of the old nail holes in the Douglas fir rails and in yellow pine rail #16 gives no suggestion as to what the lumber might have been used for." In explaining the importance of the nail holes, however, Koehler provided a formula to demonstrate the impossibility of matching up rail 16 to any other place but one on this earth. "By the laws of chance it would take a world much vaster than our own to provide a coincidence of those four nail holes matching accidentally four other nail holes with which they had no connection."

He began by figuring out that there could be ten thousand nail holes in a board that size. The first nail hole could be placed over any other nail hole in another piece of wood. But the second would now become one in ten thousand; the third, one in ten thousand times ten thousand less three; the fourth, times another ten thousand minus four. And since only one board out of ten thousand would have four nail holes in those exact places, the chance of being wrong now would be written so: $1/10,000,000,000,000,000$.

Very impressive. If, however, the board was identified as having been used to cover a common space—say, as one of many attic boards, don't the odds diminish somewhat? The boards next to rail 16, if nailed into similar supports, would have nail holes placed so as to hit a joist in essentially the same area—hardly a matter of chance. The total area where nails could be driven usefully thus shrinks dramatically, particularly when one thinks there were only four nail holes, not fourteen or forty. A carpenter working on several attics, moreover, might habitually drive his nails in approximately the same place, board after board, house after house.

Koehler did not, he says, tell New Jersey authorities about his calculation of the odds, only that "whenever you get a suspect look around his premises for a place indoors where there are empty cut-nail holes, and possibly some boards to match with the ladder rail."

Koehler then set himself the task of finding out where the lumber had come from, particularly in the side rails. Rails 12 and 13, from the bottom section, were from a tree commonly known as North Carolina pine, although it grew in other states. Rails 14, 15, and 17 were Douglas fir. By comparing planer marks on the edges and faces of the wood to those produced by cutter heads in use in a specific mill, he hoped to trace the wood back to where it had been dressed.

Koehler learned from planer manufacturers that marks like those on rails 12 and 13 were "comparatively rare in Eastern lumber mills." He sent letters to 1,598 lumber mills in the South, where North Carolina pine was dressed for shipment to lumberyards across the nation, describing the marks. This particular planer, with six knives on the edge cutter, and eight in each face cutter, had a small defect that left a distinguishable mark on the wood, plainly visible under certain light conditions. Only 142 lumber mills answered his letter, a return rate of less than 10 percent. On August 23, 1933, he wrote about his disappointment: "In all, I have received samples from only eight firms, which is surprisingly few. I thought I would get samples from considerably more."

One edge of the stock from the M. G. and J. J. Dorn Company in McCormick, South Carolina, however, showed defects in the planing "similar to but not so pronounced as those on one edge of rails 12 and 13."[56] There were eight knife cuts every .93 inch on the faces, and six cuts every .86 inch on the edges. The match was close enough to warrant a personal visit. "Uncanny?" he mused. "Say, it almost made you feel the ancients who believed in trees as gods were not so wrong. In Fraser's Golden Bough it's all worked out, just how savages the world around developed a superstition that the basis of all life, fertility, somehow was centered in trees. To them an oak was sacred; but for me— had I been less a scientist—a pine might have seemed to keep within its fibers strange and vengeful properties."[57]

Koehler's trip to South Carolina produced a list of some forty-seven carloads of North Carolina pine lumber shipped north between September 1929 and March 1, 1932, any one of which, or any part of one carload, might have boards bearing the special markings left by the planer defect. Of course, the problem was further complicated because the blades were periodically sharpened every few days. Pinpointing wood like that used in the ladder was more difficult than pulling out a single jackstraw from the jumbled pile. Koehler put it differently: "I do not see just how I mustered patience for the job that lay ahead. How to chart a pinwheel's flaming circles would seem, at first, as simple as the thing I had to do."

There was one other clue, however. The birch dowels that the builder had used to hold the ladder segments together fascinated Koehler. "A smooth and glossy surface had been worn on each, and from their roundness I had half decided they must have been turned out to serve as handles for some kind of toys." He was able to discover that several kinds of birch handles were made in Massachusetts factories. "When I went there the manufacturers were forced to shrug their shoulders." So, he says, he left that line of research and went back to the rails and rungs. That was not quite what happened, however, and the search for the dowels' original use formed a key element in Koehler's pursuit of the kidnapper, a path that did ultimately end in frustration—yet set out assumptions that guided investigations in another direction.

"My Siamese twin through all those times," writes Koehler, "was Detective Bornmann." Months before the discoveries at the Dorn Company in South Carolina, Bornmann on his own believed he had discovered pine stock at a lumber company in Trenton, New Jersey, that was close enough to warrant careful investigation. This was wood that had been shipped north from the Dalton Lumber Company of Norfolk, Virginia. He thought Dalton was in a position to be of service, "owing to the fact that their stock contains the same characteristics or defects found on rail #13."[58] There was apparently no follow-up to this investigation, or at least if there was it left no paper trail.

Bornmann soon came to believe he could identify the markings by sight. Together, he and Koehler began an intensive search on November 10, 1933, just after the latter came north from the South Carolina mill. The best result, obviously, would be if they could find a lumberyard that still had in its possession some of the wood from the Dorn Company, along with Douglas fir shipped from the West Coast. On November 16, 1933, they began the day at the National Lumber Company, 3541 White Plains Avenue, Bronx, New York. Why the lumber sleuths had not started their search there is hard to explain. The National Lumber Company was located at the nexus of all the activity in the kidnapping—practically on the corner of Gun Hill Road and but a few blocks from Woodlawn Cemetery.

Yes, said the manager, he had received a small shipment of the North Carolina pine in a mixed carload in late November 1931. None of it was on hand anymore. It had all been sold in small lots for cash, and the company kept no records of those sales. How many sales? Well, that was very hard to say, but around five hundred. Moreover, the National did not handle Douglas fir.

Another lumberyard nearby on Webster Avenue did handle Douglas fir, but it did not match up with the ladder rails in any way.

The two went on to Poughkeepsie and Germantown, New York, but with no better luck. Then it was back to the city, and then up to Connecticut, and even as far as Boston.

In New Haven, Connecticut, they visited a lumberyard that still had some of the Dorn Company North Carolina pine. Much of this wood did have a narrow indentation like that on rails 12 and 13, but it was somewhat closer to the edge. Finding out that some of the lumber had been used on a house close by, they discovered that practically every piece had the marks. "This shows that a defect in one of the planer knives may persist through perhaps a whole carload and undoubtedly through many thousand board feet before it is remedied by resharpening." It might, therefore, also show up on more than one carload, particularly if it was a mixed load, with various consignments to different outlets. And if the specially marked wood showed up at more than one lumberyard, what then? How would they go about trying to trace its purchasers?[59]

On November 27, Koehler and Bornmann stopped at the Kings County Lumber Company, located in Ozone Park on Long Island. Here they found samples of Dorn Company pine shipped on December 3, 1931. These samples were taken from bins that had been constructed to hold other lumber. The pieces showed the best match so far, with similar defects on one edge to what had been seen on rail 13. Although there were problems with the matchup, Koehler pursued the trail of this lumber to locations where it had been used in houses, carefully measuring the markings. Evidently, there were other factors that might account for tiny variations, things about the lumber-dressing process his single-day in McCormick, South Carolina, had not completely resolved. How many of these did it take to ruin an identification?

Later in the day, at the Brooklyn Consolidated Lumber Company, they discovered a company that handled both Dorn Company North Carolina pine and Douglas fir. But all this wood got mixed up with shipments from other places, "and they could not tell which was which as they were handling millions of feet of 1 × 4″ N.C. pine at that time."[60]

So far all the lumberyards were dead ends. But two days later—perhaps spurred by the thought that if some of the wood had been used for building bins at one place, why not at another?—they returned to the National Lumber Company. Lo and behold, there it was: a sample sticking out from the end of a bin that very nearly matched both the planer marks on the face and the cutter defects on the edge! But not completely.

> One glance showed that the defect we were looking for was present on the edge and that the stock had been dressed at the same speed as the pine ladder rails #12 and 13. Comparison later with a piece of one of the rails showed the planer marks to be practical[ly] identical.

> The sample from the bin also showed a defect in the planing of one of the faces which also was found to be present on the rail. There, however, was another defect in one of the knives

that dressed the same face which did not show on the ladder rail. Therefore, the ladder rail must have been dressed before this piece from the bin and could not have come from a subsequent shipment.[61]

In other words, there was an additional mark from a defect in one of the knives, a mark not present on the ladder rail. Again, they were faced with the question: how many variations are permissible to identify wood in the ladder rails as coming from stock delivered to the National Lumber Company? Planer marks on Douglas fir boards found at the same company, Koehler wrote, "although not very clear corresponded fairly well with those on rail #15."[62]

A week later, on December 6, 1933, Koehler visited another lumberyard, Butler Brothers, on East 201st Street and Harlem River Drive, to look at some Douglas fir wood that had red paint on it like that found on rail 14. The planer marks looked very much like those on the ladder rail, but those on the edges did not show up clearly enough to be at all certain.[63]

At this point Koehler thought he had enough evidence to bring to the attention of Colonel Schwarzkopf and his chief assistants. We do not know precisely what was said at this meeting in Trenton, on December 8, 1933, but Koehler records, "Further plans and the necessity of keeping our work quiet were discussed."

We can gain a pretty fair idea of what was discussed by subsequent developments. The next day Koehler stopped at another Butler Brothers yard to ask if it handled plywood with a hardened face—such as one might want to use in a radio cabinet or in another piece of furniture— or "as was used in the box for the money."[64]

Now it became clear where Koehler thought the search was leading.

In the afternoon we had a conference with Lieutenant Keaten. The importance of keeping our work quiet was again stressed. The possibility of the birch dowel having been used as a wand in a gymnasium was discussed. The fact that the dowel was not very dirty but had been handled a great deal as is shown by the film on it, indicated that it probably was handled by fairly clean but sweaty hands. It was decided that we had better look up some of the manufacturers or dealers in gymnasium apparatus.[65]

The following day, December 10, Koehler and another state trooper visited a company that sold such wands, and found out they were usually made from maple and came in different diameters and lengths. On December 11, Koehler had a "surprise," as he informed Captain J. J. Lamb that evening in a handwritten note on Hotel Lincoln stationery.

Dear Captain Lamb:

It has seemed to me for some time that rail no 16 was a piece of tongued and grooved stock taken from the interior of an old building. I believe it was tongued and grooved because both edges were hand sawed and hand planed; it came from the interior because it shows no sign of having been exposed to the weather for any length of time; and it came from an old building because it has cut-nail holes in it. Such lumber might have been used to seal the inside of a barn against cold. But where in New York City would one find a barn?

Today I had a surprise. I took the elevated up to where Condon lives to see what that section of the city looks like. Unfortunately I left his address in my room at the hotel so I couldn't tell which his house is and I didn't want to ask anyone but I knew in which block it is because I looked it up on a map just before I left.

I was surprised at the old buildings in that block. I saw one garage that apparently was a remodeled barn, because it was too large for a garage, although I can not be certain, of course. There may have been other old barns in that block, but I did not want to "rubber" too much and it was getting dark, so I can't tell.

Anyhow those buildings in that block look old enough to have been there in the horse-and-buggy age, and very likely there were barns, and barns ought to be sealed with matched or tongue and groove stock in this climate.

You see the connection? Of course, I may be all wrong, but it seems to me there are enough possibilities there to give the matter further attention, unless we get good reasons for thinking otherwise.

If that board was taken from the interior of a building and we can locate that building, the spacing of the nail holes should indicate just where it was taken. I have the distance between the nail holes in my notebook.

The note concluded with the theory that Koehler would now pursue over the next several months.

What I think happened is this: Those fellows stole 4 pieces
of fir lumber and stole or bought the 14 foot piece of pine.
When they worked on the ladder one of the pieces of fir went
wrong on them. It may have had a serious defect in it which
they did not see sooner, or it may have split in working it
up. They either did not have time or they did not want to
take the risk of getting another piece of 1×4 so they took this
piece of old lumber and cut it to the right width and used it
instead of the fir.[66]

The targets of the search had become John F. Condon and, as the last
paragraph says, "those fellows" who had stolen the lumber, or purchased part of it, and worked on the ladder.

Koehler continued to seek the origins of the dowels, believing
that they were cut from school wands—another possible connection
to Condon. And regarding the possible theft of the Douglas fir boards,
he was particularly interested in a storage yard owned by the Cross,
Austin & Ireland Company, at East 150th Street and Harlem River Drive,
a discontinued site. But Koehler never discovered any Douglas fir that
was a creditable match for the ladder.

Not until he became a prosecution witness did Koehler explain why
the nail holes in the Douglas fir had led him back to Cross, Austin & Ireland: because that company sold large amounts of lumber for construction purposes. But even if the ladder were built (as it probably
was) no more than a month or two prior to the kidnapping, the plane
marks on the Douglas fir were not nearly so distinctive as those on the
North Carolina pine. Wood shipped much earlier could well have been
used in the ladder. Indeed, it would eventually be Koehler's view that
the Douglas fir came from one of three lumber mills on the West Coast.
It even occurred to the expert that the ladder might have been cut in
one location and nailed together in another. In his many letters to
Schwarzkopf, elaborating on these theories, Koehler always used the
plural *they* to refer to the builders, not *he*.[67]

The mixture of woods suggested that some had been purchased
and some scavenged from various places. Then there was the evidence
noticed by all the examiners that the ladder had been in soil other than
at Highfields, and indications it had been planed down more than once
to make sure it nested right. Finally, there were the dowels. It seemed
unlikely this particular piece of wood had been purchased new. No
material like it was ever found.

Far beyond the normal range of a wood expert, Koehler looked for
other clues. He studied the fingerprints on the ladder brought out by

the silver nitrate solution. One near the end of a rung suggested it was probably placed there before the rung was nailed onto the ladder. He pursued the point in his next letter to Trenton, suggesting that perhaps he had a better view of the prints than anyone else who had studied them.[68]

Trenton was not impressed. Koehler was advised that "[the police] already have the photographs of all these finger prints," and he need not go to "the trouble of doing any additional work on this particular phase."

Some months later Koehler rethought his conclusion about where the rails had originated, impressed by increasing evidence that the rungs might have come from wood delivered to the Triangle Lumber Company on Long Island, not the National Lumber Company in the Bronx. The Long Island company was only about eight miles from Ozone Park, where the Queens County Lumber Company had received the next shipment of North Carolina pine from the Dorn mill. "The N.C. pine rails Nos. 12 and 13, might after all have come from the Queens County Lumber Company because the Dorn Company . . . had informed me previously that they sometimes dress more stock of a certain size than they can get into a car, and then they hold over the surplus in a shed until they get another order for the same size."[69]

Then came a remarkable musing—and admission. It revealed a cautious Koehler, not fully satisfied with his conclusions. This Koehler disappeared. He would not appear later at the trial or turn up in his published articles on the case.

I wrote to them [the Dorn Company] recently asking if their records showed whether they held over any 1 × 4 after dressing the car for the Bronx, but they replied that their records did not show anything one way or the other. However, their records do show that the 1 × 4 sent to the Bronx was dressed after other stock that was loaded in that car, which makes it more probable that some 1 × 4 might have been left over than if it had been dressed first. I raised an objection to that in my report because the sample we collected at the National Lumber and Millwork Company *has a planer defect on it that does not occur on the [ladder] rails which means that the rails were dressed before that sample.* It might be possible that both were dressed toward the very last and the lumber used in the ladder went to the Queens County Lumber Company, Ozone Park, L.I., although it is not very probable.[70]

The next thing Koehler turned his attention to was some faint writing on rail 15, which he made out to be "Henebier III." He searched directories from principal cities all across the country but could not find the name. The name Bier did appear in Bronx, Manhattan, and Brooklyn directories, however. Perhaps it was a contraction of Henry E. Bier. A Henry Bier lived on West 163rd Street in Manhattan, and a Henry Bierman resided on Laurel Avenue in Brooklyn. It might even have been the name of a boat.

> It is not a far stretch of the imagination to conceive of such a contraction of a person's name might be used for the name of a boat. I still have the boat idea in mind, because I can't see any other likely connection for the 'III' that follows the name on the rail. The fact that the criminals mentioned some places up the Sound and an 18-foot launch shows they were nautically minded. An ordinary land-lubber does not mention the length of a boat in feet, but one familiar with boats thinks of a small boat in terms of so many feet in length and of a large boat in terms of so many tons of displacement.[71]

Koehler's efforts to locate the ladder's origins had run aground, and he was left just as puzzled as Colonel Schwarzkopf and J. Edgar Hoover, who were always ready to blame each other for the impasse in the Lindbergh case.

7 CONFRONTATIONS

Mr. Hoover stated he was out with Winchell for a little while last night, . . . and at that time he had been "button-holed" by a couple of the New Jersey representatives, who stated they wanted him to get one thing straight, namely, that they had "done the job." Mr. Winchell told Mr. Hoover that he felt that if we didn't begin to "pass some stuff out" and take some credit ourselves, the other organizations would try to keep this credit from us.

—Agent E. A. Tamm, September 21, 1934

Walter Winchell loved to fan the flames of discord. It was meat and potatoes, or, in his case, ink and influence. But with Schwarzkopf and Hoover there was no need. They heartily disliked one another. As frustrations grew, so did the intensity of their animosity. President Roosevelt even got involved, calling Hoover to the White House for a little chitchat about where the Lindbergh case was going. The FBI director laid out the details in masterful fashion, not forgetting, of course, to point out that Colonel Lindbergh seemed to prefer the Treasury Department's Special Intelligence Division to his own men. Roosevelt promptly ordered all information turned over to the Justice Department. Henceforth, said FDR's instructions, Lindbergh investigations would be handled there. Hoover could not have asked for anything more.[1]

Dealing with Colonel Schwarzkopf was another matter. When Hoover complained the bureau was still being kept largely in the dark, unable to get information about suspects, or the true facts about evidence such as fingerprints, Schwarzkopf replied testily that the director was "quite definitely in error." He had all the information the state police had. Nothing had been withheld. "Naturally, it is my duty to protect the evidence and this I have done and will not permit any of it to get out of my control."[2]

It was impossible to work with the FBI men, Schwarzkopf complained to Agent Thomas Sisk, because of their standoffish attitude. Several times he had asked agents to go along with his men on investigations, but they said they would participate just as "observers." Well, fine, Schwarzkopf retorted, then they need not come at all. He could go out on the street and get anyone at all to "observe" the investigation.[3]

Just at this moment, and for some time past, there wasn't much to observe. The flow of ransom bills had come to a halt in February 1934. Some investigators believed newspaper articles about recovered bills had scared off John with "a running account of his activities." In the past he seemed to be spending the money frugally, budgeting himself for the long haul. Usually, as well, this person took care not to call attention to himself—with the one famous exception, the five-dollar bill tossed at the Greenwich Village movie cashier on November 26, 1933.[4]

The New York City Police Department inevitably became a target in this contest, subject to efforts by each side to enlist support against the other. In June 1934, Schwarzkopf visited New York police commissioner John F. O'Ryan to encourage him to support a joint complaint to the attorney general of the United States. The FBI had mishandled ransom money, insisted the colonel, by keeping it from other agencies, and, in general, behaved in an arrogant manner. O'Ryan refused to go along. "[The New York police] were going to remain neutral," he said. Schwarzkopf replied that he would go to Washington and lodge the complaint in person. There were rumors floating about, moreover, that Lindbergh was going to see the president to support the New Jersey side.[5]

The New Jersey State Police were using "under-handed tactics," Sisk reported, even "trying to embitter Dr. Condon toward the Division." They took Condon down to Hopewell the other day, "patted him on the back and treated him like a king." The idea was to convince the old man that if any FBI agent wanted him to identify pictures or go someplace, a state trooper should be there. The ploy backfired, however, as Condon deferred to the FBI. Only if it was OK with them, he said, delighted at the fight for his favor. "They were trying to do with Dr. Condon the same thing they have accomplished with Colonel Lindbergh," grumbled Hoover. "It looks as though they are trying to 'freeze us out.'"[6]

Lindbergh did contact Hoover with a request that a New Jersey state trooper be present whenever there was a conference with Lindbergh about anything. It had gotten to the point where Hoover and Schwarzkopf had begun to accuse each other of lying about the physical evidence, for example, over whether there were or were not latent fingerprints found on the ransom notes. Hoover's men claimed there were, while the New Jersey authorities said no. For some reason, the fingerprint evidence seemed to be the most sensitive of all in Trenton.[7]

A meeting did take place in Attorney General Homer Cummings's office on June 19, 1934, attended by Hoover, Cummings, Schwarzkopf and his aides, as well as a New Jersey senator and congressman. Hoover insisted their complaints were ill founded and the result of a noncooperative attitude on their part. Cummings interjected that he had seen all the correspondence, and it was true, he said, the New Jersey State Police had refused to supply the FBI with information it had requested. He wanted no more bickering, and Colonel Schwarzkopf would have to understand cooperation was not a one-way street. Then Schwarzkopf and Hoover were sent off to another room to come to some arrangement about future cooperation. They did so, but it was hardly a kiss-and-make-up session.[8]

The new cooperative spirit had yet to be tested when the ransom bills started to resurface. On August 20, 1934, the New York City Federal Reserve Bank reported finding a ten-dollar gold certificate. Eight days later two more bills showed up. The Federal Reserve Bank had put on eighteen additional clerks to aid in spotting ransom bills, and here, at last, were the first solid results. But investigators were still stymied, because the smaller branch banks had not picked them out. "It was obvious that the neighborhood and branch banks were making no effort to detect the Lindbergh ransom money," complained Thomas Sisk. "With this condition existing, there was no opportunity to procure a description of or gain any information as to the identity of the person or persons passing the ransom money."[9]

Someone out there—whether John or someone new to the game—was spending the money again. Forget about five-dollar bills, Sisk ordered the banks; they were probably all spent by now. This man was walking around peeling off ransom bills just about anyplace he pleased. There would never be a better opportunity to move in on him—and improve the bureau's image. Concentrate on the gold certificates, he said; find out who this man was.

On September 12, 1934, Walter Winchell made a prediction in his *Daily Mirror* column: "The federal men are convinced that they will break the most interesting crime on record—the Lindbergh snatch. A squad of hand picked aces still are working on it—24 hours every day." The G-men would have cracked the case earlier, Winchell went on, if they had been called in at the start. Only after the New Jersey boys bungled the job did the bureau finally get its chance. Prohibition had given G-men a bad rap as snoopers enforcing an unpopular law. It might take some time for that reputation to fade away, but, Winchell predicted, "the lads are sure that the breaking of the Lindbergh case would do more to reinstate them in the public heart than anything else."[10]

Winchell knew exactly what was going on because Hoover had put him on his special list to receive inside information. Reading his column, one would have thought he had just come from a briefing in J. Edgar's office or, more likely, had just finished a timely phone call. A former vaudeville dancer with no journalistic training, Winchell had somehow put himself at the center of things during the Depression, trading in secrets of the rich and famous, giving Mr. and Mrs. America a brief glimpse of what they were *really like* under those furs and top hats. He was, in turn, courted by the high and mighty because of their fear of being exposed—or neglected. Winchell had a permanent table at the Stork Club, where he held court and passed out benedictions. Owney Madden and J. Edgar Hoover were both welcome to pull up a chair.

Winchell reaped $7,500 a week for his radio broadcasts alone, plus other huge sums for his newspaper column and, most recently, Hollywood films. J. Edgar Hoover had not missed the rising star over Broadway. What a powerful influence Winchell could have on behalf of the bureau, and for Hoover personally in the jockeying for position as the New Deal changed the relationship between the federal and state governments. Winchell had been invited to the White House that summer to give Roosevelt his views on Nazi activities—and, to the amazement of practically everybody, they got on famously. Unlike many other columnists, Winchell was fervently pro–New Deal. His employer, William Randolph Hearst, didn't like Winchell spouting New Deal views, but was too smart to try to stop him.

Hoover quickly noticed Winchell's popularity with the White House and invited him to FBI headquarters for a private showing of his Dillinger trophies. Bank robber John Dillinger had made local cops look bad, very bad, escaping from jail once with a "pistol" made from a bar of soap and colored black with shoe polish. After Special Agent Melvin Purvis shot the gangster to death in an alley outside a Chicago movie theater, Hoover kept the desperado's death mask on his desk to show favorites like Winchell.

Cemetery John, however, looked to be a very different sort of operator. Excitement ran high as nine ransom bills were discovered in neighborhood banks during a three-week period in August and September. How to figure this guy? Was he suddenly strapped for funds and willing to run the risk of passing the bills? Maybe he was just smug and feeling secure.[11]

No one wanted to think it might be somebody new. Whoever it was, this guy was willing to argue with a clerk in a fruit market about making change for a six-cent purchase of a head of cabbage, or brag to a gas station attendant that he had a hundred more ten-dollar gold certificates at home. The clerk, Salvatore Levantino, described the man as about five-foot-ten, slender, with an athletic build and a facial shape very similar to Jafsie's description of Cemetery John. Sisk telephoned FBI headquarters in Washington at once. "[Levantino] gave a perfect description of the fellow John," including what he was wearing, "a powder blue suit and a new gray hat."[12]

The customer shook his finger at him menacingly when Levantino hesitated to make change for such a small purchase. "How about those eyes when he shook his finger at you?" asked Lieutenant Finn. "No sparks," said the clerk, "no fire, no shake in voice—like so many fellers when they get mad. . . . Eyes just cold all the time."[13]

When agents looked at the original list of ransom bills, they noticed something else important: "these bills have been showing up right in order and they can almost tell the serial number of the next bill which will show up." That meant "[the kidnappers] still have the money and are passing it." In the area of Eighty-seventh Street there were literally hundreds of produce stores. No wonder the bill passer liked to operate there. Sisk organized teams of plainclothes detectives and FBI agents to roam the area looking for a nattily dressed John pinching melons or, even better, pulling a bill from his wallet.

Hoover was not satisfied. "I want more men assigned at once," the director ordered, "and every bit of pressure put to this." Tell Sisk every team should have an FBI agent so as to ensure equal rights to the capture. E. A. Tamm sent out the word. "The director knows," he admonished Sisk, "from sources of information that are open to him that these fellows are playing along with us just so they will be in on the kill and if they can jump the gun on us when the crash comes, they will probably not hesitate to do it."

Each day from 9 A.M. until 7 P.M., plainclothes men walked the neighborhood streets of the Yorkville area, ducking in and out of fruit and vegetable stands waiting for John to appear and offer ten or twenty dollars for a bunch of lettuce or a few onions.[14] Eventually, the patrol grew to forty-eight "customers" hanging around produce stands, obviously never satisfied with anything they saw.

"Our man was easily scared," acknowledged Finn. "We had learned that. The moment a word was breathed about the ransom bills showing up in the banks, he was off the spending business for weeks, perhaps for months. That's why we had asked the newspaper and radio people to lie low."

On Sunday night, September 16, nevertheless, Walter Winchell used his radio show to berate bank tellers. "Boys," he scolded, "if you weren't such a bunch of saps and yaps, you'd have already captured the Lindbergh kidnappers."[15]

"I'd have given a year's pay check to be able to reach out and cut him off," Finn exploded. "Somebody was spilling the beans."[16]

On Monday, the Lindbergh case broke wide open. That morning a bank manager at the Corn Exchange branch on East 125th Street found a ten-dollar gold certificate in a stack of bills deposited the previous weekend. Unfortunately, the teller who took it in had been suffering from appendicitis and could barely get through the day—let alone pay attention to some particular person.

"Another blind alley," groaned Finn. But when he turned the bill over, "something like a flash of lightning struck." He saw 4U-13-41 written on the back. Could he be that lucky? It looked like a car license number. While Finn called the Motor Vehicle Bureau to make sure, the tellers found three deposit tickets from gas stations. The nearest one was the Warner-Quinlan Oil Company on Lexington Avenue, between 127th and 128th Streets.

Yes, it was a license number. It had been issued to Bruno Richard Hauptmann, 1279 East 222nd Street in the Bronx. Remembering he had interviewed six hundred people, Finn asked as calmly as he could, What was this man's description? Reading off the driver's license, the man at the bureau told him he was five-foot-ten, with blue eyes and light brown hair, and weighed 180 pounds. He was born in 1899 in Germany and gave his occupation as a carpenter.[17]

At the Warner-Quinlan station, Walter Lyle, the manager, recognized the bill as one he took in from a man about 10 A.M. on September 15, the previous Saturday. This man looked to be about thirty-two years old, Lyle said, five-foot-eleven, and 165 pounds. He had a light complexion and was of the "Scandinavian type." He asked the man whether he wanted his gas tank filled. No, he said, just five gallons of ethyl. The total came to ninety-eight cents. All this time, however, the man stood outside his car, in plain sight of both Lyle and another attendant, John

Lyons. Lyle then asked if he wanted his oil checked, too. "Never mind," the man replied, taking out a white envelope from an inside coat pocket. "Neither the bill nor the envelope were folded, and Lyle did not notice anything else in the envelope." So much, then, for Shoenfeld's pet theory all the bills would be found creased in the same way.[18]

When Lyle saw the ten-dollar gold certificate, he started to protest that the banks weren't taking gold certificates anymore. "Sure they do," the man replied. "I have a hundred more of dese at home in the house." Then he drove off. Worried about getting stuck with a bad bill, Lyle jotted down the license number on the back. "At last, after more than two years," Finn exulted, "Jafsie's John had unwittingly boasted of his ill-gotten wealth." Why had this man—why would anyone—boast about possessing a hundred illegal gold certificates? It was almost as if the fellow was saying, "I'm here, come and get me." Yes, but did he say a hundred bills or a hundred dollars—the limit for possessing gold certificates after Roosevelt's order? That was never clarified.[19]

With Special Agent Sisk, Lieutenant Arthur Keaten of the New Jersey State Police, and two other officers, Finn set up his surveillance posts near Hauptmann's house. Hauptmann, his wife, Anna, and one year-old son, Manfred, lived in a five-room apartment on the second floor. Downstairs lived Max Rauch, the landlord, and his mother, Pauline. Another couple, Victor and Louisa Schuessler, also rented from the Rauches. The house was located in a sparsely settled section of the Bronx. In fact East 223rd, the next street back, was as yet nothing more than a dirt road. Approximately fifty feet from the rear of the house was a single-car garage. One could drive due west for a few minutes—little more than a mile, actually—straight along 222nd Street and arrive at the gates of Woodlawn Cemetery.

The Hauptmanns had lived at this address in the second-floor apartment since October 1931. It had a sitting room, two small bedrooms, a kitchen, and bath. Their son, Manfred, was born on November 3, 1933. When they moved into this house, there was no garage. Their landlord said if Hauptmann would build one on an adjoining plot, he would supply the lumber and allow him to use it rent free for the time they lived there. Hauptmann agreed. It was a small garage, with not much room for anything but his Dodge car and a narrow workbench.

When the police arrived at their lookouts, the car was not in the garage. In fact, Hauptmann would not return home until the middle of the night. As more police kept arriving to join in the "posse," the neighbors became suspicious of all the strange men standing around in groups of two or three. Detectives walked up to the garage itself and peered in. Two others crossed the lawn of a nearby house—bringing an irate woman to the door with a dog. Opening the screen, she "sic'ed" her dog on the offenders, "resulting in considerable confusion and noise." The woman also called the police; in a few minutes a precinct car pulled alongside Sisk's vehicle, flashing a light inside. Finn produced his badge, and the locals went away. But now they were curious, and police cars roamed all through the neighborhood.[20]

When the suspect had not returned by 1:30 A.M., it was agreed to give up for the night and return the next morning. As the men departed, Sisk pulled aside Agent William F. Seery and told him to proceed to the nearest subway station, as though he were going home for the night, then come back immediately and continue the surveillance. All night long New Jersey and New York police drifted back as well. J. Edgar Hoover was on his way from Washington as well to be in on the "kill," whether it turned out to be a Dillinger affair or simply a dramatic arrest.[21]

Daylight came, and the besiegers held a council of war. They decided not to storm the house. "1279 East 222nd Street might be such a little fortress," said Finn, "that our only chance of getting into it would be to shoot our way in—which, of course, was the last thing we wished to do in this particular case." From the information already gathered about Hauptmann, his lack of a police record, why should they think Hauptmann was Pretty Boy Floyd or Machine Gun Kelly? "Who was Richard Hauptmann?" Finn asked himself. "What was his background? Who were his associates? Did he have a family? A child? I dismissed the last idea as an impossibility."[22]

Finn's rumination about Hauptmann's family well illustrates the police's preconceptions about their suspect. They must have been surprised at discovering the Lindbergh kidnapper might be an ordinary man living quietly, tucked away in a far corner of the Bronx, and not a professional gangster. A few minutes before nine in the morning, a nattily dressed man in a bluish gray suit and patterned tie emerged from the house and went to the garage. The police "tails" were ready to follow him wherever he went; they hoped he would drive to a produce stand or gas station, where he could be easily nabbed. But there was another surprise. He now spent most days buying and selling stocks at the Steiner, Rouse Company, a brokerage firm on Eighty-sixth Street in Manhattan. Steiner, Rouse was a favorite of German Americans, who often gathered across the street at the Yorkville Boerse, which offered *Gute Deutsche Küche* (Good German Cuisine), and where, FBI reports had it, patrons played card games and engaged in a lively trade in U.S. gold certificates at premium prices as much as two or three dollars over face value.[23]

As Hauptmann headed downtown that morning, September 19, 1934, however, none of the cars tailing him had any idea where he was going. But he was going there at a fast clip, forty miles an hour in heavy morning traffic, according to an FBI report on the "chase." He was constantly looking in his rearview mirror, the report went on, and appeared to be trying to "shake" his pursuers. Nervous that he might make a run for it, they decided to force him over and make the arrest.

Was this a classic gangster car chase, then? It depends on one's interpretation of various reports. The FBI report is disputed by other accounts. Finn described Hauptmann, for example, as a "methodical daredevil in his driving, just as he had been a methodical daredevil in the kidnap[p]ing of the child, the arranging of the ransom, and the spending of the ransom money." And again, either Hauptmann sped through several red lights when he thought he was being followed, or he gauged his time perfectly to go through the green lights along the way; either he stopped because a city sprinkler truck or a milk truck blocked his way, or he was forced to the curb near 178th Street.[24] Or, finally, according to the FBI, Hauptmann stopped for a red light on Park Avenue, and three cars surrounded him. Guns drawn, police and FBI agents piled out to rush the Dodge. Lieutenant Keaten rushed to Hauptmann's car and pulled him out, said the FBI report. Or was it a different New Jersey police officer, Detective Sargeant John Wallace? According to another report, Wallace jumped from his car, raced around to the passenger door of the blue sedan, slid into the passenger seat, and stuck a gun in the suspect's ribs.[25]

"If he made a move for a gun, we were ready to grab him," reported Finn. "But he made no move. Those cold blue-gray eyes described by Levatino and Cecile Barr looked calmly back into mine."[26]

"Get out of the car," Finn ordered. They patted him down for weapons. Then they took out a wallet from a back pocket. "It contained— what do you think?—one twenty-dollar gold certificate of the ransom money." Dr. Shoenfeld had predicted that would be the case: "Finn, when you land your man, you'll find he's the kind of fellow who'll have just one bill in his pocket."[27]

Finn's description of the actual find is misleading, for he did not tell readers that the wallet also contained other bills, a five and four ones. Shoenfeld had also predicted they would find the bill folded over exactly like the one tossed at Cecile Barr at the movie theater on November 26, 1933. The author Jim Fisher regards this as an "extremely important point" for "Hauptmann would later assert that he had no knowledge of the ransom money prior to August 1934." Finn told the Bronx grand jury on September 24, 1934, however, only that the bill was found in a "side compartment" of the wallet. In his pretrial deposition, moreover, he did not mention how the bill was folded, or if it was. Finally, the other arresting officers who saw the bill removed from the wallet make absolutely no mention of this "extremely important" point.[28]

Finn took charge right away; after all, this was New York City. Much to the annoyance of the FBI and New Jersey police, he insisted that they wait right there before taking Hauptmann back to his house to begin a search for more money. No one was to move the suspect, Finn insisted, until Inspector John C. Lyons got there. The struggle for the blue ribbon was under way in earnest.[29]

When Hauptmann asked what was going on, he was told that the bill was counterfeit. Did he have any more? Hauptmann insisted he had only good money, but yes, he did have more; he had $125 more in gold at home. There was some confusion, as well, about this statement, over whether he meant to say he had that much in gold currency or coins. Finn's recollection was that he said he had accumulated the money over several years. "I have now to use this money to buy the things for my family—I have not been working."[30]

Handcuffed to Detective Sargeant Wallace, Hauptmann was taken back to his house, where police began a search through all the rooms. They tore apart a mattress in the bedroom, ransacked drawers, found a tin box Hauptmann had mentioned containing some gold coins—but no gold certificates.

Somehow, the police had slipped Hauptmann into the house and up to his apartment while Anna was outside playing with Manfred. When she was brought in by police, Anna asked her husband what had happened. "Did you do something wrong?" Richard said, "No." But he also said he had been arrested. She turned to the police. What is the matter? she demanded to know, looking from one to the other. "You'll find out soon enough," one of the detectives said and took her out of the room.[31]

Hauptmann confirmed that a shoebox found by police contained shoes he had purchased for his wife with another of the gold certificates; but now he was insisting what he had told Walter Lyle had to do with coins, not bills. He answered questions slowly, in heavily accented English that was often hard to understand.

Something very important happened next. Hauptmann was in the kitchen, still handcuffed to Wallace. The only other person there was Inspector John Lyons, who was now in charge of the house search and interrogation. Lyons asked Hauptmann about the gold certificates, and then—for the first time—where he was on March 1, 1932. "He stated that he did not know."[32]

FBI agents also heard Hauptmann say that morning, before he was taken to police headquarters on Greenwich Street, that he was not regularly employed, was uncertain about dates of when he last worked on a steady job, but thought it was at the Majestic Apartments in the spring of 1932. In later interrogations Hauptmann claimed he worked the day of the kidnapping. By then he had become desperate to place himself at the apartments—anyplace but Hopewell, New Jersey. So much has been written about the work evidence that his original uncertainty about where he was on the day and night of the kidnapping has been passed by. FBI agent Leon Turrou would write, "His groping confused answers gave the impression that he had blundered into our arms without a prepared alibi."[33]

Turrou also believed Hauptmann had a "low bovine mentality," however, and that explained his cumbersome behavior. Having dealt with "Public Enemies No. 1" over the past several years, it was clear that police and the FBI were somewhat nonplussed by the stolid German carpenter, who, when confronted with the contradictions in his story, simply hopped birdlike down the fence to the next post. There he would sit until they threw the next question, forcing him to move again.

He made no admissions, however. "We continued to puncture his story at every turn," wrote Turrou. "We wanted a confession. We questioned him until our heads reeled, but we never got it."[34]

It was thus hard to resist the temptation to stretch Hauptmann's answers or gestures into a confession of sorts. Even Agent Sisk, who was among the more judicious of the investigators, succumbed. At the trial he testified that during his first interrogation Hauptmann had been sitting near a bedroom window. When he thought nobody was looking, he got up and looked out toward the garage. "He did that four or five times," said Sisk, "[got] up a little from his chair and look[ed] out the window."

Alerted by his nervousness, Sisk asked, "What are you looking at when you are sneaking those looks out the window?"

"Nothing."

"Is that where you have the money?"

"No, I have no money."

Going to the garage, Sisk found two floorboards that seemed loose. Prying them up, he used a shovel to dig in the soft earth below. About a foot down his shovel hit a crockery jug covered with mud. Empty except for two or three inches of water in the bottom, the jug reminded Sisk that some of the recovered money had a distinctly musty smell. "We questioned Hauptmann as to that jug," Sisk testified at the trial. "He denied knowing anything about it, but the next day when we questioned him, he admitted that he had that money in there three weeks before he was arrested."

Immediately, Hauptmann was on his feet. "Mister, Mister, you stop lying. You are telling a story." Sisk's trial testimony telescoped everything. When he found the crockery jug, no stash of ransom money had as yet been discovered. When over $13,000 of the money was found the next day in the garage, Hauptmann claimed it came from a wet shoebox left for safekeeping by a friend and business associate, Isidor Fisch. If the prosecution could not come up with an alternate explanation for why that should be, then there was only Hauptmann's explanation left. Hence the dramatic outburst when Sisk testified that Hauptmann had admitted putting ransom money in the jug.[35]

At the trial Hauptmann could not deny he had hidden the money in the garage. After drying it out, he said, he placed it inside an empty shellac can. What upset him about Sisk's testimony, then, was not the discovery of the money but his suggestion that Hauptmann had been fidgeting over the discovery of the crockery jug. It undercut his whole defense—even though it was not clear Sisk's trial revelations moved the court very much one way or another.

Who was right? The FBI agent's testimony can be checked against other evidence, including the records made at the time, which, he said, were identical to his sworn evidence in the Flemington Court House. Leon Turrou supported his account—up to a point. "Agent Sisk dug up the fresh ground and approximately one foot underground found a large jug of a cylinder shape, about 10″ high and about 8″ in diameter. This jug had about an inch of water at the bottom of it and had a piece of cloth fastened around the top so that it could be pulled up easily. Examination failed to reveal any money was contained therein. When Hauptmann was questioned as to what it was doing in the garage, he denied any knowledge of it, but from the circumstances it appeared highly possible that the money had been hidden in this jug at one time."[36]

But Lieutanent Finn disputed the FBI. He wrote later that Hauptmann was not on a chair near the window, but rather deposited on a bed in the center of the room—handcuffed to Detective Sergeant Wallace. Had he kept popping up and down to look out the window, so, too, would the detective. "Wallace was in no mood to furnish comic relief," wrote Finn.[37]

There is no indication from any interrogation records, of the police or FBI, that Hauptmann ever admitted to anyone that he placed the money in the jug. He never varied from the original "Fisch story." In general, Sisk is among the most reliable of the investigators, but there are unanswered questions. For example, once Hauptmann had taken the water-soaked bills out of the jug, why did he bother to rebury it? Why not toss it away? There was never an explanation, and Sisk was not cross-examined on the point.

At least we know for sure that no money had yet been found when police took Hauptmann to the police station at 156 Greenwich Street. Questioning began at 3 P.M. He did not have a lawyer present—in these pre-Miranda days it was not required if the arrested person demanded it—and would not have one for more than seventy-two hours.

"What is your full name?"

"Bruno Richard Hauptmann."

Hauptmann explained that he had started life in Germany as a carpenter, worked for a time as a machinist, entered the army during the First World War at age seventeen, and served for nearly two years. After the war there were no opportunities for decent work, and so he decided to come to America. After two unsuccessful tries at stowing away, he managed to get into the country in 1923 by hiding away in the coal bunker or behind the engines for ten days, eating little more than bread and water and a few scraps of food thrown out by the ship's cook. He walked off the ship, SS *Washington,* right past guards on the lookout for illegal immigrants, and into uptown Manhattan. There he met a "German fellow on the street," Fred Aldinger, who took him home, and he began his new life.[38]

He worked for some time as a dishwasher and then found small carpentry jobs, eventually joining the union to get full-time employment. He married Anna in 1926. It soon emerged that he had worked in New Jersey, around Lakewood, and later close to Freehold—not more than an hour's drive from Hopewell.

Inspector Lyons led the questioning, but crowded into the room were Colonel Schwarzkopf and key aides, Captain Lamb and Lieutenant Keaten, as well as Sisk and another FBI agent who stood in the background with Lieutenant Finn. Much to the annoyance of J. Edgar Hoover, Finn was already claiming to be the man who caught Hauptmann single-handed.

The questioning continued, zeroing in on the evidence: "Did you ever work in the National Lumber Company?"

"Yes." Hauptmann was quite forthcoming about his continuing relationship with the National Lumber Company, one that extended back several years. "I used to buy my lumber over there."

"And you used to buy lumber there on many occasions?"

"Yes," he bought lumber there in 1930, in 1931, 1932, 1933, and even this year, 1934. He had worked regularly in 1930 in the Langenbacher cabinetworks making furniture. And then for another contractor building houses. At this early stage, Hauptmann presented himself as a hard-working, frugal immigrant making his way toward middle-class status. He and Anna had worked hard, he said, and saved their money so that in 1931 they felt able to take a two-month vacation trip to California, sharing the costs with his good friend Hans Kloppenburg.

When he came back from that trip, he worked on a contract basis for the National Lumber Company. He would show up at the lumber-yard, and if a job came in, he would go out to the location with the necessary supplies. But he kept looking for steady work and found it at the Majestic Apartments in the spring of 1932. He got the job through an employment agency.

"Spring 1932 you were working on the Majestic [Apartments]?

"Maybe I make a mistake in dates, I can't remember, I didn't keep books of this, but it was Spring 1932."

By now, Hauptmann had obviously thought about what he had told Lyons back at his house, but, interestingly, he still did not claim to have been working on March 1, 1932. So twice he made no effort to pinpoint his whereabouts on the day of the kidnapping. The absence of any real alibi is striking; for if someone he had carried out the crime of the century, he might well have concocted a good story about where he was every minute of the day. Hauptmann baffled police officials. Was he just a clumsy blunderer, stumbling along a path with freakish good luck, or an ingeniously clever man who had gotten careless? His demeanor gave no clue as he sat there hour after hour answering questions with little show of emotion—except when someone talked about his duty to Anna or Manfred. Then there were tears. But no confession.

"When did you leave that job?" Lyons went on.

"I guess in April."

Couldn't he be more specific?

He had worked there only for a couple of months, he said, and left either in April or in May. Pressed, Hauptmann eventually claimed he had worked on the day of the kidnapping. Yes, he now remembered, he had started in February 1932 and worked every day until he quit. He was on the job from early in the morning until late in the afternoon, five or six o'clock. "There was nothing in his face to tell us that he wasn't innocent," Turrou later remembered. "It was distressed and tired, but clean of guilt."[39]

The questioners took a break to talk about how to proceed while police and federal agents began the process of checking the details he had told them so far.

When the interrogation resumed, Lyons went after the work alibi: "In 1932, in May, you left that job. Where did you go then?"

"I went back to the lumberyard again. . . . Sometimes I got little jobs for myself, repairing doors, windows, etc."

"Were you still working in the National Lumber Company?"

"Very seldom, because in 1931 I went to play the stock market."

The stock market? Where would an ordinary carpenter get the money to play the stock market? Where did he have his account? What stocks did he buy? How much did he invest?

He had started with $2,000, he said, but he could not remember the first broker's name.

Well, then, what was the greatest amount he had ever invested?

Somewhere between $20,000 and $25,000.

"What year was that?"

"I guess it was two years ago, or last year. The market went up, but there was a debit balance."

Two years ago, of course, would have been right after the Lindbergh ransom money was paid to Cemetery John! Now things were moving. Was that where he got $20,000 to invest in the stock market? Either that, or this guy really was a clever fellow—cleverer than most who had lost their shirts.

Now it was time to talk about the gold certificates. Hauptmann readily admitted to having gold certificates in his possession, up to $300 at one time. He was keeping gold as a hedge against inflation. But when President Roosevelt called in all the gold specie and certificates, he realized that it was useless to continue hoarding, and began to spend them. The one they found on him was the last of the lot.

Why did he tell the gasoline attendant a few days ago that he had a hundred more at home?

Well, said Hauptmann, the attendant must have misheard him. He meant to say he *used* to have a hundred at home.

OK, maybe he said that, but he could not get around the problem that *all* of the gold certificates he had been passing in recent days had been Lindbergh ransom money.

Maybe they came from the same batch at the bank when he went there to exchange money, suggested Hauptmann.

Lyons was incredulous: "You do not expect us to believe that, do you?"

There was no answer.

Well, said the inspector, there was one way Hauptmann might clear himself. Would he be willing to give them some handwriting samples?

Yes, he agreed; "it'll help me get out of this thing."

Handwriting identification is a very tricky enterprise—both for the accused and the accusers. It is a little like asking someone to take a lie-detector test; the first hope is to scare the subject into a confession. "He knew we wanted to get a sample of his handwriting to check against the ransom notes," wrote Special Agent Turrou, "and he managed to disguise his style." But no one can disguise his or her writing in precisely the same way in successive attempts. Clever as one might be, natural traits "will become evident through any camouflage."[40]

That conclusion is the basis for handwriting analysis and testimony of experts. There are three comparisons to make. Passages dictated to a suspect are called "request writings." Samples of older writings obtained from the suspect's home or some other source are known as "conceded writings." Then there are the "questioned writings," in this case the ransom notes.

It was never entirely clear in the Lindbergh case whether the suspected disguise used by the ransom note writer extended to a purposeful effort to implicate someone with a German background, or the occasional insertion of German words resulted from pressures of the moment, a reversion to familiar usage.

To minimize the chances of error, a composite of the ransom notes—designed by Albert D. Osborn—was dictated to Hauptmann, and he began writing: "Cross the street and walk to the next corner and follow Whittemore Avenue to the Sound. Take the money with you. Come alone and walk. I will meet you. The boy is on the boat. It is a small boat 28′ long. Two persons are on the boat. They are innocent. You will find the boat between Horseneck Beach and Gayhead, near Elizabeth Island."

When he got to the sentences "The boy is on the boat. It is a small boat 28′ long," Hauptmann wrote, "the boy is on the boat it is a schmal boat 28 feet lonk." The original ransom note read, however, "the boy is on Boad Nelly. it is a small Boad 28 feet long." The "N" in Nelly was written "И"—as if in a mirror—and the rest of the word was written in a print style. Lyons no doubt had hoped Hauptmann would put *Nelly* in—betraying his guilt. He had not. In the second and third dictations, the inspector told him to write *Nelly* and made some other changes. Perhaps he would write *Nelly* with an inverted *N*—almost as good. He did not. Hauptmann wrote in the second, "the boy is on the boat Nelly it is a smal boat." The *N* was written in script. On his third try, Hauptmann wrote, "the boy is on the boat Nelly it is a schmal boat 28 feet long."[41]

Later in the evening, after midnight, however, police would order him to print several capital *N*s. And these letters did look like the *N*s in the ransom notes, including the address on the sleeping suit package. And there were other similarities between these first request writings and the ransom notes, including Hauptmann's writing *the* when the dictation was *they*. Here was a singular quirk, not easily explained as a common error for someone whose original language was German.

The author Ludovic Kennedy argues that in the postmidnight sessions Hauptmann was told to write words exactly as they were spelled in the ransom notes. His friend Hans Kloppenburg remembered it that way, too. Brought to the police station for questioning, Kloppenburg was also given a writing test. "I had to copy it the way it was spelt." We do not know how many sheets of writing Hauptmann filled in the early morning hours of September 20, 1934. But the misspelling of *they* as *the* occurs on the very first page of request writing. If the spellings were being rigged at that point, why would Hauptmann have been told to spell *small* as *schmal,* since it was correctly spelled in the ransom note? Or why was he told to spell *boat* correctly, when it appeared as *boad* several times in the ransom notes?[42] The experts had difficulty with these issues.

Meanwhile, Hauptmann's interrogation was interrupted by the arrival of taxicab driver Joseph Perrone. There was as yet no solid evidence against Hauptmann. If the cabbie stepped forward and said, yes, this is the man who handed me the note for Condon, that might in itself break down Hauptmann's defenses and get him writing a confession, not just handwriting samples.

"Now, Joe," Lyons greeted Perrone, "we've got the right man at last. There isn't a man in this room who isn't convinced he is the man who kidnapped the Lindbergh baby." Over the past two years, Perrone had identified a score of men—vastly different from one another—as the one who gave him the note. But this time was different. He was on trial as much as Richard Hauptmann. "Inspector Lyons," reported Sisk, "practically coerced Perrone into identifying Hauptmann."[43]

Step by step, Lyons led him through his original story of the encounter with the man who came running up to his cab the night of March 12, 1932. Watched by more than a dozen top police officials, Perrone followed every lead the inspector gave him. By the last prompt, Perrone had fully grasped what the situation was—and where it could lead him next in terms of reward and fame.

"How long were you talking with him?"

"About seven to ten minutes."

Seven to ten minutes—an aeon of time for a secure identification! Everything was in place.

In walked three men, Hauptmann in between two beefy New York policemen. "On March 12, 1932," the inspector addressed Perrone again, but this time so Hauptmann might see how hopeless his denials were, "at about 8:30 P.M. you were driving a taxicab in the vicinity of Mosholu

Parkway and Gunhill Road. Did anybody accost you at that time? Do you see him in this room?"

Perrone marched over to Bruno Richard Hauptmann and put his hand on his shoulder. "Yes. That's the man."

Is there anything else about this man? asked Lyons.

Perrone now knew his lines well: Yes, his voice and manner of speech. "It was exactly as he spoke to me on that night." A fleeting glimpse had become a prolonged close-quarters conversation—a positive ID. Even if Hauptmann did not now confess, the police had secured a very valuable witness—an identification process in reverse. They had identified Hauptmann to Perrone. Many faces had paraded across the cabbie's memory. Now, with Lyon's help, only one remained.[44]

When Hauptmann was taken back to the interrogation room, Lyons began asking him about possible acquaintances. What church did he go to? Lutheran. Had he ever attended a spiritualist church? No. Then, a little later: did he know someone named Peter Birritella? No. Had he ever met Betty Gow or Violet Sharp? No. How about a man named Junge? No. Even with a good suspect in custody, the names from the first weeks of the investigation had not been entirely forgotten. For now, it seemed, the police had many more questions than answers.

Hans Kloppenburg, Hauptmann's good friend, corroborated, in a way, his story that he did not make a habit of reading the *Bronx Home News*—where Condon's letter had appeared. Hauptmann said he sometimes found it on the steps and took it inside the house, but he did not like the newspaper and seldom read it. Kloppenburg said he saw it on the steps on occasion, and that the Hauptmanns took it in when they found it there. On the very day Condon's letter appeared, the paper was on the steps, and Hauptmann retrieved it, so he could have written the response that triggered the ransom negotiations. Was it just another stroke of luck for the kidnapper?

There were more questions for Hauptmann about the gold certificates, but police were stymied because they had not found any more ransom money inside the house.

Lyons then dictated a new passage to a very weary Hauptmann, who had already been under interrogation for twelve hours.

> We were not near Smith Hall where the robbery took place between 6 and 12 by our time. During all the time I was out of the house but later came home. Did you not write letters to New York sending back anything that was stolen from Mr. Conway? Police keep those letters and papers; they will be good for something later maybe. One of the letters said

"Dear Sir: Thank you for the bills and for your money. We will send back the bills later perhaps, where shall we send them, the address we lost. Be at home every night so you will hear from us, you cannot tell when it will be."

Albert D. Osborn's accompanying instructions admonished those administering the test to remove each sample after the suspect completed his writing. The suspect should write the passage with different pens, because the ransom notes might have been written with a stylographic pen as "the traces of nib marks in the paper are apparently entirely lacking in these communications."[45] This potentially significant observation about the ransom notes was never followed up. No pen was ever introduced into evidence at the trial.

At the trial, however, the prosecution's handwriting experts presented an argument based upon the hyphenation of *New York* as *New-York* in the request writings, the conceded writings, and the questioned writings. In the request writings that night at the police station on Greenwich Street, Hauptmann wrote *New York* both ways on the sheets of paper that survive. He wrote *not* as *note* at least once, but more often correctly. He wrote *money* correctly every time, although it was misspelled in the ransom notes. On the other hand, he wrote *night* as *nihgt* every time! What were the chances that an individual would exhibit two idiosyncrasies exactly like those of the ransom note writer?

In response to an inquiry by handwriting experts about the late-night sessions at the police station, Colonel Schwarzkopf later admitted, however, if in a backhanded way, that when Hauptmann asked how to spell certain words correctly he was given instruction. "Occasionally when he was stuck as to spelling," the colonel wrote one prosecution expert, "and would ask how to spell a word he would be told; in general, however, he was told to spell it as best he could. He was not given any instructions as to the forming of any of the letters." Schwarzkopf's efforts to glide over embarrassing questions about the way in which the handwriting tests had been done do not encourage full confidence in either the methods of the police or the validity of the tests. Why spell any word for him? How many corrections does it take to spoil the broth? And yet there seems no pattern at all. If the police were trying to give the handwriting experts reasons to name Bruno Richard Hauptmann as the author, why not have him misspell *money* or consistently make other mistakes like those in the ransom notes?[46]

A guilty suspect would try to change his writing, always hoping to confuse the issue. If there were things beyond his control, such as an inability to write certain words correctly, these would seemingly be a dead giveaway. But when the writing samples from the first two ses-sions were presented to Albert S. Osborn and his son, Albert D. Osborn, they could not reach a decision as to whether Hauptmann had written all of the ransom notes or any of them. They demanded more—espe-cially examples of Hauptmann's printing to compare against the address on the package containing the sleeping suit. From the sheets still avail-able in the archives, it is impossible to tell if police ordered Hauptman to print the inverted *N* over and over, along with the hyphenated *New York* and *New Jersey*. On this point, Colonel Schwarzkopf had made a categorical denial—Hauptmann was given no instructions how to form "any of the letters." There is some evidence, nevertheless, that photo-stats of the ransom notes were available and that both Hauptmann and Hans Kloppenburg were instructed to copy them, or parts of them, such as the address on the aforementioned package.[47]

Even when these samples were delivered to the Osborns, father and son, they were still not quite ready to stand up and be counted like the forthright cabbie Joe Perrone. At 4 A.M. the younger Osborn called police headquarters, asking for Colonel Schwarzkopf. They talked for several minutes. When he hung up the phone, the colonel had bad news to report, according to Agent Sisk. "It doesn't look so good. He says that when they first looked at the specimens he thought they were the same, and that there were some striking similarities, but after examining them for a while he found a lot of dissimilarities . . . and he is convinced [Hauptmann] did not write the ransom notes."[48]

In the search for concrete evidence against Hauptmann, the main focus was the ransom money. There must be more of it, somewhere. Hauptmann's safe deposit box had been opened, but there was nothing there except some insurance documents and other legal papers. A team of detectives and FBI agents returned to 222nd Street and ransacked the apartment once again. Still nothing. Back out to the garage. After searching for over an hour, one of the detectives found two packages of gold certificates hidden in a compartment between two uprights on the south wall. One contained 100 ten-dollar bills, the other 83 ten-dollar bills, wrapped in newspapers, the *Daily News* for June 25, 1934, and the *Daily Mirror* for September 6, 1934.[49]

Nearby on the same wall they found an old shellac can concealed behind a cross-board. Inside, underneath some rags, were more pack-ages of bills wrapped in the same newspapers. There were twelve such packages of ten- and twenty-dollar bills. Altogether, the bills—all of it Lindbergh ransom money—totaled $13,760.

Among the first to be told about the discovery were the Osborns. The FBI agent present at the discovery, Leon Turrou, gave them the news. "Within an hour Mr. Osborn [Albert S.] called the undercover squad headquarters," Turrou wrote in a contemporaneous memo, "and advised that he and his son had positively decided that Hauptmann had wrote the ransom letters." There was a great sigh of relief at Greenwich Street. As Turrou recorded the scene, "There was . . . laughing as to the ability of handwriting experts, it being pointed out that the Osborns did not make the identification until after the money was found."[50]

"I do not know what opinion was rendered or expressed by Mr. Osborn Sr. prior to the discovery of the ransom money," added Sisk. "However, I feel sure from conversations with Lt. Finn and Col. Schwarz-kopf that he did not give a positive opinion that Hauptmann wrote the ransom notes until after the money was discovered." The Osborns, of course, *had* now rendered their opinion—and what they said would carry great weight with other handwriting experts, many of whom had learned their craft at the Osborn "school," and all of whom knew them by reputation.

But why were there so many packages, all of approximately the same size? Hauptmann's explanation, when confronted with this damn-ing evidence, was that the money had originally been given to him in a box for safekeeping by his friend Isidor Fisch, just before he left for Germany the previous December. With Fisch's approval, he had placed the shoe-sized box on a high shelf in the kitchen closet and pushed it back out of sight. He had no idea it contained money. In fact, he forgot about it, until three weeks before his arrest, when a heavy rainstorm caused leaks in the closet ceiling. While cleaning up the mess made by the rain, he noticed the box had started to come apart, and he saw the money sticking out.

What was he to do? Fisch had died from tuberculosis the previous March. He decided not to tell Anna about his find, said Hauptmann. She would get too excited. So when she was not around, he took the bills out to the garage and put them in a basket, which he hung from the ceil-ing of the garage. It took several days for the money to dry out. Then he wrapped the bills into separate packages and hid them in the places where they were found.

"Then you never disturbed this package until three weeks ago?"

"It was in the closet. I was looking [as] the rain was coming down. . . . I looked at the package, I didn't tell you yesterday because it sounds so funny."[51]

Well, where had Fisch gotten this money?

Fisch had asked him to come into business with him sometime "around 1932." "I ask him how much money you have Fisch. I said I have only One Thousand Dollars. He said, 'Listen I have $27,000.00.' I didn't ask him where he got it."

"Did he tell you where he had it?"

"He said he got most in furs."

They had agreed to go into business as partners in fur trading and on the stock market, sharing in the profits and losses from each endeavor. According to Hauptmann, at the time of his death Fisch owed him a total of $7,000. It had been $5,000, but then Hauptmann advanced him $2,000 more for the trip to Germany to purchase additional furs overseas. When word came of Fisch's death, Hauptmann began searching for the furs that he had been told were in storage prior to sale. He looked all over New York but could not find them.

So Fisch had lost plenty on the money he gave Hauptmann to invest when the stock market went down. Hauptmann had to come up with some story like this, because he knew that the police would soon see the accounts, and the many unexplained sums—with no records of how much Fisch advanced him to invest on his behalf. It was an amazing performance. In breathtaking fashion, Hauptmann had explained it all: how he came to have the money from Isidor Fisch, and why he felt he had the right to half the money he found. He had no idea, of course, that it was Lindbergh money. Best of all, he had dropped a hint that Fisch had mysterious sources of capital and had defrauded him out of "good" money.

Hauptmann had said Fisch owed him $5,000, which was, apparently, undistributed profits from the sale of furs. Interrogators could not understand why Hauptmann would advance Fisch an additional $2,000: "At that time he owed you Five Thousand Dollars?"

"Yes but extra money he made in furs."

And during another "conversation" with Hauptmann, Inspector Henry Bruckman raised the same question. Hauptmann said that Fisch had told him he had purchased various furs, Hudson seal skins and silver fox, for a total of $21,000. "When he learned that some of these transactions appeared to be fictitious," Hauptmann told Bruckman, "he felt he had a just claim against Fisch." Fisch also gave him several sums for a one-half interest in Hauptmann's stock account. All these transactions were in cash. They would go into the toilet of the brokerage house Steiner, Rouse, where the money was turned over. Hauptmann would take it home, place it in a wooden box, and then later invest it in the stock account.[52]

If Hauptmann was to be believed, then, the Fisch story had several parts. The two men had formed a partnership based almost entirely on mutual trust. Hauptmann advanced sums for the purchase of furs, over $5,000 he claimed in a letter to Fisch's brother. For his part, Fisch was supposedly making big purchases and selling the furs for huge profits. Hauptmann never saw much of this, as the sums Fisch gave him for investment in the stock account came from Fisch's share of the profits.

According to this accounting, then, Hauptmann had left his share in the fur side of the business to buy more skins.[53]

The final chapter began when Hauptmann loaned Fisch $2,000 to go to Germany to buy additional furs. When his partner died, Hauptmann discovered the fur transactions had been fictitious all along. All there was were the four hundred skins Fisch had left in suitcases at the Hauptmann's apartment. Fisch had been giving him money to invest from other sources, loans, apparently from gullible people, having convinced him that his investment in the furs would pay off big in the future.[54]

The $2,000 loan to Fisch remains the most intriguing, and unanswerable, question of all the transactions. Indeed, as police kept asking, why would Hauptmann make such a loan if he had not seen any of the promised profits from the fur trade? When asked about that, he kept repeating he told Fisch to put the earnings into merchandise. What if, instead, Hauptmann actually owed Fisch the $2,000, and probably more, as payment for money Fisch gave him to invest? Then, when Hauptmann found out about the fictitious transactions, he realized he had an opportunity to turn things around into a supposed debt owed him by Fisch's family, and could try to collect. Instead of mutual trust, it looked very much like they were running con games on each other.

However that may be, on the afternoon of September 20, 1934, Hauptmann had much more to worry about than a failed con game. The handwriting experts had weighed in after the money had been discovered. Standing before newsreel cameras with his son, Albert S. Osborn nervously fingered a sheet of paper, turning it from side to side. On it was a brief report, which he read aloud: "I have examined a large number of writings by one Richard Hauptmann, including his automobile registration cards, and have compared this writing with the writing of the Lindbergh Kidnap[p]ing notes, and in my opinion all of the kidnap[p]ing notes were written by Richard Hauptmann. I think the evidence is clear and unmistakable and sufficient in amount so that a most positive opinion can be given."[55]

Messages sent to Germany, meanwhile, turned up information that Bruno Richard Hauptmann had been imprisoned twice for crimes, once for armed robbery involving women pushing baby buggies, and again for breaking into the mayor's home by using a ladder to climb into the second story. Although not all the records were yet available, it also appeared that he had not been working at the Majestic Apartments on March 1, 1932; he didn't start there until three weeks later on March 21, and quit on April 2—the night the ransom money was paid.

Confronted with the accusation he had been lying about being at work, Hauptmann made an interesting statement.

"You are sure you were working on the 1st of March. You are sure you were there?"

"I was on the 1st of March there."

Hauptmann had in fact showed up that morning at the Majestic with his tools ready to work. No one disputed the point. What if he had been asked to stay that day?

Hauptmann's arrest had been kept out of the newspapers for twenty-four hours. The discovery of the money set off an avalanche of sensational stories, some of them inspired by police and FBI officials. It was as true, then as it is today, that the first step in a successful prosecution or defense is to win the battle in the press. By the time Hauptmann had obtained a lawyer-spokesperson on Saturday, September 23, the battle had already been lost.

Typical was the following *New York Times* story reporting on his arrest and the money found in his garage.

> Bruno Richard Hauptman, the blonde-haired, tight-lipped carpenter and former German Army machine-gunner who was arrested yesterday for possession of $13,750 of the ransom money turned over to the kidnappers in the Lindbergh case, was a mystery to his neighbors. . . .
>
> In 1932 Hauptmann suddenly gave up his work as a carpenter, much to the astonishment of his neighbors. Most of the persons living in the block were afraid to question him as to the source of his income, but those who did got the scant information that he was "making good in Wall Street."

About a year ago, related a nearby delicatessen owner to the reporter, Hauptmann came into the store: "He seemed to have taken over the family shopping. One day he gave me a $10 bill and I looked at it, the way you look at all big bills when you own a place like this. But he didn't seem to like it. Neither he nor Mrs. Hauptmann ever came into the store after that."[56]

Others quoted in this story commented more favorably on Hauptmann's character, but by and large the picture presented here and elsewhere was of a mysterious alien—someone to stay clear of—who had unexplained wealth at his command. "I remember," said one of the more than six hundred persons who stood around outside the Hauptmann's house on 222nd Street, "that he said something one night about making good money in Wall Street. I didn't pay much attention, of course, but now that I come to think of it, if Hauptmann was making money in Wall Street at that time he must have been about the only one who was."

Crowds also jammed the streets around the Greenwich Street station. Late in the afternoon a squad car pulled up in front of the police headquarters. A tall, erect man with white hair emerged.

"Jafsie!" someone shouted. "It's Jafsie!" And the crowd started chanting his name. As John Condon climbed the steps to the entrance, another shout went up: "Jafsie will burn him!"[57]

FBI agent Leon Turrou, who had accompanied Jafsie on his journey to the police station, waited with him in a small room while a lineup was arranged. "Don't worry, son," Condon had assured him. "If he's the fellow I met I'll know him. If I live a million years I'll know him." Then he tilted his head quizzically, and whispered, "Now look here, describe this suspect you've got."

Turrou drew back. "I'm sorry, Doctor—I can't tell you that. The whole point to this is that you pick him out by yourself."

"Why? Just tell me why. That's nothing but a fool notion."

Turrou did not think so at all. "I was convinced that Hauptmann had a very close connection with the crime, but I could not hazard a guess as to whether the man whose footprints were found beside the broken ladder and the man whom Dr. Condon had met on two occasions and to whom he had given the ransom money were the same." Upset by Condon's ploy, Turrou was downright cynical about the lineup. "It wasn't much of a deception. The detectives were shaved, bright-eyed six-footers. Hauptmann looked like a midget who had wandered through a Turkish bath for two sleepless days and nights."[58]

Condon scratched his head and squinted at the lineup, now extended to thirteen men. He later claimed he had recognized Hauptmann immediately upon entering the room but was offended by the whole scene as his eye ran down the line of "broad-shouldered, florid-faced, bull-necked chaps who could not by any stretch of the imagination have been confused with the man I had described, over and over, as John."

Among them stood the slender, sallow-faced Hauptmann. All around the room stood the defenders of law and order, including the recently arrived J. Edgar Hoover, who had just made it in time to join in the last round of questioning. "This was no orderly procedure of justice," Condon grumbled to himself. "It was the bustling chaos of a madhouse. And a man's life was at stake."[59]

Very well, he would upset the apple cart. Suddenly Condon yelled out, "Tenshun!" The policemen obeyed instantly, while Hauptmann remained slumped and defeated. What followed bordered on farce. Jafsie began putting the men "through a series of complicated drill maneuvers, marching them around, right flanking, left flanking, in a voice sharp and military."

Finally, Inspector Lyons could stand no more. "Stop, Dr. Condon!" he shouted. "Enough!"[60]

With Jafsie it is always difficult to determine what is genuine and what is dramaturgic. Genuinely offended by the setting, he also knew he was on stage again. He walked up and down the line three times, finally pausing before Hauptmann. Could he "eliminate" several men? he asked Inspector Lyons. Puzzled, Lyons asked whom he wished to "eliminate"? Condon selected Hauptmann and three of the detectives, and asked that they step forward. As in so many other instances in dealing with Jafsie, one had to be an expert in Lewis Carroll. He meant *select* or *pick out,* not *eliminate.*

Standing directly in front of Hauptmann, he addressed the group: "When I saw you I gave you my promise that I would do all that I could for you if you gave me the baby. The only way in the world that I think you can save yourself at all is to tell the truth."[61]

What was going on here? Did Condon hope to trump the police by obtaining a confession then and there? He wrote out a note and gave it to Hauptmann. "Read it out loud," he commanded. Hauptmann read: "I stayed already too long. The leader would smack me out. Your work is perfect."

"I could not quite hear those last three lines." Read it again, louder, he demanded.

Condon then asked the four men to hold up their hands. Cemetery John had a lump at the base of his left thumb, a very special thing Jafsie had put into his descriptions, along with the hacking cough. He had even drawn a picture of Cemetery John's hand to show police what it looked like. "Hold your palms up, hands up," ordered Lyons. Condon carefully examined the hands of each man, but none showed a lump at the base of the thumb. Where had it gone?

Then he walked up to each one. "What is your name?" "Did you ever see me before?" All four answered, "No." Condon stood as close to Hauptmann as he could get, face-to-face. Flinging his right arm toward the prisoner, he pointed his index finger at his face. "Are *you* sure that you never saw me before?"

"No, I never saw you before," replied Hauptmann in quiet tones.

"You don't remember me—speaking to me?"

"I can't say that I can."

The German's refusal to acknowledge ever having seen John F. Condon before seemed to disturb the old man. How could anyone who lived in the Bronx not know him by sight?

"How long do you live in the Bronx?

"Nine years."

"Nine years up there; you don't know me?"

"No."

What did any of this dialogue have to do with the kidnapping? Condon tried something else. He stood beside Hauptmann, looking at the side of his face. "You have nothing to say to me at all?"

"No."

"Why?"

"I don't know what to say."

Inspector Lyons did not know what to say, either, but he wanted to cut off the old man's pointless rambling. "We're tired," he said, putting a hand on Condon's shoulder. "We want to go home and sleep. We deserve it. Now, do you know any of these men or don't you!"[62]

"I would not say he is the man."

"You are not positive?"

"I am not positive."

"Do you recognize the voice?"

"The voice was husky."

Before Lyons could stop him, Condon had moved off on a new tack. "Have you gotten a little stouter, lately than you were?

"No, I am practically the same."

"Did you ever run in races?"

"No."

"Can you climb pretty well with your hands?"

"I used to do it in school as a child."

"In gymnasium?"

"Yes, gymnastic school."

How long this would have gone on if Lyons had not put a stop to it can hardly be imagined. "Dr. Condon. Is that the man?"

"He is the one who would come nearer to answering the description than anybody I saw. You gave me no hint and I picked him out. He is a little heavier. . . . I couldn't say he is not the man."

"It looks like him?"

"Yes."

"But you cannot identify him?"

"No, I have to be very careful. The man's life is in jeopardy."

With that, Condon spun on his heels and stomped out of the room, leaving a startled and angry bunch of police muttering curses at his back. Turrou followed him out. "I won't identify him for those insolent morons!" Condon exploded.

"But *have* you seen him before, Doctor?" The agent asked.

"No," he said. "He is *not* the man." FBI agent Sisk noticed that Condon seemed to be in a daze, rambling on about how everyone would mistrust him now, "but he wouldn't have it on his conscience, "no matter what they think." He told Turrou that the man in the lineup must be a "brother of John." Hauptmann was much heavier than John and had different hair, different eyes. Then he spun out for the agent a truly fantastic tale: "The real John was killed long ago and the money was taken away from him by his confederates. He intimated that the real men who are responsible for the kidnapping and the murder of the Lindbergh child are now somewhere in Long Island around Bay Shore."

Police kept Condon in custody after the lineup, until midnight—probably to give the old school principal time to reconsider his behavior. After all, he knew what detentions were about, didn't he? He paced back and forth for a time, then sat slumped in a chair with his chin on his chest. "I guess you know that my life isn't worth two cents," he told Turrou. "Hauptmann's accomplices are going to kill me."[63]

Outside the station, Inspector John J. Sullivan tried to put the best face he could on the results of what had happened when Condon confronted the police's prime suspect.

Did Dr. Condon identify Hauptmann? asked reporters.

"Not positively," said the inspector.

"You mean he wasn't sure?"

"That's it." It was an identification "in part," Sullivan said, and Condon had agreed to stay to give a statement to District Attorney Samuel J. Foley of the Bronx in connection with a possible extortion or grand larceny charge.[64]

Condon was taken to Foley's office, all right, but despite being shouted and sworn at, he did not produce a statement that could be used for an extortion case. Jafsie did do some talking, however, giving the Associated Press additional reasons why he had not identified Hauptmann—along with another far-out story about a kidnapping gang that may have included Isidor Fisch and two others, one of whom was a woman. John had a wracking cough, Jafsie told reporter Francis Jamieson, and Hauptmann had no cough. There were definite similarities, especially in speech patterns. "It is two and a half years since I saw John. My memory is not good sometimes and in a case of this importance I want to be sure. Hauptmann was cunning, and whenever I questioned him about anything he felt might lead to a trap, he evaded me. I would like to talk to him in a room with no distractions after he has been shaved and dressed as I saw John that night." [65]

Meanwhile, Condon left police with a wild-goose chase, or might it be a serious lead? Hauptmann was associated in the fur business with Fisch, he said to the reporter, and together with a third man, Henry Uhlig, played cards and frequented beer gardens. The latter two and a woman went to Germany. Only the woman and Uhlig came back. "Fisch lies buried in a cemetery at Leipzig. They ought to disinter his body and find out why he died. He was there only a short time before he died. Perhaps he died from natural causes or he may have been poisoned."[66]

Condon also told Leon Turrou that he had studied Fisch's photograph, and it now seemed to him that he saw "a party strongly resembling the features and description of Isidor Fisch pass the car in which he and Al Reich were sitting." A woman aided him in finding John at St. Raymond's cemetery, Condon continued his embroidery on his latest version of the kidnapping events. She was a mysterious blonde who appeared out of the shadows to say, "This is Whittemore Avenue." Then as he walked along the hedge toward the cemetery, she vanished.[67]

Unpredictable—even unbalanced—as he was, the prosecution had to have Condon's testimony. He would get his chance to see Hauptmann alone, later, in the Flemington jail. It was of some interest that Jafsie seemed to know so much so quickly about Hauptmann's social habits, especially his card playing and close friendship with Isidor Fisch.

Frustrated by the Condon performance, which, it almost seemed under the circumstances, was a triumph for Hauptmann, police took their prisoner to another room after the lineup, where, according to yet another FBI agent, E. A. Tamm, "they gave this fellow a real going over and punched him in the back and twisted his arms and legs and gave him hell." Agent Sisk was present and ordered all FBI men not to participate in any way in the beatings. Sisk managed to speak to Hauptmann alone and "endeavored in every possible way to obtain some admission of guilt" and to learn if any others (like Fisch?) were involved, but it was no use.

He insisted he had nothing to do with the Lindbergh kidnapping. But what about the work records? Sisk persisted. They showed he did not work at the Majestic Apartments that day, March 1, 1932. Hauptmann said the records must be wrong. "I tell you I am innocent. You don't believe me."

"You quit your job on April 2, 1932," Sisk retorted, "the same day the Lindbergh ransom money was paid to a man answering your description and then you are arrested 2½ years later and you have in your possession part of that same ransom money. Doesn't that strike you as a little bit too much of a coincidence? Do you expect anyone to believe that? Would you believe it if our positions were reversed?"

"No," Hauptmann replied. "I would not believe it."

"Well, then, you're a self-confessed liar."

"Yes. But what do you expect me to do? What can I say?"[68]

Sisk thought Hauptmann was admitting he was a liar, but was he doing that or simply agreeing it was a difficult story to believe? After all the questions and various forms of coercion, there was no confession. Nor would there ever be.

Any halfway decent lawyer could hogtie Joe Perrone, and, if not soon cured, Condon's obstinacy might become a real problem. It wasn't even possible to shut him up for a while as police gathered evidence. Talking to a reporter for the *Daily News,* Condon insisted that "the finding of the money and the actual kidnap[p]ing were entirely separate matters." Standing on the front porch of his house, he added, "I'll never be vindicated until my work is complete." Well, was Hauptmann the man who got the money? "I can't talk. Really, I never said I was positive. All is in abeyance now. . . . I did say I'd know that voice anywhere—that's true. But I meant if I heard it under the same circumstances."[69]

J. Edgar Hoover picked up on the line that Isidor Fisch's role deserved investigation. He thought the identification of Hauptmann was pretty solid, but he had in mind "that possibly Fisch was involved with Hauptmann in the outside work." What Hoover cared most about, however, was that the bureau get its share of the credit. If he had not hurried up to New York, he told associates, "the Division would not even have been mentioned." All day long there had been disagreements among the three police agencies, and his time was filled up with newspapermen, motion pictures, radio broadcasts until three in the morning. He wanted to talk with Sisk "to see if there is anything [the bureau] can begin to pass out 'underneath,' in order to get some of the credit."[70]

While Hoover worried about getting some of the credit, Bronx district attorney Samuel Foley interrogated Hauptmann: "I want to ask you some questions about this board, you know it is from your closet in your house, don't you?"

"It must be."

8
IN DISTRICT ATTORNEY FOLEY'S OFFICE

I am grateful and glad to see the police cooperating so closely with the Federal forces. I hope the apprehension of this one man will lead to the arrest of all those responsible for the kidnap[p]ing and murder of the child.

—MAYOR FIORELLO LA GUARDIA, September 22, 1934

B ronx district attorney Samuel J. Foley felt confidant he could break through the expressionless mask on Hauptmann's face and obtain a confession. After nearly two days of police questioning, and a severe beating while handcuffed to a chair, the suspect still held out. Richard was brought into his office shortly after 4 A.M. on the morning of September 21, 1934. Now it was Foley's turn.

"I want to get this case cleared up once and for all," began the young district attorney, who was almost the same age as Hauptmann. "It's been a headache for over two years."[1]

Hauptmann sat across from his desk in a deep-cushioned swivel chair, waiting to hear what came next. Foley's aides kept running in and out of the office to brief reporters about the latest revelation. "Sometimes," one aide told a reporter, "Mr. Foley would say: 'Remember your wife and baby.'" But Hauptmann replied every time: 'I do, I do; but I don't know.'"[2]

Alternating between good cop and bad cop, Foley patiently waited for his opportunity to lead Richard to the confessional. Come on, Richard, he urged, you know your explanation of where you got the money is ridiculous. No one's going to believe it. You have no chance with a Bronx County jury. It will convict you of extortion without even leaving the jury box. Then they'll take you down to New Jersey to stand trial for kidnapping and murder. God only knew what would happen there. This was the last chance to tell the truth.

Hauptmann shook his head slowly. "I am innocent, I tell you I am innocent."[3]

All right, then, they would go back to the beginning. What about those arrests in Germany, and how long it had been since he last worked? He had been living off his earnings on the stock market, Richard repeated, but he had lost a lot of money in the last year, probably $4,000.

Foley shifted to another subject: "Do you recall the taxi driver, Perrone, being brought in to see you?

"Yes."

"Did he identify you as the man who gave him the letter to take to Doctor Condon?"

"He couldn't identify me."

"Did he identify you, yes or no?"

"No."

"What did he say?"

"He said yes, but he did not see me before; I did not see him."[4]

What about this money, then? When did he find it in the closet?

About three weeks ago, said Hauptmann. The rain was coming through the ceiling in the broom closet, and he looked up and remembered the package.

How was it wrapped? asked Foley. In oilcloth?

No, in a light gray paper, a little bit heavier than newspaper, and then with brown paper around the outside of the box.

"This money in the box was wrapped around twice with grey wrapping paper and it was in a cardboard box and the cardboard box was in brown wrapping paper that was wrapped around one and a half or two times?"

"Yes . . ."

"And you tell us that the money in that box, wrapped up itself in wrapping paper, came through its own wrapping paper and the shoe box and all this paper outside and stuck out from the end of the box?"

"Not hanging out."

"Stuck out; that's your story, is it not?"

"I don't know exactly . . ."

"That seems a little silly to you now?"

"No."

Maybe it had leaked down through the closet on more than one occasion, he suggested, as if Foley must know the true story, and the box deteriorated over time. Richard and Anna had both complained for over a year about the leaks in that closet, leaks that had caused rain-water to pour down through the closet ceiling onto the floor.

Foley knew that was true. Just before Hauptmann was brought into his office, their landlord, Max Rauch, confirmed the complaint and his nonchalant attitude. "I never attended to it. I told the plumber but he did not show up. I think she spoke several times of it."[5]

Hauptmann's caginess was at least a match for Foley's persistence. When you were arrested, why didn't you tell the police about the money in the garage? the D.A. asked.

"I was thinking of it and I find when I was arrested they told me that it is ransom money from Lindbergh, and I figured how can I explain it, so I did not say anything about it."

"You realize yourself that the story sounds silly?"

"Yes."

"And your story is that you discovered the money after a rain had wet the box it was in?"

"Maybe it was wet a couple of times already."[6]

Finally, Foley's patience ran out. If you don't open up and talk now—he thrust his finger at Hauptmann—there would never be another chance. "The minute the door of this room closes on you, you're gone, you're sunk, and I will never talk to you again. The only time you will see me is in front of a jury."

"But I can see you're just an animal," he sneered.

> You don't care what happens to your wife and baby. You don't care about anything. You're the lowest human being I ever had before me, and I've had a lot of bad ones. Why, the other night down at the police department, a mob were trying to get at your wife to hang her. That poor woman has put up [with] so much from you. You were taking this blood money from this kidnapping and having a good time with a lot of fast women while your wife was visiting her people in Germany. Now you have a chance to redeem yourself, to do one decent thing in your life, and you won't do it.[7]

Foley emerged from his office boasting to reporters he had an "ironclad" extortion case. It was all bravado. Condon had deflated the police buildup by hesitating to make a positive identification. So far only Perrone's hand on Hauptmann's shoulder at the Greenwich police station connected Condon and the suspect—and it was a pretty light grip for an indictment. "The best developments so far in questioning our prisoner," the D.A. declared, "have been the discrepancies."

Reporters were not so sure that was nearly enough: "The inquiry conducted by authorities of the Bronx has failed to develop any direct evidence linking Hauptmann the former German machine gunner who had $13,750 of the ransom money, with the kidnapping or murder of the child. Mr. Foley characterized his own investigation as a 'fishing expedition.'"[8]

J. Edgar Hoover had little use for Foley's methods or his press conferences. The director had his own ideas about how the interrogation should be conducted. His men had wanted to take Hauptmann off somewhere—away from all the publicity—and make him write the ransom notes. He might break down and confess. There was no question of Hauptmann's guilt, Hoover said, but from what he saw, the man was a "'tough' individual, cold and calculating." There was strong circumstantial evidence, yes, but the matter of establishing the murder and kidnapping would take some time. He thought it might take two months to get a case ready even for extortion. While New Jersey and New York authorities were saying nothing about it, Hauptmann's fingerprints had not matched up to any found at the scene of the kidnapping. Sisk had made an urgent request for a comparison, saying that Hauptmann was only being held at the outset of the investigation on a "shot-gun charge" and not for kidnapping. No identification can be effected, replied Hoover the next day.[9]

Meanwhile, Hoover continued working on his most pressing issue: the FBI image. Paramount News wanted to film an agent standing in front of a map showing locations where the kidnapper had passed ransom money, holding up a miniature ladder and a miniature ransom money box. "I asked Mr. Clegg," wrote a pleased Hoover, "if he thought Mr. Sisk or Mr. Seery should be selected to make the talk. He stated that while Mr. Seery has more 'pep' and enthusiasm, he has somewhat of an Irish accent. . . . I stated that I want to be sure that there is the proper intonation to convey the idea that our men are keen, on the job, and well educated." Clegg suggested Sisk and Seery be given "try-outs" in front of the camera. Then let Paramount News decide. "I told him this would be perfectly all right."[10]

Despite Hoover's doubts, Foley wanted to present his evidence to a Bronx grand jury as soon as possible. He had at least fifty witnesses, he told reporters, leading off with "Dr. John F. Condon, who acted as intermediary for the return of the Lindbergh child." Then there was Colonel Henry Breckenridge, news reporter Gregory Coleman, taxi driver John Perrone—"who received $1 to carry one of the cryptic negotiation messages to Dr. Condon's home"—the gas station attendants, and three employees of the banking house of J. P. Morgan, who made up the ransom money. And after they testified he would bring forth the police investigators—forty or more—who had worked on the case.[11]

Hyperbole, prosecutors learn early, is always the best strategy. Create an impression of an almost endless line of accusers just outside the courtroom eager to testify, and intimidate the defense. Flood the press with leaks about sensational evidence. Foley knew the routine, but he had some problems with this one. Condon could not be allowed to reprise Falstaff in the courtroom; another farcical performance like that at the Greenwich station, and even a tame grand jury might laugh out loud. But how to get an indictment without him? There was the rub. Foley would have to finesse the situation a bit, employing other testimony to get around the old man's quirkiness.

Getting around John F. Condon was not easily done, as others before and after Sam Foley came to understand. The D.A. had publicly dismissed Hauptmann's claim that he had received the money from Isidor Fisch as a case of dead men tell no alibis. But Jafsie persisted in stirring the Fisch plot. "While District Attorney Foley termed Fisch only a friend of Hauptmann," Condon told reporters, he believed officials would be derelict not to "order Fisch's body exhumed and an autopsy performed to determine if his was a violent death."[12]

Reporters kept pestering Foley with questions not only about Condon's vacillations but also about newly forgotten aspects of the investigation. What about reports that Hauptmann had deposited $2,980 under the name J. J. Faulkner? He knew nothing of the deposit, said the D.A., nor did he know anything about the suspect's fingerprints being compared with those found in the Lindbergh home. Did he think the prisoner would break down and confess? "Not for the present." With that point, at least, J. Edgar Hoover agreed: "He is the coolest customer I have ever seen."[13]

By now, Anna Hauptmann had recovered from her initial shock at her husband's arrest and the disclosure that he had hidden Lindbergh ransom money in the garage, to become her husband's unstinting champion. Detained for questioning at the Greenwich Street station, she had heard an ugly crowd scream awful things, "Kill her! Stone her." Outside Foley's office, she declared Richard had told the truth about the money. Fisch was the liar. He had claimed to own a bakery, and they had learned he never did. "I think he kidnapped the baby. That's why he went back to Germany. He was afraid of being caught. I don't care if the whole world thinks my husband is guilty. I'll never believe he had anything to do with it."[14]

But reporters challenged her about where Richard was the day of the kidnapping. "I supposed he was at work. It's so long ago now that I

wouldn't remember." Wasn't she curious, then, about where he was getting his money? "Of course, and I asked him about it. He told me he was
making money in the stock market." For the rest of her life, Anna regretted making such remarks, especially her first answers about where he
was on March 1, 1932. After telling Inspector Henry Bruckman that she
could not remember if Richard had been home on the night of March 1,
1932—it was so long ago—she realized it was a Tuesday night—and on
Tuesday nights she worked and her husband picked her up from work.
At one point during the various interrogations, Anna used the word *usually,* something prosecutors seized upon, but she insisted she meant
always.

Anna admitted she had never known about any package Isidor
brought into the house or about her husband's supposed discovery of
the money. But she was firm on two other points. First, rainwater continually came into the apartment at various places, and their landlord
had not done anything about it for over a year. "It will get all rotten," she
told the landlord, "and it is your house, Mr. Rauch." Second, the shelf
where the box had supposedly been was very high and very deep. She
kept a little tin box for coupons up there but did not reach into the rear
of the shelf. It was too hard. "If I wish to get up I would have to stand on
a chair."[15]

"We have taken statements from Hauptmann and his wife concerning their activities that night," insisted Foley at his next press conference.
"We have lots of evidence to disprove their alibi. Mrs. Hauptmann's tactics are obvious." An extortion case against Hauptmann presumably
would rest on his whereabouts not on the night of March 1, 1932, but on
the night of April 2, 1932—not proof of participation in the kidnapping
but proof of where he was when the money was paid—yet there was
never any real line drawn between the two in Foley's comments. Prove
Hauptmann had no alibi for March 1, 1932, and his case was made.[16]

Anna's former employer at the bakery where she had worked
during that time, Christian Fredericksen, turned up, meanwhile, in the
huge crowd of "sightseers" outside the Hauptmann house, numbering
as many as ten thousand at times. He had pushed and squeezed his way
through to the front, where he encountered two FBI agents. Fredericksen was more than eager to tell them what he knew. Richard had driven
Anna to work at 6 A.M. the day after the kidnapping. And he also recalled
that Richard had said they were home the previous evening and had
heard nothing about the kidnapping.

This was hardly helpful to Foley. If Christian Fredericksen insisted
that Anna was at work that night, it would lend her story credibility—
and firm up Hauptmann's alibi. Fredericksen was a very excitable man,

the FBI agents reported, with a heavy accent. He apparently believed Hauptmann had nothing to do with the kidnapping—and wanted to help. "Whether his thoughts on this matter are propelled by honest motives is hard to say, but the information obtained from him, and his personality is such that very little credence can be given to any information which he might have to offer." In other words, he was a potential danger.[17]

District Attorney Foley realized he needed to get to Fredericksen and his wife, Katie, before their story solidified into a concrete alibi for the night of March 1, 1932. On September 24, 1934, the day the grand jury began taking testimony, he summoned the Fredericksens to his office. From the outset he made it plain that he was going to test their memories on every point. When Katie said, for example, that Anna had quit on June 22, 1932, Foley immediately challenged her even on that minor question: how could she be sure that was the date? "Because I keep books."

He had picked the wrong question to start things off, but he had only begun. When did Mrs. Fredericksen last see Anna? Yesterday. Why did she go to Anna's apartment? She was anxious to console her. Foley pushed Katie to admit that she could not have known if Richard came for Anna on the night of March 1, 1932, as he usually did, because that was the night she took off each week. Yes, that was true, she was not there, said Katie. Nor had she been present early the next morning when, her husband said, Richard brought Anna to work. Do you even remember what year it happened? he challenged.

"Yes, it was 1932."

" I don't know, I am asking you if you remember it or was it 1931?"

"1932."

"Positive about it?"

She read about it two years ago in the newspapers.

"Do you remember that definitely?"

"Well I should be thick if I don't know it."[18]

Foley had done his best to put doubts in Katie Fredericksen's mind about almost anything that had happened to her over the past two years, but especially about whether she actually knew that Anna was there that night. He suggested Anna had coached her on what to answer. But this was hard going. Did Richard *always* call for Anna the nights she worked so late? How did Katie know this if she was not there? Equally important was another question. How did the Fredericksens know that Anna worked that night; did Mrs. Fredericksen never change her nights off? Indeed, Foley believed that Katie might concede doubts on that point; and that could be the best way to undermine the alibi. Katie persisted, however. Who else was there to run the shop if Anna was not there?

What Foley did not know was that Katie Fredericksen had another reason for insisting that Anna had worked that night. It was a secret. Anna knew about the secret but would never reveal it. Katie was having an affair. Katie Fredericksen also introduced something about Isidor Fisch that Foley really did not wish to hear. She had called on Anna, she said, soon after Manfred's birth, to take the baby a gift. Also there that night was Fisch, who was to leave for Germany the next day. When she got up to go, Katie offered him a ride to a subway station. During the drive, Fisch asked if she would like "to go downtown and raise the roof some place." Katie did not know whether he was joking or not, but Fisch pulled out some bills to show he was serious, "We could spend that for a good time." Katie looked at the money and laughed. "You go broke before you come to Germany."[19]

Fisch's failed flirtation might come up again later if Katie Fredericksen testified that he was flashing a wad of money on the eve of his departure for Germany. Although Fisch was supposedly penurious, this brief encounter suggested he had another side: he was someone who had money to burn—someone who could, indeed, have left behind for safekeeping a shoebox crammed with gold certificates. Katie was so pro-Hauptmann, it would be hard for anyone to assess what actually went on in her car that night, and whether the money Fisch waved under Katie's nose—if that happened—revealed anything more than traveling funds he was carrying around prior to departure.

Prosecutors worked hard to cast doubts on Katie Fredericksen's calm assertion that Anna worked every Tuesday night. If Anna worked that night, unless she was part of the kidnap scheme, she would have remembered the coincidence of the kidnapping and her husband's non-appearance. She would have remembered having to go home alone in the dark, a long walk on a cold and rainy night, and, no doubt, giving her husband a piece of her mind when he came in late—if he came home at all.

In a nearby room, meanwhile, Assistant District Attorney Edward F. Breslin questioned Christian Fredericksen about what he had told the FBI agents. Yes, he said, Anna's late nights were the days his wife took off to do housework or go to the movies. Breslin tried the same tactics, challenging him on minor points to create self-doubts about his certainty on major points. He did elicit from Christian that Richard did not call for Anna every single night, and that when that happened she would become annoyed and say something like, "I can't understand why he didn't come. He could at least call up because we have a telephone."[20]

The Hauptmanns did not have a telephone, so Christian was wrong about that. But Breslin's question about "every single night" deliberately blurred over the question of Richard's routine on the two nights she worked late. That was the key question.

Christian did not claim he personally saw Richard in the bakery the night of March 1, 1932, but it took several questions to get him to admit also that he could not swear Anna had worked that night.

"Do you remember whether she was there?"

"Yes, she must have been there, because she always late on Tuesday because my wife goes out that day."

"You have no definite recollection that your wife was off that Tuesday night?"

"She was always off Tuesday night."

"You have no definite recollection that your wife was off that Tuesday night?"

"No."

After several more questions on other subjects, Breslin came back to the principal task of instilling doubts in Christian's mind: "So that you couldn't swear that he was there or that she was the night before the kidnapping because you don't know whether they were or not, that right?"

"Yes."[21]

Poor Christian Fredericksen. By the time Breslin had finished with him that day, he was no longer talking about what Bruno Richard Hauptmann had supposedly said the morning after the kidnapping, and he was no longer even sure if Richard came to pick up Anna any night! On October 29, 1934, in another statement to police, Christian said, "He used to come and take her home. I can't say that he took her home that exact day—there were times Hauptmann did not come and Anna would say, 'I can't understand why he don't come.'" A little later in the same interrogation, Fredericksen amended his statement yet again. Now it was, "There were lots of nights he did not come."[22]

Neutralizing the Fredericksens was a significant achievement for Foley's office, with implications far beyond the extortion case.

The day Foley and Breslin quizzed the baker and his wife, Hauptmann appeared at arraignment proceedings. He had been brought to court in an armored truck with bullet-proof glass. As he was led into the courtroom, spectators jumped up onto the benches to get a better view. Standing there before the magistrate in the same wrinkled suit he had on the day of his arrest, he had already become an exhibit—something lacking full human identity. In front of the bench, Hauptmann stared straight ahead, never to the left or right. He blinked when flashbulbs went off; otherwise he remained almost perfectly still. For the first time there was someone at his side, James M. Fawcett, a lawyer Anna had secured on the advice of a friend, but his client seemed hardly aware of his surroundings.

Back in his jail cell he wept continuously, said his keepers. Special guards frequently peered in through a small opening in the cell door, always on the alert to "any attempt by Hauptmann to do violence to himself." There were also news bulletins about the food he ate, and what movies were playing outside the jail. "For breakfast he ate oatmeal, and followed it with buttered bread and coffee." If he looked out the small window of his cell to the rear, he could see the signboards of the DeLuxe Theatre on Tremont Avenue, where a double feature was playing, *Whom the Gods Destroy* and *Murder in the Private Car.*[23]

Inspector Henry Bruckman, Bronx chief of detectives, provided Foley with the evidence he needed for the grand jury to finesse the Condon problem. Bruckman's discoveries tightened Perrone's identification into a viselike grip on Hauptmann's future. "Bruckman is of German extraction," read an FBI description, "large, often loud spoken and very brusque." But what made him really detestable to the FBI was his determination to keep its agents out of the way while he collected the crucial evidence for Foley to present to the grand jury.[24]

On the second morning the grand jury was to meet, the inspector took two police carpenters to Hauptmann's apartment for yet another search. Detective Lewis Bornmann of the New Jersey State Police arrived shortly thereafter. They were prepared to take the place apart, both garage and apartment, board by board if necessary, to find evidence to convince the jurors to return an indictment; then Foley could stake his claim to try Hauptmann in New York.

Foley had an idea that Hauptmann might well have other caches of money tucked away someplace, a secret wall compartment or some other hiding place. The Hauptmann residence had been gone over several times already in the five days since the arrest, including several searches of the attic, a hard-to-reach place accessible only by crawling up through a narrow hatch in the linen closet. Nothing significant had been found anywhere. But the police carpenters were there to make sure a truly thorough search was carried out this time.

Bruckman went to a closet in the room used for Manfred's nursery. It was a small, unlighted place. In fact, Bruckman had to wedge himself inside and then use a flashlight to see. Come over here, he suddenly called to Bornmann, take a look at this! On the inside of the clothes closet door, near the upper hinge, was written in pencil:

$500
1928 B-00007162A
" B-00009272A.

At first they thought they had found notations of ransom bills. The last four digits were the same as those of ransom bills of five- and ten-dollar denominations. That proved not to be the case, but they continued to search. On the upper-left inside casing of the door, they saw, "in what appeared to be Hauptmann's handwriting, '2974 Decatur' and underneath it the numbers '3-7154'." What a find! Here was Condon's address and phone exchange.[25]

Special Agent F. E. Wright was also there, and Bruckman turned to him and warned that he was not to telephone the New York FBI office about this discovery. If he did, Bruckman would know how the information "got out," and from that moment the case would become "an exclusive Bronx County matter." Publicity, he added, "would kill the case." Then the carpenters dismantled the closet door, and off Bruckman went to Foley's office with the clincher.[26]

When he returned, he had a change of heart about publicity, inviting numerous reporters and two photographers inside to see where the evidence had been found. He made sure everyone knew how to spell his name.

Agent Wright discussed these doings with T. H. Sisk:

Sisk: "Well, Mr. Wright, do you remember telling me that Bruckman walked straight to that number as though he knew right where it was?"

Wright: "Well, he found it pretty quickly."

Sisk: "He walked right up to it, I mean as though he knew it was there and then made it known that he had found something. . . ."

Wright: ". . . he seemed to walk right into the room and head directly for the closet where the number was found."[27]

Such speculations were enlarged into a full-blown tale of planted evidence by the writer Anthony Scaduto, and further drawn out by Ludovic Kennedy, both of whom credit the story told of *New York Daily News* writer Tom Cassidy, that he wrote the numbers and letters on the inside of the closet and closet door, in order to get a scoop. All this had to be worked out beforehand with Bruckman, of course, who would miraculously discover the vital evidence. What supports this tale? These authors contend, first, that the house had been searched many times and no one had discovered the writings; so how was it that Bruckman could walk in, cross immediately to the closet, and, presto, shine a light on the most important evidence yet found? Even Bornmann's terse report says nothing about the length of time it took to find

Condon's address scrawled in this dark recess. Second, why, since there was no telephone in the apartment, have the number written down there—when it could be found anywhere there was a public phone? Even Condon dismissed the closet door evidence as unbelievable.[28]

One could add to these arguments the pressing nature of finding evidence to secure an indictment, or, to put it differently, how to provide a Condon connection without Condon's appearance. On the other hand, it could be argued that previous searches were too hastily done, as FBI agents complained, and that Hauptmann chose that place precisely because it was unlikely anyone would find it there—including Anna. The Cassidy story itself may have grown out of Bruckman's boasts to the reporters he invited into the house.

Whatever one decides about the amazing serendipity of Bruckman's discovery, when Foley showed Hauptmann the closet boards the D.A. was delighted at the initial response. He fully expected another denial, like all the others. But, no, Hauptmann admitted the writing must be his! This interrogation began at noon on September 25, so Bruckman had indeed been busy that morning getting to the house, finding the writing, ordering the carpenters to dismantle the closet, and finally reaching the D.A.'s office with his evidence in time. Displaying the board to Hauptmann, Foley asked if he recognized it from his closet, and with his handwriting on it.

"Yes, all over it."

Hauptmann did not know which closet the boards came from, however, or, from this first glance, what was written there. Foley asked him to read it to the stenographer.

"I can't read it any more."

"Who rubbed it out? Can you read the address on it?"

"2974. I can't make out the first. I read the number down below, 37154."

"What else can you read on that board that you wrote yourself?"

"I can't read—that is 'a', 't', 'u' and a 'r'. Another one I can't make out."

"That's Dr. Condon's address, isn't it?"

Foley had played his trump card. Hauptmann had acknowledged the writing must be his, and that the numbers and letters spelled out Condon's phone number and his address on Decatur Avenue. "That's Dr. Condon's address, isn't it?" repeated Foley.

Hauptmann went silent before finally answering the only way he could. "I don't know."

Foley knew he had him cornered. "Why did you write it on the board?"

"I must have read it in the paper about the story. I was a little bit interest and keep a little bit record of it, and maybe I was just on the closet, and was reading the paper and put down the address."

"How did you come to put down the telephone number on there?"

"I can't give you any explanation about the telephone number."

So, Foley pressed on in a mocking tone, he was reading the newspaper in this closet and stopped to write down the address and number?

Well, said Hauptmann, trying to recover his grip on a crumbling ledge, he put newspapers on the shelves in that closet, and one time he must have noticed the address and written it there. "I followed the story of course, and I put the address on there."

"That's why you marked it on the door?"

"That's the only explanation I can give."

At this point Foley suddenly stopped talking about the writings on the closet door and launched into a long series of questions about whether or not he had been well treated, had been allowed visits from his wife and child, cigarettes, and private consultations with his lawyer without anyone present. And the answers he gave, Foley said, were of his own free will without coercion? Was that all true?

"Yes."

Foley had interrupted himself to ask about the treatment Hauptmann had received to ensure that the suspect would not later insist he had been coerced into giving those answers.

Did he wish to add anything? asked the D.A.

Yes, he felt sure the bill numbers were those of a $500 and $1,000 bill, money Fisch had given him to invest. Hauptmann had recovered enough by this point to put down some foundation for a new ledge.

Foley let that pass for the moment. Did he remember the day he wrote the memorandum on the board?

No, he did not.

"You remember that you did write it?"

"I must write it, the figures that's my writing."

"The writing is yours too, isn't it?"

"I can hardly read it."

"From what you see of it, it is your writing, isn't it—it is your figures and your writing?"

"I really can't remember when I put it on."

"Regardless of when you put it on, it is your figures and your writing, isn't it?"

"The writing I can't make out so very clearly, I don't know."

"Do you know who rubbed it or tried to rub it out?"

"No."[29]

Now he was trying to backtrack, to limit what he recognized as his writing to the bank note numbers. This was the first money he got from Fisch, he said.

When was it he got those bills? Foley challenged.

Around March of 1931.

"You have already said you didn't know Fisch until 1932," someone else interjected.

Then Hauptmann made a cryptic admission: "Well, I'm now in the bag."[30]

Obviously, serial numbers of such large bank notes were safer for him to admit to since they could have no direct connection to the ransom money, unlike Condon's address and phone number. But if he admitted to any writing at all on the closet door, saying the serial numbers had to do with funds received from Isidor Fisch was not going to get him out of the bag. He was deeply confused by now and was contradicting himself with almost every sentence.[31]

Foley returned to the question of Condon's address. When did Hauptmann put the address on his closet door, before or after he put the serial numbers there?

The only thing he could say was afterward.

"It was after the kidnapping wasn't it?"

"Yes."

"Was it before the ransom was paid?"

"No, I guess it was after."

"What makes you think so?"

"After that the whole paper was full of Dr. Condon."

"It was full of him before too, wasn't it?"

"Yes, it was full too."

"That doesn't really help you fix it then, does it?"

"I really can't give you any date when I put it down."

"You don't know whether it was before or after the ransom was paid, do you?"

"No."[32]

A clever kidnapper would have denied the writing at the outset. Instead, Hauptmann had fumbled around trying to separate the bill numbers from the address—with disastrous results. There is a police adage that truth wanders and lies stand still. One also has to account for the way questions are phrased—often to confuse—and the way police stenographers record answers—often to satisfy superiors. But clearly Hauptmann had damaged himself by not making a firm denial when the board was put down in front of him with its barely legible writing. Foley's question "Do you know who rubbed [the writing] or tried to rub it out?" could have elicited another response, along the lines of, "If I wrote it, I would have rubbed it out—completely." Inspector Bruckman had had to use a flashlight to find the writing; presumably Hauptmann would have had to illuminate it as well. Why bother to do that and then make such a botch of it?

Elated by his success, Foley told reporters, "The case has been completely broken. When I said before that it was ironclad that was true. But today there was brought down here by Inspector Bruckman . . . a board from inside a clothes closet with handwriting partially smudged and obliterated with Condon's address and phone number on it."[33]

Moving from the press conference to the Bronx courtroom, Foley introduced Bruckman to the grand jury as his star witness. Bruckman was an imposing figure over six feet tall. He fit the bill.

The D.A. had Albert S. Osborn, the handwriting expert, to back up Bruckman. But compared with the inspector's lucid account of coming upon the closet inscriptions, Osborn appeared almost inarticulate. A guilty person, he began his testimony, could not disguise his or her handwriting in the same way twice. If that were so, however, when a guilty person disguised request writings, they would not look like the disguised writings in the ransom notes, would they? Well, the answer was to look for individual characteristics that run through all the writings, conceded, request, and questioned. Here is his effort to explain his conclusion that all the writings were by the same person.

> About these request writings many of them are writings that we don't have the quantity that we have here, here we have also certain writings that were not written by request, if that were not so it would be impossible to connect this writer, but it is my opinion here the evidence when absolutely ample and sufficient here upon which to base the most positive opinion that this writer who signed those papers as Richard Hauptmann was the man that wrote the ransom notes.[34]

Fortunately, Osborn was not asked to diagram his sentences. He seems to be saying that in this case there is a large quantity not only of request writing but also of conceded writings. Without the latter it would be impossible to connect the writer with the ransom notes. When he first saw the conceded writings, "It was like meeting an old friend." A member of the jury asked if Hauptmann's recent writings checked with the ransom notes. "The recent writings are request writings, the request writings check with the older writings but it is a fact that the recent writings are disguised writings." To decipher that sentence, like his other longer statement, required a grammarian, not a juryman. Another puzzled member of the panel asked simply if it were possible to disguise writing. "I say that some of those writings, request writings I would say that there are parts that are successfully disguised and they had been written over for three or four times in different matter and of *course we have the handwriting of the automobile registration if we didn't have that we could not tell.*"[35]

Efforts were made to find someone else for the grand jury besides Cecile Barr who could identify Hauptmann as having in his possession ransom money long before August 1934, when he admitted he had started spending the gold certificates. Lieutenant James J. Finn went back to witnesses who had received ransom bills and had given descriptions of the man who tendered the money. "None of them except Cecile Barr," he said, "was able to identify him."[36]

Colonel Lindbergh's appearance also highlighted the hearings. "In the best manner of fiction," read a newspaper story about Lindbergh's latest dramatic flight to New York from California where he had been staying with Will Rogers, "the unraveling of America's most notorious kidnapping brought the bereaved flier and the accused father—Hauptmann, too, has a little son—closer to a climactic meeting."[37]

Foley only asked Lindbergh about the trip to St. Raymond's Cemetery to pay the ransom money and then turned him over to the panel for questions. "I think that is the skeleton that is essential to the case," he said, and sat down.

Did Colonel Lindbergh observe anybody in the vicinity that night?

"Shortly after we first stopped the car opposite the florist shop, a man walked by who I feel sure was one of the actual group of kidnappers or connected with them, he again came back on the opposite side of the street just before Dr. Condon returned after having paid the money." Lindbergh saw this man twice and also heard "the voice of one man at a distance." In response to another question, Lindbergh added important details about the mysterious lookout. "During the time he was nearest enough to see him very clearly, he covered his face, rather part of his face with a handkerchief and as he passed he looked first at Dr. Condon and then inside the car at me."

Would he recognize this man?

"I can't say that definitely . . . I am not certain."

Would he recognize that voice?

"I can't say positively." While he remembered it very clearly, "it would be very difficult for me to sit here and say that I could pick a man by that voice."

Did the colonel receive any impression about whether it was a man of foreign extraction?

"It undoubtedly was," he answered. "It was a very distinct foreign accent, the voice simply called to Dr. Condon, saying 'hey doc' but there was a very distinct accent."[38]

Lindbergh's testimony pretty well closed out the proceedings. An indictment was returned quickly, and when Hauptmann pled not guilty he was remanded to custody to stand trial with bail set at $100,000. Foley and other officials were not quite satisfied with the colonel's grand jury testimony, however. There were too many uncertainties that needed to be resolved. It was reported, for example, that "federal agents" wanted to show Lindbergh pictures of Isidor Fisch, to see if he could recognize him as the man with the handkerchief. Inspector Bruckman did his best to discourage undue discussion in the press about the second man at St. Raymond's Cemetery, but the best way to counter such unwanted speculations was to keep the focus on Hauptmann.[39]

The grand jury indictment was a foregone conclusion once Lindbergh appeared—even though he had hedged on the voice identification. Other evidence presented there was hedged later, before the case went to trial in Flemington, New Jersey. Another handwriting expert, John F. Tyrell, for example, called into question one of the car registrations—which Osborn had cited as essential to establish the ransom note writer—and it was dropped. The writing on the closet door was not presented at the trial, because, said New Jersey prosecutors, Hauptmann had initially conceded the point. The real reason was a desire not to open a door for defense rebuttals. So Bruckman's discoveries were never subjected to any evaluation beyond his original feeling that—at a glance—the handwriting looked like the suspect's, and Hauptmann's quickly recanted concession to Foley.[40]

The day Lindbergh testified, Lewis Bornmann was still hard at work searching through the house and garage with the two police carpenters. His first report on that day's activities noted that he had first visited the attic. "Nothing of value was found with the exception of several small pieces of wood and shavings and several cut nails that may possibly have a bearing on the case." But out in the garage, he noticed that on the right-hand wall one of the supports showed signs of having been removed and replaced. When the carpenters took off this two-by-four, Bornmann discovered that five holes had been bored into it on the side that faced the wall. Inserted into each of these holes were tightly wadded rolls of ten-dollar gold certificates. The money totaled $840.[41]

In another slot, tucked into the wood, was a small, automatic pistol, nickel plated, and stamped "Liliput," fully loaded with seven bullets.

Bornmann hastened to get this new treasure trove to Foley. The detective ended his report by saying, "No further evidence was found this date with the exception of several pieces of ponderosa pine which were later turned over to Arthur Koehler for comparison with that used in construction of the ladder."

Foley brought Hauptmann back into his office to stage another confrontation. With a newspaper covering the two-by-four, he asked, "Richard, is there anything concealed in or about your apartment that you haven't told us about?" When Hauptmann said no, the D.A. pulled off the paper and said, "I ask you now to look at what has been ripped out of the garage and brought down by the detectives."

This time he had a quick answer. "I told my lawyer about it."

"You didn't tell me about it."

"It didn't make any difference any way."

"Why not?"

"Because there was a little pistol there." The money, he said, came from the same box, the one Fisch had left behind.

"What did the pistol have to do with the money?"

"Nothing, but I was afraid about the pistol." He had had the gun for years but never used it. There was no good reason for putting the money in there, other than it "just got loose." He apparently had decided to distribute the money around the garage in various places, in packets of about $1,000 to $2,000. Why he should have taken such care with these bills, hollowing out small holes, remained a mystery. He was just afraid the illegal pistol would be discovered, and that was why he hadn't come clean.[42]

With Hauptmann tying himself in knots so handily, it seemed unnecessary to do anything else but wait for New Jersey to finish its preparations to seek extradition. "We are making no issue of defendant's alleged previous criminal record," the Bronx D.A. told the court, but he wanted bail set at $100,000 because of his responsibility to New Jersey, which was carrying on its own investigation. "As far as we are concerned," Bruckman told reporters, "our case is complete. All we are doing now is cooperating with New Jersey officials in an attempt to strengthen their case."[43]

That cooperation included trying to straighten out Colonel Lindbergh's memory. Condon's continuing failure to say once and for all it was Hauptmann he had met those two nights at Woodlawn and St. Raymond's had been a trying problem for the police, but Bruckman and Bornmann had done much to alleviate the strain with their discoveries. Foley had skirted the issue before the grand jury, allowing the panel members to ask about Lindbergh's ability to recognize the voice. But with the indictment in hand, it was time to move on to the next step. Do you think, he asked Lindbergh, if you had a chance to see and hear Hauptmann, that would refresh your memory? It might, was the reply.

At 9:30 A.M. on September 27, Lindbergh drove from Englewood to Foley's office, accompanied by several of the D.A.'s staff. Wearing sunglasses and with his cap pulled down over his face, he entered the building and went up a private elevator to the sixth floor. There he joined a roomful of detectives. Hauptmann was brought into the room and seated in the center. Foley ordered him to say "Hey Doc, over here" several times at different distances and different levels of loudness. He was "put through his paces, sitting and standing, talking and in repose." This performance lasted about ten minutes. After Lindbergh was safely out of the building, Foley's aide, Charles Brodie, told reporters about the confrontation. "Asked if Colonel Lindbergh had identified Hauptmann in any connection, Mr. Foley declined to answer."[44]

The next day, however, the *New York Times* informed readers, "District Attorney Samuel J. Foley of the Bronx made it plain to reporters that Colonel Charles A. Lindbergh had not identified Hauptmann in any sense on Thursday when the aviator, disguised in a cap and dark horn-rimmed glasses, studied the prisoner for ten minutes in a room crowded with investigators."[45]

Reporters were not the only ones kept in the dark until after Lindbergh's visit to Foley's office; FBI agents as well were kept out of the room. "They refuse to discuss matters with us," complained Sisk, "and then give it to the newspapers." As for the staged encounter, all another agent could report was, "Only God and Schwarzkopf know what he found out, if anything."[46]

"There are two sets of rules," E. A. Tamm went on, "one for them and one for us. They reserve the right to go out alone on any big tips or leads that look good but we are not supposed to go out on any lead alone even though it may be insignificant." After Bruckman's discovery of the writing on the nursery closet door, FBI agents had been kept out of the Hauptmann house while Bornmann and two police carpenters searched for more evidence. When Special Agent Wright sought to accompany them inside, he was told there would be no Department of Justice men present, unless he obtained a New York plainclothes man to accompany him. Wright informed his superiors, who immediately ordered him to return to the house and make it plain he was to be admitted. Now there was a phalanx of New York's finest guarding the entrance. "You can't get in," snapped their sergeant, "and I don't want any of your back talk."[47]

FBI agent Tamm described the investigation at this point as "a three ring circus and no ring master," and recommended Hoover begin to withdraw from the case, while the director himself said that the thing Attorney General Homer Cummings was happiest about was that the bureau was "coming out with dignity and not a part of any side-show."[48]

Determined not to be shut out, and, if necessary, to pick up the pieces of a bungled investigation, the FBI had not only pursued the fingerprint angle; even as Bruckman and Bornmann were hard at work for the grand jury, agents were conducting their own search of the apartment. "Although no one knows about it, we have two fountain pens taken from Hauptmann's apartment," wrote Hoover, which were now being examined to see if there was any connection with the ransom notes. They had also picked up specimens of handwriting, used for FBI identifications. There were also notebooks, memorandum pads, and other miscellaneous articles—"which fact is known only to the Division."

"Our agents," Hoover went on in this remarkable statement to Justice Department officials, "are the only ones who asked Hauptmann about the alibi, and although the others were present, they seemingly paid no attention [to] the questions asked by our men. We are therefore under no obligations to them, because if they don't have this information it is their own fault."[49]

One can only wonder whatever happened to all this evidence, especially the fountain pens. The Osborns had contended that certain of the notes were written with different pens. Did these pens answer that question? No pens were ever presented by the prosecution at the trial. Did Hoover keep them back, or was it that they did not fit the prosecution's case?

Almost every day there were sensational new stories in the press, most, if not all, inspired by police tips and revelations. One story emanating from the warden of the Ohio penitentiary declared that a convict had received a coded letter from Hauptmann in late 1931, which said, "Will kidnap Lindbergh baby. Hope for me." The convict, a man named George Paullin, had earlier claimed that he knew about a German couple who were involved as accomplices, and received a trip to New Jersey to help in the original search for the baby. Foley labeled Paullin's tale a "bust," but it filled newspapers for several days. There were also stories that Hauptmann had given his landlady, Pauline Rauch, Lindbergh notes in payment of the rent. Her daughter, Mrs. Laura Urvant, absolutely insisted that was so. Police should dig up the whole lot around the house, she said. "I just have a hunch they will find some of the money there." She knew the Fisch story was not true, because she had met Isidor at a party at the Hauptmann apartment and saw him frequently. He never had any money.[50]

The biggest story came out the day after Lindbergh's visit to Foley's office. The headline in the *New York Times* read: "BLADE MADE BY HAUPTMANN FOUND HIDDEN IN HIS CELL; INSANITY PLEA IS FORECAST." According to that paper, a guard had taken the prisoner's breakfast to him on a tray at 7:45. Prunes, bread, and coffee. Half an hour later, the guard retrieved the tray. A check of utensils revealed that a large pewter spoon was missing. Guards took Hauptmann to an adjoining cell, strip-searched him, and, finally, called a plumber, who discovered pieces of the spoon in the basin drain and in the toilet. About half an inch of the spoon's cup had been sharpened into a blade. Hauptmann had rubbed the piece against the bars of his cell, declared Foley, either to make a weapon to use in an escape attempt or to do harm to himself. He would leave it up to others to say which.[51]

Sheriff John Hanley, however, expressed doubt that the spoon had been sharpened at all, and noted that the various pieces had been disposed of in places where Hauptmann could not have recovered them for either use. The guard on duty, moreover, whose assignment was to look through the four-by-eight-inch opening in the steel door at frequent intervals, reported seeing no unusual activity. Unperturbed, Foley told reporters to "use their imagination" about what the prisoner intended to do with the blade. Defense lawyer Fawcett added to speculations by announcing that he intended to have Hauptmann examined by a psychiatrist. He would not comment about whether that presaged an insanity plea.[52]

A suicide attempt implied a guilty conscience. Foley and Fawcett almost seemed to be in agreement on that point. Oddly enough, the only dissenter was Walter Winchell. The columnist never doubted Hauptmann did it, and did it alone. But he laughed at those who took seriously the tale of the purloined spoon. "Remember that big hurrah about that spoon they found in Hauptmann's cell? How they found the spoon broken in parts and hidden behind a sink or something? And it was feared Hauptmann was getting ready to sharpen the thing either to saw a bar or slash his wrists? Well-hooey! It never happened—they never found such a spoon!"

"Oh, you must be wrong," Winchell mimicked a reader's shock, "'—I saw the picture of it in broken pieces in all the newspapers!' Pshaw! It looks to me like one of those instances where someone went to fantastic extremes to snatch a little publicity—by hanging onto the tail of a kite flying across page one." If anyone knew about tails on flying kites, it was Walter Winchell.

Fawcett had his client examined three times by doctors. The first time, on September 24, Dr. Thurston H. Dexter confirmed that Hauptmann had been severely beaten in an effort to make him confess. About a dozen plainclothesmen in the Greenwich station, he said it was, right after Condon failed to make his identification. These men showed him his own hammer, put the lights out, and struck him in the head, on his arms and legs, and in the stomach. Where was the money? What he had done with the baby? He was still in considerable pain at the time of the examination. "I conclude from this examination," wrote Dr. Dexter, "that he had been subjected recently to a severe beating, all or mostly with blunt instruments. The injuries resulting from this are general and include the head, back, chest, abdomen and thighs."[53]

Dr. James H. Huddleson conducted the psychiatric examination on October 3 and 5, together with physicians from New York and New Jersey. Hauptmann told them early on that in childhood he often added an *e* to words at the end. Even today, he said, "if I don't think on it, I do it." During the war he was gassed and struck in the head when a shell landed on his helmet. He was unconscious for a long time. Even now when he closed his eyes, he got dizzy. "I can't hold any balance." Here was an interesting pairing. He had explained why he wrote some words the way they appeared in the ransom notes; and he suggested a reason why he would not be a likely person to climb up a ladder on a dark night into a blackened room.

He related his arrests—"I'm ashamed of it"—and how he came to the United States. "Everything was behind me." He wanted to save up $500 and go to California to be with his sister; instead he got married. He had started school but quit after a short while. "I read fairly, but I am very weak in writing." After giving Hauptmann several tests, the examiners concluded that there was indeed "marked evidence of dizziness," which called for further tests. During the second examination, doctors found a lack of coordination of the upper extremities that did not suggest a person able to scramble up and down a ramshackle ladder at night, in and out of the nursery with a thirty-pound child under one arm. The physical tests at this second session raised more issues about how well Hauptmann could keep his balance when his eyes were shut, although there was some question about his tendency to exaggerate the difficulty.[54]

"The most noticeable facts of the examinee's attitude were his low voice, sometimes practically inaudible, his apathy and low level of interest throughout, his failure to show any excitement, resentment, grief, or any other emotion to the extent that would be expected in a man of his experience and mental capacity."

In the second exam, Hauptmann elaborated on his crimes in Germany. On one occasion he and some other fellows were shooting off a pistol in the woods, he said, and a woman came along pushing a baby carriage with packages in it, and they took some food from her. They used the pistol to scare her. On another occasion they broke into a house to steal some securities. "I didn't have any money. We decided to get some." And then there was his attempt to sell stolen goods. He had been in prison and escaped. "[Getting caught would have] spoil[ed] my whole life. I had to start a new life." In postwar Germany this was far from unusual; it was the time of the Spartacists, the *Freikorps,* and young men wandering around without jobs and desperately anxious to escape a future that looked bleaker each day. Some left Germany. Many joined a growing movement led by an inexplicably charismatic man named Adolf Hitler.

What about the story he had tried to commit suicide? "I only got a laugh about it." The warden had come to his cell and said, "I have to fix the toilet, it doesn't run right." He was put in the next cell, and then after a time they asked, "What did you do with the spoon?" They told him there was a spoon in the toilet. "That's all I know about it." The doctors asked him if he was sure the guard had not given him a spoon that morning at breakfast. "I don't know."

Once again Hauptmann explained how he got the money from Isidor Fisch, and why he had not wanted to reveal the hiding places. He knew he would never be able to spend any more of the money. "I didn't want to have a pistol charge against me. What would the $800 be to me?" He related once more why he felt entitled to spend the money: "because I was interested in his fur account, and there wasn't any furs." What about the numbers on the closet door? "One time Isidor gave me money, I always keep money in the house; I marked down what he gave me." How much money did he keep in the house? "$4,500. Always in the house. I got a good place." Here was a new wrinkle. Yet if he had $4,500 in a "good place," how had he come by that money? The money reserve would come up again at Hauptmann's trial in New Jersey, when it sounded like a newly invented piece of his story.

What Fawcett made out of all this we do not know, but there was never any attempt to enter an insanity plea. And why, if the tests revealed serious physical weaknesses, were they never repeated, or used by the defense?

Bruno Richard Hauptmann's arrest on September 19, 1934, had led to a quick indictment for extortion. New Jersey authorities announced plans to extradite Hauptmann to face murder charges. "The American public wanted his conviction," wrote FBI agent Leon Turrou, one of the arresting officers. "Not since the Kaiser's submarines had sunk the *Lusitania* had its blood lust been so aroused. . . . It was unthinkable that he be not guilty."[55]

The special New Jersey prosecution team that went to New York to initiate extradition proceedings knew that—all other evidence of guilt aside—it had only a theory of how the child died. An extortion indictment in New York, ironically, did not help matters in that regard; it only kept Hauptmann in Bronx County jail. In Washington, D.C., U.S. attorney general Homer S. Cummings pointed out the difficulty. The new federal kidnapping law which carried the death penalty—the "Lindbergh Law"— did not apply. It had been enacted after the abduction. New Jersey's kidnap law, dating from 1831, specified a maximum penalty of life imprisonment. That meant, noted Cummings, New Jersey would have to try Hauptmann for first-degree murder if it wanted to impose the death penalty. A death that occurred during a robbery constituted such a capital offense. In Hauptmann's case, the charge carrying a death penalty, paradoxically, would not be kidnapping, but the theft of a three-dollar sleeping suit!

But now, J. Edgar Hoover was saying he did not believe one man could have done it alone. On September 26, for example, the FBI director predicted swift arrests of Hauptmann's accomplices. "Things look very good," he said. And reporters wrote:

> It became known that Mr. Hoover and his men felt that Hauptmann's connection with the case did not include climbing the ladder into the Lindberghs' Hopewell residence. Department experts pointed out that the ladder, found outside the house after the disappearance of the child, was of such construction that it probably could not support Hauptmann, who weighs 170 pounds.
>
> "It is possible that he did the job alone, but it is not probable," Mr. Hoover said.
>
> The late Isidor Fisch, implicated by Hauptmann, is understood to have been of lighter weight than Hauptmann. Department officers have been seeking data through fingerprint impressions and other means in an effort to ascertain just what part, if any, Fisch, who died in Germany, might have had in the crime.[56]

This sort of comment caused consternation for New Jersey attorney general David Wilentz, named to head the prosecution. He needed to prove that the German carpenter from the Bronx had driven down to Hopewell by himself on the rainy night of March 1, 1932, unloaded a makeshift ladder he had constructed out of odd pieces of lumber, placed it against the wall, and climbed up to the nursery. If someone handed him the child, the case for premeditated murder began to cloud over. Since the kidnapper had sent a sleeping suit in order to obtain the money, ergo, he must have stolen the garment. And if death occurred in the act of stealing the child's sleeping suit, whether in the crib or climbing down the ladder, a case could be made for felonious death, a capital offense. This would even finesse the question of how the baby died, intentionally or by accident. But the New Jersey prosecutors still worried how this would all play out at a trial.

Wilentz could argue, and was advised to do so, that New Jersey law defined kidnapping as a special kind of theft, involving "any person who shall kidnap or steal, or forcibly take away any man, woman or child." But then the defense would no doubt argue in rebuttal that kidnapping, often as not, was a group endeavor. What was Hauptmann's degree of involvement? Was he simply the man who wrote the notes and was in charge of the payroll? The way the garage money had been packaged suggested such a possible line of defense. Already there were speculations that Hauptmann was only one of those responsible, and perhaps not even the one on the ladder or alone in the dark at the baby's crib![57]

Governor A. Harry Moore was surprisingly reluctant to say when he would give the word to proceed with the extradition. Would it be as soon as next week? he was asked on September 24. Not unless something definitely connecting him with the actual crime develops, he replied. "Of course, a break may come at any time. We could easily make a mistake by taking hasty action. The extradition process will be slow. It may take a week, two weeks, a month or more. New Jersey wants to have an airtight case before it goes ahead. It doesn't want to bungle the biggest case in America."[58]

There had been enough of that already, a cynic would say. Despite the evidence gathered from Hauptmann's house, there was still no witness to put him in New Jersey the night of March 1, 1932. The Fisch story, moreover, had not been effectively disproven. Walter Winchell had some free advice for New Jersey authorities: "I'd do all I could to keep Dr. Condon from rambling and qualifying and hedging, once he has made a positive statement. . . . The case against Hauptmann is declared airtight, if Dr. Condon is having one of his good days. . . . Some of the authorities are worried. Said one: 'If we put him on the witness stand and it is one of his bad days, God help us.'"[59]

New Jersey officials labeled such assertions ridiculous. They had the ransom note left in the nursery, they said, and experts had affirmed that Hauptmann wrote it. "This, the authorities argued, obviated the necessity for supporting evidence to demonstrate he had been in the State at the time the crime was committed." Perhaps that was so, but no one wanted to go into court wielding only a few lines on a piece of paper. District Attorney Foley finally said, on September 30, that he did not know what the New Jersey authorities intended, or whether they would be ready to extradite before the extortion trial began.[60]

In Washington, D.C., William Stanley, an assistant to Attorney General Homer S. Cummings, sent Hoover a copy of an article by a legal expert, Thomas S. Rice, that had appeared in the *Brooklyn Daily Eagle.* He might find it interesting, said Stanley. If he were leading the defense, the article read, he would begin his argument with the hasty actions of New Jersey authorities in allowing the child to be cremated without a proper examination and identification, "when they knew the day might come when they would put a man on trial for his life and have to rely upon such a weak identification." He would point to the perfect timing of the kidnapping, and the long period of preliminary observation necessary to make it a success. And then there was the ladder. "I would ask why such a clever carpenter and cabinetmaker built a ladder that would break. The one thing on which the most mutinous or disaffected of communistic carpenters does sound and solid work is the ladder he himself is to use. . . . We all make mistakes but that broken ladder does not sound like Hauptmann. . . . New York had better keep him for awhile until those hurdles are leveled."[61]

Hoover also received advice that he ought to have someone make sure Dr. Phillip Van Ingen, the Lindbergh family doctor, would reaffirm his identification of the body. Hoover's correspondent, a friend of Van Ingen's, thought that he needed careful treatment as he was rather shy, and no doubt would prefer to talk off the record. "I stated," noted Hoover, "that of course we want to prove murder; that it will probably be very difficult, and for that reason I had recommended that the matter be turned over to the Bronx temporarily."[62]

New Jersey had to do something fairly soon, or temporarily might become permanently. That was Attorney General David Wilentz's assignment.

9 MR. WILENTZ
BUILDS HIS CASE

So help me God, I'm telling the truth and only the truth when
I say I seen that man coming out of the woods back of the
Lindbergh place. I seen him twice. I ain't dreaming I seen him.
I really seen him and may God strike me dead if I ain't telling
the truth.

—MILLARD WHITED, October 1934

David Wilentz's family had brought him to the United States as an
infant from Russia just at the turn of the century. He was already
famous in his home state for a special talent in political organization when Governor A. Harry Moore asked him to become attorney
general. "He is 39," the *New Brunswick Daily Home News* began its description of the man suddenly put on the front pages of newspapers
around the world, "small and alert, olive skinned, with sleek black hair
and dark eyes of a gleaming softness. His manual gestures are deft, his
facial expressions, not too deliberately studied, are designed to bul-
wark his words. He knows the value of dress, though his sartorial incli-
nations are Broadway rather than Bond street. He is what is commonly
known as a 'meticulous dresser.'"[1]

In October 1934, Wilentz's most pressing problem was that he
needed an eyewitness for the extradition proceedings against Hauptmann. One reason, indeed the main reason, for the delay in New Jersey's
extradition case had been the absence of an eyewitness who could put
Bruno Richard Hauptmann on the Lindbergh estate around the time of
the kidnapping. Colonel Norman Schwarzkopf admitted that his men had
shown Hauptmann's photograph to hundreds of people near Hopewell,
"but none was certain enough of the identification to justify a trip to
New York to view the prisoner."[2]

Did Schwarzkopf really mean to say, asked reporters, he had no one who actually saw Hauptmann? "I can't help what the impression is," said the colonel. "I stand by that one statement." What about D.A. Foley's statement he had a "mystery woman" available to testify, someone who would definitely link Hauptmann to the kidnapping and murder? "He has indicated to me that there is an additional female witness available," responded Attorney General Wilentz. "I venture no opinion as to the term 'mystery woman.'"[3]

"The people propose to go to trial [on October 11]," Foley told Judge James Barrett, "unless some special rights of the People of the State of New Jersey would interfere with the setting of that date." Barrett ruled for Foley: "The date for trial is set for October 11." The only way for New Jersey to avoid being shut out—an intolerable situation—was to get an indictment for murder. And for that, Wilentz needed his eyewitness.

Foley was fed up with New Jersey, FBI agents reported from New York. The state's officials could not make up their minds what to do, and he could not get anything from them. When he asked for evidence, they stated they did not know the answer and would have to find out where to get it—and then never did. Hoover believed Hauptmann's defense attorney, James Fawcett, would fight hard to block extradition and might actually succeed "if they do not have any more evidence in New Jersey than has been indicated." Of course "public opinion" might force Governor Herbert Lehman's hand to "go ahead and order the extradition." But once the extortion trial got under way, Foley would never agree to it. The Bronx D.A. had done the "right thing," said Hoover, by refusing to listen to Governor Moore's pleas for delay.[4]

But at this moment Hoover was also furious with New York's finest. Inspector Bruckman had locked out one of his agents while police carpenters ripped up floorboards searching for evidence. Hoover threatened to withdraw all his men immediately. Bruckman's superiors apologized and promised better cooperation in the future—but no one offered to tell the FBI director what the carpenters had found.[5]

A couple of days later the *Washington Herald* ran a story asserting that New Jersey authorities had once arrested Hauptmann—and let him go. It reminded Agent Sisk of an incident the night Hauptmann was brought in to the Greenwich Street police station. Standing beside Sisk was Captain Lamb of the New Jersey State Police. When Lamb saw the prisoner, he grabbed Sisk's arm and groaned, "[I am the] unluckiest fellow that had ever lived," as he "had had that fellow up before." Pursue the matter, Hoover ordered, "for if that is true it is a serious thing and puts them in an awful bad light." The agent should "get as much as he can in order that we might have it up our sleeve if they ever get nasty with us again."[6]

A surprise statement from Trenton interrupted these backstage maneuverings. State troopers had located a man in a Pennsylvania logging camp said to have seen Hauptmann "prowling about" near the Lindbergh estate a "bare fortnight before the famous flier's son was kidnaped and slain." His name was Millard Whited, and, at the time of the kidnapping, he worked a small farm in the vicinity of Hopewell. Now he hauled wood for a living.

No one had any idea where he had gone after leaving his old shack on the Wertsville Road, neighbors said, but troopers found him in the logging camp near New Hope, Pennsylvania. Had he seen any pictures of Hauptmann in the newspapers? He did not buy newspapers, Millard answered. He did not read very well. They would come back, Trooper Joseph Wolf told him, with several large photos. When they did, Whited recollected that this man "looked exactly like" someone he had seen near his home before the kidnapping, but he couldn't say "positively" without seeing Hauptmann face-to-face.[7]

Well, that certainly could be arranged. On the night of October 4, 1934, troopers picked up Whited and took him to Trenton headquarters. Having thought things over for forty-eight hours, Whited began to feel a little uncertain about what his duties as a good citizen required. "I cannot go," he said, "I haven't got the clothes and things to go over to New York with." "I am not going to waste my time driving to New York and spending what little money I have to go to New York," he repeated. "We will take you over," said Lieutenant Keaten. But what about my lost work? Whited asked. You will be paid what you said you earned hauling wood, Keaten promised, thirty-five dollars a day.[8]

Millard Whited might be an illiterate hillbilly, but he could read faces well and calculate things in his head pretty close. Nothing definite was said about the $25,000 reward, except that it would be split up among "them."

Driven to the Bronx County jail, he picked out "the second man on the right" in an eleven-man lineup—Bruno Richard Hauptmann—as the man he had seen on the road sometime between the eighteenth day and the last day of February, "near as [he] could tell" sometime between 11:50 and 12:20 P.M.

Whited said he remembered the incident well. This man stepped out of the bushes on the Wertsville-Hopewell Road, wearing a gray slouch hat and a light suit of clothes, with a coat hanging on his arm. "I don't know just what kind of a coat it was on account of this being a narrow road, I only noticed him because he was a stranger in this section."[9]

Whited drove past and got a good look because his window was rolled down. "He walked with his hat pulled down over his eyes and a frown on his face." Intrigued, Whited kept watching in his rearview mirror as the man looked up and down the road, sort of like he didn't know which way to go. Four or five days later, he saw him again, between 4 and 5 P.M.—standing at a crossroad nearer to the Lindbergh estate. He had on the same clothes and everything, and, just like the first time, he was looking up and down the road, like he was trying to decide which way to go. "I was making about ten miles an hour, [so] I had a good opportunity to look him over."[10]

He was unusually sensitive for an untutored witness: he explained why he had noticed the man—a stranger in the neighborhood—and, even better, described his menacing expression—suitable for a lurker planning a kidnapping. And, best of all, he had happened on him twice! He made only one slip in this recital: "I am positive that this is the man who I talked to the Detectives about in March 1932." There is no record of his ever having talked to anyone, uniformed state troopers or detectives, in March 1932 about seeing anyone near the Lindbergh house. Only his word. And when he was asked in late April 1932, "Have you noticed any persons walking through the woods in the vicinity of the Lindbergh Home before March 1, 1932 that acted in a suspicious manner?" Whited answered firmly, "No I have not."[11]

In Washington, Attorney General Homer Cummings had feared that New Jersey, lacking conclusive evidence, might go for a deal. "The Attorney General," Hoover reported to an associate, "feels pretty strongly about the New Jersey situation, and is very fearful of negotiations with Hauptmann on a money basis, which he thinks will reflect on any agency which is in on the case." It was coming down to put-up-or-shut-up time. New Jersey grand jury hearings were scheduled in Flemington for October 8, 1934—three days before Foley's trial for extortion was supposed to start.

The big news out of New Jersey was not Whited's appearance, however, but Colonel Lindbergh's testimony at the Flemington grand jury hearing. Newspapers reported that Wilentz had suddenly changed his mind about calling Lindbergh, only a few hours before the hearings began. "Wilentz vouchsafed no explanation of the change in his plans.[12] The reason was that Lindbergh had now identified Hauptmann as the man who called out, "Hey Doc," the night the ransom was paid. That's all it took. Millard Whited's starring role would come at the extradition hearings in New York.

It took less than a day for the Flemington grand jury to return a murder indictment, paving the way for the extradition proceedings. Shortly after the jurors began deliberations on the eyewitness and ear-witness testimony, an urgent message came out from the jury room: What was the score in the World Series game between Detroit and St. Louis? Hunterdon County prosecutor Anthony Hauck rushed out to get an answer. The score was tied, he reported back. Maybe they would get home in time to listen in.[13]

Colonel Lindbergh's dramatic testimony, which had lasted less than ten minutes, made it easier for the jurors to get back to the World Series, but it actually did not bear directly on a murder indictment. It "proved" only extortion. Prosecutors thus went off to New York with lots of loose ends still poking out of their briefcases.

J. Edgar Hoover did not think much of the Flemington proceedings. In fact, he was downright insulting about Jersey justice. The indictment and the continuing row between New York and New Jersey, he told a superior at the Department of Justice, made it a perfect time to bow out of the case. "Some of the evidence that was produced in New Jersey yesterday," he said, "is apparently 'phoney.'" In another memorandum that same day, he added that he was "somewhat skeptical" of "the testimony of Lindbergh relative to recognizing the voice. . . . While there is no doubt that Hauptmann is guilty, I want to have confidence in the evidence."[14]

On the other hand the Department of Justice could make a big splash right now, said Hoover, because it was a perfect time to release the accounting report prepared by its expert, J. A. Genau. The department had pieced together a key part of the puzzle and found that Hauptmann had no way to explain at least $26,000 in deposits. And when this was added to $14,500 found in the garage, plus $5,000 attributed to Hauptmann, you had over $45,000 of the ransom money. The accounting report impressed Agent Clegg sufficiently to make him believe that it was, after all, a one-man job. "There are logical reasons which would point to the presence of someone else," Clegg believed, "but there are an equal number of logical reasons why there is only one person." And the money deposits headed the list.[15]

But could one assert beyond reasonable doubt that the $26,000 was actually ransom money? If it was, Hauptmann had successfully laundered it, or the brokerage houses simply missed it. Hoover admitted as much: "The source of the money cannot be determined from the accounts, and none of it can be identified as ransom money, although it might well have been." A prepared statement for Attorney General Cummings to use announcing Agent Genau's report had to be amended,

204 THE CASE THAT NEVER DIES

as well, where it referred to the $5,095 located before Hauptmann's arrest, by deleting "which funds had been expended by Hauptmann in various parts of New York City or in some instances had been exchanged for other currency." The FBI had been unable, Hoover noted, to prove that Hauptmann expended this money.[16]

Even with the caveats and deletions, however, the statement Cummings then gave out at the Department of Justice made it seem conclusive that, first, all but a few thousand dollars of ransom money could be traced directly to Hauptmann, and, second, and no less important, the FBI had been the only agency to have the resources and ability to produce such a report. Thus it was a perfect time, as Cummings also announced, for the FBI to withdraw in honor. Hoover had even toyed with the idea of giving the statement first to Foley, a final little bit of nastiness to Schwarzkopf and New Jersey, but thought better of the idea.[17]

Meanwhile, David Wilentz said he felt comfortable with what he had from Lindbergh. "We consider that the best identification so far is that by Colonel Lindbergh himself—the recognition of Hauptmann's voice as the voice he heard in the Bronx cemetery the night the ransom was paid." The media agreed. The *New York Times* headlined the voice identification: "COL. LINDBERGH IDENTIFIES HAUPTMANN BY HIS VOICE; MURDER INDICTMENT VOTED."

> Numerous attempts have been made by friends of the colonel and by some officials to get from him a public statement setting forth his belief that Hauptmann is the kidnapper. He has steadfastly refused to do so.
>
> With the announcement of his identification, it is assured that he will be one of the State's most important witnesses in the murder trial that Hauptmann faces in Flemington.[18]

FBI agent Leon Turrou would write in his memoirs, however: "Many, including myself, thought it remarkable that Colonel Lindbergh, sworn to truth, could recognize a voice heard for a few moments in a dark wood after a lapse of two years. It was all the more surprising since the colonel's accusation was not weakened by the slightest shade of doubt. I think his cold unhesitating recital loaded with stark drama convinced the jury more than anything else."[19]

Still, and whatever one thought of the credibility of his identification, Lindbergh had not seen Hauptmann in New Jersey. So the spotlight was on Millard Whited when the New York extradition hearing began on October 16, 1934, the week after the Flemington indictment. Wilentz led him through his story of seeing the man with the topcoat over his arm. Only now the man with "a strange face . . . stepped in front of me." He had a better view, in other words, than if he just passed him in a car, as in his original statement. Hauptmann's defense attorney, James Fawcett, wanted to know what else made Whited pay such close attention. Well, the stranger "had a look as though he was surprised or [had] something on his mind."[20]

"Do you see that man in the court room?" asked Wilentz.

"I do."

"Will you indicate him?"

"Right there." Whited turned in his chair and raised his arm to point at Hauptmann.

"Will you walk down to him, with the court's permission?"

The cadaverous Whited rose from his chair and started toward the defense table. Deputies leaned back as he passed, as if afraid to be touched by this gaunt figure delivering a summons from hell itself. The courtroom buzz grew louder as Whited moved closer to where Hauptmann sat staring straight ahead. Justice Ernest Hammer commanded the crowd to silence. For a second Whited stood behind Hauptmann, then tapped him on the shoulder. "Hauptmann gulped, his face was blanched," a New Jersey reporter wrote. "His eyes stared straight at his accuser. Deep-set, they flashed, glared."[21]

Back in the witness chair, Whited's aura shrank considerably. In place of the backwoodsman who eked out an honest living, there appeared a sly fellow, eyes darting around, trying hard to remember what he said five minutes earlier. Asked when he first revealed that he had seen a stranger prowling the roads before the kidnapping, Whited testified that he had told police about it early on the morning of March 2, 1932. Fawcett could not know this was suspect testimony. So he probed another issue. Had Whited seen newspaper pictures of Hauptmann *before* the state trooper came to see him a few days ago? Did that help him identify his client?

Well, replied Whited, he knew there had been pictures in the paper, but he hadn't seen them. "I'm here and I'm there and I'm everywhere and I hear folks talking."

He hadn't seen them?

No, he hadn't.

Well, persisted the defense attorney, could he have identified Hauptmann if a trooper had not shown him a picture?

"I am not saying one way or the other," Whited blurted out before catching himself. "I said that is the face that I saw on the mountain."[22]

If you never saw that picture, Fawcett repeated, you could still pick out the prisoner?

"Yes."

Even if the defense attorney had had access to the police reports for March 2 and April 26, 1932, and had known that Whited's story about telling the police he had seen a stranger lurking around in mid- to late-February had never been told to anyone until a few days ago, it probably would have done little good.

Fawcett brought forward witnesses who knew Millard Whited's reputation. Asked what his reputation was in the Hopewell community for veracity and honesty, one of Whited's cousins replied, "Not much."

"Well, is it good or bad?"

"Bad."

Two others Fawcett called said the same thing. Attorney General Wilentz immediately demanded to know from one of them, E. J. Nens, whether he and Whited had quarreled. "Some time ago, yes, sir," came the answer. Wilentz had what he wanted and sat down, but Fawcett asked what the quarrel was about. "He bought some lumber in the neighborhood and didn't pay for any of it."[23]

The other star witness was Albert S. Osborn. After Osborn identified Hauptmann as the writer of the first note, Wilentz centered his attention on a phrase in a subsequent note of March 5, 1932, "Why did you ignore our letter which we left in your room." This note and another one promising to send the sleeping suit as proof the baby was in his hands, declared Wilentz, "are an admission and confession on the part of Hauptmann that he was in the baby's room the night of the kidnap[p]ing."[24]

Fawcett, of course, took issue with premise that Hauptmann had written the ransom note. Unlike the grand jury hearings, where Osborn had had no challenge to his methodology, at the extradition hearings the defense attorney asked him exactly which of the requested writings and conceded writings he had used to reach the conclusion that Hauptmann was the author of the ransom notes. Fawcett wanted to show that the expert had taken a letter here, and a word there, to make the argument.

Osborn responded to Fawcett's observations by noting that on several occasions in the conceded writings and the ransom notes, a misplaced *h* occurred. In a driver's license application, the German had written *light* as *l-i-h-g-t*. In a ransom note, *right* appeared *r-i-g-t-h*. In another ransom note *the* was written *h-t-e*. Then there was that odd *x* written as almost a double *e*, only back-to-back. He had found in both the conceded writings and the ransom notes this "peculiar letter which I had never before seen written by anybody."

Fawcett went after these assertions, suggesting that the *x* in question was common to German writing.

No, said Osborn, he had examined "thousands of specimens of the writing of Germans" and had failed to find a "single example of it." There he was on very weak ground. His boast that he had examined thousands of specimens of German handwriting and never seen an example of an *x* written that way did very little for his reputation. The *x* in question was from a script style known as Suetterlin, created by a Berlin graphic artist, and which was taught from 1915 to 1941 in German schools. Someone more familiar with German handwriting would never have made such a comment—especially not under oath.[25]

The expert also said the writing was Hauptmann's because in the ransom notes the *i* was *never* dotted, and the same was true in the request writings. But in the favorite examples from which he took certain characteristics, the license and car registration applications, the *i* was more often dotted than not. Little wonder Osborn objected strenuously to being handed exhibits one at a time and asked to explain his procedures. At one point Justice Hammer had to rap for order when the audience laughed as the expert puzzled over a certain exhibit, unable to tell whether it was marked *J* or *Y*. Osborn's plight amused the courtroom even more when the stenographer said the marking was actually a *G*.[26]

Fawcett produced Anna Hauptmann and the Fredericksens as witnesses, but there was still only Anna's word that Richard had picked her up that Tuesday evening after work.

The defense attorney also tried to introduce evidence that Richard had worked at the Majestic Apartments (also called the Majestic Hotel) during the day of the kidnapping. He had subpoenaed a timekeeper from the company, Reliance Property Management, one Edward F. Morton. When his name was called out, however, he did not answer. Instead, the company had sent an assistant treasurer, Howard Knapp, who effectively became Wilentz's witness. To Fawcett's astonishment, Knapp declared that records for the first two weeks of March 1932 did not exist. "Our records do not indicate that any such records exist at this time," he said, adding after a pause, "or at that time, either."[27]

Fawcett could not believe what he had heard. This firm employing over 100 men had no payroll records? He pressed the question again: "You have no payroll records before that date?"

"Nothing before that on the Majestic apartments."[28]

Knapp's testimony upheld police investigations that Hauptmann had begun work on March 21, 1932, and quit on April 2, 1932—the day the ransom was paid.

Wilentz then produced two checks issued to Hauptmann, one for $36.67 dated March 31, 1932, and a second for $6.67, dated April 15,

1932. To Wilentz, the checks proved that Hauptmann had worked only eleven days in March and two days in April, and that his rate of pay had been $100 a month. But which two days in April did he work? The time sheets do appear to have been tampered with in order to show that he had not worked on Saturday, April 2, 1932, the day the ransom was paid, and had, in fact, resigned instead two days later on Monday, April 4, 1932, after he got the money.[29]

If he worked every day until April 4, except for the Saturday, then the paycheck should have been for $10.00, not $6.67. On the other hand, if he put in a full day on April 1 and 2, as he said he did, and resigned at the end of April 2, the check was right. The more important date, of course, was March 1, 1932; newly discovered records indicate he did not work on that date—although he did show up at the Majestic Apartments early in the morning prepared to work. The prosecution, however, wished to demonstrate also that he had not worked on April 2, and that became a much more complicated matter.

When Hauptmann took the stand at the extradition hearing, he did not claim that he had been working on March 1, 1932. "Well, that is one thing I can't exactly remember," he said. And then in response to a follow-up question: "If I worked for the Majestic Hotel before March 1, then I was working on March 1 on the Majestic Hotel. That I am positively sure."

When Attorney General Wilentz cross-examined, he jumped on that statement at once as contradictory to what he had told the arresting officers. "You told them, did you not, that you were working on that date at the Majestic Hotel?"

"I did."

"You did tell them that?"

"Yes."

"Why did you tell them that, if you didn't know that to be the fact?"

"They didn't give me any chance to think at all."

"Didn't give you any chance to think, and that is why you said yes?"

"Yes."

"You could just as well have said, 'I don't know,' couldn't you?"

Fawcett was on his feet: "I object." Justice Hammer sustained the objection.

Although neither Wilentz nor Fawcett knew it, the very first answer Hauptmann had given to police was, in fact, that he did not know where he had been on March 1, 1932. At the time he was handcuffed to Detective John Wallace in his kitchen, and Inspector John Lyons had put the question. Wallace said in his report, "He stated he did not know."[30] Taken to the Greenwich Street police station, Hauptmann had had time to think about the matter—a lot of time during the questioning—and it was then that he tried to insist he had been working on March 1, 1932.

Wilentz would make contradictory statements, himself, about the work records, claiming in one instance that police had the records in their possession, and in another that the police at no time had possession of the payroll records. In the first place, the payroll records and the time sheet records were two different entities. On October 27, the attorney general insisted there had been no tampering with the payroll record. "The police at no time had possession of the payroll," he said. "I am sure there are no erasures on it." Did he mean the time sheets or the payroll records? Two days later, on October 29, an unsigned receipt in the New York City Police Department listed payroll records for March and April 1932 as having been received by New Jersey authorities from Bronx assistant district attorney Edward Breslin.[31]

Was Wilentz simply hoping Hauptmann would make another claim to having been at work on March 1, 1932, when he had records to show he wasn't? We simply do not know what records were at the attorney general's disposal when he pressed Hauptmann to make yet another claim that he had been working on March 1, 1932. Howard Knapp's claim at the extradition hearing that there were no such records for the period before March 15–31, 1932, was untenable, and so were police claims that they were missing. The payroll records covered in the Breslin receipt do not contain an entry for "Richard Hauptmann" before March 15 or after April 2, 1932. Why, then, if they were available to police, were they not used at the hearing or the trial? The simple answer has to be that the German carpenter dropped his claim that he had been working on that day, beginning with his answer to Fawcett: "Well, that is one thing I can't exactly remember."[32]

Hauptmann also made the statement, in response to Wilentz's questions, that his pay rate was $80 a month, not the $100 he had been promised, thereby laying the basis for a later claim that he resigned for that reason—and not because he had suddenly struck it rich. The check amounts for $36.67 and $6.67 cannot be easily accounted for in that way, because the $100 rate breaks down to $3.33 per day, or eleven days in March and two in April. But perhaps he had been told his pay would be less in the future.[33]

When Wilentz challenged him on the money hidden in the garage, Hauptmann asserted that it had not been found as the result of a search, but that he had told an Inspector Ryan, or Lyons—he could not remember the name—about the money. It was the morning after his arrest, he said, and this man asked him if he had any more money in his possession. "I didn't speak right away. He said to me, 'Do you want to speak to me alone?' I said, 'Yes.' I finally told them I had another $14,000 in my garage."

Flabbergasted, Wilentz asked if he did not lie, then, when he told police the $14,000 was the last of the money at his house.

Hauptmann admitted he had not told the truth about that cache hidden in holes drilled in a board in the garage.[34]

His story still was that he had not told the truth about the last $870 found in the garage because he feared police would find the small pistol hidden next to the money in another of the holes.

"Was it loaded?"

"I guess the magazine, there were some bullets in."

"That wasn't a hunting gun, was it? You didn't use that for hunting, did you?"

"Yes, I did."

"Show the court about the size of it with your finger, your hands. . . . What would you say, about four or five inches in length?"

"I guess three to four inches."

"What calibre?"

"I don't know the calibre."

"You don't know the calibre?"

"I really don't know it."

"It is what they call a comrade gun, isn't it? Isn't that what you call it over in Europe, a comrade gun?"

"No, I don't know."

"Isn't it the sort of gun that you can hide between your fingers, if you are asked to hold your hands up, so that the person can't see it?"

Fawcett objected, and the objection was upheld by Justice Hammer. But the New Jersey attorney general had scored his points: Hauptmann was an alien; he was a machine gunner in the German army in the Great War; and he was in possession of a weapon used to deceive Americans, an "I surrender" pistol.[35]

Hauptmann denied he had written the ransom notes or anything else except some bank note numbers on his closet door. He also stated he had not been in or around Hopewell on March 1, 1932.

Then Fawcett asked him, according to press reports,

"Did you murder the child, Charles Augustus Lindbergh . . . [?]"

"No," interrupted Hauptman, as calm as though at his carpenter's bench.

". . . on March 1, 1932, or any other time?" Fawcett finished.

Charles Lindbergh, Jr., with his mother, Anne Morrow Lindbergh, and his grand-mothers, Mrs. Dwight Morrow, standing, and Mrs. Lindbergh. Photo courtesy of the Library of Congress.

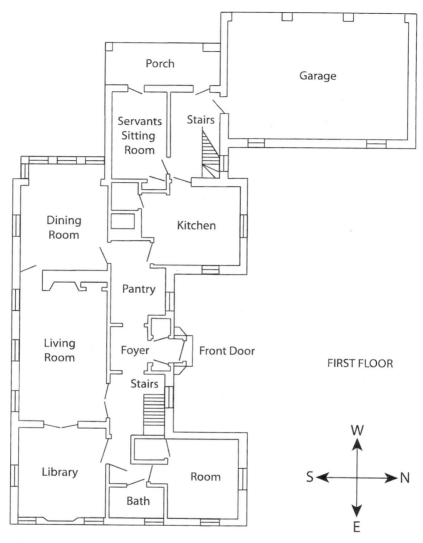

Floor plans of the Lindbergh home. Illustrations by Erin Gardner Myers.

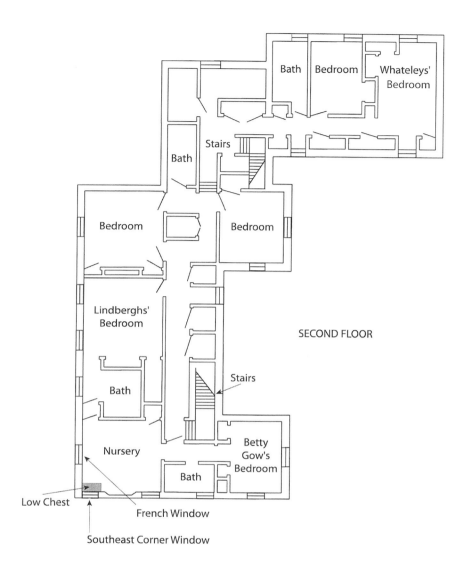

Bath

Bedroom

Whateleys'
Bedroom

Bath

Stairs

Bedroom

Bedroom

Lindberghs'
Bedroom

SECOND FLOOR

Bath

Stairs

Nursery

Betty
Gow's
Bedroom

Bath

Low Chest

French Window

Southeast Corner Window

Charlie's crib showing a sunlamp that seemed to disappear after the kidnapping. Photo courtesy of the New Jersey State Police Archives (NJSP).

Betty Gow, Charlie's nursemaid, was the first suspect along with boyfriend "Red" Johnson. NJSP.

The nursery window showing an untouched beer stein on left, trunk, and narrowness of window, which would have made entrance and exit difficult. NJSP.

The window lock on the nursery window must have been left unclosed, providing one of the mysteries about the possibility of inside help with the kidnapping. NJSP.

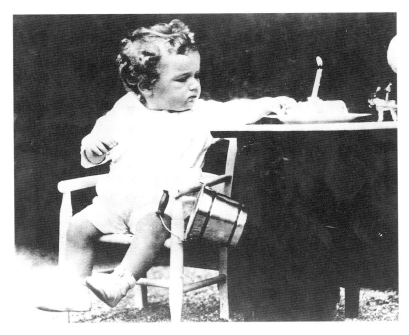

Charles A. Lindbergh, Jr., on his first birthday. This picture was used on the poster distributed at the time of the kidnapping. Questions arose about why there were no later photographs available. NJSP.

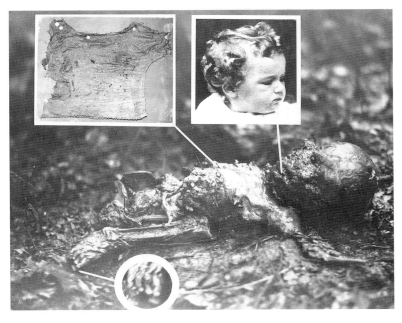

Charlie's corpse and some of the points used for identification. NJSP.

Inspector Harry Walsh was the key interrogator in the early stages of the investigation after Charlie's body was found. Some blamed him for Violet Sharp's suicide. NJSP.

Isidor Fisch with an unknown woman. Fisch was a man of many guises, who appeared to some to be unlucky at everything he tried, and to others a mysterious man who dealt in hot money. NJSP.

Richard (back row, left) with several friends. This picture contrasts with descriptions of Hauptmann as stolid and unemotional. NJSP.

Hauptmann in prison. The look shown here was the one he adopted throughout the trial. NJSP.

The flamboyant Edward J. Reilly, chief defense attorney for Hauptmann. NJSP.

C. Lloyd Fisher with Hauptmann. Fisher proved to be his strongest champion. NJSP.

Amandus Hochmuth, who said he saw Hauptmann's car go into a ditch the morning of the kidnapping. NJSP.

Charles Lindbergh on the witness stand. His testimony alone was enough to convict Hauptmann. NJSP.

Prosecutor David Wilentz holding a copy of one of the ransom notes. His style kept defense witnesses off balance. NJSP.

The ransom note illustrates the kidnapper's distinct signature. NJSP.

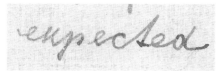

The letter *x* in ransom note two, compared to Hans Müeller's *x*, showing that there was nothing unique about this way of writing *x*. NJSP.

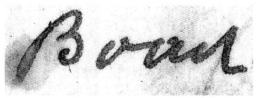

"Boad" from Evidence Page

Close-up of D/T

"Bread" found on last page of notebook

Boad from evidence used to link Hauptmann to the crime. Note the *d* and *t* in Hauptmann's handwriting, in his notebook. NJSP.

Arthur Koehler with the ladder. The wood expert astounded jurors with his precise conclusions about the wood, and how the ladder was constructed. NJSP.

Detective Lewis Bornmann with the kidnap ladder. Bornmann's discovery in the attic hung the ladder around Hauptmann's neck. NJSP.

Rail 16 placed in Hauptmann attic beside other floorboards. NJSP.

Judge Thomas Trenchard, who presided at the trial, and whose charge to the jury was criticized then and later. NJSP.

Mickey Rosner and his lawyer, Edward Aronow. Rosner was the Lindberghs' contact with the New York underworld in the first days after the kidnapping. Corbis.

Dr. John Condon posing in a store window with replicas of the evidence presented at the trial. NJSP.

Jafsie on stage. Condon's career as witness-in-chief continued into the post-trial era, as he devised a monologue on law and order for audiences on the East Coast. NJSP.

The base from the table with the writing. NJSP.

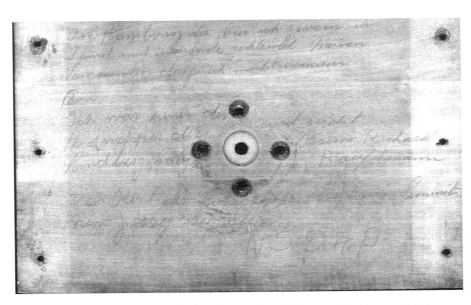

The table found in 1948, with the German inscription on the base containing a confession to the Lindbergh kidnapping. NJSP.

"I never murdered," said Hauptmann firmly.

"That is all," the lawyer concluded.

Wilentz was on his feet. "Didn't you build a ladder and put it up against the Lindbergh house?" said the attorney general, "and didn't you go up that ladder into the house and murder the child?"

"No," he shouted, half rising from his chair. Then he became again the stolid, monosyllabic carpenter. It was his only outburst in five court appearances.[36]

The testimony over, Justice Hammer took a brief recess and then announced his decision. Unlike a regular trial, the extradition hearing placed the burden of proof on Hauptmann to show conclusively that he was not in the state the night the crime was committed. He had failed to do so. Hammer adopted, for purposes of the extradition, Wilentz's argument that the ransom notes did provide evidence—if not a confession—that Hauptmann had been in the baby's room that night. As for Whited's crucial testimony, Justice Hammer noted that it had been weakened by attacks on his credibility, but under the liberal rules of evidence that obtained at such hearings it added weight to the appealing state's claim. Yet, he added, "I do not regard this statement as setting forth a rule of evidence for the guidance of a trial court which later may consider the same evidence." With that final word, Hammer remanded Hauptmann to the custody of New Jersey officials.

Fawcett made a final effort to prevent Hauptmann's extradition to New Jersey, producing two witnesses who, he argued, could prove that the accused had been working a full day at the Majestic Apartments on March 1, 1932. All that could be established, however, was that an employment agency had secured such a position for him, and that he did report for work that morning—only to be told he was not needed that day. David Wilentz brushed aside the witnesses Fawcett presented as of no consequence. The handwriting was enough to convict, he said. He believed that the crime was a "one-man job." New Jersey was no longer seeking any accomplices.[37]

Late Friday afternoon, October 19, 1934, Wilentz arrived at the Bronx County jail to give Sheriff John Hanley the necessary court papers for Hauptmann's transfer to New Jersey authorities. At 8:43 P.M. Hauptmann was ushered out of the jail through a crowd of onlookers to a waiting police car driven by Captain J. J. Lamb. Ten minutes later the car with its motorcycle escort had crossed the George Washington Bridge; and at 10:22 P.M. the small caravan with sirens screaming reached

Flemington, New Jersey. Outside the courthouse ten state troopers formed a corridor to the rear entrance near the jail. "Spectators reached on tip toes and craned their necks, huge flares for the cameramen filled the corridor with smoke and a ghostly white light, and the good natured troopers locked arms to prevent anyone from breaking line."[38]

Hauptmann's car halted momentarily and waited for Wilentz, who had followed in another car, to lead the way into the jail. Shackled between two troopers, the prisoner kept his head lowered as they moved swiftly into the jail. Told he could have anything he wanted to eat, he asked only for black coffee. "In the restless fashion of a caged animal, he paced nervously in his 10-foot cell, which is more modern and commodious than his recent quarters in the Bronx jail. With measured steps, he traced and retraced the length of his compartment, the door of which is always open into a bullpen, facing six empty cells, which is 30 feet long and four feet wide. At the end of each short journey, he would turn quickly around to his left and change the posture of his head as he started again over the same short span."[39]

That first Sunday afternoon of his New Jersey imprisonment, October 21, local officials counted cars passing the Soldier's Monument near the courthouse at a rate of 836 per hour. Inside the jail, Sheriff John N. Curtiss and Warden Harry O. McCrea had already taken turns before Paramount, Universal, and Hearst Metrotone newsreel cameras. The two were especially proud of a special cage they had designed to hold Mrs. Hauptmann when she visited her husband. Built by a local Flemington man who had just finished Governor Moore's summer lodge nearby, it was two feet square and six feet tall, enclosed on three sides and across the top with fine mesh screening. A projection at the top prevented the cage from being pushed closer than one foot to the bars. Hauptmann had been separated from all but verbal communication with Anna.[40]

On Wednesday morning Hauptmann was led into the courtroom itself to stand in front of Judge Thomas W. Trenchard to answer the indictment. "I plead not guilty," he responded in clear tones with only a slight trace of an accent. The attorney general suggested they begin the trial on November 14, but defense attorney Fawcett protested he could not be ready for another month after that. It would be distasteful to begin then, said Wilentz, so near the Christmas holidays. Very well, replied Trenchard, the trial would start on January 2, 1935, "at 10 o'clock in the forenoon in this courtroom."[41]

With that, the proceedings were over. Richard swung around in his swivel chair at the defense table, smiled faintly at Anna sitting nearby, and said in a low voice, "I'll see you later."

A surprise awaited Hauptmann back in his cell. There was Jafsie, eager to talk to him.

Condon had been troubled by his failure to identify Hauptmann that first night in the Greenwich Street station. On October 5, he had told Agent Turrou that he hoped it could be arranged for him to see Hauptmann privately for about half an hour. That would "dispense all remaining doubt in his mind." "Dr. Condon pointed out that he is considerably aggrieved over the fact that he failed to identify Hauptmann." It was all the police's fault, he said, and he would prefer to work through the FBI.

But he added something David Wilentz did not wish to hear at this stage—or at any stage of the trial. "Dr. Condon further advised . . . that he studied the photograph of Isidore [*sic*] Fisch which appeared in the newspapers and that it is his belief now that when on March 12, 1932, he went to meet 'John' at the Woodlawn Cemetery he saw a party strongly resembling the features and description of Isidore [*sic*] Fisch pass the car in which he and Al Reich were sitting."[42]

Turrou relayed Condon's request to Wilentz. The attorney general was happy to use this opportunity to bring home to John Condon a full realization of the stakes involved, and the role he had to play if justice was to be done at the forthcoming murder trial. So on Tuesday October 23, two New Jersey state troopers picked him up at his Bronx home, along with Gregory Coleman, his amanuensis from the *Bronx Home News,* and delivered them to the attorney general's home in Perth Amboy, "for the purpose of going over Dr. Condon's activities in regards to the Lindbergh case."[43]

In Condon's account of the meeting, the conversation opened with Wilentz saying, "I'm glad to see you, Doctor Condon. Frankly, we're somewhat puzzled concerning your status as a possible witness." Did he or did he not say he had identified Hauptmann?

"I did not say that I identified him"

Wilentz's face dropped, wrote Condon, and he said, "Well, that's that."

But wait a minute; this was John Condon, master of the art of perplexity: "Nor did I say I did *not* identify him."

"I don't follow you."

This allowed the old pedagogue to spin out his sticky rationale for withholding a "declaration" of identification until the proper time and place—the trial.

"Wilentz nodded," wrote Jafsie. "Serious of face, he had been following closely my words, my reasoning. He extended his hand. 'Doctor,' he told me, 'I don't have to tell you the value of the service you have rendered the State. I see your view of it, and it is a very just view. You have my word of honor that I shall hold in strictest confidence what we have discussed here.'"[44]

How much of this dialogue ever happened that way, in those words? Perhaps only Wilentz's opening and closing statements. In between, where Condon talks about fair play and the difference between an identification and declaring an identification, the attorney general would have brought him up short with some down-home talk about real differences, those between indictments and convictions. Any shadow of a doubt about the identification would allow the defense to sneak accomplices in through the crack and ruin the case. Condon must be firm. He considered Colonel Lindbergh a great hero, didn't he? And he was honored to be associated with him, through these tragic circumstances, wasn't he? He did not ever want to lose the world's most famous aviator's respect, did he? Well, now, the colonel had identified Hauptmann's voice; if Condon failed on the witness stand, justice would be denied, and the colonel and Mrs. Lindbergh left distraught. It was fine with Wilentz if Condon wanted to keep his "secret," for the time being—in fact it was useful—the old codger would have his shining hour, just so long as it didn't cast a shadow over the state's case. Whether Wilentz used those words, or some other expression, he certainly would have made the point that Condon could not go on and on playing the game as he had that first night in the Greenwich Street police station, and practically every day since.

Troopers took Condon and Coleman home that night and came back the next day to escort them to Flemington to see Hauptmann. Wilentz would be there along with Hunterdon County prosecutor Anthony Hauck to get a quick report.

The scene inside the Flemington jail—like every other stage Condon played on—had aspects of the surreal and moments of bathos. The state police record made by Trooper Hugo Stockburger is only two pages long and no doubt records the things most important to Wilentz out of an hour's conversation. Nevertheless, it is the most contemporaneous. In it, Condon begins, "You have seen me before?"

"I saw you once, this is the second time."

"What is your name, what does your mother call you?"

"Richard."

Allowed to sit with Hauptmann on a bench outside his cell, Condon jotted down some words on a piece of paper. "Do you remember these two words I wrote in German letters, they made trouble for me. The New York Police called me wacky and screwy, do you know what that means.

I have never found it in the dictionary." Where this was all leading is impossible to say, but it suggests an effort at a coded message. Condon rambled on about the night he met him in the park, continuing to scribble words as he talked about four stages of the negotiations. They had agreed to use "John" as an identification, he said, almost as if instructing Hauptmann on his lines for the trial.

On he went with a soliloquy about how he got involved. "I told him," Condon said of his first conversation with Lindbergh, "if it was his brother I wouldn't do it but for the baby I tried to get the baby back." Then this plea: "I am not afraid of the police or anyone, although the whole world is against me. Fingers are pointed at me, there he goes he passed the ransom money. I am not one of the ordinary crowd, I am an educated man and was a professor in college."

Condon then offered an odd "apology," that may well have led Hauptmann to believe he would not testify against him. "John, I don't mean to call you John, I went to Canada when there was 20 inches of snow, to the swamps of Mexico and to Los Angeles. I have spent my money. If you tell the truth I will help you and I am not going to ask anyone for help. I have suffered a lot, my wife is crying every day."[45]

To anyone within hearing distance, this fustian tale of a truth seeker braving challenges almost beyond human capacity must have seemed astonishing—and deadly threatening to the case if uttered on the witness stand.

Whatever the old man hoped to accomplish, in the guise of either teacher or priest, Hauptman's only answer was that he had nothing to do with the Lindbergh crime. "If I know anything about it I would tell for the sake of my wife and baby."

Condon persisted in his effort to bring Hauptmann to the confessional: "John, is there anyone higher?"

"What do you mean, higher?"

Higher, it turned out, meant Al Capone, not God. "Did you ever hear of him?" *Al Capone?* What was Condon doing reintroducing Al Capone at this stage?

Hauptmann replied he didn't know gangsters, and, curiously, "if I had something to do with it I wouldn't be here today." He would not be awaiting a murder trial, in other words, because he would have told about all the others who were involved.

The conversation then turned to the money found in the garage and, finally, Condon's address and phone number in the closet. How did it get there?

"That's what I always do," Hauptmann replied. "I was following up the case like everybody and wrote the [phone] number on the board."[46]

Hauptmann had reversed himself yet again. This was the explanation he had blurted out during his arrest and then denied at the extradition. Only the bank note numbers were in his writing, he testified there. Now he was back to the first explanation.

He must have told Anna about his slip, because the next day when she came to visit him in his cell he was a bit sheepish about the exchange: "I did not talk much to this man."

"You must have talked considerably as he was here over an hour."

"I did not tell this man anything that I had not said before."

A little later, Anna came back to the closet writing: "You have this habit of marking telephone numbers and things on the wall."

"Yes. I do those things without thinking."[47]

Condon, ironically, never believed this and never understood how his phone number got on that closet board.

Jafsie's account of the Flemington jail encounter was filled with mawkish admonitions. Hauptmann should think of his friends in Germany, his wife and baby, and, most of all, his mother. "Her heart would hold more peace if that son would speak, would tell the truth—even though the truth might be ugly. Do you want her to go on suffering, Richard; wondering what her boy has done and why he has done it? It would be far better, for her sake, to speak. Now. "[48]

At one point, according to Condon, Hauptmann said, "I will tell you the truth. But tell me first, do you want to see me burn?" Here was a strange reprise or postscript to Cemetery John's question at the Woodlawn Cemetery—"Would I burn if the baby is dead?" It startles the reader because nothing like it can be found in the trooper's minutes of the conversation.

Condon would insist that his pleas brought tears to this lonely man, "a beaten shell of his former self; his ego a smashed, bleeding thing." Peace and happiness were near, if Hauptmann would but reach out and seize them. Silence followed. "I took a handkerchief from my pocket reached forward and brushed from his face a tear that clung there."

Thus the prisoner assumed a penitent's pose before God, Condon related, placing both clenched fists against his breast. He spoke softly: "I am glad you came to talk with me. You have lifted a great weight from me, here."[49]

There is only one sentence in the trooper's record that even resembles this exchange. It is Hauptmann's response to a Condon question about whether he was glad to see him. Yes, came the reply, it felt good to talk to someone. (None of the guards were allowed to talk to the prisoner. Moreover, lights were kept on in his cell day and night, and there were constant searches—as many as twenty-five to thirty a day.)

"It's about time for you to leave, Doctor." It was a jailer rattling the cell door, Condon wrote. He broke the spell. Hauptmann had been so close to confessing. He would have succeeded, he asserted, were it not for some ignorant bumpkin. But the confession Condon wanted would not have been welcome to New Jersey authorities. If Hauptmann had "talked," giving names and particulars of accomplices who had received shares of the ransom money, it would have played havoc with the case they were developing.

"Well," the impatient attorney general demanded when they returned to his office from the jail, "is he the man in the cemetery?"

"I'm still not ready to declare my identification," answered Condon. "I will do that at the trial."

"You'll do that right here and now!"

"A man's life is at stake."

"What are you afraid of, Doctor—Hauptmann's accomplices? There aren't any, but if there were, we'd protect you."

"I am not afraid, I just want to be sure. We're dealing with a man's life."

Wilentz jumped to his feet. "I have a mind to toss you in jail. Get him out of here."[50]

Statements made to the press bolster this account. The attorney general first explained to reporters that Jafsie's visit was merely part of a "general round-up of all witnesses," and he would not reveal what had transpired beyond the comment that the conversation had concerned only notes exchanged with the kidnapper prior to the ransom payment. A day later, however, Wilentz told reporters he was bound by an agreement not to say what the result had been. "I can say this—from the general tone around the Attorney General's office and the State Police headquarters you ought to be able to surmise."[51]

In a ghostwritten autobiography produced largely to stir sympathies during the post-trial appeal process, Hauptmann claimed that during the conversation Condon jumped up and shouted to Wilentz, "I will not testify against this man." The old man had to be quieted down, wrote Hauptmann, and from that point forward his conversation did not make any sense. The interview left everyone in a state of confusion. A visitor to the prison cell, Harry C. Whitney—whose actual status in the case was never completely determined—came away to tell reporters that although Hauptmann said that Condon had made the identification, he was sure that if they were able to meet again, the old man would see that he was "not the man he gave the money to."

Fawcett immediately denied his client had said any such thing, and sent an associate to Flemington to encourage Hauptmann to repudiate any such statement. "No," Hauptmann told this man, Condon had not said he recognized him. Instead, he explained, "[Condon told me] the police ha[d] been bothering him a great deal and had cast their suspicions on him and that he would like to straighten out the entire case, and he asked me if I could throw any light on the situation."[52]

Anna worried not only about what her husband had told Condon, but also about what he was saying to the lawyers. "I would not trust him too much," she said of Condon. "I have heard a lot about him from our friends." One of the troopers who recorded this conversation noted that Hauptmann had said, "[Condon] made a very good impression on me." Reporters had asked her, she said, what was going on with Condon. "There is something fishy about this," she told Richard. Hauptmann then gave more details about the conversation, especially how he denied he had ever met with the Lindbergh mediator on a bench near Woodlawn Cemetery. "He called me John several times." And then he remembered something else. Condon had said that the newspapers were reporting that he had sold a boat to Hauptmann. "That's ridiculous," scoffed Anna, "you shouldn't talk to anyone except your lawyer and he has told you so many times."[53]

Anna's conversation, abbreviated in the trooper's notes, offers several intriguing hints about what actually took place. Why did she say, "I would not trust him too much," or, "There is something fishy about this," if Condon had not at least implied he *would not* testify against Richard? And again, the hint that Condon and Hauptmann had known each other in another context was dangerous territory for everyone.

A few days later a New York policeman came to see Hauptmann about names in his notebooks, and he had helped him out with proper spelling. "He is going to interview all the people mentioned in that note book. That's all right, I have no enemies except one, Condon."[54]

A week after the interview Condon had still failed to say publicly whether he would identify Hauptmann or not. Was Condon now his "enemy" as a result of the visit, or was there a prior relationship between the two that had been altered by that visit? It is conceivable that the trooper who recorded the exchange substituted *enemy* for another word. Still, there are other possibilities. If Hauptmann knew he was not Cemetery John, Condon's silence had made him an enemy. If Condon knew him as an accomplice, his silence was a betrayal.[55]

Hauptmann had slipped badly when he failed to deny that the writing on the closet door was his—put there for the feeblest reason one could imagine. It was hard to believe that he had followed the case closely for any other reason than to be in contact with Jafsie to set up a rendezvous for ransom negotiations. He need not have answered the question at all or could simply have repeated what he had testified in open court, that only the bank note numbers were in his hand.

But Condon could not accept that explanation: "The ransom money in the cans, the ransom money in the holes in the joist, the revolver in the plank! All of these things, found months later at the kidnap[p]er's place, I can understand. But to this day I cannot bring myself to accept the written telephone number and address in the kidnap[p]er's closet, despite the fact that he, himself, admitted that he wrote them there."[56]

Condon's question to Hauptmann about the closet writing, and his response to the answer, is close to the heart of the matter. He explains in *Jafsie Tells All* that some newspapers accused him of an intimate relationship with Hauptmann because his private phone number was on the accused man's closet door. But that was not so. It was the published number that was there. Condon's question, nevertheless, could also be read as an accusation to the man awaiting trial that he had involved him in the crime. Suppose for a moment that Condon's involvement was a bit more complicated than he had ever admitted to anyone. Inspector Harry Walsh, for example, had repeatedly questioned Condon's vow to be fair to Cemetery John if the child were safely returned to its mother's arms.

Throughout *Jafsie Tells All* Condon returns again and again to the unsolved mysteries of the case. "How much of Hauptmann's stories to me of a gang," he asks, "of accomplices—was true, how much false?" When did Hauptmann—not Cemetery John—ever tell him anything about accomplices? While this could be nothing more than a ghostwriter's error, it is perhaps instead a Freudian slip.[57]

While Wilentz pondered what he might expect to hear from Condon when he finally got him on the witness stand, Anna discharged James Fawcett as her husband's attorney and hired in his place Edward J. Reilly. ("He's out," Reilly told reporters. "I'm in.") Apparently, the episode of the conflicting statements about what Richard had said to Condon was the final straw. Anna came into the Flemington jail flushed with what she thought was good news: "Do you remember a case in New York where a woman smuggled a gun into the jail to her husband and he tried to shoot his way out of jail and killed a guard and someone else? The lawyer who defended the woman in that case is the one we turned the case over to yesterday." He had won that case. If he could win that one, where the evidence was overwhelming against the defendant, he could best a young attorney general who had never tried a murder case.

"What did Fawcett say about it?" questioned Richard.

"I saw Mr. Fawcett yesterday and told him about it and he said Mrs. Hauptmann I done my best and I told him that his best wasn't good enough. The other lawyer told me that you should have never come over to Jersey."[58]

They talked again the next day about the change, with Anna continuing to try to bolster both their spirits. "You know," Anna said, "the Attorney General Wilentz is so angry because we changed lawyers."

"I should think he would be, Fawcett was too friendly towards Wilentz. I thought that right along."[59]

Reilly, now in his early fifties, had defended more than two thousand important cases in his career. "His flair for the sensational and dramatic," the *New York Times* reported, "has become a tradition." Known as the "Bull of Brooklyn" because of his courtroom style, and, more recently, as "Death House Reilly," the lawyer had been offered to Anna as part of a deal by representatives of William Randolph Hearst. If she would agree to give exclusive interviews throughout the trial to Hearst columnist Adela Rogers St. John, the attorney's fees would be covered. Hearst never expected—or wished for—Reilly to win the case. "In this trial," he instructed St. John, "I am sure we can produce a flame of nationwide indignation that will deter other criminals."[60]

Actually, Anna had little choice. The Hearst offer helped to make it possible for her to move with Manfred to Flemington, so as to be close to Richard during the trial. She had made critical miscalculations at the beginning—perhaps most grievously when she left the house to live with her niece, Maria Mueller, only a day or so after the arrest. She even asked permission from the police before she did so. The police had no objections at all. Permission was readily granted, and Detective Bornmann leased the apartment days later. He became the gatekeeper and kept everyone out, FBI as well as defense lawyers.

If money were no object, Richard and Anna would have picked the most famous criminal lawyer of them all, Clarence Darrow. Anna read an article about Darrow's recent press statements while he was visiting in Atlantic City. New Jersey had a very weak case against Hauptmann, he said—at least for murder. "I haven't seen anything there is to indicate murder, have you? Just the fact that Hauptmann had the money on him," the aging master of courtroom oratory went on, "doesn't prove that he had anything to do with the murder. It . . . was a good basis for extortion, but I don't see anything else there."[61]

Reading this, Anna apparently wondered if Darrow would come to Flemington. So did Richard. "How about that criminal lawyer from Chicago you were telling me about the other day?"

"I only read an article in the newspaper," she replied.

"I wonder if we could get him to sit in on the trial," Richard persisted.

Anna changed the subject—her way of discouraging false hopes. They had no resources to hire Darrow, even for a day. Besides that, Lloyd Fisher, Reilly's nominal associate on the defense team, had quietly interviewed Darrow and concluded he was no longer up to the strain.[62]

Anna steered her conversations with Richard to supposed signs the New Jersey case would finally collapse. She had received a letter from a woman, she told her husband, which demonstrated that the handwriting expert Osborn was not reliable. This woman had employed the expert to identify her husband's handwriting in a divorce trial, and he had failed. She had even sent a newspaper clipping along to help.[63]

Meanwhile, there were newspaper stories about the discovery of evidence that would definitely tie Hauptmann to the kidnap ladder.

10 VISIONS OF A LADDER

> When the love of truth and the desire for justice combine in the slow uncovering of a deep mystery, you have a masterpiece out of real life surpassing the best that fiction can do.
> —*New York Times* editorial, January 25, 1935

Arthur Koehler had every reason to feel good about his work. After all, he had traced pieces of the ladder to a Bronx lumberyard a year before Bruno Richard Hauptmann's arrest. Now if the police could find him the missing pieces of the puzzle, he would do the rest. "Congratulations on success so far," he wrote to Captain J. J. Lamb. Concentrate your efforts now on rail 16. "That is the one that has the cut nail holes in it and has both edges dressed by a hand plane as if cut down from a wider board." It "may have been taken from a local structure accessible to the maker of the ladder, possibly because something may have gone wrong with a piece of 1 × 4 that originally had been secured for the purpose."[1]

Koehler's letter sent Detective Lewis Bornmann to Hauptmann's attic to find wood that matched rail 16, with results that far exceeded anything Attorney General David Wilentz could possibly have hoped for when he began assembling his case.

There was never any question of who should carry out the assignment of searching for wood that matched rail 16. The obvious choice was Lewis Bornmann—Koehler's "Siamese twin" in the previous search.

At 9 A.M. on September 26, 1934, Bornmann said he and Bronx detective Maurice Tobin, along with two police carpenters, squeezed their way into the attic and made a "thorough search." This "first" report ends, however, in anticlimactic fashion.

Nothing of value was found with the exception of several small pieces of wood and shavings and several cut nails that may possibly have a bearing on the case. These were retained . . . and later turned over to Arthur Koehler, wood technologist of the U.S. Forest Products Laboratory who is now at the Training School, West Trenton, for comparison with the wood and cut nail holes in the ladder used in kidnapping the Lindbergh baby.[2]

"Nothing of value was found"—seemingly a clear statement. Bornmann filed two other reports covering the events of that day; all three reports were backdated—a not uncommon practice in the midst of an intensive investigation. But in this instance the discrepancies in the reports leap out at the reader. The "first" report cited above, for example, could not have been written on September 26, 1934, because Koehler was not in Trenton, but at home in Madison, Wisconsin, on that date.

The backdating of reports makes it hard to determine when Arthur Koehler first saw the "pieces of wood" Bornmann supposedly found on September 26. He did not arrive in Trenton until September 28, so it could not have been earlier—but how much later was it? If nothing of value was found after a "thorough search," something prompted Bornmann to return to the attic—perhaps several times, and perhaps alone—and to submit additional reports covering the same search the same day. It may have been that a phone conversation with Trenton jogged his memory about cut nail holes in rail 16. But whatever sent him back, his second report disclosed a major discovery.

In the second "special report" Bornmann does not explain when he entered the attic, and merely asserts that while searching for evidence he noticed the last board on the far side of the unfinished flooring in the attic was not the same length as the others. The floor consisted of twenty-seven one-by-six-inch pieces of North Carolina pine tongue-and-groove roofing, approximately twenty feet, one-half inch long, running east to west, and nailed to the joists with cut nails.

Originally, that is, there were twenty-seven boards that length. But someone had apparently removed an eight-foot length from the last board. He could see the nail holes in the joists where it had been taken up, he said, as well as a small quantity of sawdust between the joists, and a mark on the next board where the saw had cut into it slightly.

Bracing himself in a squatting position, Bornmann stated, he used his bare hands to pull up the remaining length of the board from the joists, even though fourteen face nails secured it. Why he thought to handle potentially crucial evidence in such a crude fashion, and especially with two carpenters standing by, has never been explained.

Not surprisingly, it broke off at a knot about two feet from the end. After this damage was done, he finally ordered the carpenters "to remove the cut nails which had been used to fasten this board to the joist, these to be turned over to Mr. Arthur Koehler for comparison with the nail holes on rail #16 of the ladder."[3]

"I . . . removed a section about 9 foot long from this particular board," Bornmann explained, "and being familiar with the various kinds of wood used in the construction of the ladder and as the flooring appeared to be of the same type wood as one of the rails in the ladder, this particular section was removed to be turned over to Arthur Koehler, Wood Technologist, who is now at the Training School, for a more thorough examination."

What if Bornmann's first trip to the attic had not been on September 26, but a day or so earlier? In that case, the sequence of reports makes better sense—at least chronologically. Bornmann would have delivered the loose nails to Captain Lamb, who fitted them into rail 16 and ordered him back to the attic the first thing the next day. But is it not equally possible that the discovery of this board came several days *after* September 26? The carpenters who accompanied him that day remembered the date. But the detective may have made many unreported trips to the attic as well—for several days running. Having rented the apartment from the Rauches after Anna left, he controlled all the comings and goings. Defense attorneys for Hauptmann were never allowed access to the attic until well after the trial was over.

Bornmann proved extremely reticent about admitting he had gone into the attic looking for wood. At the trial, he would say simply he was looking for "evidence." Asked why he had taken the carpenters up into those narrow confines, he would protest, "not for boards. We were looking for money." Yet the search ended abruptly after only one board out of twenty-seven had been removed.[4]

It was a logical idea to look for money, certainly, as there was plenty of space under the attic floorboards and elsewhere. A person could hide many things from the prying eyes of a landlord or nosy neighbors. But the crack detective, who discovered so many other crucial pieces of evidence, does not tell us about removing any other boards at all. That is why Bornmann also insisted at the trial he was the first person to visit the attic—to make the story plausible.

Finally, however, in a 1983 interview, Bornmann admitted outright that looking for wood to match the ladder rail was his primary "objective" in going into the attic, even if he still did not admit it was a directed search. He said he knew what kind of wood to look for from his previous searches with Koehler. Here was a whole attic full of it. In other words, it *was* a directed search, and that was why he was so reluctant to talk about it at the time.[5]

Unaware of Bornmann's great discovery, Agent T. H. Sisk thought the ladder was the weakest link in the prosecution case for a one-man job. There must have been others involved, he told Attorney General Homer Cummings. The ladder was too short—as it was put up against the wall—for one person to have handled the task of getting in and out of the window. Besides, Hauptmann weighed too much at the time of the kidnapping. Then there were the two lookouts giving signals at each of the cemeteries. These were logical conclusions, Cummings agreed, but not conclusive.

While all the ripping and pounding went on, Bornmann kept the FBI out of the attic along with everybody else. J. Edgar Hoover pointed this out in a 1936 letter to New Jersey Governor Harold Hoffman. In the early searches of Hauptmann's residence, he wrote, it was ascertained that a board was missing from the floor of the attic: "No representative of this Bureau was, however, present in the attic of the Hauptmann residence when, on September 26, the segments of the ladder used in the kidnap[p]ing were compared with the boards in the attic floor."[6] His agents had complained about being excluded from the attic that day—and were skeptical about Bornmann's keen powers of observation. Police had scoured the apartment looking for the origins of rail 16 without any luck, they wrote, including nine searches of the attic. (Bornmann denied that other police investigators had searched the attic before he had.) Yet the discovery had not been made until after the FBI had been denied access to the apartment.[7]

No tests of any kind were made while the board was still in place. We do not even know exactly how long the section was that Bornmann removed. The carpenters squared off the end where it broke at the knot; then days later, after he had supposedly taken it down to a closet on the second floor of the house, it was cut down again to less than seven feet in order to fit into a car for transport to Trenton. There were trucks and other vehicles that could handle such a length, but Bornmann apparently wanted to see if it could fit inside Hauptmann's car—and that took precedence over evidence preservation. Why was it even necessary to see if it could fit—when sliced up—into his car if the identification would depend upon nail holes and wood grain pattern?

Bornmann's behavior is dumfounding if taken at face value. There were now three pieces of the board later called State's Exhibit 226 (S-226) at Hauptmann's trial. The largest piece, approximately nine feet in length, had been removed and cut into two pieces, leaving on the attic joists a rump section of indeterminate length between two and three feet. What finally happened to this piece no one seemed to know—or care about. Bornmann told Governor Hoffman in March 1936 that the landlord, Max Rauch, had claimed the piece left behind in the attic— plus all the other remaining twenty-six boards—as souvenirs for friends. "After the trial I had nothing more to do with the case, and as far as I knew they were still there then."[8]

Arthur Koehler, meanwhile, had arrived in New Jersey on September 28, 1934. State police authorities gave him a big buildup, reminding everyone that the expert had discovered that the National Lumber and Millwork Company in the Bronx—where Hauptmann had worked and purchased lumber—was the "unquestionable source" of some of the wood in the ladder. Prior to Hauptmann's arrest, of course, Koehler had never been quite so absolute in his judgments about the only two rails he identified. "It might be possible," he had written in one of his earlier reports, that "the lumber used in the ladder went to the Queens County Lumber Company, Ozone Park, L.I., although it is not very probable." And even the pieces from the National Lumber Company were not an exact match. At the time he wrote those words, it will be remembered, the prime suspect he had in mind was John Condon, who also lived in the Bronx not far from the National Lumber and Millwork Company, but who also had varied business interests in other parts of the metropolitan area.

What was his new assignment? reporters asked. He was in New Jersey to do what Colonel Schwarzkopf instructed him to do. "Since Mr. Koehler is regarded by the police as a vital witness for the State in the contemplated prosecution of Hauptmann on kidnapping and murder charges, he has been requested to remain at the Wilburtha Barracks, where a laboratory will be fitted up for him [by the New Jersey State Police], and not to discuss the case unless Colonel Schwarzkopf or the latter's deputy, Major Charles H. Schoeffel, is present."[9]

"After posing for three different moving picture outfits," Koehler dismissed the reporters and set to work examining wood planes and other tools brought from Hauptmann's garage.

There was no question, he concluded, but that rail 16 and two of the rungs of the ladder had been planed with Hauptmann's largest plane, which had a blade two and a half inches wide. The marks it made were exactly like those on the ladder. "It had not been sharpened or dulled further since then." He found it just mildly curious, however, that Hauptmann had used his largest plane, "when the next smaller one might have done just as well." This led him to ponder whether the notching of the rails and cutting the rungs to proper length might have been carried out elsewhere, at some "secluded spot" away from his neighborhood. That would explain why hand plane marks on the side of the ladder did not match with plane marks other places on the edges, "or with any made by Hauptmann's planes."

"Did Hauptmann take a smaller plane along," Koehler asked himself, "which was later resharpened, or did someone else furnish the plane?" Dangerous speculations these, and certainly not for public exposure. They suggested unknown accomplices and, therefore, hidden menaces for the prosecution's murder case.[10]

Any time the evidence went wandering outside Hauptmann's house or garage was cause for worry. The original examination of the ladder had revealed soil deposits not present under the nursery window. Koehler looked at soil around Hauptmann's garage—but nothing was said about this search at the trial. By that time, all these little questionings had been stuffed down a memory hole.

Koehler had apparently forgotten something he had written in his March 1933 report about plane marks on wood. At that time he had contended that rail 16 and the rungs of the ladder had to have been made at approximately the same time, "since a plane would hardly show the same pattern due to the dullness for a number of years." Now he was contending otherwise, that his tests of the dull plane found in Hauptmann's garage two years later proved "without question" that it was the one used on rail 16 and the rungs.[11]

Some time between October 1 and 4, 1934, Koehler examined the small pieces of wood and package of cut nails that Bornmann had collected from the garage and the attic. "The cut nails taken from the attic and garage fit the holes in rail #16 exactly, which indicates that the board probably was removed from some of Hauptmann's previous work either for others or for himself." But there is no mention in this report that he had seen or heard of any board taken out of the attic, whether still in Hauptmann's closet or now in Trenton.[12]

Captain Lamb must have known about it, but there was apparently a reason for not telling Koehler yet. Perhaps Lamb and Bornmann were waiting for a final confirmation that the nails matched rail 16, which Koehler did not supply until almost a week later, on October 8, 1934, the day the New Jersey grand jury handed down its indictment. When the wood expert advised Lamb the nails fit, the captain ordered Bornmann to take Koehler to the Hauptmann attic to put rail 16 down over the joists, and see if it matched up against the longer board supposedly still stored, according to Bornmann, in the closet at the apartment.

Climbing up to the attic the next day with Bornmann, Koehler first measured the holes in the joists to see if they matched the locations in rail 16. They did. Bornmann said he then went to the closet and proceeded to cut down the partial floorboard he had previously removed on September 26 to six-feet, eight and a half inches—the length of each of the ladder rails—to enable it to be taken in a car to Trenton. That, at any rate, was Bornmann's account of the day's events.[13]

Koehler's reports of events in the attic varies considerably from Bornmann's. In his account, the two arrived at the Bronx address and spent time, first, looking around the garage in search of lumber with hand plane marks matching those on the ladder. "We then climbed up the narrow closet in the hall to the attic and looked around for lumber or marks like those on the ladder." Finally, they went over to the far edge, where all of the last board was now supposedly missing, including the two- or three-foot piece where Bornmann's board had broken off. Koehler's report stated, however, that the board the detective removed from the attic had not been in the closet all this time after all! "This piece had been taken up by Detective Bornmann (except for a short end by the East wall which broke off) and taken to Troop "C" Headquarters for comparison with rail 16 because both have cut nail holes in them. The cut nails taken from the board in the attic fitted exactly into the holes in rail #16."

So the board had been in Trenton, already cut down to auto size. But had Koehler not seen it there?

> On this day we took back the piece taken up in the attic and replaced it, driving the cut nails partly back into their original positions. At that end of this board which was near the middle of the attic there was sawdust on the lath and plaster below; and in direct line with the end there was a short saw cut in the adjacent board. Both of these facts indicated that a piece had been cut off from the board right there in the attic. Furthermore the joists beyond the end of this board had cut nail holes in them from which the nails had been removed, all of which indicated that part of the board had been removed at some previous date.

> I had in my pocket note book measurements of the distances between the four nail holes in rail #16, and Detective Bornmann and I compared those distances with distances between nail holes in the joists and found that four of those in the joists corresponded exactly with those in the rail.[14]

Bornmann and Koehler cannot both be right about the sequence of events, nor about the location of the attic board on October 9, 1934. One thing is clear, however: both reports indicate that rail 16 was not taken to the attic until the day *after* Koehler "verified," according to Bornmann, that it had been removed from the attic. The first identification, then, was made without a close look at rail 16 in place abutting S-226.

On October 10, the pair returned to the attic with rail 16. All that remained, as Koehler explains, was to put it down across the joists: "By taking cut nails out of the portion of the board, which had previously been taken up by Detective Bornmann, and placing them in the holes in rail #16 and tapping them lightly with a hammer all four could be driven through into corresponding holes in the joists. The nails were not driven in completely but far enough to make sure that the distance and slant of the nails coincided exactly in the rail and joists."[15]

When they finished, one of the police carpenters took pliers and pulled the nails out once more, "which showed that they came out easily and therefore had been driven into preexisting holes."

Koehler's expertise, as he would explain at the trial, was in identifying wood samples. The preliminary attic IDs had to do with the placement of holes and the easy fit of nails. When the boards were in place— so that the nails fit into the joists—a gap of one and fifteen-sixteenths inch remained. "That much evidently had been cut off in squaring off the end of the rail. A piece two feet long must have been cut off the end of the other end. We looked for the pieces but could not find them in the attic."[16]

It must have occurred to Koehler by this time that the ladder builder had made things difficult for himself with this board. He went to this trouble, Koehler finally concluded, only as a semidesperate measure. When he manipulated the board down through the closet and out to the garage, Hauptmann left no evidence behind except the small pile of sawdust and the mark on the next piece of flooring where the saw cut was made. That was unusual, certainly. Then he cut off both ends to make his ladder rail, ripped the board lengthwise on both sides, planed it down, and carefully cut out the notches for the rungs—rather than find a more suitable board someplace else. It would have been quicker to buy a board closer to the size he needed. But maybe he did not want to be seen buying a board on the day of the kidnapping?

He had put himself to a lot of extra work, moreover, on a ladder rail that he did not need, as rail 16 was the top left side of the section never used. If Millard Whited was to be believed, Hauptmann had been roaming all around Highfields on several occasions in the weeks before the

230 THE CASE THAT NEVER DIES

kidnapping, and presumably knew how high a ladder he required. Of course, rail 16 may not have been a last-minute addition. That would explain everything except the primary question one started with: why he went into the attic to find a board.[17]

In the days following the attic experiments, Koehler went to work to match up the two pieces of wood. At first the grain gave him trouble, as the two sides did not seem to match up "clearly from one piece to the other because of the presence of a knot in the end of the piece of flooring which distorts the grain, and the piece 1-5/16″ wide which is missing between the two." But the growth rings on the ends had the same curvature and width. "Since it can be said that no two pieces of wood are the same, it is evident these two came from the same piece." Planer marks on the flooring and the rail, moreover, were of the same width.

Did Bornmann somehow, either alone or in collusion with others, contrive to fake the rail 16 evidence? Anthony Scaduto and Ludovic Kennedy have presented extensive arguments that he did, while other writers, such as Jim Fisher, have denied the possibility. Police throw-down evidence of all sorts (especially in this period) occurs far too often not to want to examine all possibilities. Once the money was found in Hauptmann's possession, both the inclination and pressure to produce other evidence was all but overwhelming. One remembers how the money discovery seemed to have influenced the Osborns, for example.[18]

Could such a clever piece of fabrication have been carried out in ten days—or even ten years? Photographs and evidence from the original examinations can be used to show the grain patterns match, and the nail holes match those in the joists. Where could anyone—even those far more skilled in wood uses than Bornmann—have located such a board? A tongue-and-groove board would have to be found somewhere, which had the same grain pattern and the same ring growth, taken to the attic, and nailed into the joists.

This would seem to be a "Mission Impossible" assignment.

It is fair to conclude, however, that here is an instance where logic and physical evidence are at odds. To select a board from his own attic to complete an unneeded section of the ladder, or to select a board so difficult to use for any purpose, seems unreasonable behavior. But, then, kidnapping one of the most famous children in the United States hardly bespeaks a "reasonable" frame of mind or someone averse to taking great risks. A mix of arrogance and stupidity might explain it. At the same time, how do we account for Bornmann's behavior in managing the attic searches? He went up there expecting to find a board to match rail 16. The story about the search for more ransom money was hooey. Finally, there was the delay in revealing this startling discovery to Koehler.

Speculating about the attic board has kept many researchers up late at night. But numerous things seemed to fall in place once Bornmann made his discovery.

The most important new finding had to do with the chisel. Whereas in 1933 Koehler noted that he could not identify what size chisel had made the notches for the rungs, he now insisted he could identify a chisel mark on—*of all the rails*—rail 16!

After careful reexamination of each recess, he found one, the second from the bottom, had been made with a three-quarter-inch chisel—the same size as the one left behind with the ladder some seventy-five feet away from the house, and the same size as one of those not found in Hauptmann's toolbox. He could not really say "missing"—as in taken away—because no one-inch chisel was found there either. By December, however, in pretrial reviews of the ladder evidence he was about to give, this single chisel mark had multiplied into an opinion that a three-quarter-inch tool had carved out *all* the recesses.[19]

Obviously, he could not say at the trial that only one recess had been made with such a chisel. That would sound ridiculous. The immediate question would be why had the ladder builder used his chisel only once—on the unneeded rail—then brought that precise tool down with him to give police a clue? But between them, Attorney General Wilentz and Koehler neatly finessed the problem.

> Q: What sized chisel was used in the construction of this ladder, if you know?
> A: A three-quarter inch chisel was used in chiseling out recesses for the rungs.

He saved himself from perjury here by saying "used" instead of "exclusively used." If he had concluded one recess had been made with a three-quarter-inch chisel, he apparently could sleep nights on a conclusion that all of them were.

The attorney general and his witness had teamed up in a performance worthy of Blackstone the Magician—the most famous conjurer of the day. Calling for Hauptmann's toolbox, the attorney general pretended as if they had never even peeked in there before that very moment.

> Mr. Wilentz: Will somebody open this chest for me?
> Q: Do you know what sizes of chisels make up a carpenter's chest of chisels?
> A: As a rule a good carpenter's tool chest should contain a quarter inch chisel, half inch chisel, three-quarter inch

chisel, one inch, and one and a half, and possibly two inch chisel. . . .

Q: Tell us what size chisels there are there. Take your time, Mr. Koehler. Can I help you here?

A: There is a quarter inch chisel, a half inch chisel, and an inch and a half chisel.

Q: Is there any three-quarter inch chisel in the chest that was found in Hauptmann's home? . . .

A: No.

Putting away the chisels, Koehler displayed a photograph to explain how he had determined that rail 16's recesses had been made by a three-quarter-inch chisel. Like Blackstone, Koehler the Scientist used patter to distract everyone, including the jury. Pointing to the picture, he declared: "This is the picture *of one of the recesses* for the rungs in rail 16. *These recesses* were chiseled out and *this shows a mark made by the chisel,* one side of the chisel went down there and then there is a right angle turn here."

The quick switch back and forth between the singular and plural thus allows him to argue that all the recesses were made by one three-quarter-inch chisel. The illusion is complete. "That three-quarter of an inch chisel, in other words, fits perfectly into that mark made by that chisel." Wilentz provided the clincher in brilliant lawyerly fashion: "Of course you don't know what three-quarter inch chisel made the mark." And Koehler replied, "No."

But had the witness used the chisel found with the ladder to test his finding on the photograph? Yes, he had. Would he show this to the jury with the ladder, please. "I want you to walk along nice and slowly and indicate to each juror . . . one at a time, and I wish you jurors in back would please lean forward. We need a little more light. Is that the ridge you are talking about right in there?" Yes.[20]

The story of the chisel does not end there, however, with Koehler's slow walk in front of the jury box. Shortly after the trial, Koehler's article "Who Made That Ladder" appeared in the *Saturday Evening Post.* In it he recounted how he had identified the marks left by the "guilty" chisel.

The man who used the ladder in the Lindbergh yard dropped it from his hand or pocket. There were right-angled lines on the ladder just where the chisel made its bites. It was a doubly guilty tool, because not only had it helped to make the ladder, but it had been brought probably for use as a burglar's jimmy and, possibly, to crush a baby's skull. *For all my cold and calculating science I could not touch it without a sense of horror.*[21]

After discussing other evidence, however, Koehler came back to the chisel in an almost casual way, waving aside objections with a shrug. Any carpenter, he wrote, would have recognized the chisel as having come from the same manufacturer as others found in Hauptmann's toolbox. "But if you insist, I'm willing not to count the chisel in the final score of compromising circumstances, because there were others more important."[22]

Indeed there were. But Wilentz had encouraged his expert witness to involve the jury in a moment of high drama.

This is a good place to refresh our memory about the chisel found at Highfields. It was discovered on the ground near the ladder seventy-five feet away from the house. The first investigators believed it had been brought there to jimmy open the shutters and/or lever up the window. The shutter on the nursery window was warped, however, and there were no chisel marks on the casing. The window's lock mechanism would have made it impossible, anyway, to pry it open from the bottom. But if the window was left closed but not locked, getting purchase still would have been difficult—unless one knew ahead of time and brought the chisel for that purpose. That raised the question of how a kidnapper would know the window could be raised from the outside without ever having been in the house. A chisel would do no good against a locked window, and he would be faced with breaking the glass to gain entrance.[23]

For some reason, moreover, the chisel apparently was not brought into the Lindbergh house at the same time as the ladder, and processed for fingerprints, but left outside in the elements overnight. This "signature" clue thus becomes all the more difficult to explain. If the ladder was too heavy to carry any farther, the chisel added no weight to the kidnapper's burdens. If he dropped it accidentally when he dropped the ladder, he had made no effort to recover it. Too nervous? Perhaps.

But there was another, far more dramatic reason, for concentrating the jury's attention on the chisel. Wilentz planned to argue that it could have been used as a murder weapon. That would clear up so many difficult issues about why it was brought there—if not really explain why it was left behind. Proving the chisel had made the cuts for the ladder rungs was only preliminary to this larger purpose.[24]

Throughout the pretrial period, Koehler had continued to seek still more evidence from the ladder. He was unsuccessful in locating wood for the rungs that Hauptmann might have purchased, although he did obtain more wood from the National Lumber and Millworks that he believed to be a match with the wood in rails 12 and 13. Hauptmann, he discovered, had purchased quantities of wood from several other lumber companies late in 1931, none of which matched. Koehler also had police dig up samples of dirt from around Hauptmann's garage, apparently for a test to see if the soil there matched traces found on the ladder. If Hauptmann tried it out next to his garage, and the ladder broke, then the explanation for rail 16 became obvious.[25]

No evidence of such a match was ever presented at the trial. During these investigations, Koehler revisited the Cross, Austin & Ireland Lumber Company to ask about a supposed visit by a man reputed to be Hauptmann on December 14, 1933. According to the manager, William J. Reilly, Hauptmann and another man attempted to pay for a forty-cent purchase with a ten-dollar bill "yellow side" down. After they were asked for something smaller, the men offered a five-dollar bill. When the cashier went to get change, she opened the door where Koehler and Bornmann sat studying purchase records. This gave the customers a fright when they caught a glimpse of the wood expert and the policeman, causing them to depart without the wood. Reilly tried to catch up with the men, Koehler wrote in a contemporary report, but all he could see was the license plate on the car, "which he said agreed with that on Hauptmann's car when arrested, although how that can be is not clear since the two occurrences were in different years."[26]

When it came time for Koehler to write his self-congratulatory article in the *Saturday Evening Post* a few weeks after the trial's conclusion, the story had changed dramatically, beginning with the foreman's name, which now became Riley. "I now will exercise a privilege of the movies and tell what afterward was unfolded." The car was now a small green car, and the license plate definitely belonged to Hauptmann. "According to Riley one of the two men was—and I will now use his name—Bruno Richard Hauptmann." Riley and his assistant identified Hauptmann from a newspaper photograph, Koehler went on. "It is possible that my badge may have glinted from beneath my coat that day as Hauptmann looked into the cubby office where we sat."[27]

Neither Koehler's testimony about the chisel, nor his sudden turnaround on the story of events at the lumber company, indicates he was wrong about the attic board. There are credibility issues here, nevertheless. Aside from all other questions, moreover, if another man accompanied Hauptmann when there was an attempt to exchange a Lindbergh ransom bill, and both fled in panic at seeing Arthur Koehler's badge, that would indicate a conspiracy of at least two individuals.

While Koehler and police officials traveled back and forth to the Bronx and environs searching for more wood, taking new photographs of the attic, and digging up earth samples, Walter Winchell came back onto the scene with a distorted account of the attic discovery. In the *New York Daily Mirror* on December 10, 1934, Winchell claimed he had learned a piece of wood from Hauptmann's attic floor had been nailed to the side of rail 16 to give it extra support. "A patch of wood used to strengthen one part of the crime-ladder fits exactly into the place in the attic floor."

Winchell's column stirred up a flurry of comments and misleading denials. "Oh, my God!" protested a supposedly infuriated David Wilentz. "Why did you make that public? It was to be my closing line in the summation."[28]

The *New York Times* carried emphatic denials of the columnist's revelation. "There is absolutely no truth in the matter," Koehler said, while Wilentz claimed he had seen no reports from the wood expert and did not expect to "until tomorrow." These were less than candid comments. Wilentz's denial is less sweeping, as befits his professional responsibilities.[29]

The *Hunterdon County Democrat* reported, on the other hand, that Wilentz would neither confirm nor deny the columnist's assertions, but the state's attorneys were said to be concerned about "leaks," a backhanded way of confirming the story. The New Jersey paper also noted a cryptic comment made a week earlier by Wilentz's chief assistant, Anthony Hauck. "Important new evidence" had been found, said Hauck, definitely tying "Hauptmann to the electric chair." A piece of wood cut off from a rung in the ladder had been taken from the wall of the apartment. The identification had been made through nail holes and grain patterns.

Defense attorney Frederick A. Pope expressed both surprise and skepticism. "If this were true it would have been disclosed months ago. I do not believe it is true because I am satisfied that Hauptmann had nothing to do with the kidnapping."[30]

Another defense attorney, Lloyd Fisher, walked across the street from his office in Flemington to the county jail to ask Hauptmann about the report. "Richard," Fisher said, "I read a story in the paper today where the State claims that they found a piece of wood in your house which fits with parts on the ladder."

"It's impossible," Hauptmann said laughing, "that's a lot of nonsense."
"I didn't believe it."[31]

Searching for more wood to convict Hauptmann, police also interviewed his landlord, Max Rauch, and Rauch's mother, Pauline, as well as past and present tenants of the third apartment in the house. Both Max and Pauline reported suspicious doings in the garage, and lights on while Hauptmann worked behind closed doors. The landlord remembered some sort of wire running from the apartment to the garage, but the one he produced for examination led only from the bedroom to the living room. Rauch also noticed something else he thought funny: Anna Hauptmann would watch the garage when her husband was away, and he would always close the door when he worked inside, parking his car close up against the entrance.[32]

Neither Rauch ever saw Hauptmann carry anything down from the attic to the garage, or observed him either test or move a ladder in and out of the car—much as they obviously disliked their tenant. The two other renters—Donato Scarola and his wife, and Victor Schuessler and his wife—never saw anything suspicious. Scarola left near the end of February 1932, but he observed Richard building the garage until the time he and his family moved. The Schuesslers moved in during August of that same year, so of course they would not have seen him at work on the ladder. Schuessler knew the garage was kept locked, on the other hand, but told police he had gained entrance several times using a penknife. Richard had even given him permission to use the garage on other occasions. Schuessler and his wife also had keys to the apartment when the Hauptmanns went to Florida on vacation because Anna had asked them to water her plants. The Schuesslers spent several evenings with the Hauptmanns in their apartment. "[Victor Schuessler] never saw anything around the house or garage that would lead him to suspect Hauptmann of being involved in any crime."[33]

Criminals do not advertise their doings as a rule. But where the landlords saw Richard as a suspicious character, his fellow tenants did not mark any particular behavior as indicating he was hiding something. There was a very expensive Stromberg-Carlson combination radio-Victrola Hauptmann had purchased on April 29, 1932, for $396. Where did the money come from for that? The truck driver who delivered the set at first remembered being paid in gold certificates. "Look at all the gold backs," he said he told his helper. But when he was questioned again after identifying Hauptmann at the police station, he changed his mind. Only some of the money, he now recalled, had been in gold certificates.[34]

Testimony at the trial was produced to suggest he had a hidden cache of money in the radio set, but Schuessler and his wife had permission to be there alone when the family was away. No one, landlord or neighbor, had ever seen a ladder under construction; no one heard any sounds coming from the attic.

Police also found a pair of high-powered binoculars. These were traced by the serial number to a purchase made by a Mr. C. Tihy, on September 27, 1932. The sales slip recorded that Tihy paid $126 for the glasses and gave his address as 127 East Eighty-fourth Street. No such place existed. An apartment house stood at 125 East Eighty-fourth Street—but no one there had ever heard of a tenant named C. Tihy.[35]

Hauptmann used various aliases when he first came to the United States. Did he also invent C. Tihy to get rid of ransom bills? Some months later, of course, another man with a fictitious address, J. J. Faulkner, boldly walked into a bank, exchanged $2,980 in Lindbergh gold certificates, and walked back out onto the street and disappeared. C. Tihy and J. J. Faulkner might have been only two of the aliases Hauptmann used to assist him in laundering money. Tihy is a rare last name, an odd choice for an alias. It is known in Slovakia, France, and Ireland. Tihy could be a sort of play on words, Tee-hee, but there is at least one other curious thing about this name. Civil War records reveal that a C. Tihy from New York City served in the Civil War, something that would have been known to a history buff.

Hoover remained skeptical about the ultimate success of the prosecution—a feeling heavily colored by his dislike for all things New Jersey. After Assistant Prosecutor Joseph Lanigan approached Agent Sisk for help in providing information on anything the police might have missed in the investigation, Sisk went to Hoover, who warned him against spending too much time in Trenton. The director especially didn't want Sisk spending overnights there. He should tell Lanigan that he had to get back to New York to attend to a seriously ill wife. The FBI should provide all of its reports, said Hoover, and be willing to provide witnesses at the trial—but its staff should not sit in on strategy sessions. "New Jersey officials might be trying to get us into a position where they could pass the blame, or at least part of it, on us, in case they were unsuccessful in prosecuting Hauptmann." He most certainly did not want "them" to be able to say they had "the advice and guidance of representatives of the Department of Justice."[36]

New Jersey prosecutors were fairly confident at this point, but Whited's testimony had become something of a problem. Whited was under assault from his own family. His brother, Edward Whited, had been quoted in newspapers as saying that Millard was a very unreliable person. Trooper John R. Genz sought out Ed to see if he would recant and change "his story around so that it would not go against his brother in court." Well, he might, said Ed. Give him a few days to think about it, and he might be willing to provide one that would "contradict" what he gave to defense attorneys.

Edgar Lenz had been around to see him recently, Ed went on. Lenz was another one who had challenged Millard's lifelong acquaintance-ship with the truth. Lenz had been telling him, Ed Whited said, that he ought to stick to his story, "because before this case is over they will be able to make plenty of money for themselves." Like Millard, brother Ed was no slouch when it came to seeing the main chance. What were the police offering? he implied. The trooper promised to come back and see him in a day or two.[37]

Trooper W. O. Sawyer was out and around the vicinity of Hopewell at about this same time. He interviewed a man, Jonathan Voorhees, who was on the panel of jurymen drawn for the trial. On the pretext of trying to locate a man who used to live thereabouts, Sawyer tried to find out what he could about Voorhees's ideas on witnesses. Like the others, he "would doubt very much the veracity of this man's [Whited] testimony." With so many having expressed doubts about Whited's tes-timony, the state definitely needed another witness to place Hauptmann and the ladder in the vicinity.[38]

One suddenly appeared. Tipped off that a Hopewell man named Frank Story had heard about someone seeing a man operating a vehicle with a ladder in it near the vicinity of the Lindbergh home on March 1, 1932, police went to his home on November 28, 1934. Yes, it was true, Story told them. Amandus Hochmuth, a German immigrant and retired New York security guard, had recounted the incident to him. Hochmuth now lived with his daughter and son-in-law in a house on the northwest corner of the Wertsville Road, leading to the Lindbergh estate.[39]

Troopers Sawyer and Genz proceeded to the house and began interviewing the eighty-seven-year-old Hochmuth, gradually leading up to questions about Hauptmann. After about an hour and a quarter of talk about various topics to see how he did, they asked if he had seen a picture of Bruno Richard Hauptmann. No, he had not. They produced pictures, and Hochmuth looked them over very closely. "He looks like the man," he said at last. Sawyer asked what he meant, and Hochmuth gave the following account.

On the morning of March 1, 1932, a car turned the corner onto the Wertsville Road. It turned too fast and slipped into a ditch. The driver had to adjust the ladder inside the car before he tried to drive out. While he was doing that, Hochmuth got a good look at him. He had on a dark blue sailor cap, he said, with a shiny peak. The old man thought he could identify him if he saw him again. He hadn't come forward before because he feared the publicity and thought if he identified the man with the ladder, "it would be the cause of the man going to the electric chair and he did not want to do that."[40]

Hochmuth's daughter and son-in-law were not pleased about Amandus's dawning sense of duty to come forward with this dramatic story—which would get more dramatic with each telling. Efforts to interview him again on December 12 and 19 failed, because Harry Plump, the son-in-law, refused to let the two troopers see the old man. Sawyer recorded that he made several attempts on both dates, without success. Harry Plump "dominates him completely."[41]

Finally, on December 20, Hochmuth was persuaded to go to the Flemington jail to view Hauptmann. The prisoner told one of his attorneys, Lloyd Fisher, that the old man paced back and forth in front of his cell with a feeble step for about forty minutes, never saying a word. As soon as newspaper reporters learned about the "mystery visitor," they asked Warden Harry O. McCrea what was going on. McCrea replied disingenuously that he "had no idea who the man was," who the two men were that accompanied him, or even who signed the pass for him to get in. Perfectly aware of the game prosecutors had played with Condon, Lloyd Fisher told reporters he would make another protest to the attorney general, demanding that henceforth Hauptmann be inspected only in a lineup or in the presence of his lawyers.[42]

Hauptmann's guards rejected Fisher's accusations. The trooper in charge, Lieutenant A. L. Smith, said that Hauptmann had not been interviewed by anyone, "but that some unknown man had merely looked at him, and that there was nothing that would necessitate the presence of counsel." McCrea and Smith might not have known the name of the "mystery visitor," but everything else they said about the visit was simply a lie. Hochmuth was brought there to fix in the old man's mind the face to identify on the witness stand.[43]

After he had had time to study Hauptmann, Hochmuth was taken to Trenton to see Captain Lamb. He said he had been walking out from the house to the barn when he saw the car go into the ditch; he got a good look at the man from about thirty feet away. The man had on what looked like a yachting cap with a shiny bill. It happened around 8 or 9 A.M., he thought, but it could have been later because it was so long ago. In any event, it was before lunch. Early morning was not so good for the prosecution, because it would have been unlikely (*very* unlikely) Hauptmann could have gotten there by that time. Why anyone would have arrived so early on that day, and risked being seen for an entire afternoon—or even longer if he was there at 8 or 9 A.M.—could not be explained. "The man I saw today," affirmed Hochmuth, "looks exactly like the man I saw in the car that morning but his face was a little more ruddy and might have been a little heavier." Anyone could make a mistake, he repeated, but he was "almost positive" about the man. He was also "almost positive" that the car they showed him at headquarters was the car. "The reason I did not tell the investigators who questioned my family shortly after the kidnap[p]ing about the car with the ladder is that I did not want to get mixed up in it and I did not want any publicity in this matter."[44]

But Hochmuth's affirmations were as shaky as his signature. Before he could be sent into a courtroom, Assistant Attorney General Robert Peacock had to coach him along, using the "firing squad" principle. If Amandus did his duty, in other words, he would be only one of several witnesses who saw Hauptmann that day. He was not the one doing the condemning; they all were. When he repeated his story to Peacock on January 6, 1935, he was not walking to the house from the barn that day, but stationary on the back porch of the house. When he saw the car go into the ditch and noticed the ladder, he now remembered, he said to himself, "What is that—has Lindbergh got window cleaners?" (The similarity to Ben Lupica's comment on window cleaners is striking.)

Why do you say that? asked Peacock.

Because he looked like it with a ladder in his car.

Very well, about what time was that?

"I think it was about ten o'clock or something like that."

This was not quite late enough, so Peacock rephrased the question for him: "It was between ten and twelve o'clock, before you had your lunch in the forenoon?"

"Yes."

It all went well until Peacock asked if he had seen the man again since that day.

"I can't exactly say I have seen him."

"Is Hauptmann the man who was in that car?"

"I saw a picture that resembles him very much."

"You would say Hauptmann was the man?"

"I can't say that. I can't say that. The face that looked and stared—he looked up at me—it was a red face—the features were the same—he looked as if he had seen a ghost—he stopped and looked at me for about fifteen seconds."

When Hochmuth started toward the car, the man got the car going.

"You have seen Hauptmann at the jail?"

"I could not say exactly."

Peacock began to lose patience, telling Hochmuth that he was going to be asked that question and he would have to say yes or no.

"I can't say it was or I can't say it was not."

"What could you say?"

"It resembles him. That face I saw was red as if the blood had come out on his face. I suppose he was afraid he would tip over and grabbed for the ladder. The ladder was kind of slipping. I have seen several going into the ditch."

This was going nowhere except into the ditch. But that was the only car you ever saw with a ladder go into the ditch, Peacock tugged at Hochmuth's memory, trying to pull the testimony back onto the road.

Yes, that was true.

Well, was he almost positive, then, about his identification?

"It is hard to say. It is a case of life between death and life."

They wrestled with several more questions without Peacock getting a firm hold on where his witness was going. He tried going back to the subject of the car, but Hochmuth was no longer sure about that either. "I think it is the same car, but I did not see the whole of it, don't you see."

"What do you mean," said an exasperated prosecutor, "you did not see the whole of it?"

"The car—the ditch in the field obstructed my view."

At last Peacock decided they had to refresh Hochmuth's memory. And there was also the likelihood that if he sat in the courtroom, the state's other witnesses would push him in the right direction. "Suppose you went to Flemington and sat in the court and studied Hauptmann for a while—do you think you would be more sure of your identification?"

"Well, I really hate to identify him."

"Why?"

"Because I am not quite sure. In the prison there I saw him standing up. Well, you see there is a difference looking up that way and looking down that way."

Peacock had another idea. He produced one of the photographs, which seemed to ease Hochmuth's mind somewhat. "What do you say about that picture?"

"That looks very much like him." It looked like the face of the man in the car, only a little thinner—and his eyes were staring. "They looked to me like blue eyes. I have been rehearsing that in my own mind."

So, Peacock said, "You can say that man you saw that day in the car is exactly like the man you see in the picture?"

"Yes."

"Now, if you sit in court probably you can say that the man in the car is the same man as the one you see in court."

Switching tactics, Peacock then asked Hochmuth if someone had told him not to identify Hauptmann.

"Well no, not exactly." His family had said he should stay out of it. But that was no way for an old soldier to behave, one who had fought in the Franco-Prussian War and still had his pride. "I know what I am doing." And yet: "You see it is pretty hard on a man like me—my age— to say that is the fellow."

Peacock reverted to the "firing squad" principle to give the old man strength. "You must remember this. We know he is the man. We know other people saw him in that neighborhood. People right up above you saw him there. We know a man saw him because he gave a description of him that night, the same night of the day you saw him."

Hochmuth rallied bravely, showing he knew about Lupica. "There is another man who saw the car as far as I know—that student. He saw the car more. The way I heard that he saw the ladder in the car, too."[45]

At last he understood his duty. So Amandus Hochmuth put Hauptmann in a car with the supposed kidnap ladder on the day of the crime.

A few months after the trial, a check of New York City Public Welfare records disclosed that Hochmuth had had two physical examinations in 1932, in June and August. They both recorded that when he applied for aid, he was found to be "partly blind . . . frail," with "failing eyesight due to cataracts."[46]

11 THE SEARCH FOR ISIDOR FISCH

> But if it is contended that his best friend, Fisch, . . . was a
> party to it with him . . . let them bring the grave of Isidor
> Fisch alongside of all the other graves they have brought into
> this courtroom, if it is any consolation and comfort to this
> party, if it is any consolation and comfort to him, let them
> bring the dead in here; if he helped Mr. Hauptmann, and there
> isn't a scintilla of evidence that he did, that doesn't excuse
> Hauptmann, not a bit.
>
> —DAVID WILENTZ, closing statement at the trial of
> Bruno Richard Hauptmann

Standing before newsreel cameras in back of the jail, Edward J. Reilly pronounced himself well satisfied with the setting for the trial of the century. "I have found Flemington very friendly. . . . It is a beautiful town and its residents are congenial. I have been here only a short time but I know I should like to live here." He had just come from seeing his client, Reilly went on, and found him "cool, calm, and collected and with the appearance of an innocent man."

Reilly also liked the Fisch story about how Hauptmann had found the ransom money spilling out of a wet shoebox in his closet. And why not? No one could prove otherwise. Fisch was dead. With John Condon's erratic behavior, an inexperienced prosecutor, and simple countryfolk sitting on the jury, this trial could turn out to be his grandest triumph ever. Not that he believed Hauptmann innocent. But he was willing to believe he had a chance—or pretend for the cameras that he did. Reilly was more P. T. Barnum than anybody else, and he looked like "Rich Uncle" on that new *Monopoly* game, dressed in morning coat and spats, with a boutonniere. (Devised by an unemployed weaver living off his wife's earnings in nearby Germantown, Pennsylvania, *Monopoly* successfully captured the edgy mood of the time, where fate depended on a single roll of the dice.)

"We are starting from scratch in this case," said Reilly. But where would he find anything to prove Hauptmann's story?

Hauptmann had been told about efforts to convince Whited's brother, Ed, to change his story. He had laughed at the discovery of "wood" taken from his apartment for the ladder. He and Anna concentrated—especially at her urging—on perfecting the Fisch story. Visiting him on November 17, 1934, she said the lawyers wanted him to try to remember anything that would help. "Do you remember the time when you and I and Fisch went to the Radio City to see the picture, 'Alice in Wonderland,' and on our way to the theater he pointed out an old house to us, which didn't look so good from the outside, but we could see through the windows women who were dressed in evening gowns?"

"I think I do, wasn't that on Fourth Avenue? Didn't he tell us that his boss used to stop there?"[1]

Isidor Fisch's supposed double life was Reilly's starting point, but Hauptmann could supply precious little information to his lawyers about his erstwhile friend's life and associations. Police investigators and those working for the defense did learn that Fisch led a highly compartmentalized life, keeping friends walled off from each other. Some knew him as a man who moved money around from one enterprise to another; others pitied him as an impoverished young man on the verge of tuberculosis.

In December 1934, John Condon took a car trip to Miami, making sure, as always, that reporters did not lose track of his whereabouts. When they "found" him eating dinner in a Palm Beach coffee shop, they told him that the defense had asked the court to provide a theory of the child's death. Condon remarked, "No one saw Hauptmann kill the baby. I don't think they can convict him."

He was in Florida, he said, "checking up" on information he had received in some of the 2,500 letters sent him that pointed to Orlando and Miami. He planned to interview people in several Florida cities, to obtain "local color" that might lead to new clues.

Condon was next seen at Al Capone's home on Palm Island, where, he explained to reporters, he had tried to give Mrs. Capone "good news—unusually good news." She was not home at the time of his visit, so he had to leave word with a servant that he would phone the next morning. "It is based on a letter," he said, "that I received from a woman whose identity I cannot make public at this time."[2]

Why Condon the superpatriot would be concerned about reliev-
ing Al Capone's family of any anxiety about the Lindbergh case would
surprise anyone not already accustomed to Jafsie's Munchausen
personality.

Returning home, however, he discovered that New York and New
Jersey police officers were waiting on his doorstep. "He just went to
Miami for a little vacation and rest," he assured them. "Nothing in particular" took him there. Newspaper reporters had pestered him, but he
had told them "nothing in reference to the Lindbergh Case." The Florida
venture had proven, he said, that none of the gangsters mentioned in
connection with the crime had anything to do with it at all. While he
expected new efforts to discredit him and his testimony, he knew that
his behavior had been beyond reproach. "I have been true to the promises made to myself." Let the courtroom ordeal—dreadful as it might
be—begin, he said. He was ready.[3]

Condon's trip south had other implications for the trial, however.
His various statements suggested that when it actually came to it, he
might once again back off an identification. And what if he suggested
that Isidor Fisch was the lookout, as he had done in private conversations with FBI agent Leon Turrou? Who could really say?

To protect themselves against any possible contingency, police
quietly sought information about the possibility that Condon and Hauptmann had met before the encounter with Cemetery John that night in
Woodlawn Cemetery. Condon's real estate office on City Island at the
corner of Beech Street and King Avenue had a view of nearby Hunter's Island, where Hauptmann often played soccer and picnicked with
friends months before the kidnapping. Hauptmann kept a canoe he
purchased in the summer of 1932 at Dixon's Boathouse, not far from
Condons' place. He never had occasion to visit the boathouse, Condon
insisted, even though he had been a part-time resident of the island for
forty years.[4]

The owners of the boathouse told police that Hauptmann would
drive there in his car, sometimes with two or three others, and row
over to Hunter's Island, returning at nightfall. They never saw Condon
at their end of the island. More important, they had never seen Hauptmann at their boathouse before the day of the kidnapping. City Island
is a small place, nevertheless, easily traversed by car from end to end
in a few minutes. Condon was a great walker, who boasted he had
searched the country high and low for Cemetery John. He sought out
the company of young men and held court wherever and whenever he
could. He talked with sailors and ship workers about Red Johnson at
various locations—and yet police were supposed to believe he never

encountered or even observed the young men canoeing across from Dixon's Boathouse to Hunter's Island?[5]

And he never saw Cemetery John in a restaurant on the island, either? Rumors that Condon and Hauptmann frequently came together to a place called Bunnie's Fry Shop proved false, but the proprietor, Preston Parry, told police that while he could not remember Hauptmann ever eating there, Condon did almost every day he was on the island. He would come into the restaurant, said Parry, and if no one noticed him immediately, he would call out—"Mr. Bunnie, I see where they have found some more of the Lindbergh ransom money." That would get the customers' attention, and Condon would launch into one of his mini-orations. If you want my opinion, Parry told police, "Dr. Condon is just a big faker."[6]

The results of the police investigations of Condon's life on City Island did not rule out, of course, the slim possibility that they had met at some other locale before the kidnapping. When Hauptmann first came to the United States, he worked out at a boxing club in Manhattan. Condon's fondness for the sport, and for athletic young men like his City Island friend and associate Al Reich, a former professional boxer, might have thrown them together at some point.[7]

However that may be, Condon's meddlesome comments littered the highways from Massachusetts to Florida. What would happen when he sat down in the witness chair and "Death House" Reilly asked what he was doing at Al Capone's house? Or why he told reporters that he doubted Hauptmann could be convicted of murder? In any other case such a witness would crumple up under cross-examination like an empty bag of hot air; but this was not any other case, and Condon was a nonpareil master of braggadocio. If he even faltered on the witness stand, however, the Fisch story would gain a measure of credibility.

So the search for Fisch became a high priority for both prosecution and defense.

Isidor Fisch came to the United States from Leipzig, Germany, in 1925, when he was scarcely twenty years old. Upon his arrival, he went to live with the family of Herman Kirsten, his former boss back in Germany, and continued to work in the fur trade as a cutter. Also living there in rented rooms were Karl and Gerta Henkel and Fisch's friend from the old country, Henry Uhlig. Sometimes he made as much as sixty to eighty dollars a week. Although he had first thought he would return to Germany, after seeing what the new world had to offer, Fisch and Uhlig both filed papers for U.S. citizenship. According to Uhlig, they had made out very well here. Despite ups and downs, "Isidor and I worked fairly regularly all those years." Isidor saved his money and "always had a lot laid away for any jobless period." Moreover, he "watched his pennies" to such an extent that he often appeared poverty-stricken.[8]

Never robust, Fisch was a small man about five and a half feet tall, and weighing hardly more than 140 pounds. His friends said he looked a lot like the entertainer Eddie Cantor. Police investigations of Fisch's short, unhappy life revealed, however, that he was indeed a man of many guises, appearing to some who knew him as a naive person with nothing to hide other than a string of failed ambitions, while to others he was known to be clever and cunning, forever borrowing from Peter to pay Paul, and not averse to joining up with more experienced con men in various schemes such as the Knickerbocker Pie Company.

In the summer of 1929, Isidor took ill with what was diagnosed as pleurisy, but very likely was the first stages of the tuberculosis that would cause his death five years later. Constantly under a doctor's care, he could not seem to regain any of the weight he had lost during the initial onset of the disease. He became determined to get away from the cold, dampish fur-cutting room, which was contributing to his poor health.

Then, early in 1931, January or February, Uhlig and Fisch returned home from a movie about midnight to find a man name Schleser waiting for Isidor. He had a business proposition for Fisch. Did he want to become a partner in a new bakery to be called the Knickerbocker Pie Company?

Charles "Charlie" Schleser had dabbled in many enterprises, including making sausages and buying and selling real estate. In the former enterprise, he might have encountered the Morrows' butler, Septimus Banks, during the period in the late 1920s when Banks was on his own in the catering business. Schleser made quite a record for himself in real estate. All his associates knew him as a gambler—for big stakes. His office partner was one Joe DeGrasi, a short stocky man, with a dark complexion, a cast in his left eye, and a decided limp. The firm they worked for, the United Land and Development Company, dealt exclusively in New Jersey properties, particularly in the vicinity of Plainfield, about forty-five miles northeast of Princeton on main routes.

Both men were arrested for swindling a woman, Mrs. Glynn, out of $2,000 on a shady real estate deal. A very busy man, Schleser had at least four charges on a rap sheet, including one for passing bad checks and two for grand larceny. After getting out of prison, he decided real estate was not his game and moved into the kitchen to try his hand at making pies. But he did not abandon his old ways. A new associate, Lamber Brush, the original founder of the pie company, told police that

Schleser had considered suicide because a woman he had fleeced out of $5,000 had lodged a complaint with the police. It was rumored his friend DeGrasi had slipped off to Europe with the money and Schleser's wife. True or not, they were soon back together.[9]

Why did Schleser think Fisch would have the money to invest? Perhaps he knew that Fisch had property in Freeport, Long Island, he could mortgage, or could borrow from Karl Henkel's mother, Auguste Hile, who had taken a special liking to him. Fisch had repaired her fur coat, and they became great friends—so much so that she would entrust nearly $4,000 to him to invest for her in various enterprises, and appoint him her agent to collect debts.

Fisch had at first offered $800 as his stake in the pie company, but Schleser said that was ridiculous—"he could not for a moment consider it." So he must have had some idea Fisch could come up with more—a lot more. He was right. Within two weeks Schleser had obtained $3,000 from the Fisch connection, half from Fisch's friend Erich Schaefer and half from Fisch. The $1,500 Isidor gave Schleser was paid over in three $500 bills. It was the beginning of a new career for Isidor—entrepreneur.

The Knickerbocker Pie Company lasted only eight months before it went bankrupt—supposedly because of the "terrific competition" in the pie business.[10] Lamber Brush told an FBI agent that Schleser had "hoodwinked" Fisch. Charlie Schleser was a "trickster very capable of successfully putting over a shady deal and undoubtedly closely identified with the criminal element." He was a small man with gray hair and glasses, said Brush, thirty years old, five-foot-nine or so, who weighed around 140 pounds. Several times while the pie company was in operation gangsters had visited the premises and gave every indication of being intimate with him. According to Brush, "it was Schleser's boast that he could get gang assistance at any time should he need it." Then there was Joe DeGrasi's candid explanation of how he and Schleser had operated in the real estate business. He dug up the "suckers," he told Brush, and turned them over to Schleser, who was the office man "and who would put through the deals by which several people were victimized."[11]

John T. Hewitt, another of the original partners in the pie company, gave yet a different story of the company's demise. He had invested $4,000, he told police, and got out after losing $1,000, which sum Schleser and Brush agreed to repay—but never did. These two kept the books, which at times were strewn across the floor of a basement office. Fisch hung around Schleser all the time, he went on, and was the company's "angel," and Schleser's prey. "Hewitt stated that Schleser was a conniver and a faker."[12]

When Fisch came around, said a former employee of the Knicker-bocker Pie Company, it was a sort of standard joke that "[they] all would be paid." If Fisch was the company's financial angel, his wings were much too fragile to keep it aloft for very long. But what else went on at that address? Fisch may well have learned about money laundering there.

After the pie company went under, nevertheless, Fisch contin-ued his close association with Schleser in an idea for a company to make electric signs, named the Solux Manufacturing Company. Under Schleser's tutelage, Fisch set out to raise $3,000 to launch the venture, borrowing from many of the same people as before, and adding new investors—sometimes offering as security shares in the defunct pie company.[13] On November 1, 1932, he wrote to one of his backers, the father of a friend, asking him not to lose faith in his trustworthiness: "I have certain plans which I will eventually work out. The whole summer I engaged myself in saving up a certain amount of money for the pur-pose." There was a good opportunity now to make real profits. "I buy my merchandise on credit and with that money I am able to do some-thing else in order to derive a profit."[14]

Fisch lived near the poverty line, but there was always a good deal of money floating around. His "good friend" Charlie Schleser would hardly have stayed close to Fisch were it otherwise.

A new partner was taken into the Solux firm, Albert B. Kurtz, Schleser's lawyer and friend. Kurtz felt that the only way for the com-pany to make an impression was to have a fine home office—his office, remodeled. So out into the world of eager investors went Isidor Fisch to find the first $1,000 to pay for the remodeling and some secondhand machines. Apparently, this time the Fisch-Schleser relationship suffered. When Fisch brought the $1,000 check from his pigeon, and the company directors took it to the bank, Schleser was given $600 to put in his safe. The temptation was too great for the latter, who skipped out with the dough to raise more capital at the racetrack—or some other gam-ing place. When his colleagues caught up with him, Schleser was prop-erly contrite—and promised to cover the money within a month. He got a job driving booze trucks, Kurtz told Detective Hausling of the New Jersey State Police, "and later brought back several hundred dollars into the concern." Fisch and his friend Erich Schaefer were not pleased, however, and they came into the office daily to demand all of their money. This was around April of 1932, lawyer Kurtz informed Hausling, who failed to notice this amazing coincidence with the ransom payoff date and Schleser's new funds.

Out of these failed enterprises, nevertheless, there developed a strong friendship between Fisch and Schleser. Indeed Charlie began to see himself as Isidor's protector. Things went from bad to worse after the company's demise, Schleser told investigators, but even more so for Fisch, who was at times reduced to living in a wooden shack in the rear of a friend's house on Coney Island. He refused Schleser's offers to come live with him, so Charlie said, and, at times, slept on benches in Grand Central Station. At one point he rented a room on East 127th Street but was evicted in the spring of 1933. Schleser ran into him on the street, and he was so weak he almost fainted on the street until they got some food in a nearby restaurant.

According to Schleser, Fisch was so depressed that he renewed previous threats to commit suicide. Finally, with a few dollars he raised here and there, he purchased a ticket to return to Europe, where he subsequently died of tuberculosis.

Schleser had never heard of Hauptmann, he told police after Richard's arrest, and "protested vigorously" against the attempt now to blacken Fisch's character, "and stated that his desire to right this wrong was his reason for having come forward with the story just narrated." Schleser's brave leap into the fray to rescue Isidor Fisch's reputation certainly deserves attention.[15]

In fact, it attracted a great deal of attention. On December 5, 1934, New York detective Max Leef had an enjoyable conversation with Schleser—who was more than happy to go to Trenton to tell Attorney General Wilentz all about his good friend Isidor Fisch. Schleser had, he said, indisputable evidence about where Fisch was on the night of March 1, 1932.[16]

Wilentz welcomed Schleser's detailed account of Isidor Fisch's ongoing struggles to fend off the gales of poverty and illness. Fisch never took any real salary from either the Knickerbocker Pie Company or the Solux Manufacturing Company, Schleser said, only a few dollars from time to time to stay alive. "I always felt that he was one of the most upright and honest men I ever met in my life."

Although their business association ended in December of 1931, he claimed, they remained close friends socially. Through Fisch, for example, Schleser made other friends—such as Karl and Gerta Henkel, a couple who lived in the same apartment house as Isidor.[17] Henkel had worked for a time as a driver for the Knickerbocker Pie Company. But Schleser was no doubt happy to become acquainted with the Henkels in a more lasting way, not least because Karl's mother, Auguste Hile, was, as noted earlier, one of Fisch's most generous and constant financial backers.[18]

Auguste Hile was not one of those who believed Fisch was poverty-stricken. If she had, she probably would not have given him the money to invest on her behalf. She recalled later that she had seen him in December of 1932 in a restaurant "and he had many gold bills in his pocket book."[19]

Schleser told Wilentz, nevertheless, that he saw Fisch every day except for Sundays and holidays until the end of June 1933. Sometimes he saw him twice a day. Oh, yes, and sometimes Fisch came to his house in the evenings.

Well, asked Wilentz, did he seem to you to be a man of means?

"Why, he was just fading away from sheer worry," said Schleser, "because he wanted to be able to get into some sort of business which would enable him to pay his debts."

Did he have new clothes?

"The poor boy, he wore one hat, a white hat, and it was black and both of us didn't have money to have his hat cleaned, until one day in the summer of 1933, it was a terrible hot day, I had a dollar to spare and he went into a store and bought a hat for forty-five cents, he got a straw hat."[20]

Isidor Fisch led a highly compartmentalized life; that much was clear. Detectives looked up John Mohrdieck, who had been one of the signers of Fisch's petition for citizenship, and discovered that he and his mother had invested with Fisch, and so had their friends. Mohrdieck put up $634 and received as collateral "Certificate No. 5" in the name of Isidor Fisch for ten shares of the Knickerbocker Pie Company. Fisch cautioned Mohrdieck not to tell anyone about this deal, as it was special, and only Gerta Henkel and Erich Schaefer knew anything about it. "If the manager of the baking company found out about it, he wouldn't like it."[21]

All this time Fisch lived in the cheapest room in Selma Kohl's boardinghouse, constantly falling behind in his $3.50 rent payments. Gerta Henkel fed him a little bologna and tea when he was out of money. And yet he spent his days convincing people to invest thousands in businesses without a prospectus, or any prospect of success in the middle of the Great Depression. The story of Isidor Fisch belongs among the Broadway legends of Damon Runyon. "Always try to rub against money, for if you rub against money long enough," he wrote, "some of it may rub off on you."

His passage to Germany was paid for by contributions from several people, with enough left over so that he could repay some of his debts. His friend Erich Schaefer contributed $35, but the biggest amount came from his newest business associate, Bruno Richard Hauptmann, who gave him $2,000 so that they would not have to sell a stock of furs they (supposedly) owned together.

Erich Schaefer was probably Isidor Fisch's most loyal supporter in life and death, even more so than Charlie Schleser. He never met Hauptmann either—but at least he heard about him from Isidor. Isidor was practically penniless, insisted Schaefer—but this man Hauptmann had begged to go into business with him, offering him all kinds of money, as much as $5,000 to $10,000 to start out in the fur business. But Isidor always turned him down, having no desire to "hook up" with this interloper. He and Isidor had an arrangement, Schaefer claimed, and this would mean a three-way split. Indeed, this was the reason—or at least one of the motivating factors—that Isidor returned to Germany, to get away from Hauptmann's entreaties, and to see if his brother, Pinkas, could provide credit for six months so that they could start out "on this side."[22]

When Assistant Attorney General Robert Peacock prepped Schaefer before the trial, his witness remembered something else. Isidor had marveled at Hauptmann's ability to beat the system. "Here is a man," Schaefer heard him say, "without practically any education whatever, who is able to live without working, and take trips and things and really enjoys life, just through the stock market."

Fisch presented several faces to the world. Here was yet another— the face of a man who turned down all this money so as not to offend a dear friend. If so, it would be the first time Fisch had refused money for one of his ventures. Schaefer's purpose in telling this story seems transparent: he wanted to put (ransom) money in Hauptmann's hands, but keep Fisch clean of all connections with the tainted money.

Schaefer also knew something about Fisch's other friends. At the Henkels', he said, Fisch met a man they called "John, the bootlegger," who was also a friend of Hauptmann. Henkel and "John, the bootlegger," often went hunting in New Jersey. And the three were planning a trip to Maine.[23]

Gerta Henkel had known Isidor Fisch from their childhood days in Leipzig, and now they were both living in the same house in New York City. According to Karl and Gerta in their first statements to police, they introduced their new friend from Hunter's Island, Richard "Dick" Hauptmann, to Fisch in their apartment in early August 1932. Later, at the trial, Gerta would say that she now agreed with Hauptmann's testimony that the two were *re*introduced in their apartment, having previously met on Hunter's Island, where the German community in the area often went for outings. It was a little joke between them.[24]

It was no joke, however. The timing of the meeting between Richard and Isidor assumed great importance at the trial. The prosecution insisted that Hauptmann's claim to have met Isidor Fisch weeks earlier in March or April of 1932 was a made-up tale to explain how he got the money to invest in the stock market soon after the ransom was paid. Hauptmann had said the day after his arrest that he thought he had received two large-denomination bills from Fisch *in 1930,* a $500 bill and a $1,000 bill to invest in the stock market. And that accounted for the serial numbers found written in pencil on the interior of his closet door. Once police discovered that the serial numbers did not match any of the ransom bills, they lost interest. Perhaps they should have checked further.

Charles Schleser, it should be remembered in this context, told the police that in January or February of 1931, Fisch brought him three $500 bills to invest in the Knickerbocker Pie Company, and when the Solux Company got started there was a $1,000 "check" deposited in the bank for start-up—Fisch's money Schleser used to gamble and never paid back.

At the trial and after his conviction, Hauptmann insisted that he had, indeed, met Fisch in March or April of 1932. He was "pretty sure" it was March, out on Hunter's Island. Fisch was sitting there with another person speaking German. The other fellow was blond, a bit younger, and spoke with an Austrian accent. At the end of the conversation, Hauptmann said to Fisch, "I will take you to the Subway Station. It is about an hour to walk."[25]

Hauptmann's various claims—he even said he believed Isidor had been spying on him before they met—cannot be proved. The state's contention that Gerta Henkel was lying when she testified that her original statement was wrong, and that she had reintroduced them in her apartment, however, also cannot be proved. She had not gone to Hunter's Island before July 1932, and therefore could easily have been unaware of prior contacts—especially given Fisch's obsession with keeping his friends in the dark about his doings.

It is also true that Fisch had many Viennese friends. One of them, Henry Gewurz, first met Fisch in 1927 at the Viennese Jewish Social Club, located in the Bronx on 163rd Street. Gewurz told police that Fisch generally "hung out with a clique of about 20 members." Just a few days before he left for Germany, Fisch told this man that he was going there to get cured of tuberculosis and would return when he was well. Fisch appeared to be "dumb looking," he added, but was actually a shrewd businessman. "Gewurz states that he saw Fisch several times in the fur district in the company of a tall blonde man." Hauptmann could have learned about the "tall blonde man" after his arrest, but Gewurz's statement stands on its own as a confirmation that Fisch had such a friend, and that he was frequently in his company.[26]

But if he did meet Fisch before the summer of 1932, how serious could their relationship have been? He did not tell Anna, for example. The problem is a complicated one from Hauptmann's point of view. If he knew Fisch then, from March or April as he insisted, that would allow him to claim that some of the unexplained money invested in the stock market came from Fisch. No record exists that such was the case. They were operating at this time on the basis of a "gentleman's agreement," Hauptmann would say. It should be remembered that, according to Charles Schleser—also backed up by Henry Gewurz—during this period Schleser was meeting daily, sometimes twice a day, with Fisch. Were these all simply social visits?

It is interesting that Hauptmann never specifically claimed he received any money from Fisch as a result of these earliest supposed contacts. On April 8, 1932, Hauptmann deposited $600 into a brokerage account with the firm Carlton and Mott at 170 Broadway. No money was withdrawn from any of his other savings accounts to explain this sum. He also deposited into a joint savings account smaller sums totaling $408 that month. No doubt some of this was Anna's salary, and perhaps some from funds he might have earned from small carpentry jobs after he quit his job at the Majestic Apartments. But the bulk of the money cannot be explained that way.

Over the summer and into the fall of 1932 there are other large expenditures, nearly $400 for a Stromberg-Carlson radio/Victrola, $109 for a canoe, and a series of cash deposits in old accounts plus a new one he opened at the Mount Vernon Trust Company. This is also the summer that Anna went to Europe for several weeks.

Perhaps the most interesting "connection" to Isidor Fisch, however, can be found in a statement of William Mulligan, an employee at the brokerage firm of Steiner, Rouse on East Eighty-sixth Street, where Hauptmann moved all his stock holdings on August 8, 1932. Mulligan reported that Hauptmann had come in that day to open a new account by transferring two sets of securities from his previous firm: five hundred shares of Curtis Wright and one hundred shares of Warner Brothers. At the moment these airplane and movie stocks were low-priced, but good enough to open an account. When Mulligan asked him some questions about his finances, and whether he rented, Hauptmann said no, he lived in a private home he owned himself. He also said he had no bank accounts; he was afraid of the banks and had withdrawn his money. When Mulligan asked what business he was in, he received the following reply: "He told me he was a fur trapper and dealer, that he was accustomed to traveling around through the West, trap and buy skins in Oregon and Washington and then on his way back, he would stop off at St. Louis and dispose of them."[27]

Why all these stories? Did Richard Hauptmann look like a man who traveled all around the West checking fur traps? He had to invent something, obviously, if he planned a new career in the stock market. He could not very well say he was unemployed.

Mulligan's superior shrugged off any doubts about Hauptmann's credentials since he was not asking for a loan, merely to establish an account with open orders to sell, and was in no hurry to receive the money. Besides, Hauptmann seemed acquainted with several other clients, German Americans who made up a large number of Steiner, Rouse customers.

That said, Hauptmann's choice of occupations suggests his acquaintance with Isidor Fisch was more than casual. It is highly unlikely, furthermore, that such an idea would dawn on Hauptmann after just one meeting at the Henkel apartment.

Meanwhile, Richard had begun to boast about his killings on the stock market to friends, including Otto and Louise Wollenberg. Anna confided to Louise that they had saved nearly $12,000 at the time they took a lengthy trip to California in the late spring of 1931. Richard took them over to Hunter's Island, and while there he said he had made a lot of money in stocks, sometimes $2,000 a week. If he had not been on the island one day, he said, he could have made $50,000. They could always find him, he said, at Steiner, Rouse just down the street from their apartment.[28] Richard seemed especially determined to impress the Wollenbergs with his ability to beat the workaday life of others. He thought nothing of paying forty dollars for two tickets to the Jack Sharkey–Max Schmeling heavyweight championship fight.

On January 1, 1933, the Wollenbergs were introduced to Isidor Fisch at the Hauptmann apartment. Otto had been drinking all night. "Who is that little shrimp there?" he asked. "That guy is worth thirty-thousand dollars," Hauptmann replied. "He is my partner in furs and in the stock market. We have an agreement that we go half and half on everything."[29]

Untangling the business arrangements between Fisch and Hauptmann is an almost impossible task. Hauptmann's books are the only source, and it is by no means clear that the entries reflect the true state of affairs. The books, said Special Agent Genau in his report, were kept in a manner that afforded him the information he desired to keep, yet prevented others from learning much of his business. Hauptmann always maintained, when questioned, that his money to invest in stocks came from savings, Isidor Fisch, and profits from furs. And when questioned about his losses, he would always say, as well, that Fisch had lost a lot of money in stocks. Agent Genau ended his report with this conclusion: "The source of the $26,016.00, which represents the total of all cash deposits to the several brokerage and bank accounts of Haupt-mann and his wife as detailed hereinbefore in this report, cannot be determined from the brokerage and bank accounts available."[30]

Hauptmann's greatest difficulty was explaining how he could have put the money into the stock market and still have had plenty to invest in the purchase of furs. Fisch's method of operations in his previous ventures, borrowing to invest in pies, using stocks in the defunct com-pany as collateral for the next round of borrowing, apparently worked with Hauptmann—right up to the last when he borrowed $2,000 to go to Germany so that he supposedly would not have to sell their furs at a loss.

Fisch's fur business was at least partially an illusion from the begin-ning. He apparently allowed Hauptmann to know only enough to keep him happy. It took the police only a few days after Hauptmann's arrest, on the other hand, to discover that Fisch knew very little about buying and selling furs, at least according to professionals in New York who could find no record of an Isidor Fisch trading furs in the city.[31]

At Selma Kohl's house, an investigating officer, Sergeant William Kelly, was referred to Margaret Helfert, who used to know Fisch and now lived across the street. And she had an amazing story to tell. About three weeks before Fisch left for Germany, he had asked her to type up two bills on the letterhead of a firm, Klar and Miller. These bills were for furs supposedly sold to Isidor Fisch, one for $6,000 and another for $11,000. There was no firm by the name of Klar and Miller in existence. Helfert also told Kelly that sometime after Fisch died, she met Haupt-mann on Hunter's Island. He asked if she had made out these bills. Informed that she had, Hauptmann came to her apartment with his account book, which showed items for $6,000 and $11,000. He also told her that he had given Fisch $7,000.[32]

Hauptmann's astonishment that Fisch was not who he seemed to be—a fur trader with good connections—may not have been genuine. He would have to be awfully naive not to have checked up on someone he supposedly entrusted with thousands of dollars from a shrinking stock market account. One explanation might be that he did, indeed, receive thousands of dollars from Fisch to invest in the stock market, although the records of such funds are absent from Hauptmann's account books with one or two exceptions. As for profits from the fur-trading partnership, the Genau report concluded that Hauptmann's fig-ures showed a net profit of $6,637 from May to November of 1933. These profits, however, were on furs purchased from the nonexistent "Klar and Miller Bros." Hauptmann's books also showed that the final purchase of furs totaled $21,900 on November 3, and that at the time of Fisch's departure from New York for Germany the following month, these furs remained unsold.[33]

Hauptmann's statements and his books—if taken at face value—showed that the partnership had outstanding some $17,463 in furs, half of which "belonged" to each man. Richard said that when Isidor left, he paid over to him $2,000. The $2,000 can be established beyond doubt, as the money was drawn from Hauptmann's stock account. But Genau could not figure out anything else from Hauptmann's books that would establish the terms of the fur partnership, or its purchases and sales: "As already stated, it appears that this record book was maintained in a manner which apparently afforded the owner such information as he desired to preserve and denied to all others access to this same information so that . . . the entries can neither be substantiated nor proven to be fictitious."[34]

If Hauptmann was receiving "hot money" from Fisch, it is remarkable that none of it had ever shown up in a bank where Steiner, Rouse made its deposits. If, on the other hand, Fisch was getting Lindbergh bills from Hauptmann, and laundering them somehow through fictitious fur deals, what became of the money going in that direction? Selma Kohl remembered only one package of furs coming to Fisch in the time that he lived with her; but she also remembered Hauptmann coming to his room nearly every day. "He had a lot of company," she added—a comment that did not interest her interrogator, Assistant Attorney General Robert Peacock, busy preparing the case against a solo kidnapper.

Gerta Henkel related that Isidor got very nervous waiting for Richard, pacing up and down, looking out her window to see if he were coming down the street. Sometimes, if Richard did not come, he would go away alone in the morning. "Where you go, working or what?" she would ask him. He said he was going to the stock market, Gerta reported, and sometimes he and Richard would go together.[35]

So Hauptmann and Fisch *were* in business together. The $2,000 advance Richard provided Isidor to pay for his ticket was not charity. Erich Schaefer might have believed Isidor was actually trying to escape from Richard by slipping off to Germany, but that was an unlikely story from a man trying to put distance between Fisch and Hauptmann—just as Charlie Schleser did, perhaps for very different reasons.

Then there is Fisch's career as a "hot money" vendor, documented in a number of affidavits obtained by defense lawyer Lloyd Fisher after the trial. In one of them, a blond-headed man taller than Fisch, known only as Fritz, sought to act as a go-between to arrange a sale in a billiard parlor on the corner of Eighty-sixth Street and Third Avenue. The would-be buyer backed off when he saw who the seller was. "I . . . told

Fritz that Fisch was already indebted to me for borrowed money, and that I did not believe any of Fisch's stories." Fritz made an appearance in another deposition, again working in partnership with "Izzy" on the corner of Eighty-sixth Street. This time Fritz tried to convince the prospect the money could be passed anywhere by giving him a five-dollar bill to buy cigars. The man used the bill, kept the cigars, and turned down the offer. No deal, he said, seventy-five cents on the dollar was too much. If Izzy changed his mind about the price, he should let him know.[36]

None of this money was ever said to be Lindbergh ransom money, although the second failed deal occurred soon after the kidnapping. Fritz's appearance as Fisch's front man recalls Hauptmann's statement that when he first met Fisch on Hunter's Island, a blond man who spoke German with an Austrian accent accompanied him. Over and over again, one finds Fisch determined to keep his friends far apart from one another. When one is engaged in the sort of enterprises Isidor undertook, this was good business practice as well.[37]

Hauptmann last saw Fisch when he took him to the boat for his trip to Germany on December 6, 1933, a few days after a farewell party. Who did he want to invite to the party, Richard had asked him, maybe a girlfriend? No one, he answered, ask your friends. "It is funny," Hauptmann told an interviewer in prison, "why not invite your friends?" But Isidor said no. All right, replied Richard, he would invite Hans Kloppenburg, the Henkels, and Henry Uhlig, who was going to Germany with Isidor. No, said Fisch, if those people came, he didn't want any party. "It was the funniest thing in the world," but Richard went along with him. Hans Kloppenburg showed up anyway, as it was the usual night, the first Saturday of the month, for their "musicale," and Richard had forgotten to tell him not to come.[38]

Previously, Isidor had dropped off two satchels and four hundred sealskins, which he said were worth six dollars apiece—a vastly inflated estimate. These sealskins were presumably to establish his trustworthiness as he departed for Germany. The night of the party, December 2, 1933, Richard said Isidor brought in a little package, about the size of a shoebox, tied in string, and told him to keep it in a dry place. He would get it when he came back. No one else at the party saw the shoebox, except Hans Kloppenburg, who was standing by the door. When Richard asked what was in it, he said he got no real reply. So he assumed it contained important papers or perhaps photographs that should not get wet. Then he forgot about it.[39]

That was the beginning of the Fisch story. Reilly's inability to produce a coherent account of Isidor Fisch's multiple schemes to raise money made the whole idea that Hauptmann later discovered the box, months after Fisch's death, sound ludicrous. Richard could not really explain how water from a leak in the closet could penetrate the layers of wrapping paper, exposing the money one rainy afternoon in mid-August 1934. The prosecution harped on the notion that Isidor Fisch was a purely innocent victim of Hauptmann's desperate efforts to wriggle free from conviction and the death penalty. A first-rate defense team, with equivalent funds to the state's deep pockets, would have served a very different Fisch to the jury.

News came from Germany a few months later that Fisch had died of tuberculosis. His brother, Pinkas, wrote Richard that Isidor had told his family that "the stocks and the merchandise [he left behind] would amount to quite a bit of money." His letter set off a search for Isidor's treasure that led Richard and Henry Uhlig around New York to find out what had happened to the bakery, and where the missing furs might be stored. The search was still going on almost up to the day of Richard's arrest in September 1934. In those weeks and months a series of letters went back and forth between Hauptmann and Pinkas Fisch. Beneath the studied politeness was a wary probing by both sides.

Pinkas reassured Richard he was fully aware they were close friends and business partners. He intended to maintain that relationship for the sake of his brother's memory and asked for details about the several business enterprises Isidor had mentioned, such as stock speculations and silver fox furs. In his last few hours, Pinkas went on, Isidor had tried to tell them something else but lacked the strength. It was true that Isidor had been unable to speak very much as his illness progressed because the tuberculosis had spread to his larynx. Whether he had anything more to say is doubtful, although the Fisch family took note of his anxious efforts to send some message to his friend Richard. It is certainly possible that Pinkas hoped to extract useful details from Richard by suggesting his brother was about to reveal the whereabouts of hidden resources.

But Pinkas must have been stunned by Richard's response. Richard said he had put up his stocks, had loaned money to Isidor for the purchase of furs, and had provided $2,000 to fund the trip to Germany. In all, Isidor owed him at least $7,500. He had also discovered, he wrote Pinkas, that Isidor had borrowed nearly $4,000 from a woman named Mrs. Hile. Isidor had told him about his $10,000 investment in a baking concern; but when Richard tried to find out about the company, he discovered it had gone bankrupt. Finally, did Pinkas have any idea about where the furs that Isidor claimed he had bought with Richard's money might be—furs that supposedly were valued at over $21,000?

If Pinkas had been attempting to con Richard, he got back more, much more, than he bargained for. Richard then tried to persuade Pinkas that the best way to settle these matters would be for the Fisch family to give him the power to go to Isidor's safe deposit box in search of documents to lead them to the missing furs and any other assets. Pinkas responded, once again, that his brother had not been able to talk very much. "I am sorry that I cannot name the storage place of the merchandise. I asked Isidor about this half an hour before his death but he answered in broken and indistinguishable words that he could not tell me." All he could do was give Richard some possible names. Pinkas said, however, that he did know about Mrs. Hile, and that Isidor told him the loan had been repaid except for interest. Apparently, then, there had been a discussion in some detail about finances—despite Isidor's rapidly declining state of ill health. Pinkas ended this letter by stating he intended to come over personally for some weeks to resolve the whole business but was not sure when he could get away, because he needed permission of the Reichsbank to get the necessary funds, an oblique reference to Nazi restrictions on bank accounts owned by Jews.[40]

Pinkas had commissioned Henry Uhlig, Isidor's childhood friend now back in the United States, to join in the search for the furs and other assets. His sister, Hanna, also believed that "her brother must still have money over there." When Uhlig got together with Richard, the latter was beginning to realize that Isidor had conned him into believing there were furs somewhere in storage waiting to be sold at profits of 20 to 30 percent. Richard's books showed that the partnership had made some $6,000 in previous sales, but where those funds went (if they existed) was never determined.

Isidor had left with Hauptmann some four hundred sealskins, it will be remembered, telling him they would bring $2,000—a story apparently intended to keep Richard from asking too many questions. When Richard found out that there were no other furs anywhere else in New York, he told his wife, "If Isidor's brother comes I won't give them to him, I will sell them because he cheated me for all my money." One evening Henry Uhlig came over. "Look at the furs," Richard said, "you are a furrier. . . . I am going to sell them now anyhow. I will get over $2,000 on those and this helps me a little for what Isidor cheated me." Uhlig picked up one of the furs and threw it at him. If you get a dollar for one of these, he said, you would be lucky.[41]

Even Isidor's closest friends had no idea what he had done with any money from the sales of furs. Erich Schaefer's mother, Mary, wrote Pinkas that no one knew what he had done the last three months before he left for Germany. "He must have taken the money which he received for the furs and played the stock market." When Uhlig and Hauptmann went out in search of the safety deposit box, they stopped at the office of attorney Louis Blitzer, a lodge brother and friend of Isidor Fisch for many years. Richard was now claiming that Isidor owed him $14,000, a combined sum of funds advanced for stocks in a bakery, for furs, and for various supposed transactions in the stock market. He had no evidence to support any of these claims.

It did appear that Isidor had become involved in trying to start up yet another "bakery," but—in this whirligig he had set in motion in 1931 with Charles Schleser—nothing was ever what it seemed to be. What Blitzer took to be a new company probably was Isidor's effort to recycle the stocks one more time.[42]

Could it be another coincidence that Richard had settled on $14,000 as Isidor's debt to him? When he explained how he found the money, and why he did nothing to inform the Fisch family of his discovery, Richard always justified his actions as simply taking what was rightfully his after Isidor had left him holding an empty bag with no silver fox or any other furs left in sight beyond the cheap sealskins. His first letter to Pinkas Fisch contained a detailed inventory of the phantom furs. When they couldn't be found, he had a claim to the $14,000 Isidor had left for safekeeping.[43]

Since we do not know, and never can know for sure, which of these possibilities is the real Fisch story, there is little to be gained by further speculation. What we do know, however, is that it is not possible to take Isidor Fisch for simply a poor, struggling young man. Henry Uhlig wrote to relatives in Germany soon after his return to the United States sounding like a man whose eyes had suddenly been opened. He was, after all, as Pinkas had said, Isidor's childhood friend and had made the last trip back on the boat with him. When Pinkas commissioned him to find out about his brother's finances, Uhlig found out instead that Isidor had borrowed all over "from fools who gave him money on his word." He borrowed to buy furs that did not exist, and he borrowed against the defunct baking company's stock as late as a few months before he left for Germany. Uhlig told his family not to talk about these matters—"There is still much more about this matter but it is disgusting."[44]

Uhlig had become a good friend of Richard Hauptmann in the aftermath of the search for Isidor's lost fortune and even planned a hunting trip to Maine at the time of Richard's arrest. Given what he knew about Isidor's behavior, he did not find Richard's story about finding the money ridiculous at all. "I believe," he wrote again to Germany, "that

Isidor bought this money from some vagabond (as he knew many) with the money he had borrowed from these people, in order to speculate with it, as they were gold certificates." According to this thesis, Fisch left it with Hauptmann because he discovered that he, in turn, had been caught in one of his own snares—and left with money he could not spend. The police had asked Uhlig whether he had noticed that Isidor had much money. Nothing else. "The police do not want to know anything about Isidor because, as one says here: dead men tell no tales."[45]

"What a swine Isidor proved to be!" Uhlig went on. Only recently, with Richard's arrest, did he realize how "much worse" Isidor's scheming had proven to be. He had persuaded Richard to go into the fur trade. "He was always boasting that he had $29,000 from Hauptmann." Did not Uhlig stop to wonder where in the world Richard would have found $29,000 to invest in such a way? Was Richard, as Uhlig said about the other lenders, one of the fools who took him at his word? Exactly how much money did Isidor Fisch receive from Richard Hauptmann? Was it $29,000, $14,000, $7,500, or just $2,000 for a final trip home?

As anxious as Henry Uhlig was to portray Richard Hauptmann as one of Isidor Fisch's innocent dupes, Charles Schleser was determined to prove Fisch innocent of any and all wrongdoing—even if it meant infiltrating the Hauptmann camp. This plan was hatched when Schleser met with Attorney General Wilentz in Trenton on December 6, 1934. Schleser told Wilentz that after Hauptmann's arrest he saw Karl Henkel's name in the papers and remembered that Henkel had been a driver for the Knickerbocker Pie Company. He also told the attorney general that he hadn't been able to earn a cent for about a year, and so he called on this old acquaintance to see if he could borrow $400. Why should he expect Karl Henkel to loan him money? Wilentz might have asked that question; but it was really a defense attorney's question. When he went to the house to see Karl, Schleser continued, on the night of November 23, only Gerta Henkel was there. While he was waiting for Karl to return, other friends stopped by, including Hans Kloppenburg.

And did they discuss the case?

Yes, said, Schleser. All those people who came there that night believed Hauptmann innocent, and that Fisch supplied the money found in the garage. Gerta Henkel, especially, said that Fisch was nothing but a crook of the worst kind.

One can imagine Wilentz's excitement as he put the next question: What did you say in respect to all that talk?

"Due to the fact I felt I should state nothing by [*but?*] the truth in the affair, I haven't disclosed anything of my inner talks concerning Fisch."

Perfect! Schleser could not be more suited to find out all he could about the Hauptmann defense plans.

Schleser left that first night without seeing Karl Henkel. But the next day they met at Schleser's "office." "I felt I better go out of the office and talk where we could be undisturbed and it was about 10:30 or probably 11 o'clock in the morning then, and we went to a cafeteria and sat there discussing matters pertaining to Hauptmann and Fisch up to about 3 o'clock in the afternoon." And, oh, yes, he almost forgot: "I approached him with reference to a loan."

And what did he say to that?

"He said he has no money right now, but he knows people who have a lot of money and he is going to see them and if possible he is going to get money from them."

Prosecutors must deal with unsavory characters—or more crimes would never be solved, or criminals brought to trial. Charles Schleser had just admitted he was blackmailing the friends of Richard Hauptmann, but he was useful. He had an entrée into the inner circle. Wilentz could never put him on the witness stand for fear the loan "request" would blow up in his face. But the attorney general needed to know the details. What did they say? He asked.

Karl Henkel kept putting him off, finally tell him to go see Reilly. What would I have to say to him? Schleser had replied. "I can tell nothing but certain things Mr. Reilly might not like to hear."

But was he still in contact with Henkel and the others? Wilentz asked.

Yes.

And did they want him to say that Fisch was borrowing money all over the place to put together funds to hire some gangster to do the kidnapping?

Yes.

"[But you did not] furnish any special help because you are convinced that Fisch was not only not dishonest, but that you were then and are now convinced that Fisch is an upright and honest man?"

Yes.

A perfectly satisfactory ending for a *very* satisfactory interview leading to Schleser's eager agreement to go back to the Hauptmann circle to find out all he could about defense plans. Wilentz thus obtained from Schleser confirmation that Hans Kloppenburg was going to testify about seeing Fisch bring the small package into the house, and that they were lining up people to refute the handwriting experts. Interestingly, Schleser was the one who had picked out the funny-looking *x* as a damning piece of evidence. If the prosecution could prove the notes were in Hauptmann's hand, "nothing in this wide world will be able to save his neck," Schleser had told Hauptmann's friends, and he "considered that *x* written by the same hand." Kloppenburg and the others laughed that off. Many Germans wrote the *x* that way, he said. "If they think they are going to convict him on this handwriting they have another guess coming."

Who was Schleser trying to impress with this rendition of his conversation at the Henkels' apartment? Picking out the *x* demonstrated, at least, that he had studied the notes carefully, and also Hauptmann's handwriting. Perhaps Schleser was dropping hints about how his testimony, if he were called, could benefit the state.[46]

On December 10, just four days after this first interview, Schleser was back in Trenton, this time talking about his alibi for Fisch's whereabouts on the night of March 1, 1932. It seemed that Schleser had been scheduled to call upon some people that night, Mr. and Mrs. Henry Jung, but he had been ill for two days and could not make it. When Isidor stopped by to see him that evening, Charlie asked him if he would help him out and go in his place. The appointment was important because it had to do with a $700 note that fell due that very night, and he needed to make arrangements to pay off the debt to the Jungs in installments. Isidor agreed to do the favor, and the Jungs were completely surprised to see this total stranger show up. Schleser could not resist embellishing the story. "They had a few drinks and later made some tea and had a bite and they liked Fisch so much that he often visited them after that."[47]

Schleser's alibi for Isidor Fisch was almost too convenient, too fully imagined, and too perfect not to be suspicious. It supposedly proved where Fisch had been the night of the kidnapping, at least part of the time, but, just as Hauptmann's alibi about how he received the money depended on a dead man's silence, so, too, did Schleser's statement about where *he* had been that night depend on the same sealed lips.

If Schleser were involved, would he have volunteered so often and so completely to help the prosecution? He might well have. There are many reasons for a criminal to try to get close to police working on a case, ranging from ego gratification to some of Dr. Shoenfeld's favorite sorts of psychoses.

When Schleser met with Wilentz on December 10, the attorney general gave him new instructions: the next time he met with the Henkels he should try to convince them that he had been very badly treated by Fisch, and that he shared their opinion of him. This he did at a meeting at the Henkels' apartment the following day. The day after that, Schleser related all the details of the conversation and how the Hauptmann "clan" planned to drag in Anne's brother as a feebleminded young man who had threatened to harm the baby, who, according to rumor, was himself feebleminded. They planned also to make much of Violet Sharp's suicide. Reilly had secured a letter in which Violet supposedly warned of danger to the child. In addition, there was the sudden death of Olly Whateley in May 1933. The butler, who was living alone at Highfields while his wife was in England, had been taken ill with a stomach ailment. He died a few days later of peritonitis. Both deaths, Hauptmann's defenders were going to claim, were suspicious and somehow linked to the kidnapping.[48]

At a final interview with Assistant Attorney General Robert Peacock on December 17, Schleser related his interview with Reilly, during which he had kept pressing the defense attorney to find out if the defense team wanted to call him to testify. He had used as bait some receipts Fisch had given him for stock in the failed Knickerbocker Pie Company. Whether Reilly understood the game being played or not, he gave no promises about testimony. He asked Schleser to produce samples of Isidor's handwriting and said, "[I'll] arrange to take care of you."[49]

(Two years later, in January 1936, Governor Harold Hoffman's special investigator, H. C. Keyes, interviewed some neighbors of Schleser's, who told another Fisch story: Isidor had brought a small package to the Schlesers' house a few days before he left for Germany, explaining it contained bonds. When Charlie's wife peeked into the package, she saw money, and that alarmed Isidor, who took it back saying he would leave it with someone who would ask no questions, his good friend Richard Hauptmann.)

Schleser boasted of his "Dave" and "Charlie" relationship with Wilentz. From their first meeting, Schleser was kept pretty close to the prosecution. It is entirely possible that Schleser hinted about telling the defense that Fisch had come to him with a mysterious package. "This man Schleser is a slippery person," concluded Keyes. "It is obvious that if Schleser was at first inclined to help the defense to the extent of calling at Reilly's office, that what he had to testify was helpful to the defense." It may be, after all, that Schleser offered to tell this story in court for $400—or more—and was turned down because somebody smelled a rat. In any event, Schleser and Karl Henkel were not discussing the merits of apple versus blueberry pies for more than five hours that Saturday in November.[50]

There is one final point to the Fisch story that did come out in time for the trial, a United Press report of January 10, 1935. An enterprising reporter had discovered that Peter Birritella's church was diagonally across the street from where Isidor Fisch had resided. There was a pattern of coincidences linking Fisch's neighborhood to people connected with the Lindbergh tragedy:

> [Birritella's] church is less than a block from the filling station where the ransom note that finally trapped Hauptmann appeared. Only a few blocks away was a speakeasy in which Septimus Banks, Morrow butler, known to be friendly with Miss Sharpe [*sic*], spent much time. "Open meetings" of the Rev. Birratella's [*sic*] flock were held on Thursdays, Miss Sharpe's day off. When Miss Sharpe swallowed poison a few days after the baby's body was discovered, police disclosed she had been nervous when first questioned. Had she heard the prophecies of Mary Cerrita or had she information she feared she might divulge, was the question arising today.[51]

"If Isidor Fisch had not died in Germany," Richard told his wife in the Flemington jail, "I would not be here behind the bars, and you would not be standing out there. How I trusted him with everything, never thinking I could get in a position of this kind." The first sentence leaves one impression, but the second is more ambiguous—and always will be. What was the "everything" he had entrusted to his friend?[52]

12 JUDGE TRENCHARD'S COURTROOM

We have been regaled by so many prison pictures, so many crime and detective and district attorney pictures that, as the day dawdles on and one would-be juror after another is questioned, challenged, rejected, it begins to seem like a picture. Presently the reel will end, and Minnie Mouse and her white shoes take the screen.

No. This is real. This is the court house of Flemington; the Hauptmann trial is in progress.

—novelist KATHLEEN NORRIS, *New York Times,* January 2, 1935

"Oyez! Oyez! Oyez! Oyez!" intoned the court crier. "All manner of persons having business with the Court of Quarter Seasons—Oyer and Terminer . . . , let them draw nigh and they shall be heard." Outside the courthouse a colorless winter sun illuminated milling crowds of people anxious to glimpse even a coat sleeve or a hat on one of the rich and famous being ushered through the doors to their privileged seats. Judging by the number of automobiles barely crawling along the streets and strung out for miles along the roads leading into town, more than sixty thousand people had come to Flemington to be part of the spectacle.

Squeezing between the crowd and deputy sheriffs guarding the doors, hawkers offered newspapers, miniature working models of the ladder, and even locks of hair. It was reminiscent of a medieval fair complete with relics from the martyred saints. One raspy voice stood out above the others. "What's your name?" asked a reporter. "They calls me 'Pushcart,'" the man replied, grinning, and resumed his bellow. No one could decipher what he was saying, but he was the envy of the other hawkers, especially the weak and timid voices of local paperboys recruited for special duty.

Inside the courtroom, the bustle and hum was like a pre-theater crowd waiting for the curtain. Reporters occupied 150 of the 500 seats available. Walter Winchell was there, of course, proclaiming to all near and far that he had pushed the police into tightening the ring around Hauptmann. So were Gabriel Heatter and Damon Runyon. The novelists Nora Roberts and Edna Ferber, as well as the British writer Ford Madox Ford, had found places near the oak rail separating prosecution and defense tables from the audience. Those who could not get seats lined the walls.

When the door to the left behind Judge Thomas Trenchard's desk opened, all eyes turned to see the accused man. Almost unnoticed near the back of the room stood Anna, straining like all the rest to see her husband guided to his place between a local constable and a state trooper.

Dressed in a brownish gray, double-breasted suit with a pocket-handkerchief, he looked like a young businessman, and not at all like someone on trial for his life. It was an ironic parody of Richard's lost ambitions. Reaching the defense table, he shook hands with attorney Lloyd Fisher, and the two chatted for a moment or two before he sat down. Fisher and his client had already forged a lasting bond. Also seated at the defense table were Edward Reilly, resplendent in formal cutaway and fawn-colored spats, as well as Frederick Pope and Egbert Rosecrans, both descendants of Union generals in the Civil War. Pope readily admitted to his young law clerk, Sam Chiarvalli, that he had joined the defense team for publicity. They all did, Chiarvalli asserted. But that did not matter. "Sam," Pope told him, "there is no doubt in my mind that this poor guy is being railroaded."[1]

A few minutes later Colonel Charles Lindbergh appeared at the rear of the room and strode briskly to his place at the prosecution table. Dressed in a light gray suit and blue striped tie, Lindbergh stopped to talk with David Wilentz before sitting down to busy himself with a large three-ring-binder notebook one of the prosecutors handed him. Sitting with David Wilentz were Hunterdon County prosecutor Anthony Hauck, Assistant Attorneys General Robert Peacock and Joseph Lanigan, and Judge George K. Large, a very prominent local attorney originally invited to be part of the defense team. Taking out a notepad from his jacket, Lindbergh began jotting down notes. He did not once turn his head to the defense table a few feet away. Neither man looked at the other.

Three days earlier, before the trial started, the *New York Evening Journal* had reported Lindbergh's request to sit with the prosecutors: "Col. Lindbergh was granted the extraordinary privilege during the hoax trial of John Hughes Curtis [the man who had falsely claimed to be in touch with the kidnappers], but it was believed unlikely that Supreme Court Justice Thomas W. Trenchard, who will preside, would permit such a thing in this case."[2]

But Trenchard did permit it. Reporters also noticed something else, even more unusual. "It was observed that Colonel Lindbergh was carrying a pistol in a shoulder holster. Although his coat concealed it most of the time, it was visible when he leaned forward to consult with the lawyers at the State's counsel table." Rumors he had recently received death threats had been denied by spokespersons. Before the kidnapping, he had received threats against himself and his family, "mostly from cranks and persons obviously disordered mentally, but no such letter has been received for a long time." The colonel had carried a pistol for five years and was considered an expert small-arms marksman. How that justified carrying a weapon into a court of law was not explained further.

At precisely 10:10 A.M. on January 2, 1935, Judge Thomas Trenchard rapped his gavel for the first time. As the questioning of prospective jurors began, Lloyd Fisher hoped to turn the opening courtroom scene to his client's advantage by calling attention to the extra precautions in Hauptmann's guard and Lindbergh's ill-concealed weapon. Fisher pointedly asked Charles Walton if he would be influenced by the fact that the prisoner was "surrounded by State police in the courtroom." Oh, no, Wilentz protested. It was not a fact that the prisoner was surrounded, there was only the one constable and a state trooper. Judge Trenchard was also unhappy. "There was no justification at all," he reprimanded the defense lawyer, "for asking that question." Fisher's strategy was clear: he hoped to portray his client as somewhat bewildered by it all, wondering why he was there—and not back beyond the oak rail watching the real culprit go on trial.[3]

Charles Lindbergh stared intently at each of the prospective jurors when the questioning resumed, as if trying to see inside their minds and hearts. The selection complete, David Wilentz rose—"May It Please the Court." Trenchard nodded. Just at that moment Anne Lindbergh entered the courtroom, evoking little gasps of wonder and sympathy.

On the day of the kidnapping, Wilentz began, the Lindbergh child was a normal, happy, jovial tot—blue-eyed, curly headed, blond haired— who spent the day playing with his family. That very night the child was killed. "The state will prove to you jurors that the man who killed and murdered that child sits in this very courtroom—the gentleman in the custody of the Sheriff's guards right in the rear of the distinguished members of the Bar who make up the defense counsel."

Walking back and forth, pounding a fist into his other hand, at times scornful, at times imitating a German accent, Wilentz imbedded details into the jury's consciousness. "Why," he declared in mock wonderment at one point, "he used Lindy's money to buy Sweepstake tickets with! What do you think of that?" By juxtaposing the terrible crime with such frivolous, arrogant behavior, Wilentz described the vast chasm that separated Hauptmann from everyone else in the room, from common human decency. The accused man was something low and alien that had come unbidden into American society to do this evil thing. Observing the prisoner, Kathleen Norris agreed that Hauptmann was—"an outsider, not possessing in his make-up any of the yeast that is America, not understanding."[4]

Colonel Lindbergh heard the voice of Hauptmann that night at St. Raymond's Cemetery, Wilentz went on, the night the ransom was paid. "Hey Dok-*tor*," the man called. "Hey, Dok-*tor*," repeated Wilentz, giving Hauptmann a scornful glance. It was a crucial moment in the trial, but Wilentz was probably the only one in the room who understood fully why that was so. Wilentz tried here at the outset to put all the confusion about the voice identity to rest. "In the still of the night you could have heard it for two blocks and particularly in the vicinity of the Bronx."[5]

By locking in what was heard in his opening statement, the attorney general effectively ensured Condon's visual identification as well. The old educator would have a hard time, indeed, doing anything else when he appeared on the stand after Colonel Lindbergh had testified that the voice calling out "Hey, Dok-*tor*" at St. Raymond's was Hauptmann's voice.

Wilentz then described the discovery of Charlie's "horribly decomposed" body "in that hole, the grave that Hauptmann had placed for it." A truck driver—"some colored gentleman"—answering a call of nature was horrified at the sight and rushed off to tell somebody. "And pretty soon, pretty soon, Colonel Lindbergh and Betty Gow and others had turned the body of that child faceup. The moisture in the ground had still preserved the face a little bit, so that it was white when it was turned up, and twenty minutes after the air struck, it had turned black."[6]

Neither Colonel Lindbergh nor Betty Gow had been present when the body was turned over, but Wilentz sacrificed accuracy to the need to affirm the identification of the body against rumors that the one found in the woods near an orphanage was not really Charlie's. It would not be the only time truth was bent to serve justice in Trenchard's courtroom. Wilentz described a scene that never occurred to convince the court that Lindbergh and Gow had seen the body before the face had turned black and less easily recognizable. "Anybody that knew that child, any member of the family," asserted Wilentz, "would know right away that was the 'Little Eagle.'"

"He came there with his ladder," Wilentz said of Hauptmann's preparations, placed it against the wall, and entered the Lindbergh home "with the intent to commit a battery upon that child and with the intent to steal the child and its clothing." Now came his first theory of how Charlie died. "As he went out that window and down that ladder of his, the ladder broke. He had more weight going down than he had when he was coming up. And down he went with this child. In the commission of that burglary, that child was instantaneously killed when it received that first blow. It received a horrible fracture, the dimensions of which when you hear about it will convince you that death was instantaneous."[7]

Despite this statement, the prosecutor really did not have a coherent theory about how the child had died. All through the trial the prosecution doodled curlicues around the question of how the kidnapping was actually accomplished and in what way death occurred.

Wilentz told the jury how Hauptmann had quit his job on the day the ransom was paid, and lived thereafter "a life of luxury and ease." Now, said the prosecutor, he could take a trip to Florida, now he could have a boat on Hunter's Island, and now he could buy a $400 radio in the midst of the worst depression in modern times. Not only that; now he could now "speculate and gamble with thousands and thousands and thousands of dollars." He poured money into various accounts. "Forty-five hundred dollars in the account of Mrs. Schoenfeld or whatever her name is, the wife, the maiden name, the delightful wife of Mr. Hauptmann." Wilentz stumbled over himself here, confusing Anna's maiden name, Schoefler, with Shoenfeld—the name of the psychiatrist who had claimed he could identify Hauptmann's personality and motive for the crime from the ransom notes, and who now sat in the courtroom helping the prosecution by providing the attorney general with hints about what would break down the defendant's psychological defenses.[8]

Wilentz paid little attention to Freudian motivations, however, preferring Mammon. His passing reference to Anna as "the delightful wife" of the accused was interesting, finally, not as a tribute to her character but, once again, as a condemnation of the lone person responsible, and for whom there could be no other judgment but guilty.

"We demand the penalty of murder in the first degree." Curiously, he did not say "penalty *for* murder," but *"of* murder." Normally, one would say *for* murder, thereby establishing the crime *as* murder (along with the perpetrator), but not *of* murder, which is a slightly ambiguous statement implying *as if* murder or *as bad as* murder.

Reilly immediately moved for a mistrial on the grounds that Wilentz had not delivered a proper opening statement, but an inflammatory and impassioned appeal designed to stir up the jury's emotions before the trial started. Trenchard denied the motion but did remind the jury— at Reilly's urging—that the purpose of an opening is to "tell the jury what the evidence will show." Wilentz had gone far beyond that, obviously.

All through the opening statement, Hauptmann had been staring straight at Wilentz, motionless, but he stirred at the attorney general's next words and braced himself as if for a hard blow. "The state calls Anne Lindbergh." As she walked to the witness stand, her husband half rose from his chair at the prosecution table to offer encouragement.[9]

There would be some surprises for the attorney general before she finished her testimony. Wilentz began by leading Anne through the events of that day: the baby's cold that had prompted her to stay over for another night at Hopewell, her afternoon walk when she paused outside the nursery window to throw pebbles up to the window, and the muddy conditions outside where she left footprints along the wooden walk.

Then the prosecutor asked Anne to tell him about the child: "Was he a normal child?

"He was perfectly normal."

"Healthy?"

"He was very healthy."

His cold was much better that afternoon, Anne said, than it had been for the last two days.

"Was he able to talk yet?"

"He talked."

"To what extent, Mrs. Lindbergh?

"I don't remember any particular conversation on that afternoon."[10]

It was an ambiguous answer, but no one took special note. Rumors about the baby's health, however, had arisen from the very first day of the kidnapping, stemming, in the first instance, from the apparent lack of fingerprints in the nursery or on the ladder. When Colonel Lindbergh ordered the body cremated immediately after the discovery and a brief autopsy, questions about the identification, as well as the health of the child, began to spread.[11]

The child's health, however, was a troubling matter for the prosecution. Hence the attorney general's immediate concern to have his first, and most sympathetic witness, Anne Lindbergh, dispel the rumors by her testimony. If fragile health accounted for Charlie's death from the short fall, a jury might not return a verdict of murder in the first degree. Here, once again, arose the related problem that the jury might not fully understand that while kidnapping did not carry the death penalty yet in New Jersey, a death that occurred as a result of a felony—even stealing the sleeping suit—was a capital offense. Who could say that at some point Hauptmann's attorneys might not attempt to raise the health issue to cloud both issues? They might offer a deal, a guilty plea for kidnapping if the murder charge were dropped. Throughout the trial, from Anne's testimony to the summation, such a situation was a major prosecution concern.

Wilentz, perhaps, need not have even raised the issue, but it was always good to get on the record that the kidnapper had struck down a perfectly healthy child who would never have a chance to enjoy life.

The next series of questions posed by the attorney general went off in an entirely different direction. These concerned the thumb guards. And in this instance Anne was not so helpful to the prosecution. Wilentz had hoped to have her say that she placed on the child the thumb guard later found in the drive near the entrance to the estate or saw Betty Gow, the nursemaid, do it. That would make it clear there had been no chance for anyone else to carry it out from the house after the kidnapping and place it on the gravel road in the opposite direction from the footprints and ladder. But Wilentz could not lead Anne the way he would lead other witnesses—including her husband.

"How was it fastened?"

"I did not put it on . . ."

"Well, do you know?

"[Continuing] myself."

"Did you see it done that night?"

"No, I don't remember seeing it done. I know the thumb guard and I have done it myself."

"Do you know whether—"

"But that night I did not put it on."

"Did you see it on though after it was put on?"

"I don't remember seeing it on."

"You don't remember. . . . Mrs. Lindbergh, will you tell us whether or not you recognize that as being one of the thumb guards the child had on, one of the thumb guards that was used for your child?"

"Yes."[12]

With this double-barreled question, Wilentz neatly stepped out of the hole he had dug for himself while trying to get Anne to say she had seen the thumb guard on Charlie. He practically reversed what Anne had actually said. She did not say that, yes, the thumb guard was on the child that night—had in fact said she could not remember. She agreed only that, yes, it was one of the thumb guards normally "used for your child." A skillful defense attorney would have brought that out for the court to ponder, along with the idea that others were alone with the child that night.

Inadvertently, Wilentz had stirred memories he really did not wish to have present in the room. Anne's repeated insistence that she was not the last person to leave the nursery—Betty Gow followed her out a few minutes later, after seeing that the baby was safely asleep—raised unsettled issues about which window had been left open, whether the thumb guard had been left off to ensure the baby slept soundly, and even whether or not he had been pinned down to the mattress as usual.

When Betty Gow discovered the child was not in his crib, just after 10 P.M., Anne rushed in to the bedroom but did not notice if any of the windows were open, nor did she see any note on the windowsill. The remarkable thing about that was that in her first statement to the police, Anne had said when she went into the room the light was on. Others would say the window where the kidnapper entered the room was up several inches. Anne's testimony could have occasioned some difficulty for the prosecution's case, particularly in regard to any inside help the kidnapper might have received.

Wilentz himself opened the door a bit to such speculations: "On the night when you walked into that room did you observe whether or not the room had been changed, its appearance had been changed at all from the time that you had seen it at 7:30?"

"I saw no change in the room at all. I noticed no change."

"Did you notice the bedclothes?"

"The bed clothes were apparently untouched, as though the child had been taken out. The pins were still fastening the bed clothes to the mattress."

Wilentz put yet another question that could have opened doors for the defense: "Had you had pins affixed from the bed clothes to the mattress?"

"I left the baby before he was completely put in for the night."

So as with the thumb guards and the window, Anne never saw the pins fastened. That left one final question hanging in the air: "Now, when you went in there who had preceded you in there, do you know?"

"As far as I know only Miss Gow."

Over and over again, Anne Lindbergh had refused to follow Wilentz's lead. Most of the other witnesses had been prepped by the prosecution. In Anne's case, however, Wilentz had seen no need. Emotion and sympathy, he gambled, would prevent Reilly from even exploring the questions. He was right. "Take the witness," Wilentz said, as if offering a dare. "The defense feels the grief of Mrs. Lindbergh requires no cross-examination," replied the honorable Mr. Reilly in his most gracious manner.[13]

Reilly could have asked follow-up questions, not in cross-examination style but as if gently trying to help Anne remember the night better so that they could all be clear about certain things. She might have been able to clarify the thumb guard matter, whether or not the pins were normally placed so close together, and to talk a little about the bedclothes not being disturbed.

The contrast between Anne's behavior on the stand and her husband's eagerness to follow Wilentz's lead was quite striking. Charles Lindbergh sat with crossed legs in the witness chair, elbows resting lightly on the arms, hands clasped on his lap. Occasionally, he would lean forward, a slightly quizzical look on his face, as if trying to understand fully the import of the questions being asked. He recited his arrival at Highfields near 8:30 P.M., their dinner together, a brief conversation with Anne in the living room—when he heard the noise he had first identified as the sound of slats from an orange crate falling off a chair in the kitchen—and his entrance into the study, where he sat writing until Betty Gow rushed downstairs to ask him if he had the child. Under Wilentz's guidance, Lindbergh readily agreed that the sound he had heard could have been from a ladder outside near the nursery window, even though the kitchen was in the opposite direction.

Lindbergh's memory on this point was important because it provided evidence that the kidnapping had taken place shortly after 9 P.M., during the interval that the colonel had prescribed that the child was not to be disturbed, from 7 to 10 P.M. He was now willing to say definitely this was the time, apparently, although his friend Major Thomas Lanphier had once told FBI director J. Edgar Hoover that Lindbergh had surmised the kidnapping had occurred earlier.

Responding to Betty Gow's agitated question if he had the baby, Charles rushed upstairs to the nursery, where, like Anne, he first noted the state of the bedclothes. "The bed clothing in the crib was in such condition that I felt it was impossible for the baby to have gotten out himself. . . . The clothing was standing—the bed clothing was standing stiffly enough so that the opening where the baby had been was still there, the clothing had not collapsed."[14]

If the child had been yanked out of the bedclothes by a stranger, a juror might have wondered, why did both Anne and Charles take special care to say that they noticed the bedclothes had hardly been disturbed?

Lindbergh was the first to see the note on the windowsill and gave instructions that no one was to touch it or enter the nursery. He took his rifle from the closet and rushed outside to look for the child. Local police arrived in answer to the butler, Olly Whateley's phone call, and then state police, and at last—after more than two hours—the envelope was opened.

Wilentz then guided Lindbergh through the often-bizarre negotiations carried on with the aid of Dr. John Condon, until finally the narrative reached the night of April 2, 1932, when the two arrived in the vicinity of St. Raymond's Cemetery with the $70,000 demanded by the kidnapper for Charlie's return. In all previous statements, including his recent one to the Bronx grand jury, Lindbergh had described a man who passed by the car where he sat waiting for Condon to make contact and come back for the money. But Wilentz wanted nothing to do with this mysterious person who kept part of his face covered with a handkerchief and seemed to peer into the car window. For the state's purposes, he had disappeared as if he had never existed. "You heard a voice hollering, 'Hey, Doctor,' in some foreign voice, I think, as you referred to it," the attorney general prompted. "Since that time have you heard the same voice?"

"Yes, I have."

"Whose voice was it, Colonel, that you heard in the vicinity of St. Raymond's Cemetery that night, saying 'Hey, Doctor'"?

"That was Hauptmann's voice."[15]

Lindbergh then said he had heard the same voice in District Attorney Foley's office in New York after his grand jury testimony. He had testified at that hearing, it will be remembered, that he could not be expected to pick out the voice after more than two years.

Wilentz then picked up the health issue again. "Except for a little cold and except for the fact that one of the toes overlapped the other or so the child was perfectly normal?"

"Perfectly normal."

Reilly had promised reporters he would have plenty of questions to ask Colonel Lindbergh. His first question was "Are you armed, Colonel?"

Prosecutors objected that the question was not material and Judge Trenchard agreed, but Lindbergh intervened to say that he did not mind answering the question. Wilentz withdrew his objection, and Lindbergh announced that he was not armed.[16]

It was not a good beginning. Reilly next tried to impress upon the jury Lindbergh's surprising—if not negligent—lack of attention to background checks on the household employees. He did not make out much better there. What about Olly Whateley? Had Lindbergh looked into his prior employment?

He spoke with him for maybe a half hour or an hour. That was all.

"Beyond that did you go any further?"

"Beyond that I never go any further."

What about Betty Gow? "Did you make any effort to learn her background?"

"I don't know. That may have been done. I personally only talked to her. Mrs. Lindbergh may have looked into her background."

Did his attitude change after the kidnapping, and did he then pursue the question of the servants' background?

Not personally, he replied. "I placed my confidence in the police."

"Did you not make any effort as a father to find out the background of the people that were in the house the night your child was snatched away?"

Prosecutors again objected, but this time Trenchard let the questioning go on.

"I placed my entire confidence in the police and followed their suggestions from that time on. I tried to cooperate in every way that I could."[17]

Reilly was finally onto something here, but he muffed it. By asking about background checks, he had got Lindbergh to assert that he followed police suggestions and cooperated in every way he could. That was not true. Lindbergh had controlled every move until the discovery of the body. He had thwarted efforts to have lie-detector tests given to the servants and made unilateral decisions at key points, employing underworld figures to find out if he could make contacts with the kidnappers that way, and, most of all, allowing John Condon to pursue the negotiations without police participation.[18]

Reilly let Lindbergh off the hook and moved on to ask if it was not true federal agents had never seen the actual ransom notes.

"Oh, no, I don't believe that is so. No. I know that is not a fact."

An FBI observer at the trial picked up on this answer. Lindbergh might not have remembered, but the FBI had never seen the notes. In fact, the ransom notes were still a point of contention. "I never saw the notes," commented Hoover, "and in fact we asked for exact copies of same but N.J. sent us mutilated copies."[19]

Reilly tried hard to get Lindbergh to admit it was possible someone entered the front door while they were at dinner, and received the child from one of the servants, slipping out again into the night. No, it was not possible, said Lindbergh. There was no carpet on the stairs. Anyone coming in or going out would have been heard. Reilly could well have pressed that question—a prosecutor certainly would have. If one were listening for a sound like footsteps on the stairs, his answer could be accepted uncritically, but surely someone (especially wearing socks over his shoes as was often surmised) would not make so much noise. There was also a second staircase in the rear of the house, but the defense counsel did not press that issue, either.

Instead, Reilly shifted to the bedclothes and the likely restlessness of a two-year-old with a cold. "Didn't you think it strange, Colonel, that the child would be put to bed suffering from a cold, no matter how slight, after being rubbed with Vicks, at seven o'clock or half past seven, and nobody entering the room or the nursery to look at that child until ten o'clock at night?"

Lindbergh explained the household routine of leaving the child's sleep undisturbed during that period.

Reilly asked if it were not likely the child would turn over, disturbing the bedclothes in various ways to get more comfortable. And what if he got too warm?

"If the baby got very warm, we would hear about it immediately."

"He would call out, would he not?"

"I believe so."[20]

The point Reilly hoped to establish was that if Lindbergh could detect noises on the stairway, how, indeed, could an intruder have managed the kidnapping without making more of a sound than what Lindbergh called orange crate slats falling to the floor. Therefore, the crime had required aid from someone familiar with the routine, able to move about silently—and, above all, without allowing the child to wake and call out for help. Wilentz pondered these questions as well, and, as we will see, came up with a theory in his summation to the jury.

There followed a sharp exchange over the kidnapper's ability to manage the ladder and the child for a distance of seventy-five feet from the nursery.

"How much would you say this ladder weighed?"

"Three sections, I would say, would weigh, very roughly, 35 or 40 pounds, somewhere in there."

"An ungainly thing to carry, wasn't it?"

Lindbergh saw where this was heading, and snapped, "He could carry it under one arm."

"One arm?" Reilly pursued.

"He could."

"But you would have to disconnect it?"

"It was in three sections."

"You would have to disconnect it and fold it in three sections to carry it this way, put your arms through the rungs, take it off."

Reilly had him in an awkward corner for the moment. And Lindbergh's answer was evasive: "I do not know how many different ways it could be carried."

"You did not see any indications it was dragged along the ground, did you?"

"I do not recall that; I do not remember seeing any drag marks."[21]

A muddy night, a man burdened with a ladder under one arm, and a child weighing about thirty pounds under the other—was this a likely scenario?

Reilly then asked about the colonel's use of underworld figures, implying he might have been trying to divert the investigation as far away from the household as was possible. The defense had to be very careful here, because of Lindbergh's status as the nation's greatest hero.

Going after Condon was a bit easier. Had he ever considered, Reilly suggested to Lindbergh, that the "master mind might insert an ad in the paper and answer it himself?"

"I think that is inconceivable from practically any practical standpoint."

"You think it is?"

"As a matter of fact, I tried to consider it with every individual who has been connected in any way with this case, exempting no one, whether there was any connection."[22]

Lindbergh's effort to show that despite Reilly's insinuations, he had considered everyone a suspect, provided the defense attorney with a springboard to get into the story of John Hughes Curtis. At the Curtis trial, Lindbergh had testified he had no reason to doubt Curtis had actually been in touch, directly or indirectly, with the people responsible for the kidnapping.

When Reilly asked Lindbergh about this testimony, Wilentz became very agitated. And Judge Trenchard challenged the premise. Reilly's question, he said, assumed there was evidence the Curtis story was true, but that was not the case. No, Reilly explained, the point was to ascertain Lindbergh's belief at the time of the Curtis trial, for it bore directly on the attorney general's assertions that the defendant was the lone kidnapper and killer. "I believe on cross examination I have a right to find out whether or not Colonel Lindbergh was not of the belief as recently as the Curtis trial that it was a group of people and that he has only swung around to this belief against the defendant since the apprehension of the defendant."

Wilentz was not to be outfoxed. Before Lindbergh answered that question, he demanded, he should be asked at the same time who he now believed was responsible. Reilly protested—Lindbergh had already testified that the voice he heard at St. Raymond's Cemetery belonged to Hauptmann—but to no avail. So he put the question this way, not realizing he was about to undo all his work thus far: "Colonel, I will ask you, as suggested by the Court, and I assume that your answer will be that the defendant, you believe now, is guilty of the kidnapping; is that correct?"

Lindbergh turned to Judge Trenchard, "Shall I answer?"

"Yes."

"I do."[23]

Reilly's critics have scored him for asking this question—*above all other mistakes he made*—for it allowed Lindbergh to make another identification, one he could not challenge. The defense lawyer had managed to turn one of his best arguments—that Lindbergh had believed all along in the gang theory—into a prosecution accusation against his client. Newspaper headlines said, "COL. LINDBERGH NAMES HAUPTMANN AS KIDNAPPER AND TAKER OF RANSOM; COOL IN 3-HOUR CROSS-EXAMINATION." Reilly's efforts to lay the groundwork for his defense theory through questions about the bedclothes, the ladder, Condon's self-initiated role, and the colonel's belief there was a gang involved until the time of Hauptmann's arrest, washed out with the tide like so many footprints.

The FBI observer at the trial reported, "Everyone was amazed that Reilly did not attempt to cross-examine Colonel Lindbergh at all about Lindbergh's identification of Hauptmann's voice." But it would have been a tricky business after the previous exchange. "A long ray of sunlight played on the pale countenance of Bruno Richard Hauptmann," wrote one columnist, as court adjourned for the day. "The ray singled out the accused man and his face showed a sign of relief, after listening for hours of testimony which may send him to the electric chair."[24]

After a weekend recess, trial testimony resumed on January 7, 1935, when Betty Gow took the stand. Reilly had promised he would keep the nursemaid in the witness chair for a long time, and soon thereafter he would produce a bigger sensation than Lindbergh's accusation—the names of the actual kidnappers. Betty had seemed nervous listening to the proceedings, constantly fiddling with the purse in her lap. But Wilentz quickly established Betty as a sympathetic figure, filled with great affection for her ward.

She said she had left the nursery shortly after 8 P.M., satisfied that Charlie was sleeping soundly. In fact, she would remark to Anne downstairs that he had gone to sleep rather quickly. Just on to 10 P.M. she looked at her watch and said, "I must go to the baby."

Then Wilentz asked the key question: "When you got in there, what did you find?"

"I found things exactly—I didn't put any light up, but let the door of the room open so that the light from the hall would come in."[25]

That was her routine, she never put the light on so as not to startle the baby, but she had to pause here to rethink, "I found things exactly . . ." Catching herself, Betty picked up the story again. She had closed the French window and turned on the electric heater. Going to the crib, she realized she could not hear Charlie breathing. "I bent down, felt all over for him and discovered he wasn't there." After learning Mrs. Lindbergh had not taken him to her room, she went downstairs to find out if he was with the colonel. Alarmed, Lindbergh rushed upstairs, saw immediately the child was gone, and declared to his wife, "Anne, they have stolen our baby."

Prosecutor Robert Peacock had prepped Betty beforehand so she would be able to describe the scene after the room search had been completed, when the women sat waiting for police to arrive. "We did not speak," Betty recalled for Peacock. "No one said anything. I just could not speak to Mrs. Lindbergh about it."

"Was Mrs. Lindbergh praying?"

"No. She was sitting in absolute silence."

"The three of you were sitting in that room and Mrs. Lindbergh was praying—she was in an attitude of prayer—hand on her forehead?"

"She does not show emotion."

"But at that moment she was looking to someone higher for help— I am not going too far when I say that, do you think?"

"No, you are not."

"Am I going too far when I ask you to testify the baby had gone and Mrs. Lindbergh, Mrs. Whateley and I sat in silence and Mrs. Lindbergh sat in an attitude of her hand on her forehead as if in prayer? Isn't that exactly what happened?"

"Yes."

"Tell me that scene in that room."

"After Whateley called the police, Mrs. Whateley and I joined Mrs. Lindbergh in the sitting room. We sat there very quietly. Mrs. Lindbergh sat with her hand to her forehead in an attitude of prayer—all hoping that we could get the baby back soon."[26]

During direct examination at the trial, however, Betty amended the lines Peacock had so carefully supplied and rehearsed with her earlier. Asked what went on in the sitting room while the women waited for the police, she said, "Well, I guess we were all praying for the safe return of the baby." Was anything said? "We didn't speak." Betty was not going to single out Anne as the only one moved to prayer, and leave herself open in any way to Reilly's expected efforts to portray her as disloyal.[27]

Of more import, Peacock had asked her if she thought it might have been possible for someone to spirit the child down the stairs to the outside without being seen. Where Lindbergh would testify that it was not at all a practical possibility, Betty was unsure. "The only time it could possibly have happened would be when they were both in the dining room and Mrs. Whateley was in the kitchen."

Peacock did not want to go down that path any farther and asked whether it was a windy night.

"Yes, a very bad night."

Had she heard any noise?

"No."

A crash of any kind?

"No."

Did she observe the mud tracks going toward the crib?

"No. I did see the sheet was soiled with dirty hands—brownish dirt."[28]

None of these were fruitful avenues for the prosecution. Why, for example, were the bedsheets smeared with brownish dirt and yet there were no other prints left in the nursery? In her original statements and now again, Betty mentioned the bedsheets. But no one else ever talked about them.

Reilly badly overplayed his hand with Betty, winning no friends by hovering over her—a florid bully browbeating the young woman who had been Charlie's almost constant protector. Why had she come to the United States without ever applying for citizenship? What was the real nature of her relationship with the sailor Red Johnson? How much had the prosecution paid in "costs," $650 was it, to bring her over from Scotland for the trial?

These accusations tended to crowd out any substantive points in his cross-examination. Concentrating on his favorite theory that the kidnapper could not have used the window on the southeast side of the nursery to enter and leave, Reilly asked if Betty had ever tried the windows. They were new, he said. "Were they rather stiff?"

"I don't recall."

Wasn't it a fact that one would have to open that window from the outside, and that the shutters—even if not closed tightly—were drawn in as far as they would go? And with the exception of the little warp that made it impossible to fasten completely, they were closed?

Yes, she agreed, this was all so.

Then came two questions that Betty did not answer truthfully.

"You had never given any indication to any person in the world that that room was the nursery, had you?"

"No."

"Nobody had ever questioned you about where the nursery was or where the crib was or where the baby slept, had they?"

"They have not."[29]

But we know she had been there when Red Johnson was shown around the house. In fact, Johnson readily admitted to police that he had been in the Lindbergh house on three occasions before the kidnapping.

When she discovered the baby was gone, Reilly asked, did she turn on the light?

"No, I didn't."

Who was the first person, then, to turn on the light?

"Colonel Lindbergh, I believe."

Betty's answer did not accord with Anne Lindbergh's testimony that she found the light on when she entered the nursery. Why was she so insistent she had not turned on the light? A cleverer defense attorney would have pressed the question, trying to find out if her denial was connected to a desire to make sure that no telling clue had been left behind.

Leaving that question unexplored, Reilly turned to her discovery of the thumb guard in the gravel driveway near the entrance to the estate on April 1, 1932, the day before the ransom was paid. He challenged Betty to explain how in the world the thumb guard could have remained there for all that time—a whole month—without having been discovered. Had he pressed her on the discrepancy about the lights in the nursery, he could have linked that to the thumb guard by asking whether she had found it instead on the floor of the nursery after the kidnapper left and then deposited it where it was found.

Reilly did make much of the idea that the thumb guard was not only a relatively large piece of apparel, with long shoestring-like ties, but also "shiny." He took it to the jury box.

Wilentz strongly objected to that adjective: "It is not shiny; therefore, I object to the question."

"I will leave it to the jury whether it is bright and shiny."

"No, you needn't leave it to the jury. It is not bright and shiny; that is my view."

"And it isn't muddy, and it isn't rusty."

Trenchard intervened. If Reilly left off describing its brightness, he said, that would satisfy the attorney general.

Betty Gow quickly caught on from Wilentz how to handle this increasingly troublesome situation—just as other witnesses for the prosecution would take their clues from him later.

When did you last see the thumb guard? Reilly asked.

The day she found it, she replied.

"Nobody cleaned it so far as you know?"

"It was in a much muddier condition when I picked it up than that."

What did she mean by saying that, Reilly fairly shouted, when she had already said during direct examination that it was in exactly the same condition?

"It can't possibly be in the same condition," she shot back, "when it has been handled by people."

"Now you are a very bright young lady, Miss Gow, aren't you?"

"I am," she rejoined—to laughter and applause.[30]

Pert Betty had shown Reilly a thing or two—or so, at least, reported the press as well. No tormenting bully would get her down. The fact was, of course, that Reilly had cornered her. Her answer that recent handling had removed all the dullness and dirt hardly sufficed as an explanation for why this object had gone undiscovered for so long. Kathleen Norris wrote, nevertheless, that she had impressed all the reporters in the courtroom by her defiance of Reilly's overbearing truculence. "I had suspected she was proud; she showed that she could actually be haughty. . . . No question seemed to faze her, and once or twice there was the sharpness of actual reproof in what she said."[31]

But proud and haughty Betty collapsed upon leaving the courtroom. In the Flemington atmosphere this, too, was taken as a sign of her candor.

Had she told the whole truth—according to the court's oath, or by any other standard? She had lied about whether she ever told anyone about the location of the nursery. She had lied when she told the court that Lindbergh had turned on the light in the nursery, unless Anne's repeated statements about it being on when she rushed into the room were in error. She did nothing to clear up the confusion about which window had been left open—a crucial matter that pertained to the way the kidnapper entered the room. And, finally, there was a contradiction between Betty's statement to Robert Peacock a few days before she took the stand, and what she said again under oath. In the Peacock interview, Betty said, "Upon my arrival [at Highfields] I found he had quite a cold which apparently had gone to his chest." By late that afternoon, she had explained to Peacock, he was "somewhat better" with a normal temperature. Yet at the trial, she said, just as certainly, that the cold was "very slight."[32]

Every one of these questions was a crucial matter for both sides in the trial. The kidnapper's familiarity with the layout of the house, and the Lindbergh routine, was assumed by the first investigators. The same was true of the window. Only the shutters on that particular window were warped and could not be closed. Had the light in the nursery been turned on by someone inside the house in order to check for and eliminate clues? And—the least explored—the child's condition: a chest cold in those days was always a serious matter for concern, but no local doctor had been called. Was there some reason for that?

Since Violet Sharp and Olly Whateley were dead at the time of the trial, and Red Johnson was not called back from Norway, hardly any of the "downstairs" people of the Morrow/Lindbergh estates were ever heard or cross-examined, except for Elsie Whateley. It was Betty's voice the jury heard tell much of the story—and beneath the pert responses it was not a truthful voice.

A sharp defense attorney could have bundled these questions into a rather large package of doubts for the jury to ponder. Reilly was not that man. And now he faced the acknowledged master of befuddlement, Dr. John F. Condon, "Jafsie," the Man of Mystery.

Condon had teased the press—and the prosecution—right up to the eve of his appearance in the courtroom. Would he, or wouldn't he? Prosecutors felt 95 percent sure he would, but with Condon the other 5 percent sometimes counted more. He could bend words into pretzels, and he loved his newfound career as witness-in-chief—so much so, in fact, that after the trial he would take it to store windows and the vaudeville stage.

In black derby and free-flowing fur-trimmed black coat, Jafsie swept into the courtroom like the grand duke of Liechtenstein—if ever there were such a person. Powerfully built and weighing over two hundred pounds, he had the lithe movements of a much younger man. He made an imposing figure in the witness chair and actually appeared to grow stronger and more alert as the day wore on.

Wilentz led him to the first dramatic moment when Condon saw the man waving to him through the gate to Woodlawn Cemetery: "Who was the man you spoke to then between the gates?"

"John as given to me by himself."

"And who is 'John'"?

"John is Bruno Richard Hauptmann."[33]

His "distinct tones rang out through the court room" three times during his testimony to accuse Hauptmann; each time, he raised and lowered his arm in an executioner's stroke, drawing out the moment to its fullest. Once, however, he referred to the accused as "Bruno Rudolph Hauptmann."

After Condon "visited" him in the Flemington jail in late October, Hauptmann had released a statement to the press through his lawyers. "I earnestly wish this gentleman would make a full statement," it read. "Not only do I wish this in my interest but also in the course of justice. Because he is holding the key in this case and with it the key of my cell."[34]

Now Condon had made his full statement. (Until that moment, Anna Hauptmann told her friends, she and Richard had really thought the trial would end in a not-guilty verdict.) When Reilly challenged him, Condon launched into a rigmarole about how there were two parts to an identification, in order to explain his behavior at the Greenwich Street police station: first came the knowledge that the suspect was the right person, but to complete the process there had to be a "declaration" of the identification. It was mumbo-jumbo, but Condon got away with it.[35]

Condon's various descriptions of Cemetery John had varied in details, an inch in height, five or ten pounds in weight, a shade or so in hair color, the shape of the eyes—but overall were reasonably close. From his descriptions, political cartoonist James Berryman had drawn a picture of Cemetery John that had many similarities to Hauptmann. Still, there were questions, such as the lumpy spot at the base of Cemetery John's thumb—a prominent part of Condon's description. And there was Condon's comment at the Greenwich police station that Hauptmann was not Cemetery John but looked like he might be his brother.

When Reilly pursued the lineup fiasco, asking Condon if he had not, in fact, denied Hauptmann was the man he had met in the two cemeteries, the state's key eyewitness evaded the "trap" with miraculous faith in the trustfulness of his listeners. "I never said it was or was not."

"Because you know you are not sure?"

Oh, no, that was not the case at all. "I made the distinction between declaration and identification. The identification meant what I knew mentally, the declaration meant what I said to others. There isn't a man who breathes who has ever heard me say that was the man but one." When Reilly tried to get him to explain this uncommon English usage, Condon accused *him* of trying "to divide the identification and declaration and denial, [to] make it appear as though I was dishonest and I am not." He turned to Judge Trenchard to ask if he had been too "severe" with Reilly. Trenchard assured him he had not.[36]

His show of outraged anger at Reilly's "accusations" had brought him Trenchard's sympathy, and general approval in the courtroom. It was a truly amazing performance, and it had only just begun.

Wilentz turned to the conversation with "Cemetery John." What had Condon said to Cemetery John?

He had asked him for proof—some way of knowing he had been in the nursery that night. "The baby was held in the crib by safety pins."

Who said that, Wilentz wanted to make sure, John?

Yes, John.

And did you have them with you? asked Wilentz.

Yes, he had removed them from the crib and then asked Colonel Lindbergh afterward, "what they call French leave."

In other accounts he had said he showed the pins to Cemetery John first and then asked what they were. But he did not even need the pins if this was the correct sequence in the dialogue.

"Please give me a chance," he said he told John. "I promised Mr. Lindbergh, Colonel Lindbergh and Mrs. Lindbergh, to help them get their baby. That is what I am out for[,] nothing else."

And what did he say in return? Wilentz pursued.

"Nobody else shall ever get the baby but you, and you can put that baby's arms around Mrs. Lindbergh's neck." And he had believed him.[37]

The conversation, one might suggest, was less about Cemetery John's identification as the kidnapper than about Condon's proof that he had been in the nursery himself. He had the pins and the toys, and asked for a chance to prove *himself*. Their talk on a park bench near the cemetery went on and on, according to Condon, who wrung out of John a "confession" that his mother would not like what he was doing, and that he feared he would "burn" if the child was dead. School principal and naughty student, the most familiar of situations for Condon, with ultimate power in the master's hands. "Please give me a chance," Condon recalled his words—a surprisingly intimate form of address to the kidnapper or his agent.

But why should Condon have been the one, when a ransom note had been sent to Colonel Henry Breckinridge's office and a channel established that way? One explanation could be that, knowing the child was dead, the kidnapper had fears that Breckinridge could not be trusted (or persuaded). It would be hard to imagine anyone saying such outrageous things to the experienced Breckinridge—whose knowledge of human nature went beyond schoolchildren, and who had, it ought to be remembered, cut short the "séance" with Peter Birritella and Mary Cerrita to warn them that a week's delay would be too long.

That first conversation in Van Cortlandt Park near the cemetery had to last long enough to win over Condon, who could then persuade Lindbergh.

On cross-examination, Reilly zeroed in on Condon's letter to the Bronx newspaper with its limited circulation, as compared to one of the large dailies. "Didn't you do that because you knew at that time that the kidnapping band were waiting for your letter in that paper?"

"No, sir."

Well, then, if you did not know the kidnappers, why should you have imagined they were anywhere near to where the *Bronx Home News* might be seen? They could have been in Texas, or Mexico, or anyplace.

"Yes."

"And yet if they were you expected them to see the *Bronx News,* did you?"

"Yes, sir."

Reilly then tried to get out of Condon that he had seen the signature before he called the Lindbergh home.

When the kidnapper's response arrived, what did he do?

He called, Condon said, but he did not open the inside letter until told to do so by the person answering the phone.

If that were the case, why should he have thought it was any more than a crank letter?

"That writing would make me take notice of it, yes, sir."

But when questioned closely, Condon seemed to admit he opened the inside letter first. The letter "had the symbol on the night I telephoned and I telephoned *from that letter* in my hand to Colonel Lindbergh."

Reilly moved in to capitalize on Condon's seeming contradiction: "And when the Colonel came to the phone didn't you tell the Colonel, 'I have a letter with the same symbols on it as the note left in the nursery,' and didn't the Colonel say, 'If you have come out?'"

"No, sir. This is what I said. I said, 'Colonel, I do not know whether this is important or not, but there are what I might call a secantal circle, that is, one circle cutting in the other, the same as a secant cuts through a circle,' and I said, 'Is it important? Shall I bring it down to you?'" And he was told to come down at once.[38]

In redirect examination, Condon attempted to clarify this by saying that he had been instructed to open the inside letter and then saw the letter with the signature symbol. In one sense, of course, whether Condon opened the inside letter before he called or not hardly makes any difference. It is the way he answered the questions that causes one to wonder if a trip had not been planned first, and the letters designed to provide the opening for his entrance onto the kidnap scene. Condon's various explanations for why he got involved in the search for the child were a confusing mixture of braggadocio and possibly something else.

The *Bronx Home News* had been his outlet for patriotic screeds for years previous to the events of March 1932, so it was only natural that he would choose to put himself forward as Lindbergh's would-be rescuer. He must have known that it was unlikely he would get a response, and certainly never expected to find himself chosen by the kidnapper to carry on the actual negotiations.

That is all very understandable, except that we do not know how many responses Condon received to his original letter offering to add $1,000 to the ransom if the kidnapper would turn over the child to him for its safe return, nor why, if he had not seen the symbol—and did not know what it meant—he picked out that particular one. By the time Reilly finished, practically everyone was confused. No surprise there.

And so it went all through the cross-examination. Had Condon ever told anyone that Cemetery John was a Scandinavian? No, but he had told people several times that John *said* he was a Scandinavian. This was not true. During his interrogations by Captain Harry Walsh he had insisted, vehemently so, that he made him out to be not a German but a Scandinavian. He also said that Cemetery John coughed a lot, revealing a serious pulmonary condition. In his trial testimony, however, he said that John coughed only once.[39]

On other difficult questions, moreover, Reilly started getting a string of, "I don't remember's," in response to such questions as whether he had told neighbors on City Island in April 1932 that the kidnapping was done by a gang of four or five people, and much more recently, whether he had told an acquaintance in a restaurant that the child had been brought back to the location where it was found. "I don't remember having said so."

When was it, then, that he claimed to have seen "Hauptmann" from a city bus?

Well, said Condon, it was in August 1934, the latter part of the month, but he was not sure of the date. He had not made a note of the date, or the bus number, or anything else.

"Did you call out to the chauffeur, 'Get that man'"?

"'Get the man?' No, it was none of my business."

"None of your business?"

"No, sir."

"To get the man?"

"For me; no sir."[40]

If Condon actually recognized Hauptmann in a fleeting glance from a moving bus as the man he knew from the ransom negotiations, how was it possible that he could not make an instant identification in the police station only a month later?

Several times during his testimony Condon referred to the accu-sations against Red Johnson and Betty Gow. He had often said that one of the reasons he got involved was to clear an innocent man. Reilly asked if he knew that Johnson had called Gow the night of the kidnap-ping. He did, he said, he knew it that night. Condon's snappy assertion jolted the prosecutors. The next day, under Wilentz's guiding hand, he amended his testimony to say that he learned later such a call had been made. But the next question caught him off guard again. How did he learn about the call? asked Wilentz. From "John," he said, after their talk at Woodlawn Cemetery. This was equally bad. Wilentz interrupted to try to steer him away from the subject. "Go ahead," said Reilly, "I have been waiting to hear this." The prosecutor gave him a hint, suggesting the newspapers might have been the source. Condon at last caught on but could not leave it alone. Yes, he said, "it came to me from general gossip and the newspapers."[41]

Reilly's efforts to point out all the different accounts Condon had given from the time of the kidnapping to the trial met with little suc-cess—at least in the contemporary press. The jurors enjoyed the old man's battle of wits with the chief defense counsel, a man they gener-ally loathed anyway for his lord-it-over manner. Reilly suggested that Condon had boasted before the trial about how successfully he would handle a cross-examiner. You are enjoying your place in the sun, he said, are you not? No, said Condon, I feel sad about it. A perfect answer. He then explained why he had prepared so carefully: "because I found insidious snares in every single place that I went, in order to trap me and make fun of me and ridicule me, and they haven't succeeded."

Reilly had been happy to let Condon ramble on, hoping that the jury would see how his brain really functioned at its most extravagant level, blithely concocting rationalizations. But Wilentz stepped in time and again to warn him just to answer the question and be content. "On each reproof of this kind, Dr. Condon would nod his head at the prose-cutor and promise not to do it again."[42]

After Condon left the stand, prosecution and defense both tried to put a spin on his testimony. Reilly claimed that he would now show that it had been Isidor Fisch who received the ransom money. "We had a very satisfactory day." Judge George K. Large responded for the prose-cution that Condon had made an excellent witness, proved that he had been dealing with Hauptmann, and showed the entire world he was not in any way connected with the kidnapper.

Curiously enough, the prosecution then proceeded to produce a wit-ness who placed Hauptmann in the same room with Condon. This was a chancy maneuver from one point of view—how wise was it to suggest they were in contact outside of the cities of the dead? Hildegarde Olga Alexander, a twenty-six-year-old lingerie model, claimed she saw the defendant standing about fifteen feet away from Condon in the telegraph office of the Fordham station of the New York Central Railroad one evening in March 1932. She could not pinpoint the night in question, but it was sometime after Condon's role had become known publicly but before the ransom was paid. When and how Alexander learned of Condon's role when no one else did was not explained. But her testimony was interesting, nevertheless, because she saw Condon arguing or talking very loudly to someone nearby. "He was very excited." Hauptmann, she said, was watching him very intently. The station was practically empty, she said, except for those three men. Reilly's cross-examination tried to demonstrate that she was very unfamiliar with that particular railroad station and had no reason to be there at all.[43]

Lloyd Fisher added to reporters that it was extremely unlikely, furthermore, that she could possibly have known about Condon's role. She was not telling the truth. Prosecutor Wilentz characterized Alexander's testimony, on the other hand, as revealing that Hauptmann had shadowed Condon while the negotiations were going on, and, by doing so, also demonstrated that none of the people the defense wanted to tie in, Olly Whateley, Isidor Fisch, Red Johnson, or Betty Gow could be implicated in the kidnapping.[44]

Perhaps because Alexander was a "surprise" witness, but one of those taken to Hauptmann's cell in Flemington to view the defendant before testifying, the defense did not have an effective response, except for Fisher's observation. The defense missed an opportunity to pose questions about the other person Condon was arguing with in the station, as alluded to several times by the witness. Why was he there in the station telegraph office when, supposedly, Colonel Breckinridge was living in his house keeping watch over the schoolmaster? The timing of the "sighting," early evening around 6 P.M., makes it likely that this was one of those days when he lectured at Fordham University in the afternoon. Even so, why there were no other observers of Condon from the Lindbergh camp during these convenient times remains difficult to understand.

Two other witnesses, meanwhile, had identified Hauptmann. First was Amandus Hochmuth, the Franco-Prussian War veteran. Like Alexander, Hochmuth had been ushered into the Flemington jail to get a good look at Hauptmann before the trial. He then testified that he was outside his daughter's house in the forenoon of March 1, 1932, when a car came around the corner at a good speed and skidded into a ditch. He was not more than twenty-five feet away from the car, he said, and the driver looked out of the window at him. "He glared at me as if he saw a ghost."

How long did all this take? asked Wilentz.

About fifteen seconds, was the answer.

What did you see inside the car? Wilentz then asked.

"I saw something; some of the ladder."

Reilly moved to strike that out as calling for a conclusion. But Judge Trenchard, as usual, granted the prosecution considerable leeway so far as witness conclusions were concerned.

Wilentz then asked Hochmuth to identify Hauptmann as the man he saw on March 1, 1932, which he did dramatically by getting down from the witness chair and walking over to place his hand on Hauptmann's shoulder.

When Reilly began his cross-examination he kept hammering away that Hochmuth had been prompted over and over again to recognize Hauptmann by state troopers, who kept constant tabs on him. Hochmuth testified that he had seen the dirty, green car around noon. (Hauptmann's car was dark blue.) This testimony, of course, had been drilled into him, as his initial statements to the police had placed the time as much earlier. Reilly repeated that it was around noon on March 1, 1932, "is that so?"

"It was a clear day." (Of course it was not a clear day at all, but a rainy, windy day, and Hochmuth could only see the driver through a car window.) He also claimed to be sitting on the porch all during this time—apparently waiting for cars to slide into the ditch.

Reilly tried to raise the question of Hochmuth's eyesight, but not having the medical reports available, which showed that he suffered from cataracts in both eyes, he could do little when Judge Trenchard appeared to support the witness's claim that his eyes were "all right." Reilly asked him what the driver was wearing.

Hochmuth thought he saw a dark shirt.

"You think he had a dark shirt on?"

"All I took in was his red face and the glaring eyes."

"I see. He had a red face?"

"Yes."

"Like mine?"

"A litttle more red."

"A little more red than mine?"

"Oh, yes."

It must have been very red, indeed, to be redder than Reilly's. This man's appearance on the day of the kidnapping supposedly made a tremendous impression on the old war veteran—that red face and glaring eyes—yet he testified that he had failed to mention it to anyone, not even his daughter or son-in-law.

"Nobody in the world," Reilly said, "knew what you were going to say, is that so?"

"Exactly."

It was a preposterous statement, and Reilly tried to make that evident to the court. Had he been taken to the jail by a state trooper recently?

Yes, said Hochmuth, several days ago.

"You saw the defendant, Hauptmann, there, didn't you?"

"I saw a figure in there, but I couldn't see him."

"Didn't they have you in there thirty minutes?"

"Maybe so."

"There was nobody there but the defendant, was there?"

"That's it, and two troopers."[45] Two troopers, one in mufti, the other in a uniform with a yellow stripe down each leg, said Hochmuth.

Finished with his time in the witness chair, Hochmuth met Hauptmann face-to-face in the corridor. The old man reached out and touched the shoulder of the defendant for a second time that day, saying "I am sorry for you, young man."[46]

Hochmuth's daughter agreed that he had kept his testimony secret from the family. But she wondered why police and prosecutors would ask an "old man like him to tell a story about something he did not know anything about." She told reporters about his eyesight and remarked that he never saw Hauptmann pass their house at all. They held him for three days at state police headquarters, she said, until one day when he called and said he would be home soon. But then they placed a guard over him and took him to New York. "I know what I know," Hochmuth still insisted. "I've seen what I've seen."[47]

The next important eyewitness who knew what he had seen was Joseph Perrone, the taxi driver who received the kidnapper's note for Condon on the night of March 12, 1932. Unlike Hildegarde Alexander and Amandus Hochmuth, he was no surprise to anyone. Perrone had identified Hauptmann as the man who came running out at him with his hand raised as he drove down Gun Hill Road near Van Cortlandt Park. Before Hauptmann's arrest, Perrone had identified several others as the man. And now he readily admitted to Reilly that it was dark along that road except for the few lights from the park, and that he had been going along at a pretty fast rate. "Yes, I was. I wouldn't say too fast."

The man had no idea that you would be coming along that road at that time, near eight o'clock, did he?

"I don't know how he ever came running to me."

And then, Reilly went on, you testified that you stopped under a big arc light—and that was where the man came up to his window?

"Yes, sir."

Actually, Reilly then got him to admit, it was an ordinary street lamp on a pole across the road.

And did Perrone wear glasses?

Yes, he had to wear glasses at night for nearsightedness.

The man was wearing a fedora, pulled down in front?

"Turned up in the front."

It wasn't down, then, like men usually wear such a hat?

"No, no sir."

Aware he had answered too quickly, Perrone corrected himself and said it was the "custom" of that particular kind of hat to wear it pulled back in front. If Perrone's man was Cemetery John, the custom changed quickly, in less than two hours, when Condon encountered him outside Woodlawn Cemetery. Perrone didn't notice, on the other hand, whether the man's hand had been bare or covered, and claimed not to know anything about whether fingerprints would have been left on the envelope.[48]

Reporters asked Hauptmann during a recess what he thought about Hochmuth and Perrone. The former, he said, was simply mistaken. Perrone was a liar. "To give him a note like that I came out under a big light with my hat pulled back? I would be crazy."

Another ID witness Wilentz offered at the trial was Cecile Barr, a ticket-seller at the Sheridan Square movie theater in Greenwich Village. Wilentz had also used her at the extradition hearings. Barr had received a five-dollar Lindbergh bill on November 26, 1933. When she was first questioned a few days later about the man who had passed the bill, she said she had taken special note because the bill had been folded over three times and literally thrown at her in the cashier's cage. This rude patron, who was thirty to thirty-five, slender, about five-foot-eight or five-foot-nine, with light brown hair, had been wearing a dark soft hat with the front pulled down. He was, she had said then, "apparently American." The description fit Hauptmann, except no mention was made of an accent. Detective F. J. Ruggiero interviewed Barr again on October 2, 1934, showing her a photo of Hauptmann, "and she partially identified same."[49]

When she was questioned in Foley's office the next day, she added that she particularly noticed his long chin line. To make sure, Barr was taken into a courtroom, where she could observe Hauptmann for a period of time. She was ready then to appear at the extradition hearing.[50]

The man who gave Cecile Barr a five-dollar bill on the night of November 26, 1933, she repeated twice in her trial testimony, had his hat "pulled way down" over his forehead.

Reilly asked Barr how long it would take to sell a ticket and make change. Less than thirty seconds?

She had noticed the man because of the way he tossed a folded-up bill at her, she said. But she seemed uneasy when Reilly pressed on the matter of time.

"That is about as long as it took to sell the tickets. . . . ?"

"To sell the tickets?"

"Yes."

"(No answer)."[51]

The defense attorney then asked if she knew anyone in New Jersey. Only the state trooper, Corporal Horn, she said.

When had she met him?

When he called at the theater in October 1934, to tell her that he was taking her out to Flemington.

Never before?

No, never before.

As it happened, Corporal William Horn had been one of the policemen who questioned her for some time shortly after November 26, 1933, about the five-dollar ransom bill she received that night. She had talked with the trooper for a considerable length of time—in the daylight—but had no recollection of that meeting.

Actually, it had been Wilentz who first asked about Corporal Horn, apparently counting on the witness to remember him from that occasion, but she did not, and he quickly changed the topic. Reilly was caught off guard as much as Wilentz by Barr's failure to remember Corporal Horn.

The prosecutor asked her one last question to reinforce her credibility: Did she remember what picture was playing that night?

"Oh, yes, sir, Walter Winchell's *Broadway Looking Through a Keyhole*."

Laughter broke out, and Judge Trenchard had a very hard time restoring order. Amid the hubbub, Reilly tried to make himself heard. "Just a minute," he said. "Just a minute. I want to recall her." But Cecile Barr had left the witness stand, and the defense apparently forgot all about its wish to question her again about her memory for faces.[52]

When Millard Whited supposedly saw Hauptmann twice, lurking around roads near the Lindbergh estate, he had again changed the way he wore his hat. Now it was "just tipped a trifle forward." Whited added new details to his previous statements. He had been no more than six feet away on one occasion and eight feet on the other. What was most remarkable, however, was that there seemed to be no car anywhere around.

Wilentz then asked if he had reported these sightings to anyone the morning of March 2, 1932.

Yes, he certainly had, to a party of police who had come to his house, a group that included Colonel Lindbergh as well.

When confronted with evidence later that he had never given out such information, Whited insisted he had been told to keep it quiet! He also testified that he was not promised payments of $35 a day for his missed time—something he would admit later in post-trial questioning, as well as that he believed he had been promised up to one-third of the $25,000 reward money.[53]

Lloyd Fisher cross-examined Whited for the defense, asking first if he would recognize someone through a photograph.

Whited was not sure what he meant.

Well, if he saw a picture of himself, he would recognize it, would he not?

"Not some of them."

Whited's innate shrewdness belied his appearance as someone who had stumbled into the case out of a simple desire to do right. Fisher fenced with Whited through several pages of testimony, always hearing "to the best of my knowledge" whenever he approached too close to the many contradictions between the Bronx extradition hearings and what Whited was now telling the court. Fisher did manage to squeeze out that Whited now placed the sightings of Hauptmann much closer to the Lindbergh house than before, that he was not at all sure of the exact days he saw the stranger on the road, that he had told only one or two of the men who came to his house the early morning of March 2, 1932, about the mysterious stranger on the road.

Whited's reputation—even more than his memory—made him a poor witness to send a man to the electric chair. After the trial this would emerge in even more disturbing clarity.

Prosecutor Wilentz's final question ought to have been an embarrassment for the state in defense appeals: "Are you in any way interested in this case except as a resident of the county?"

"No, sir."

When Millard Whited stepped down, the state had presented its most useful eyewitnesses. Hochmuth and Whited were the only ones to put Hauptmann in the vicinity of the Lindbergh estate, although another man, Charles Rossiter, put him near the Princeton airport; Cecile Barr was the only one to have recognized him as presenting a ransom bill before August 1934; Hildegarde Alexander the only witness for the state to have seen Hauptmann and Condon together; and Condon the only person ever to have spoken with Cemetery John. But, above all of these witnesses, in the jury's memory it was Colonel Lindbergh's voice identification that carried the most weight. If Wilentz could prove that Hauptmann had written all the ransom notes and built the ladder—then the case for extortion became a sure conviction for murder. The eyewitnesses might have problems getting that hat placed right, but the "scientific" evidence could not be refuted, could it?

At the conclusion of these first days of testimony, the FBI observer, T. H. Sisk, thought conviction was a sure thing. Colonel Lindbergh had made a fine witness, said Sisk, the "finest he had ever seen." Reilly, on the other hand, seemed "rather poorly prepared." The judge had been splendid thus far. And, as Sisk said, the defense "has no money to effect an appeal."[54]

Certainly, it had had no money, either, for expert witnesses to counterbalance the $30,000 paid to the prosecution handwriting team.

TRIAL BY EXPERTS

The most brilliant performances in the witness chair should be credited to the handwriting experts and the wood specialist. Their testimony was a treat to the jury. The question as to which side of the case they were on disappeared. The perfection of their work submerged both prosecution and defense.
> —CHARLES F. SNYDOR, juror no. 4, June 1935

"Intimate" knowledge of wood is a type of specialized training that police officials cannot be expected to have," Arthur Koehler wrote after the trial, "but it serves to show how technical experts along various lines can often assist law enforcement agencies in tracking down and convicting criminals."[1]

Koehler was too modest. Prosecutors found experts indispensable not merely because of the scientific work they performed, but also, perhaps even primarily, if they were frank about it, because they put an added burden on the defense financially. Judge Trenchard refused to allow Reilly or any other member of the defense to put in the record how much the state of New Jersey was paying its corps of handwriting experts, but the total was something over $30,000—ten times what the defense had available for all of its witnesses and attorneys' fees.[2]

The effort to refute the handwriting experts and Arthur Koehler's wood testimony was beyond Hauptmann's means, even if there had been witnesses with sterling credentials willing to testify. Outrage at the crime made it unlikely the defense could find a great number of experienced expert witnesses willing to spend the time to look beyond newspaper headlines—and the prosecution made sure that a constant stream of stories about new evidence against Hauptmann made their way speedily into the press.

"Well, at last you have the man in New Jersey," Albert S. Osborn wrote Schwarzkopf after the extradition hearings, "and I think that everyone breathes a sigh of relief. I do not remember of any defendant in any case that I have been in who has so little sympathy from anyone. I suppose it is because he kidnapped a baby and especially a Lindbergh baby."[3]

Police turned to Osborn for names to fill out the roster of experts. Osborn warned Colonel Schwarzkopf to keep the defense in the dark about the inquiries. The colonel understood perfectly. Of each man Osborn recommended, the colonel asked, "[Are you] willing to work with us?" And the recruitment letters all contained this closing:

> The nature of the case requires that we ask you to keep this request strictly confidential for the present. When you testify in court, of course, your connection with the case will become known, and we will be glad to see that you are given full credit and publicity for your accomplishments. Until that time, however, it is essential that your connection with the investigation be kept strictly confidential.
>
> Hoping we will be privileged to have you associated with us in this matter, and thanking you for the courtesy of your consideration, I beg to remain,
> Very respectfully yours,
> H. Norman Schwarzkopf [4]

As the doyen of American handwriting experts, Albert S. Osborn had great influence among the specialists. Indeed, who would want to go against him—especially in this case? One of the recipients, Harry Cassidy, wrote back, "It might be of interest to you that I have always had better success before small town and country juries than with those of larger cities. Have never appeared as a witness north of the Mason-Dixon where the folks don't know me."[5]

James Clark Sellers was anxious to know the conditions surrounding Hauptmann's request writing, "so that [he could] take those things into consideration in arriving at [his] final conclusion." Colonel Schwarzkopf replied that "occasionally when [Hauptmann] was stuck as to spelling and would ask how to spell a word he would be told; in general, however, he was told to spell it as best he could. He was not given any instructions as to the forming of any of the letters." In his trial testimony, however, Schwarzkopf would stoutly deny having provided any "help" in this regard to the question: "Is the spelling his own?" he replied, "Yes, sir."[6]

Occasionally, of course, could mean any number of things but not a flat denial. Schwarzkopf had not commented at all upon the length of questioning before the writing began or the total number of pieces obtained. In other words, as the defense brought out, none of the experts knew what actually went on at these sessions. Detective Philip Creamer, for example, told Assistant Prosecutor Robert Peacock something in a pretrial deposition that did not jibe with Schwarzkopf's assurances to the experts. He had dictated to Hauptmann several paragraphs from a magazine, *Spring 3100*—perhaps as many as fifteen. These writings were never heard of again.[7]

To their credit, the experts were anxious to see more of Hauptmann's writings contemporaneous with the kidnapping. They were also anxious to see the originals of the "questioned writings" or "anonymous letters" (ransom notes) to compare with the request writings, because, wrote Cassidy, "many of the photostats are not as good as they should be." Still, these handicaps did not prevent the experts from arriving at a firm conclusion. As Sellers put it, "I am irresistibly led to the conclusion the anonymous letters were written by Hauptmann." He did warn there were "many dissimilarities which the defense can no doubt make capital of, but they are greatly outweighed by the really identifying similarities."[8]

The experts conducted a lively correspondence in the weeks before the trial concerning what documents should be included from Hauptmann's conceded writings, and which ones were not useful. John F. Tyrrell was concerned at one point that a 1933 passenger car registration form not be used, because too many words, *Sedan, Gas, Yes,* and the figure *4*, did not fit well with the exhibits they were preparing. "As for the expense book, my opinion is that it had better be definitely mislaid. Hauptmann knows that you have it, that his German friends wrote in it, his attorney may call for it. In the event he secures it the net effect will be—well, less desirable even than if the state had introduced it."[9]

Albert S. Osborn agreed with Tyrrell, so the car registration and the expense book were both ruled out. That was too bad, Osborn wrote to Prosecutor Joseph Lanigan, because the middle two pages included the word *Boad,* which the kidnapper had written in his final note supposedly explaining where the child could be found. They might tear out those pages, but it would be "dangerous": "we would be accused of using what was favorable to our contention and excluding the rest."[10]

Tyrrell also raised a question about the now well-known writing—Condon's address and phone number—on the wood panel found in the Hauptmanns' closet. Would that be used? Schwarzkopf wrote back that the "Attorney General is not considering this point because Hauptmann himself admitted this writing." Hiding in this brief reply, however, is a big elephant of a question. It is not really a response, to begin with, for the issue has to do with a comparison to the "questioned writing." That Hauptmann admitted during interrogation that the writing must be his really has nothing to do with this matter. If the *experts* presented the writing on the wood panel as identical to that on the ransom notes, they would open the way to a challenge that could undermine a vital part of the case. But if a *police officer* testified about the writing on the wood panel, on the other hand, all the defense could do really was offer a new Hauptmann rebuttal.[11]

Harry Cassidy also had a question about some individual letters. The peculiar small *x* that occurred in the ransom notes and on car registrations in 1931 and 1932, was not in Hauptmann's later writings, as one would expect from a person steadily learning to write standard English. And then there were the small *k*s. It was because of this letter, Cassidy said, that he needed to see still more of other Hauptmann writings. When those *k*s could be found before or after the writing of the ransom notes, the case would be complete. He thought it highly unlikely that the distinctive *k*s appeared only in the ransom notes. It would not change his testimony if none were found elsewhere, but discovering others would materially strengthen it and that of the other experts. "I have heard eloquent pleas by defense attorneys on reasonable doubt theories sway weak jurors which were based on much less tangible evidence than these dissimilar '*k*'s."[12]

Anna had warned her husband not to say anything about the handwriting! "Don't even admit that it looks like yours. Just say you didn't write it." Richard nodded his head. Two days later she was back at the jail with a new thought: "Why don't you tell them that you want to re-write all of these letters that they have, using the same words, etc., to prove to them that you could not have written them?"

"I am willing to do that."[13]

Richard's offer—if made—was never taken up. Even following the trial, while in the state prison death house in Trenton, he continued to puzzle about the handwriting. "I can't understand it," he said he told his lawyer at the time of the extradition hearings. "It looks exactly like my handwriting." He maintained, of course, that it was not his handwriting, but perhaps someone who knew German as a native could have copied his individual quirks. After all, he told Detective Ellis Parker, now investigating the case again, in June 1935, all Germans mix their words up unless their English is perfect.[14]

The prosecution hoped to demolish all these theories with a phalanx of distinguished experts from all over the country. Albert S. Osborn, the first to testify, said that he had originally examined the ransom notes in May 1932 and concluded then that the same person wrote them all. He saw seven or eight connections—several outside the study of handwriting itself—the most important of which was the signature, "a peculiar and ingenious device that appeared on the lower right hand corner."

That accomplished, Osborn turned to linking the request writings with the ransom notes and conceded writings. This was the heart of his testimony. He found that the first note (the nursery note), and the first lines of the second note were written with great deliberation. The rest of note two and those that followed were written somewhat more freely but, in his opinion, by the same person. The assertion that the ingenious signature was proof they were all written by the same person distracted everyone's attention while he slid by any argument that the differences in penmanship could be accounted for by a collective effort and not a single author.

The unique signature, after all, only meant that the author of the letters had access to the method for making the circles and holes. It might be mystical but was not necessarily the creation of one mind. Osborn here was slipping into Dr. Shoenfeld's territory to find the secret of the ransom notes. He read backward, in other words, from one signature to one writer, who eased up and wrote more naturally after the nursery note and part of the second note.

From that conclusion he moved to an analysis of the request writing by itself. One could tell genuine, honest writing, he said, from that produced by a guilty man by noting differences after at least three rounds of dictation. "And that is exactly what we find in this request writing. In one instance we find it [the differences] on the same sheet of paper. In my opinion, these request writings—I mean the ransom notes— are disguised writings; part of the request writings are disguised writings, and the writer didn't have but one disguise." One has to follow Osborn's syntax with great care because it is very easy to become lost along the way.

Some portions of the request writing, he argued, were in the "style" of the ransom notes and others in the "style" of Hauptmann's conceded writings. Thus the request writings are the linchpin between the ransom notes, at one end, and Hauptmann's ordinary, everyday penmanship at the other. Apparently, one is to accept that he stopped suddenly in the middle of the page and shifted from ransom note style to what he used when not engaged in criminal activity. Remember, Osborn believed he had but one disguise.

Osborn explained that he made his comparison from bits and pieces taken here and there from the request writings. He did not tell the court how many pieces came from which samples. It would be an easy task, argued the defense, to choose letters from a large group of writing samples to match letters in the ransom notes.

Actually, back in 1932, Osborn had written a lengthy supplemental report on the nursery note and the second note, posing the question whether the differences could be accounted for by the use of two different pens. One pen might have been a fine-pointed pen and the other a stylographic pen. He also found differences in the ink; the ink used in one of the later notes was more like that in the nursery note than any of the others. "This ink is of a peculiar character and shows red with a heavy deposit when looked at at an angle."

His 1932 supplemental report also challenged his 1935 testimony on a very vital point: Osborn argued in testimony that a disguise must be sustained with great care and deliberation—hence the need to dictate a passage, take it away quickly, and require that it be done a second and a third time, for eventually the writer's efforts to maintain his disguise will fail him. But in 1932 he could not explain the ink smears in the first note, unless it had been written hurriedly "under unusual conditions, in an automobile, for example," where it would have been impossible to use a blotter as in the later notes.[15]

Osborn zeroed in on the peculiar small x that appeared in the ransom notes, and on certain contemporaneous Hauptmann writings, car registrations in 1931 and 1932. "It isn't German, it isn't roundhand, it isn't Latin script." In this case, as noted before, Osborn's knowledge of German writing failed him. The peculiar x was known as Suetterlin, taught in German schools from the time of World War I. "If we had only the request writing we wouldn't have these x's at all," Osborn testified. "There are some words with x's in the request writing but not that x." Harry Cassidy, remember, had noted the same thing and put it down to Hauptmann's growing command of English. Clark Sellers had written in a pretrial report, finally, that it was the x that had convinced him Hauptmann wrote the ransom notes. The x occurs five or six times in the ransom notes.[16]

The handwriting experts had gathered around the x like hounds treeing a fox. But was it really that damning? In addition to German students, other Europeans who learned to write during the pre–World War I period were trained to make the script x in that fashion. For example,

Alexis Carrel, Lindbergh's longtime mentor on both medical and eugenic–related issues, signed his first name by making the *x* in that fashion. Carrel was French.[17]

Listening to the elder Osborn testimony, Hauptmann had shown "signs of emotion." "Although the prisoner's facial expression stayed about the same, his breathing was labored to such an extent that it was very noticeable," reported a guard. "I also observed a different expression in his eyes, which might be described by using the word frightened."

Osborn stepped outside the courthouse after direct examination, to tell the members of a press conference some things they might not know about handwriting expertise. "Handwriting," he informed reporters gravely, "is like a woman's appearance—character can be told from both." He had made some notes, he went on, about the ransom letter writer's personality and characteristics—all gleaned from the handwriting. Even in these "pre-feminist" days, it would have been interesting to hear Nora Roberts's or Edna Ferber's comments on this assertion. Wilentz disdained the defense experts as nothing more than graphologists—entertainers who read ink lines instead of lifelines. Osborn's claim to tell character from handwriting came pretty close.[18]

Back on the witness stand, Reilly began cross-examining by asking how many specimens the expert had examined before Hauptmann's arrest.

Over a hundred.

Had he ever examined Isidor Fisch's handwriting?

Yes, he had.

The last question was as important as the answer because it suggested police had not ruled out Fisch as a suspect, despite public announcements to the contrary.

Asked if he had made a comparison of two of the other ransom notes with the nursery note, Osborn gave a surprise answer: "I haven't compared any of the ransom notes directly with the nursery note. . . . None of them are compared that way."

Well, would he not agree, anyway, that the phrasing was a little clearer in a subsequent note than in the first one?

"I would say that it is a little clearer than the nursery note, and perhaps a little more freely written than some of the others, but it is essentially the same."

Was this one disguised, too?

"They are all disguised to a certain extent; that is, that they are not natural free writing."

So we learn, finally, that while Hauptmann had but one disguise, apparently there were shades of that disguise, despite Osborn's prior insistence that portions of the request writing were in disguise and portions were not—like black and white.[19]

Elbridge Stein, the second expert, brought out the x factor as well. All the defense could do, with Lloyd Fisher cross-examining, was to show that Hauptmann wrote his xs two ways in the conceded writing. But in the earlier examples—at the time of the kidnapping—he had ended the word *Bronx* on a license application with an x that looked much like those xs in the ransom notes; while in the last two applications, it became, as Stein said, a common, garden variety x.[20]

Fisher hammered hard on this pick-and-choose process: "Now, how many words are there, total number of words, on all the ransom notes?"

"I can't tell you."

"How many words are there, total, on the request writings?"

"I can't tell you that."

"How many separate words have you photographed?"

"I don't know that."

"Well, have you photographed ten percent of them, ten percent of the words?"

"I'd be doubtful. Maybe I did, but I wouldn't know."[21]

Fisher also tried to get Stein to admit that difficult words in the ransom notes like *hazardous* were almost always spelled correctly, whereas words like *not* and even *be* were often botched, as if the writer were trying to pretend to be semiliterate. Harry Cassidy, when he got on the stand, had the answer for that one: the writer must have used a German-American dictionary. Sure, enough, Attorney General David Wilentz quickly came up with a German-American dictionary taken from Hauptmann's apartment. Concerned that the defense had found a soft spot, the prosecutor "disclosed" to the *New York Times* that Hauptmann was an avid, indeed, indefatigable "dictionary student." In the one they found, "a great number of the words were underlined." What words he did not say. But he promised the state would produce this book in court. "We are prepared to show that Hauptmann was a dictionary student," said Wilentz, "even though the handwriting experts did not know about it except from their studies of the writings and the letters."[22]

The book never appeared, perhaps because it might not show that the underlinings were the right words, or perhaps because of the difficulty of telling whether Richard or Anna Hauptmann drew the lines.

There was another line, however, a very short one, the hyphen the ransom note writer put between *New* and *York,* that the experts tied to Richard's conceded writings. Defense attorney Frederick Pope questioned John F. Tyrrell on that point, trying to get him to concede that Albert S. Osborn had wrongly asserted the hyphen was unique to

Hauptmann's writings. Well, he had never seen it that way, either, said Tyrrell. "Of course," he added, "I live in Wisconsin." Pope handed him several examples of such a hyphen, some of them written by Germans, some not. There was even one, said the defense counsel, in "plain old garden variety of American handwriting." Tyrrell insisted that it was probably an "Americanized" foreign hand. But the point had been made.[23]

Pope then tried to turn the tables on the experts by getting Tyrrell to concede that the misspelled words, as well as some of the incorrect grammar, made up the actual "disguise" in the ransom notes. If those things were corrected, he kept pressing the expert to say, then the letters would be in almost perfect business form.

This line of argument flummoxed Wilentz for a moment. "Now, if your Honor please," he addressed Judge Trenchard, "we don't want counsel's admission that these are made for the purpose of disguise, because we deny through our experts, we know nothing about it, we rely upon the experts, and their contention is that it is not a disguise, and therefore we neither ask nor want nor accept the admission."

After a great deal of back-and-forth between the three men, with Wilentz doing all he could to object to and deflect Pope's questions, came this final remark from the expert: "Well, there are various grades of businessman." Tyrrell would not admit that the broken spellings were part of a clever disguise, but Pope had again made the point that the writer had to be educated enough to spell the big words correctly—or at least to know where to find them—or, by implication, a third possibility, someone had dictated the ransom notes to the writer.[24]

Albert D. Osborn took the stand and asked to see the wrapper from the package containing the sleeping suit, the one sent to Condon as proof the kidnapper had the child. The curious thing about the package was that it bore two addresses, one printed, and, almost next to it, the other in longhand. Osborn called the court's attention to the "second address" written in longhand. This writing, he testified, "truly" depicted the ransom notes. The writer let down his disguise somewhat here, Osborn said, and it looked like the request writing—that portion of it where the defendant had written in a hand that resembled his conceded writing. Lloyd Fisher was on his feet to object. Your honor, he said, Condon had clearly testified that he had no clear recollection of any second address on the package, and, he could have added, thought the writing might be his own. Somewhat taken aback, Judge Trenchard ruled there was testimony "that this envelope, in one fashion or another, came from the hands of the defendant." It was obviously a close call. Trenchard's ambivalent comment, "in one fashion or another," hardly supported Osborn's contention. "Of course, after a while," Trenchard addressed Fisher, "you are going to cross-examine and you may then bring these matters up." Fisher would, indeed, return to the subject, because Osborn had backhandedly suggested Condon as the author of the ransom notes![25]

At the beginning of his cross-examination, however, Fisher took Osborn back to the x question. He got him to admit that there were no peculiar $x$es in the request writing, and that Hauptmann obviously knew how to make a common x, so if the writing on the wrapper looked like the defendant's conceded writings, did it also look like the request writings? But, try as they might, the best the defense team could ever do with that x problem was to say he had written it both ways. They failed to bring out effectively that Germans had been taught earlier in the century to write the x in that fashion.

Lloyd Fisher delighted, however, in pointing out to Albert D. Osborn that contrary to what his father had said, the hyphen in *New York* was not uncommon at all: "Did you hear him testify that in all his experience he had never observed a hyphen between the words 'New' and 'York'?"

"Well, I can't recall his testimony now."

"Well, can you remember that part of it, Mr. Osborn?"

"Yes, I think he said that. . . . If you say he did, I will take your word for it."

"Don't take my word for it. Take the record, Mr. Osborn. . . . Do you remember his saying it?"

"I think he said it. This is as far as I will go."

Albert D. Osborn then said that in twenty years *he* had never seen the hyphen used that way, either.

Fisher produced five envelopes, all with the hyphen placed between *New* and *York*. "Now you have gone twenty years without seeing such a thing as that, haven't you?"

"I am afraid I have."

"And in five minutes you have now seen four or five of them?"

"That is right."

All this was leading up to an envelope sent from Germany that had a hyphen between *Bronx* and *New York*. Asked to identify the writer on the return address, Osborn read "I. Fisch." Osborn dismissed the show-and-tell game, insisting all Fisher had done was demonstrate that a few people put a hyphen in that place. So what? The hyphen was only "one of a hundred connections between Hauptmann and these ransom notes."[26]

But Fisher scored another point the younger Osborn could not quite throw off with a glib response. Osborn had used the wrapper on the sleeping suit in dramatic fashion to assert the author of the longhand writing was Hauptmann. John Condon had testified earlier, however, that he was not sure who wrote that address—maybe himself. Now Fisher drew out the implications of the contradiction.

Here, first, is what Condon said in response to the attorney general's question: "I notice that there are two names, one Mr. Condon, and Dr. John F. Condon. Were they both on there at that time?"

"That I couldn't remember. I think not. That looks like my writing."

"On the side here?"

"Let me look again"

"Yes, take a look (handing to witness)."

"That looks like mine. I am not sure (Examines Paper). I couldn't say."[27]

Wilentz wanted confirmation that both addresses on the package were the handiwork of the person who sent the sleeping suit. But he didn't get it.

Fisher led into the point he wanted to make by asking Osborn about difficulties in comparing the figures or numbers.

Not at all, said the expert. He picked up the wrapper and pointed to the way the *2* had been made. It was a distinctive *2*, he said, like those in Hauptmann's writings.

An avid tennis player, Fisher then drove a sharp backhand down the line: "Now, you are assuming that Dr. Condon testified that this was on this envelope when it [was] received by him, is that correct?"

"I am not assuming anything about Dr. Condon, I know who wrote that."

"Are you assuming, do you know that Dr. Condon said in his testimony that he wasn't sure whether this lower part was on there when he received it or not?"

"I did—"

"Did you hear his testimony?"

"I didn't hear it, I didn't read it."[28]

Osborn's unwavering certainty that the two addresses had been written by the same man depended—as did much of the other handwriting evidence—on the selection of certain letters from the large number of request writings. There were more request writings than the prosecution used, but they never surfaced at the trial and have never turned up. The *x*s, however, came from the ransom notes alone—except for one or two in the conceded writings. Unlike the request writings, the conceded writings used by the experts made a very small bundle, indeed.

There was one piece of handwriting evidence, especially, that the experts did not discuss—under prosecution instructions—the wood panel in the closet. Since Hauptmann had originally conceded during interrogations and at the extradition hearing that the writing there must be his, Schwarzkopf had told them there was no need. Instead, New York police inspector Henry Bruckman testified at the trial about discovering that evidence. Upon arriving at Hauptmann's apartment that morning, the day the Bronx grand jury handed down its indictment, Bruckman called the police carpenters together. "I wanted to give them the benefit of such knowledge as I gained during the course of the investigation, and I went there for the purpose of directing their attention along certain investigational lines." Walking almost immediately to the small closet, he backed in, squeezing around so as to face the inside doorframe. There was no lightbulb in the closet, but he saw a smudge on the trim. Putting on his glasses, he examined the mark closely and could make out telephone numbers.

Challenged by Reilly, Bruckman said he had no difficulty seeing the smudged writing because it was around eleven o'clock and the room was well lit. (In other statements, however, he had said he needed a flashlight.)

Did he know Condon's phone number himself? Reilly asked.

"Frankly," said Bruckman, "I must admit that I did not know it. It had slipped my mind."

Reilly then asked if he were the first policeman to go into the closet.

Yes, he assured defense counsel, he was, though this was six days after the arrest, adding, in answer to another question, that he had previously carried out similar inspections on the other closets. But not this one for some unknown reason.

Alas, for Bruckman, one of the carpenters there that day, Maurice Tobin, testified at the trial during cross-examination that the inspector had not gone into any other closet. It began with the following exchange.

"Now, so far as you know," asked Frederick Pope, "were these numerals, contained on this board, submitted to the handwriting experts?"

"That I couldn't say."

"How many other closets were there in the Hauptmann house that were examined by you men?

"I believe there were two more besides this one here that we speak of now."

"Did Inspector Bruckman squeeze into both of these closets?"

"He did not."

"That is all," Pope said, then paused. "Just one second. The only one he did squeeze into was the one the figures came out of?"

"That is all I know of."[29]

At the trial, Hauptmann recanted his admission that he had written the numbers on the closet trim; and for years after the trial, Bruckman's discovery would be hotly contested. But the state had felt no need to prove the handwriting was his, and thus the experts were spared cross-examination on the question.[30]

What can one say, finally, about the handwriting testimony? There were more than five hundred pages of testimony from the handwriting experts, much of it highly technical and tedious, yet, according to newspaper reports, the jurors listened avidly as one after another of the witnesses held up detailed charts to demonstrate the similarities. The defense team tried all sorts of things to refute the findings. Handwriting experts had no board qualifying examinations to pass, they asserted, so they could just hang up a shingle and declare themselves open for business. ("Professor," a defense counsel "mistakenly" addressed one expert, knowing he would be corrected.) More seriously, the defense pointed out that handwriting experts often appeared on opposite sides in trials—sometimes with terrible consequences for an innocent party.

Lloyd Fisher would protest that defense witnesses had only one day to examine the documents during the trial. But the prosecution had assembled an A team. Reilly had leftovers to pick from—and was not very good in finding any experts even so. Indeed, the defense appeared amateurish and almost clownish. Reilly had lined up his "experts" for pictures, standing in front of them beaming like a proud homeroom teacher, full of boasts about how well they would do on the stand. But had this bunch been given a month of Sundays to study the papers, they still would have been no match for the Wilentz team. Only one or two even showed up for the trial. Without access to Colonel Schwarzkopf's pretrial correspondence, demonstrating the extended time the prosecution experts had to examine the documents, the conferences in Trenton, the choice of what to choose and what to "mislay," it could hardly have been otherwise.

After the handwriting experts, Wilentz planned to put wood expert Arthur Koehler on the stand and let him astonish the jury by demonstrating how the left rail on the top section of the ladder had once been nailed to the floor of Hauptmann's attic. Getting the ladder admitted into evidence had been the prosecutor's biggest challenge. The defense claimed there was no evidence linking the defendant to any ladder left at the scene. Where had it been ever since that night? How many times had it been taken apart and rebuilt? How many people had handled it?

Detective Bornmann had been summoned to recount the discovery he made in the attic, but that was not enough. Twice it was offered in evidence—and twice refused by Trenchard. Finally, on the third try, the judge cleared the way by ruling that Amandus Hochmuth's eyewitness testimony provided the missing link. "I feel constrained to admit the ladder in evidence," Trenchard said, sounding a bit uncertain of his precedents. If the ladder had not been admitted, the state's case would have been put in jeopardy. But Trenchard had not allowed that to happen. And so, with a sigh of relief, Koehler at last was duly sworn as the state's ladder specialist.

The federal wood expert had kept full notes of his researches and experiences, beginning with his original findings in 1932 and 1933, right up to the opening of the trial. His speculations he kept to himself. He pondered why, it will be recalled, Hauptmann had used a very large plane to work the narrow edges of rail 16 and two of the rungs. "It seems logical," he also mused, that the ladder had been taken to some secluded spot for testing. Why? Because some of the plane marks did not match with any found in the garage. "Did Hauptmann take a smaller plane along, . . . or did someone else furnish the plane?"[31]

Neither one of these conclusions—that he had taken the ladder out for testing, or that "someone else" had furnished a plane—was what Wilentz wanted Koehler to talk about in the witness chair. Nor did he want him to quote from his 1933 report on the ladder, and particularly not this section: "The construction of the ladder in general is very crude, showing poor judgment in the selection of the lumber and in the design of the ladder, and poor workmanship. For a job that was to pull down $50,000, it showed poor foresight." Nor this one: "The chisel used in making the mortises for the cleats evidently was a sharp chisel, since it cut the wood smoothly across the grain and left no scratches. It is not even possible to determine the width of the chisel used." Nor this one either: "The spacing of the old nail's holes in the Douglas fir rails and in yellow pine rail #16 gives no suggestion to what the lumber might have been used for."[32]

In his final summary report before the trial, Koehler changed several things but again concluded that the ladder had not been "intended for general use." The rungs, for example, were made of comparatively soft wood and were oddly spaced at twenty to twenty-one inches apart, as compared to twelve inches in most ladders. And there was more about the workmanship: "Coarser nails were used than should be for driving into the edge of the thin rails, as a result the rails were split in a number of places." In short, he concluded, the ladder did not appear to be made by an "Expert Carpenter," as had been reported in the papers.

Frederick Pope, who would handle the wood evidence for the defense, did not even want to allow Koehler to express an opinion—as a scientist—about the relationship between the board from the attic, State's Exhibit 226, and rail 16, the left side rail on the top section of the ladder. He protested that Koehler might indeed be able to identify types of wood, but when it came to detective work, he said, his judgment was not to be taken as authoritative. Throughout the trial, of course, the defense would have no chance to visit the attic and had to rely on photographs supplied by the prosecution to the court. The defense protested that a claim was being made that the photographs represented the true situation in the attic before Koehler or Bornmann ever got there. And indeed that was the case. The photographs were not evidence but an interpretation of evidence.

Trenchard ruled against the defense on both points, and Koehler was doubly certified as scientist and detective. The nail holes in rail 16, he began, fitted exactly into the joists under Hauptmann's attic floor. There did not exist and could not exist another board anywhere with cut nail holes, spaced exactly like these were, the same distance apart, the same direction from one another. One of the nail holes in the rail and in the joists was at an angle—and yet when cut nails were pushed through all the holes, that nail went into the joist perfectly, as did the others, without manipulation. When the ladder rail was placed down on the joists, moreover, it was perfectly square to the board next to it. He went on to talk about other ways in which he had determined that rail 16 originally came from a board on the attic floor, including planing marks and matching growth rings.

Well, Wilentz asked him, how, then, did he account for the gap between the two boards when they were both in place? One witness, he added, had said it was about one-half inch. (It was not one-half inch but more like one and one-half inches.)

Koehler replied that the board had been cut off a second time to square the future rail for his ladder, but he could still extend the grain pattern through the gap with confidence.

After finishing with the boards, Wilentz brought Koehler to a consideration of the three-quarter-inch wood chisel that had been found the morning after the kidnapping. The state had two uses for the chisel: to persuade the jury Hauptmann had cut out the recesses for ladder rungs, and to suggest to the jury the chisel might be the murder weapon.

Defense Attorney Pope, unaware of Koehler's 1933 conclusion that it was not possible to judge the width of the chisel used to make the recesses, gave away part of the first point by objecting that the chisel found at the Lindbergh estate had been discovered forty miles from Hauptmann's garage. Unless it had been found with Hauptmann's tools, he insisted, there was no point to testimony about an ordinary three-quarter-inch chisel.

But the state turned the argument: a three-quarter-inch chisel "missing" from a set in Hauptmann's toolbox had very probably traveled with the ladder forty miles to Hopewell.

When Pope seemed to concede the rungs had been fashioned with that size chisel, he opened himself up to Judge Trenchard's comments: "It was found, was it not, under the southwest window of this nursery?"

"Somewhere on the Lindbergh property." The defense attorney interrupted, and added, "I don't remember where. It is an ordinary three-quarter inch chisel."

Too late. Trenchard tied the chisel to the crime with obiter dictum—"Where the ransom note was left, which has been traced to the defendant."

"We don't agree to that." Pope tried vainly to catch up.

"I know you don't, but I am telling you what the evidence tends to show."[33]

Pope should have challenged Judge Trenchard's comment that the chisel had been found under the window. He failed to do so, and here was yet another instance where lack of knowledge about Hauptmann's attic and the crime scene hurt the defense cause immeasurably. The chisel had been found out in the field, near where the ladder had been left, not under the window. Photographs taken the next morning show clearly the location. Pinpointing the correct spot might not undermine state contentions, but it certainly would have raised questions about whether this, or any other, chisel had been brought along to lever open the nursery window or bludgeon a child in its crib. Pope's docility stemmed from ignorance, Trenchard's comments from his basic sympathies.[34]

Koehler no longer believed it was impossible to identify the size of the chisel used to chip out the recesses to hold the rungs. After careful reexamination of each recess, he had discovered before the trial began that at least one had been made with a three-quarter-inch chisel, the second from the bottom on rail 16. The more he looked, the more he found. In his last pretrial reviews of the ladder evidence, this single chisel mark convinced him that a three-quarter-inch tool had carved out *all* the recesses on rail 16. "It will be recalled that the mark of a ¾" chisel was found on one of the ladder rails and that no chisel of that size was among Hauptmann's tools."[35]

Koehler testified that planing marks on the ladder corresponded exactly with those that one of Hauptmann's planes produced on pieces of wood he brought into court. Planing a test piece of wood, the expert placed onion paper over the surface and rubbed it with a pencil, the same technique generations of kids had used to obtain Lincoln like-nesses from pennies. He had done it himself, he said, adding a folksy touch to his testimony. He then rubbed the onion paper over the ladder rung and showed the results to the jury. Identical!

When Pope cross-examined him on this point, he asked if the wit-ness had measured the marks in three dimensions. If the plane were held at a different angle to the surface, he suggested, a different pattern could be produced.

Measuring plane marks in three dimensions was not necessary for identification purposes, replied the witness, although he agreed that the distance apart within the marks "varied with the angle to which the plane is held while being passed over the wood."

Had he ever reached a conclusion about markings this way before? Pope asked.

"Yes."

"When?"

"Oh, at various times."

"And for what purpose?"

"To compare the marks on wood with those made by a plane."

"Was that done at various times during the pendency of this investigation?

"Even previous to that."

"And did you ever testify in court before in your life as to the plane markings on a piece of wood?"

"No."

Pope could not know how close he might have been here to a very important discovery. He should have asked again about tests during "the pendency of this investigation," for Koehler had been making many comparisons of plane marks for this case, rejecting those that did not fit. Obviously, he had experimented with angles in doing these tests. But since Pope did not ask, Koehler did not say how many of Haupt-mann's planes he had tested or how many pieces of wood he had re-jected. In evidence bins at the New Jersey State Police Museum, there exist several pieces of wood, each marked as to its suitability, with a notation on one that it should be discarded. In his postarrest reports, remember, Koehler had mused about the reasons why a seemingly over-size plane had been used on the rungs and why none of Hauptmann's planes matched some of the other marks. The prosecution also pre-sented at the trial a wooden bracket taken from the Hauptmann garage, with the telltale plane marks on the side facing the wall. That bracket had been in police hands since the arrest, of course, and it was always a puzzling piece of evidence, particularly why, again, Hauptmann had used an oversize plane and why, again, on a place, like the ladder rungs, where planing seemed unneccessary.[36]

The *New York Times* reporter assigned to the trial, Russell B. Porter, wrote that Hauptmann "seemed crushed" by Koehler's testimony; folding and unfolding his arms across his chest, crossing and uncrossing his legs, he seemed even whiter than usual. His reactions to the day's testimony were different from anything before in the trial. In place of his ordinarily impassive face, the look upon his face, wrote Porter, "could only be described as bewilderment. Whether innocent or guilty, it was evident that he had never before comprehended the vast amount of scientific knowledge and research at the disposal of modern society in the investigation of crime."[37] The witness had given the inanimate evidence the loudest voice in the courtroom and certainly mesmerized Porter as well.

The only place Koehler's testimony did not exactly fulfill the attorney general's fondest hopes came in redirect questioning, when Wilentz sought to ridicule defense arguments that a competent carpenter would not have made the kidnap ladder. Koehler had from the very first labeled the ladder a crude piece of work, except for dowels used to fit it together. But even this was clever, rather than prudent, creating weaknesses that caused it to break. "Let me ask you," said Wilentz, "does this ladder look like the work of a $100 a month carpenter?"

"Well, I don't know just what kind of carpenter work that would be."

A bit of a surprise, that answer, so the prosecutor took Koehler back through another discussion of the dowel pins and notches for rungs. But he still would not get the right answer.

"Is this the work of a carpenter of some sort or other?"

"It might be a very rough carpenter."

"Well, a jeweler wouldn't make this ladder, would he?"

"No."

"It would have to be somebody that knew something about carpentry, isn't that it?"

"Well, something about it, yes."

Impatient with Koehler's equivocal answers, answers that seemed to say that while he could prove the board came from that attic, he could not venture an opinion about whether Hauptmann had actually built it, Wilentz finally pointed directly to the recesses for the rungs and demanded to know, "Is that the work of a carpenter, good or bad?"

"Yes; used carpenter's tools."

Wilentz had suddenly found himself locked in a test of wills with his own witness. "Never mind whether he used carpenters' tools; does it appear like the work of a carpenter?"

"I would say that anybody working with wood would be a carpenter in a sense."

Finally, Wilentz stopped himself—realizing he was making matters worse. "I am not arguing with you about it. I just want to know. My recollection is that you stated that a man weighing about 175 or 180 pounds could go up that ladder without it breaking." But when he came back down with an extra thirty-pound burden, "would not that ladder break? What is your opinion?"

"I couldn't say."

Koehler did agree the greatest stress would be around the dowels. But then, he ruminated out loud, it might break at several points, even at the top rung as the kidnapper stepped out of the window.[38]

It had been some time since the jury early in the trial had heard testimony from State Trooper John J. Sweeney and others about the problems connected with gaining access and coming back down again. This is a good place for us to consider what Sweeney had to say. He testified about a ladder experiment that had been carried out two days after the kidnapping. Its purpose was to demonstrate that even an older man like Sweeney could manage the climb, maneuver himself in and back out the window onto the ladder—causing it to break. As science, the experiment was ludicrous from beginning to end. When he arrived at the Lindbergh estate, his first assignment was to put the ladder together and push it up against the nursery wall. "I put the three sections of the ladder together with the help of a couple of troopers. . . . We put the foot of the ladder in the indentations that was made in the mud." By placing the ladder exactly in the indentations, Sweeney and his colleagues were destroying more evidence—the depth of the holes it had made with the weight of kidnapper. Indeed, as Colonel Shwarzkopf testified, several ladders were placed in those holes during the initial investigation, with troopers scampering up and down, driving the holes deeper. He estimated that the holes were about two inches deep but did not seem to know when that measurement was taken. Schwarzkopf apparently had no interest in measuring that depth as part of an effort to figure out the weight of the kidnapper.[39]

Sweeney did not use the actual kidnap ladder, moreover, to make his climb, and the experiment was carried out in broad daylight. The window was open, and the shutters were drawn back. This is important. It suggests that police either assumed that the window had been open the night of the kidnapping, or knew their experiment was faulty. If the former, the experiment explained why there was no chisel mark or any other mark on the outside of the window. (That hardly helped the prosecution argue against an inside partner for the crime, but the defense did not capitalize effectively.) To make his entrance, Sweeney had had to put his hand at least partly *inside* the window to gain purchase. In the initial investigations, it should be remembered, no one had seemed sure whether that window had been left open or whether it was found open when Betty Gow discovered the child missing.

Sweeney testified that in his role as the intruder, he had exited feet first, stepping up to the windowsill and then after getting his legs out, sitting there for a moment before pivoting around to the ladder, probing for the top rung. He also testified in cross-examination that he did not close the window—another difference from the actual condition of the crime scene. Sweeney was not wearing gloves during the experiment, a significant point because it was always assumed that the kidnapper had left no fingerprints because he did wear gloves. But if that were so, how much more difficult would it have been to open and close the window—how much dexterity was lost?

Reilly asked the witness, "And what would you do with your right arm?"

"Hold on to the window case."

"What did you do with your left arm?"

" Hold on to the window sill."

" Both arms were busy."

"Yes, sir."

Jurors might wonder after this exchange what had happened to the child while Sweeney was fishing around with his legs in the dark trying to find the top rung of the ladder. Wilentz tried to ease their minds: "You told counsel that you put one hand on the window sill and one hand some other place—I forget, it doesn't matter so much—was it difficult to come out?"

"No, sir."

"Did you use the two hands because you had to?"

"I think so."

"Could you have come out with a package?"

" I could."

" With any greater difficulty or with the same ease?"

"Well, I would have to lay the package down."

Sweeney was proving something of a problem here, but Wilentz pressed on. "On what?"

"On the window sill."

"And then as you balance yourself, what would you do?"

"Pick it up."

Sweeney was an apt pupil under such tutelage. But the verbs switch back and forth here. It is not *did* you come out with a package, but *could* you have come out with a package. It is not what *did* you do with the package on the sill, but what *would* you do. "Pick it up," he said when the light finally dawned. Sweeney never came down that ladder, or any ladder, with a package. But Wilentz neatly clouded the issue by switching the verb tense back again: "So that—and in coming down the ladder, could you then come down the ladder, one hand coming down the rungs and the other hand with a package?"

"I could."

"Did you have any difficulty at all about it?"

"No sir."

The defense had one last shot at clearing up the confusion. "You never went up this ladder and went into the window, did you?"

"No sir."

"You never went out the window with a bundle in your arm and swung on to this ladder, S-32 [the kidnap ladder]?"

"No."[40]

Sweeney did not fall, either.

Nor did he leave, apparently, any footprints going up or down. Indeed, all the footprints that tracker Oscar Bush had noticed the night of the kidnapping had disappeared by the time of the trial—save the one Trooper Nuncio DeGaetano had measured with his flashlight near where the ladder had stood. Three troopers testified about the footprint: DeGaetano, J. A. Wolf, and Detective Lewis Bornmann. When asked if they had done anything to preserve the print from being destroyed, they all said that efforts had been made to keep people away from the area, were vague about any photographs that might have been taken, and knew absolutely nothing about whether a plaster of paris mold had been taken.

Reilly questioned Bornmann about whether he had tested the size of the print against Olly Whateley's shoe that night.

He had not.

Well, was that because he knew what size the butler's shoe was?

"I knew he hadn't been out there."

"How did you know he wasn't out there?"

"I had his word for it."

"Oh, you took his word for it? You took the word of the man who has since died that he hadn't gone outside the house, is that it?"

"That is correct."[41]

In fact, a plaster cast was taken of this footprint. The *New York Times* reported on its front page on September 28, 1934, that a gymnasium shoe found in Hauptmann's garage was to be taken down to Trenton for comparison with the mold. Only recently, the archivist at the New Jersey State Police Museum, Mark Falzini, discovered documentary references to the molds, one taken at St. Raymond's Cemetery and the other at the estate. The inventory reads, "Two plaster of paris casts of footprint," and in pencil, "One taken at Hopewell & the other at St. Raymond's Cemetery."[42]

In evidence crates at the museum are two pairs of Hauptmann's shoes. If they had fit the molds, would Wilentz have passed on the opportunity to have Hauptmann step into the kidnapper's footprints?

Trooper Archie Stinson, who had a falling-out with Schwarzkopf and was forced to resign in 1935, wrote Governor Harold Hoffman in early 1938 to tell him about a meeting in a Flemington judge's office the day the trial began. Present were David Wilentz and Assistant Prosecutor Robert Peacock, along with Schwarzkopf and various other officers of the state police. "These gentlemen were having an argument regarding whether there was one or more footprints underneath the window from which the child was kidnapped. Yet all of these men, when they went on the witness stand against the victim testified that there was one footprint found. No mention was made during the whole trial of the fact that they had traced someone from the Lindbergh home several hundred feet into the woods in the rear of the Lindbergh home."[43]

Stinson had a grudge against Colonel Schwarzkopf, so one might doubt both his motives and his memory. But Schwarzkopf had written a Boston city councilman a month after Hauptmann's arrest, and three weeks after the *Times* reported that his gym shoe had been taken to Trenton for comparison, to explain why bloodhounds had not been used the night of the kidnapping. By midnight, he wrote, there were more than fifty newspaper reporters and photographers on the grounds, by daybreak over four hundred. "This group had overrun the whole property and had even trampled *the few footprints which existed, despite the fact that boxes and boards had been layed [sic] over them to protect them.* Under the circumstances, bloodhounds would only have tracked the courses of newspaper reporters. Another fact that would have made trailing exceedingly difficult was the inclemency of the weather, it being a windy and rainy night."[44]

But where had the intruder fallen, as Wilentz suggested in his opening statement, to avoid leaving more footprints below the window on that "windy and rainy night"? Clearly, this required some thought, and in his summary Wilentz offered up several alternative scenarios of how the child died to explain the footprints that weren't there.

So, in the end, there were two parts to the ladder evidence to consider. First, there was that supplied by Arthur Koehler, who testified about tools and nails, wood grain and plane marks; and then there was Trooper Sweeney (assisted by his colleagues) reenacting in daylight the kidnapper's ascent and descent from the nursery—and assuring the court, under Wilentz's careful tutelage, that it *could* be done, although he had not done it.

Between them, and with the expert testimony on the nursery note, the attorney general had confidence the jury would see Hauptmann (and no one else) on the ladder.

14
CROSS EXAMINATIONS

The prisoner on this date was very despondent, did hardly any sleeping, but paced up and down with tears in his eyes. He ate no full meals. Immediately after the interview with his wife, attorney Reilly made a final effort to have this man confess, and upon being unsuccessful left for New York.

—Record of A. L. Smith, Flemington guard detail, February 14, 1935

The courtroom assembly had waited nearly a month for Reilly to call "Bruno Richard Hauptmann." As he walked to the stand, he still seemed an enigma. What made this German carpenter tick? After Hauptmann's direct testimony was over, Wilentz asked reporters if they noticed the absolute lack of feeling. "There was no change in his face or manner. When he talked about the Lindbergh child he talked as if he were discussing dollars and cents."[1]

Psychiatrist Dudley Shoenfeld, however, had his own take on what drove Hauptmann to this heinous crime. Previously, he had believed the "singnature" revealed his homosexuality. Now, he thought otherwise. Richard was only a boy of seventeen, he told reporters, when he was forced into the army. He resented the military discipline that had instilled a sense of inferiority; but as a patriotic German he admired his fatherland's "Red Knight," Baron Mannfried von Richthofen—the greatest of all German aviators killed in the war. Choosing Colonel Lindbergh, then, was more than greed; it was an act of vengeance against a usurper. Wasn't he now reading in his cell a biography of von Richthofen, and hadn't he named his son Manfred?[2]

But both Wilentz and Shoenfeld agreed Hauptmann was an alien—someone unwanted in the United States. His guttural accent said it all.

Although he had worn the same suit of clothes every day, the *New York Times* noticed for the first time when he sat down to testify that the colors he wore, gray and blue, were those of World War I German army uniforms. With Hitler's brutal regime ruling Germany—and making itself more hated everywhere else—Hauptmann represented for many inside and outside the courtroom the once and future enemy.

Lloyd Fisher opened for the defense by trying to bring the jury's thoughts back to the everyday world. Was it likely, he asked, that a man about to commit a kidnapping would take his tool kit to the Majestic Apartments expecting to go to work?

Reilly tried to impress on the jury that Hauptmann would never have made such a clumsy ladder in the first place: "Now, how many years, Bruno, have you been a carpenter?"

"About ten years."

"You have seen this ladder here in court, haven't you?"

"Yes."

"Did you build this ladder?"

"I am a carpenter."

The courtroom exploded in laughter—one of the few times not at Hauptmann's expense.

Step down from the witness stand, Reilly then said, and appraise the workmanship.

"Looks like a music instrument."

Wilentz acted as if had not heard the defendant. "What is it?" he asked.

Reilly answered for Hauptmann. "He says in his opinion it looks like a music instrument." Turning back to his witness, he asked him to explain why he said it looked like a music instrument.

"To me," Hauptmann replied, "it [doesn't?] look like a ladder at all. I don't know how a man can step up."[3]

Reilly had his client's account books brought in, and Hauptmann made a great show of examining all the entries to try to demonstrate he did not suddenly become flush after the ransom was paid but moved money around—sometimes the same day—or invested large sums of cash Isidor Fisch had given him. He did not open separate accounts because Fisch wanted it that way. Maybe he kept his own record, said Hauptmann, but of course no such documents ever turned up. That arrangement supposedly lasted until November 1, 1933, when they made a "clean table" and each put up $17,500 in a new joint endeavor.

To make it all fit, he now claimed that he met Fisch long before the "introduction" in the Henkels' apartment sometime in August 1932. On

May 9 of that year, Hauptmann testified, he gave Fisch two sums of money: $430 to purchase furs from his bank accounts and an additional $170 from a very special place. That last $170 "came from the $4,300 I left home. I got home, I mean." He had stashed away money, week by week, during the prosperous years of the 1920s before the Great Depression until he had over $4,000 in a secret hiding place under linens in a trunk.[4]

He had never revealed his secret to Anna because he was hoping to surprise her by buying a house. He liked to surprise his wife in this fashion, as he had when he purchased the Dodge automobile for $700 back in 1930. When he found the Fisch money, he had not informed Anna about that, either, because she would get too nervous about it.

Reilly asked him to explain, nonetheless, where the $3,750 came from that Hauptmann used to purchase a mortgage on January 1, 1933. Well, he replied, $1,750 came from the trunk, $800 from the bank, and $1,200 from the fur account. And that, "Made up them $3,750." While the magical trunk seemed like something out of Grimm's fairy tales—the more Hauptmann took, the more was there—police learned from the bank that none of the mortgage purchase money had been gold certificates.[5] Indeed, inability to trace any of the ransom money directly to Hauptmann before August 1934, while it did not make the magic trunk any more believable, had proven frustrating.

On and on the recitation of Hauptmann's finances went, however, including his testimony that when President Roosevelt called in gold certificates, he had deposited $1,250 in that very currency.

Nobody came around the next day, said Reilly, and told him he had deposited "gold Lindy notes, did they?"

"Nobody came around, because there was $50 gold notes and I guess two or three hundred dollar gold notes, too."

He had been saving these gold certificates, he told the court, as a hedge against inflation—like that which had occurred in post–World War I Germany. They were, he said, the last of the $4,300 in the trunk.[6]

Hauptmann's finances left one mystified. There is no indication the jury understood the recitation, any more than anyone else who had tried to figure them out. FBI agent Genau had concluded that the defendant's ledgers were designed to allow him to understand what was going on, but no one else. At the trial, Treasury agent William Frank said, on the other hand, that he could account for nearly $49,950 of the ransom money. Hauptmann's cash assets and stocks totaled no more than $203 on April 2, 1932, asserted Frank. Over the next two years, he invested more than $16,000, and this sum plus the $14,600 found in the garage and his other expenditures made the figures come out almost perfectly—only $50 off.

Frank's testimony and cross-examination had gone on interminably, as Reilly tried to wring out a concession from the accountant that he had exaggerated investments and double counted deposits. Back and forth they batted decimal points and zeros, for nearly one hundred pages of dialogue—the last ninety-nine of which would have glazed over the most attentive juror's eyes. In almost all of these accountings, moreover, the J. J. Faulkner deposit and other recovered monies were always added in as funds Hauptmann controlled, though that had never been proven. If, for the sake of argument, one subtracted those sums, and the $14,000 Hauptmann said he got from Fisch, the balance sheet had to be radically adjusted.

Wilentz knew Frank's addition and subtraction were a little too perfect—besides boring the daylights out of everyone. So he would do something about that.

"I notice that there are hundreds of shares of Curtiss-Wright," he said to Frank.

"Yes, sir."

"That is aviation stocks, isn't it?"

"Yes, sir"

"Airplane stocks."

"That is correct."

After some questions about stocks in general, Wilentz came back to Curtiss-Wright, observing that by May 1933, Hauptmann still had hundreds of shares in the company.

"Do you know," he prompted Frank, "what business Colonel Lindbergh is in?"

The court had heard enough about airplane stocks, protested Reilly. Frank's list contained many varieties of investment spread across Wall Street opportunities. "I say it is merely an attempt to get again before this jury, in an improper way, the fact that the Colonel is interested in aviation."

Wilentz accepted the accusation: "That is the intention, but not improperly. That is the intention."

For once Trenchard sided with the defense, sustaining Reilly's objection. But not before Wilentz repeated that Hauptmann had bought hundreds and hundreds of shares in aviation companies. The defendant's interest in airplane stocks "indicates some connection and thought as to the man who was the most prominent in aviation in the world." It was for the jury to decide what it all meant.[7]

But what did it all mean? As Reilly continued extracting the details of Hauptmann's financial dealings, they suggested money-laundering operations. Ten days after purchasing the $3,750 mortgage, he deposited another $1,400 in the bank. Reilly asked him where he got it.

"This money Isidor Fisch said I should put in the bank, in the stock account. But my account was strong enough to carry his buying. So I didn't put it in the stock account; I put it in my bank. That's just the same as mine."[8]

No one checked up to see if that were true. Here was an instance, nevertheless, that might indicate if he were telling the truth; if he had enough money that day to cover Fisch's investment, there might be a lot more to the partnership than anyone suspected. A few weeks later Hauptmann opened bank and stock accounts in Anna's name. He had done this to protect his funds against a potential lawsuit, he said, resulting from an accident he had in which a man named Alexander Begg had been injured. But it may have provided him with a cover for further dealings with Isidor Fisch. It may have been, in fact, their joint account in all but name. In this regard, it is worth noting that on the day Richard learned Isidor had died in Germany, he took $2,700 from this account to purchase stocks. Did that mean he could now do as he pleased with the money? Perhaps. And then there was the frantic search for Isidor's assets Richard and Henry Uhlig undertook, a quest that uncovered nothing but an empty safe deposit box. The search may have been an effort not only to discover furs and hidden funds—but also, even primarily, to remove incriminating evidence.[9]

In closing his direct examination, Reilly sought sympathy for his client by asking him to tell the court about his beating at the police station and the ordeal of writing the dictation over and over again into the early hours of the morning.

Hauptmann now faced a much more grueling two-day ordeal by cross-examination. He had been arrested for armed robbery after the war, hadn't he? began the prosecutor. Yes. And put in prison? Yes. And he escaped? Yes. And he made three attempts to enter the United States illegally? Yes. "You sneaked in the last time." And at the time of his arrest he was in communication with his mother about whether the coast was clear for him to return to Germany, wasn't he? Yes, he had plans to return to Germany, but only, Hauptmann insisted, so he could come back to the United States legally. He wasn't running away.

So far things had not been going all that badly. But things were about to change, beginning with the ladder. Wilentz pretended he was offended. Hauptmann must have been coached to say such things about the ladder, and he chastised him for mocking references to the state's prime exhibit. A music instrument indeed! The assault had its desired effect. "You see you are not smiling anymore, are you?" said the prosecutor.

"Smiling?"

"It has gotten a little more serious, hasn't it?"

"I guess it isn't any place to smile here."

"'*I am a carpenter.*'"

"I am."

"That was funny, wasn't it?"

"No, sir, there is nothing funny about it."

"There is nothing funny about it? You had a good laugh, didn't you? Did you plan that in jail there, did somebody tell you to give that answer when I asked you about the ladder, to stand in front of the jury and say, 'I am a carpenter'?"

"No, sir."

"You thought that out yourself?"

"No, I didn't think a thing about it."

Wilentz continued hectoring Hauptmann, trying to force a violent response. "You have got a peculiar notion about will power, haven't you?"

Frederick Pope objected, "Well, I think this has gone just about far enough."

Wilentz withdrew the question and asked for a recess. Pope readily agreed to a recess and suggested they should all come back "into a courtroom" afterward.

"What do you mean by that, Mr. Pope?" Judge Trenchard snapped.

Abuse of the witness, Pope said, risking Trenchard's wrath.

Offended by the suggestion he had allowed the prosecutor to step over the limits, Trenchard rebuked Pope, not Wilentz.[10]

"Now I want to show you a little book and ask if it is yours," began the most dramatic exchange in the cross-examination. "Is that your handwriting? Take your time about it. Look at it."

Hauptmann should have sensed the trap from Wilentz's solicitous urge "[to] take your time about it."

But in he walked: "Yes, that's my handwriting."

"Take a look at this word particularly. Tell me if that is your handwriting, that one word there."

Hauptmann sat deathly still, staring at the word.

"Or did some policeman write it?"

"I—I can't remember every word I put in here."

"Just the one word, that's all. There are only a few words on the whole page. That one word; tell me if that is your handwriting."

"It looks like my handwriting, but I can't remember I ever put it in."

Judge, jury, reporters, everyone strained forward as if to look for themselves at what was in the little book. Wilentz teased out the suspense as long as he could.

"You can't remember what?"

"No, no."

"Don't mix it up now. Just stay with that word there for a minute; two dollars and fifty cents. You see that word."

"Yes."

"Alongside of it?"

"Yes."

"Are they your figures?"

"They must be my figures."

"They must be your figures. Now let's get to this word that you use."

"Yes."

"Yes. That is your word then, isn't it?"

"I can't remember if I ever put it in."

"Well now, this isn't a joke. You know either it is your handwriting or it isn't. Is it your handwriting?"

"It looks like my handwriting."

"Now, tell me," Wilentz boomed out, "how do you spell 'boat'?"

"B-o-a-t."

"Yes. Why did you spell it b-o-a-d?"

B-o-a-d, was the way the kidnapper had apparently spelled *boat* in the final note telling Colonel Lindbergh he would find the child on the *Nelly.*

Hauptmann tried to buy time: "You wouldn't mind to tell me how old this book is?"

"I don't know how old it is. You know; I don't know."

"Let me see it."

Turning it over and flipping through the pages, Hauptmann said the book was probably eight years old.

"All right. Why did you spell b-o-a-d?"

"Well, after you make improvement in your writing."

"All right. So that at one time you used to spell 'boat' b-o-a-d?"

"Probably eight or ten years ago, and I am not quite sure if I put it in."

"All right," Wilentz said. "At one time you used to spell 'boat' b-o-a-d, didn't you? Isn't that right?"

"No, I don't think so.

"Eight years ago, six years ago, ten years ago, whenever it was, you used to spell 'boat' b-o-a-d, isn't that right?"

"I don't know."

Was this the moment Hauptmann might actually break down and confess? "Although no one in the crowded courtroom could tell whether Hauptmann was innocent or guilty, his look of terror was easy to read."[11]

"You tell the truth now. Didn't you spell it in there?"

"Now, listen. I can't remember whether I put it in there."

Fisher and Pope both objected. Wilentz was flogging the witness.

"Well, it isn't twice objectionable," the prosecutor said with a smile, relishing the moment.

Trenchard ruled for the defense, so Wilentz took another angle.[12]

"But the word 'boad' in there," he went on, "you won't say that it is not in your handwriting, will you?"

"I wouldn't say yes either."

"The reason you don't say yes or no is because you know you wrote 'boad' when you got the fifty thousand from Condon, isn't that right?"

"No, sir."

"Boad Nelly. Look at it," Wilentz said, handing the ransom note to Hauptmann.

"No."

"Do you see the word 'boad Nelly'?"

"I see it, certainly."

"Same spelling?"

"Same spelling."[13]

The little expense book was four years old. It contained a list of expenditures on the Hauptmanns' 1931 California vacation, including the notation of $2.50 for a boat ride. Richard's fate dangled on one letter—on evidence the handwriting experts had feared to introduce because the little book contained a variety of writings that were not Hauptmann's. But the attorney general had thrust it at the accused with the zeal of a seventeenth-century New England judge scourging the Devil's agent from the land. It was far more damning than all the charts, all the plane marks, and all the account analyses.

If Richard had done as the prosecutor suggested, and taken his time, he would have noticed differences in the way the word was spelled in the ransom note and in his little book. In the little book, what looked like a spelling error was actually the way Germans had been taught to write final *t*s on words, while the ransom note *boad* is written with an *o* next to an *l* to fashion a unique *d*. Why he testified against himself on this crucial point is very hard to understand.[14]

There were no more big shocks. But between April 1932 and his arrest in September 1934, Hauptmann agreed he had made only a few hundred dollars as a carpenter. Where, then, did all this money come from to buy stocks, purchase a fancy radio, a canoe, and field glasses?

From a trunk he kept in the big closet off the living room, hidden in with the bedding and clothes.

"Was the trunk locked?"

"The trunk was locked."

"Who had the key?"

"I got a key."

"Did your wife have a key?"

"No, sir, the last year we lost the key, we got to break up [open] the trunk the last time."

"Featherbeds in there, and your wife didn't have a key?"

"No, sir."

"Clothes in there and your wife didn't have a key?"

"No, sir."[15]

Wilentz was incredulous. Anna never looked there? Twice a year from 1929 to 1934, someone replaced the winter clothes with summer clothes, and then summer clothes for winter clothes; and supposedly his wife never once burrowed into this trunk to find anything, never even touched it?

Well, Wilentz moved on, when he found the other money poking out of that wet shoebox, how did he feel?

"I was excited."

"Did you say anything, did you holler out, 'Anna, look what I found,' or anything like that?"

"No, I did not."

You did not! "Didn't she work and slave in a bakery and bring to you when you and she got married, her earnings and her savings?"

"That has got nothing to do with them $14,000 at all."

We see, as Wilentz saw, his dilemma. If he said he had told Anna about the money, he would endanger both her and Manfred. So he had to insist she never saw anything, however weak the trunk story appeared to the court.[16]

Richard's frequent use of the word *them* throughout his trial testimony, and his statement he had been planning a trip to Germany for more than a year *already*, gave Wilentz the opportunity to call attention to such phrases in the ransom notes. In one of the later notes, for example, the writer had said that Colonel Lindbergh should pay attention to the "singnature," especially "them three holes." On trial for his life, Hauptmann kept saying "them" when he referred to amounts of money.

Once he found this "wet" money, Wilentz asked, why did he put part of it into holes he drilled into a large piece of board? Police found it there along with a larger carved-out space that concealed a small pistol.

He had never planned it that way, said Hauptmann; the holes were originally intended for tools. And he hadn't told about the hiding place because he feared the pistol would be found, knowing it would lead to his deportation as an illegal immigrant.

Wilentz summed up his cross-examination: "You concealed the truth from the police; you concealed the truth from the Supreme Court Justice; you concealed the truth from your wife; you concealed the truth about your board; you have concealed the truth about everything in this case, haven't you?"

"No sir."

Well, when he was arrested, hadn't he said he had only a few gold certificates and coins back at home—money he was still saving as a hedge against inflation? But police discovered the can with the packages of money, nearly $14,000, behind a shelf.

No, he testified, soon after his arrest he spoke privately to a man named O'Ryan, who wore no uniform and might have been a detective, and told him about the money hidden in the garage. (General John F. O'Ryan was New York City police commissioner at the time.) He told O'Ryan, he said, about the money hidden on the south wall before it was discovered.[17]

Wilentz called General O'Ryan as a rebuttal witness. Hauptmann had just testified that he told the commissioner where the money could be found beforehand, said Wilentz, was that correct?

"No, that is not correct."

The prosecutor repeated the question to emphasize that the defendant had lied yet again, lied so many times it was not possible to say he ever told the truth. "The moneys were discovered without any information from him then, is that it?"

"Oh, yes. The money had been found before he told me about where the money could be found."

Well, this second answer was not so definitive, was it? While O'Ryan's carefully worded second answer did not confirm Hauptmann's claim, it also did not confirm police assertions that Hauptmann had not told them about the money before *he* knew that it had been discovered.[18]

Finished with money, the prosecutor brought out the board Inspector Henry Bruckman had found in the closet—the one on which Condon's address and phone number had been written. During his interrogation, and later at the extradition hearings, Hauptmann had admitted, albeit ambiguously at times, that the writing must be his. He now repudiated those statements. "I wouldn't make any notice on the inside of a closet where you have no chance to stand to write or read, it is impossible."[19]

Frederick Pope dismissed Wilentz's performance as "theatrical" but told the press that if his client were convicted, the defense would appeal in part on the grounds that the prosecutor stimulated the audience to ridicule with statements such as "My God, don't you ever tell the truth?"[20]

Wilentz was much gentler with Anna Hauptmann. She testified that on the night of March 1, 1932, her husband came to the bakery sometime around seven, a little before, maybe, or a little after. He stayed there with her until they both left around nine, and went straight home. She knew he had come that night because it was her late night at work. She also remembered the night of April 2, 1932, the night the ransom was paid, because they always had a musical evening the first Saturday of the month. Hans Kloppenburg, a close friend, was also there that night. The third crucial night, November 26, 1933, was Richard's birthday. It was only a few weeks after Manfred's birth. Her niece was there that night, as well as Isidor Fisch. So Richard could not have been down in Greenwich Village buying a ticket to a movie. Basically, that was her testimony, along with a rebuttal of prosecution insinuations that Richard had been seeing Greta Henkel ever since her 1932 trip to Germany.

Hadn't she told police at the time Richard was arrested, asked Wilentz, that it was too long ago to remember what had happened on March 1, 1932?

That was so, she admitted, but when someone then asked her if she remembered the night of the kidnapping, she said she did; it was a Tuesday, her late night.

What about the closet shelf where Fisch's box of money was supposed to be? asked Wilentz.

She had never looked there.

"So you cleaned the first shelf, and you cleaned the second shelf, but you never cleaned the top shelf?"

"No, I didn't use it."

"You don't really mean that, do you, Mrs. Hauptmann?"

"No, I didn't use it."[21]

She had testified she was in another room the night Fisch supposedly brought the shoebox. Reilly had tried to get her to say she had seen the box, but she would not. Wilentz's purpose, on the other hand, was to suggest she would lie to save her husband, not only about the box but about Richard's failure to pick her up at the bakery.

Reilly then produced Elvert Carlstrom, who insisted he had seen Haupt-mann in the bakery that night. He was frequently there, but he remem-bered that night especially because it was his birthday, and he decided to treat himself to a nice dinner after working all day in New Jersey. He knew the place and was quite familiar with the blond woman who worked there, though he did not know Anna's name. When he saw Haupt-mann's picture in the newspapers, he recalled that he had seen him sit-ting there that night. It was not a large place, Fredericksen's bakery and deli, so this was important testimony.

The prosecution had somehow neglected to check previously on the possibility there might have been several witnesses who saw— or did not see—Hauptmann in Fredericksen's. But, then, Anna did not seem to remember the customers that night, either. Unless Carlstrom's story was broken, the prosecution would have real trouble. Wilentz sent a squad of detectives to New York to find out everything they could about Carlstrom—and why he had come forward at this time. Wilentz's cross-examination strategy, switching back and forth rapidly between subjects, using long questions in hopes of producing confusion, was all the more effective with witnesses like Carlstrom who were not native English speakers.

The prosecutor tried to discredit Carlstrom's memory. You saw him only once?

Yes, only once, Carlstrom replied.

Not expecting much of a challenge to his heavy sarcasm, Wilentz erred when he asked, "You would remember him as long as you lived, wouldn't you?"

"I do."

"Certainly. Was it his eyes?"

"No, it was—"

"What was there about him?"

"Because he was laughing at me in the bakery."

"Yes. All right." (Whenever Wilentz was surprised, "all right" popped up—a classic verbal pause while he figured out how to divert attention from the testimony.) "He was laughing at you. But what was there about him that impressed itself upon your mind so that you would remember his face as long as you lived?"

Carlstrom surprised him a second time. "Because I got mad at him and when I got mad at somebody then I remember the face."

Wilentz kept asking over and over, trying to recoup, finally getting him to say something he could grab hold of to try to discredit his memory. "What kind of eyes did he have?"

"I think he had blue eyes, if I am not mistaken."

"If you are not mistaken, he had blue eyes. If you are mistaken, he had other eyes, is that what you mean?"

"That is not what I mean."

"Were his eyes deep set or were they out like yours or like mine?"

"They were deeper set. I guess they were deeper than yours."

"How about yours?"

"I can't see my eyes."

Carlstrom's answers had made him a good witness. So Wilentz shifted to questions about the various places where he had lived since coming to the United States, demanding to know details about each one, not just the street address but whether the building was brick or frame, how many stories it had, if there was a janitor, an elevator. All through this extraordinary grilling, the defense did not challenge its materiality, asking only that Carlstrom be given a chance to answer completely. Wilentz asked him at one point whether he had ever seen anyone go up to the third story of one of the places he lived for five months. Carlstrom hesitated, not sure if he had. That was all it took for the prosecutor to challenge his credibility. Finally, as Wilentz went on and on bullying him over insignificant questions, and interrupting his answers to pile on more opportunities for the jury to hear a nervous foreign accent, Reilly asked somewhat deferentially that the witness be accorded the same courtesies prosecution witnesses had enjoyed.

"Never mind about the courtesy," Wilentz snapped in frustration. "May I suggest, if your Honor please, I don't need any scolding from counsel."

Reilly denied he was scolding, and repeated that the prosecutor had not allowed Carlstrom any opportunity to think about his answer. The witness, he said, "should be treated in a gentlemanly fashion, and not browbeaten and broken down this way."

At this point, Judge Trenchard intervened with blatant favoritism. "I don't see anything irregular about his examination." He then overruled another defense objection on the grounds that Carlstrom's statements had "been of such a wavering nature that it does seem as if the Attorney General ought to be permitted a reasonable latitude in testing the accuracy of such testimony."

The prosecutor continued hammering on the point that Carlstrom had not decided to come forward until very recently, having seen a picture of the defendant and Reilly together, implying his tale was nothing more than opportunism.

Carlstrom had been living with a family on Long Island in September 1934, when he realized from newspaper arrest reports that Hauptmann was the man he had seen in Fredericksen's that night.

"Who did you tell it to?

"I told it down in the kitchen."

"To who?"

"Mrs. Strauss was there and her brother-in-law and another fellow."

"And what did you tell them?"

"I remember now that I said that I saw in the newspaper that the waitress' husband was arrested and then told them there that I remembered I saw him in the restaurant on March 1st."

"You think it over. There is no question about that being true?"

Yes, it was true, but Carlstrom then said he had not seen a picture of Hauptmann until later; he made the identification instead from newspaper descriptions. "I don't think I saw his picture at that time."

"Why, you told us before you saw it in September, didn't you?

"Not his picture—yes, I saw—"

"What?

"I saw his picture in September, I guess I did."

But, said Wilentz, he had originally testified, hadn't he, that the first time he recognized the man was from his picture with Reilly a few weeks ago? Wasn't that so? It was not so; he had not testified that way. Wilentz slipped that in without it being picked up by anyone. What he had said, instead, was that he had seen many pictures of Hauptmann in the newspaper, but the one with Reilly made him sure. "That's the one," he recalled his thoughts, "I recognize the man." Why this discrepancy? Wilentz wanted the jury to believe there never had been an identification until someone got to him.

Carlstrom hedged for another reason, however. He had not wanted to get involved because he knew there would be questions about that night—about what he did after he left the bakery. He had spent the rest of the night with a prostitute, from 1 until 5 A.M., and was afraid if he came forward he would be incriminated in an illegal act, an especially dangerous situation for someone not yet a citizen.

Wilentz turned "incrimination" on its head in a parting shot: "You weren't with Mr. Hauptmann that night between one and five, were you?"

"I was not."[22]

Police had in their hands several statements from the Strauss family confirming Carlstrom's testimony that he had recognized Hauptmann as the man he saw soon after the latter's arrest. But Carlstrom's reluctance to explain why he had not gone to police right away undermined its impact.[23]

Wilentz put on the stand a rebuttal witness, Arthur Larson, who said he and Carlstrom had been in Dunellen, New Jersey, that night, sleeping in an upstairs room of a house where they worked. But Larson then admitted he did not know if March 1, 1932, had any special meaning for Carlstrom. He had pinpointed the date because the next day he had gone for paint supplies and read the newspapers. Reilly elicited that New Jersey detectives had brought Larson into court so he could hear Carlstrom's testimony before he went on the stand.

Wilentz also called Carlstrom's employer, Oscar Hilbert Christiansen, but he proved less than a perfect witness.

Reilly objected to calling Christiansen to corroborate a rebuttal witness. There were strict rules against it. If the defense then called somebody to corroborate Carlstrom's presence, he said, "[they] would go on indefinitely."

No longer any surprise, Trenchard disagreed. The witness could be asked "whether or not he can tell from an examination of his books, whether or not Carlstrom, *if that is his name,* was there on that night." An absentee owner, Christiansen lived in New York. He came nowhere near New Jersey on March 1, 1932. The judge was insinuating Christiansen's opinion—and, worse, a factual impossibility—into the trial.

Wilentz was happy to take the insinuation, of course, and try to make more out of it.

What were Carlstrom's hours of employment supposed to be?

No specific hours, replied Christiansen. He was supposed to take care of the fire.

Wilentz tried again. "Was that to include day and night?"

"That I don't know."

"Was the fire to be taken care of at night?"

"As long as the fire was taken care of, I didn't care if he left there or not."[24]

Another witness, Louis Kiss, also saw Hauptmann in the bakery that night. Hauptmann came in from the outside, said Kiss, accompanied by a large German shepherd dog, and walked over to Anna. Speaking in German, he told her that "somebody want to take away the dog." Richard often walked the baker's dog while he waited for Anna to finish work. Kiss remembered the incident because the dog ran around the room in an excited fashion, and because the man was speaking in German. He remembered the night because it was exactly one week, he said, after he had to take his child to the hospital, on Washington's Birthday.

Kiss was followed to the stand by August Von Henke, who recalled that he was in the vicinity of the bakery that night looking for his missing dog. Seeing the baker's dog, he mistook it for his own and got into a loud argument with Hauptmann, threatening to have him arrested for dognapping![25]

These two witnesses, who had never met, tied in nicely. Wilentz attacked Kiss's testimony because the witness had said it was exactly one week after Washington's Birthday, pointing out that that day was February 22. In leap years, one week later would be February 29, not the first of March. Wilentz did not dispute he was there one of those nights, however, and if he saw Anna and Richard, it would have to have been the night she worked late, Tuesday, March 1, 1932. Wilentz also attacked Kiss and Von Henke as shady characters, whose activities during Prohibition included making rum for sale to friends and running a speakeasy.

There was no reason to believe that Carlstrom, Kiss, and Von Henke were any worse witnesses than Hochmuth and Whited. Indeed, there is some evidence later uncovered by Lloyd Fisher that Wilentz worried about his attempt to discredit Kiss, and tried to pressure him into changing his testimony.[26]

Reilly did much to discredit his best witnesses, himself, by putting on the stand a string of poseurs and nincompoops. Fisher despaired at this conduct. Reilly picked his witnesses by reading "so-called fan mail." Some of them were well-meaning enough. "More often they were just plain damn fools."[27]

By far the worst was Philip Moses, who had first turned up one evening at Fisher's office in Flemington claiming he was Hauptmann's savior. Fisher's secretary chased him out. But the very next day Reilly announced, to everyone's amazement, that this Moses would prove to be the turning point in the case. While he waited his turn to go on the witness stand, Moses went around town signing autographs, "The man who will save Hauptmann—Philip Moses." He traded them for cans of tobacco. The first question Wilentz asked on cross-examination was whether he signed autographs, and then if he was a songwriter. Moses immediately produced a song and recited the lyrics. Did he also do imitations? Delighted his talents were being recognized at last, Moses responded by going into a Will Rogers act.[28]

Hauptmann stood to lose his life because of Reilly's P. T. Barnum display and complained bitterly to Lloyd Fisher: "Reilly make a damned fool of us all by such monkey shines as he had today with that taxi-man Moses." Worse: "He lowers me in the eyes of the jury."[29]

From the outset the defense had demanded the right to inspect the ransom notes. It was not until after the trial had started that the state agreed to allow such an examination, over *one* weekend at the Hilde-brecht Hotel in Trenton. The prosecutors promised that the defense team could have them in privacy for a whole day. Reilly, meanwhile, had been boasting he had lined up the greatest handwriting expert in the world, someone who lived in Vienna. More than that he would not say.

Fisher and Pope arrived at the hotel about ten in the morning of the designated Saturday to find Reilly and prosecutor Joe Lanigan toasting one another with applejack at the bar. As they moved on to the lobby, a reporter pointed at two of the "damndest looking figures that ha[d] ever assailed [his] eyes." Aren't these your experts? the reporter said with a smirk. "My God," said Fisher, "I hope not." But they were, indeed, Reilly's specialists. One was an elderly gentleman, wrapped up well in an overcoat, although the temperature in the lobby was quite warm, at least seventy-five degrees. Remnant tufts of white hair came down over his collar. "He had on glasses with exceedingly heavy lenses," Fisher later recalled, "and when I introduced myself and put out my hand to shake hands, he pulled his hand up but missed mine by almost a foot." With him was a young fellow, barely into his twenties, if possible, a stranger looking creature still. About five-foot-three, he had a perfectly blank face and a pompadour hairstyle. "He had on a coat of one pattern and trousers of another, and the coat reached practically to his knees. It was many sizes too big for him and his hands were lost in the folds of the sleeves." They reminded one of characters from Charles Dickens.

Accompanied by a small posse of state troopers and stenographers, the ransom notes finally arrived. Reilly paraded his experts into the room where the materials were set out on a table. Colonel Malone, the tufted elderly gentleman from the lobby, and his sidekick, the pie-bald Mr. Myers, called Fisher aside. They could not look at the notes, Myers whispered, until they had been paid $500. Told there was not that much money in the world, and that, so far as Fisher was concerned, they were not worth five cents, they departed, "the old man tottering along with one hand on his cane and one on Myers's arm." Fisher never saw either of them again.[30]

Then there was Reilly's world-class expert, the great Hilda Braunlich from Vienna, who actually lived in New York. A graphologist with no expertise at all in identifying authorship, she fit right in with the rest.

The only one who even qualified as an expert was John M. Trendley from Missouri, who nevertheless would concede on the stand that he had once made a dreadful mistake because his mind was on a load of bananas he had coming into his fruit stand, which he feared would spoil before he finished testifying.

"This, then," despaired Fisher, "was the crew that was to [do] combat with $33,000 worth of hand-writing testimony, that is, testimony that was paid $33,000 but that actually billed the State of New Jersey for more than $50,000. There wasn't a single one of them, in my opinion, barring Trendley, who could have qualified."

Still, the state took no chances. Despite the promise that the defense experts could confer in privacy, the troopers and stenographers hovered close by. "It was utterly impossible for these people to even converse in a whisper without being over-heard by representatives of the State." They had been in the room for about thirty minutes when Reilly herded them all out to the large Colonial Dining Room, where moving picture cameras had been set up, and still photographers in large numbers stood waiting for their appearance. All told they had about three hours, at most, with the documents. "Fred [Pope] and I, thoroughly disgusted, left."

Afterward, Wilentz repeated the story to the jury that Malone would not testify because he was convinced the writer was Hauptmann. Fisher asked him not to continue to do this as a matter of fairness. Neither Malone nor Myers had even seen the documents, Fisher said, demanding $500 first. If Malone had refused to appear because the defense had no money, a suddenly generous Wilentz said, the state would pay him his fee. All day long that Saturday, Joe Lanigan continued to order drinks for anyone who cared to step up to the bar. He ran up a bill of about $83, which the state refused to pay. Joe gave it to his good friend Ed Reilly, who submitted it to Anna Hauptmann, and she paid.[31]

As soon as John Trendley seated himself in the witness chair, prosecutor Lanigan objected to his qualifications as a witness. Producing court records from other cases, Lanigan sought to demonstrate that Trendley had once contradicted his own testimony, had broken off testifying in order to save a carload of bananas, and had boasted of his ability to forge signatures.

Trendley readily admitted these errors. Since he had testified in nearly four hundred court cases over forty years, said Reilly, the few mistakes he had made hardly disqualified him. Lanigan had had an ample opportunity to investigate Trendley, Reilly pointed out, whereas the defense was kept in the dark about some prosecution witnesses until five minutes before they were presented to the court. Even so, the defense attorneys had been able to get information on Albert S. Osborn's mistakes. It all went to show that handwriting analysis was not a science but an informed opinion.[32]

Whether such a statement helped the defense was doubtful. The parade of prosecution experts with their charts seemed to defy opposition. Joe Lanigan, in fact, suggested Trendley had prepared no charts because he knew he would look ridiculous if he did. In big cases, Lanigan asked, do you use charts and photographs?

Yes, certainly, replied Trendley.

"Yet, in a case like this you prepared no charts, did you?"

"How could we when you wouldn't surrender nothing?"

"Who?"

"You. You didn't even want to let me look at the original."

"When was that?"

"When I was down at Trenton for two days and got two hours on them."

Lanigan tried to turn the point to his advantage by belittling Trendley's testimony as based on only two hours' examination, and appearing surprised that he had spent so little time with the original documents. It was a deft stroke, of course, but only because the jury had no way of knowing what went on at the Hildebrecht Hotel that weekend while Lanigan ran up the tab for drinks at the bar.[33]

Trendley did hit some soft spots in the prosecution testimony, nevertheless. Albert S. Osborn had admitted that he had not compared the ransom notes to one another and had picked out only *is* from the nursery note on his chart to compare with Hauptmann's writing. "In your opinion," demanded Reilly, "would that be sufficient to send a man to the electric chair?" Lanigan objected, and the defense attorney did not demand an answer. Trendley did get to answer Reilly's key question about the nursery note, however. There were, he agreed, changes in form, effect, and pressure midway in the letter. "That writer had great trouble writing that letter." This tallied with Osborn's original 1932 report speculating that the nursery note might have been scrawled in a car, something that the prosecution did not wish to talk about at the trial. Such questioning about the nursery note might leave the impression that the experts really did not know who wrote that note—or, indeed, if it might have been written by more than one person.[34]

Trendley also zeroed in on the *k*s that had troubled Harry Cassidy, among others. The defense witness observed that there were some thirty-nine *k*s in the ransom notes, written over a two-week period, none of them looking like the *k*s in Hauptmann's hand in the request writing. The ransom note *k*s turned to the left, whereas none of those in the request writing did. "I think that is the most outstanding characteristic in this whole case of the ransom letters, that a man two years after—if Hauptmann wrote those letters, he would have to disguise all his letters and he couldn't carry 26 letters in his mind while he was writing, he was bound to put some of the characteristics in." Trendley's ability to spot the *k* difficulty would have given his testimony much greater weight had the Schwarzkopf correspondence been available to the defense. (See chapter 13 for a discussion of that correspondence.)[35]

Reilly finally asked Trendley about the xes. Was it not true that a great many people living in areas under "Teutonic influence" before World War I wrote the letter that way? Yes, and, moreover, while Hauptmann's xes resembled those in the ransom notes, they actually belonged to different "family" groups. "They wouldn't harmonize [if] put together as one group."[36]

The defense called Ben Lupica, the student who had seen a man in a dark suit and black fedora, driving a 1929 Dodge with New Jersey license plates, at the foot of the road leading to the Lindbergh house. He now testified that he had seen only *two* sections of a ladder stretched out across the back of the front seat, diagonally from left to right. The car was either black or dark blue. He also testified that the man "resembled Hauptmann." Lloyd Fisher also elicited that Lupica had been scheduled to testify for the state but was informed that the prosecution had "more positive" witnesses and did not need him.

The ladder itself also came under question from one of the last defense witnesses, Charles de Bisschop, a lumberman from Massachusetts who tried to demonstrate that the admitted gap between rail 16 and the State's Exhibit 226 could not be filled in with the drawings Koehler had produced to show they were pieces of the same board.

Koehler was put back on the stand to defend his argument, and said that in addition to all the other things, the center beading from the mill planing was identical in the two boards. Frederick Pope defied him to show that center beading varied from boards planed in North Carolina or South Carolina. But Pope was more interested in Koehler's assertion that his drawing represented factually what the rings looked like in the missing gap. At first Koehler insisted that it was not just his opinion but science. His drawing represented the way the grain markings matched up. He had no doubts whatsoever. Pushed to the limit, however, Koehler blinked when Pope asked if he really wanted to say to the jury that his drawing would look exactly like what the missing block would reveal.

"I said when those rings are connected up like that, there is nothing inconsistent about that pattern."

"Well then, it is a matter of opinion, isn't it, based on what you see?"

"Yes."

Well, said Pope, that is what we have been trying to get at for most of an hour.[37]

Hans Kloppenburg then testified that he had been at the Hauptmann apartment on April 2, 1932, because that was their music night—the first Saturday of every month. Kloppenburg, moreover, was the only witness Hauptmann had who said he saw Isidor Fisch deliver a box a few nights before he sailed for Germany in December 1933. "It was about five to six inches high," Kloppenburg said, "and seven, eight wide and the length was about 14 inches."

When the attorney general cross-examined Kloppenburg, however, he stumbled all over himself in trying to avoid answering whether he had seen Fisch go out the door without the package. Kloppenburg's agony shows right through his testimony.

"I am sure that he left it in the kitchen and he didn't take it."

"Well, you didn't see him go home, did you?"

"No—Well, I maybe."

"So you don't know what he took home with him, do you?"

"Well, I don't know."

"Well, that is what I want you to say then if you don't know."

"No, I think I saw him."[38]

Wilentz carefully circled around the date of April 2, 1932, using answers Kloppenburg had given previously to the Bronx district attorney. At that time Kloppenburg had said it was too long ago; he could not remember any specific dates in either March or April 1932 when he had seen Hauptmann. Kloppenburg had made that statement of his own free will, Wilentz reminded him. In October 1934 he had said of his own free will he could not remember seeing Hauptmann on the night of April 2, 1934. "What caused you to change your mind and come to this court and swear differently from the statement you gave to the police?"

Kloppenburg said he remembered later about the jokes they all told that night, since it was the day after April Fool's, and then he recalled it being the musical evening.

Wilentz suggested that "this story about Saturday night parties" was just too convenient and was intended to establish an alibi. Kloppenburg had been unable to remember until he thought things over after being in the D.A.'s office. "Isn't that the reason Mr. Hauptmann picked out the first Saturday night to get the money from Condon so he would have you to establish the alibi?"

"That's a very funny question," replied Kloppenburg.[39]

In fact, it was. It even suggested, if the attorney general was not careful, that everyone in the house that night was guilty—and he didn't want to do that. No one except Hauptmann had ever seen the package after it was supposedly placed on the kitchen closet shelf.

Shortly before the trial began, however, Lloyd Fisher received a letter from Gustave Miller, a plumber the Hauptmanns' landlady, Pauline Rauch, had employed on several occasions down to the present. Miller had remembered that in the Hauptmanns' apartment in July 1934 he had had to deal with a water leak—more than a leak, with water gushing down through the ceiling and all over the floor. As Miller related to reporters, "Hauptmann didn't seem bothered by my going into the closet. I noticed a lot of things on the floor that were all wet, but I can't call to mind any shoe box like Hauptmann talked about."[40]

But that was not all. Miller had first come to the house in 1931 to check on the boiler in the cellar. While he was down there he noticed that the place looked like a junkyard; jam jars and other stuff were all over the place. Why don't you put up some shelves? he told Pauline's son, Max. "Well, I can get some boards from the attic floor," replied Max. "The tenants up there don't use the attic." Not too long after this trip to the house, he was called back to deal with a toilet. This time he noticed several boards in the cellar, rough flooring boards about six or seven feet long. They had nail holes in them as if torn up from something. Thinking of the boards, he asked again about the shelves. "Well, Mr. Miller, I don't seem to get the time," replied Max Rauch.

Improbably, the plumber was also in the Hauptmanns' apartment on the day of the kidnapping, March 1, 1932. He worked there practically all day, he claimed, at least from 11 A.M. to 4 P.M., trying to repair a stopped-up sink. The Hauptmanns were not home. He was again in the neighborhood about 10 P.M. He saw a light on in their apartment.

"I'm telling nothing but the truth," Miller said about his subpoena, "and I don't care what kind of questions Mr. Wilentz shoots at me." On the stand, Miller told of finding the water all over the floor of the closet in July, 1934 and climbing up to the attic to see if he could find the source of the trouble. He walked across the boards up there, holding a candle to aid him in the dim light through the window. As he walked, he looked down, but there were no boards missing or half-boards.

Wilentz belittled everything Miller said, getting him to admit that he failed to notice anything else in the attic such as rugs or a radio. He also mocked Miller's suggestion that the cellar boards looked like they might have come from the attic.

"Now you saw a board down in the cellar one day?"
"Right."
"A piece of wood."
"Yeah."
"It didn't have anybody's picture on it, did it?"
"No."[41]

Wilentz tried, finally, to have Miller admit that he had his own suspicions about Hauptmann and had told police it would be a good idea to search the drainpipes for money. When Reilly objected, the prosecutor withdrew the question.

Miller's memory that he had been in the Hauptmanns' apartment on the day of the kidnapping was never questioned on the stand. It ought to have been. Did he keep records, and had he consulted them? Agent Wright of the FBI questioned Miller just two days after Hauptmann's arrest. Miller told Wright he had met Hauptmann about a year and a half earlier—which would have put the date in the fall of 1932, not the early spring. But, then, he had not said he talked with Hauptmann that day, only that he was in the apartment. He added that he had been in and around the garage, and even in the light of what he now knew, had never seen anything suspicious.[42]

As the trial moved into its final days, the defense called Colonel Norman Schwarzkopf back to the stand. Lloyd Fisher led off with a series of queries about the ladder, particularly the manner in which it had been examined for fingerprints. Schwarzkopf did not remember how extensively the side rails had been tested or how many photographs had been taken. Were the tests to see if anyone could have actually gotten in and out of the nursery, asked Fisher, conducted as quickly as possible with the ground in about the same condition? "Was there any test made to see how heavy a man would have to be or how light he could be to drive the bottom of the ladder two inches in the ground?"

"No," Schwarzkopf replied. "The holes that were there were the holes that were used in the experiment."

"You put them right in the same holes, you didn't move an inch to one side or another, or make an experiment to see what weight would force the ladder down in the ground two inches?"

"No."[43]

Fisher turned to the Squire Johnson report on the ladder, the first careful examination by any sort of "expert," and the one that concluded a left-handed person had built it. Schwarzkopf dodged all around the question whether he had received the report before finally admitting, yes, it was one of many. Wilentz immediately objected to questions about the report: he could not cross-examine a report. Fisher responded that he could subpoena Johnson to see what he had to say in person, but the prosecutor was not interested—and there was no other way for Fisher to make the ladder testimony into a "he said, she said" contest between Johnson and Koehler.

There was the testimony of Dr. Erastus Mead Hudson on the ladder. Hudson testified for the defense that he had seen only one hole in rail 16, not four, when he examined it for fingerprints a few days after the kidnapping. Newspaper photographs taken before Hudson got to Hopewell do indicate there were four holes, however. His expertise on fingerprints, nevertheless, surpassed the abilities of the state police at the time of the kidnapping, for he employed a silver nitrate process used in Europe to bring out hundreds of readable prints. "Almost every square inch of its surface was ridged with palm- and fingerprints, some fragmentary, a few overlapping, another few blurred, but many complete and clear. Closer inspection showed fingerprints on the ends of the rails and *even under the rungs where they had been nailed down.*"[44]

Koehler had noted the same thing, it will be remembered. Hudson's examination, moreover, had been conducted before the ladder was taken apart and reassembled, as it was so many times. He had expected, when Hauptmann was arrested, to be called back into the case—and eventually to testify for the prosecution.

When he heard about the arrest, he called an officer he knew at the Trenton barracks. "We got our man," he was told.

"Were his prints on the ladder?"

"No."

"Then you'll have to look further."

"Good God, don't tell us that, doctor!"

Hudson learned something worse. When Hauptmann's prints were not found on the ladder, someone in state police headquarters ordered all the fingerprints washed off. Expecting to be a prosecution witness, Hudson found himself in an ambiguous position. Schwarzkopf had refused to make it public that Hauptmann's prints did not appear on the ladder. "I wrote him to the effect that if he did not make this public I would see fit to do so, at the same time stating the opinion that if Hauptmann had made the ladder from six to eight months prior to the kidnapping his prints should be on it."[45]

Hudson's threat produced an invitation from the attorney general, who said he wanted to talk to him about becoming a state witness. Hudson nixed such a meeting unless Wilentz was prepared to "clarify the fingerprint situation." Told he could expect no such announcement, Hudson called a friend at the *New York World Telegram* and released the story the day before the trial began. Hudson finally concluded that his experience made him wonder "whether other opinions so glibly and profoundly asserted by experts before the Hunterdon County jury were in truth more accurate."[46]

Wilentz called rebuttal witnesses to dispel any lingering notion that Isidor Fisch had anything to do with the crime. Reilly had claimed all through the trial that the $14,000 in Hauptmann's garage was only part of what Fisch had available. His witnesses testified to seeing the latter with money to burn. Wilentz had gone to great lengths to refute this assertion by bringing members of the family over from Germany to dispute Hauptmann's account of their relationship. Henna Fisch testified through an interpreter that all her brother had was about $500. Reilly did get her to admit that the family had no idea what Isidor might have had in the United States. Still, she insisted, he certainly did not reveal he had any hidden riches.

The prosecution also presented witnesses, however, to show that Isidor Fisch was at the apartment of Henry and Erna Jung throughout the evening of March 1, 1932. The first was Joseph O. Levenson, a real estate dealer who said he had known the Jungs for a number of years, but admitted he had been to this apartment only once before and never would be there again. He just happened to be there that night and met Fisch, whom he would never see again. Under cross-examination Levenson could not remember what sort of night it was, rainy or clear. Just dark, he said. Yet he could remember the only previous visit he had made to the Jung apartment because it was a Sunday afternoon and it was a pleasant afternoon.

Levenson apparently piqued Reilly's old warhorse instincts. How had he come to be a witness? Reilly wondered.

A detective Leef showed up at his office, Levenson said.

"A strange man out of the clouds dropped into your house and said, 'Come down to Flemington, and testify,' is that it?" Wilentz protested, "He didn't come out of the clouds." Judge Trenchard remonstrated mildly, but Reilly was off and running. "And he tells you about something that happened in Jung's house in 1932, right?"

"He asked me about it, if that was so."

"Yes, but you hadn't told him."

"No, sir, after he asked me I answered the question."

He just dropped in, then, said Reilly, while you were just sitting there, and told you something about somebody you knew nothing about.

"That is right."

"And you expect us to believe that?"

Erna Jung testified next. She explained that she remembered the night of March 1, 1932, because there had been business dealings that evening. She and her husband had expected to receive some money in payment of a loan they had made. Present there, in addition to Joseph

Levenson, were several people, including a Mr. Boehm and a Mr. Lutz. About 7:30 P.M. Isidor Fisch arrived. He stayed the whole evening until nearly midnight.

On cross-examination Reilly asked what it was about that particular night that made her remember Fisch was there.

Well, because he came in the place of someone else who was ill.

The witness apparently was a bit nervous, because Reilly asked if she thought it was funny to come down to testify.

"No."

Who was this person that sent Fisch in his place?

Charles Schleser. She remembered that it was a foggy night, but she could not recall what it was like on any other night around that date.

How was it that she had become a witness?

"Because I know Mr. Fisch was in our house that night."

And when did she remember that?

When she saw his picture in the newspaper.

Oh, and when did she first see that?

"Well, when the trial was going on, I suppose."

"During this trial?"

"Since Mr. Hauptmann insisted that he had the money from Mr. Fisch and I said, 'That is Mr. Fisch.' Since that time we have been mentioned Mr. Fisch's name." It turned out, however, that this was not the first time the Jungs had seen his picture in the paper, or so she now said. She had seen it five or six times going all the way back to the time of Hauptmann's arrest. But she admitted to Reilly she had done nothing about this the first three times.

Well, then, the business that night, was it with the realtor, Mr. Levenson?

No, he just came to visit. "He plays chess and he came up to play chess with my husband."

That was strange. Levenson and Henry Jung must not have been too serious about chess, since he had only been there once and never came back. Nor is it usual to schedule a chess night with a roomful of people. Levenson had arrived, according to Erna Jung, at approximately the same time as Fisch, when they were finishing dinner. By this point in her testimony, she was looking around the courtroom for help. And Reilly had to prompt her several times to look at him.

So what happened when Levenson arrived, did they play chess?

No, they just talked for a while, talked about this man who owed them money, "and as soon as the door opened, about eight o'clock, Mr. Schleser didn't come, it was Mr. Fisch came in."

He had nothing to do with the business either?

No, but he was a friend of Mr. Schleser's.

Did he play checkers or chess, too?

No, there were no games that night, because the Jungs expected friends. But they just talked business. The more the witness talked, the stranger that evening became.

Reilly wanted to know when they had another party like this, and she guessed, maybe the next Saturday. Asked again what time Levenson arrived, she backed it up to maybe seven o'clock. If they had been finishing dinner when Fisch arrived, Levenson apparently caught them right in the middle of eating.

At this next gathering, who was the first to arrive?

Schleser, around eight.

Did she always write down the time a guest arrived?

No, but Schleser had come to apologize for sending Fisch when he had been ill. Going back to the Fisch visit, Erna Jung now admitted she did not look at the clock when Isidor arrived or when he left around midnight.

Reilly now began to hypothesize about what had happened. Max Leef had apparently gained information from Schleser that the Jungs would have documents in their house bearing the March 1, 1932 date, and that these would confirm Fisch's presence there because he had stood in for Schleser settling the business affairs. And, as it turned out, it was indeed Schleser who had brought Detective Leef to their apartment.

All this happened just a few weeks earlier. But no one would ever know what went on during this conversation between someone who was a convicted criminal and accomplished con artist and Leef, who had also become one of Fisch's stoutest defenders, and Henry and Erna Jung.

She had never met Leef before?

No.

Nor contacted District Attorney Foley?

No.

"Then out of—I will withdraw that. [Laughter.] In walks Mr. Leef, is that right."

"Yes."

It also turned out that Erna Jung had met members of the Fisch family during her stay in Trenton. Wilentz had seen to it that she met these fine people. Reilly caught her looking around for help, looking for Wilentz. "Don't look down there, please," he said. "Of course I can understand why you are looking down there, but we will pass that for the minute. After you talked to [Pincas] Fisch last night you decided to come over here today and tell this story, is that right?"

"I was here yesterday all day long."[47]

Henry Jung followed his wife to the stand. He explained at last the "business" that had been conducted that night. Schleser had promised to settle some debts, and that night there were seven or eight papers signed in the Jung apartment. Fisch had come at half past seven and left around eleven, not midnight as his wife had said. Schleser paid only part of what he owed. Actually, there were more like a dozen notes drawn up that night, only one of which was paid—by Isidor Fisch. But even that one Jung did not return.

Reilly feigned surprise. You mean to say, he said, that Fisch would pay a note and not get it back?

Then came this strange revelation: "Mr. Schloesser [sic] didn't sign those notes. They are only signed by Boehm. Mr. Schloesser paid me." Well, of course, he didn't. Fisch paid that night.

Reilly asked when the notes were made out.

March 1, 1932.

Was he sure about that?

"I am sure about it."

"Look at these notes and see if the ink isn't almost still fresh on these notes?"

Wilentz objected: "Just a minute. The tone of counsel's voice won't change the ink, if your Honor please."

Reilly: "It may impress it upon the witness."

Henry Jung did not deny how the notes looked. "I will tell you them notes mean money to me. I keep them in a clean place."

Did anybody witness the notes?

"Mr. Levenson made them out."

If one tries to recapitulate the whole scene that evening, the result is completely baffling. And it got stranger still. The investigation apparently began, according to Jung, when Leef found some receipts he signed among Fisch's effects. These receipts were all made out to Fisch, even though it was Schleser who owed Henry Jung the money. Where were these notes now? Jung thought they must be in the possession of the court.

"No," Reilly fairly shouted at him, "we are testing your memory, Mister, you are the man who was there."

"I can see that too." Jung examined a book he had brought. "That is May 26th, 1932, a $10 receipt was signed." What about the rest? "That is about all; that is all, $10 receipt."[48]

Reilly kept hammering away at the hapless witness. The dates on the notes, even the sums, were hardly clear to anyone. Jung could not even explain why he had in his possession two notes, one for $700 and another, on a different date, for $725, if they involved the same loan of $700.

From the time of Hauptmann's arrest, no one had been more energetic in trying to distance Isidor Fisch from the crime than Charles Schleser. He had even spied on the Hauptmann family and friends for Wilentz. The Jungs' apartment turned out to be a perfect solution. Max Leef obviously liked the idea. Beyond that we cannot go—except to note that if the perfect alibi had been found (albeit after the trial began) for Fisch, who was there to ask about Schleser's indisposition and illness?

Charlie Schleser was the missing man at the trial—but, as we will see again in the next chapter, he had hovered close by in the Trenton hotel where Wilentz had housed his witnesses.

Now the trial was over except for the summations. Reilly led off, telling the jury the prosecutor was right; there could be no doubt this was the crime of the century. No one could fool them: "You will have it howled in your ears. . . . There isn't any doubt about it, and I am not here to fool you." But if they faced this thing straight on, didn't it come down to plain, ordinary horse sense? "So I am appealing to your common, ordinary David Harum inherent American horse sense, that you gathered from this part of the country and which has been inherent since the days of the Revolution."

It might have helped his case had he struck such a pose earlier in the trial. But this statement, at this time, probably only made him seem more the city slicker talking down to his country cousins. Still, he went on in this vein. He had marched with his detachment of sailors in the parade welcoming Lindbergh back from his flight across the Atlantic. No one held the colonel in higher esteem than he did. But they shouldn't rush to judgment when there was no evidence. Reilly then hit at what he considered the biggest contradiction in the case. The state wanted everyone to believe that this man who was clever enough to leave no fingerprints would sit in Woodlawn Cemetery discussing all the angles of the case for nearly an hour and a half with his face exposed—at once the careful mastermind and the perfect fool.

Hauptmann could not have known the Lindbergh family was staying in the Hopewell house that night, moreover. But the servants knew it. Reilly pointed once again to Betty Gow, whose background, he suggested, was unknown to everyone, including the family who hired her to take care of the new baby. Then there were the other servants. "I don't know anything about these people, but I say the circumstances point absolutely along a straight line of guilt toward that butler and the servants who were disloyal to Colonel Lindbergh."

Here was a sick child, and yet Betty Gow left it alone for two hours, from eight to ten. "Do you believe that? Well, if she did, it was part of the disloyal plan by which that baby was taken out of that house." (Reilly's intonation and his use of the phrase "Do you believe that?" would come back to haunt the defense when Judge Trenchard adopted it in his charge to the jury.) The women on the jury, Reilly said, would know that a sick child would be restless, not likely to be sleeping soundly when an intruder entered. It would wake up before the person reached the bed.

Reilly then went through the supposed way the kidnapper entered the nursery, climbing the ladder with gloves on. "He reaches up and he finds that the shutters are just closed together. He opens the shutters, one back and the other back. Now how long do you suppose two loose shutters would stay back with a gale howling? They would be banging, banging, banging, back and forth. But nevertheless, with those shutters banging back and forth and a gale blowing, this man has to take himself by his two hands, and I don't see how he could get above the second section of the ladder, because he would have to hold on to the side of it, and he would have to hold on to the wall as he went up, to steady himself; but finally he is on the top rung now, and he is reaching three feet through the air, gripping the bottom of the window sill, of a house he had never been in, of a house where he doesn't know who is inside the room—and any fool would know that a Colonel of the United States Army would have a gun somewhere around and put a bullet through your heart."

Hard enough to get in, how would the kidnapper get over to the bed and yank a child out without some noise being made—then make his way back out, feeling with one leg for the ladder, which then supposedly broke and hurled the man and child to the ground, leaving no marks in the mud?

Reilly then argued that the ladder was a plant; it was never up against the wall. But to argue this point, he had to deny the existence of footprints leading away from the house. Here was a curious agreement between the prosecution and the defense, because footprints did not fit in with either case as presented to the jury. Yet they were there. They were seen by the original investigators, and tracked by Oscar Bush the next morning, leading off to the lane in back of the house.

Then Condon entered the case, Reilly continued. "Condon stands behind something in this case that is unholy," he said. There was first of all this peculiar concern about Red Johnson, a man he had never met, yet supposedly before he became involved Condon had heard about the accusations against Johnson from several people he knew, sailors.

Johnson was being wrongly suspected. Condon searched out these opinions, visiting every single shipyard up and down Long Island Sound. He claimed he found out that Johnson was just not that kind of fellow.

But he slipped up on the stand. When Reilly asked if he knew about Johnson's phone call to Betty Gow, he was caught off guard and said, "I knew that the night of the kidnapping."

Condon had been so particular about Red Johnson, but when the second taxi driver came to the house bearing the note directing him to the vicinity of St. Raymond's Cemetery, nobody bothered to take his name, let alone put him under custody. Condon said he was too excited. And so while the others could see this was no ordinary cabbie, he was allowed to drive away into the night.

Reilly told the jury that the state's witnesses were basically opinion witnesses, who had testified for a fee.

Finally, he reached August 1934, when Hauptmann spent ten or fifteen of the ransom bills. "He doesn't change his name, he doesn't move out of his house; he doesn't move out of the city; he doesn't go back to Germany; he doesn't go to Mexico; he doesn't go to another State—but he starts to spend ten or fifteen of these bills in his own neighborhood, where anybody can check him—buying a pair of shoes for his wife, buying gasoline, and when the man said to him, 'Have you any more home?'—instead of saying to the fellow, 'Now, don't bother me, I just got that from a cigar man down the street,' evasive or crooked, he said, 'Sure, I have got ten or twelve or a hundred more at home'—and the man writes down his automobile license." And if he suspected anything amiss by the gas attendant's question, why didn't Hauptmann return home and take the rest of the money to some other hiding place outside the Bronx?

His list of questions went on. Why would he be crazy enough to put Condon's phone number and address inside a closet where it was so dark one could hardly see, when he could simply go to a telephone booth and look up the phone number? Or memorize it? "Of all the plants that were ever put into a case, this board on the inside of a closet is the worst example of police crookedness that I have seen in a great many years." And who was it who found the writing? One of the ordinary policemen searching the apartment? No, it was big husky Inspector Bruckman, the chief inspector of the Bronx and, he might have added, D.A. Foley's urgent emissary the day of the grand jury hearings.

Using the state's own witness, Whited, Reilly said that the prosecutors had Hauptmann out looking over the grounds a week or two weeks before the kidnapping. If that were so, of course, he would have realized that he did not need three sections of a ladder to gain entrance to the nursery, for the third section would stick up in the air over the window. Nevertheless, he went home and set to work—and built three sections anyway, carrying the ladder down to Hopewell—for what purpose? "He crawls up into his attic and tears up a board and takes it downstairs some place and saws it lengthwise and crosswise and every other wise to make the side of a ladder, the upper joint of which he never used or never needed."

Reilly wrapped up his summation: "This case is too perfect from the prosecution's viewpoint and what they produced here. There isn't a man in the world with brains enough to plan this kidnapping alone and not with a gang—that master mind wouldn't be a carpenter—and then sit down and make the foolish mistake of ripping a board out of his attic and leaving the other half of it there to make the side of a ladder, a portion of which he never used. You have got to use horse sense, and you have got to use common sense."[49]

Now it was Wilentz's turn for the final word. As the attorney general began his summation, he noted the jury's state of fatigue and practically apologized. "You know, I really hate to take all this time with the jury." But that was the way things were done. The defense had had its chance, and now the state would make its final plea.

There was a misconception about the state's duty that he wanted to clear up right away. "Please don't get the idea that the State has got to prove everything that it starts out to prove, everything beyond a reasonable doubt. That's a joke." Just because the state alleged a fact, and then was not able to prove that fact, or even several facts it alleged, that was not a reason to acquit. He would come back to that point later, he promised.

Meanwhile, he wanted to say that even the kidnapping and murder of the Lindbergh child would shrink into insignificance in comparison to the crime that would be committed if Hauptmann were set free. "That would be the crime of the century." "To let him roam the streets of this country and make every woman in her home shudder again; that would be a real tragedy, an American tragedy."

From the beginning it was known, Wilentz said, that the kidnapper was someone of German descent, and that the writer of the notes was a carpenter. This was no crime by an amateur, but by someone with "ice water in his veins instead of blood." Someone who had a criminal record. Wilentz acknowledged that he would have to show that Hauptmann was in the room that night—but, he asserted, experienced criminals did not bring movie cameras along so someone could record the deed.

It was said the child would have awakened, but he thought it possible a stranger could get into the room. Still, "This fellow took no chance on the child awakening. He crushed that child right in that room into insensibility. He smothered and choked that child right in that room. That child never cried, never gave an outcry. Certainly not. The little voice was stilled right in that room."

Wilentz then gave the jury a series of options to satisfy any doubters about a first-degree murder charge and that one man acted alone at a critical moment. Apparently, the attorney general had not told his associates what he was going to say, for only a short time before he spoke Assistant Prosecutor Anthony Hauck had repeated the state's opening assertion that the child had died in a fall from the ladder. But now Wilentz offered a new explanation: "The smudges on the bedsheet cry out evidence of the fact that Betty Gow testified to, the fact that the child didn't cry out when it was disturbed. Yanked—how? Not just taken up, the pins are still left in the bedsheets. Yanked, and its head hit up against that board—must have been hit. He couldn't do it any other way."

Or there was a second possibility: "Did he use the chisel to crush the skull at the time or to knock it into insensibility? Is that a fair inference? What else was the chisel there for? To knock that child into insensibility right there in that room."

This sort of performance is known as a variance. And it could have led to a mistrial. One issue would be whether the evidence as presented could be read to justify a change in the summation. The coroner's report that the child died from an external blow was inconclusive as to how the injury was sustained. Wilentz therefore felt free to speculate. He banked on public sympathy rather than legal precedents to sustain his approach if defense lawyers appealed.

As for the defense attorneys' charge that they had been denied access to Hauptmann's attic, Wilentz responded by calling them cry-babies. "The poor boys, we wouldn't let them—terrible thing, we wouldn't let the defense do this and we wouldn't let them do that." They had seen anything they were entitled to see. "The only trouble I find is that we have treated this fellow entirely too well."

"If I had my choice I wouldn't get in the same room [with Hauptmann]. I wouldn't become contaminated, I wouldn't want to breathe the same air."

Then Wilentz came back to the attic. Why did they need to get up there, anyway? There were pictures; Anna Hauptmann knew what was up there. Even so, a visit to the attic was agreed upon, but on the day the defense wanted to examine the attic the attorney general was sick and couldn't make arrangements. They could have gone up any other day. This assertion, of course, had no basis in fact but was designed to deflect criticism stemming from the state's refusal to allow the attic to be entered and studied, or the ransom notes to be evaluated effectively, by the defense.

> Who would be the type of person that would take a child and murder it? Who could there be?
>
> Why, men and women, if that little baby, if that little, curly-haired youngster were out in the grass in the jungle, breathing, just so long as it was breathing, any tiger, any lion, the most venomous snake would have passed that child without hurting a hair of its head.
>
> Now what type of man, what type of man would kill the child of Colonel Lindbergh and Anne Morrow?
>
> He wouldn't be an American. No American gangster and no American racketeer ever sank to the level of killing babies.
>
> And let me tell you, men and women, the State of New Jersey and the State of New York and the Federal authorities have found that animal, an animal lower than the lowest form in the animal kingdom, public enemy Number 1 of the world, Bruno Richard Hauptmann; we have found him and he is here for your judgment.

Wilentz was still a bit afraid the jury might decide not to convict because it had not been shown that Hauptmann was the lone perpetrator. "So far as Hauptmann is concerned he could have had fifty help him; if he participated in this murder that's all you have got to deal with. He can bring Violet Sharp's corpse and body and lay it right alongside of him if he wants; he can bring Isidor Fisch's grave from Germany and put it alongside of him. That doesn't help this defendant in this case a bit. If he participated in this crime, he is guilty, and it doesn't matter whether six, ten, or fifty helped him."

As he finished, Wilentz pointed to the scale of justice hanging over the judge's bench. "Did you ever see that scale, the American scale of justice? Here is how it hangs now (indicating), way up there is the testimony of the State of New Jersey, way down in its lowest ebb is Hauptmann, Hauptmann, dangling on there, dangling on the hope and on the straw, right at the bottom of that scale, hoping that one juror, one juror may do it, may do it for Fisher, may do it for Reilly, may do it for somebody else, hoping that he will get life imprisonment instead of death."

Reminding the jurors that a recommendation for mercy and life imprisonment might mean Hauptmann could be out in fifteen years, Wilentz challenged them not to be afraid to ask for the death penalty. "We have proven it overwhelmingly, conclusively, positively. Now, jurors, there is no excuse, you would never forgive yourself if you didn't do it, you wouldn't be happy, you wouldn't feel right, honestly you wouldn't. You have got a chance to do something for society that nobody else in the entire county of Hunterdon will ever have an equal chance and you have got to do that, you have got to do it." They could take courage from everyone, the federal authorities, the Bronx police, the New Jersey State Police—and of course "Colonel Lindbergh who was here." "If you believe with us, you have got to find him guilty of murder in the first degree."[50]

Judge Trenchard's charge to the jury was really like a debate rebuttal speech to Reilly's summation. Was there any reason, indeed was there upon the whole "any doubt in your mind as to the reliability of Dr. Condon's testimony?" As to the defense argument that the crime was perpetrated by a gang, with the help or connivance of some of the servants, Trenchard was scornful—using Reilly's own phrase. *"Now do you believe that?* Is there any evidence in this case whatsoever to support any such conclusion." Trenchard came back to the money issue, and where Reilly had attempted to downplay any money Hauptmann invested in stocks soon after the ransom was paid, the judge pointed out that after the delivery of the ransom money, "the defendant began to purchase stocks in a much larger way and to spend money more freely than he had before. . . . The defendant says that these ransom bills, moneys, were left with him by one Fisch, a man now dead. *Do you believe that?"* No one except the defendant, not even his wife, ever saw the shoebox on that shelf. As for the ladder: "There is evidence from which you may conclude, if you see fit, that the defendant built the ladder, although he denies it. Does not the evidence satisfy you that at least a part of the wood from which the ladder was built came out of the flooring of the attic of the defendant?" Trenchard then gave Amandus Hochmuth's testimony his blessing, calling it "highly significant." He saw the dirty green car with a ladder, driven by the defendant, carom off into a ditch. "Do you think that there is any reason, upon the whole, to doubt the truth of the old man's testimony?"[51]

The case went to the jury with Trenchard's words supplying the final dose of courage Wilentz hoped they would show in the verdict. After the trial was over, Captain Russell Snook of the New Jersey State Police wrote handwriting expert Clark Sellers to describe what happened the last day at Flemington. Judge Trenchard's charge was a "master-piece." The defense team entered their technical objections about the inflection of his voice when he would say, "Do you believe *that?*" And Sellers could imagine why the defense objected to Trenchard's inflections. Even Snook thought they were "particularly significant and interesting."[52]

The jury went out about 11:15 A.M., climbing the steep stairs to the deliberation room, where Snook had carefully laid out all the exhibits, especially the handwriting exhibits. Graffiti going back to the Grover Cleveland era covered (and still covers) several walls, cartoons and limericks depicting that president in scurrilous fashion, along with outraged assaults on his low tariff policies. Surrounded by all this, they began to weigh Bruno Richard Hauptmann's fate.

Downstairs, meanwhile, newspaper reporters who had "chiseled" their way in after Trenchard cleared the courtroom milled around with the lawyers. The room reeked of tobacco smoke, except when someone could stand it no longer and raised a window on the frozen atmosphere outside. In the legal library behind the bench, a crap game started in the afternoon. Lloyd Fisher was in the game, along with Walter Winchell, and Dr. Shoenfeld, and others. Schwarzkopf and Wilentz stood aside, worried that at the last moment things might not go well. A source inside the jury room kept them pretty well acquainted with what was going on.

There was no doubt in the jurors' minds about Hauptmann's guilt. But there were several ballots about whether he should receive life in prison or death. On the first, there were three votes for life in prison. About 10:15 P.M. the sheriff entered the room to ask if they should be locked up over night. No, the foreman answered, they had reached a verdict. There was a brief delay while Judge Trenchard was summoned. Captain Snook wrote Sellers: "The old bell in the tower started to toll its death notes and I understand that the court-room scene was a very tense one. I was outside at the jury-room door when the jury came out. Their faces were haggard and some walked with staggering steps. They tell me that Verna Snyder almost broke down as the poll of the jury was taken." The attorney general and Colonel Schwarzkopf feared that some might collapse before the verdict could be given. During all this time Hauptmann's face was expressionless, with the exception of an occasional blinking of one eye.

Guilty. Death.

As he was led away, ashen-faced and with terror in his deep-set eyes, he did not glance toward his wife, said a reporter. "She looked at him with red-rimmed eyes, but did not weep."

Colonel Lindbergh had been there for the judge's charge to the jury but had returned to Englewood in the afternoon. Charles and Anne heard the verdict on the radio. "We went into the drawing room," wrote their guest, Harold Nicolson, a British writer who had been commissioned to write Dwight Morrow's biography. "The wireless had been turned on to the scene outside the court-house. One could hear the almost diabolic yelling of the crowd. They were all sitting round . . . Anne looking very white and still. 'You have now heard,' broke in the voice of the announcer, 'the verdict in the most famous trial in all history. Bruno Hauptmann now stands guilty of the foulest . . .' 'Turn that off, Charles, turn that off.'"[53]

Charles took Nicolson aside into the pantry. "I don't know," he told him, "whether you have followed this case very carefully. There is no doubt at all that Hauptmann did the thing. My one dread all these years has been that they would get hold of someone as a victim about whom I wasn't sure. I am sure about this—quite sure. It is this way . . ."

Charles was speaking to him, Nicolson recorded, but the writer believed that he intended his review of the evidence for Anne—to ease her tension. Nicolson agreed that the conviction was an absolute necessity, for if Hauptmann had gone free in the face of all that circumstantial evidence, "then all the gangsters would have felt a sense of immunity." The Lindberghs' sacrifice had, finally, saved the nation, so it seemed.

"Poor Anne—she looked so white and horrified. The yells of the crowd were really terrifying. 'That,' said Lindbergh, 'was a lynching crowd.'"

"Hauptmann was a magnificent-looking man," Lindbergh added as a sort of coda. "Splendidly built. But . . . his little eyes were like the eyes of a wild boar. Mean, shifty, small and cruel."[54]

"The tremendous responsibility imposed on the Hunterdon County jury was shouldered without flinching," David Wilentz told reporters outside the courthouse. "The nation is indebted to these courageous men and women."

"This is a cry for blood," Lloyd Fisher said, half to himself. "It is the clamor of the crowd on no matter whom."[55]

One man gave no interview that night. "The prisoner was returned to his cell. He did not collapse, but was very badly shaken, and cried practically all night, with no sleep." Reilly came to him the next day to see if he was ready to confess, "and upon being unsuccessful left for New York."[56]

"Our own nightingale will be singing soon because the grass is beginning to take on its verdant coat of green," Snook ended his letter to Clark Sellers, "and the buds are beginning to burst open, although we have not yet had any real warm weather. We feel confident, however, that Spring is just around the corner for us."

15
THE GOVERNOR AND THE MAN IN THE DEATH HOUSE

[Governor Hoffman] stated that he had been misrepresented in the Hauptmann matter, and had been improperly represented as a friend of Hauptmann. He indicated that this situation had reached the stage where on the previous day a cartoon had appeared in a leading New Jersey newspaper showing Hoffman holding out his arm with his hand placed on Bruno Richard Hauptmann's shoulder, with a caption indicating that there was a friendly connection between the two.

—Memorandum of conversation with J. EDGAR HOOVER, January 18, 1936

S hortly before midnight on January 15, 1936, the manager of the Hotel New Yorker knocked on the door of J. Edgar Hoover's suite. New Jersey governor Harold Giles Hoffman was a guest in the hotel, explained Mr. Andrews, and had expressed a desire to have a confidential talk—that night—with the FBI director. Of course he could not refuse to see the governor of New Jersey, Hoover told Andrews. He would be glad to talk to him.

A few minutes later the hotel manager was back with Governor Hoffman. Introductions made, he departed, leaving Hoover and his confidant, Clyde Tolson, alone with the governor. He needed help, Hoffman began. He had decided to reprieve Hauptmann for thirty days, in the hope the condemned man might "break" and possibly implicate others in the crime. But he was in a rather peculiar position in this case, inasmuch as he could not call on his attorney general for assistance— because Wilentz would not agree to have the FBI investigate further— and he felt he could not secure any aid through the New Jersey State

Police. Indeed, he had very little confidence in its commander, Colonel Norman Schwarzkopf.

He believed, said Hoffman, it was quite possible that the kidnapping-killing of the child was a separate operation from the extortion. There were wide discrepancies between what John Condon—and Colonel Lindbergh himself—said in the New York courts and what they then said in Flemington. Hoffman reviewed the case in detail from the time Mickey Rosner acted as an intermediary with the underworld through Hauptmann's arrest and the discovery of the wood evidence in the attic.

For nearly three hours into the early morning Hoover listened as the governor spelled out his reasons. Governor Hoffman must know, the FBI director said, that the bureau's official connection with the case terminated once New Jersey state officials went to trial; but he would certainly be interested in information the governor deemed worthy of further investigation. Had the governor discussed these points with the state police? Hoffman grunted. The state police had a closed mind and wanted nothing to do with his evidence.[1]

Hoover probably wondered if Hoffman had any idea about *his* distrust of and dislike for Colonel Schwarzkopf. Hoover had his own doubts about some of the evidence, but having hurried to New York to claim the lion's share of credit for the arrest, he was hardly in a position to repudiate the outcome. Besides, he believed the man was guilty. Still, he would watch Hoffman's progress with no little interest, knowing it would discomfort Schwarzkopf.

Unknown to Hoover, however, the governor had also met with David Wilentz earlier in the evening. Informed that Wilentz was dining with friends downstairs, the governor asked him up to his suite. "It was a long, earnest, important talk." Hoffman floated his plan for getting a confession, and Wilentz supposedly agreed to give it a try. Hoffman would see Anna Hauptmann in the morning to persuade her to tell Richard he must now speak the truth—or face death the next day. He did not tell Wilentz, however, what he later told Hoover: he had already decided upon a reprieve regardless of what might happen as a result of his conversation with Anna.[2]

Arriving in Trenton on an early train, Hoffman summoned Anna to a secret meeting in a hotel room. When he told her what she was expected to do, Anna exploded, beating him on the chest with her fists. *"No! No! No!"* she screamed. "Dot isn't so! Richard did tell the truth! He is telling the truth." Finally, she calmed down and listened to him explain. The attorney general had agreed that if Hauptmann told everything he knew—even if he had acted alone—he would join in the governor's effort to have the sentence commuted to life imprisonment. "You must go to the prison this morning. You must see your husband. You must tell him that he can save his life. You must tell him that you want him to tell the truth."

"No! No! No! I couldn't do dot! He vould turn his back to me. He vould think dot the last von in the world to know that he is innozent should think, too, dot he haf commit this crime."

Would she at least see if her husband would talk to the attorney general and himself and answer some questions? "Maybe Richard will say something to help. He might even say something that will save his life."

That she would do, but she would not say to him that he must tell the truth. "I know dot he has always told the truth dot he did not do dis terrible thing."

An hour or so later she called Hoffman from the prison to tell him Richard would be glad to see the attorney general. "But, Gofe'nor the story is just the same; he haf told eferything he knows—nothing more he can tell."

Hoffman then called Wilentz to tell him what had happened. "The hell with it, Harold," came the reply. "If that's still his attitude, I'm damned if I'm going to do anything to help him." The governor put down the phone and went to his office in the state house. "In an atmosphere charged with threats of impeachment and other forms of political extinction, and with reporters swarming around like bees, [Hoffman] announced that [he] was granting a thirty-day reprieve to Bruno Richard Hauptmann."[3]

Hoffman was a Republican who had survived the Democratic sweep in 1934. Ironically, one of his first acts had been to reappoint Judge Trenchard, so he could continue to preside at the trial. Hoffman had had a meteoric political career and was barely into his forties. A charismatic speaker who stirred deep emotions and engendered strong loyalties, he was, according to political pros, a real "comer," a possible vice presidential candidate in 1936. Like so many others, Hoffman would become enmeshed in the Lindbergh case and never disentangle himself. At the end his political career would be in shambles.

Although he had been kept informed of events since Hauptmann's arrest, Governor Hoffman had not been engaged in the early efforts to reverse the decision at Flemington. Judge Trenchard had set the original execution date for mid-March 1935. Hauptmann's lawyers immediately began work on their first appeal. Reilly was shoved aside when he dragged his feet. It would only be courteous, Reilly had said, to await Wilentz's return from a posttrial vacation in Florida before proceeding.

Fisher and Pope exploded. "When our man is scheduled to die the week of March 18th, we should not be wasting time waiting for Mr. Wilentz to return from Florida. . . . if we were to follow Reilly's suggestion, he would be dead and buried."[4]

Hauptmann's petition to the Court of Errors and Appeals automatically delayed the execution. When attorneys' statements were heard, Egbert Rosecrans argued for the defense, stressing Wilentz's inflammatory summation. Why hadn't there been an objection at the time? asked the judges. Reilly was chief counsel, replied Rosecrans. "We may have been neglectful and we may have been ignorant, but that doesn't make any difference. The trial judge should not have allowed these things to go on. Because counsel did not object is no excuse."[5]

Rosecrans could have gone much farther down this path, but Trenchard's sterling reputation no doubt gave him pause. There was, for example, the judge's complacency on the bench when Wilentz browbeat defense witnesses, his obiter dictum argument with Pope over where the chisel had been found, his repeated "Do you believe that?" challenges in his summary, and—perhaps most of all—his silence about Wilentz's last-minute options for the jury to find Hauptmann guilty of first-degree murder. Singly or collectively, these might not add up to judicial error, but they certainly denoted a hanging judge.

Fisher got Sheriff John Curtiss to allow newsreel cameras into the jail, so the nation could see and hear his client proclaim his innocence before he was transferred to the death house in Trenton. That would put a stop to press speculations about an impending confession now that he faced the chair. But when Fisher showed up with the Paramount News team, state police guards tried to convince Curtiss he was making a big mistake. The sheriff did not back down but allowed Hauptmann only one minute to make his statement.[6]

Hauptmann's high-pitched voice seemed far off and detached, as if he were only going through with this to please his attorneys. "I want to tell the people of America that I am absolute innocent of the crime of the murder. My conviction was a great surprise. I never saw the Lindenbergh [sic] baby and I never received any money. I want to appeal to all people everywhere to aid me at this time. A defense must be raised to carry my appeal to a higher court. Before God, I am absolute innocent. I have told all I know about the crime."[7]

Hauptmann's demeanor had always been a problem. On one occasion he told Fisher: "I don't know what to do. If I break down, they will all say I was guilty, and if I fight with my heart and fight with my soul and don't break down, they'll say I am cold-blooded and just the sort of person to commit this crime. I am torn with emotion and almost crazy."[8]

On the morning of February 16, 1935, a caravan of police cars slowly made its way to the Trenton State Prison, where a crowd of five hundred had gathered to await the condemned man's arrival. The cars pulled up to the fortresslike building adorned with effigies of serpents, rams, eagles, and kneeling human figures. As he emerged, dressed in a suit for the last time, Hauptmann paused to give photographers a chance to take his picture. "Everything's fine," he assured them with a smile—almost as if arriving to begin work on some important business project. "I am innocent," Hauptmann said in a clear voice.

For the first time, publicly, he accused Isidor Fisch of the crime. "Funny," he said to reporters, "but at first I don't think Fisch could do the kidnapping to get the money. But later I do. He can't do it alone either. No. He can't."[9]

That same day in New York, Betty Gow forced her way through a crowd up the gangway of an ocean liner docked at the Panama Pier. Unable to locate her stateroom in the tourist-class deck, Betty panicked and soon found herself cornered on the first class deck. A middle-aged woman wearing glasses elbowed herself to the front. "Let's have a look at her," she called out, grabbing Betty's arm "Let me alone," Betty cried. Yanking her arm away, she struck the woman in the face with her fist.[10]

Betty Gow never returned to the United States. The first suspect, along with boyfriend Red Johnson, Charlie's nursemaid remained single and alone the rest of her long life in Glasgow. She spoke only once of the case that had blighted her fortunes. "Reilly went too far," she said. "To insinuate that I knew more about the tragedy than I made known to the court was most unjust."[11]

Never called to testify at the trial, Red Johnson returned to Norway, where he married a high school sweetheart. But according to their daughter, he became an alcoholic, with periods of depression. He also had problems with his nerves and would "turn a stiff face at the sight of a police car." For two years after his return, an unmarked car constantly followed Johnson. On one occasion two men jumped out of the car, having sighted Red with one of his nieces, and demanded that the blond little girl be undressed to prove she was, in fact, a girl. "When he put his mind to it," Johnson's daughter recalled recently, "he was very skillful and could accomplish things. For example, he built a house for his parents—all by himself." Gossip about Lindbergh money followed him the rest of his life every time he made a purchase, and townspeople where he lived always remembered "Rødejonsen."[12]

Dr. Dudley Shoenfeld, the psychiatrist who had "diagnosed" the kidnapper through the ransom notes, and who had sat through the trial every day offering advice to Wilentz on what tactics to use to break down Hauptmann, now asked that he be kept alive to serve as a subject in the study of the criminal mind—but he needed to confess. Unlike Lloyd Fisher, who estimated he saw Hauptmann over three hundred times in the Flemington and Trenton jails, Shoenfeld never had an opportunity to interview the accused man. Nevertheless, he felt qualified to argue to Governor Hoffman that he must make it clear to Hauptmann there was no hope—no hope at all unless he confessed.

Eleanor Roosevelt, meanwhile, told reporters she was "somewhat perturbed" about a conviction based purely on circumstantial evidence. She was not in sympathy with Hauptmann, she said, but worried about what might happen to an innocent person in a similar situation. It was a very cautious comment but drew immediate fire from a Long Island district attorney, who asserted juries might take her comments too seriously and refuse to convict guilty persons. In Florida, Wilentz declined to comment. "Mrs. Roosevelt is the wife of the President, isn't she? I have no comment whatever."[13]

The jurors had quickly formed themselves into an association, the "Hauptmann Trial Jury Association." The first order of business was to discuss plans for a nationwide tour on stage. "It would be very dignified and nice," said jury foreman Charles Walton, who expected to earn $500 per week for the duration of the three-month tour. "We can all use the money." Preliminary plans called for the jurors to parade on stage, single file, and cast their ballots—again and again, night after night. "Hauptmann," read a newspaper report, "will be found guilty as charged from the stage of theaters in New York, Chicago, Kalamazoo and other points." They would all go, it was said, including Mrs. Verna Snyder, the 291-pound housewife from little Centerville, who was supposed to make $300 a week. Some would be leaving the confines of Hunterdon Country for the first time. Husband Fred Snyder, the village blacksmith, said, "It will help broaden Verna." The tour never took place, as, after a little reflection, its sponsors thought better of the idea.[14]

Jafsie actually got on stage, appearing first in Trenton, New Jersey, for three performances a day at the Gayety Theatre, combining violin renditions and impersonations with a lecture on Justice Department activities. But the seventy-seven-year-old Bronx educator-turned-criminologist faced a tough crowd the first night. "The audience didn't take too kindly the efforts of 'Jafsie' and toward the end of his act some even heckled him." Upset, Condon remonstrated that he had not taken on this new assignment "for money or notoriety" but to defend J. Edgar Hoover against unjust criticism.[15]

Anticipating some unjust criticism himself, Colonel Schwarzkopf told reporters, "I have gained a friend. There is nothing I wouldn't do for Colonel Lindbergh—there is no oath that I wouldn't break if it would materially help his well being." A strange statement for the head of a police organization to make. Sworn to uphold the laws of New Jersey, Schwarzkopf apparently made the remark to justify his actions in not having Lindbergh followed to the payoff rendezvous. "We knew that the ransom money would be paid on the night of April 2, 1932, but we did not make any official or unofficial move to trail the collector of that money. We stayed clear of that cemetery. I have never regretted my decision on the night of the kidnapping when I felt that the child must be found and that we should do nothing official to hinder that possibility." Schwarzkopf's startling admission raised serious questions about the role the New Jersey State Police had played that night, and later, in squelching all efforts to discover the kidnapper's accomplices (if there were any) in order to bring closure to the case for Colonel Lindbergh's sake and that of his family. "Colonel Lindbergh is the finest man I have ever known," Schwarzkopf declared. It was a remarkable "confession," for if this kidnapper got away with it once, who was to say he would not do it again? Yet most agreed Schwarzkopf had done the right thing.[16]

When J. Edgar Hoover sent Schwarzkopf a telegram about an accumulation of five-dollar Federal Reserve notes in the Philadelphia Federal Reserve Bank, moreover, he learned just how anxious the New Jersey authorities were to write finis to the Lindbergh case. The bureau did not intend to examine these forty-nine thousand bank notes, said Hoover. Did New Jersey have an interest in doing so? Schwarzkopf replied immediately. "This department contemplates no examination of notes referred to in your telegram this date. *Suggest that any identified notes be taken out for destruction.*" The search for Lindbergh ransom money was over. As it happened, other bills had turned up, including a ten-dollar gold certificate.[17]

While the court deliberated over the summer—a decision was scheduled for sometime in the fall session—Hauptmann's defenders gained an important new ally, Governor Harold Giles Hoffman.

Unknown to his critics, Hoffman had been interested in the case from its beginning in 1932, when he was New Jersey's commissioner of motor vehicles. A frequent visitor to his office in those days was Ellis Parker, grizzled chief of detectives in Burlington County. Shunted aside by Schwarzkopf and the state police the morning after the kidnapping, Parker never forgot or forgave. And he did have a stunning reputation for cracking supposedly unsolvable cases. Parker was obsessed with showing them all a thing or two. Eventually this obsession would get him in deep trouble—really deep trouble as the first person charged with kidnapping under the federal Lindbergh Law.

Parker kept nudging him along, assuring Hoffman he had a line on the real criminals. He would tell Hoffman every time he dropped by the commissioner's office that Schwarzkopf was a fool. One day, he confided that he had received a telephone call from someone who promised he could produce the child.[18]

Parker's "informant" was Paul Wendel, a disbarred attorney and convicted perjurer who claimed to be acting as an intermediary. The detective suspected Wendel was himself part of the gang, but played along to find out all he could.

In two letters to Hoffman late in May 1932, Parker also claimed the corpse found in the woods was not the Lindbergh child. Proof? Colonel Schwarzkopf had issued a statement that it was "not proper" at this time to take up a collection for a memorial at the spot where the decomposed body had been found. A few days later, Parker wrote that he was "positively certain" he was onto the right culprit. "His mental condition is such, that he cannot be forced. Twice he has taken Anna [Bading, Parker's secretary] for a short ride. I firmly believe he wanted to tell her, but that his heart failed him." Curiously, Wendel had asked what would happen to Parker if the baby were delivered to him for return to the Lindberghs. Would *he* be arrested? Parker assured him no one would dare, because Governor Moore had given him a personal letter. Wendel was really asking about what would happen to him, Parker suggested to Hoffman. "There is only one thing I can do and that is, to play him until such time as he will give it up."[19]

Parker was convinced as well that Condon had a key role in the kidnapping beyond being the intermediary; and he tried to have the FBI introduce him to Jafsie so they could have a long private conference. The detective told Hoover's chief assistant that he was convinced male menopause was the reason for the kidnapping. "Men passing through a certain period of life, as well as women, are subject during that period, to mental disturbances which might and often do cause those who have hitherto been of good character to commit heinous crimes."[20]

Condon was a little past that stage, surely, but Parker's favorite suspect was Paul Wendel. He was still on Wendel's trail when Hauptmann was arrested. "Harold," Parker insisted, "they've got the wrong man."

Even if Hauptmann did not confess and give up his accomplices, the ongoing Parker investigation seemed to offer Hoffman a good chance to crack the case and cash in politically. During the trial a very odd thing happened, further confirming Hoffman's belief that the rumpled backwoods detective with a corncob pipe was about to break wide open the crime of the century. Out of the blue, Jafsie, fresh from his tour de force on the witness stand, showed up in Mount Holly, Parker's home base, along with his faithful sidekick and bodyguard, ex-pugilist Al Reich. Condon deposited himself in White's barbershop for a shave and accolades. Ellis Parker, Jr., came into the barbershop to see the great and mystifying Jafsie in person. Condon had been waiting for his father to show up. "Tell your father that silence is golden," Condon said. Ellis Junior tried to draw him out. What did he mean by that? Jafsie smiled his Cheshire cat smile. "I'll be back after the trial to talk over the case with your father."[21]

Their paths apparently never crossed, but Hoffman had confidence enough in Parker's investigative techniques to send him on a risky mission inside the state prison to interview Hauptmann. The warden at that time was Colonel Mark O. Kimberling, a good friend of Governor Hoffman's who would succeed Schwarzkopf as head of the state police. Kimberling admitted Parker to Hauptmann's cell on two occasions at night, even though prison rules proscribed such visits except for attorneys and spiritual counselors.

At one session, on June 5, 1935, Hauptmann described meetings with a "carpenter," apparently a Czech, in October or November of 1931, and how he, Hauptmann, had given him a written "application" for a position. They met in some library, where the mysterious Czech dictated what he was to write. He never saw him after that. As for March 1, 1932, Hauptmann said he had reported for work at the Majestic, and, when there was nothing for him that day, returned to the agency that had gotten him the job. Then he went to Radio City and walked around until about six o'clock, when he returned home.

He first met Isidor Fisch on Hunter's Island at the beginning of March—"I am pretty sure"—not later in the year. Another man, an Austrian, had accompanied Fisch, and Hauptmann took them in his car to the subway. The next time they met was three weeks later.

Parker shifted to the question of fingerprints. Hauptmann related that the police had taken set after set during the hours after his arrest. They took at least forty sheets of prints, coming back on at least two occasions because they said the prints were "no good." They even took prints of his knuckles. He talked to his lawyer James Fawcett about this, asking him if they could transfer his prints onto a piece of wood. Then it came out, he said, that there were no fingerprints at all.[22]

Hauptmann insisted that when Condon had visited him in the Flemington jail in October, 1934, he had jumped up at one point and cried out, "I will not testify against this man," or "No, I can't testify." According to what Hauptmann told Parker, Condon took a piece of paper and drew crossing lines, dividing the sheet into four parts. In one corner he drew a picture of the bench at Woodlawn, in another corner he put the money, and in the third a picture of the child. The fourth he left open. Hauptmann did not understand his meaning, so Condon made it clear. The missing person in the fourth corner was the key. Did Richard know who got the money? Who got the child?

Everyone always asked him about the rest of the money, Hauptmann said. If the accountants were right, and he had spent $49,000 of it, why did they do that? Lloyd Fisher also affirmed that immediately after his conviction, Hauptmann had been asked again about the money. "A very unusual thing happened when I returned to my cell after the verdict," Hauptmann had told Fisher. "Lieutenant Smith came to my cell and said to me, 'Bruno, if you will tell what you know about the other $35,000 of the ransom money—we know you didn't commit this murder, but we think you know something about the rest of the money—if you will tell us where the rest of the money is, we will see that you get a break.'"[23]

Hauptmann told Parker the police had coerced the identifications made during the New York extradition hearings. When they brought Millard Whited, the semiliterate woodcutter, into the room, he said, Hauptmann was placed in a lineup with two cops. Whited did not respond quickly enough, so a detective gave him a shove and pointed at Hauptmann. As for Amandus Hochmuth, when they brought him to the Flemington jail, he stayed for half an hour. There must have been at least a half dozen others they trooped through that jail.[24]

Parker's reports of this conversation, and his insistence he was still on the trail of the real kidnapper, counted heavily with Hoffman even as the Court of Errors and Appeals closed another door.

On October 9, Hauptmann's tenth wedding anniversary, the court panel unanimously reaffirmed the Flemington verdict. "The defendant's handling of the money makes clear his guilty connection with the enterprise. . . . It is inconceivable that Fisch, if he had this money, would have left it in defendant's custody in the manner claimed." Obviously, they didn't know Fisch very well. He was perfectly capable of doing that. Whether he did or not was another question.[25]

"To be sure, Richard had been caught with the money," Fisher admitted, "and a devil of a lot of it, too. Also, it was difficult to believe his involved story about Isidor Fisch and the shoe box—although, after spending many hours talking with Richard and many dollars of my own money investigating Isidor, I was convinced that it was true." Even if one believed Hauptmann knew it was hot money, said Fisher, he should have been tried only for possessing stolen property—or perhaps extortion.[26]

Lloyd Fisher prepared a new appeal to the Supreme Court for a review of the decision, but chances there were scarcely any better. At least it postponed the execution date again.

Yet another dissenter—in secret—was Colonel Mark Kimberling, warden of the state penitentiary.[27]

Kimberling came into the governor's office in early October 1935, at a time when Hoffman's desk was piled high with tax troubles, political troubles, and every other kind of headache. "Governor," said the warden, "Hauptmann has asked to see you."

"*Me* see Hauptmann, Mark?" Hoffman replied. "What for?"

"I don't know exactly, Governor. But he keeps asking for you."

Then came another message, this one from Charles Curtis, former vice president of the United States under Herbert Hoover. "Governor, are you looking into this Hauptmann case?" There were a lot of funny things about that case. "I've read a lot of the testimony, and it doesn't seem to me that he was adequately represented—or that he got a very fair deal." Curtis asked Hoffman to talk to Evalyn Walsh McLean, the wealthy Washington woman who owned the famous Hope Diamond. Gaston Means, another con man claiming to be in touch with the real kidnappers, had fleeced her out of $100,000. She still had an interest in the case, nevertheless, or perhaps particularly so, and joined Curtis in urging the governor to intervene.

So when an evening engagement was canceled at the last minute the night of October 16, 1935, Hoffman telephoned Kimberling. "Mark," he said, "I'm coming down to see that fellow. Will tonight be O.K?" It was. Hoffman made another call, this one to Anna Bading, who was in full evening dress at the time attending a meeting of the Eastern Star. She broke away and met the governor at Kimberling's residence. They walked from there to the prison, turned right inside the gate, and entered the death house. "As the door opened, the beam from a prison guard's flashlight fell directly on the chair in which Hauptmann was later to die."[28]

Telling Anna to sit down on a bench beside the electric chair, Hoffman passed through the door to Hauptmann's cell. Would he hear a confession implicating Hauptmann's accomplices? He did not know what to expect. The prisoner was on his feet. "Governor, vy does your state do to me all this? Vy do they vant my life for something somebody else have done?" Let him take a lie-detector test, he pleaded. "Vy won't they use on me that—and on Doctor Condon also use it? They haf too some kind of drug, I haf heard. Vy don't they use on me that drug? And on Doctor Condon use it too?"[29]

No carpenter made the ladder, Hauptmann said, certainly not one with the skills he possessed.

He then talked about the footprints at St. Raymond's Cemetery and outside the Lindbergh home. Now he knew why they had taken all his shoes—to see if they fit plaster casts of the footprints. "Vy did they not produce at the trial the impression of which they cast a model? Vy? They cannot say that my foot has become larger or smaller?" Defense attorneys did not know that the state police had, in fact, taken a plaster cast of a footprint found at Hopewell, as well as one at St. Raymond's. But Hauptmann was right.

He held no brief for Hauptmann, Hoffman would write, but as the conversation unfolded, it put "new doubts in [his] mind and aided in fashioning a firm resolution to search out, within the limits of [his] resources and ability, the truth—and the whole truth—in this mysterious, challenging case."

When he left, he had to pass again through the death chamber. "When the door opened, that chair, covered with a piece of white muslin and resembling a seated ghost, could be seen by the occupant of Hauptmann's cell. At least six men had shuffled past the German carpenter, some of them silent, some sobbing, some shrieking, to be strapped in that chair."[30]

As ex officio chair of the Court of Pardons, the governor still had only one vote, however, and not the power to commute the sentence. When he became seriously involved in the Lindbergh case in 1935, Hoffman probably did calculate the political odds for and against. It was true, on the one hand, that the state—and nation—had cheered Hauptman's conviction; but if few thought Hauptman totally innocent, quite a number wondered about accomplices and his degree of guilt. If Hoffman could "crack" the case, he would have succeeded where the entire mechanism of law enforcement had failed!

Ellis Parker was at work, meanwhile, checking out a story that George Steinweg, a ticket-broker, had taken in gold certificates from Isidor Fisch on November 14, 1933, in payment for steamship tickets and travelers' checks. Steinweg claimed to Parker and other investigators that he had sold some of the certificates to a business associate, who eventually faced questioning by police when he deposited the money, and was made to write "J. J. Faulkner" over and over again. Steinweg said he had talked with bank officials, who confirmed the whole story, especially that they were ransom bills, but the deposit never appeared on any list of recovered money.[31]

This interview and other evidence seemed to confirm that Fisch had money with which to purchase the tickets before he received cash from a check given to him by Hauptmann later in the day. These were peripheral bits and pieces that might, at most, chip away at the outer circle of evidence surrounding Hauptmann as he awaited execution.

Lloyd Fisher had become an almost daily correspondent, supplying the governor with affidavits that offered further evidence about Isidor Fisch's finances and his dealing in hot money.

The most interesting of these affidavits was a statement from Oscar Bruckman, a driver who knew Fisch from the days of the Knickerbocker Pie Company, and who had testified at the trial for the defense. During that period, he said, Fisch and his partners, Charles Schleser and Lamber Brush, took weekend trips out of town, leaving him in charge of the business. But in his affidavit he went beyond the question of Fisch having plenty of money on his person to describe an instance where Fisch had tried to have him take a pistol and act as an armed bodyguard while he collected a large sum of money. Bruckman would not take the pistol but agreed to meet Fisch outside the bank he had designated for a rendezvous. Fisch never showed up, however, and later told Bruckman he had made the deal by himself. On another occasion Fisch told him he had sold stocks and had obtained some hot money he needed to get rid of outside of New York. If Bruckman would drive him, he could get rid of the money and Bruckman could make a lot more than he did driving a cab. For some reason, Reilly had not been interested in putting Bruckman on the witness stand.[32]

The affidavit, said Fisher, would demonstrate something "[the defense has] been trying to develop all summer long, and shows conclusively that Fisch was a crook and had been engaged in crooked deals for a number of years. Second, the time fixed as the time of the pistol episode coincides with the approximate time of the passing of the ransom money."

Hoffman had been interested in Hauptmann's comments about a lie-detector test, and his challenge to Condon to take one. Could such a thing be managed? The original so-called Lie-Detector was the invention of William Moulton Marston, who had three degrees from Harvard University: an A.B. in 1915, a law degree in 1918, and a Ph.D. in psychology in 1921. Apparently his wife, Elizabeth, triggered the idea in his mind simply by saying that when she got mad or excited her blood pressure seemed to climb. Out of that idea he developed his truth machine, which measured blood pressure changes when a subject gave false answers.

Failing to convince federal authorities during World War I that he had a way to expose spies, after the war Marston continued his efforts to publicize his methods, claiming at one point that he had successfully tested ninety-seven out of one hundred suspects in Boston. In a 1923 murder trial, defense attorneys attempted to introduce his findings to clear a man named Frye. The judge ruled against admission of the testimony. The circuit court agreed that "expert testimony" had to be deduced from a well-organized scientific principle, "sufficiently established to have gained general acceptance in the particular field in which it belongs."[33]

The Frye "rule" lasted for seventy years, with most—but not all—courts rejecting testimony based on such tests. Improvements, meanwhile, to the Lie-Detector, renamed Polygraph, provided additional measurements besides systolic blood pressure, such as heart rate, breathing rate, and galvanic skin response. If the courts rejected the Polygraph, the American public, as always, was fascinated with the supposed wonders of technology to reveal the deepest secrets of human experience. Marston's efforts to publicize his methods even brought a letter of inquiry from FBI director Hoover. In 1935 the FBI purchased a Polygraph from one of his competitors, Leonarde Keeler, who worked out of Northwestern University.

Keeler had actually succeeded in having a test on one of his subjects, a Cleveland man sentenced to serve ten years for robbery, admitted in an appeal. In this case, the judge and attorneys for both sides had agreed test results could be introduced at a new trial.

When an FBI agent interviewed Keeler, the expert informed him that Anna Hauptmann had been to see him to try out the Polygraph for herself. Unfortunately, the trial test had been leaked to the newspapers and trumpeted as more proof of her husband's guilt—if not, indeed, her own. An unauthorized report said she had been caught at the outset lying about her age and abruptly called off the rest of the test, saying her attorneys would object. When she discovered the machine actually detected lies, in other words, she was afraid for her husband.

The facts were quite different. Keeler had started his test by using cards. It was a standard pretest in which the operator asks the subject to take a card with a number, and respond no every time, including when the operator calls out the correct one. When the subject tells a "lie," the reactions are measured. Keeler determined she was a good subject. But when he moved on to the Lindbergh case, she took the apparatus off, saying she must consult her attorneys. Still, as Keeler told the FBI agent, she remained very anxious to have her husband tested. Keeler was equally—if not more—eager to conduct the examination and said he would be glad to have the FBI present at the time. Referred to Hoover, the agent's report of Keeler's invitation brought a stinging rebuke. "Under no circumstances," scrawled the director on this memorandum, "will we have anything to do with the test of Hauptmann."[34]

Governor Hoffman, however, had contacted William Marston after his visit to the death house, and together the two of them tried to think of a way to persuade Judge Trenchard and the attorney general to allow such a test. Both adamantly opposed the idea.

Hoffman also wanted to pursue the idea of giving Condon a lie-detector test as well, showing Marston the evidence he had collected about Jafsie's various accounts of his meetings with the extortionist. Two agents were appointed to seek out Condon and ask him to take the test. They pursued him to Massachusetts, where Jafsie had now taken his "act" back on stage in hopes of a friendlier audience. The ads read: "Now available for personal appearances in vaudeville or motion picture theaters—'JAFSIE' Dr. John F. Condon. Most enigmatic, colorful, and widely publicized personality in America, Condon recently played to terrific grosses in Boston and Lynn, Mass."[35] An Associated Press photo showed Condon in the window of a Lynn department store, posing with replicas of the ladder and other evidence. But Marston's agents could not catch up to him there. Traveling from Massachusetts all the way to City Island, they arrived in a secondhand violin shop, where they at last encountered a man who said he was Condon's vaudeville agent. No, he was not there, said the man, and he could not be reached. Too bad, came the reply; he would lose a lot of publicity from all the front-page stories about his taking a lie-detector test. All of a sudden, a grizzled gray-haired man appeared from an alcove screened by an American flag. "What's that?" cried Condon. "Here you—let me talk to these men."[36]

Once the terms were explained—a confidential report to Governor Hoffman before any newspaper release—Jafsie backed off in a hurry. He said a number of seemingly crazy things: "I will take a Lie Detector Test. But not until Bruno Hauptmann is dead." And: "I'll take a test if Hauptmann will bring back the Lindbergh baby." And: "I'll make a deception test if Hauptmann will tell why he sent me down to the swamps of Florida to look for Colonel Lindbergh's child." Finally, Condon said he would like to meet Dr. Marston. "I like to meet all famous people. But I'll tell you what's the matter with these modern psychologists." Then in a stage whisper: "They don't know what the twelve apostles are in the mind!"[37]

Marston's men were not the first to be thwarted by the fabulous Dr. John Condon.

Hoffman could find no way, either, to manage a test of Hauptmann. If Marston were listed as Hauptmann's attorney, no one would believe the test results. Besides, the newspapers were onto the story. In response to their questions, Hoffman declared: "Dr. Marston is a scientist of high standing. I should like to have him give Hauptmann a Lie Detector test." It was not to be.

"I hope even yet," Marston wrote after Hauptmann's execution, "to find a living human being whose mind contains information about the Lindbergh kidnaping. If such a person exists, his secret knowledge can be read like print by the Lie Detector. If he can be examined before his pulse circulatory system is stilled by those who wish to bury the facts in an officially prepared grave, I predict some startling disclosures."

Until then, Condon had won. "Jafsie was laughing at New Jersey legal summonses from a distance—he went on a sudden trip to the Panama Canal with the consent and warm approval of Attorney General Wilentz."[38]

Why had Hauptmann asked for the test? Perhaps he thought his willpower would overcome any machine. Hadn't he resisted all efforts to make him confess? The police then and now use lie-detector tests to bluff accused persons into confessions, but Hauptmann's plea, backed by the governor, seemed to unnerve state officials. FBI director Hoover had wanted no part of a lie-detector test.

Famed aviator Amelia Earhart would write to Governor Hoffman, however, urging him to have Hauptmann tested with a new "truth" drug, scopolamine. She had thought a long time about the question—probably realizing it could jeopardize her relations with the Lindberghs. But she thought that its use in this case would "hasten by decades" all sorts of scientific advances in the courtroom.

> Please understand I do not criticize the conduct of the Hauptmann case or the personnel connected with it. I do not plead for, nor condemn, the man himself. I do not here question the society in which kidna[p]ping may be a profitable venture. However, the purpose of this letter is to question the society which steadfastly turns its face from the light yet demands a life in its ignorance. Were the stakes not so great and the means to be sure not at hand, the situation might not be so serious. A painstaking effort to reach by Scopolamine to the bottom of a hideous internationally known chain of events, would be a contribution to civilization. Whether or not it affected the sentence of the man in the New Jersey State Prison, it would still demonstrate to the world

American sincerity and American belief that no stone should
be allowed unturned in the search for justice.

The governor replied that he was in thorough agreement with her
views and had asked for any "scientific" test months earlier, but had
failed to persuade the court.[39]

So Condon sailed off to Panama at the end of December 1935—not only
with Wilentz's blessing but with a state police chaperon—for a long
vacation with his daughter, Myra Hacker. She also served as gatekeeper,
protecting him against himself when he talked to reporters—or at least
attempting to. Just before sailing, the old master seized one last chance
for publicity. He had been offered up to $250,000 to change his testi-
mony, he said. "I told Hauptmann in his cell that I do not want to see him
burned now," he went on, "but I am under attack and I must resist." He
had done his duty, carried out the oath he made the night he slept in
the nursery. "This is not the fight of Condon against Hauptmann. This is
the fight of Hauptmann versus the state of New Jersey."[40]

Liberty editor Fulton Oursler had worked closely with Condon on a
"Jafsie Tells All" series, soon to appear in his magazine, and was shocked
at his sudden departure. "It seemed odd to me that Condon had left the
country without a word of explanation without even a telephone call of
farewell. For months we had worked closely together in the preparation
of his story."[41]

Curious about what had precipitated this voyage to Central America, where Governor Hoffman (or anyone else) would have difficulty
getting to him, Oursler remembered that Hauptmann had issued a
statement from the death house just after Thanksgiving. "I call upon Dr.
Condon to tell the truth. He holds the key to my cell." Oursler wondered
what this meant. Was Hauptmann about to confess and name Condon
as his accomplice? "The very fact that it was so vague was disturbing."
The editor decided to call Attorney General Wilentz to see if there
had been any developments that would make publication of the articles
unwise or embarrassing. Assured there were none, Oursler still felt it
best to consult directly with Condon about "Governor Hoffman's sudden activity."[42]

Oursler had previously asked Condon if there was any basis for
Hauptmann's claim that Jafsie said he could never testify against him.
No such thing had ever transpired, replied Condon. "The Attorney Gen-
eral and another gentleman were listening to me and I never said any
such thing. I declared my identification of the accused to the 'Attorney
General,' who deemed it prudent to hold the secret until the day of

the trial. I am quite a big target, but well equipped." This was authentic Jafsie-speak.[43]

But Condon obliged Oursler's desire for a talk to clear up these points before he left the country and even took his editor on a walking tour of all the sites where Jafsie had engaged Cemetery John in those fateful negotiations. Not only that; Condon promised he would show Oursler "new evidence" of Hauptmann's guilt. The major piece of this evidence was a story that a cabinetmaker named Samuelsohn, the man who constructed the wooden box to hold the ransom money, had cut the wood for the kidnap ladder—to Hauptmann's precise specifications! Condon took him to see Samuelsohn, and to hear this fantastic story, which, if true, would completely negate all the evidence presented at the trial that Hauptmann's tools had been used to make the ladder. When Oursler then visited Condon in Panama, Myra Hacker was adamant that he not publish anything about the Samuelsohn story. But, said Oursler, it was your father who took me there, and who told me that he thought it was important and should be investigated. The episode reprised events of years past when Jafsie could not remember who had made the box, suggesting it had been a man, Frank Peremi, who had died before the date of the kidnapping. Samuelsohn was now eager to take credit for the box—and the ladder. What a strange turn of events.

"My father will think as I think and say as I say," she snapped. "We do not wish anything about Samuelsohn published. We do not believe that story." Oursler read her the notes Condon had supplied after his interview with Samuelsohn. "We do not wish that published," she reiterated. "Mr. [Thomas] Sisk of the Department of Justice investigated the story. He says there is nothing to it. That is gospel for me." It was not for Condon, however, who now repeated he thought it ought to be investigated. When Oursler came away from this interview, he later wrote, his mind was "occupied with a new mystery." Something had happened to make Condon stop talking. "Of all the human beings I ever knew, he had been the most talkative. His conversation was incessant. Now the mighty flow of it had dwindled to a tiny frightened stream."[44]

Oursler had no doubts about Hauptmann's guilt and regarded Condon with a large measure of respect. Still, he wondered about a few things.

People say, Oursler recalled his conversation with Jafsie in Panama, that you tell different stories day after day, and often one does not agree with the other.

"That's true."

Jafsie looked off into the distance, reported Oursler, and lifted a forefinger like a clergyman.

"I did that deliberately. I did it at the request of the two colonels—Lindbergh and Breckinridge. It was part of a deliberate plan to mislead the defense." He rambled on about how the defense claimed he was muddleheaded, senile, wacky. But his testimony convinced the jury he knew what he was talking about. Then he pretended to let Oursler in on a big secret. Cemetery John had told him at Woodlawn the first note was left in the crib, but that did not sound right. So he asked Colonel Lindbergh. Yes, it was, declared Lindbergh—and that proved he was negotiating with the right man!

Oursler tried hard to swallow this tale. He knew that Lindbergh had sworn in his testimony the note was found on the windowsill. What was one to make of this "discrepancy"? he asked himself. It was the only time he ever caught Jafsie's "memory off guard." He usually remembered events with astonishing precision, especially in small details. But this was far more than a discrepancy, for the location of the first note had to be known to the person who left it there. If it had not been left on the windowsill, who moved it there from the crib? However much inclined to honor Condon's veracity, he could never quite satisfy himself on this point. Condon had said, moreover, he deliberately told different stories at the behest of the "two colonels," to confuse the defense. But when he first gave his varying accounts of the meetings with Cemetery John, there had been no arrests—and no defense.[45]

In a rambling, almost incoherent, letter to the *New York Times* titled "Trading Men!" Condon declared that in all wars there was a "fair exchange of prisoners." In this case, however, the United States had lost its "National Hero" to a foreign power in exchange for Bruno Richard Hauptmann. Lindbergh's decision to leave the country and take his family to England had shocked many people and further inflamed opinion against the man who had caused this loss. Condon's letter sought to take advantage of that new surge by reminding a national audience how he had accepted Colonel and Mrs. Lindbergh's "invitation" to restore the baby and then to "run down the cowardly knave who climbed a ladder which the carpenter had planned and submitted to the cabinet-maker," both of whom he knew, "and which ladder the heartless carpenter nailed together in three sections, to carry out his nefarious scheme." He ended by warning New Jersey courts to stand firm against efforts to have Hauptmann's sentence commuted, and with a bitter xenophobic screed.

> Will the Courts stand as a tribunal, only to be swept out of power by an individual for the sake of political aggrandizement, or will the representatives of the people stand firm and

defy gangsterdom, or individual marauders while we trade National Heroes like Col. Charles A. Lindbergh and his family for the discarded miscreants of other Countries who lie, cheat, kidnap and murder, depending upon the loot and spoils to serve as a cache to free them from the toils and meshes of the law.

But, at least, Colonel Lindbergh had told him he would remain a citizen. "He will return in triumph to us and U.S. May God speed that return."[46]

About this same time, Hauptmann also wrote a letter, addressed to his mother but intended for Governor Hoffman as well, and therefore for the public. Warden Kimberling warned Hoffman that it made "some very interesting comments on the case" and was quite likely to receive heavy press coverage in Germany, "placing [New Jersey officials] in an embarrassing position for having released it from the State Prison." He did not want to take the responsibility alone. Hoffman decided it should not be released. Forty years later, in 1977, the letter was found in a small cache of Kimberling's papers and made public.[47]

The letter revisited all of Hauptmann's previous arguments about the footprints not fitting his shoes and the absence of fingerprints, but focused on Condon's role. Why was it he had changed his mind after the visit to the Flemington jail, when Condon supposedly sprang up in anguish declaring he could not testify against him? It was a riddle to him. "Now the gentleman . . . sits in the shop window with a ladder in his hand for advertisement. How this seventy-year-old man can still sleep with peaceful conscience, I truly cannot understand."

Throughout the six weeks of the trial, Hauptmann went on, the prosecution had contended that the ladder broke when the kidnapper attempted to climb down from the nursery with the child. But in his summation, after all the testimony had been taken, and after Reilly had completed his final remarks, "so that there was no more opportunity to refute it, the prosecutor changed the whole view." Hauptmann doubted "that such a thing has ever been in history before."[48]

But despite this irregularity, the U.S. Supreme Court refused to review the New Jersey Court of Errors and Appeals' decision.

A few days after his meeting in the New Yorker hotel with J. Edgar Hoover in mid-January of 1936, Governor Hoffman wrote to him asking for specific items pertaining to statements by Condon. When Hoover put his men to work trying to discover if there had ever been a complete statement taken from Jafsie, the report he got back from the New

York office was that no such statement existed. "It is inconceivable," Hoover raged, "that such should have been the case." In his reply to Hoffman, however, the director admitted no such thing. He said that his men had conducted over a hundred interviews with Condon at one time or another, and that copying them all would be too great a task. Most of the transcripts of these interviews should already be in New Jersey State Police files. If necessary, he could provide summaries of the important points covered. So the governor never learned the bureau had not sat Condon down for a nice long tête-à-tête.[49]

Working closely with his friend Warden Kimberling and others, meanwhile, Hoffman drew up a list of questions for Schwarzkopf to answer. One key question was what role did Charles Schleser play in the case? Hoffman also asked Schwarzkopf to turn over for his use state police reports of the investigation on practically every angle of the case. Among the items he requested was a plaster cast of the single footprint police claimed to have found outside the nursery. He was told there was only a photo. But that was not the case. At one time such a cast had been in existence and was reported in an inventory of evidence made in the 1950s—as we have already seen.[50]

While Hoffman was seeking information about Schleser from Colonel Schwarzkopf, a note arrived for the state police commander signed Ottilia Haerber. This woman had been a witness for the state at the trial, testifying that Isidor Fisch had been in her house the night the ransom was paid. But now she had misgivings. Her mind would not be at ease, she wrote, until she told what she knew: "A partner of the late Isidor Fisch, guilty of several shady deals, also falsifying handwriting, was in a hotel in Trenton for 8 days at the expense of the state, although he was not called on the witness stand." She asked Schwarzkopf to send a detective to see her, someone who spoke German, and she would explain her suspicions.[51]

Two men were eventually sent to interview Haerber—*after a two-week delay*—and she explained that the man she saw at the hotel in Trenton was Charles Schleser, who was accompanied by a lawyer. He and Fisch were always together around the time of the kidnapping and ransom negotiations, she told the investigators, and Schleser, especially, had appeared very suspicious and nervous. Her impressions of Fisch and Schleser had been aggravated, the detectives recorded, because they had swindled her out of $250 in a pie bakery deal. She had met Schleser through Anna Stotz, a former roomer in her house, who now supposedly worked as a maid elsewhere in the city. A visit to the apartment house failed to find Stotz, and there this perfunctory investigation came to an end.[52]

But what a stark contrast with things she had said before when she confirmed Fisch's presence in her home the night the money was paid to Cemetery John. Once again Hoffman was to learn nothing about a potentially vital question remaining after the trial. He knew he could not count on Schwarzkopf or Hoover to give him anything that might discredit their investigations. To assist him in his search for new clues, the governor proceeded to hire a number of private detectives, including Leon Hoage, whose letterhead promised he could solve any case: "A MYSTERY—IS SUCH ONLY SO LONG AS A FEW SIMPLE FACTS REMAIN UNKNOWN."

Time was fast running out, however. The governor's reprieve was only for thirty days—and legally he could not extend it a day longer. In the vote of the Court of Pardon and Appeals, Hoffman's vote was the only one favoring commutation of the sentence. That vote, and recent revelations that he had visited Hauptmann in the death house, made him the target of an indignant press—and the outrage of governors in many states. Wilentz had publicly expressed the belief that the governor's actions aroused false hopes in Hauptmann's mind; he would never confess so long as he thought such a powerful man stood between him and the chair.

Stung by the criticism, Hoffman launched a counterattack on his critics. On January 26, 1936, he wrote Schwarzkopf a public letter expressing dissatisfaction with the whole investigation. Hauptmann's fate, he insisted, was almost the least important feature of the case. He had no interest in him as an individual and had never expressed an opinion as to his guilt or innocence. "As Governor of the State of New Jersey I direct you, with every resource at your command, to continue a thorough and impartial search for the detection and apprehension of every person connected with this crime. You will acknowledge receipt of this letter and will report to me, in writing, at least once weekly, the steps being taken by your organization and coordinating agencies to prosecute this investigation."

He attached to the letter a long list of statements and queries about the evidence, many drawn from advance copies of Condon's sensational "Jafsie Tells All!" series in *Liberty*. The articles boosted circulation to more than a quarter million and served Hoffman's cause because Condon said it could not have been a one-man job. Now he could quote the state's star witness back at Schwarzkopf and Wilentz. "I do not believe that this crime was committed by any one man, and there is ample evidence, direct from the record, that the chief witnesses and those [who] were engaged in the prosecution share my belief."[53]

Schwarzkopf sent a series of innocuous reports that addressed none of Hoffman's concerns and revealed nothing about such items as the

Schleser investigation. As always, the governor was on his own, except for Lloyd Fisher and his own private investigators.

Together with Prosecutor Anthony Hauck, Fisher and Governor Hoffman interviewed the semiliterate logger Millard Whited on February 22, 1936. After warning him that anything he said might be used against him later, the governor led off by asking about the night of March 1–2, 1932. Some people came to visit you, he said, wasn't that correct? They had, acknowledged Whited. To Hauck's dismay, Whited immediately became confused by the next question as he tried to keep his answers in line with his court testimony. Why didn't he tell the police that night about the stranger he had seen lurking around the area before the kidnapping? At first he invented a second visit only two or three days later. It was then, he said, he told police he had seen Hauptmann on two occasions near the time of the kidnapping. The reason he had not told about the encounters in his only official statement to the police on April 26, 1932, was to help the police. "They [the original police investigators] asked me to please keep it a secret. I never told no one, not even my wife."

One of these troopers he promised to help was a "Joe Wolf," but he could not remember the name of any others with him on this unreported second visit. A few minutes later Whited abandoned this second meeting, asserting he had described the man he saw around Hopewell near the Lindbergh estate during the very first police interrogation. The confusion grew as Whited added in more visits by plainclothesmen; they were the ones who badgered him into making the April 26, 1932, statement denying he had seen anyone suspicious around the Lindbergh place. He had remained loyal to his first interrogators, he boasted, while "them fellows there was trying to frame the state troopers, was trying to butt in on what the state troopers was asking me."

Whited chased himself around this mulberry bush several times while trying to catch up with the last story he had told only a few minutes—or even seconds—earlier. He had contended, near as one could figure out, that his April 26, 1932, statement saying he had not seen anyone suspicious around the time of the kidnapping had been given under duress—the result of constant pestering by men who had not identified themselves properly as state troopers.

Hoffman finally asked if he had not felt uneasy providing a statement containing false assertions.

"Well, I did not—it seems to me, to the best of my knowledge there is a little in there that does not sound just right, but it has been so long ago that it is a hard matter for a man to go back and remember word for word just exactly what he said."

What about the reward he had been promised for identifying Hauptmann? Someone had evidently promised Whited that he would receive a third of the $25,000. "Governor," Hauck interrupted, "I do not want to interfere, but what I would suggest about this statement is this—it is only a suggestion." But as the questioning went on, it developed that Whited had asked for a down payment before he would go to New York for the extradition hearing. "I told Joe Wolf I needed money at that time." After he hollered enough, another trooper brought him cash in Lambertville, $35 or $40. Eventually, he got $150 to cover expenses.

But he said at the trial, Hoffman reminded him, that he only received a dinner and no cash at all.

"I know it."

"Did you lie about it?"

"I absolutely thought that was my business, what I got out of it."

It soon dawned on him what he had admitted, so Whited ran back the other way around the bush. He had said he got nothing but dinner because he had not yet been paid at the time of the trial testimony. "I had been promised but I hadn't gotten nothing." He didn't understand, he said, that the question had been whether he had been promised some money. Indeed, he now said he didn't "fairly understand" a lot of the questions at Flemington. "Listen," he said, tired of chasing himself, "I think, Mr. Fisher, I think this: I think the best thing for me to do is to keep quiet until Mr. What's-his-name gets back."

"Mr. Who gets back?"

"Mr. Wintzel."

"Mr. Wilentz?"

"Yes."[54]

Wilentz did not turn up at the governor's office to offer Whited any help that day, but Hauck reported what had happened and the two prosecutors denied that the logger said the things he did. "Wilentz has said that he thinks the Governor must have misunderstood Whited," Fisher wrote Hoffman, "and Hauck has denied that Whited said many of the things that I know he did say." But the transcript spoke for itself. The state's loyal witness had been making a number of boasts and promises, meanwhile, that he was about to come into a large sum of money after Hauptmann's execution. "This fellow would sell his own mother's life away for thirty-five cents."[55]

As the waiting game continued, Evalyn McLean launched her own project. She called upon Samuel Leibowitz, Clarence Darrow's successor as the top defense lawyer in the land. Leibowitz had represented "Scarface" Al Capone and the head of "Murder Inc.," Albert Anastasia, as well as the Scottsboro boys, young blacks falsely accused of raping two white women in Alabama. Only one of his eighty clients had ever "walked the last mile."

Evalyn McLean felt sure he would listen to her. He did listen but shook his head. No one could save Hauptmann—and he certainly didn't want to try—unless the carpenter confessed his part in the crime and named the others. McLean might have forgotten that Leibowitz had commented almost daily during the trial for the *New York Evening Journal* and had broadcast over station WHN. "Dr. Condon has strapped Hauptmann into the electric chair," he had written. "When he sees the chair he will talk." He would name all his confederates before he died.[56]

Someone had to be there that blustery night to hold the ladder, he told her. Maybe the baby was killed when the person inside tried to throw it out the window to someone waiting below. But however it happened, he could do nothing unless Anna Hauptmann asked him to see her husband. She would tend to that, she promised. Criminologist Robert Hicks would serve as her go-between. Anna regarded Hicks as a friend, and with his encouragement she agreed to ask Leibowitz for help.

What changed her mind? Perhaps simple despair. Feeling helpless as the final days of the reprieve flashed by like a subway express train, she must do something. But it may also have been that Evalyn McLean had not quite presented the situation accurately to Hicks. She may have presented it as a somewhat ambiguous proposition. As her own views were closer to those of Lloyd Fisher than Samuel Leibowitz, she could have implied that here was Hauptmann's last opportunity to convince a very important lawyer he was innocent.

Lloyd Fisher learned about Leibowitz's first visit to the death house from the newspapers—and was flabbergasted. Anna had wrongly assumed he had been consulted. And she now knew as well that she had been wrong about Leibowitz's willingness to hear Richard's arguments and work with him on that basis. "You see, Hauptmann," he had said, "I'm not paying any attention to all of these so-called eyewitnesses who pointed you out as the man seen around the Lindbergh grounds shortly before the child was kidnapped. I don't believe that after two years their identifications are entitled to much consideration, but how can we get away from all of these other things that stand out like so many red lights in the dead of night, and that cry out, 'Guilty, guilty, guilty.'"[57]

"I asked Richard," Fisher wrote Hoffman afterward, "just what in the hell he thought could be accomplished by having a man in there who had indicated he thought Richard was guilty?" It was something beyond his control, Hauptmann replied with a forlorn shrug. "I didn't know he was coming here. My wife spoke to me about it, and I told her not do anything until she consulted you and Judge [Frederick] Pope."

Well, the only thing to do now was to let him come back, said Fisher. Otherwise it would look as if they were afraid of the Great Defender. The second time he came, Anna accompanied him. When they left the prison, Leibowitz emerged brimming with confidence. "I have had a very gratifying interview with Bruno in the presence of his wife," he told reporters. "He broke down and cried like a child. I am coming to see him again on Sunday."

"Did he confess?"

"I have no comment."[58]

At 3 A.M. the next day, Fisher's phone rang. Robert Hicks was calling on Anna's behalf. Would he come to see them about the Leibowitz situation—now, at once? You two created the situation, he snapped at Hicks, and you must live with it. He was not about to go anywhere at three in the morning.[59]

A few minutes later he relented. However they had gotten themselves into such a mess, he could not abandon his client. Let Leibowitz play out the string, he told them.

Leibowitz, meanwhile, called Fisher asking him to a meeting the next night at the Towers Hotel in New York. Governor Hoffman also accepted his invitation to talk about strategy. Leibowitz led off by saying they had to break down Hauptmann's extreme egocentricity. That was the only way. It had led him to rob the mayor of his hometown; it had pushed him to stow away three times before reaching the United States; and finally, it had driven him to steal the child of the most famous man in the nation to "satiate his demonical craving for the spotlight."[60]

Outraged, Fisher accused Leibowitz of knowing Hauptmann was innocent but refusing to admit he could be wrong about what he had said. He wanted Hauptmann to confess to satisfy *his* own ego, and nothing else. Leibowitz retorted that Hauptmann would have confessed a long time ago had it not been for Fisher's wrongheaded approach. "You are his prop, his crutch. He is leaning on you to save his life." Hoffman finally got the two of them to stop shouting at each other, and Fisher reluctantly agreed to back up Leibowitz's efforts to break down Hauptmann's resistance.

But if Hauptmann still protested his innocence, Fisher asked, what then? "Will you then tell the world that he is innocent?" "Yes," said Leibowitz, at least according to Hoffman's account. "But don't worry about that," he said with a smile. "When I get through with him you'll find out that he is guilty. He'll be crying for mercy."

In Fisher's account, however, Leibowitz gave no such promise to tell the world Hauptmann was innocent. All he said was if Hauptmann withstood the examination, and if Fisher convinced him his chances were practically nil, "it will certainly go a long way toward convincing me that this man isn't guilty." And in a third account, by Leibowitz's biographer, he went on to say he had one move left in that case. "His one weak spot is that boy of his. If Hauptmann can be made to understand that he is going to the chair and that everyone has washed his hands clean of him, if an hour before he is to walk 'the last mile' to the chair, you will take his child into the cell and let him feel that kid's arms around his neck, I tell you he'll break down and tell the truth; he'll name his accomplices."[61]

Did Leibowitz really think—could anyone really think—that such a "last move," the ultimate psychological "third degree," would wring the truth out of Hauptmann? What would a confession under such circumstances really prove?

When Fisher and Leibowitz went together to see Hauptmann, the New York attorney pulled out all the stops. For more than four hours, Leibowitz hammered away at Hauptmann, pointing at the death chamber a few feet away and drawing mental pictures of the chair, describing the smell of burning flesh. He ridiculed all of Hauptmann's explanations and kept asking him to tell him how he really "thought" the crime had been committed. After each telling point, he would say, "Isn't that so, Lloyd?" And Fisher would say yes, according to their agreement.

It was no use. Hauptmann would not break—and Leibowitz was worn out with the effort. He had ruptured a small vein in his eye. At last he announced he was ready to leave. As they departed, Hauptmann called out, "If I can help you any more in this case, Mr. Leibowitz, come back and see me," adding as they walked away, "you know I got lots of time."[62]

Outside the prison, Liebowitz issued a statement announcing he was through with the case. He praised Fisher and other defense attorneys for doing their best, then delivered a crushing blow. Nothing had changed his opinion an iota about Hauptmann's guilt, and he had not come into the case to defeat the ends of justice. "I know that Lloyd Fisher has done everything that is humanly possible for his client. He is a splendid lawyer and will continue to exercise his talents and energies to the utmost in his client's behalf. But I for one have refused to associate myself as this man's lawyer."[63]

It was a low blow couched in flowery words. The next day Fisher saw Hauptmann to tell him the news: Leibowitz had announced to the press that he thought Hauptmann was guilty, and that he wouldn't have anything more to do with the case. It was exactly what he had warned his client would happen. "I know," said Hauptmann, "but I thought I had convinced him I was innocent."[64]

The campaign to bring Condon back would have to take priority now, as the execution date had been set for the week of March 30. Even as Leibowitz argued himself blue trying to convince Hauptmann he must confess, the prisoner was handing Warden Mark Kimberling a note asking that efforts be made to inform Condon that he would like to see him again. "I believe I can prove to him that I am not the man he dealt with."[65]

Hoffman had continued to call for Condon's return from Panama. "He should be made to explain the discrepancies between his original statements given to police authorities and his trial testimony, as well as an explanation of his statements made since the conviction . . . Dr. Condon's conduct and his conflicting statements warrant far more than the cream-puff type of questioning to which he has been subjected previously."[66]

At last, word came that Condon was on his way back from Panama. He was aboard the Grace Line's *Santa Inez* scheduled to dock in Brooklyn on March 17, 1936. The day before his arrival Wilentz conferred with Hauck and Colonel Schwarzkopf. Afterward, the attorney general said nothing in Condon's testimony implicating Hauptmann had been refuted or attacked, and whatever opinions he had about others in the crime were not relevant or even legal evidence. Condon had indicated, on the other hand, that he would see the New Jersey governor in New York— but only if Wilentz was also present.[67]

Fisher suddenly dropped what he hoped would be a bombshell. He had a new statement from Hauptmann that he had frequently seen the educator on City Island, both before and after the kidnapping! If this were so, he went on, then Jafsie's identification must be put in doubt. "Hauptmann says he saw Dr. Condon from time to time, never, however to speak to him. It follows that Dr. Condon must have seen him. How, then, could it have been that Dr. Condon never recognized him and caused his arrest in all those two years unless it is true that Hauptmann is not the man who got the ransom money? I would like to ask Dr. Condon that question."[68]

This was a new development, certainly, in the enigmatic dialogue between pursuer and pursued—and something of a role reversal. Hauptmann had claimed the first night at the Greenwich Street police station, and again at Flemington, that he had never seen Condon before his arrest. Yet here he was saying he saw him frequently before and after the kidnapping at City Island. Would not such an admission provide evidence that Hauptmann had spotted Condon as a likely intermediary, useful to complete his negotiations?

Hoffman sent word to Condon that he would be glad to meet him anyplace in New York City, and he would welcome Wilentz's presence. "I am sure you will cooperate in every possible way with an honest endeavor to clear up doubts that are entertained by thousands of people and to bring to the bar of justice all persons who may have had anything to do with the commission of the crime."[69]

Condon responded after consulting with his new counselor, David Wilentz. In a lengthy summation of his role in the Lindbergh case from the beginning, he said that the only suitable place for such a meeting would be his home. He would only entertain written questions and would only provide written answers. Assertions that he had been inconsistent in any of his previous statements were false and malicious lies, as were stories that he had fled the country to avoid questioning. "The occasion of my departure last January after a conference with your Attorney General was alluded to as possessing some malign significance," he complained.

For these reasons, he could not imagine the governor could conduct a fair examination unless the rules had been stipulated beforehand. "Although you have apparently usurped the functions of the courts and the duly constituted investigating officials, and despite your unfairness, I have, nevertheless, decided to permit you to confer with me at my home as above indicated." The conditions, obviously, would have allowed Wilentz to vet all the questions and answers, and to be present to make sure Condon did not throw a boomerang—such as the explanation he gave Oursler about Samuelsohn, or, on another occasion, when he tried to convince the editor that Lindbergh had deliberately misrepresented where the nursery note had been found to insure that Condon was dealing with the right man.[70]

There would be no confrontation between Condon and his accusers, as there was no way to compel his cooperation. But Hoffman had one or two final moves to make.

On March 23, William Lewis, a former trooper now working as one of the governor's investigators, had a conversation with the chief of detectives of Cape May County, Jesse Souder, himself a former trooper. Souder informed Lewis that he knew that Detective Sergeant Lewis Bornmann had framed the rail and ladder evidence. He knew this, he said, from an informant inside the state police, who would go public with the information if Schwarzkopf was not reappointed as head.[71]

This was not really a "new" development so far as the governor was concerned, because defense lawyers had argued hard throughout the trial that there was something very wrong with the ladder evidence. Fisher had sought access to the attic from the time the trial opened, as Wilentz and Schwarzkopf had tossed the issue back and forth as if playing a game of monkey in the middle, never really saying no but always managing to avoid allowing him or any other member of the defense team from going up there—especially not without Arthur Koehler present. Frederick Pope had had no luck, either, in gaining access to the Lindbergh home when he and Harry Walsh had attempted a visit after the trial. They did manage to examine the window and saw no chisel marks, which, Pope insisted, would have been there had the chisel had been used to wedge open the window. A three-quarter-inch chisel, furthermore, would have been no use in opening shutters on the Lindbergh nursery window if they had not been warped.[72]

With private detective Leon Hoage standing by, as well as Colonel Schwarzkopf and several aides at the Wilburtha State Police School on March 24, 1936, Hoffman tried to elicit from Bornmann the first full account of his discovery in the attic. It was the first time the governor had had a chance to see rail 16 and its supposed source, State's Exhibit 226, put end to end. Hoffman started off quietly enough, asking how the board had been pulled up. "Did it come pretty hard when you pulled it?" To a certain extent, said Bornmann, who then caught himself, "but it only had those few nails in"—This was dangerous territory; there were fourteen nails in 226.

There were many more questions to follow about Bornmann's leverage, how he managed the feat, bent over in an awkward position perching on the joists. The board broke at a knot, he pointed out, and that part was left in the attic. A strange way to handle vital evidence, particularly for someone who had worked closely with a wood expert, and even more particularly with two New York police carpenters standing by with proper tools. The nails had to be hammered out and then extracted by pliers. He took the remaining nine feet downstairs and put it in a locked closet. The nails he took back with him to Trenton. They fit the holes in rail 16. Returning to the attic with Arthur Koehler, they tried to fit the nails through the holes in rail 16 into the joists. Another perfect fit. This, of course, had been the heart of the testimony given at the trial.

What caused him to notice that board (S-226), over at the far end of the attic floor? asked Hoffman. Bornmann explained, "I was looking for some yellow pine that could have been planed down, and that wood in the attic seemed to be what I was looking for." He alone had worked with Arthur Koehler during the search for the wood that had been used for the other rails in the ladder, so it was not surprising that others who might have been up there searching for money (as he said he was that day) would not have been so quick to notice the odd one out, a half-board sawed off at a joist. But his answer to Hoffman also suggests that he consulted with superior officers in Trenton between visits to the attic and was sent back on a mission to find a missing link to Hauptmann.

Indeed, in a 1982 interview Bornmann said that although he was looking for more ransom money, the search for a matching board was "primarily [his] objective." Bornmann did not even know, finally, or care about what had happened to the piece left in the attic. He thought the landlord, Max Rauch, might have disposed of it by selling off pieces for souvenirs.[73]

The next day at three o'clock in the afternoon Hoffman's secretary, William Conklin, called Fulton Oursler to invite him to be present when the governor fired "his big gun in the Hauptmann case." It would prove conclusively, said Conklin, that he had been framed. On the morning of March 26, then, four cars arrived at the house where Richard and Anna had lived. Oursler's taxi got there first. Next came Lloyd Fisher and a man who had worked as a press agent for the recently assassinated Huey Long. What he was doing there was anybody's guess. But Fisher was fairly bubbling over with excitement. "This is a shot that will be heard around the world," he proclaimed. "We have unmistakable evidence that the state has framed Hauptmann and that the evidence of rail sixteen is of absolutely no value whatever."[74]

The third car arrived, bringing Attorney General Wilentz, Anthony Hauck, Sergeant Bornmann, and Arthur Koehler. The last to arrive was New Jersey license number 1. Inside were Governor Hoffman, a wood expert from the Department of the Interior, Arch Loney, Detective Leon Hoage, and Professor Alan Hazeltine, a chemist.

The ascent to the attic began, although the first man up, Loney, broke one of the supports in this narrow passageway. Oursler quipped that Hauptmann's ladders had a habit of breaking, which cost him a scowl from "his friend" Governor Hoffman. Hoage joined Loney, and the two men immediately began taking various measurements.

Still downstairs were Fisher, Wilentz, and Hoffman—arguing, as usual, about Condon. Oursler interrupted their discussion. Condon was thoroughly honest and reliable, the editor declared. Hauptmann had killed the baby with his own hands. But, he admitted, there were still some nagging questions the governor was justified in trying to clear up. It was the furthest he would ever go to satisfy his conscience about those strange "memory" lapses Jafsie had suffered concerning the nursery note, or the even stranger story about Samuelsohn's account of how the ladder had been cut out to Hauptmann's specifications.[75]

"I consider this an outrageous proceeding," Wilentz protested. "I am here only to protect state troopers against intimidation." Obviously, he had been warned Bornmann was Hoffman's prime target. "If you think that son-of-a-bitch Hauptmann is innocent, why don't you turn him loose?" Wilentz kept pressing the point. "You are encouraging him in his son-of-a- bitch attitude of not confessing."[76]

The argument raged on in the attic. Hoffman, all two hundred pounds of him packed on a short, square frame, somehow managed to squeeze himself upward through the narrow passage to join the rest, bent over and shuffling about as best they could. His aides were assaulting Koehler from all sides, brandishing tape measures, and kneeling down to sight along the boards. With more people in the attic than had ever been there at one time, the hubbub of noise and dust would have driven termites to seek shelter below.

Perhaps the most dramatic find of the morning escaped immediate attention. Leon Hoage's tape measurements revealed that Arthur Koehler's original floor plan of the attic had been in error. Koehler had plotted out the attic to show that the carpenters who first laid the attic had placed twenty-seven boards exactly in the right place so that the distance from the eaves on both sides was precisely eleven feet, four inches. His document was yet another "proof" that Hauptmann had taken a board from the attic to build the ladder. Hoage found, however, that with the twenty-seven boards in place, the distance from each side *was not* equal; it varied by at least four or five inches. Confronted with this challenge, Koehler blithely repudiated his own floor plan, telling Hoage, as recorded in his memorandum of the attic meeting, "there was no reason why a rough floor in an attic should be centered." Of course not, but Koehler had said it was. And he had testified on the basis of such measurements in a capital case where a man was on trial for his life.[77]

Someone got the windows open at this point to let in some badly needed fresh air, and saw scores of reporters outside who seemed to know more about what was going on than those inside.

Hoffman's aides had a long list of other challenges to Koehler's testimony, however, and the purpose of the meeting quickly became clear. Arch Loney called Koehler an ignorant four-flushing son-of-a-bitch. Hoage charged that rail 16 could not have been a part of the original attic floor because even when one accounted for the supposed planing, it was still too wide. Koehler simply denied that was the case. The dimensions did not differ, he insisted. The argument over width went on for an hour.

Next there was the question about the number of nails in S-226 and rail 16. Hoage asked Koehler how many surface nails there were in the other boards; when the wood expert from Wisconsin started to look, Hoage raised his voice—"don't look!" Wilentz turned on the governor's man like a wildcat. Who did he think he was? "I'll be goddamned if you're going to talk to Koehler that way." (During the trial Wilentz had talked that way to defense witnesses, time and again, while Judge Trenchard never raised a gavel.)

That board was the first one laid, Koehler said, and therefore, since all the others would be pushed up next, it had to have many more nails than the others, all driven through the surface. The governor's group argued as one that no board needed that many nails, even if it was the toeboard. There were twenty-four nail holes in the joist where the board—or boards—had been. Moreover, there were many more nails driven through S-226 than rail 16, even accounting for their different lengths. How is one to account for the difference? The possibility that rail 16 was fabricated evidence loomed up so that it could be plainly seen even in the dust and tumult, if one wanted to look.[78]

Koehler had testified at the trial that a carpenter would cut the wood flush along the joist. But the group up in the attic could now see that the wood was cut so that a little bit hung over the joist. Someone in the governor's party then challenged Bornmann's account of how he ripped up the board by hand. How could he have done that with tongue-and-groove flooring? Because of drying and shrinkage, Koehler said, pointing to other areas of the floor where "many of the boards in the floor had shrunk enough so that the tongue was completely exposed." His assertion did not prove that had been the case, especially given the number of face nails Bornmann had to overcome, and still did not excuse the improper handling of potentially crucial evidence. In addition, if the argument was that the first rail had been a toeboard hammered in with twenty-four nails to ensure over-all snugness, how was it that so many of the other tongue-and-groove boards had since separated because of "shrinkage"?[79]

Then came a special test with a piece of cardboard designed to show that the nick in the board next to S-226 could not have been made as the prosecution said it had because the angle was all wrong. Wilentz took the cardboard and tried to show that it could be twisted to prove anything. Why was there no nick, if the carpenter was so constrained, down at the end of where rail 16 had supposedly been removed? All these demonstrations, however, dragged out as they were over several hours, were preliminary to the grand finale when Hoffman himself pushed the original nails into the holes and they would not go down flush to the surface. Oursler wrote: "The temperature in that room, which had seemed 120 degrees, suddenly felt like zero. I felt a chill down my back. Nobody said anything—there was nothing to say. Hauck did say to one man in a low voice—'This is pretty god-awful. We had a strong enough case without this.'"[80]

Wilentz recovered from the shock fairly quickly, nonetheless, and demanded that the joists be sawed off and sent to some laboratory to examine the nail holes. Feeling triumphant, Governor Hoffman was more than happy to order a carpenter to the scene to cut off six so that twelve holes could be examined.

Meanwhile, Hoffman ordered Bornmann to go downstairs so that he could confront him directly. "I want you to tell the truth about that board. Do you still say that it was nailed down solid when you found it?" Bornmann stuck to his guns. Wilentz, however, was worried. "For God's sake if there is anything wrong up there that I don't know about, tell the Governor and let's get it over with."[81]

Bornmann swore he had told the truth about everything that had happened up in the attic when he discovered that one board had been cut off. "I had told him the truth and nothing but the truth and that I could pull the switch right now on Hauptmann with a clear conscience." With that statement the attic debates came to an end, and the combatants descended to their cars with the joist pieces for the trip to Columbia University. When the joists were cut open, all the nail holes were shown to be the proper depth to accommodate the cut nails. For some reason, fibrous material had clogged the bottom and prevented the nails from going in all the way.

Hoffman had counted on his dramatic demonstration to persuade Wilentz to join him in a new appeal before the Board of Pardons. Not now. Koehler came away boasting that this new visit—in the presence of his harshest critics—to the place where Hauptmann had sawed out his final board had more than ever convinced him that rail 16 came out of the attic. Hoffman had obviously banked too much on the nail demonstration. He tried to recoup something from *l'affaire mansarde*, telling the press the evidence showed that the nails had been driven recently, whereas if they had been there a long time the holes would be clear when the nails were removed. Moreover, the holes showed little evidence of oxidization, which should not have been true if they were there a long time.

Bornmann had claimed, it will be remembered, that the nails had come out easily when he removed the remainder of board twenty-seven with his bare hands, and that was why he could pull it up without damaging the tongue or groove; but Koehler, trying to explain why the nails had not gone in all the way during the attic test, noted that the holes had been clogged with "wood fibers" and other gritty material. In other words, pulling out the nails would not have been so easy. Questions like these did not trouble Arthur Koehler, but they continue to haunt the ladder evidence even today.[82]

It turned out that all the evidence Hoffman had gathered was of little use, because Judge Trenchard ruled that no new evidence could be presented to set aside a trial verdict after six months from the time of the conviction—a deadline long since passed.

"Suppose," Hoffman had asked in disbelief, "that at the last minute a condemned man is shown to be innocent. Is there no way in which his case can be reopened?"

"I am bound by the law," Trenchard had replied.

Other legal authorities believed, however, that if such evidence were forthcoming, a new trial would have to be granted.[83]

Anthony Hauck was concerned enough about the governor's maneuvers to prepare legal papers to try to prevent him from granting any further reprieves—for any reason. The execution was set for March 31.

All that was left was Ellis Parker's nearly forgotten investigation of Paul Wendel. Parker had been chasing the fifty-year-old disbarred attorney and convicted perjurer since 1932, sometimes even pretending to use him as his own special investigator. Wendel had spent time in a mental hospital, so playing roles might not have been something new. In any event, letters sent in code from Wendel to Parker's secretary, Anna Bading, had carried this game of cat and mouse, or seduction and betrayal, down many a blind alley. Parker could never quite corner him.[84]

On February 14, Parker had given his new "deputies" the go ahead to apprehend Wendel in New York City, where he was living in the Hotel Martinque. Pretending to be mobsters angered that the Lindbergh kidnapping had curtailed their activities, Parker's deputies dragged Wendel off to another hotel room, and later to a basement, and questioned him for several days demanding a confession. Kept in the dark most of the time, Wendel had no idea if he ever would be freed. It was hardly surprising that he "confessed," filling twenty-five pages with details. He told how he had supposedly watched the house, climbed up the ladder (which, oh, yes, he had made specially), and then escaped out the front door. He took the baby to a tenement in Trenton and kept it there until early May. Meanwhile, he collected the money. Alas, one night the child fell out of a makeshift crib and struck its head on the bare floor, causing a fractured skull. Worried about getting rid of the money, Wendel gave all or some of it to Isidor Fisch to sell. Fisch could not get rid of it safely before he departed for Germany, and left Hauptmann to hold the box.[85]

Parker mailed the confession to the Board of Pardons. When Wilentz discovered where Wendel was being held, he demanded the prisoner be surrendered to police custody. Once safe, Wendel immediately repudiated the confession. Still, the issue was before the Mercer County grand jury on the day Hauptmann was to die.

On the morning of Tuesday, March 31, 1936, Hauptmann wrote his last letter to Governor Hoffman. He wanted the governor to know, he said, that he was not guilty of this crime. "I offert myself to any test what science may offer,—but I was beging in vain. I did this, not to force the prosecution to put me free, but only to convince the world that I am innocent."

"Why did, and does Dr. Condon hide so many thinks he knows[?] It is not for the cource of justice that this man say everything. Why did Dr. Condon say in my cell, he can not testify against me[?] My God Dr Condon and your witnesses, did you ever realize what you did[?] For a short time I will stand before a higher judge, you will live a little longer, but you never can leave this world whit a happier inner feeling as I do." As for Wilentz, "God will be judge between you and me."[86]

Later in the day, Hauptmann was taken to the holding cell next to the execution chamber. His head was shaved, and his pants slit where the electrode would be fastened. Then he was left alone in the bare cell. He began weeping. Warden Kimberling appeared at his cell. He had heard Hauptmann had not eaten for twenty-four hours. He should eat something, said Kimberling, he could order anything he liked. Hauptmann replied bitterly, "Send it to Condon."[87]

The crowd outside had reached nearly 10,000. Armed guards sat or stood on the prison roof as searchlight beams illuminated the whole area. The witnesses were now inside being frisked for cameras. They had expected to be directed into the death house chamber. But nothing happened. They waited until Kimberling finally arrived to tell them that there would not be an execution that night. Sent back outside, they disappeared into the crowd. Lloyd Fisher brought Anna the news the sentence had been put in abeyance while the Mercer County grand jury met to consider the Wendel confession. "I knew it! I told you so!" she said to the attorney.[88]

A new execution date was set for Friday, April 3. But neither Anna nor Richard seemed to believe it possible that the execution, halted at the last minute, could actually be carried out at any date in the future.

The grand jury sat all day Tuesday and Wednesday, then abruptly adjourned without a decision. This left Kimberling in limbo. Wilentz advised him the sentence must be carried out, barring action by the Board of Pardons or another reprieve by Governor Hoffman—who had already announced he would not grant a second stay.

At this last minute there was a telegram from Clarence Darrow to Governor Hoffman and the Court of Pardons. He said that he had received communications from countless numbers of persons in all classes congratulating him on his opposition to the "extreme sentence."

> Unexceptional disapproval of present attitude of Jafsie heretofore so eager and free to occupy the limelight but now in this crucial hour prevented by Wilentz coming forth with any possible further light on the situation. It seems unprofessional to demand immediate death of Hauptmann. In the face of such widespread public disapproval Hauptmann should be entitled to retrial with sincere desire for fair play.[89]

The crowd was smaller the night of April 3, 1936; only about five hundred showed up, perhaps because they, like Anna and Richard, believed there would be another reprieve. Executioner Robert Elliott arrived at the prison about 4 P.M. It was a cold, blustery afternoon and night, Elliott later remembered. "I dreaded this assignment more than any other. Though it was generally believed that more than one person was implicated in the crime, none but Hauptmann had been found. I wondered whether justice would best be served by snuffing out the life of this man."[90]

Elliott had been approached by representatives of the press with various schemes by which he could signal Hauptmann's entrance into the death chamber and the exact moment of his execution. "I have in my pocket a check for $10,000 made out to you, Mr. Elliott," one told him, if he would cooperate in providing a "small service." There would be no risk to his reputation if he did so.[91]

Lloyd Fisher was the last to see Hauptmann, except for his spiritual advisers, Reverend Werner and Reverend Matthiesen.

"Hello, Richard," Fisher said.

"I can see by your face it is bad. Have you talked with the Governor?"

"Yes, and his hands are tied."

"Does this mean it is the end?"

"Yes Richard, it is the finish."

"I can't believe it. I can't believe they will kill an innocent man. . . . Can't you talk to the Governor again?"

Fisher repeated there was nothing the governor could do. "If there is anything you know, anything you could say that would help you, please tell me. I can still stop this thing if you can say anything that will help clear the mystery up."

Hauptmann looked shocked. "Lloyd, you know there is nothing more I can say. You above any one, you who know me best, know there is nothing I can say. You know there is nothing I know about this crime, about any part of it."

"Yes I believe that, Richard. Good-bye."

The spiritual counselors took over. Hauptmann requested John 14 be read him. Then he said, "I am at peace with my God. I am so happy. I have no hatred against anyone, not even Wilentz. I only wish I could face Condon at this minute. Please take good care of my wife and baby. Thank the Governor and the Warden and Mr. Fisher."[92]

Minutes later, Bruno Richard Hauptmann was led into the death chamber. He was wearing a gray-blue shirt, open at the neck, and khaki trousers with dark stripes along the sides. Out of his sight was a huge clock, held by a guard to show the exact time of the execution. The prisoner walked with shuffing steps like sandpaper to the chair. Kimberling had told the witnesses it was about eighteen feet from the door to the chair. It should take about seven paces. Hauptmann took long steps, noted a reporter; it only took him six paces. He actually walked past the chair, seemingly in a daze, and had to be turned around. Pushed down, his hands gripped its broad arms, and he sat staring straight ahead as Elliott placed the electrode cap on his head and adjusted the mask.

Reverend Matthiesen began the death prayer in a loud, firm, monotonous voice. He continued reading, placing himself directly in front of Hauptmann as the executioner turned the large wheel.

"A wisp of smoke came through Hauptmann's shaven head, then another and another. Matthiesen continued to recite the prayer for the dead. He spoke in German. He spoke precisely. Each syllable was distinct."[93]

It took a few minutes before the doctors placed their stethoscopes on Hauptmann's chest and agreed: "This man is dead."

Escorted through the crowd by burly police, executioner Robert Elliott was the first to leave the death house, holding his hat down over his face. Lloyd Fisher came out looking puzzled, as if searching for someone he knew, someone to hear his vow: "I will clear the name of Bruno Richard Hauptmann if it is the last thing I do." Pale and worn, Warden Kimberling was almost the last one out of the death house. He stood there quietly and answered questions, a cigarette dangling in his left hand between two fingers.

"Hauptmann did not say anything either before he was brought out or when he entered the death chamber," he announced. "He died very game."

"How many jolts did he get?"

"Two, I think. I'm not very sure." He corrected himself: it had been three.

"Did everything go all right?"

"Yes, oh yes. I mean I guess so."

"What took so long?"

"There was a little delay in going to the death house and then a little delay in determining death. There were seven doctors and each took his turn examining the body. Dr. Wiesler thought he detected a flutter of the heart and they wanted to make certain."

"What time did he get the first jolt?"

"He got the first er—er jolt, as you express it, at 8:41."

"Did he show any signs of fear?"

"No. He died game."[94]

16 THE PALATE OF MORTALS

Today's victory flatters the palate of mortals—
Yes, but tomorrow it must
Sour, sicken, and turn to an old deep-grown reproach.
—EURIPIDES, *Andromache*

hree days before Christmas, 1935, Charles Lindbergh, his wife, Anne, and their three-year-old son, Jon, left New York on a freighter. By the colonel's orders no one came to the dock to see them off. No other passengers were on the ship. As they left the harbor, Charles stood on the deck bareheaded and saluted the Statue of Liberty. When they arrived in England, they were beginning a very different life that would embroil Charles in the dark maze of prewar international politics.

"After six months in England with nothing to do," writes Anne's biographer Susan Hertog, "Charles was once again the hero poised at the edge of history. The Germans, in a sense, had reinvented Charles in the image he had come to expect. And the Nazi leaders, masters of pageantry and drama, understood how to use his political power for their ends. Charles was eager to be of 'use' for a cause and a culture that transcended his own."[1] Within two years Lindbergh would allow himself to be used by German leaders to herald the Third Reich's vast fleet of bombers and fighters in such a way as to discourage opposition to Hitler's political aims.

In the American press, meanwhile, there had been much finger-pointing about who drove the Lindberghs into exile. "It is extremely distressing and discouraging," intoned a hypocritical William Randolph Hearst, "that this grand country of ours is so overrun with cranks, criminals, and Communists that a splendid citizen like Colonel Lindbergh must take his family abroad to protect them against violence."[2]

Widely regarded as the pivotal case for determining whether the United States had the ability to govern itself, the Lindbergh kidnapping focused the nation's attention on the seeming power of the underworld to dictate its own terms—Capone's release, say, for the return of the child. Of course, while the crime was typical of the era, it turned out to be instead something very different: a freelance operation. That did not lessen its shock value.

Hauptmann's arrest and trial shifted the focus somewhat to nativism and threats from without—just as one reporter noticed that Hauptmann's daily attire matched the colors of German World War I uniforms. His conviction was never in doubt. Much as he disliked Edward Reilly, Lloyd Fisher knew that no defense attorney, no team of defense attorneys had it included Clarence Darrow or Daniel Webster, could have changed the outcome. After attending Hauptmann's funeral, Fisher wrote: "It was a two million dollar funeral. Not that the man, whose funeral it was, belonged to the two million dollar class. On the contrary, he had only recently taken the pauper's oath. It was the great State of New Jersey and greater state of New York and still greated United States of America that had spent this sum to turn a human being into a wisp of smoke and a jar of dust."[3]

John Condon lamented Lindbergh's absence but promised the nation there was still hope for his return. "Col. Lindbergh told me that he would remain a citizen of the United States. He will return in triumph to us and U.S. May God speed that return." He wrote to the *Atlantic Monthly* to tell the editor that he had written a poem about his entrance into the Lindbergh case, to be divided under several headings starting with "My Reasons for Aiding," and then "My publication to Make Contact," "The Contact with the Kidnappers," "My Meeting with 'John' (the Kidnapper)," and finally, "Giving the Money." He also proposed an article, "Organized Crime and the Government." "Are you interested?" he asked. "What am I offered?"[4] It would appear, from these headings, that Jafsie never gave up on the idea that there had been a gang.

However that may be, Condon's verse, "O Lindy Come Back Home " was too much for one anonymous critic. "Your so-called poem . . . is a lot of slush. . . ." "If you knew the real feelings of the American people, you would pipe down. You did nothing—as far as the public feels except foolishly hand over $50.000 and got nothing for it. But you got what you love so much; 'PUBLICITY'."

Condon forwarded the message to "Jay Edgar Hoover, Chief of G-Men," asking for protection. The old schoolmaster's complaints about threatening mail finally led Hoover to send an agent to determine if there had been any violation of federal statutes involved. The "Doctor's condition, both physically and mentally, had deteriorated a great deal during the past year," his wife told the agent, and that "the members of his immediate family have little or no control over him."[5]

Yet even before Hauptmann's arrest Lindbergh had expressed several doubts about Condon's encounters with Cemetery John. He questioned the prompt reply Condon received to his letter in the *Bronx Home News* and had difficulty believing the story about how he caught up to Cemetery John at Woodlawn and persuaded him to sit beside him for nearly an hour. He held a gun in his pocket aimed at John, said Condon, demonstrating their positions, and John also had him covered. After the arrest, all these doubts disappeared as Lindbergh testified with absolute certainty it was Bruno Richard Hauptmann's voice he heard that night at St. Raymond's Cemetery.[6]

FBI agent R. G. Harvey had pointed out still more Condon discrepancies, including his inability to give an accurate description of the woman who came to the bazaar to warn him about publicity, and his curious vagueness about the mysterious taxi driver who delivered the second note. What sort of person was Condon, anyway? Obviously, the kidnappers trusted him—but what else was there to know about this man? Did he know Cemetery John from some other encounter? Was he selected, therefore, because he could keep a secret, or did he just stumble into the case, a naive do-gooder who found himself, much to his surprise, a trusted emissary of the preeminent national hero? Because Condon changed his story so many times, no one could ever answer these questions.[7]

"The Lindbergh case lifted Dr. Condon out of a placid existence and the role of village character into a complicated and troubled existence as 'Jafsie,' with the fierce light of international publicity focused sharply upon him," noted the *New York Times*. Eventually, he got his wish for Lindy's return to the United States. He met Lindbergh one last time at an America First Rally in April 1941, after Lindbergh came home to lead the fight against U.S. intervention in World War II. Condon died of pneumonia on January 2, 1945, ten years to the day after the trial of the century began.[8]

One cannot take leave of John Condon without feeling there is always something more—or something missing—that would clear up at least some of the mystery surrounding this man. In an interview with Trooper Samuel J. Leon on June 26, 1934, Condon explained yet again how he became involved in the Lindbergh case. If the defense had had access to this interview, Condon's time on the stand would have been much more difficult for him and the prosecution. He had written the letter offering $1,000 for information, he told Leon, and received a reply in the mail that read "something like this:—'Go see Col. Lindbergh and see if he will use you as a go-between. He will know that this is the right party because he will know by the signal on this letter as we left the same signal on the baby's crib.'" [9]

The actual letter he received had not told him to "go see" Colonel Lindbergh, and the language sounds much more like an oral instruction—in anticipation of a letter—than it does a letter. In this version, Condon is also told beforehand about the peculiar signature. It may be no more than yet another of the endless permutations of the "Condon Story," or, it could be argued, it explains better than any of the others how Condon knew which letter to open and take to show his cronies.

An FBI report of an interview with Condon and his daughter, Myra Hacker, a few days later, on July 12, 1934, brought forward two versions of what happened on the night of April 2, 1932, when the ransom was paid. Myra told the agent that *"they had all previously discussed the fact that he [?] should be given a liberal tip."* And she thought her father had done so. When the knock came on the door, she saw the party through the glass, noted that he was young, slim, and Italian-looking, and *"was not dressed like a taxi driver."* Her father took over to answer the door, and she retreated to another room. In this same interview, Condon said the man *"was dressed like a taxi driver."* He even said he did not remember his daughter being there that night. And so we have only Condon's word that the man had arrived like Joe Perrone. If Condon gave the messenger a tip, obviously, he would have been asked to explain this in greater detail, and why he had not asked for his name. By forgetting about Myra's presence, Condon could claim (to his own satisfaction, at least) that his interpretation of events was the only correct one—as he was able to do with the meetings at Woodlawn and St. Raymond's. [10]

Finally, what is there to say about John F. Condon's role? It appears likely, after reviewing all the evidence, that he was never entirely truthful about his role in the kidnap negotiations. When he came into the case remains a question, and his various reports of both phone conversations and the cemetery exchanges raise more problems. That his unchallenged testimony on these points and others sent a man to the electric chair places a dark shadow over the verdict to this day.

David Wilentz had handled Condon better than anyone else, both before and during the trial. Wilentz never tried another murder case. But the Lindbergh kidnapping launched his career as one of New Jersey's most powerful lawyers and power brokers. He founded a legal dynasty whose clients numbered among the state's top business concerns, and, when gambling became legal, included Atlantic City's casinos. At ninety-three, he continued to practice law and after spending several hours at the office, died quietly in his sleep on July 6, 1988.[11]

On October 6, 1981, Wilentz had walked into a conference room at New Jersey State Police Headquarters, where Governor Brendan Byrne was announcing an executive order opening ninety thousand previously secret documents in response to Anna Hauptmann's law suit charging wrongful execution. Byrne said the state had a "moral responsibility to respond," but he was confident the prosecution had acted correctly in the Lindbergh case and the jury verdict was just. Off in one corner as Byrne spoke, Wilentz examined the ladder. "This is the first time I've seen it since the trial," he said. "Nothing I know of could possibly support an allegation that anything was suppressed."

"I tried the case," he went on. "I presented whatever evidence the state police and the FBI had. I did what you would expect someone who was the prosecutor would do." Asked about Hauptmann's request for a lie-detector test, Wilentz said, "I never heard of it." At that point, Colonel Clinton L. Pagano, the superintendent of state police, interrupted in timely fashion to say, "I think he had one at that time." Governor Byrne agreed. And that ended the press briefing. No one checked the record. Ironically, given that false statement, Byrne then said he hoped opening the files would ensure that questions surrounding the case "will not be kicked around for years and years to come."[12]

Pressure to open state police records had followed the discovery of former governor Harold Hoffman's Lindbergh case files in a Perth Amboy garage many years after his death. It was this discovery that provided the immediate stimulus for Anna Hauptmann's unsuccessful suit against the state of New Jersey. If these documents had been left in the custody of some state agency, it is well worth wondering whether Governor Byrne would have been so willing to open state police files— and risk having questions "kicked around for years and years to come."

Threatened with impeachment, and generally condemned by fellow state governors, for his late-night visit to the death house to see the condemned man and listen to his story, Hoffman remained convinced until his death that more than one person must have been involved in the crime.

Hoffman's later career after leaving the governorship included a term as motor vehicle commissioner. He was suspended from that position in 1954, when an investigation turned up evidence he had embezzled the state out of $300,000. Soon after this discovery he was found dead in a New York hotel, supposedly of a heart attack, but a confession was found close by.

Hoffman's last duty in regard to the Lindbergh case had been to disburse the $25,000 reward posted by the state for the capture of the kidnapper, giving him the opportunity for a few parting shots at his critics. On January 15, 1937, Hoffman embarrassed the state legislature by revealing it had never actually passed a bill appropriating the money. "There also seemed to be some doubt as to whom the money should be paid even though it were available." Law enforcement agencies had suggested to him the courts should decide the matter. "Perhaps," said Hoffman, "they are not quite sure that the 'persons furnishing information leading to the detection and conviction' of the murderers of the Lindbergh baby have yet been found."[13]

There were plenty of claimants. For example, a freelance minister from Oswego, New York, wrote, "I was born with a caul or veil, and have the power of Prophecy. . . . I told in detail just where the man could be found in New York City and they must have followed the instructions for he was found in the location I mentioned."

Paul Wendel wrote Hoffman that he had read in the newspapers the governor was having trouble in dividing up the reward. He deserved it all, claimed Wendel, because he had held out against Ellis Parker's efforts to make him confess and take Hauptmann's place on death row. "Yes, honestly, I believe that my family and I are entitled to the $25,000 because I was the one who refused to let Bruno Hauptmann go free, thus backing up the Courts of the United States and saved New Jersey respect."[14]

Hoffman eventually made the choices. William Allen, the black truck driver who first saw the body on May 12, 1932, received a very large sum, $5,000. An entrepreneur had snapped Allen right up after his discovery for a Coney Island sideshow. It was a brief engagement, and Allen was never paid anything. Attempts to take the show on the road to New England failed; and the truck driver said he had been told it upset the Lindberghs, so he got out.[15]

The largest payout, $7,500, went to Walter Lyle, the gas station attendant who had jotted down Hauptmann's license number on the back of a ten-dollar gold certificate. Lyle's coworker, John J. Lyons, suddenly decided that he deserved a large share of the reward, because, he said, Walter had not called attention to the bill. Instead, said Lyons, he had been given the bill as part of his week's pay—and *he* was the one who asked the bank teller to check the bill.

When an FBI agent had interviewed them, he had said, "If you're right about this description and we get the man, you boys ought to be taking a trip to Europe." But Lyle continued to insist he should receive the whole $25,000. Suppose, grumbled an unhappy Lyons, that he had not checked it at the bank. "I could have used it to pay my rent, or stuffed it in a mattress at home. It's only because I turned it over to the bank five minutes after I got it that they got Hauptmann." Hoffman awarded Lyons $1,000.

Actually, the teller had never paid attention to the bill. It was William Strong, a bank officer, who noticed it and called the police. He received $2,000. FBI agent Thomas Sisk thought he should have received much more. If Strong had not picked out the bill from those that came across his desk, Hauptmann might not have been caught. Yes, Lyle had put the license number on the back, but it was easily rubbed off. It had been Strong who took the time to check the bill against the ransom list. He should get 75 percent of the award. Lyle had no idea that it was a ransom bill; he just wanted to protect himself. Sisk's real fear, of course, was Lieutenant James Finn's claim that because the New York police had circulated the ransom bill numbers to gas stations, Hauptmann had been caught. That was simply not true, insisted Sisk; only some of the gas stations had been put on special notice—and besides, Finn had withheld the numbers of the gold certificates. Sisk wanted to make sure the reward percentages did not put the New York police above the FBI in the final accounting.[16]

Hoffman awarded $1,000 each to Cecile Barr, Amandus Hochmuth, Millard Whited, and Joseph Perrone. When he gave Hochmuth his check, he asked him to describe a nearby vase with flowers. The old man said he saw a woman's hat. Hoffman had also been informed previously that Joe Perrone had been warned that if he did not identify Hauptmann, he would be arrested as an accomplice.

The remainder of the money Hoffman ordered paid to William F. Cody ($2,000), a banker who discovered the bill Cecile Barr took in; Charles Rossiter ($500), a lesser eyewitness; and the rest, at $25 each, to the approximately one hundred tellers who located and identified ransom money.

John Condon did not put in a claim.

Arthur Koehler received nothing. As a government employee, Koehler was not permitted to take reward money—something he apparently forgot when he wrote Hoffman on November 17, 1937, to say he did not know it was necessary to make a formal application for part of the reward. But now that he knew, he felt he should receive a substantial share for identifying the wood in the ladder that had come from South Carolina. That discovery, in itself, he argued, should have been sufficient to nab Hauptmann if the police had been more rapid in their investigation of employees of the National Lumber and Millwork Company. Then there were the hand plane marks, which, he said, matched up exactly to tools in Hauptmann's kit. And there was rail 16. Acting on his information, police had discovered the place in Hauptmann's attic where it had been before becoming part of the ladder. Finally, he said, he had determined that the chisel found with the ladder at Highfields "was of the same make and pattern" as a one-quarter-inch chisel in Hauptmann's toolbox.

Whether Governor Hoffman noticed or not, on this final point Koehler was in fast retreat from his trial testimony, where he had claimed that marks on rail 16 had been made by a three-quarter-inch chisel, and strongly implied it had been the one "left" near the ladder. Now all he would say was that the chisel was of the "same make and pattern" as those of other sizes in Hauptmann's tool chest.[17]

Perhaps the most recent attic experience had left him a somewhat chastened expert. Yet no one has ever been able to demonstrate that rail 16 was fabricated evidence.

As in so many instances in the Lindbergh case, the debate about rail 16 pits logic against forensic evidence, a major reason for its enduring interest. But the confrontation in Hauptmann's attic left many lingering questions even about the forensic evidence. As for logic, one is left to wonder, why, if Hauptmann had observed the Lindbergh house on several occasions, he would make a ladder in three sections, when he needed only two? Rail 16 was on the upper section—the one not used. Why, for that matter, make such a poor ladder for the crime of the century?

Criminals are not usually noted for foresight, it might be argued, or they wouldn't get caught so often. But there were indications the ladder had been in soil not found in the ground at Highfields, that it had in fact been tested before being used. If rail 16 was a last minute substitution for a broken piece, therefore, when was it made? Did Hauptmann return that morning from the Majestic Apartments in a rage that work he had been promised had been denied—at least for several days—and he now faced having to tell Anna some hard truths about their finances? And so he decided the crime must be committed that very day. But the ladder was broken or not quite ready. He hurried to the attic to saw off a board at the far end, maneuver it down the narrow opening, and take it to the garage, where he had to ripsaw it down both sides, plane it, and then, at last, nail in the rungs. All this for a board that otherwise would have cost no more than fifteen cents. Putting the ladder in his car, he headed for Hopewell, arriving in time for Amandus Hochmuth to see him around ten, or eleven, or, at least, before noon.

Here is a crucial crossover point between forensic evidence and eyewitness testimony. Hochmuth's assertion that he saw the glaring, red face of Hauptmann as his car slid into the ditch (or nearly did so) would explain the emergency nature of rail 16, but only if Hauptmann arrived late enough for him to have completed all the preparatory tasks that day. Hence the effort to persuade the old man that it was late morning or noon, not earlier, as he originally said, when he saw the car and driver with the ladder.

Ben Lupica saw the car with a New Jersey license plate much later, of course, but that sighting reduces the urgency of using an attic rail because nothing else was available, and repeats the question—why a board from the attic? And why drive around in the vicinity all day—just to be seen? Or to spy on the house? A cautious man would presumably not purchase a single piece of wood on the day of the kidnapping from a local lumberyard.

Hauptmann built the garage after he moved to 222nd Street in October of 1931, so it is unlikely that the ladder could have been started many weeks before the kidnapping. Going out that final day to purchase a quantity of wood—not just one board—would have been hardly any more suspicious than recent purchases of a similar nature.

Consider, in this regard, that Koehler's identity of the wood in rails 12 and 13 had faded into the background. It was never definitive, remember, and was made at the time Koehler was focused on Condon. A much greater risk was entailed, therefore, in taking wood from the attic, which Hauptmann would have had to carry downstairs and out to the garage with the landlady, Pauline Rauch, present. The expert wood testimony remains, nevertheless, the most suggestive circumstantial evidence that Hauptmann committed the actual kidnapping. It was, in many respects, the perfect piece of evidence.

Albert S. Osborn was the dean of handwriting experts in his time. The Osborns, father and son, were paid $11,000, on bills totaling $17,000. There are several points to make about Osborn's reports, however, that suggest less than absolute certainty that all the notes were written by the same person. Osborn talked several times about the possibility that the first note was written under great stress, perhaps in an automobile outside Highfields waiting for an opportunity, yet he also insisted that a disguise must be a planned and careful operation. Hauptmann had only one disguise, he stated, which he used throughout the notes. Despite this statement, Osborn admitted that there had been no effort to compare the notes one to another, but only to the conceded and request writing. Other aspects of the handwriting testimony also bear consideration, beginning with the way Osborn and Schwarzkopf lined up the "team," cautioning each member not to reveal his status as a prosecution witness. And after his direct testimony, Osborn boasted to reporters about his skill at identifying character traits from handwriting. Inside the courtroom, meanwhile, the prosecution ridiculed defense witnesses as graphologists. Their star witness, however, was not only a graphologist when he chose to be, but also a detective.

Thus, on November 6, 1935, Osborn wrote to Colonel Schwarzkopf that he felt it not improbable Hauptmann had hidden more of the money someplace else. New Jersey authorities, as we know, really did not want to hear such a thing from Osborn, having "proved" in court that the accused had disposed of more than $49,000 of the money. Schwarzkopf had himself told J. Edgar Hoover he was not interested in screening any more bills. But Osborn thought he was on the track of Hauptmann's real accomplice: Anna. Hauptmann would probably tell his wife about the rest of the money, he urged Schwarzkopf, once his final appeal had been turned down. As soon as that happened, Anna Hauptmann should be followed day and night. "I have a suspicion that some of the money may have been buried, perhaps in a cemetery or park, or somewhere else. . . . My thought is that if for a week or two Mrs. Hauptmann could be constantly shadowed, it might lead to some valuable information."[18]

Schwarzkopf assured him he would take the suggestion seriously. It might be too late, anyway, replied the handwriting expert. The "interested party" seemed to have plenty of money. "It is reported that she rides away in taxicabs whenever she wants to go anywhere." If nothing else, Osborn had revealed his total ignorance of Anna Hauptmann's financial situation. Just as the discovery of the money in the garage had finally decided him about authorship of the ransom notes, what he had heard about Anna's spendthrift ways influenced his detective work.[19]

There were many reasons to conclude that Hauptmann had a hand in writing the notes, including idiosyncratic usages such as *them* before a number, a trait that came up in testimony as well as in the notes, or the addition of *already* to end statements. He also wrote a form of the letter *x* in both the ransom note and certain conceded writings that his defenders could never really get around very successfully. But the clincher at the trial had been Wilentz's dramatic "discovery" of *b-o-a-d* in the little expense account book, and Hauptmann's misguided and halting effort to explain it away.

As convincing as these traits were, there are some missing forensic pieces. Wilentz used the little book, but the handwriting experts had warned him about selective evidence, and the handwriting on the boards in Hauptmann's closet was also not subjected to expert analysis. The ink was never traced, moreover, either the blue or the red ink, to any in Hauptmann's house. FBI agents took away several pens from his apartment, while Albert S. Osborn suggested that some of the notes might have been written with a particular type of instrument. No pen was produced at the trial. There were several suggestions about how the "singnature" might have been made. Nothing was introduced at the trial.[20]

Wilentz was equally successful in his presentation of the money issue. He brought out the strange tale at the trial of a hidden cache in a trunk—which Anna supposedly never saw—and a jumble of explanations about Isidor Fisch's peculiar desire not to have any of his transactions with Richard recorded, transactions that supposedly allowed Hauptmann to invest large sums in the stock market, and to claim that his friend suffered heavy losses on these moneys. That request, if Fisch made it, would not have been out of character. In some ways, the "Fisch story" about how Richard got the $14,000 found in his garage was more believable than the various explanations he gave for the money he had been spending ever since the night the money was paid to Cemetery John in St. Raymond's Cemetery. And yet, with the exception of the five-dollar bill a man threw down at Cecile Barr, the ticket-seller in the booth at the Sheraton Square movie theater, no one ever identified Hauptmann as a ransom-bill passer until the last flurry in August and September of 1934. And there were bills passed after his arrest, including a ten-dollar gold certificate.

How was it that none of the money Hauptmann brought to Steiner, Rouse was ever picked up as Lindbergh ransom bills? Nor was money he used to make the purchases of an expensive radio-phonograph, binoculars, and a canoe—the three items prosecutors cited as showing the Hauptmanns lived a life of luxury during the Depression—ever identified as ransom money.

Speculations about the ransom money in Hauptmann's possession, and where he could possibly have obtained the money otherwise to invest sums up to $26,000, made an argument, which Governor Hoffman seized upon, for trying to find out if there were other participants in the kidnapping. Lingering in the back of such theories were the serial numbers of those two large bills found on the closet door trim, one for $500 and another for $1,000, which Hauptmann said he had received from Isidor Fisch. Once the bills were identified as not part of the ransom, police lost interest. That was too bad. Perhaps they were a real clue about Hauptmann's involvement in money laundering or currency speculations—but after his arrest and the discovery of other evidence besides the money, no one wanted to risk a successful prosecution to bring accomplices into the case.

Because under New Jersey law kidnapping was not a capital offense, the prosecutor feared any doubts about Hauptmann's sole guilt would deny him the verdict he desired. So no matter how difficult the means of entry to the nursery, the sighting of lookouts at each of the cemetery meetings, the "coincidence" that this was the first time the family had remained in Highfields, other investigations ceased once Hauptmann was arrested.

Yet only a week after Hauptmann's arrest, Henry Breckinridge recalled an incident—"[it occurred] just about the time I received the kidnap letter addressed to me." Photographs of Isidor Fisch in the papers had caused him to remember a man who visited his office. This man burst in, saying that the Lindberghs must deal with "us." The two of them discussed the case, and the stranger displayed considerable "mental and emotional excitement" the whole time. "He engaged in a long mysterious conversation all around the point but never coming to it." He had a peculiar glint in his eyes and informed Breckinridge that the needs of science must be served over and above human life. "I recall very vividly the sensation of apprehension felt when talking to him." Nevertheless, Breckinridge put his safety second to "stringing this man along," and he took him out for a bite to eat. The man came back a day or so later, but his conversation was so vague as to be almost incomprehensible. Breckinridge could not believe he had anything to do with the case, but wanted to keep his door open to all possibilities. And, for that reason also, he did not ask the police to put him under surveillance.

"The individual was educated, intelligent, looked like a Jewish student—frail constitution, wore glasses, talked with little or no foreign accent, but was obviously a foreign type." He stood about five-foot-six, weighed about 120 pounds, and was between twenty-four and twenty-eight years of age. He had black hair and wore eyeglasses. If Breckinridge had asked a police artist to draw a portrait of this man, the resemblance to Isidor Fisch would indeed have been striking.[21]

This was not the only odd occurrence about this time. Breckinridge and Mickey Rosner had hosted the famous séance put on by the Reverend Peter Birritella and Mary Cerrita, Sunday afternoon, March 6, 1932. Cerrita told Breckinridge to be in his office the next morning. And he did receive a note there from the kidnapper which indirectly referred to Breckinridge's warnings about Anne's condition. The appearance of the young man who also talked "all around the point" filled the gap before Condon's letter appeared in the *Bronx Home News*. A researcher into the case, Robert Purdy, recently pointed out that the third ransom note, moreover, the one Breckinridge received at his office, could not have been mailed by Hauptmann, as he was several miles away at the time it was posted from Greenwich Village.[22]

Mary Cerrita may have been the woman who met with Condon at his home just prior to his sending the letter to the newspaper offering himself as go-between, as well as the messenger at the bazaar. Jafsie's vagueness about both encounters contrasted sharply with his ability to recognize Hauptmann as Cemetery John though he never saw him in daylight. Cerrita recalled of the séance that she said at one point, "I see initials. They are like a light. They are J.F.C."[23]

Birritella and Cerrita never missed a chance to plug their ESP credentials, and this sounds just like that, an afterthought from the other world. Still, police officials became very interested in them, and Reverend Birritella's brother John, who had credentials as a chauffeur. Once again, Condon's vagueness about the second taxi driver stirred speculation that the Birritellas continued to be involved as messengers. Their phones were tapped, and revealed that when they were not communicating with the other world, they ran a pretty effective con operation.[24]

It should be recalled that the Temple of Divine Power, the spiritualist church run by Reverend Birritella, was diagonally across the street from where Isidor Fisch lived with the Henkels in Selma Kohl's boardinghouse. The church was also on the same street as a restaurant frequented by Septimus Banks and the Warner-Quinlan gas station.

Then there was Charlie Schleser, an accomplished con artist on a much larger scale than the Birritellas. He and his friend Joe DeGrasi tried a little of everything, from New Jersey real estate to baking pies, often relying on Isidor Fisch to provide funds. There is evidence that the dough at the Knickerbocker Pie Company went into money laundering rather than blueberry pies. Fisch managed to borrow quite a lot of money to keep the enterprises afloat for a time. Schleser might well have spotted John Condon at City Island in his real estate office during the time they were both in the business.

However that may be, Schleser repaid his debts to Fisch, posthumously, by providing an alibi for Isidor's whereabouts on March 1, 1932. He also served as an informant for Wilentz, reporting on the defense Anna and Richard's friends planned for the trial—after his appeal for a "loan" was rejected.

If there was a conspiracy to kidnap the Lindbergh baby, it was very likely planned, as the ransom notes said, for some time. That would allow contacts to be made to observe the habits of the family, including, perhaps, information from the servants. Violet Sharp's vagueness about her "date" the night of March 1, 1932, might have been the result of a fear of other investigations. Red Johnson had a less than compelling alibi for that evening, and Olly Whateley apparently did not recognize him on the phone when he called Highfields.

Schleser and DeGrasi were certainly better acquainted than Richard Hauptmann with New Jersey locales from their real estate days. Con men, they were used to deceptions in which one party has no idea about the activities of others involved. Also as con men, they would be aware of the human weaknesses of someone like Jafsie, itching to be part of something grand and noble. There are missing links, obviously, but no more than in the theory that Hauptmann acted alone.

Wilentz advanced several theories about Charlie's death at the trial. The first was that he died as the result of a fall when the kidnapper's ladder broke. In his final summary, on the other hand, he said that Hauptmann struck the child or smothered it. He abandoned the original argument and risked an appeal for a variance because of the need to prove first-degree murder, committed by one man.

It seems unlikely that a fall into the soft mud under the window would have caused death. But what if that *had* been the cause of death? Was there any reason that such a fall might have killed Charlie? There might have been. Charlie's picture on the poster circulated to the public before the body was found was one taken when he was a year old. Why were there no recent photographs? Pictures taken in the nursery, as well as drawings by the police, show a sunlamp that disappeared from the room soon thereafter. Anne's newspaper appeal to the kidnappers on March 3, 1932, specified not only his diet but a special medication as well, "fourteen drops of viosterol, a vitamin preparation, during the day." The primary use for this supplement is to prevent rickets. The dosage here was equivalent to a bottle of cod liver oil. And, finally, there was the way Charlie was pinned to the bed, narrowly spaced at the neck, which hardly allowed him to move his head and body during sleep. Did this all add up to a serious condition known as craniotobes, or brittle bones of the skull?

Al Dunlap, a popular detective magazine writer of the day, first explored the viosterol angle in an article, "Was the Body of the Lindbergh Baby Really Found?" He argued that the near skeleton found in the woods was not Charlie but some other child's decomposed corpse, put there to divert the investigation from kidnapping to murder. Why do that? What difference did it make? "If a body had not been found, how much more money would Colonel Lindbergh have had to pay out?"[25]

This passing remark implied that Lindbergh had reason to believe the child was dead, even though he knew the body was not that of his son. But Dunlap believed the kidnappers had placed another body there to quiet the furor for the time being—intending to reopen negotiations later. Dunlap set out to prove it was not Charlie's body by beginning with the supposed problem of the skeleton's length. In the autopsy report it is set down as thirty-three inches. But in the kidnap circulars the boy was said to be only twenty-nine inches tall. How could that be? The baby could not have grown four inches after death! Well, of course not; the answer was that the circular had it wrong. The child's height at his last medical examination had been recorded by Dr. Philip Van Ingen, as approximately two feet, nine inches, or thirty-three inches. The doctor noted, however, that he had had some difficulty in getting him to stand up straight.[26]

Van Ingen also attended the autopsy at the morgue in Trenton to look at "what was left," but found it impossible to go beyond agreeing that the measurements of the body and other details about the teeth, the way the little toe on the foot that remained curled inward, and "the general appearance of the head" all corresponded with what he knew about the Lindbergh child. Afterward, it was reported that he could not say for sure it was the baby, even if someone offered him $10 million. When prosecutors asked Van Ingen about the identification just before the trial, he still would not commit himself to a positive identification. "I told them I could not say that."[27]

Al Dunlap used the autopsy report for another purpose, however, to claim that the body was not Charlie's, and thereby opened a significant set of issues. Besides the imaginary discrepancy in the child's height, Dunlap reported the "skull was larger than usual. . . . the circumference of the cranium is *apparently greater than would be found in a child of this age.*" In addition, the fontanel was not closed, being about one inch in diameter, while it should have been completely closed in a child that age. "According to the Fischer Laboratories in Chicago," he wrote, "the fontanel should not be more than three quarters of an inch in diameter at the end of the first year." Other physicians had told him, Dunlap went on, that rickets might account for such a condition, and, indeed, the child's diet was known to be that "given for a child so afflicted, but this is a common condition and was by no means so severe in the case of the Lindbergh baby, as is clearly shown by his photographs and his ability to stand and walk at an early age."[28]

Instead of proving his case, Dunlap really established that the body *actually was* that of the Lindbergh child. The enlarged skull, or, as fully reported in the autopsy, this "unusually high and prominent forehead and cranium, apparently greater in circumference than would be found at this age," was noted again by Van Ingen in his pretrial deposition: "He had a square head which went with a moderate rickety condition."[29]

Prosecutors were not anxious to hear more about this "moderate" case of rickets, so the subject was dropped. Defense attorneys would have been very much more interested. The autopsy, furthermore, described the toes of the remaining foot as more than the little toe simply curling inward, that the second toe lapped over the big toe completely, and the next toe almost covered the big toe as well. Lindbergh's decision to have the child cremated immediately, while perfectly understandable as a way to avoid exploitation (pictures from the morgue were soon circulating anyway, one finding its way to John Condon), did inevitably raise speculations about the health of the child.

Did concerns about Charlie's health cause Lindbergh to keep the investigation under his personal control until the body was found? Observers as varied as Mickey Rosner and J. Edgar Hoover noted his unwillingness—even stubbornness—when it came to interrogation of the servants. Only Colonel Schwarzkopf, who declared that there was nothing he would not do for Lindbergh, appeared unconcerned about his behavior. Schwarzkopf saw his duty after Hauptmann's arrest to bring closure for the sake of his new friend's family. So did practically everyone else, whether for Lindbergh's sake or to secure a first-degree murder conviction.

Leads were not followed up if they involved a challenge to Lindbergh's management in any way, beginning with the question of the warped shutter. On the morning of March 2, 1932—the day after the kidnapping—the Penn's Neck station received a call from a David Watson of Newtown, Pennsylvania. Watson, a contractor on the Lindbergh house, reported that he had read accounts of the warped shutter on the nursery. He had hung the shutters himself, he said, and asserted, "It would be impossible for them to be warped now." It would have happened when they were being hung, and he would have fixed them at the time. He would be happy to talk to the state police at any time. There is no indication anywhere that Watson's assertion was tested by questioning the servants—even though the implications of what he said were enormous.[30]

In fact, Corporal Joseph Wolf's initial investigation said only: "There was a window on either side of the fireplace (both were regular sliding windows). The catch also shutter [*sic*] on left window were securely fastened. The window on the right of fireplace was closed but not locked and looking out the right hand shutter was open and the left half closed." And that "Mr. Lindbergh immediately visited the nursery and found the right hand window in the east wall of the nursery was unlocked and the right half of the outside shutter was open."[31]

Lindbergh's truculence at the beginning of the investigation contrasted strongly with his eagerness to clear up the voice identification at St. Raymond's after he told the grand jury in September 1934 that he could not be expected to pick out a person by that method. Then there was his abandonment of the idea that the "lookout" at the cemetery indicated a conspiracy, and his willingness—as contrasted with Anne's testimony—to follow Wilentz's lead at the Flemington trial.

In sum, everyone walked around on tiptoe throughout the investigation rather than press the hero to answer difficult questions—or to allow anyone connected with him to provide answers.

Let us suppose for a moment that the kidnappers had some sort of inside information that the baby would be in Highfields that night. Suppose, further, that the information had been obtained on a promise that no harm would come to the child. In that case either the inside informant had been betrayed, or the death of the child came as a genuine shock to the perpetrators when the ladder broke. That would explain, perhaps, Violet Sharp's suicide, and why the money was never divided up, as some of the original gang decided to back out. Condon's visitor at the bazaar set up an appointment for later in the next week and perhaps never showed up—although that is not entirely clear. Her mission may have been to assure Jafsie that negotiations were still on—the result of a discussion about what to do now that the baby was dead and the likelihood of the body's discovery was growing greater each day.

Pull on these loose threads, and they come away easily. It has not proven possible to weave into a tight pattern any of the theories spun out over the years since the night Charlie was taken from his bed. And yet they constitute a continuing challenge to acceptance of the final verdict.

New evidence continues to emerge. In 1948, a man named Elmer Bolliard, in Plainfield, New Jersey, was repairing a small table he had purchased a decade earlier. As he turned it over, he saw pencil writing on the brace used to support the tabletop with the pedestal. It was in German. Translating the "message" caused a shock—it was a confession by someone who had participated in the Lindbergh kidnapping! The anonymous author claimed he was part of the gang, "and not Bruno Richard Hauptmann." The rest of the money, the writing said, had been buried in Summit, New Jersey. It was signed NSDAP—the initials of the Nazi Party. The writing demonstrated a solid familiarity with the German language, but police regarded it as nothing more than a hoax, and there matters rested for many years afterward.

The table brace with the writing was stuffed in with other Lindbergh evidence and forgotten. Police did take photographs of the message, however. They were looked at from time to time, first by one of the organizers of the police files on the case, Dolores Raisch, and then by another researcher, Steve Lehman, who found the newspaper articles on Bolliard's discovery. It was another researcher, Siglinde Rach, who realized that the first few lines in the message were from an old German sailors' folk song. Finally, two days before Thanksgiving 2002, archivist Mark Falzini found the brace itself in a storage crate in the police museum warehouse, which had not been inventoried for years.

Examining the actual piece of wood, Falzini thought that the screw holes in the table brace looked as if they might correspond to those in the ransom note "singnature." And what an insight that has turned out to be. Putting a strong light under the brace, Falzini placed the first ransom note over the holes. Then the next, and the next. All eleven matched up perfectly, both singly and on top of one another. The chances against such a perfect match would seem to be astronomical. One could not maneuver the notes and the holes in the brace even a millimeter and still have a perfect fit.

Bolliard's table has become central to further discussions about the Lindbergh case. Already a television station in Florida has featured the table in an investigative series. Researchers on various aspects of the case have raised questions about the possibility of a hoax; but after viewing the table, they come away more than half convinced Falzini's discovery has changed the terms of the whole question of innocence and guilt. One researcher, a wood expert, noted that not only do the holes match up perfectly, but the edges of the paper correspond almost exactly with the edge of the brace. It even appears that the handwriting on the notes begins exactly where there is a change in the wood coloration, as if the author was using that discoloration as a margin.[32]

There are other inquiries pending into possible DNA tests on the ransom letters' envelopes. If Hauptmann wrote all the notes, or only some, or even none, such tests would go far toward resolving the matter. But even then the issue of multiple authorship might not be completely resolved, nor the possibility the notes were dictated by one person to another. So far the New Jersey authorities have refused permission for such testing, insisting that the fragility of such valuable historical documents cannot be compromised. Few historians, however, would object to a few snips of paper being cut out of the envelopes.

"Those who believe [Hauptmann] was innocent also think he was railroaded," writes Jim Fisher. "Does it necessarily follow that all wrongfully convicted defendants are innocent? In American jurisprudence, the chief goal of a trial is not truth, but justice. Hauptmann may arguably have been denied justice, but was he guilty?" Of course if this is the only question one is to consider, everything else goes by the boards. It makes no difference, then, that the eyewitnesses were coerced or cajoled, that the defense was denied access to the ransom notes except for one brief session and to the attic until after the trial was over, or that the prosecutor's summation contained a selection of causes of death so that the jury might feel comfortable with at least one if they felt uneasy about pronouncing a death sentence because of a fall from a ladder.[33]

There was no doubt Hauptmann would be convicted. But the state wanted him sent to the electric chair. No other punishment was enough. It was predicted he would confess in the last hour before he entered the death chamber. To explain why he did not, defenders of the verdict have accused him of being in some way less than human—or exactly as David Wilentz described him in his summation to the jury. The effort to exclude any possibility of accomplices bordered on a mass personality defect itself, with the prosecution and the media displaying all the symptoms of a compulsive-obsessive. Capital punishment intensifies those defects, requiring prosecutors to portray the accused as subhuman, and substituting vengeance for justice.

The Lindberghs never returned to Highfields. Four years after the trail, the writer Paul Gallico drove down the road to the house in the middle of winter. "It stood atop the hill, bleak and tragic," he reported. "Snow as half a foot deep on the ground. At first there was no sign of life behind the staring windows. Grayish curtains still adorn the downstairs window frames. Then dogs began to bay. A woman appeared at an upstairs window and made note of our car registration. It was the wife of the caretaker. . . . They live alone there. Strangers are not welcomed."

In mythic terms, Hauptmann's execution satisfied a need to reclaim that which had been stolen away—from the Lindberghs and the nation—but Highfields was left alone and barren of life. Today, however, the house has a new life as a state institution, a halfway house for delinquent boys. And we as a people continue to debate the ethics and effectiveness of capital punishment as restitution and deterrent. How much simpler it would have all been if he had just confessed—some might say. But Illinois governor George Ryan had some pertinent things to say on that point when he announced a moratorium on executions in his state. "Our capital system is haunted by the demon of error, error in determining guilt and error in determining who among the guilty deserves to die."[34]

Notes

INTRODUCTION

1. Interview with Louise Lennahan, May 16, 2003.
2. Anne Morrow Lindbergh, *Locked Rooms and Open Doors: Diaries and Letters of Anne Morrow Lindbergh, 1933–1935* (New York: Harcourt Brace Jovanovich, 1974), 14.

ONE. SUDDEN FAME

1. Charles A. Lindbergh, *"WE"* (New York: G. P. Putnam: 1927), 225–226.
2. Walter Ross, *The Last Hero: Charles A. Lindbergh* (New York: Harper and Row, 1976), 147; Lindbergh, *"WE,"* 241.
3. Charles A. Lindbergh, *The Spirit of St. Louis* (St. Paul: Minnesota Historical Society Press, 1993), 482.
4. *"WE,"* 276–279.
5. A. Scott Berg, *Lindbergh* (New York: Berkley Books, 1998), 162–163.
6. Ross, *Last Hero,* 143.
7. Joyce Milton, *Loss of Eden: A Biography of Charles and Anne Morrow Lindbergh* (New York: HarperCollins, 1993), 149–150.
8. Berg, *Lindbergh,* 197.
9. Susan Hertog, *Anne Morrow Lindbergh: Her Life* (New York: Anchor Books, 2000), 142.
10. Berg, *Lindbergh,* 229–231.
11. Milton, *Loss of Eden,* 189–190.
12. Charles A. Lindbergh, *Autobiography of Values* (New York: Harcourt, 1978), 130.
13. Berg, *Lindbergh,* 224, 349.
14. Anne Morrow Lindbergh to Evangeline Lodge Lindbergh, February 7, 1932, Anne Morrow Lindbergh, *Hour of Gold, Hour of Lead, Diaries and Letters, 1929–1932* (New York: Harcourt Brace Jovanovich, 1993), 224.
15. Stanley Hamilton, *Machine Gun Kelly's Last Stand* (Lawrence: University of Kansas Press, 2003), 8.

16. Ibid., 11.
17. Ibid., 9.

TWO. BETTY GOW'S JOURNEY

1. Hertog, *Anne Morrow Lindbergh,* 158–159.
2. Statement of Charles Henry Ellerson, April 12, 1932, Statements File, New Jersey State Police Museum (hereafter: NJSP).
3. Statement of Betty Gow, March 3, 1932, Box 24, Harold Giles Hoffman Papers, NJSP.
4. Ibid.; R. D. Brown, report on Betty Gow, July 8, 1932, Box 6, Classification 7-1, Record Group 65, Records of the Federal Bureau of Investigation (hereafter: FBI).
5. Trial transcript, microfilm copy, New Jersey State Library, Law Library, 120–121; *New Brunswick Daily Home News,* June 28, 1932.
6. Statement of Finn Henrik Johnson, March 8, 1932, Statements File, NJSP.
7. Hertog, *Anne Morrow Lindbergh,* 151.
8. Sven Petter Myhr Naess, "Interview with Else Marie Bing: Daughter of Fin Henrik 'Red' Johansen," September 4, 2003, available at NJSP. Report to Harold Hoffman from Winslow Humphrey, March 3, 1936, Box 12, Hoffman Papers. Red and Betty had been warned on several occasions by officers in Palisades Park about parking after hours, most recently at 4 A.M. on January 1, 1932, when they were taken to headquarters and reprimanded. Red had to register as a disorderly person, a polite euphemism, to save the Lindberghs embarrassment. On Red's venereal disease, see also Trooper Lewis Bornmann, and Detective Frank Carr, "Finn Henry Johnson," May 28, 1932, Box 3, ibid.
9. *New York Times,* March 7, 1932.
10. On Betty's ambitions, see Detective Frank Carr and Trooper Lewis Bornmann, "Information on Betty Gow," June 15, 1932, Box 25, Hoffman Papers.
11. FBI File, 62-3057, 62, NJSP; T. H. Sisk, "Setting Out Details of Trip over Crime Scene . . . ," October 27, 1934, Investigative Reports, NJSP.
12. FBI Summary Report, 62-3057, 62, NJSP.
13. Statement of Charles Henry Ellerson, March 11, 1932, Statements File, NJSP; Jim Fisher, *The Lindbergh Case* (New Brunswick: Rutgers University Press, 1987), 23; FBI Summary Report, 62-3057, 67, NJSP; minutes of a conference held on May 18, 1932, in the office of Colonel H. Norman Schwarzkopf, Captain John J. Lamb Collection, J-6, NJSP; interview of Ambrose J. Titus and his wife, by Trooper Lewis Bornmann, March 12, 1932, Box 11, Hoffman Papers. Ambrose Titus doubted that he would recognize the man, as "his memory [was] not so good." But Titus did say that he was about forty years old, five-foot-nine, with a slim build and thin face. He wore a dark suit, brown overcoat, and hat. This description was somewhat close to later descriptions of the kidnapper.
14. Statement of Finn Henrick Johnson, March 8, 1932, Statements File, NJSP.
15. Minutes of conference, May 18, 1932.
16. Statement of Anne Morrow Lindbergh, March 11, 1932, Box 1, Hoffman Papers; trial transcript , 61–62.
17. Marguerite Junge diary, undated, courtesy of Steve Lehman. Wahgoosh plays a significant and interesting role in the Lindbergh case in the sense that

descriptions of the dog's behavior tend to follow interpretations of how the crime took place. Thus authors who see the kidnapping as an inside job, ask readers why the dog did not bark that night. Authors who believe otherwise explain the dog's silence as caused by the wind howling outside and his bed being located at the other end of the house. See, for example, Gregory Ahlgren and Stephen Monier, *Crime of the Century: The Lindbergh Kidnapping Hoax* (Boston: Branden Books, 1993), 14, 55, 63; George Waller, *Kidnap: The Story of the Lindbergh Case* (New York: Dial Press, 1961), 4–5; Fisher, *Lindbergh Case,* 24–25.

18. Statement of Betty Gow, March 10, 1932, Box 3, Hoffman Papers.

19. Lupica gave several statements about what he saw that evening. They are remarkably consistent in identifying the car as blue or black, a 1929 Dodge, with a New Jersey license plate. See investigation report by T. H. Sisk, December 8, 1933, Box 22, Hoffman Papers; deposition of Sebastian Benjamin Lupica, January 28, 1935, Box 11, ibid.; statement of Sebastian Benjamin Lupica, September 9, 1933, Statements File, NJSP; FBI Summary Report, 62-3057, 114–119, NJSP.

20. Statements of Anne Morrow Lindbergh, March 11 and 13, 1932, Box 1, Hoffman Papers; statements of Betty Gow, March 3 and 10, 1932, Statements File, NJSP; trial transcript, 323.

21. Statement of Anne Morrow Lindbergh, March 11, 1932.

22. Trial transcript, 70–71.

23. Statement of Betty Gow, March 3, 1932.

24. Statement of Anne Morrow Lindbergh, March 13, 1932.

25. Statement of Marguerite Junge, March 7, 1932, Box 13, Hoffman Papers; statement of Adele Marguerite Junge, April 13, 1932, L File 73, NJSP; statement of Elsie Mary Whateley, March 10, 1932, Statements File, NJSP; statement of Betty Gow, March 10, 1932; statement of Finn Henrik Johnson, March 8, 1932. Of these accounts, only Marguerite Junge's first statement indicates that Betty showed any annoyance at Red's telephone call. Her husband, Johannes, tried very hard to pin down the call for police as to both the time it was made and from what location. Statement of Johannes Junge, March 9, 1932, Statements File, NJSP.

26. Statement of William Boland, April 15, 1932, Statements File, NJSP; statement of Marguerite Junge, March 7, 1932; statement of Finn Henrik Johnson, March 8, 1932.

27. Statement of William Boland, April 15, 1932, Statements File, NJSP.

28. Anne Morrow Lindbergh to Eleanor Lodge Lindbergh, March 2, 1932, Anne Morrow Lindbergh, *Hour of Gold, Hour of Lead,* 226–228. Anne's hearing problem was discussed by Major Thomas Lanphier, a close friend, a few days after the kidnapping. J. Edgar Hoover, "Memorandum for the File," March 19, 1932, FBI Records.

29. Statements of John Kristofeck and Joseph Kuchta, March 2, 1932, Statements File, NJSP.

30. Statement of Finn Henrik Johnson, March 8, 1932.

31. Anne Morrow Lindbergh, *Hour of Gold, Hour of Lead*, 227; on the ladder placement, see T. H. Sisk, "Bruno Richard Hauptmann," October 27, 1934, Investigative Files, NJSP.

32. Leon Hoage, "Definite and Valuable Clues—Overlooked in the Lindbergh Case," undated, copy in Box 1, David Wilentz Collection, NJSP.

33. These conversations are compiled from various statements to the police made by Betty Gow and Elsie Whateley. Statement of Betty Gow, March 10, 1932; statement of Elsie Mary Whateley, March 10, 1932; statement of Betty Gow, January 1, 1935, Robert Peacock Collection, NJSP.

34. Hoover, "Memorandum for the File," March 19, 1932; *Chicago Daily Tribune,* April 11, 1932; statement of Betty Gow, March 10, 1932; Anne Lindbergh, *Hour of Gold, Hour of Lead,* 227. Before her diary was published containing this passage from her letter to her mother-in-law, detective writer Alan Hynd published an article, "Everyone One Wanted to Get Into the Act," which contained the following sentence: "Lindbergh himself was a great one for practical jokes that often scared the hell out of people. A few months before, he had taken the baby from the crib, hidden him in a closet, and thrown the household into an uproar for twenty minutes." The article was reprinted in Alan Hynd, *Violence in the Night* (New York: Fawcett Books, 1955), 9–60.

35. Robert Thayer, untitled memorandum, March 3, 1932, Box 28, Hoffman Papers.

36. Testimony of Betty Gow, trial transcript, 314; statement of Anne Morrow Lindbergh, March 11, 1932.

37. Testimony of Betty Gow, trial transcript, 275; statement of Trooper Frank A. Kelly, March 16, 1932, Statements File, NJSP.

38. Jim Fisher has Lindbergh feeling the night air seeping into the room from an open window in *The Lindbergh Case,* 23, without providing a source for the statement. Betty Gow's "tour" is recorded in two memoranda by Nuncio DeGaetano, March 3 and March 9, 1932, Box 29, Hoffman Papers. Lewis Bornmann testified about Lindbergh's uncertainty, trial transcript, 363.

39. Statement of Colonel Charles A. Lindbergh, March 11, 1932, Statements File, NJSP; Frank J. Wilson and Beth Day, *Special Agent: A Quarter Century with the Treasury Department and the Secret Service* (New York: Holt, Rinehart and Winston, 1965), 65.

40. Wolfe's comments are quoted in an article by detective writer Al Dunlap, "Bungling the Lindbergh Kidnapping Case," a copy of which is in NJSP. In this article Wolfe claimed not to have seen *any* footprints, or that is what Dunlap understood him to say when he may have meant he did not see any leading back to the window, a point corroborated by Williamson in a conversation with a news reporter. See Laura Vitray, *The Great Lindbergh Hullabaloo: An Unorthodox Account* (New York: William Faro, 1932), 38. The book is filled with inaccuracies, but the accounts of Wolfe and Williamson's impressions tally well with those from other sources.

41. Statements of Harry H. Wolfe, March 16, 1932, and Charles E. Williamson, March 9, 1932, Statements File, NJSP; trial transcript, 220–221.

42. Memorandum by DeGaetano, "Activities of the Undersigned on March 1, 1932," March 3, 1932, Box 29, Hoffman Papers.

43. The first quotation is taken from DeGaetano's report of March 3, 1932, the second from an additional report by DeGaetano, March 9, 1932, also in Box 29, Hoffman Papers. Bornmann made a similar report, March 9, 1932, Statements File, NJSP.

44. Joseph Wolf, "Major Initial Report," March 1, 1932, Investigative Files, NJSP.

45. Observations of state troopers, recorded in Tommy Bonsall to Jim Burke, undated (1938), Box 33, Hoffman Papers.

46. The note is from a copy in the NJSP. The originals of the notes are available. This note is a typesetter's nightmare, so it is hardly surprising that variations appear from book to book on the case. The printed version presented here represents only an interpretation, as well, of some of the oddly penned letters.

47. Jim Fisher, apparently building on earlier accounts, writes that Major Charles Schoeffel paused to ask Lindbergh whom he wanted to see the letter, thereby chasing Wolfe and Williamson out of the room. *Lindbergh Case,* 18. He gives no source for this statement. The story perhaps originates in Sidney B. Whipple, *The Lindbergh Crime* (New York: Blue Ribbon Books, 1935), 11. Whipple does not provide a citation, either. Laura Vitray, however, a reporter like Whipple, writes that five persons were present: Wolfe and Williamson, Kelly, the fingerprint man, Lindbergh, and another state police officer. *Lindbergh Hullabaloo,* 39–40. And, finally, the FBI Summary Report (62-3057, 46, NJSP) has Lindbergh sharing the note with Whateley!

48. The stories appeared in the first two papers on March 3, 1932, and in the *Trenton Times* on March 2, 1932.

49. Fisher, *Lindbergh Case,* 13.

50. Lloyd Fisher, "Can Any Reasonable Man Believe That the Mystery is Solved?" unpublished article in Box 4, Hoffman Papers.

51. *New Brunswick Daily News,* March 2, 1932.

52. The Lindbergh search party is documented in several reports: DeGaetano's of March 3 and 9, 1932; N. J. Nelson, "Secondary Major Report," March 2, 1932, Secondary Reports File, NJSP; Bill Conklin to Harold Hoffman, February 27, 1936, Box 8, Hoffman Papers. Whited's statements are of particular importance, given his later role at the Hauptmann trial.

53. *New York Times,* March 3, 1932.

54. Statement of Trooper Lewis Bornmann, March 9, 1932, Statements File, NJSP.

55. *New York Times,* March 3, 1932.

56. Statement of Trooper Frank A. Kelly, March 16, 1932, Statements File, NJSP.

57. Lewis Bornmann, "Investigation of Oscar Bush," March 13, 1932, Reports File, NJSP.

58. Vitray, *Lindbergh Hullabaloo,* 56–57.

59. Ibid.

60. Ibid., 106–107. For a discussion of Bush, and a complaint about the way he was treated, see Wayne D. Jones, *Murder of Justice: New Jersey's Greatest Shame* (New York: Vantage Press, 1997), 36.

61. *New Brunswick Daily Home News,* March 3, 1932.

62. Hoover, "Memorandum for File," March 19, 1932.

63. Ibid.

64. Ibid. The story of Betty's abortive interrogation was leaked to the *Chicago Daily Tribune,* April 11, 1932.

65. Leon Turrou, *Where My Shadow Falls: Two Decades of Crime Detection* (Garden City, N.Y.: Doubleday, 1949), 107.

66. Naess, "Interview with Else Marie Bing."

THREE. MICKEY ROSNER'S GAME

1. Statement of Morris Rosner, May 14, 1932, Box 28, Hoffman Papers.

2. Statement of Robert Thayer, May 16, 1932, Box 11, Hoffman Papers; William Helmer, *Public Enemies: America's Criminal Past, 1919–1940* (New York: Checkmark Books, 1998), 34, 49.

3. There are various accounts of how it was decided to contact Rosner. Some have Congresswoman Ruth Pratt, Thayer's mother-in-law, initiating the contact, while Thayer himself claimed it was his own idea. See FBI File 62-3057, 142, NJSP; statement of Robert Thayer, May 16, 1932.

4. Statement of Robert Thayer, May 16, 1932.

5. Ibid., Robert Thayer, untitled memorandum, January 2, 1933, Statements File, NJSP; statement of Morris Rosner, May 14, 1932.

6. Robert Thayer, untitled memorandum, March 3, 1932, Box 28, Hoffman Papers.

7. Ibid.

8. Morris Rosner, untitled manuscript, March 3, 1932 (1933), 30–31. A copy of this manuscript is in Box 22, Hoffman Papers.

9. Ibid., 40; statement of Robert Thayer, May 16, 1932.

10. Rosner, untitled manuscript, 2.

11. Helmer, *Public Enemies,* 37–38, Rosner, untitled manuscript, 3–4; Robert Thayer, undated handwritten notes, Robert Thayer Papers, Library of Congress, Washington, D.C.

12. Statement of Morris Rosner, May 14, 1932; Rosner, untitled manuscript, 4.

13. Statementof Morris Rosner, May 14, 1932.

14. Statement of Robert Thayer, May 16, 1932.

15. Robert Thayer, undated handwritten notes, Thayer Papers.

16. Rosner, untitled manuscript, 48; Vitray, *Lindbergh Hullabaloo,* 147–150.

17. Earnest Kahlar, *Ransom Kidnapping in America, 1874–1974/The Creation of a Capital Crime* (Cardondale: Southern Illinois University Press, 1978), 63.

18. Walter Lippmann, "The Underworld: A Stultified Conscience," *Forum,* February 1931, 65–69.

19. Thomas Doherty, *Pre-Code Hollywood: Sex, Immorality, and Insurrection in American Cinema, 1930–1934* (New York: Columbia University Press, 1999), 151.

20. Robert J. Schoenberg, *Mr. Capone: The Real—and Complete—Story of Al Capone* (New York: Quill Books, 1992), 332.

21. A very useful account of the threat to Constance Morrow is in Edward Dean Sullivan, *The Snatch Racket* (New York: Vanguard Press, 1932), 3–12.

22. Thayer, untitled memorandum, January 2, 1933.

23. The statement is reproduced in Waller, *Kidnap,* 24–25.

24. Ibid., 25. Emphasis added.

25. Noel Behn, *Lindbergh: The Crime* (New York: Onyx, 1995), 78, 99, 102; *New Brunswick Daily Home News,* March 7, 1932.

26. *Trenton Times,* March 2, 1932.

27. Sergeant C. J Campbell, memo, "Investigating Kidnapping of Col. Lindbergh's Son," March 2, 1932, Reports File, NJSP; Waller, *Kidnap,* 19; "Investigation by Lieut. Arthur Keaton . . . ," September 30, 1932, Reports File, NJSP.

28. *Daily Mirror,* May 12, 1932.

29. Classic Film Scripts, *M, a Film by Fritz Lang,* introduction and translation by Nicholas Garnham (New York: Simon and Schuster, 1968), 32–33.

30. Ibid., 46.

31. Statement of Morris Rosner, May 14, 1932.

32. The problem, as always with the ransom notes, is that different readers interpret the handwriting either to emphasize or to minimize the spelling errors. This is especially true when it comes to *d*s and *t*s and *th*s. Although the renderings are subjective, my own choice is to record what the words look like to me, and provide this and other explanations for the rationale in endnotes.

33. Statement of Morris Rosner, May 14, 1932.

34. Rosner, untitled manuscript, 12.

35. Ibid., 13.

36. Ibid., 14–16.

37. Ibid., 25–26.

38. Ibid., 21.

39. Ibid., 24.

40. *New York Times,* March 7, 1932.

41. From a newspaper clipping fragment, dated March 7, 1932, NJSP.

42. Diary entry, March 6, 1932, Anne Morrow Lindbergh, *Hour of Gold, Hour of Lead,* 231–232; Thayer, "Saturday," undated handwritten notes, Thayer Papers.

43. Alan Hynd, "Untold Facts in the Lindbergh Kidnapping," *True Detective Mysteries,* January 1933, 34–37, 97. Emphasis added.

44. Testimony of Salvatore Spitale, June 2, 1932, Bronx Grand Jury, Bronx District Attorney Files, NJSP.

45. 89.118 to Lindbergh, March 7, 1932, Thayer Papers.

46. Frederick L. Collins, "Before the Body Was Found She Said the Lindbergh Baby Was Murdered," *Liberty,* April 4, 1936, 39–41; Breckinridge, "Memorandum of Henry Breckinridge Re: Birritella Séance," Folder 15, Wilentz Collection. The accounts that follow are taken from this memorandum, Mickey Rosner's recollections, and the Collins article in *Liberty.*

47. It also sounded like a "message" John F. Condon, "Jafsie," would receive from a mystery woman several days later at a bazaar.

48. As it turned out, Saturday, March 12, 1932, was the date that John F. Condon met Cemetery John in Woodlawn Cemetery.

49. See Collins, "Before the Body Was Found."

50. From the original at NJSP. Once again, however, deciphering the letter is a matter of subjective judgment about letters, especially *d*s and *t*s.

51. Frank Wilson's report, November 11, 1933, SI 6336; Birritella investigation, Investigative Reports, Binder 1, NJSP; telephone intercepts, Box 26, Hoffman Papers.

52. Collins, "Before the Body Was Found." We will come back to the Birritellas, and their possible role in the kidnapping, in the final chapter.

53. Schoenberg, *Mr. Capone,* 328.

54. Elmer L. Irey, as told to William J. Slocum, *The Tax Dodgers* (New York: Greenberg, 1948), 68; John Kobler, *Capone: The Life and World of Al Capone* (New York: Da Capo Press, 1992), 345.

55. Irey, *Tax Dodgers,* 68; Wilson and Day, *Special Agent,* 58.

56. Robert Thayer, "Written at 11 A.M.," March 12, 1932, Thayer Papers.

57. Frank Wilson, "Undercover Man: Inside the Lindbergh Kidnapping," *Colliers',* May 10, 1947, 71–75.

58. J. Edgar Hoover, "Memorandum for the Files," March 14, 1932, Folder 29, Wilentz Collection.

59. May 2, 1932, 13; the idea that Capone masterminded the kidnapping lingers and is most recently given a fictional treatment in Max Allan Collins, *Stolen Away: A Novel of the Lindbergh Kidnapping* (New York: Bantam Books, 1991).

60. James Whitaker, "Capone Bargains for Baby," *Daily Mirror,* March 9, 1932. Emphasis added.

61. Untitled memorandum, March 22, 1932, Schwarzkopf Collection.

62. Robert Thayer, untitled memorandum, January 2, 1933, Statements File, NJSP; Rosner, untitled manuscript, 64.

63. Thayer, untitled memorandum, January 2, 1933.

64. Ibid.

65. J. Edgar Hoover to H. Norman Schwarzkopf, November 16, 1932, with attachment, and V. W. Hughes, "Memorandum for the Director," November 17, 1932, both in Box 7, Classification 7-1, FBI Records.

FOUR. MAN OF MYSTERY

1. St. Clair Mckelway, "Profiles: Goodbye, Mr. Jafsie," *New Yorker,* December 29, 1934, 20–25; Lloyd Ultan, "The Bronx in History," http://www.bronx.com/6_96historyarch.html.

2. T. H. Sisk, Report, October 27, 1934, FBI files, copy at NJSP.

3. John Condon, *Jafsie Tells All: The Inside Story of the Lindbergh-Hauptmann Case* (New York: Jonathan Lee, 1936). 11, 13.

4. Ibid.

5. Ibid., 18; the letter itself may found in the NJSP, dated March 7, 1932.

6. Condon, *Jafsie Tells All,* 22.

7. Ibid., 22–23. As usual in transcriptions of the ransom notes, there are minor differences from one author to another.

8. E. J. Connelly to J. Edgar Hoover, June 23, 1932, Box 6, Classification 7-1, FBI Records.

9. Statement of John F. Condon, May 14, 1932, and statement at Lindbergh investigation, May 20, 1932, both in Bronx District Attorney Files, NJSP.

10. Statement of Robert Thayer, May 16, 1932, Box 11, Hoffman Papers.

11. As in all the notes, it is impossible to separate some spelling errors from difficulties in the handwriting caused by haste or hitches in writing style.

12. Statement of Robert Thayer, May 16, 1932.

13. Testimony of Henry Breckinridge, September 25, 1934, before the Bronx grand jury, Bronx District Attorney Files, NJSP.

14. Statement of John F. Condon, May 14, 1932, Bronx District Attorney Files, NJSP.

15. Ibid.

16. Grand jury testimony, May 20, 1932, Bronx District Attorney Files, NJSP. Emphasis added.

17. Condon, *Jafsie Tells All,* 49.

18. Coleman explains these contacts and subsequent events in his grand jury testimony, September 24, 1934, Bronx District Attorney Files, NJSP. There is an unsigned partial manuscript, titled "Vigil," in Box 1, David Wilentz Collection.

It is probably the work of Coleman, the only reporter with hour-to-hour access to Condon during this period. The project had to be abandoned because early on, the author wrote what he expected would be the happy conclusion to Condon's "Vigil." "While the police of the entire nation were engaged in their search, Dr. John F. Condon, for 46 years a school teacher, was quietly carrying on negotiations which resulted, today, in the solution of the case. His home at 2974 Decatur Ave., near Moshulu Parkway, was the nerve center for the entire dealings with the abductors" (2).

19. Statement of John F. Condon, May 14, 1932, Bronx District Attorney Files, NJSP.

20. From transcripts of telephone conversations with Mrs. Condon and John F. Condon, on March 11, 1932, Box 4, Hoffman Papers; statement of John F. Condon, May 13, 1932, Statements File, NJSP.

21. Transcripts of telephone conversations, March 11, 1932, Box 4, Hoffman Papers; and Condon, *Jafsie Tells All,* 56–60.

22. Statement of Joseph Perrone, May 21, 1932, Statements File, NJSP.

23. Ibid.

24. Ibid., and statement by Joseph Perrone, May 22, 1937, L File, NJSP.

25. Letter from NJSP.

26. Condon, *Jafsie Tells All,* 70.

27. "Vigil," 12.

28. Summary Report, 62-3057, 5, NJSP; Ludovic Kennedy, *Crime of the Century: The Lindbergh Kidnapping and the Framing of Richard Hauptmann* (New York: Pengin Books, 1996), 101, 135; Fisher, *Lindbergh Case,* 57. Fisher gives no details of the man's appearance. He might have been someone named Joe DeGrasi, an Italian who had fled a robbery prosecution by returning to his native land, but who apparently returned to New York in the spring of 1932. DeGrasi was associated with shadowy doings of the Knickerbocker Pie Company, along with several others who would become involved with one phase or another of the investigation of the kidnapping and Bruno Richard Hauptmann. See, for example, the investigative report by E. A. Hausling, November 22, 1932, Investigative File 1602, NJSP, where he is described as "about 32 years of age, dark complexion, short and stocky, stout, cast in his left eye."

29. Statement of Robert Riehl, July 19, 1932, Statements File, NJSP. Every Lindbergh researcher owes an eternal debt to the archivist Mark Falzini for providing a compendium of the different versions Condon related of his meetings with Cemetery John, no two alike. There is no satisfactory way of dealing with this. I will refer to that compendium, trying to be as specific as possible to an individual source, without constantly pointing out inconsistencies. The compendium is available at NJSP, along with, of course, the original documents.

30. Condon's familiarity with the area was quite striking, as his observations of activities at the shack indicated. Trial transcript, 750–751.

31. Statement of John F. Condon, June 26, 1932, grand jury testimony, May 20, 1932, Falzini compendium.

32. Interview with John F. Condon, reported in a newspaper clipping, May 24, 1932, NJSP.

33. Cemetery John quote from "Vigil," 17. As this is the first report, chronologically, of the conversation, it may be the most accurate. In other versions, Cemetery John says the blanket was pinned to the mattress, and in still others

he describes the pins without Condon having produced them. See Falzini compendium.

34. Condon, *Jafsie Tells All,* 185–186. It should be noted that Condon's account here accords with the prosecution's speculations as to various ways the baby might have been killed, and that it was written three years after the events.

35. The version in Condon, *Jafsie Tells All,* and Condon's May, 1932, grand jury testimony, are put side by side in the Falzini compendium. In an attempt to clear up the "mystification," as Condon puts it, he explains in *Jafsie Tells All,* 91, that he had asked Norwegian residents of City Island about Johnson's character. That only raises the question, however, of when Jafsie queried these people. Is he telling us that he knew about Johnson's good character before the kidnapping, or that he took time before he was involved, or during the negotiations, to go to City Island to find out? I should like to thank Siglinde Rach for calling this point to my attention.

36. Indeed, in his very first report upon leaving Cemetery John that first evening, Condon told Al Reich, who had driven him there, "the fellow had a thin face and was coughing." Statement of Al Reich, May 13, 1932, Statements File, NJSP. The fullest statement of the coughing "observation," is "Investigation of Dr. John F. Condon," June 2, 1932, Statements File, NJSP. On other contradictions, see an unsigned memorandum to Governor Harold Hoffman, "Re: Dr. John F. Condon," undated, Box 21, Hoffman Papers.

37. Kennedy, *Crime of the Century,* 102; Condon, *Jafsie Tells All,* 41.

38. All quotations in this section, unless otherwise noted, are taken from a compendium of Condon statements on the sleeping-suit episode, compiled by Mark Falzini and available at NJSP.

39. It has been argued that someone had inside information, conveyed to the kidnapper, that Lindbergh had been contacted by a friend of shipbuilder John Hughes Curtis, who claimed to be in contact with the real culprits down south in Baltimore, and eventually, Cape May, New Jersey. Hence Cemetery John's anxiety to reestablish his bona fides in this fashion.

40. John F. Condon, "'Jafsie' and the Ransom Money," *Liberty,* February 15, 1936, 12; he edited this sentence in *Jafsie Tells All,* changing the word *exquisite* to *extreme* (103). Still, there is a voyeuristic overtone here that is not completely removed by the change. Condon, moreover, liked to chastise others when they failed to grasp that he always spoke in precise ways to convey subtle distinctions.

41. Condon, *Jafsie Tells All,* 104.

42. Minutes of a conference held in Schwarzkopf's office on May 18, 1932, NJSP. Emphasis added. In a lengthy note, Fisher, *Lindbergh Case,* 433, considers evidence that the suit had been misidentified. He leaves the question open, while leaning toward the idea that it was the real suit. Lab tests revealed several kinds of stains on the suit, consistent with the chemical makeup of the Vick's salve rubbed on the baby's chest that night—but it was a common medication and had probably been used on Charlie several nights in succession or on other occasions.

43. Fisher, *Lindbergh Case,* 66, citing Condon, *Jafsie Tells All,* 109. The quote from Lindbergh I cite is the only Lindbergh statement on that page referring to the timing of the payment.

44. "Vigil," 30–31.

45. F. X. O'Donnell, "Memorandum for Special Agent in Charge E. J. Connelly," March 25, 1932, Box 3, Classification 7-1, FBI Records.

46. Ibid., 32.

47. Condon, *Jafsie Tells All,* 121–122.

48. Alan Hynd, "Untold Facts in the Lindbergh Kidnapping," *True Detective Mysteries,* February 1933, 53, 104. Hynd's veracity is always a question, but it tallies closely with the one given to the FBI, "Report Made at New York City," March 8, 1934, by J. E. Seykora, Box 21, Hoffman Papers.

49. Coleman, "Vigil," 36.

50. Condon, *Jafsie Tells All,* 129.

51. Fisher, *Lindbergh Case,* 68–69.

52. Ibid., 74.

53. Frank Wilson to chief, Intelligence Unit, Bureau of Internal Revenue, November 11, 1933, SI-6356-M, NJSP.

54. In "Vigil," it is stated that the money was made available immediately to Condon, along with a note authorizing him to pay $50,000 if he saw the child; box details in Condon, *Jafsie Tells All,* 64–65; in statements to the police in mid-May, however, Condon makes up a fictitious second letter to him, instructing him on the dimensions of the box he was to make. See Box 33, Hoffman Papers.

55. J. J. Manning, reports of September 15 and 29, 1933, Box 6, Classification 7-1, FBI Records.

56. Jones, *Murder of Justice,* 103–104.

57. Statement of Betty Gow, May 12, 1932, Statements File, NJSP.

58. Irey, *The Tax Dodgers,* 75.

59. J. M. Keith, "Memorandum for the Director," April 6, 1932, Box 3, Classification 7-1, FBI Records; T. H. Sisk, "Memorandum for Mr. Tamm," July 12, 1934, Box 15, ibid. The New York police cover was a highly confidential operation unknown until this document was discovered.

60. FBI Summary Report, 62-3057, 194, NJSP.

61. Ibid., 34. The long list of descriptions, and nondescriptions, of the second "taxi" man were put together in a report for Governor Harold Hoffman, undated, Box 21, Hoffman Papers.

62. Emphasis added. Condon's masterful job of confusing the issue appears in the grand jury hearings, May 20, 1932, 24–26, Bronx District Attorney Files, NJSP.

63. Statement of Charles A. Lindbergh, May 20, 1932, Box 3, Hoffman Papers.

64. Ibid. This early record of what Lindbergh heard is important, given the controversy over whether he could later identify Hauptmann as the man who called out that night from a distance of more than a hundred yards. Condon, as usual, recalled the incident in a variety of ways, "Hey, Doc," one time, simply "Doc," another, and so on. At the trial, Attorney General David Wilentz made a great deal of the kidnapper's call to Condon in his opening statement, several times approaching near Hauptmann and repeating the words as if pronounced "Hey, Dok-tor." Lindbergh's early statement, therefore, is important as non-coached evidence.

65. In one version, the man practically falls over backward with generosity: "We know it's hard times like that, why certainly we'll take fifty thousand." "Investigation of Dr. John F. Condon at Alpine, N.J.," June 2, 1932, Hoffman Papers, Box 22, NJSP.

66. Thanks to Siglinde Rach for her suggestions about this note Cemetery John apparently had ready for Condon ahead of time.

67. Trial testimony, 656–659.

68. Although the account in the preceding paragraphs is based largely on Condon's grand jury testimony on May 20, 1932, it also relies on his earlier statements to police, see Condon, *Jafsie Tells All*, and "Vigil."

69. Statement of Charles A. Lindbergh, May 20, 1932, Box 3, Hoffman Papers.

70. FBI Summary Report, 62-3057, 195–196, NJSP.

71. Ibid.

72. The note, like the others, can be found at the NJSP. There are two points about this note that deserve special comment. First, as in the other directional notes, the writing is even and fairly smooth, although there are more spelling errors than in the other directional notes. Second, and more important, two spellings of *Boad (Boat)* clearly have been altered to make them appear to be errors, changing a *t* to a *d*. I thank Sigilinde Rach for calling this important alteration to my attention.

73. Turrou, *Where My Shadow Falls*, 114–115. Leon Turrou's memory of this scene may not be entirely accurate, but the general impressions he received from the conversation and exchange offer an accurate picture of the mood of the two men. Condon's sense of relief at having a burden off his shoulders, particularly the $20,000, is especially noteworthy. Other evidence suggests, moreover, that despite his public demeanor, Lindbergh had begun to have suspicions about Condon's reportage, if not anything else.

74. Irey, *The Tax Dodgers*, 78–79.

75. Turrou, *Where My Shadow Falls*, 115.

76. *New Brunswick Daily Home News*, April 14, 1932.

77. *New York Times*, April 13, 1932.

78. Ibid., April 18, 1932; *New Brunswick Daily Home News*, April 15, 1932.

79. *New York Daily Mirror*, April 20, 1932.

80. Harvey Deuell to William Conklin, undated [1936], Box 28, Hoffman Papers; *Newark Evening News*, May 16, 1932.

81. J. J. Manning, untitled report, December 8, 1933, Box 10, Classification 7-1, FBI Records.

82. H. Norman Schwarzkopf, untitled memorandum, April 7, 1932, unmarked folder, Schwarzkopf Collection.

83. Jones, *Murder of Justice*, 141.

84. J. Edgar Hoover to H. Nathan, May 16, 1932, Box 4, Classification 7-1, FBI Records.

85. For newspaper reporters at the scene, see K. Sandberg, Report 1518, Reports File, NJSP.

FIVE. INTERROGATIONS

1. Berg, *Lindbergh*, 274.

2. Ibid.

3. Lindbergh, "Outline of Information . . . ," April 20, 1932, and additional notes, April 21, 1932, NJSP.

4. Fisher, *Lindbergh Case*, 135; *New York Daily Mirror*, May 18, 1932.

5. For the scene at Highfields, see Waller, *Kidnap*, 108–111; Rosner, untitled manuscript, 160; shorthand report, April 12, 1932, Nick Blasius Notebooks, NJSP.

6. Katharine Anne Dunning, "What Jafsie Told His High School Girls: The Surprising Story of How He Revealed His Role in the Lindbergh Case Weeks before the Rest of the World Knew the Secret," *Liberty,* May 16, 1936. I am grateful to Dolores Raich for calling this article to my attention and providing a copy.

7. *New York Times,* May 14, 1932.

8. *New York Daily Mirror,* May 14, 1932.

9. "Text of Report Made in Autopsy," May 12, 1932, Box 13, Hoffman Papers.

10. *New York Times,* May 15, 1932.

11. E. Sandberg, "Unknown Subjects," July 12, 1934, Department of Justice File, NJSP.

12. *New Brunswick Daily Home News,* May 22, 1932.

13. Ibid.

14. Newspaper clipping (from internal evidence), *Berkshire Evening Eagle,* May 24, 1932, Schwarzkopf Collection.

15. Ibid., May 26, 1932; John L. Sullivan, chief, Police Department, Pittsfield, to Colonel H. Norman Schwarzkopf, May 27, 1932, NJSP.

16. Sullivan to Schwarzkopf, May 27, 1932.

17. Newspaper clipping, *Berkshire Evening Eagle,* May 26, 1932, Schwarzkopf Collection.

18. Ibid.

19. Condon, *Jafsie Tells All,* 191.

20. "Investigation of Dr. John F. Condon at Alpine, N.J., by Inspector Harry W. Walsh, Sergeant Warren T. Moffatt, Lieutenant A. T. Keaten, and Detective Horn Concerning the Kidnapping and Murder of Charles A. Lindbergh, Jr., in Hopewell, N.J. on March lst," June 2, 1932. There are three fairly full accounts of the Condon interrogation at Alpine. None appear to be complete. The first is Condon's, as related in *Jafsie Tells All,* 188–199. Condon tells us that the trip to Alpine came "shortly after" the suicide of Violet Sharp, the Morrow maid, on June 10, 1932. Fisher, *Lindbergh Case,* 164–166, pinpoints the date as June 16. The only primary-source account of the interrogation, cited at the beginning of this note, is dated June 2, 1932—eight days before the death of Violet Sharp. Copies are in various files at the NJSP, including Box 22, Hoffman Papers. There is another, brief account of instructions issued by Walsh, dated June 22, 1932, not for an examination at Alpine but for Corporal William Horn to take Condon to Newark, New Jersey, to view pictures in a rogue's gallery. Investigative Files, NJSP. It is likely Condon confused the dates, and Fisher followed his account, which he indeed says is "based upon" Condon's. See *Lindbergh Case,* 422. The official stenographic notes by police officials are relatively tame, though perhaps deliberately toned down. They are still quite pointed in demonstrating Walsh's incredulity at many of the things he is being told. By contrast, Fisher downgrades Walsh's abilities and exaggerates Condon's brilliance in turning aside all the policeman's sallies. If Condon's accounts, as further embellished by Fisher, are taken at face value, Walsh's continuing doubts about Jafsie become less creditable, while Condon's role as the "official" narrator of the Lindbergh case, on the other hand, becomes all the more creditable.

21. "Investigation of Dr. Condon," June 2, 1932.

22. Ibid.

23. Condon, *Jafsie Tells All,* 198–199.

24. "Investigation of Dr. Condon," June 2, 1932; Condon, *Jafsie Tells All,* 198–199.

25. "Investigation of Dr. Condon," June 2, 1932.

26. Ibid.

27. Ibid.

28. E. J. Connelly to J. Edgar Hoover, June 4, 1932, Box 5, Classification 7-1, FBI Records.

29. Gaglio's search for Joseph Perrone in April was confirmed by another cabbie, Albert Santella, who took Condon's friend to the restaurant; see "Statement of Albert Santella," May 22, 1932, Statements File, NJSP. Santella's statement to police also included information that the night Condon first went to Hopewell, March 9, a cabbie waited around Rosenhain's for two hours before being dismissed by Condon, who told him, "I am sorry, one of my friends has offered his car, which was Gaglio; that was the car they went out in, Gaglio's car." Condon's instructions to the cabbie to wait for that period would suggest that he expected to be asked to come to Hopewell and took care in preparing for the trip.

30. E. J. Connelly, untitled report, May 27, 1932, Investigative Files, NJSP.

31. Perrone's various "identifications" can be followed in statements he made to NJSP investigators, beginning on May 21, 1932, and continuing on January 3, 1933, March 9, 1933, April 13, 1933, May 9, 1933, and other dates, and to the FBI on various occasions, as reported by Agent E. Sandberg, September 4, 1934, all in Box 14, Hoffman Papers.

32. Statement of April 13, 1933, and undated memorandum, "Perrone," both in Box 14, Hoffman Papers.

33. The handwritten letter is in State Police Reports F-125, NJSP. Thanks to Mark Falzini for calling it to my attention.

34. E. A. Hausling, "Investigation re John Birretella," October 17, 1933, Investigative Files, NJSP.

35. Report, December 21, 1933, by Sergeant A. Zapolsky and Corporal Samuel Leon, Investigative File 601, NJSP.

36. E. Sandberg, report, July 24, 1934, Box 22, Hoffman Papers.

37. Affidavit, April 8, 1936, by Arthur J. O'Sullivan, Box 22, Hoffman Papers.

38. Supplement to FBI Summary Report, 62-3057, 4, NJSP.

39. Frank Wilson to chief, Intelligence Unit, Internal Revenue Service, November 11, 1933, SI-6336-M, NJSP.

40. Ibid.

41. Lieutenant Arthur Keaten, "Investigation of a Letter . . . ," November 21, 1932, L Files, NJSP; Keaten, "Investigation of One Jack Longsio, Whose Photo Was Identified by Dr. Condon," March 23, 1933, Investigative Reports, NJSP; Kennedy, *Crime of the Century,* 125.

42. Harry Walsh, "The Hunt for the Lindbergh Kidnappers," *Jersey State Journal,* November 17, 1932.

43. From poetry found in Violet Sharp's diary after her death, Violet Sharp File, NJSP. I wish to thank Mark Falzini for calling these poems to my attention.

44. Report of Statement by George Payne (June 1932), Scotland Yard Reports, NJSP.

45. Statement of Violet Sharp, March 10, 1932, Box 14, Hoffman Papers.

46. Walsh, "The Hunt." There are many problems with the "second interrogation," however. Walsh puts the date as April 18, 1932. The only available

transcript has the date April 13, 1932, Statements File, NJSP. In the transcript, moreover, there is no mention of Ernie's being a bus driver. And there are other important differences to be noted. It is possible that Walsh conducted another interview with Violet prior to April 13, however, at Highfields, for which no record seems to have been made available to the New Jersey State Police.

47. Statement of Violet Sharp, April 13, 1932, Statements File, NJSP.

48. Statement of Walter Phillips, M.D., Englewood, N.J., June 16, 1932, Statements File, NJSP.

49. Untitled note by Drs. Harry D. Williams and Leo Haggerty, May 21, 1932, Statements File, NJSP. Kennedy, *Crime of the Century*, 119–121, writes that Walsh conducted an interview with Violet at Highfields on this date, and that it lasted but seven minutes until the doctors intervened. According to Walsh, "The Hunt," the interview took place in the library, and it was during this time that Violet's room back in Englewood was searched. There does not appear to be a transcript of the interrogation. It is very difficult, indeed, to straighten out both the chronological and geographic evidence concerning the various interviews.

50. The transcript of this examination is dated May 23, 1932, "Hopewell, N.J.," and is in the Statements File, NJSP; Walsh, "The Hunt," however, places it at the Morrow home in Englewood. From internal evidence in the transcript, it appears that the interview was held at Hopewell. He also writes that he informed Colonel Lindbergh about the results of his questioning in order to get the colonel's approval to set up another interview. The transcript, however, has Lindbergh present.

51. Statement of Emily Sharp, June 11, 1932, Scotland Yard Reports, NJSP.

52. The accounts of Violet's last meeting with police officials come from two sources, an untitled memorandum of the conversation by Harry Walsh, dated June 9, 1932, Box 14, Hoffman Papers, and Laura Hughes's two untitled statements, June 10 and June 14, 1932, Statements File, NJSP; J. E. Seykora, untitled report, May 10, 1934, Box 14, Classification 7-1, FBI Records; J. Edgar Hoover to H. Nathan, June 21, 1932, Box 6, ibid.

53. Walsh, untitled memorandum, June 9, 1932, Box 14, Hoffman Papers.

54. Memorandum signed by Keaten, Walsh, Sergeant Warren Moffatt, and Corporal William Horn, June 10, 1932, Box 14, Hoffman Papers.

55. The Schwarzkopf "Bulletin," *New York Daily Mirror*, June 11, 1932.

56. *New Brunswick Daily Home News*, June 11, 1932. Waller, in *Kidnap*, 150–151, embellishes the story, and other authors follow his account, adding other details gleaned from newspaper articles. See Fisher, *Lindbergh Case*, 151–152, and Jones, *Murder of Justice*, 174–175.

57. Quotations from *New York Daily Mirror*, June 12 and June 13, 1932.

58. Ibid., June 12, 1932.

59. Statement of Ernest Brinkert, June 12, 1932, Statements File, NJSP; Fisher, *Lindbergh Case*, 154.

60. Statements of Ernest Miller and Katherine Minners, June 11, 1932, and Elmer Johnson, June 16, 1932, Statements File, NJSP.

61. Violet Sharp to Fan Simons, June 7, 1932, Scotland Yard Reports, NJSP.

62. Fisher, *Lindbergh Case*, argues that revelations about Violet's sexual activities "probably [explain] her suicide." His reference to the archives, however, contains a single report of such activity, and an account of an interview with an official in 1984, who assured him the files contained evidence of her

intimacy with five men during a period prior to the kidnapping (161, and foot-
note 20). The archival reference is incomplete, as A. E. Norman's report of February 10, 1936, of the affair with William O'Brien, provided by an informant who
was sure "fear of exposure of these relations prompted her to commit suicide,"
turned out to be a gossipy assumption, with no real basis. See E. A. Hausling,
"Investigation of Information . . . ," February 21, 1936, Investigative Files, NJSP.
The reference to Violet's intimacy with at least five men, as provided orally to
Fisher, cannot be confirmed by archival research.

63. Recently, famed criminal investigator John Douglas and his colleague
Mark Olshaker revived interest in the Violet Sharp aspect of the investigation.
Like Harry Walsh, they opine that one cannot dismiss "her link in the chain of
intelligence information that made the kidnapping possible." *The Cases that
Haunt Us* (New York: Scribner, 2000), 161.

64. "K-4" to Hoffman, "Re-Rudolph Anton Schultzer," January 2, 1936, Box
24, Hoffman Papers. I thank Siglinde Rach for providing me with a copy of this
document from her files.

65. *New York Daily Mirror,* June 14, 1932.

66. Hoover note on H. Norman Schwarzkopf to J. Edgar Hoover, July 7,
1932, Box 6, Classification 7-1, FBI Records.

67. Walter N. Thayer to Charles Lindbergh, January 17, 1933, and H. Norman Schwarzkopf to Robert Thayer, January 26, 1933, NJSP; J. Edgar Hoover to
Albert D. Osborn, May 21, 1932, Box 4, Classification 7-1, FBI Records.

68. J. Edgar Hoover, handwritten note, March 17, 1932, Box 29, Classification 7-1, FBI Records.

SIX. EXPERT OPINIONS: MONEY, HANDWRITING, AND A LADDER

1. *New York Daily Mirror,* March 9, 1932.

2. Thomas Fensch, ed., *Top Secret: FBI Files on the Lindbergh Baby Kidnapping,* (Woodlands, Tex.: New Century Books, 2001), 159.

3. T. H. Sisk to J. Edgar Hoover, June 23, 1934, Box 15, Classification 7-1,
FBI Records.

4. John Brant and Edith Renaud, *True Story of the Lindbergh Kidnapping*
(New York: Kroy Wen, 1932), 54–56. Thanks to Siglinde Rach for calling my attention to this neglected story of Oscar Bush's efforts to reconstruct the crime.

5. Fisher, *Lindbergh Case,* 138–139; Robert Peacock, as told to Jack
Yarmov, "Guilty as Hell: At Last, the Truth about the Hauptman Case," unpublished manuscript, 9–10, NJSP; Waller, *Kidnap,* 138–139.

6. Trial testimony, 486–512.

7. Ibid.

8. Squire Johnson to H. Norman Swartzkopf [sic], March 10, 1932, Box 13,
Hoffman Papers.

9. Ibid.

10. Squire Johnson to Commissioner Ellis, June 4, 1932, Box 13, Hoffman
Papers.

11. Ibid.

12. K. F. Kellerman to H. G. Knight, June 4, 1932, Investigative File 117, NJSP.

13. C. A. Appel, memorandum for the director, May 24, 1932, Box 5, Classification 7-1, FBI Records.

14. Arthur Koehler, "Who Made that Ladder?" *Saturday Evening Post,* April 20, 1935, 10.

15. Kennedy, *Crime of the Century,* 128; *New York Times,* April 12, 1932.

16. The rundown on the ransom bills was compiled by the Federal Bureau of Investigation and is most readily available today in Fensch, *FBI Files on the Lindbergh Baby Kidnapping,* 277–341.

17. Ibid., 318–319.

18. Waller, *Kidnap,* 201. Waller's description of Finn's map is probably the best account we have of the detective's painstaking efforts to plot out the pattern of spending.

19. T. H. Sisk to J. Edgar Hoover, June 29, 1934, Box 14, Classification 7-1, FBI Records.

20. Lieutenant Arthur Keaten, "Investigation Regarding Part of the Lindbergh Ransom," May 5, 1933, Box 4, Hoffman Papers; Keaten, "Investigation in Reference to Deposit Slips," May 19, 1933; Keaten, "Investigation Regarding J. J. Faulkner," May 16, 1933; Keaten, "Investigation," May 26, 1933; all in Box 19, Hoffman Papers; Frank Wilson to chief, Intelligence Unit, Internal Revenue Services, November 11, 1933, SI-6336-M, 22.

21. Wilson report, SI-6336-M, 22; Anthony Scaduto, *Scapegoat: The Lonesome Death of Bruno Richard Hauptmann* (New York: G. P. Putnam, 1976), 304–309, is the fullest treatment of the Giessler investigation; J. J. Manning, "Unknown Subjects," September 11, 1933, Box 3, Wilentz Collection.

22. Lieutenant Arthur Keaten, "Investigation in Connection with One J. J. Faulkner," May 8, 1933, and Sergeant A. Zapolsky, "Investigation of Lindbergh Case regarding John Faulkner of 1336 Balcom Avenue," May 8, 1933, both in File F-18, NJSP. Condon, *Jafsie Tells All,* 53.

23. Albert D. Osborn to J. Edgar Hoover, May 17, 1932; Hoover to Osborn, May 21, 1932, Box 4, Classification 7-1, FBI Records.

24. E. J. Connelley, untitled report, May 24, 1932, Box 5, Classification 7-1, FBI Records.

25. Osborn's report is included as an attachment to E. J. Connelley to J. Edgar Hoover, May 28, 1932, Box 5, Classification 7-1, FBI Records.

26. Ibid.

27. Snook, "Detailed Report," May 17, 1932, L File, NJSP.

28. See, for example, the flat statement of Elbridge Walter Stein: "In my opinion, the writer of these letters was a writer who had at some time learned to write German. . . . while there is undoubtedly German influence in the writing, it is not predominant but is somewhat eclipsed by the influence of American writing." June 24, 1932, L File, NJSP. Or the opinion of Albert S. Osborn, who wrote that the effort at disguise, particularly in the first letter, made it somewhat difficult to determine the actual nationality of the author: "Various words and forms point toward the German language and handwriting, but this does not necessarily indicate that the writer was a German but was one who wrote the German language." Supplement to the FBI Summary Report, Exhibit E, 12–13, NJSP. Wilson report, 3.

29. L. G. Turrou, untitled report, October 13, 1932, Box 7, Classification 7-1, FBI Records.

30. Ibid.

31. J. E. Dunn to J. Edgar Hoover, October 14, 1932, ibid.

32. Dudley D. Shoenfeld, *The Crime and the Criminal: A Psychiatric Study of the Lindbergh Case* (New York: Covici-Friede, 1936), 47. The account that follows is largely drawn from this book and the unpublished copy of the Leigh Matteson manuscript, "Lone Wolf vs. Lone Eagle," in Box 4, Hoffman Papers.

33. "Memorandum to Captain Oliver and Lt. James Finn," November 10, 1932, as quoted in Shoenfeld, *The Crime and the Criminal,* 51–56. Shoenfeld played an important role in the Lindbergh case from near the beginning to the end. His analysis of the ransom notes smacks more of graphology than medicine, however. Other interpretations of the symbol have been made from time to time, some seeing it as takeoff on a military insignia, or as a replica of an ancient central European cult, for example. None are really convincing.

34. E. Sandberg, "Unknown Subjects," July 24, 1934, Box 2, Lehman FBI Files, NJSP.

35. George Waller, who thanks Dr. Shoenfeld for his help in supplying information for his book, *Kidnap,* writes on 202 that "every bill was folded" this way, providing a clue "as unique as a signature." Fisher, *Lindbergh Case,* 179, picks up the theme, asserting that "each note" was folded that way, and also that Finn had discovered the pattern in the way it was tendered, by taking "a small folded bill from his watch or vest pocket and toss[ing] it onto the counter for the bank or store clerk to unfold." He provides no source for this assertion. The above quotations from FBI sources are in the laboratory report, of August 7, 1934, Box 2, Lehman/FBI Files, NJSP; and Fensch, *FBI Files on the Lindbergh Baby Kidnapping,* 285. I have italicized *some* in the first quotation for emphasis.

36. Shoenfeld, *Crime and Criminal,* 48.

37. Ibid., 55.

38. Matteson, "Lone Wolf," 114–115.

39. Shoenfeld, *Crime and the Criminal,* 53 ff.

40. Matteson, "Lone Wolf," 84.

41. Ibid., 91–94.

42. Ibid., 133–134.

43. Shoenfeld, *Crime and the Criminal,* 52. Wilson in his November 1933 report expressed his own doubts about Condon's reliability.

44. Ibid.

45. John F. Condon to Lucy Grosenbeek, March 19, 1934, Box 3, Hoffman Papers. In addition, he wrote to C. Hurley on February 27, 1934, ibid.: "If you know anything about the {Box, Boodle, Baby Bandits} 4, let me hear. If you want me to do something, let me hear. What do you wish to tell me?"

46. John F. Condon to J. Edgar Hoover, January 12, 1933, and Condon to Hoover, May 11, 1933, both in Box 42, Classification 7-1, FBI Records; Condon to Homer S. Cummings, October 18, 1933, and Condon to Hoover, October 20, 1933, both in Box 9, ibid.; and Condon to Hoover, February 5, 1934, Box 11, ibid.

47. J. Edgar Hoover to Rudolph Forster, December 29, 1933, Box 10, Classification 7-1, FBI Records.

48. T. H. Sisk to J. Edgar Hoover, June 23, 1934, Box 15, Classification 7-1, FBI Records.

49. Ibid.

50. Corporal William F. Horn and Corporal Samuel J. Leon, "Memorandum of Story . . . ," October 18, 1932, Box 18, Hoffman Papers.

51. H. S. Betts, "Report on Examination of Ladder," June 1, 1932, Hoffman Papers. This report is a summary of various findings by federal agencies.

52. Ibid.

53. Koehler, "Who Made That Ladder?" 10.

54. Arthur Koehler, "Report of Examination of Ladder for the New Jersey State Police," March 4, 1933, NJSP.

55. In addition to the sources cited, I thank Stephen Lehmann for providing me with a copy of his unpublished paper, "The Ladder," November 16, 2000, in author's possession. Lehmann raises especially significant questions about the scientific "methods" employed in the ladder investigation.

56. P 101 File, NJSP.

57. Koehler, "Who Made That Ladder?" 86.

58. Lewis Bornmann, "Continued Investigation of the Origin of the Wood Used . . . ," May 6, 1933, Investigative File 117, NJSP.

59. Koehler, "Report on Examination of Ladder . . . ," December 10, 1933. This is another diary-style memorandum. The entry quoted here is for November 22, 1933.

60. Bornmann, untitled memorandum, November 29, 1933. Entry for November 27, 1933.

61. Koehler, untitled memorandum, December 10, 1933. Entry for November 29, 1933.

62. Ibid., December 1, 1933.

63. Ibid., December 6, 1933.

64. Ibid., December 8, 1933.

65. Ibid.

66. Investigative File 117, NJSP.

67. Arthur Koehler to Captain J. J. Lamb, January 10, 1934; Koehler to Lamb, January 12, 1934; both in P 101 File, NJSP.

68. Koehler to Lamb, January 31 and February 2, 1934, P 101 File, NJSP.

69. H. Norman Schwarzkopf, memo to Captain J. J. Lamb, February 5, 1934, and Koehler to Lamb, June 13, 1934, both in P 101 File, NJSP.

70. Arthur Koehler to Captain J. J. Lamb, June 13, 1934, P101 File, NJSP. Emphasis added. The meaning here is clear. After reexamining the ladder rails on his return to Madison, the expert still had not found the minute marking that he discovered in time for his 1935 article.

71. Arthur Koehler to Captain J. J. Lamb, July 27, 1934, P 101 File, NJSP.

SEVEN. CONFRONTATIONS

1. J. Edgar Hoover, "Memorandum for the Attorney General," September 13, 1933, Box 9, Classification 7-1, FBI Records.

2. H. Norman Schwarzkopf to J. Edgar Hoover, September 2, 1933; Hoover to Schwarzkopf, September 18, 1933; Schwarzkopf to Hoover, September 25, 1933; and Hoover to Schwarzkopf, October 12, 1933, all in Box 9, Classification 7-1, FBI Records.

3. T. H. Sisk to J. Edgar Hoover, June 23, 1934, Box 15, Classification 7-1, FBI Records.

4. Waller, *Kidnap,* 209.

5. J. Edgar Hoover, "Memorandum for Mr. Tamm," June 8, 1934, Box 14, Classification 7-1, FBI Records.

6. Ibid.

7. J. Edgar Hoover, "Memorandum for Mr. Cowley," June 4, 1934, and Hoover, "Memorandum for the Attorney General," May 22, 1934, both in Box 14, Classification 7-1, FBI Records.

8. J. Edgar Hoover, "Memorandum for Mr. Tamm," June 19, 1934, Box 14, Classification 7-1, FBI Records. A lengthy memorandum was prepared for Hoover's use at this conference by Sisk, dated June 8, 1934, ibid. It details the animosity as centering on the question of fingerprints and ransom money.

9. T. H. Sisk, "Bruno Richard Hauptmann alias Richard Hauptmann alias Richard Hoffman alias Karl Pellmeier," October 17, 1934, Box 3, Lehman FBI Files, NJSP. The paragraphs that follow are largely drawn from this lengthy summary document, except where otherwise noted.

10. On Hoover and Winchell, see Neal Gabler, *Winchell: Gossip, Power, and the Culture of Celebrity* (New York: Alfred A. Knopf, 1994), 199–202.

11. Ibid., and Richard Gid Powers, *Secrecy and Power: The Life of J. Edgar Hoover* (New York: Free Press, 1987), 190–95.

12. E. A. Tamm, "Memorandum for the Director," September 7, 1932, Box 16, Classification 7-1, FBI Records.

13. James Finn, "How I Captured Hauptmann," part four, *Liberty,* November 3, 1935, 40–46. Finn's account of the interview with Levantino—as with other subjects he discusses—is much more elaborate than Sisk's FBI report.

14. Tamm, "Memorandum for the Director," September 7, 1932; E. A. Tamm to J. Edgar Hoover, September 8, 1934, Box 14, Classification 7-1, FBI Records.

15. Kennedy, *Crime of the Century,* 160–161.

16. Finn, " How I Captured Hauptmann," part 4.

17. There is considerable confusion over the sequence of events at this point. In two official statements, one to the Bronx grand jury in September of 1934, and the other in a pretrial deposition dated November 22, 1934, Lieutenant Finn states that once he saw the numbers on the back of the ten-dollar gold certificate he immediately telephone the Motor Vehicle Bureau. He says nothing in either instance about receiving at this time the information that the license belonged to a German-born carpenter. In his magazine article, "How I Captured Hauptmann," part 5, *Liberty,* November 9, 1935, 40–45, he says it was during the same phone call. He also says in this article, contrary to his sworn statements, that he first visited the Warner-Quinlan gas station before calling the Motor Vehicle Bureau.

18. Corporal William F. Horn, "Continued Report of Investigation Concerning a Recovered $10.00 U.S. Gold Certificate," October 3, 1934, Accordion File—NJSP, 18–25.

19. Finn, "How I Captured Hauptmann," part 5. Horn's interview, cited above, has Lyle saying that this was the first gold certificate he had seen since Roosevelt's proclamation, and Hauptmann replying, "No, I only have about one hundred left." In neither instance was there a need for Hauptmann to stress that he had more of the bills at home in order to get the attendant to take the money.

20. Sisk, "Bruno Richard Hauptmann . . . ," October 17, 1934, Box 3, Lehman/ FBI Files, NJSP.

21. Ibid., 24; William F. Horn, "Report of an Investigation Concerning a Recovered $10.00 U.S. Gold Certificate . . . ," September 25, 1934, Box 13, Hoffman

Papers; Walter Winchell, *Winchell Exclusive,* (Englewood Cliffs, N.J.: Prentice-Hall, 1975), 107.

22. Finn, "How I Captured Hauptmann," part 5.

23. H. H. Clegg, "Memorandum for Special Agent in Charge T. H. Sisk," October 1, 1934, Harold R. Olson Files, NJSP. Given the German experience with postwar inflation, it was a not unlikely possibility that such dealing went on, in an effort to protect savings, either in the United States or to send abroad to the old country. I am grateful, again, to Siglinde Rach for information about the Yorkville Boerse and Bruno Richard Hauptmann's possible connections there through Hans Müeller.

24. Finn, "How I Captured Hauptmann," part 5; Sergeant John Wallace, "Dismounted Patrol at Fordham Road . . . ," September 20, 1934, Box 13, Hoffman Papers; Corporal Horn, "Report of Investigation Concerning a Recovered $10.00 U.S. Gold Certificate."

25. Waller, *Kidnap,* 220.

26. Finn, "How I Captured Hauptmann," part 5.

27. Ibid.

28. Fisher, *Lindbergh Case,* 445. Fisher acknowledges the dispute about whether the bill was found folded over in such fashion, but concludes in his summation that Detective Sergeant Cornel Plebani, an aide at the NJSP Museum at the time he did his researches, "stated emphatically" that was the case. Plebani apparently did not show him any evidence to support this assertion. Finn's statements to the grand jury and his pretrial deposition are in the Foley Files, NJSP, and Box 13, Hoffman Papers. The arresting officers' statements are those by T. H. Sisk, "Bruno Richard Hauptmann . . . ," October 17, 1934, Box 3, FBI Files, NJSP; Trooper Dennis Dore, "Activity on the Hauptmann Case," November 2, 1934, Box 33, Hoffman Papers; Corporal Horn, "Report of Investigation of a Recovered $10.00 U.S. Gold Certificate"; Detective Sergeant John Wallace, "Dismounted Patrol at Fordham Road . . . ," September 20, 1934, Box 13, Hoffman Papers.

29. E. A. Tamm, untitled memorandum, October 19, 1935, Box 23, Classification 7-1, FBI Records.

30. Pretrial deposition, November 22, 1934, Box 13, Hoffman Papers.

31. This account of Anna's encounter in the room where Richard was being held is taken from her statement to lawyers on November 23, 1934, Box 25, Hoffman Papers, and Kennedy, *Crime of the Century,* 171–172.

32. Wallace, "Dismounted Patrol at Fordham Road."

33. Sisk, "Bruno Richard Hauptmann"; Turrou, *Where My Shadow Falls,* 121.

34. Turrou, *Where My Shadow Falls,* 121.

35. Trial transcript, 1587–1591.

36. Leon Turrou, "Bruno Richard Hauptmann," October 13, 1934, Box 3, FBI Files, NJSP.

37. Finn's article is cited in Scaduto, *Scapegoat,* 333–334. Scaduto's claim via Lieutenant Finn that Hauptmann was handcuffed is supported by Wallace's own record, "Dismounted Patrol at Fordham Road . . . ," September 20, 1934. Fisher, *Lindbergh Case,* 190, has Finn, not Sisk, as the man who dug up the garage and who discovered the crock, and then took it to Hauptmann to hear his denial. Finn's supposed rebuttal was: "Sure you do [know about the crock]. This is where you hid some of the ransom money. Isn't that right?" Fisher cites no source for this dialogue.

38. Transcript, September 19, 1934, 3:00 P.M., NJSP. Unless otherwise noted, the accounts of this first interrogation are taken from this source.

39. Turrou, *Where My Shadow Falls,* 121.

40. Ibid.

41. The Hauptmann "request writings" are in the NJSP.

42. Kennedy, *Crime of the Century,* 179.

43. Ibid., 177.

44. Transcript of second interrogation session, September 19, 1934, NJSP.

45. Undated form letter and instructions, NJSP.

46. H. Norman Schwarzkopf to J. Clark Sellers, October 26, 1934, Accordion Files—General Handwriting, NJSP.

47. Kennedy, *Crime of the Century,* 178–180; Fisher, *Lindbergh Case,* 207.

48. Quoted in *Hunterdon County Democrat,* February 5, 1981.

49. Wallace, "Dismounted Patrol at Fordham Road."

50. Ibid., and Fisher, *Lindbergh Case,* 447. Turrou decided later to bolster Sisk's story about the crockery jar buried below the garage floor, writing in 1949, "Another cache of gold certificates was presently dug up from the garage floor, hidden with Teutonic lack of sentimentality in a dill-pickle jar." *Where My Shadow Falls,* 126. There never was such a cache of gold certificates; Turrou's motive for the statement seems obvious, to discredit further Hauptmann's story about how the money was found. Given the FBI's skepticism about a lone kidnapper at the time of the arrest and trial, as exemplified in the contemporary reports of both Sisk and Turrou, the effort to seal the case in retrospect does him no credit.

51. Transcript of interrogation, September 20, 1934, at 4:20 P.M., NJSP. The information that follows is taken from this source, unless otherwise noted.

52. Bruckman, "Statement Dictated to Stenographer Thomas J. Riordan . . . ," September 22, 1934, Box 33, Hoffman Papers.

53. Bruno Richard Hauptmann to Pinkas Fisch, May 4, 1934, NJSP. The whereabouts of this $5,000 is a total mystery. Thanks again to Siglinde Rach for providing insight into the origins of the Hauptmann-Fisch partnership.

54. It is also likely that the Fisch-Hauptmann partnership encompassed a number of less than legal operations, such as money laundering. The secret exchanges of money at Steiner, Rouse suggest such an operation, perhaps hidden behind the Hudson seals and silver fox. Hauptmann's statements during a semipublic morning lineup add more to the story. The question, obviously, is whether they add more truth to the story.

Acting Inspector John. J. Sullivan began the dialogue with a question: "Did you ever deal in furs?"

"My friend did."

"How long?"

"Since '30."

"How did you make out?"

"Successful."

"How successful?"

"Up to 10,000."

"Did you keep any books?"

Without waiting for a reply, Sullivan went on: "They don't show how you bought and sold. How do you account for that?"

Hauptmann then launched into an explanation that no one could understand.

Sullivan ended the dialogue with a dismissive quip, "You kept no books." *New Brunswick Daily Home News,* September 21, 1934.

55. "Report of Examination of Richard Hauptmann's Writings," September 21, 1934, Bronx District Attorney Files, NJSP. Osborn's demeanor can be observed in newsreel films available at NJSP.

56. *New York Times,* September 21, 1934.

57. Scaduto, *Scapegoat,* 112.

58. Turrou, *Where My Shadow Falls,* 122–123.

59. Condon, *Jafsie Tells All,* 220.

60. Turrou, *Where My Shadow Falls,* 123.

61. Transcript of the lineup is in Box 28, Hoffman Papers. The *New York Times* for September 21, 1934, also has what appears to be a verbatim account. They vary about certain details. I have drawn on both in the paragraphs that follow.

62. Turrou, *Where My Shadow Falls,* 123.

63. Ibid., 124; Kennedy, *Crime of the Century,* 193; Leon Turrou, untitled memorandum, September 21, 1934, quoted in *New York Times,* October 23, 1977; Fisher, *Lindbergh Case,* 214.

64. *New York Times,* September 21, 1934.

65. *New Brunswick Sunday Times,* September 23, 1934.

66. Ibid.

67. Turrou, memorandum, September 21, 1934; *New Brunswick Sunday Times,* September 23, 1934.

68. E. A. Tamm, "Memorandum for the Director," September 24, 1934, Box 2, Lehman/FBI Files, NJSP; T. H. Sisk, "Bruno Richard Hauptmann with Aliases," October 29, 1934, File 1600, NJSP. Fisher, *Lindbergh Case,* 220–221, constructs an imaginary dialogue between Hauptmann and Turrou in which the suspect appears about ready to make a confession and asks the agent if he could expect some leniency if he did so. Turrou could not make any promises, because kidnapping was not a federal crime at the time of the Lindbergh case. But he promised to bring this to the attention of the state prosecutor. Hauptmann then clammed up, and the moment passed. Turrou's assertion of the near-confession came in a letter to Harold M. Olson, one of the claimants to be Charles Lindbergh, Jr., dated January 24, 1977. It was occasioned by Olson's letter to him citing Anthony Scaduto's book, *Scapegoat,* as evidence that Hauptmann had been framed. Turrou regarded it as "scandulous" that anyone should think Hauptmann had been wrongly convicted. When Olson persisted in another letter, Turrou wrote back on March 21, 1977, "Hauptmann would have confessed to me when I interviewed him in the Bronx county jail but he wanted me to assure him that I would obtain leniency for him." Scaduto's book, he charged, was "pure imagination and speculation, and as I told you before Hauptmann was justly executed for the crime he had committed. I am sorry that you think otherwise." Clearly, Olson had touched a nerve, as the higher-pitched tone of Turrou's second response indicated. In his earlier memoir, *Where My Shadow Falls,* the former agent had expressed many of the doubts later researchers felt in going over the events of the arrest and interrogations. There is no mention of the near-confession in that memoir. Nor do Turrou's 1977 recollections match well with

Sisk's contemporary memorandum of Hauptmann's adamant refusal to confess any guilt. The Turrou-Olson exchanges are in the Olson Donation, NJSP.

69. *New York Daily News,* September 22, 1934.

70. Tamm, memorandum, September 21, 1934.

EIGHT. IN DISTRICT ATTORNEY FOLEY'S OFFICE

1. T. H. Sisk account of Foley's questioning is quoted at length in Kennedy, *Crime of the Century,* 197–199.

2. *New York Times,* September 23, 1934. I have reversed the order of these quoted sentences.

3. Sisk account, in Kennedy, *Crime of the Century,* 197–199.

4. Transcript of statement of Bruno Richard Hauptmann, 4:05 A.M., September 21, 1934, Box 5, Wilentz Collection.

5. Ibid.; and statement of Max Rauch, 3:40 A.M., September 21, 1934, Bronx District Attorney Files, NJSP.

6. Statement of Bruno Richard Hauptmann, 4:05 A.M., September 21, 1934.

7. Kennedy, *Crime of the Century,* 198.

8. *New York Times,* September 23, 1934.

9. T. H. Sisk to J. Edgar Hoover, September 20, 1934, and Hoover to Sisk, September 25, 1934, both in Box 16, Classification 7-1, FBI Records.

10. J. Edgar Hoover, "Memorandum for Mr. Tamm," September 22 and 23, 1934, Box 17, Classification 7-1, FBI Records.

11. Ibid.

12. *Dallas Morning News,* September 23, 1934.

13. *New York Times,* September 23, 1934; *New Brunswick Sunday Times,* September 23, 1934.

14. *New York Daily News,* September 22, 1934.

15. Statement of Anna Hauptmann, September 21, 1934, Statements File, NJSP.

16. *New Brunswick Daily Home News,* September 24, 1934.

17. M. Breed and J. S. Kavanaugh, "Memorandum for File," September 21, 1934, Accordion File—Hauptmann Investigation, NJSP.

18. "Statement of Christian Fredericksen Taken at the District Attorney's Office, 5:40 P.M.," September 24, 1934, Statements File, NJSP.

19. Ibid.; Katie's affair was never revealed publicly by Anna during her lifetime. Confidential source.

20. "Statement of Christian Fredericksen Taken at District Attorney's Office, 5:40 P.M.," September 24, 1934.

21. Ibid.

22. Statement of Christian Fredericksen taken October 29, 1934, Statements File, NJSP.

23. *New York Times,* September 24, 1934.

24. Unsigned memorandum, December 23, 1935, Box 36, Classification 7-1, FBI Records.

25. Lewis Bornmann, "Searching of Bruno Richard Hauptmann's Home and Garage . . . ," September 25, 1934, Reports File, NJSP.

26. Unsigned memorandum, "Bruno Richard Hauptmann, with Aliases . . . ," December 23, 1935, Box 2, Lehman/FBI Files, NJSP.

27. Ibid.; and the Sisk-Wright Conversation is quoted in Kennedy *Crime of the Century*, 205.

28. Scaduto, *Scapegoat*, 252–256, 263–264; Kennedy, *Crime of the Century*, 204–206.

29. Statement of Bruno Richard Hauptmann, September 25, 1934, Statements File, NJSP.

30. J. Edgar Hoover, "Memorandum for Mr. Tamm," September 25, 1934, Box 2, Lehman/FBI Files, NJSP.

31. Fisher, *Lindbergh Case*, 226, leaves out the questions about Hauptmann's welfare, which divided the interrogation, and thus compresses the discussion of the address and the bills, and indeed does not refer to them here. By the second half of the interrogation, there is reason to believe that confusion existed, as in the question that begins, "You must remember that you did write it?" "I must write it, the figures that's my writing." Hauptmann clearly means the bill numbers, as Foley tries to clear this up. "The writing is yours too, isn't it?" Hauptmann answers, "I hardly can read it." By leaving out the discussion of the bill numbers, Fisher does not allow for confusion or Foley's concern to clarify the issue.

32. Statement of Bruno Richard Hauptmann, 12:21 P.M., September 25, 1934, Statements File, NJSP.

33. *New Brunswick Daily Home News*, September 25, 1934; Fisher, *Lindbergh Case*, 227.

34. Testimony of Albert S. Osborn, September 25, 1934, Foley Collection, NJSP.

35. Ibid. Emphasis added.

36. Deposition, November 22, 1934, Box 13, Hoffman Papers.

37. *New Brunswick Home News*, September 25, 1934.

38. Testimony of Charles A. Lindbergh, September 26, 1934, Foley Collection, NJSP.

39. *New Brunswick Daily Home News*, September 27, 1934.

40. The little-used Accordion File labeled "General Handwriting" is the fullest account of the correspondence between Colonel Schwarzkopf and the prosecution handwriting experts. See especially on these points, John F. Tyrell to H. Norman Schwarzkopf, December 7, 1934, and Schwarzkopf to Tyrell, December 6, 7, 11, and 13, 1934.

41. Bornmann report, dated September 25 and 26, Box 12, Hoffman Papers.

42. Statement of Bruno Richard Hauptmann, September 26, 1934, Statements File, NJSP.

43. *New Brunwick Daily Home News*, September 27, 1934.

44. *New York Times*, September 28, 1934.

45. *New York Times*, September 29, 1934. This important issue has become another battleground for those who have studied and written on the case. Scaduto, in *Scapegoat*, 318–322, using newspaper sources and the diary of the British author Harold Nicolson present in the Morrow home, argues that Lindbergh remained unsure after this encounter and did not identify Hauptmann's voice until October 8, 1934, a mysterious delay of nearly two weeks, making the evidence seriously questionable. Fisher, in *Lindbergh Case*, quoting the diary of a Foley secretary, Benjamin Arac, says that the identification took place on September 27, 1934. Since Fisher does not provide any specific location for this

diary, nor acknowledge it in his bibliography, it is impossible to resolve this question completely. One might ask, however, why Foley would keep such an important development a secret.

46. *New York Times,* September 28, 1934; E. A. Tamm, "Memorandum for the Director," September 27, 1934, Box 3, Lehman/FBI Files, NJSP.

47. E. A. Tamm, untitled memorandum, September 27, 1934, Box 17, Classification 7-1, FBI Records; J. Edgar Hoover, "Memorandum for Mr. Tamm," September 27, 1934, Box 3, Lehman/FBI Files, NJSP. This report relates to this particular day, unless it is misdated.

48. Tamm, memorandum, September 27, 1934; J. Edgar Hoover, "Memorandum for Mr. Tamm," September 26, 1934, Box 3, Lehman/FBI Files, NJSP.

49. Hoover, "Memorandum for Mr. Tamm, October 6, 1934, Box 18, Classification 7-1, FBI Records.

50. *New Brunswick Daily Home News,* September 23 and 24, 1934; *New York Times,* September 28, 1934.

51. *New York Times,* September 29, 1934.

52. Ibid.

53. Thurston H. Dexter, "Report of Oral and Physical Examination of Bruno Richard Hauptmann," September 25, 1934, Box 2, Hoffman Papers.

54. James H. Huddleson, "Report to Mr. James M. Fawcett, undated, 1934, NJSP.

55. Turrou, *Where My Shadow Falls,* 127.

56. *New York Times,* September 27, 1934.

57. See, for example, Harold H. Fisher to David Wilentz, September 27, 1934, L File, NJSP.

58. *New York Daily News,* September 22, 1934.

59. *New York Daily Mirror,* September 26, 1934.

60. *New York Times,* September 27 and 30, 1934.

61. William Stanley to J. Edgar Hoover, September 29, 1934, Box 3, Lehman/FBI Files, NJSP.

62. J. Edgar Hoover, untitled memorandum, September 26, 1934, Box 3, Lehman/FBI Files, NJSP.

NINE. MR. WILENTZ BUILDS HIS CASE

1. *New Brunswick Daily Home News,* December 18, 1934.

2. Undated newspaper article [October 3, 1934], Scrapbooks File, NJSP.

3. Ibid.

4. J. Edgar Hoover, "Memorandum for Mr. Tamm," October 5, 1934, and Hoover, "Memorandum for Mr. Tamm," October 6, 1934, both in Box 18, Classification 7-1, FBI Records.

5. J. Edgar Hoover, "Memorandum for Mr. Tamm," September 27, 1934, and Hoover, "Memorandum for Mr. Tamm," September 28, 1934, both in Box 17, Classification 7-1, FBI Records.

6. E. A. Tamm, "Memorandum for the Director," September 29, 1934, and J. Edgar Hoover, "Memorandum for Mr. Tamm," September 30, 1934, both in Box 18, Classification 7-1, FBI Records.

7. J. A. Wolf, "Identification of Richard Bruno Hauptmann by Millard Whited . . . ," October 4, 1934, Box 8, Hoffman Papers.

8. Ibid.; and "Transcript of Stenographer's Notes . . . ," February 22, 1936, Box 8, Hoffman Papers.

9. Statement of Millard Whited, October 6, 1934, Box 8, Hoffman Papers.

10. Ibid.

11. Statement of Millard Whited, April 26, 1932, Box 8, Hoffman Papers. The only recorded statement of an interview on the early morning of March 2, 1932, has Whited saying he had seen nothing suspicious that night.

12. Undated [October 7, 1934] newspaper clipping, Scrapbook File, NJSP.

13. Hoover, "Memorandum for Mr. Tamm," October 6, 1934; *New York Times,* October 9, 1934.

14. J. Edgar Hoover, "Memorandum for Mr. Tamm," October 9, 1934, Box 3, Lehman/FBI Files, NJSP; Hoover, "Memorandum for Mr. Tamm," October 9, 1934, Box 18, Classification 7-1, FBI Records.

15. E. A. Tamm, "Memorandum for the Director," October 9, 1934, Box 18, Classification 7-1, FBI Records.

16. J. Edgar Hoover, "Memorandum for Mr. Tamm," October 10, 1934, Box 18, Classification 7-1, FBI Records.

17. *New Brunswick Daily Home News,* December 18, 1934.

18. *New York Times,* October 9, 1934.

19. Turrou, *Where My Shadow Falls,* 127–128.

20. *New York Times,* October 17, 1934.

21. *Hunterdon County Democrat,* October 18, 1934.

22. *New York Times,* October 17, 1934.

23. *Hunterdon County Democrat,* October 18, 1934.

24. *New Brunswick Daily Home News,* October 16, 1934.

25. For an explanation of Suetterlin—the German handwriting—on the web, see: http://www.peter-doerling.de/Englisch/Sutterlin.htm. Many thanks to Siglinde Rach for pointing me toward this information.

26. *New York Times,* October 17, 1934; *New Brunswick Daily Home News,* October 16, 1934; Accordion File—Hauptmann Investigation, NJSP.

27. Scaduto, *Scapegoat,* 278–281.

28. Ibid., 279. Scaduto's treatment of the work records issue raises questions about disappearing evidence and deliberate concealment, as does an unpublished report by Michael Melsky, "Observations Concerning Missing Majestic Payroll Record Dated Week Ending March 15 1932," author's possession. The controversy is a difficult one to resolve, as will be seen as the question unfolds after the extradition hearing and during the Flemington trial.

29. Corporal William F. Horn, "Report of Investigation Concerning Search for Original Timesheets . . . ," November 5, 1934, Accordion File—Hauptmann Investigation, NJSP.

30. *New York Times,* October 16, 1934.

31. Ibid., October 19 and 27, 1934; a copy of the receipt is in Box 33, Hoffman Papers.

32. The records can be found in an envelope marked "Mr Bayliss," in Box 33, Hoffman Papers. Michael Melsky argues, however, that these records are incomplete, and he puts them in the context of a possible "bait-and-switch" ploy to convince defense attorneys at the trial that he had the records to refute a claim Hauptmann had been working that day. It does appear that the work records, at least the time sheets, have been tampered with, but there is no

conclusive proof that it was done by the police or by others working in cooperation with the police.

33. It does not break down exactly, of course, because of the differences in the numbers of days in a month, but it does appear that the work went on every single day, including Sundays.

34. *New York Times,* October 16, 1934. It is interesting, however, that FBI agent Leon Turrou recorded there was a bit of subterfuge about the "discovery" of the $14,000 in Hauptmann's garage. Turrou wrote that after the first search of the house, a conference was held, attended by police and government agents, with J. Edgar Hoover arguing for a new search despite a doubtful Colonel Schwarzkopf. "Four of us went down," he reported, "and the house, attic, and garage were gone through timber by timber." The money was found in a five-gallon gasoline can hidden in an ill-concealed compartment on the south wall of the garage. But then he wrote as well, "The rules of evidence are such that the money would not have been legally admitted by the court as evidence unless a member of the household—in this case Mrs. Hauptmann—was present. We therefore replaced the cans and called in Mrs. Hauptmann. 'Can you tell us if any money is hidden here?' I asked in German. She shook her head. 'Money? Money in this house? You're crazy. We're poor people; where would we get money to hide? Please, please, Herr Policeman, why are you holding Richard?' We went through the motions of searching and found the gold certificates for her." *Where My Shadow Falls,* 125. Turrou's memory for details was sometimes faulty, but not for such an important finding as the money in the garage. He noted that the team that went to the house on the morning of September 20, 1934, searched the entire house, the attic, and the garage—timber by timber. And yet the money was found in a very short time.

35. *New York Times,* October 16, 1934.

36. *New Brunswick Daily Home News,* October 16, 1934.

37. Ibid., October 19, 1934.

38. *Hunterdon County Democrat,* October 25, 1934.

39. Ibid.

40. Ibid.

41. *Hunterdon County Democrat,* October 4 and 25, 1934.

42. Leon Turrou, "Memorandum for Special Agent T. H. Sisk," October 5, 1934, Box 16, Classification 7-1, FBI Records.

43. Samuel J. Leon, "The Taking of Dr. Condon to Perth Amboy . . . ," October 23, 1934, File 1603, NJSP.

44. Condon, *Jafsie Tells All,* 229–231. Condon apparently conflates what happened at his two meetings with Wilentz. The elements of truth in this account probably refer to his meeting with the attorney general after the interview in the Flemington jail.

45. H. Stockberger, "Conversation between Doctor John F. Condon and Bruno Richard Hauptmann . . . ," October 24, 1934, Flemington Guard Detail, NJSP.

46. Ibid.

47. A. L. Smith, "Conversation between Mr. and Mrs. Hauptmann . . . ," October 25, 1934, Flemington Guard Detail, NJSP.

48. Condon, *Jafsie Tells All,* 233–234.

49. Ibid.

50. Fisher, *Lindbergh Case,* 267.

51. *Hunterdon County Democrat,* October 25, 1934; *New York Times,* October 25, 1934.

52. Hauptmann ms. autobiography, quoted in Kennedy, *Crime of the Century,* 235; *New York Times,* November 1 and 2, 1934.

53. Stockburger and Smith reports of the conversations between Anna and Richard, October 24 and 25, 1934, Flemington Guard Detail, NJSP.

54. H. Stockburger, "Conversation between Mr. and Mrs. Hauptmann . . . ," November 3, 1934, Flemington Guard Detail, NJSP.

55. This paragraph is the result of several exchanges between myself and Siglinde Rach about the meaning of *enemy* in both English and German.

56. Condon, *Jafsie Tells All,* 205. As usual, there are errors of fact in Condon's account. No money was found in a joist, and the discoveries occurred within days of Hauptmann's arrest, not months.

57. Ibid., 227.

58. H. Stockburger, "Conversation between Mr. and Mrs. Hauptmann . . . ," November 2, 1934, Flemington Guard Detail, NJSP.

59. Stockburger, "Conversation between Mr. and Mrs. Hauptmann . . . ," November 3, 1934.

60. *New York Times,* November 3, 1934; Scaduto, *Scapegoat,* 121.

61. *New York Times,* November 13, 1934.

62. H. Stockburger, "Conversation between Mr. and Mrs. Hauptmann . . . ," November 24, 1934, Flemington Guard Detail, NJSP; interview with Ryman Herr, Jr., April 26, 2003.

63. Stockburger, "Conversation between Mr. and Mrs. Hauptmann . . . ," October 25, 1934.

TEN. VISIONS OF A LADDER

1. Arthur Koehler to Captain J. J. Lamb, September 21, 1934, File P 101, NJSP.

2. Lewis Bornmann, "Searching of Bruno Richard Hauptmann's Home and Garage . . . ," September 25 and September 26, 1934, Reports File, NJSP.

3. Lewis Bornmann, "Searching Apartment and Garage of Bruno Richard Hauptmann . . . ," September 26, 1934, File 1600, NJSP.

4. Trial transcript, 2151; stenographic report of conference at Wilburtha, March 24, 1936, Box 13, Hoffman Papers.

5. Bornmann taped interview, June 28, 1983, NJSP; transcript, March 26, 1936; and for pointing out to me the surprisingly curtailed search for money, thanks to Troopers Anthony Ceravolo and Walter Babecki.

6. J. Edgar Hoover to Harold Hoffman, January 23, 1936, Box 6, Hoffman Papers.

7. Fisher, *Lindbergh Case,* 229. Fisher notes that the other searchers had been looking for ransom money, however, not the origins of rail 16—which is another way of saying that Bornmann was directed to look for the wood.

8. Transcript, March 26, 1936.

9. *New York Times,* September 29, 1934.

10. Arthur Koehler, "Report of Examination of Tools and Lumber from Hauptmann's Garage and House," October 4, 1934, File 117, NJSP.

11. Koehler's methodology, and this issue in particular, is discussed in Stephen A. Lehman's unpublished essay, "The Ladder," November 16, 2000, author's possession.

12. Koehler, "Report of Examination."

13. Lewis Bornmann, "Searching Apartment and Garage of Bruno Richard Hauptmann . . . ," September 25 (October 8, 1934), Box 13, Hoffman Papers; Bornmann, "Taking Mr. Koehler to the Hauptmann Home . . . ," October 9, 1934 (October 10, 1934), Reports File, NJSP.

14. Arthur Koehler, "Report of Examination of Tools and Lumber from Hauptmann's Garage and Home," October 31, 1934, File 117, NJSP.

15. Ibid.

16. Ibid.

17. Faced with this logical difficulty, it is sometimes suggested that Hauptmann set out for Englewood that day, where the higher nursery would require all three sections of his ladder—or at least his planning would—and finding the child not there, he traveled on down to Highfields. Of course this assumption requires that he could get close enough while it was still light to determine activity at the busy Englewood mansion with its two dozen servants, then hurry down to central Jersey.

18. Scaduto, *Scapegoat*, 384–391; Kennedy, *Crime of the Century*, 209–212; Jim Fisher: *The Ghosts of Hopewell: Setting the Record Straight in the Lindbergh Case* (Carbondale: Southern Illinois University Press, 1999), 125–127; at present Kelvin Keraga is studying the forensic evidence at the New Jersey State Police Museum, where the ladder and S-226 are stored. His findings should be available soon.

19. Koehler, "Report on Examination of Tools and Lumber from Hauptmann's Garage and House," October 4, 1934; Koehler, "Report on Wood in the Lindbergh Kidnap Ladder," December 20, 1934, File 117, NJSP.

20. Trial transcript, 2262–2267.

21. Arthur Koehler, "Who Made That Ladder?" *Saturday Evening Post,* April 20, 1935, 10–11, 91. Emphasis added.

22. Ibid., and see Koehler's article, "Technique Used in Tracing the Lindbergh Kidnaping Ladder," *Journal of Criminal Law and Criminology* (Jan.–Feb., 1937), 712–724. "The chisel found on Colonel Lindbergh's premises on the night of the kidnaping answered the . . . description, although there undoubtedly also were numerous other sharp ¾ - inch chisels in existence."

23. *New York Times,* March 3, 1932.

24. Photographs at the NJSP show where the chisel was found, and show it alone without the ladder on the bare ground the next morning. For these questions about the chisel, I am indebted to Anthony Ceravolo and Walter Babecki, who are familiar with investigative procedures.

25. N. DeGaetano, "Investigation of Lumber in New York City," December 19, 1934, Reports File, NJSP; Claude Patterson, "Continuation of Investigation of Bruno Richard Hauptmann," December 19, December 21, 1934, ibid.

26. Arthur Koehler, "Conference with Assistant Attorney General Peacock," November 22, 1934, File 117, NJSP.

27. Koehler, "Who Made That Ladder?" 10, 11, 84, 86, 89, 91, 92.

28. Winchell, *Winchell Exclusive,* 112.

29. *New York Times,* December 10, 1934.

30. Ibid., December 13, 1934.

31. H. Stockburger, "Conversation between Lawyer Fisher and Haupt-mann . . . ," December 10, 1934, Flemington Guard Detail, NJSP.

32. John Wallace, "Visit to the Former Hauptmann Home . . . ," November 19, 1934, and A. Zapolsky, "Continued Investigation re: Bruno Richard Haupt-mann . . . ," November 26, 1934, both in File 1600, NJSP.

33. Claude Patterson, "Continuation of Investigation of Bruno Richard Hauptmann . . . ," December 18, 1934, File 1600, NJSP; Patterson, "Continuation of Investigation of Bruno Richard Hauptmann . . . ," December 14, 1934, Accordion File—Hauptmann Investigation, NJSP.

34. A. Zapolsky, "Tracing of Stromberg-Carlson Radio Set," September 25, 1934, Reports File, NJSP.

35. William J. Grafenecker, "Investigation and Report Re: Binoculars . . . ," Reports File, NJSP. The binoculars were listed with their serial number along-side other possessions Hauptmann entered into a small book that recorded even the weight of his 1930 Dodge, and its car key number. It is possible Haupt-mann did not purchase the binoculars but received them in some other way. Isidor Fisch lived at one time on East Eighty-fourth Street and later moved to 127th Street. The fictitious address given was 127 East Eighty-fourth Street. Fisch frequented a café on West Thirty-first Street almost daily during this period, and the binoculars were sold on West Thirty-second Street. Thanks again to Siglinde Rach for this intelligence report on another "coincidence" in a case overburdened with chance and seemingly fortuitous events.

36. J. Edgar Hoover, "Memorandum for Mr. Tamm," October 29, 1934, Box 19, Classification 7-1, FBI Records.

37. Genz, untitled report, November 14, 1934, File 1600, NJSP.

38. W. O. Sawyer and John R. Genz, untitled reports, November 19 and 21, 1934, File 1600, NJSP.

39. William E. Foster, untitled, undated memorandum, Reports File, NJSP; N. DeGaetano, "Information Regarding the Lindbergh Case," November 28, 1934, File 1600, NJSP; W. O. Sawyer, untitled report, November 28, 1934, File 1600, NJSP.

40. Sawyer, untitled report, November 28, 1934.

41. W. O. Sawyer, "Patrols and Interviewing of Hopewell and Vicinity Resi-dents," December 12, 1934, and December 19, 1934, File 1600, NJSP.

42. W. O. Sawyer, "Identification of Bruno Richard Hauptmann by Amandus Hochmuth . . . ," December 20, 1934, File 1600, NJSP; *New York Times,* December 22, 1934.

43. H. Stockburger, "Conversation between Mr. and Mrs. Hauptmann," December 22, 1934; A. L. Smith to Colonel H. Norman Schwarzkopf, December 21, 1934; Smith to Schwarzkopf, December 22, 1934; and Smith to Schwarzkopf, December 23, 1934; all in Flemington Guard Detail, NJSP.

44. "Statement of Amandus Hochmuth," December 20, 1934, Box 33, Hoff-man Papers.

45. "Statement of Amandus Hochmuth, Taken January 6, 1935," Box 33, Hoffman Papers.

46. Ruth Hill, deputy commissioner, Department of Public Welfare, unad-dressed letter, June 17, 1935, Box 33, Hoffman Papers.

ELEVEN. THE SEARCH FOR ISIDOR FISCH

1. H. Stockburger, "Conversation between Mr. and Mrs. Hauptmann . . . ," November 17, 1934, Flemington Guard Detail, NJSP.

2. *Palm Beach Post-Times,* December 15, 1934; *New York Times,* December 15 and 16, 1934.

3. Samuel J. Leon, "Interview with Dr. John F. Condon," December 26, 1934, Accordion File 60-111, NJSP; *New York Times,* January 3, 1935.

4. Samuel Leon, "Investigating Life of Dr. John F. Condon at City Island . . . ," November 7, 1934, Accordion File 60-111, NJSP.

5. Ibid.

6. Samuel Leon, "Continuation of Investigation in Reference to the Life of Dr. John F. Condon . . . ," November 9, 1934, and Leon, "Report of Continued Investigation in Reference to Dr. John F. Condon . . . ," November 10, 1934, both in Accordion File 60-111, NJSP.

7. Thanks to Siglinde Rach for bringing this possibility to my attention.

8. Copy of *New York Evening Journal* article, September 25, 1934, Accordion File 17, NJSP.

9. The above two paragraphs are based on several reports in Investigative File 1602, NJSP, especially those by Detective E. A. Hausling for November 14, 15, 21, 22, 27, 30, and December 1, 1934.

10. F. X. O'Donnell, "Memorandum for the File," Investigative File 1602, NJSP.

11. F. X. O'Donnell, "Memorandum for File," September 27, 1934, Accordion File 17, NJSP.

12. E. A. Hausling, "Continued Investigation of Isidor Fisch," November 21, 1934, Investigative File 1602, NJSP.

13. E. A. Hausling, "Continued Investigation of Isidor Fisch," November 9, 1934; and Hausling, "Continued Investigation re: Isidor Fisch," December 4, 1934, both in Investigative File 1602, NJSP.

14. Isidor Fisch to W. Schaefer, November 1, 1932, translated from German by FBI agent Leon Turrou, Investigative File 1602, NJSP.

15. Hausling, "Continued Investigation of Isidor Fisch," November 9, 1934; Hausling, "Continued Investigation re: Isidor Fisch," December 4, 1934.

16. Ibid.

17. "Interrogation of Charles Schlosser (sic.)," December 6, 1934, Robert Peacock Collection.

18. Undated memorandum, "Augusta Hile," Accordion File 17, NJSP.

19. Ibid.

20. "Interrogation of Charles Schlosser," December 6, 1934.

21. E. A. Hausling, "Continued Investigation re: Isidor Fisch," November 10, 12, 1934, Accordion File 17, NJSP.

22. Hausling, "Continued Investigation re: Isidor Fisch," December 4, 1934.

23. Interrogation of Erich Schaefer, December 10, 1934, Statements File, NJSP. Erich's father, William, had somewhat less confidence in Fisch and the promises he had been making since the end of 1932 to repay what he owed him. Shortly after Isidor left for Germany, William wrote to say that he was gratified to learn that Isidor had not forgotten him, "and so we hope that everything . . . will be settled to your and my satisfaction." William Schaefer to Isidor Fisch, February 3, 1934, letter and translation in the possession of Kurt Tolksdorf, to

whom I am deeply indebted for providing access to his voluminous files on the Lindbergh case.

24. Statement of Gerta Henkel, October 8, 1934, and statement of Karl Henkel, October 13, 1934, both in Statements File, NJSP.

25. "Statement of Bruno Richard Hauptmann, Taken at the New Jersey State Prison," June 5, 1935. The interviewer was Ellis Parker, one of the persons Governor Harold Hoffman used in his post-trial investigation of the case. I am indebted to Dolores Raisch, who found this document in the Hoffman Papers.

26. Hausling, "Continued Investigation of Isidor Fisch," November 9, 1934.

27. J. A. Genau, "Bruno Richard Hauptmann with Aliases," October 18, 1934, FBI Report under file number 62-3057, 19–20, copy in NJSP. The "Genau Report" was the basic source for information on Hauptmann's finances, although it was not introduced at the trial.

28. J. E. Seykora, "Memorandum for File," October 9, 1934, Box 3, Lehman/FBI Files, NJSP.

29. Ibid.

30. Genau report, 30–31, 53A.

31. W. Kelly to Captain J. J. Lamb, September 24, 1934, Investigative File 1602, NJSP.

32. Ibid.

33. Genau report, 36–38.

34. Ibid., 39.

35. Statement of Selma Kohl, December 12, 1934, Statements File, NJSP; statement of Gerta Henkel, October 8, 1934; Milton, *Loss of Eden,* 314–315, writes that Fisch was probably engaged in laundering money, not buying and selling furs, and that what made him nervous was the word that Owney Madden had joined in the hunt for the Lindbergh kidnappers. Madden's interest in the case, however, was long over by this time. He had been sent to prison in July 1932 and did not get out until the next July, at which time he "retired" to Hot Springs, Arkansas, to run a gambling casino and "spa" for visiting gangsters.

36. Affidavits of Arthur H. Trost, June 19, 1935, Gustave Lakatis, June 14, 1935, Philip Wohrmann, December 28, 1935, all in Box 4, Hoffman Papers. Affidavit of Oscar Bruckman, January 8, 1936, enclosure in Lloyd Fisher to Harold Hoffman, undated, Box 4, Hoffman Papers.

37. There is a report in FBI files on the case that Hauptmann was often in the company of a tall, blond, German-speaking man at Steiner, Rouse. Leon Turrou, "Memorandum for the File," October 2, 1934, File 1600, NJSP.

38. "Statement of Bruno Richard Hauptmann, Taken at the New Jersey State Prison," June 5, 1935.

39. Ibid. Hans Kloppenburg's collaboration is noted in Kennedy, *Crime of the Century* 155. Until Fisch entered the picture, Kloppenburg had been Hauptmann's closest friend. Kloppenburg, perhaps naturally, always regarded Fisch with suspicion. From that standpoint, his ability to "remember" the shoebox cannot be considered simply as the disinterested testimony of a person with no stake in the outcome.

40. The letters, Pinkas Fisch to Richard Hauptmann, April 15, 1934, Richard to Pinkas, May 4, 1934, and Pinkas to Richard, June 3, 1934, are all in Investigative File 134, NJSP.

41. Affidavit of Richard Weidene, October 1, 1934, History of Isidor Fisch

File, NJSP; statement of Anna Hauptmann, April 20, 1935, Box 3, Hoffman Papers.

42. M. Breed, "Memorandum for File," September 24, 1934, Accordion File 17, NJSP.

43. I am indebted to Siglinde Rach for sharing her ideas on these points during our many discussions of the case.

44. Henry Uhlig to Mr. and Mrs. E. Uhlig, September 18, 1934, NJSP.

45. Henry Uhlig to Mr. and Mrs. Borman, October 11, 1934, NJSP.

46. Statement of Charles Schleser, December 6, 1934, Box 20, Hoffman Papers.

47. Statement of Charles Schleser, December 10, 1934, Box 20, Hoffman Papers.

48. Statement of Charles Schleser, December 12, 1934, Box 20, Hoffman Papers.

49. Statement of Charles Schleser, December 17, 1934, Box 20, Hoffman Papers.

50. H. C. Keyes to Governor Harold Hoffman, January 10, 1936, Box 10, Hoffman Papers.

51. Joseph Dunninger, *Inside the Medium's Closet* (New York: David Kemp, 1935), 170.

52. A. L. Smith to Colonel H. Norman Schwarzkopf, October 24, 1934, Flemington Guard Detail, NJSP.

TWELVE. JUDGE TRENCHARD'S COURTROOM

1. Interview with Judge Sam Chiarvalli, July 13, 2001.

2. *New York Evening Journal,* December 31, 1934.

3. *Hunterdon County Democrat,* January 3, 1935.

4. *New York Times,* January 3, 1935.

5. Trial transcript, 6, reads "Hey, Doctor," while *The New York Times,* January 4, 1935, reads "Here Dok-tor" and describes Wilentz's German accent. The "foreign accent" obviously would be much more noticeable if Condon and Lindbergh heard "Dok-tor," rather than "Doc," as Condon stated on most occasions. In Lindbergh's very first statement on the scene at St. Raymond's, however, on May 20, 1932, he used the phrase "Ay, Doctor," and described it as a foreign accent. Box 3, Hoffman Papers. Wilentz wanted no contradiction between his witnesses.

6. Trial transcript, 8–9.

7. Ibid., 2–3.

8. Ibid., 12.

9. *New Brunswick Home News,* January 3, 1935.

10. Trial transcript, 62–63.

11. In 1993, two lawyers in New Hampshire, one a veteran defense attorney, Gregory Ahlgren, the other a longtime law enforcement officer, Stephen Monier, published *Crime of the Century: The Lindbergh Kidnapping Hoax,* which argued that the crime was actually one of Lindbergh's pranks that went terribly wrong when the ladder broke. He had planned, according to this theory, to show up at the door of the house with the baby in his hands, and surprise everyone. The extortion, they argue, was a second crime, unrelated to the

accident. Thought up on the spur of the moment, it became a real crime when copies of the original "ransom note" became available to underworld figures. Ahlgren and Monier stressed Lindbergh's penchant for cruel practical jokes but made no argument that Lindbergh plotted a kidnapping, let alone the death of his child.

12. Trial transcript, 71.

13. Ibid., 74–76, and Statement of Anne Morrow Lindbergh, March 11, 1932, Box 1, Hoffman Papers.

14. Trial transcript, 81.

15. Ibid., 112.

16. Ibid., 117.

17. Ibid., 120–123.

18. Hertog, *Anne Morrow Lindbergh,* 260–261, gives an excellent account of Reilly's partially successful efforts to demonstrate Charles Lindbergh's controlling attitude during the ransom negotiations—and in general. Thanks to Bill Mooney for pointing out Hertog's conclusions.

19. E. A. Tamm, "Memorandum for the Director," January 5, 1935, Box 20, Classification 7-1, FBI Records.

20. Trial transcript, 152–153.

21. Ibid., 168–170.

22. Ibid., 188–189.

23. Ibid., 201–203.

24. Tamm, "Memorandum for the Director," January 5, 1935; *New York Times,* January 5, 1935; *New Brunswick Home News*, January 4, 1935.

25. Trial transcript, 271.

26. Deposition of Betty Gow, January 1, 1935, Peacock Collection, NJSP.

27. Trial transcript, 274.

28. Deposition of Betty Gow, January 1, 1935.

29. Trial transcript, 312–313.

30. Ibid., 322–325.

31. *New York Times,* January 8, 1935.

32. Deposition of Betty Gow, January 1, 1935; Trial transcript, 313.

33. Trial transcript, 622.

34. *New York Times,* January 10, 1935; *New Brunswick Daily Home News,* November 27, 1934.

35. Interviews with Dolores Raisch.

36. Trial transcript, 682–683, 689–691.

37. Ibid., 629.

38. Ibid., 696–697, 709–715. Emphasis added.

39. Ibid., 751–753.

40. Ibid., 790–791.

41. Ibid., 816–817.

42. *New York Times,* January 11, 1935.

43. Trial transcript, 1060.

44. *New York Times,* January 15, 1935.

45. Trial transcript, 445–462, 467–469.

46. *New York Times,* January 9, 1935.

47. Ibid., and Russell Stoddard to Governor Harold Hoffman, undated [1935], Box 10, Hoffman Papers.

48. Trial transcript, 530–537.

49. Trooper Ruggiero, "Investigation Concerning Identification of Bruno Hauptmann photo . . . ," October 2, 1934, Box 21, Hoffman Papers. Ruggerio's report details the effort to find others who might have made an identification. See also the reports by Detective Claude Patterson, October 3 and 5, 1934, Reports File, NJSP.

50. William F. Horn, "Report of an Investigation Concerning a Recovered $5.00 Bill . . . ," November 27, 1933; Lieutenant James. J. Finn to Commanding Officer, November 28, 1933; and "Statement Taken October 3, 1934," all in Box 21, Hoffman Papers. In Cecile Barr's deposition requesting a share of the reward money, she cited her description of the theater patron as the one put on circulars and noted that she furnished information that the kidnapper was either German or Scandinavian, information that was soon passed on to police officers and the public.

51. Trial transcript., 1924–1925.

52. Ibid., 1916–1917, 1926–1929. Thanks to Steve Lehmann for calling my attention to Cecile Barr's inability to remember her first encounter with Corporal Horn.

53. Trial transcript, 1984–1985; unsigned, undated memorandum, "Millard Whited," Box 33, Hoffman Papers.

54. E. A. Tamm, "Memorandum for the Director," January 5, 1935, Box 20, Classification 7-1, FBI Records.

THIRTEEN. TRIAL BY EXPERTS

1. "Technique Used in Tracing the Lindbergh Kidnapping Ladder," *Journal of Criminal Law and Criminology,* January–February 1937, 27, 712–724.

2. Lloyd Fisher, "I Appeal," unpublished article, 18, copy in Box 4, Hoffman Papers.

3. A. S. Osborn to H. Norman Schwarzkopf, October 20, 1934, L Files, NJSP.

4. Scaduto, *Scapegoat,* 376; A. S. Osborn to H. Norman Schwarzkopf, November 21, 1934, and Schwarzkopf to H. E. Cassidy, October 20, 1934, both in L Files, NJSP.

5. H. E. Cassidy to H. Norman Schwarzkopf, November 18, 1934, L Files, NJSP.

6. C. Sellers to H. Norman Schwarzkopf, October 24, 1934, and Schwarzkopf to Sellers, October 26, 1934, both in Accordion File—General Handwriting, NJSP; trial transcript, 937.

7. Deposition of Phillip Creamer, November 22, 1934, copy in Box 33, Hoffman Papers.

8. H. E. Cassidy to H. Norman Schwarzkopf, October 15, 1934, L Files, NJSP; C. Sellers to H. Norman Schwarzkopf, November 5, 1934, Accordion File—General Handwriting, NJSP.

9. J. F. Tyrrell to H. Norman Schwarzkopf, December 7, 1934, Accordion File—General Handwriting, NJSP.

10. A. S. Osborn to J. Lanigan, December 3, 1934, L Files, NJSP.

11. H. Norman Schwarzkopf to J. F. Tyrrell, December 7, 1934, Accordion File—General Handwriting, NJSP.

12. H. E. Cassidy to H. Norman Schwarzkopf, October 21, 1934, L Files, NJSP.

13. A. L. Smith to H. Norman Schwarzkopf, November 26 and 28, 1934, Flemington Guard Detail, NJSP.

14. Statement of Bruno Richard Hauptmann, June 5, 1935, NJSP. I thank Dolores Raisch, once again, for finding this very valuable document.

15. The opening portions of Albert S. Osborn's testimony, trial transcript, 960–970; Osborn, "Supplemental Report Regarding the Lindbergh Kidnapping Letters," June 1, 1932, L Files, NJSP. Osborn's 1932 notations about the use of a blotter on the ransom notes raises yet another question about the conditions under which the request writings were taken, in addition to the number of pieces obtained, and what instructions were given to the writer.

16. Trial transcript, 974–975.

17. Carrel's signature can be found at the Website http://clendening.kumc.edu/dc/pc/Carrel.jpg. I thank Siglinde Rach for discovering this fact.

18. *New Brunswick Daily Homes News,* January 12, 1935.

19. Trial transcript, 1011–1017, 1040–1041.

20. Ibid., 1109–1111, 1103.

21. Ibid., 1141.

22. *New York Times,* January 17, 1935.

23. Trial transcript, 1212.

24. Ibid., 1226–1227, 1231.

25. Ibid., 1340–1343. I thank Steve Lehman for calling my attention to this testimony and Fisher's objection.

26. Ibid., 1359.

27. Ibid., 632.

28. Ibid., 1367–1370.

29. Ibid., 1738–1740.

30. Ibid., 1740–1755.

31. Arthur Koehler, "Report of Examination of Tools and Lumber from Hauptmann's Garage and House," October 1 to 4, 1934, File 117, NJSP.

32. Arthur Koehler, "Report of Examination of Ladder for the New Jersey State Police," March 4, 1933, Box 10, Hoffman Papers,

33. Trial transcript, 2260–2261.

34. The chisel is one of the most interesting pieces in the Lindbergh case puzzle. Many writers on both sides of the issue have simply assumed that it was found under the nursery window. George Waller, *Kidnap,* 576–577, uses the Trenchard intervention to demonstrate how weak the defense challenge to Koehler was in general. Waller did not have access to many of the documents now available, and simply assumed Pope had issued a forlorn challenge. But no troopers saw it there that night when they searched the area; instead, photographs at the New Jersey State Police Museum show it out in the field near where the ladder had been found—with no indication how it got there. Thanks to Trooper Tony Ceravolo for sharing his research into the chisel.

35. Koehler, "Report of Examination of Tools and Lumber from Hauptmann's Garage and House," October 4, 1934; Arthur Koehler, "Report on Wood in the Lindbergh kidnap ladder," December 20, 1934, File 117, NJSP.

36. Trial transcript, 4236–4237. Thanks to Mark Falzini, archivist at the museum, for permitting me to witness the opening of these evidence bins.

37. *New York Times,* January 24, 1935.

38. Trial transcript, 2233–2237.

39. Ibid., 3423–3431.

40. Ibid., 2233–2237.

41. Ibid., 348–349, 357, 442–443, 362–363.

42. Undated, "List of Evidence on the Lindbergh Case Which Is Stored in a Cell in the Cellar of the Barracks." I wish to thank Mark Falzini, who discovered the document in the files, and Dolores Raisch, who had the newspaper clippings in her personal files.

43. A. Stinson to Harold Hoffman, January 16, 1938, Hoffman Papers. Reports of these prints were noted in two places. Together, DeGaetano and Bornmann traced prints "made by rubber boots or overshoes on an abandoned road which lead[s] to the chicken coop and an old abandoned house at the entrance to the Lindbergh estate. In certain sections there were also a dog's prints near those of the boots or overshoes." From there the footprints "went across the road and appeared to stop alongside some impressions that appeared to be from an automobile and then further trace ceased." A search of the abandoned house yielded nothing. The first quotation is taken from DeGaetano's report of March 3, 1932 , the second from an additional report by DeGaetano, March 9, 1932, also in Box 29, Hoffman Papers. Bornmann made a similar report, March 9, 1932, Statements File, NJSP.

44. H. Norman Schwarzkopf to Clement A. Norton, October 19, 1934, Box 21, Hoffman Papers. Emphasis added.

FOURTEEN. CROSS EXAMINATIONS

1. *New York Times,* January 28, 1935.

2. Ibid. Shoenfeld is not identified by name in the article "Air-Hero Complex Laid to Hauptmann," but it is clear who the psychiatrist is from the context.

3. Trial transcript, 2467.

4. Ibid., 2512.

5. Special report by F. W. Fay to director of investigation, Department of Justice, October 30, 1934, Box 2, Hoffman Papers.

6. Trial transcript, 2514–2515.

7. Ibid., 1886–1889.

8. Ibid., 2514.

9. The coincidence of these financial transactions, and the conclusions drawn here, can only be called informed speculation. We know that the Hauptmann-Fisch relationship was a fast-growing friendship, and that they quickly became engaged in various joint enterprises. Hauptmann's efforts to push back their supposed meeting date to account for funds that he had available to invest soon after the ransom was paid should be taken seriously, given other facets of what we know about Fisch's secret dealings, and his efforts to keep his "friends" from becoming acquainted with one another. It does not exonerate him, however, in any way. I am especially indebted here to Siglinde Rach for sharing her ideas on the Hauptmann-Fisch financial relationship.

10. Trial transcript, 2686–2687.

11. *New York Times,* January 26, 1935.

12. Trial transcript, 2544–2547.

13. Ibid., 2548–2549.

14. Mark Falzini prepared the chart that shows the crucial differences in the letters, yet another of his many contributions to the study of the case. I am grateful for his effort and his willingness to share all these findings. The *d*s and *t*s are a persistent problem in the ransom notes. There has been no adequate evaluation of the number of times words are supposedly misspelled, when in fact it is this confusion that occurs in many instances. As noted earlier, several writers have attempted to decipher the writings, and provide different versions of the notes in their books. It is a subject for much further study.

15. Trial transcript, 2608–2609.

16. Ibid., 2570–2571.

17. Ibid., 2856, 2870.

18. Ibid., 4193–4195.

19. Ibid., 2672.

20. *New York Times,* January 29, 1935.

21. Trial transcript, 2937.

22. Ibid., 2964–3066.

23. Reports from the New York City and Nassau County Police Departments, all dated January 30, 1935, were gathered by a state trooper named A. H. Albrecht, who also reported by telephone to Wilentz what they contained, and that the Strausses were regarded as a reputable family. File 1600, NJSP.

24. Trial transcript, 4106.

25. Ibid., 3074–3127.

26. Kiss provided Fisher with an affidavit recounting how a New York attorney, seeking a position in District Attorney Thomas Dewey's office, had been advised that David Wilentz had told him he would use his influence if Kiss would change his testimony and say he had been at the bakery at least an hour earlier the evening of March 1, 1932. The attorney, a man named Berko, had also threatened Kiss with jail for perjury. Kiss replied that if Wilentz himself offered him $5 million, he would throw it in his face, because he had "told the truth." Kiss affidavit, January 6, 1936. This affidavit was supported by another one, given by Desider Weidinger, February 6, 1936, who was present for the encounter with Berko. Both are attached to Lloyd Fisher to Harold Hoffman, February 10, 1936, Box 4, Hoffman Papers.

27. Lloyd Fisher, undated memorandum to Harold Hoffman, Box 8, Hoffman Papers.

28. Ibid.

29. Lloyd Fisher, undated memorandum to Harold Hoffman, "Things That Hauptmann Complained of and Things Which He Insisted Should Indicate His Innocence," Box 2, Hoffman Papers.

30. Lloyd Fisher, undated, untitled memorandum to Harold Hoffman, Box 12, Hoffman Papers. The story of Colonel Malone is important, however, because it was widely put out to the press that these two "experts" had withdrawn because their testimony would not be helpful to the defense.

31. Ibid.

32. Trial transcript, 3188–3190.

33. Ibid., 3255.

34. Ibid., 3227

35. Ibid., 3249–3250.

36. Ibid., 3251.

37. Trial transcript, 4258–4260.

38. Ibid., 3362–3368.

39. Ibid., 3374.

40. Undated newspaper clipping, "Bruno Plumber Offers Alibi for Wood Missing from Attic," File 1600, NJSP.

41. Trial transcript, 3743.

42. F. M. Wright, "Memorandum for File," September 21, 1934, FBI Summary Report, 62-3057, NJSP.

43. Trial transcript, 3428–3429.

44. E. A. Hudson, "A Scientific Verdict on the Lindbergh-Hauptmann Riddle," *Liberty*, April 3, 1937, 32–37 Emphasis added.

45. Ibid.

46. Ibid.

47. Trial transcript, 4150–4158.

48. Ibid., 4159–4171.

49. Ibid., 4700–4780.

50. Ibid., 4360–4492.

51. Ibid., 4506–4511.

52. R. Snook to C. Sellers, March 29, 1935, Accordion File—General Handwriting, NJSP. Snook's account is the only one to contain such a full account by one of the participants. It is especially valuable for that reason.

53. Harold Nicolson, *Diaries and Letters, 1930-1939,* ed. Nigel Nicolson (New York: Atheneum, 1966); Scadato, *Scapegoat,* 196–197.

54. Ibid.

55. *New York Times,* February 14, 1935.

56. A. L. Smith to H. Norman Schwarzkopf, February 13, 1935, Flemington Guard Detail, NJSP.

FIFTEEN. THE GOVERNOR AND THE MAN IN THE DEATH HOUSE

1. Clyde Tolson, "Memorandum for the Attorney General," Box 24, Classification 7-1, FBI Records.

2. Harold Hoffman, "What Was Wrong with the Lindbergh Case?" part 4, *Liberty,* February 12, 1938, 47–53.

3. Ibid., part 5 (February 19, 1938), 24–31.

4. Kennedy, *Crime of the Century,* 353.

5. Ibid., 356.

6. A. L. Smith to H. Norman Schwarzkopf, February 15, 1935, Flemington Guard Detail, NJSP.

7. Kennedy, *Crime of the Century,* 349.

8. Fisher, undated, untitled memorandum, Box 29, Hoffman Papers.

9. *New Brunswick Daily Home News,* February 16, 1935.

10. Ibid.

11. *New York Times,* February 23, 1935.

12. Sven Petter Myhr Naess, "Interview with Else Marie Bing: Daughter of Fin Henrik 'Red' Johansen," September 4, 2003, available at NJSP.

13. *New York Times,* February 24, 1935.

14. *New York Evening Journal,* February 16, 1935.

15. *Trenton Evening Times*, August 19, 1935.

16. Sid Boehm, "Faith to Lindy Sealed My Lips—Schwarzkopf," *New York Evening Journal,* February 16, 1935..

17. J. Edgar Hoover to H. Norman Schwarzkopf, March 28, 1935, and Schwarzkopf to Hoover, March 29, 1935, both in Hoffman Papers. Italics added.

18. Harold Hoffman, "What Was Wrong with the Lindbergh Case?" part 1, *Liberty,* January 29, 1938, 10, and part 2, February 5, 1938, 16–17.

19. These letters from Harry Moore to Ellis Parker, March 7, 1932, and Parker to Harold Hoffman, May 23 and May 27, 1932, along with many others, are in a special collection, Parker-Wendel Collection, NJSP.

20. H. Nathan, "Memorandum for the Director," December 16, 1933, Box 10, Classification 7-1, FBI Records.

21. Newspaper clipping, "Ellis Parker Gets 'Tip' From Condon," January 15, 1935, from Web page: http://www.geocities.com/country detective1/1930-1939/jafsie.jpg.

22. Statement of Bruno Richard Hauptmann, June 5, 1935, Hoffman Papers.

23. Lloyd Fisher, "I Appeal," part 3, "Can Any Reasonable Man Believe That the Mystery Is Solved?" 11, undated manuscript, Box 4, Hoffman Papers.

24. Statement of Bruno Richard Hauptmann, June 5, 1935.

25. Kennedy, *Crime of the Century,* 364.

26. Fisher, "I Appeal," part 2, "Of Course, Colonel Lindbergh Answered 'Hauptmann,'" 1–2.

27. Kimberling's willingness to allow Ellis Parker into the state prison to conduct secret interviews with Hauptmann became known in 1937 at the time of Parker's trial for kidnapping Paul Wendel. Obviously, Kimberling knew what the result of those interviews would be—an effort to reopen the case. *New York Times,* May 21, 1937.

28. Hoffman, "What Was Wrong with the Lindbergh Case?" part 2, *Liberty,* February 5, 1938, 16–18.

29. Ibid. Hoffman wrote he went back to the hotel after his meeting with Hauptmann and dictated the gist of what was said in a memorandum. A search for this document in his papers has been unavailing.

30. Hoffman, "What Was Wrong with the Lindbergh Case?" part 2, 19.

31. Statement of George Steinweg, October 25, 1935, Box 4, Hoffman Papers; Kennedy, *Crime of the Century,* 153–154.

32. Lloyd Fisher, undated memorandum to Harold Hoffman, with enclosed affidavit of Oscar Bruckman, January 8, 1936, Box 4, Hoffman Papers.

33. National Academy of Sciences, "William Moulton Marston, the National Research Council and Wonder Woman," http://www.naedu/openbook/0309084369/html/292.htm.

34. Reports on Anna Hauptmann's test from copies of Keeler's notes are in the NJSP. E. Coffey, "Memorandum for the Director: Visit with Mr. Leonarde Keeler," April 1, 1935, Box 22, Classification 7-1, FBI Records.

35. Newspaper clipping, "'Jafsie' Advertises in Theater Magazine for Stage Bookings," December 26, 1935, Hoffman Papers. Marston provides an account of the Hauptmann-Condon scenario in *The Lie Detector Test* (New York: Richard Smith, 1938), 78–88.

36. Caption for " 'Jafsie' on Tour," December 17, 1935, Hoffman Papers, and William M. Marston, "Exactly Why Hauptmann Got No Lie Test," *New York Evening Journal,* February 26, 1938.

37. Marston, "Exactly Why Hauptmann Got No Lie Test."

38. Marston, *Lie Detector Test*, 87–88. Marston's search never turned up any suspects or startling discoveries, but he achieved fame as the creator of the protofeminist comic strip *Wonder Woman,* whose magic lasso was taken from Aprodite's girdle. All those caught within its loop were forced to tell the truth!

39. Amelia Earhart to Harold Hoffman, April 1, 1936; Hoffman to Earhart, April 2, 1936, Hoffman Papers.

40. *New York Times,* December 14, 1935.

41. Fulton Oursler, "Jafsie in Panama Discusses New Evidence," *Liberty,* March 28, 1936, 56–63.

42. Ibid.

43. Oursler's letter and Condon's reply are from a copy in the Hoffman Papers.

44. Oursler, "Jafsie in Panama."

45. Fulton Oursler, *Behold This Dreamer! An Autobiography,* ed. Fulton Oursler, Jr. (Boston: Little, Brown, 1964), 325.

46. *New York Times,* December 30, 1935.

47. Mark Kimberling to Harold Hoffman, January 3, 1936, Box 25, Hoffman Papers. When the letter was discovered, it caused a flurry of interest in American newspapers. The *New York Daily News,* March 28, 1977, noted, "The suppression of Hauptmann's letter shows how sensitive New Jersey officials had become to criticism as the time for his execution drew near." The discovery also came near the time the first critical book on the case, Anthony Scaduto's *Scapegoat,* was published. David Wilentz, who was still practicing law at eighty, quipped that he had never written a book or tried to capitalize on the case.

48. An English translation of the letter, dated December 27, 1935, is in Box 2, Hoffman Papers.

49. E. A. Tamm, "Memorandum for the Director," January 29, 1936, and J. Edgar Hoover to Harold Hoffman, January 29, 1936, both in Box 24, Classification 7-1, FBI Records.

50. Harold Hoffman to H. Norman Schwarzkopf, January 3, 1936, with marginalia, from a copy supplied by Hope Nelson (née Hoffman); see also Mark Kimberling to Harold Hoffman, January 25, 1936, and undated memorandum to Hoffman, signed L.F.M. (Meade?), both in Box 2, Hoffman Papers.

51. Ottilia Haerber to H. Norman Schwarzkopf, February 25, 1936, Investigative File 1602, NJSP.

52. William F. Horn, "Report of Investigation . . . ," March 10, 1936, Investigative File 1602, NJSP.

53. From copies at the NJSP.

54. Transcript of stenographer's notes of examination of Millard Whited, February 22, 1936, Box 8, Hoffman Papers.

55. Lloyd Fisher to Harold Hoffman, February 25, 1936, and Fisher to Hoffman, March 9, 1936, with attachment, both in Box 4, Hoffman Papers. Another Hoffman aide, Bill Conklin, had received word from Trooper Wolf, moreover, who said that he was sure Whited had never mentioned anyone suspicious in that first interview, much less been instructed to keep any secrets. Wolf made no promise of a monetary reward, but he had delivered Whited to higher officials, especially Captain Lamb, who spent a good deal of time in private with the man. Conklin to Hoffman, February 27, 1936, Box 4, Hoffman Papers.

56. Undated clipping [January, 1935], and clipping, January 29, 1935, Box 11, Hoffman Papers.

57. Quentin Reynolds, *Courtroom: The Story of Samuel S. Leibowitz* (New York: Farrar, Strauss, 1950), 326–332.

58. Fisher, undated memorandum, "Leibowitz," Box 11, Hoffman Papers; *New York Times,* February 14, 1936.

59. Fisher, "Leibowitz."

60. Reynolds, *Courtroom,* 334.

61. Fisher, "Leibowitz"; Harold Hoffman, "What Was Wrong with the Lindbergh Case?" part 6, *Liberty,* February 26, 1938, 50–52; Reynolds, *Courtroom,* 335.

62. Fisher, "Leibowitz." For some reason, Hoffman, whose account rests on that of Fisher's, changed Hauptmann's words, adding a German accent that Fisher had not described. "Come back, Mr. Liebervitz, if you haf any more questions to ask. You know, I haf lots of time." "What Was Wrong with the Lindbergh Case?" part 6.

63. *New York Times,* February 20, 1936.

64. Fisher, "Leibowitz."

65. *New York Times,* February 20, 1936.

66. Ibid., January 29, 1936.

67. Ibid., March 17, 1936.

68. Ibid., March 23, 1936.

69. Ibid., March 24, 1936.

70. Oursler, *Behold This Dreamer,* 325.

71. William Lewis, memorandum on Lindbergh-Hauptmann case, March 23, 1936, Box 29, Hoffman Papers.

72. Interview with Frederick Pope, quoted in George G. Hawke, "Trial By Fury: The Hauptmann Trial," senior thesis, Princeton University, 1951, 122–124.

73. "Transcript of Stenographer's Notes of Examination . . . ," March 24, 1936, Box 13, Hoffman Papers; audio interview tape with Bornmann, NJSP.

74. Oursler, *Behold This Dreamer,* 336.

75. Ibid., 337.

76. Ibid., 337–338.

77. The debate that raged in the attic on this point is best followed in two documents, Leon Hoage, "Hauptmann Attic," March 22, 1936, Hoffman Papers, and Arthur Koehler, "Report of Investigation . . . , March 28, 1936, Investigative Reports, NJSP.

78. There were fourteen nails in the 136 inches of S-226, or one every 9.7 inches, while in rail 16 there were nine nails in 106 inches, or one for every 11.7 inches. In S-226 five of nine joists contained two nail holes, and in rail 16 only two of seven joists contained two nail holes. This was hardly conclusive evidence of planted evidence—far from it—but together with the story of how Bornmann ripped up the board, and had it sawed twice, it was worth further investigation. Thanks to Michael Melsky for sharing with me his conclusions on the odd "match" between S-226 and rail 16.

79. Again, thanks to Michael Melsky for discussing these issues with me and for his insights.

80. Koehler, "Report of Investigation . . . ," March 28, 1936; Oursler, *Behold This Dreamer,* 340–343.

81. Lewis Bornmann, "Questioning by Governor Hoffman," March 28, 1936, Investigative Reports, NJSP.

82. Koehler, "Report of Investigation . . . ," March 28, 1936.

83. *New York Times,* March 26, 1936.

84. The Parker-Wendel correspondence is in a special file in the Hoffman Papers.

85. Scaduto, *Scapegoat,* 235–254. Scaduto's account revived interest in the Wendel tale.

86. Richard Hauptmann to Harold Hoffman, March 31, 1936, Box 2, Hoffman Papers.

87. Kennedy, *Crime of the Century,* 395.

88. Ibid., 396–397.

89. Clarence Darrow to Harold Hoffman, undated copy in Box 2, Hoffman Papers.

90. Robert Elliott, *Agent of Death* (New York: E. P. Dutton, 1940), 192–193.

91. Ibid.

92. Fisher, undated memorandum, Box 29, Hoffman Papers.

93. *Newark Ledger,* April 4, 1936.

94. *New York Evening Journal,* April 4, 1936.

SIXTEEN. THE PALATE OF MORTALS

1. *Anne Morrow Lindbergh,* 280, 296.

2. Berg, *Lindbergh,* 345.

3. Lloyd Fisher, "I Appeal," unpublished manuscript in the Hoffman Papers.

4. Undated letter, NJSP. Thanks to Mark Falzini, who discovered this Condon offering.

5. John F. Condon to J. Edgar Hoover, July 8, 1936; Hoover to Condon, July 17, 1936; R. Whitely to Hoover, November 5, 1936; all in Box 26, Classification 7-1, FBI Records.

6. Hugh Larimer, untitled report, March 4, 1933, copy in Box 1, Wilentz Collection. Lindbergh also told an attorney, Dan B. Cowie, of his suspicions, adding that Condon had been out of his sight for several minutes at St. Raymond's the night the money was paid. Cowie to Harold Hoffman, January 13, 1936, Box 3, Hoffman Papers.

7. R. G. Harvey to T. H. Sisk, May 14, 1934, Box 14, Classification 7-1, FBI Records.

8. *New York Times,* January 3, 1945.

9. Samuel Leon, report, June 26, 1934, File 375, NJSP.

10. The underlinings were those of New Jersey State Police. Sandbergh, report, July 24, 1934, copy in NJSP. Thanks to Mark Falzini for calling this document to my attention.

11. *New York Times,* July 7, 1988.

12. Ibid., October 7, 1981.

13. Lindbergh Reward File, Hoffman Papers.

14. P. Wendel to Harold Hoffman, November 18, 1937, Box 24, Hoffman Papers.

15. Harold Hoffman to Frank J. Murray, January 10, 1938, Box 24, Hoffman Papers; J.B.C., "A Reporter at Large: Twenty-Five Thousand Dollars," *New*

Yorker, November 6, 1937, 42–50. Unless otherwise noted, the reward stories are all taken from these sources.

16. T. H. Sisk to J. Edgar Hoover, April 4, 1936, Box 25, Classification 7-1, FBI Records.

17. Arthur Koehler to Harold Hoffman, November 17, 1937, Box 24, Hoffman Papers.

18. A. S. Osborn to H. Norman Schwarzkopf, November 6, 1935; Box 15, Hoffman Papers.

19. H. Norman Schwarzkopf to A. S. Osborn, November 7, 1935, and Osborn to Schwarzkopf, November 8, 1935, both in Box 15, Hoffman Papers.

20. Henry Lee and Jerry LaBriola, *Famous Crimes Revisited* (Southington, Conn.: Strong Books, 2001), 129.

21. Henry Breckinridge, memorandum, September 28, 1934, Breckinridge's Employees F-5, Investigative Files, NJSP. Special thanks to Mark Falzini for discovering this document and calling it to my attention.

22. "Who Helped Hauptmann—Case 2?" May 28, 2003, Lindbergh Kidnapping Discussion Board.

23. Frederick L. Collins, "Before the Body Was Found, She Said the Lindbergh Baby Was Murdered," *Liberty,* April 4, 1936, 39–41.

24. Copy of court deposition by Kathryn L. B. Kallish, January 26, 1934, Investigative Files, NJSP.

25. Al Dunlap, "Was the Body of the Lindbergh Baby Really Found?" *Startling Detective Adventures,* May 1933 or 1934, 10–15, 63–65, copy in NJSP.

26. Dr. Philip Van Ingen told prosecutors that Charlie was "a rather spoiled youngster and it was almost impossible to get him to stand up straight in order to measure him." Statement of Van Ingen, November 21, 1934, Box 15, Hoffman Papers. There may have been other reasons besides being spoiled for this difficulty in measuring Charlie's height.

27. Ibid.

28. Al Dunlap, "Was the Body of the Lindbergh Baby Really Found?" *Startling Detective Adventures* (May 1933 or 1934), 64, Clipping Files, NJSP.

29. "Text of Report Made in Autopsy," May 13, 1932, Box 13, Hoffman Papers; Statement of Van Ingen, November 21, 1934.

30. Sgt. Campbell, report of telephone call (March 2, 1932), Reports of Telephone Calls, March 1, 1932–March 4, 1932, NJSP. Watson was investigated, as were all other workmen, but not until May 1933. The conclusion was that he had no information of value to offer, and that he had an excellent reputation. No one asked him about the shutters. Lewis Bornmann, "Investigation of Men Employed . . . ," May 4, 1933. File R 7, NJSP. Thanks to Mark Falzini for calling these documents to my attention.

31. Joseph A. Wolf, "Major Initial Report," March 1, 1932, Investigative Reports, NJSP.

32. Kelven Keraga, posting June 2, 2003, on http://groups.yahoo.com/group/LindyKidnap/message/5615.

33. Fisher, *Ghosts of Hopewell,* 137.

34. *New York Times,* January 13, 2003.

Bibliography

A NOTE ON ARCHIVAL SOURCES
At the New Jersey State Police Museum, West Trenton, New Jersey, are located the Records of the State Police Investigation, which include Investigative Files, Statements Files, Reports Files, "L" Files, Accordion Files, Steno Notebooks, and various other miscellaneous files, such as the Robert Peacock Collection, the Norman Schwarzkopf Collection, the David Wilentz Collection, and the Brooklyn District Attorney Files, along with donations by previous researchers and gifts from others with a long interest and/or family connection with the case, including scrapbooks, newspaper collections, photographs, and so forth.

In addition, special notice should be taken of the Morris "Mickey" Rosner untitled manuscript/memoir also at the New Jersey State Police Museum, which provides the fullest account available of the negotiations carried on in the very first days after the kidnapping. Rosner's contacts with Owney Madden, Salvatore Spitale, and Irving Bitz, as well as with Henry Breckinridge and Charles Lindbergh, are a detailed account of the effort to work through the underworld to secure the child's return. It is an invaluable source.

The largest single collection at the museum is the Harold Giles Hoffman Papers. Hoffman, who conducted his own investigation of the Lindbergh case, obtained from the state police copies or originals of many of the reports filed in the above categories. Some were never returned to their original files. He also carried on a lengthy correspondence with several figures in the case, especially C. Lloyd Fisher, one of Bruno Richard Hauptmann's lawyers. Fisher's unpublished articles are in this collection. In addition, Hoffman's private investigators sent him reports almost daily. The most active of these investigators was Leon Hoage, who worked with Hoffman on various experiments as well as other investigations into, for example, the various contradictions in John F. Condon's statements to authorities. There is also a file of correspondence with Ellis Parker, invaluable to understanding the "kidnapping" of Paul Wendel.

The museum also has in its possession a copy of George G. Hawke's senior thesis at Princeton University, titled "Trial By Fury: The Hauptmann Trial." Hawke's paper is especially useful for the interviews he had with Frederick Pope, not available in any other form. Another defense lawyer, Egbert Rosecrans, wrote a thirty-page memorandum on the case, setting forth his conclusions about how Hauptmann carried out the crime. A copy is now available at the museum.

One cannot overlook, of course, the evidence artifacts themselves, such as the ladder, various personal items taken from Hauptmann's apartment and garage, his tool box, the ransom notes, Arthur Koehler's wood blocks, the handkerchief dropped at St. Raymond's Cemetery, account books (including the famous little book with *boad* written in it). Previously, the sleeping suit, locks of hair, pieces of bone, and the thumb guard were in this collection, but all these have been returned to the estate of Anne Morrow Lindbergh.

At the Library of Congress, the Robert Thayer Papers are useful for his record of the very first days of the negotiations with the kidnapper. Also at the Library of Congress are the Henry Breckinridge Papers, which, except for one or two items of correspondence with John Condon, are disappointing.

At the National Archives, College Park, Maryland, are the files of the Federal Bureau of Investigation pertaining to the Lindbergh case. In 1932–34, Hoover's bureau was the Bureau of Investigation, but I have used the name Federal Bureau of Investigation for purposes of recognition. These papers constitute a crucial new find in documenting the investigation and the rivalry between police agencies, especially the ongoing arguments between J. Edgar Hoover and Colonel Norman Schwarzkopf.

They also contain accounts of investigations hitherto previously unavailable on a large number of subjects, such as the handwriting on the ransom notes and Hoover's efforts to promote the bureau's interests every step of the way.

BOOKS

Ahlgren, Gregory, and Monier, Stephen. *Crime of the Century: The Lindbergh Kidnapping Hoax*. Boston: Branden Books, 1993.

Behn, Noel. *Lindbergh: The Crime*. New York: Onyx, 1995.

Berg, A. Scott. *Lindbergh*. New York: Berkley Books, 1998.

Brant, John, and Renaud, Edith. *True Story of the Lindbergh Kidnapping*. New York: Kroy Wen, 1932.

Christie, Agatha. *Murder on the Orient Express*. 1934. Reprint, New York: Berkley Books, 2000.

Collins, Max Allan. *Stolen Away: A Novel of the Lindbergh Kidnapping*. New York: Bantam Books, 1991.

Condon, John F. *Jafsie Tells All: The Inside Story of the Lindbergh-Hauptmann Case*. New York: Jonathan Lee, 1936.

Doherty, Thomas. *Pre-Code Hollywood: Sex, Immorality, and Insurrection in American Cinema, 1930–1934*. New York: Columbia University Press, 1999.

Douglas, John, and Olshaker, Mark. *The Cases That Haunt Us*. New York: Scribner, 2000.

Dunninger, *Inside the Medium's Closet*. New York: David Kemp, 1935.

Elliott, Robert. *Agent of Death*. New York: E. P. Dutton, 1940.

Fensch, Thomas, ed. *Top Secret: FBI Files on the Lindbergh Baby Kidnapping*. Woodlands, Tex.: New Century Books, 2001.

Fisher, Jim. *The Ghosts of Hopewell: Setting the Record Straight in the Lindbergh Case*. Carbondale: Southern Illinois University Press, 1999.

_____. *The Lindbergh Case*. New Brunswick: Rutgers University Press, 1987.

Gabler, Neal. *Winchell: Gossip, Power, and the Culture of Celebrity*. New York: Alfred A. Knopf, 1994.

Hamilton, Stanley. *Machine Gun Kelly's Last Stand*. Lawrence: University of Kansas Press, 2003.

Helmer, William. *Public Enemies: America's Criminal Past, 1919–1940*. New York: Checkmark Books, 1998.

Hertog, Susan. *Anne Morrow Lindbergh: Her Life*. New York: Anchor Books, 2000.

Hynd, Alan. *Violence in the Night*. New York: Fawcett Books, 1955.

Irey, Elmer L., as told to Slocum, William. J. *The Tax Dodgers*. New York: Greenberg, 1948.

Jones, Wayne D. *Murder of Justice: New Jersey's Greatest Shame*. New York: Vantage Press, 1997.

Kahlar, Ernest. *Ransom Kidnapping in America, 1874–1974/The Creation of a Capital Crime*. Carbondale: Southern Illinois University Press, 1978.

Kennedy, Ludovic. *Crime of the Century: The Lindbergh Kidnapping and the Framing of Richard Hauptmann*. New York: Penguin Books, 1996.

Kobler, John. *Capone: The Life and World of Al Capone*. New York: Holt, Rinehart and Winston, 1965; New York: Da Capo Press, 1992.

Lee, Henry, and LaBriola, Jerry. *Famous Crimes Revisited*. Southington, Conn.: Strong Books, 2001.

Lindbergh, Anne Morrow. *Hour of Gold, Hour of Lead, Diaries and Letters of Anne Morrow Lindbergh, 1929–1932*. New York: Harcourt Brace Jovanovich, 1993.

_____. *Locked Rooms and Open Doors: Diaries and Letters of Anne Morrow Lindbergh, 1933–1935*. New York: Harcourt Brace Jovanovich, 1974.

Lindbergh, Charles A. *Autobiography of Values*. New York: Harcourt, 1978.

_____ *The Spirit of St. Louis*. St. Paul: Minnesota Historical Society Press, 1993.

_____ *"WE."* New York: G. P. Putnam, 1927.

Marston, William M. *The Lie Detector Test*. New York: Richard Smith, 1938.

Milton, Joyce. *Loss of Eden: A Biography of Charles and Anne Morrow Lindbergh*. New York: HarperCollins, 1993.

Harold Nicolson. *Diaries and Letters, 1930–1939*. Ed. Nigel Nicolson. New York: Atheneum, 1966.

Oursler, Fulton. *Behold This Dreamer! An Autobiography*. Ed. Fulton Oursler, Jr. Boston: Little Brown, 1964.

Powers, Richard Gid. *Secrecy and Power: The Life of J. Edgar Hoover*. New York: Free Press, 1987.

Reynolds, Quentin. *Courtroom: The Story of Samuel S. Leibowitz*. New York: Farrar, Strauss, 1950.

Ross, Walter. *The Last Hero: Charles A. Lindbergh*. New York: Harper and Row, 1976.

Scaduto, Anthony. *Scapegoat: The Lonesome Death of Bruno Richard Hauptmann*. New York: G. P. Putnam, 1976.

Schoenberg, Robert J. *Mr. Capone: The Real—and Complete—Story of Al Capone*. New York: Quill Books, 1992.

Shoenfeld, Dudley D. *The Crime and the Criminal: A Psychiatric Study of the Lindbergh Case*. New York: Covici-Friede, 1936.

Sullivan, Edward Dean. *The Snatch Racket*. New York: Vanguard Press, 1932.

Turrou, Leon. *Where My Shadow Falls: Two Decades of Crime Detection.* Garden City, N.Y.: Doubleday, 1949.

Vitray, Laura. *The Great Lindbergh Hullabaloo: An Unorthodox Account.* New York: William Faro, 1932.

Waller, George. *Kidnap: The Story of the Lindbergh Case.* New York: Dial Press, 1961.

Whipple, Sidney B. *The Lindbergh Crime.* New York: Blue Ribbon Books, 1935.

Wilson, Frank. J., and Day, Beth. *Special Agent: A Quarter Century with the Treasury Department and the Secret Service.* New York: Holt, Rinehart and Winston, 1965.

Winchell, Walter. *Winchell Exclusive.* Englewood Cliffs, N.J., Prentice-Hall, 1975.

ARTICLES

Collins, Frederick. " Before the Body Was Found She Said the Lindbergh Baby Was Murdered." *Liberty,* April 4, 1936.

Condon, John 'F. "'Jafsie' and the Ransom Money." *Liberty,* February 15, 1936.

Dunning, Katherine Anne. "What Jafsie Told His High School Girls: The Surprising Story of How He Revealed His Role in the Lindbergh Case Weeks before the Rest of the World Knew the Secret." *Liberty,* May 16, 1936,

Finn, James. "How I Captured Hauptmann." Part 5. *Liberty,* November 5, 1935.

Hoffman, Harold. "What Was Wrong with the Lindbergh Case?" *Liberty,* January 29, February 5, 12, 19, 26, March 5, 12, 19, 26, April 2, 9, 16, 23, 30, 1938.

Hudson, E. "A Scientific Verdict on the Lindbergh-Hauptmann Riddle." *Liberty,* April 3, 1937.

Hynd, Alan. "Untold Facts in the Lindbergh Kidnapping." *True Detective Mysteries,* January 1933.

J.B.C. "A Reporter at Large: Twenty-Five Thousand Dollars." *New Yorker,* November 6, 1937.

Koehler, Arthur. "Technique Used in Tracing the Lindbergh Kidnapping Ladder." *Journal of Criminal Law and Criminology,* January–February 1937.

———. "Who Made That Ladder?" *Saturday Evening Post,* April 20, 1935.

Lippmann, Walter. "The Underworld: A Stultified Conscience." *Forum,* February 1931.

Mckelway, St. Clair. "Profiles: Goodbye Mr. Jafsie." *New Yorker.* December 29, 1934.

Oursler, Fulton. "Jafsie in Panama Discusses New Evidence." *Liberty,* March 28, 1936.

Wilson, Frank. "Undercover Man: Inside the Lindbergh Kidnapping." *Collier's,* May 10, 1947.

Index

New Jersey State Police (*continued*)
statement regarding ransom note,
37; work with "Lindbergh Squad,"
33
Newton, Cleveland A., 39
New York American, 52
New York City Police, 33, 144
New York Post, 40
New York Sun, 1
New York Times, 10, 27, 29, 48
Next Day Hill, 8, 13, 15, 17
Nicolson, Harold, 357
Norris, Kathleen, 267, 270, 284

Office of Strategic Services (OSS), 34
O'Ryan, John F., 144, 330
Osborn, Albert D. (handwriting
expert), 111, 405; analysis of Bari's
samples, 125; analysis of Hauptmann's samples, 162–163, 165, 230;
design for Hauptmann's samples,
158; interest in Lindbergh case,
122; testimony, 306–308; use of
different pens, 161, 192
Osborn, Albert S. (handwriting
expert), 221, 338; analysis of
Hauptmann's samples, 162–163,
165, 230, 300, 305, 406–407; analysis
of ransom notes, 122–126, 405;
correspondence with Schwarzkopf,
299; testimony, 187, 189, 206–207,
302–304, 339; use of different pens,
192
OSS. *See* Office of Strategic Services
O'Sullivan, Arthur, 78, 85, 100
Oursler, Fulton, 374–376, 386, 388, 391

Pagano, Clinton L., 401
Parker, Ellis: and charges of bungled
investigation, 91; on Hauptmann's
handwriting, 301; investigation of
Wendel, 364–367, 392–393, 402; as
Sherlock Holmes of Burlington
County, 42; and Steinweg's story,
369
Parker, Ellis, Jr., 366
Parry, Preston, 246
Paullin, George, 192
Payne, George, 102

Peacock, Robert: discussion about
footprint, 319; and handwriting
samples, 300; ladder experiment,
115; theory of solo kidnapper, 257;
trial preparation of Betty Gow, 281,
284; trial preparation of Hochmuth,
240–242; trial preparation of
Schaefer, 252; trial preparation of
Schleser, 265
Peremi, Frank, 76, 375
Perrone, Joseph: debriefing, 78;
description of "Cemetery John," 64,
68, 81, 96–99, 125; description of
Liepold, 121; identification of
Hauptmann, 159–160, 162, 172, 174,
175, 182; as prosecutor's witness,
176; and reward money, 403;
testimony, 293–294
Philadelphia Bulletin, 30
Phillips, Dr., 107
Plump, Harry, 239
Polygraph. *See* lie-detector test
Pope, Frederick, 235, 383; access to
Lindbergh home, 387; appeal, 361;
trial proceedings, 268, 305–306,
309, 311–315, 326, 328, 331, 337–
338, 340
Porter, Russell B., 315
Prohibition, 9, 39, 40, 43, 336
Public Enemy (film), 40
Purdy, Robert, 408
Purvis, Melvin, 146

Queens County Lumber Company,
141, 225

Rach, Siglinde, 414
Raisch, Dolores, 414
ransom: payment of, 46, 67, 71, 76,
80–81, 86; raising, 75; receipt for,
81, 128
ransom bills, 118–119, 125–127, 144,
145, 147–148, 151, 182–183, 252,
258, 294, 367; defense's examination of, 336–338; go-betweens
involved, 59–60, 62. *See also* gold
certificates
ransom notes, 277; first, 27, 376;
handwriting of, 122–129, 157–162,

About the Author

Lloyd Gardner is Research Professor of History at Rutgers University, where he has taught since 1963. Gardner received his Ph.D. from the University of Wisconsin and is the author or editor of more than a dozen books on American foreign policy. His most recent book is *Pay Any Price: Lyndon Johnson and the Wars for Vietnam.*